EXHIBITION SPONSORED BY

ATHENS: THE CITY BENEATH THE CITY

GREEK MINISTRY OF CULTURE - MUSEUM OF CYCLADIC ART

EDITORS
Nicholas Chr. Stampolidis - Liana Parlama

ASSISTANT EDITORS
Dimitris Plantzos, George Tassoulas

ENGLISH-LANGUAGE EDITION:
TRANSLATION
John Leatham, Colin Macdonald, Christina Theohari

EDITING
William and Anne Phelps

COPY EDITING
Diana Zapheiropoulou

CO-ORDINATION
Dimitris Plantzos

DESIGN
Rachel Misdrachi-Kapon

DESIGN CONSULTANT
Moses Kapon

DESIGN AND PRESENTATION OF THE EXHIBITS
Moses and Rachel Kapon

PHOTOGRAPHY
George Maravelias, Socrates Mavromatis, Dimitris Benetos

DRAWINGS
Manolis Korres, Vasso Kyriakopoulou, Eutychia Draggiotou, Vivi Papandreou,
Renata Karamousketa, Petros Deuterigos, Dimitris Koutsogiannis,
Michalis Chatzigiannis, Eleni Lembesi, Stelios Daskalakis, Dimitris Koukoulas

Published in conjunction with the exhibition "The City Beneath the City", organised by the Greek Ministry of Culture and the N.P. Goulandris Foundation and held at the Museum of Cycladic Art, Athens, 29 February 2000 - 31 December 2001.

ISBN 0-8109-6725-1

Produced, printed and bound in Greece by

KAPON EDITIONS
23-27 Makriyanni St., Athens GR - 117 42, Greece, Tel./Fax: (01) 92 14 089
e-mail: kapon_ed@otenet.gr

Distributed in 2001 by Harry N. Abrams Incorporated, New York

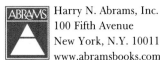

Harry N. Abrams, Inc.
100 Fifth Avenue
New York, N.Y. 10011
www.abramsbooks.com

ATHENS: THE CITY BENEATH THE CITY

Antiquities from the Metropolitan Railway Excavations

CURATORS

LIANA PARLAMA - NICHOLAS CHR. STAMPOLIDIS

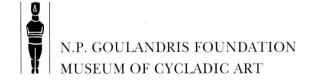

N.P. GOULANDRIS FOUNDATION
MUSEUM OF CYCLADIC ART

Distributed by Harry N. Abrams, Inc., Publishers

MANAGING COMMITTEE

LIANA PARLAMA
Director of Prehistoric and Classical Antiquities
Ministry of Culture

NICHOLAS CHR. STAMPOLIDIS
Professor of Classical Archaeology, University of Crete
Director, Museum of Cycladic Art

ISMENE TRIANTI
Ephor of Antiquities, Acropolis

BESSIE DROUNGA
Architect

DIMITRIS PLANTZOS
Curator, Museum of Cycladic Art

HONORARY COMMITTEE

His Excellency the President of the Hellenic Republic
CONSTANTINE STEPHANOPOULOS

ELISAVET PAPAZOI
Minister of Culture

KOSTAS LALIOTIS
Minister of the Environment, Town Planning and Public Works

DOLLY GOULANDRIS
President of the N.P. Goulandris Foundation

LINA MENDONI
Secretary-General, Ministry of Culture

THEODORA KARAGIORGA
Ephor Emeritus of Antiquities

EXHIBITION

MANAGEMENT AND CO-ORDINATION
Liana Parlama - Nicholas Chr. Stampolidis

ARCHITECTURAL DESIGN AND INSTALLATION
Bessie Drounga

WORK TEAM
Liana Parlama
Nicholas Chr. Stampolidis
Ismene Trianti
Effie Baziotopoulou-Valavani
Ioanna Tsirigoti-Drakotou
Stamatia Eleftheratou
Olga Zachariadou
Maria D. Theohari
Eutychia Lygouri-Tolia
Dimitris Plantzos
George Tassoulas

DESIGN - DOCUMENTATION
Nicholas Stampolidis
Bessie Drounga
George Tassoulas

SUPPORT TEAM
Petros Kalligas
Maria Tolis
Antonis Dragonas
Skopiotis Marinakis
Athanassios Katsaros
Haralambos Fameliaris
Philippia Kalli
Eleni Lembessi
Thalia Spyridaki
Philia Passadaki

CONSERVATION
Stavros Kassandris
Themis Kardamis
John Kardamis
Marios Zisis
Theone Dimitrakopoulou
Elli Kokkali
Christos Laskaridis
Polytimi Loukopoulou
Chrysa Fousseki
Anthi Hatzipapa
Athanassios Kangiouzis

CARPENTRY
Arist. Milios & Son

PAINT-WORK
Museum of Cycladic Art
conservators and support team

LIGHTING EQUIPMENT
Maria Vakirtzi

ELECTRICIANS
Nikos Vrailas
Tasos Kostis

**COMMUNICATION AND
PUBLIC RELATIONS OFFICER**
Eleni Papadimitriou

ARTWORK
DOT IMAGING Ltd.

FINANCIAL ADMINISTRATION
Athanassios Massouras

TRANSPORTATION
Athanassios S. Bergeles

INSURANCE
INTERAMERICAN S.A.

CARETAKERS - GUARDS
Miltiadis Varvaressos
Theodoros Minogiannis
Haralambos Papoulias
Stelios Papoulias
John Piskopanis
KATRANTZOS Services
and Systems Corporation

In addition to the permanent staff
of the 3rd and 1st Ephorates of the
Archaeological Service who authored
the relevant sections and entries of the
catalogue, the following archaeologists
took part in the M.R.A. excavations:
Ch. Agouridis, G. Alexopoulos,
E. Anesti, S. Asimakopoulou,
S. Giannakou, E. Giatroudaki,
V. Ghika-Palikaropoulou, N. Gurova,
N. Daliani, E. Kavraki,
G. Kassimi, T. Michalakopoulos,
G. Michalopoulos, P. Michailidou,
D. Barbouni, M. Panagiotopoulos,
K. Sarris, E. Servetopoulou,
A. Tinga, K. Trandalidou, A. Psalti.

AUTHORS

E.B.-V.	Effie Baziotopoulou-Valavani (125, 263-270, 304-313, 348-349, 352-355, 378-379, 383-390)
V.Ch.	Vasso Christopoulou (92)
S.E.	Stamatia Eleftheratou (67-84)
S.G.	Stella Ghika (65-66)
H.H.	Hara Harami (38-39, 42, 44, 46-48, 51, 60-61, 63, 93-94)
E.H.	Elissavet Hatzipouliou (119, 201, 204-206, 208-212)
P.G.K.	Petros G. Kalligas (8-25)
E.K.	Elena Kassotaki (29)
A.K.	Andromache Katopodi (95-104)
G.K.	George Kavvadias (118, 213-214, 220, 230-237, 249-262, 282-297, 303, 339, 346, 371, 376-377, 382, 393, 412-417)
T.K.	Tonia Kokoliou (179, 445-447, 450)
Ch.K.	Christos Kontochristos (49-50, 52-59, 62)
Ch.B.K.	Charalambos B. Kritzas (123, 137, 174)
Th.K.	Theodora Kyriakou (116-117, 229, 248, 298-302, 325-333, 340-345, 357, 359-370, 380-381, 420)
E.L.-T.	Eutychia Lygouri-Tolia (106-115, 183, 190, 197-198)
S.M.	Skopiotis Marinakis (30, 45, 64)
M.M.	Mavroidis Mavroeidopoulos (1-7, 26-28)
M.-Ch.M.	Maria-Christiana Mougnai (31-37)
M.N.	Maria Nikoloudi (169, 173)
V.O.	Vassiliki Orphanou (247, 391, 409, 418-419, 421-443)
I.A.P.	Ioanna A. Papaloi (40-41, 91)
L.P.	Liana Parlama (128-136, 452)
V.P.	Vasso Penna (178)
M.I.P.	Melpo I. Poloyiorghi (43)
I.P.	Irene Poupaki (85-90, 105)
N.S.	Nicholas Stampolidis (126-127, 164, 166, 170-171, 181-182, 191-192, 203, 207, 225, 227, 238, 350-351, 392, 399-401, 449, 451)
H.S.	Haris Stoupa (314-324, 334-338, 394-398, 402-407)
M.D.Th.	Maria D. Theohari (145-149, 193-196, 239-240, 411)
I.T.	Ioannis Touratsoglou (120, 175-177, 184-189)
I.T.-D.	Ioanna Tsirigoti-Drakotou (226, 271-281, 347, 356, 358, 372-375, 408, 410)
O.Z.	Olga Zachariadou (121-122, 138-144, 150-163, 165, 167, 180-181, 199-200, 202, 215-219, 221-224, 228, 241-246, 444)
P.Z.	Pantelis Zoridis (124, 168, 172, 448)

CONTENTS

The Nicholas P. Goulandris Foundation - Museum of Cycladic Art greets the 21st century and the creation of the Metropolitan Railway of Athens with the exhibition "The city beneath the city".

The uninterrupted occupation of Athens over more than six millennia, with continuous – and ever more daring – intrusive steps being taken to meet the needs of successive generations, the most recent of which is the Metropolitan Railway, alters the appearance of the landscape while eradicating traces of the past. The significance of the excavations that preceded the construction of the Railway is therefore obvious. This great engineering project, which is already changing the lives of Athenians, gave the Archaeological Service the chance to examine a total of nearly 65,000 sq.m. (6.5 ha.) lying within the modern city. It has been the largest excavation ever carried out in Athens – carried out, moreover, in a short space of time.

Important parts of ancient Athens were investigated during the excavations, conducted for the most part on the sites of Stations and Ventilation Shafts for the Railway. More than 30,000 moveable objects were brought to light. Following a necessarily strict process of selection, the Managing Committee chose about 500 objects for inclusion in the present exhibition. Our overriding criterion was the requirement that not only finds from each new station should be put on display but also the surviving evidence of the whole gamut of life led by Athenians over a period of twenty-five centuries: day-to-day existence and public life, religion and burial practices. The exhibition follows the topography of ancient Athens, making it easier for the visitor to gain a more accurate impression of the latter. We hope that in this way it answers the obvious question posed in recent years: what were the antiquities being met with during construction of the Athenian Metro?

The sheer quantity and diversity of the finds and the difficulties inherent in their display were the main obstacles in the way of what I believe to be an outcome worthy of praise, an outcome achieved through the equable co-operation by all with the Managing Committee.

I wish to stress that the Museum of Cycladic Art excelled itself and put its all into the mounting of this exhibition. I thank most heartily Professor Nikos Stampolidis, Director of the Museum, and all our loyal staff who worked unstintingly to prepare so large an exhibition within a mere six months. Our collaboration with the Director of Prehistoric and Classical Antiquities at the Ministry of Culture Mrs Liana Parlama, the Ephor of the 1st Ephorate of Prehistoric and Classical Antiquities Mrs Ismene Trianti, and the architect Mrs Bessie Drounga was both harmonious and fruitful throughout the period in which the exhibition was being prepared. I warmly thank them all for their vital contribution.

The catalogue, an indispensable adjunct of the exhibition documenting its contents, was compiled under the scholarly supervision and with the general oversight of Professor Nikos Stampolidis and Dr Liana Parlama. Apart from them, the archaeologists who excavated the several sites on behalf of the 1st and 3rd Ephorates of Prehistoric and Classical Antiquities, undertook the compilation of the catalogue entries. I congratulate and thank them all. I wish in particular to congratulate Rachel and Moses Kapon and their associates on their excellent work in producing this elegant publication.

In all our endeavours while organising the exhibition "The city beneath the city" we enjoyed the unreserved support of the Minister of Culture Mrs Elisavet Papazoi and the Minister of the Environment, Urban Planning and Public Works Mr Kostas Laliotis. Without their assistance an exhibition of this size and diversity would have been impracticable. Finally, thanks to the generous grant received from Attiko Metro S.A., which reflects their social awareness, it has been possible to implement the entire project. The Board of Directors of the Foundation and I personally thank them all most warmly.

DOLLY GOULANDRIS
President of the Nicholas P. Goulandris Foundation -
Museum of Cycladic Art

The construction of the Metropolitan Railway, a vision entertained for decades by the city of Athens, presented a great challenge to the Ministry of Culture and the Archaeological Service for it opened up the possibility of revealing a vast work of excavation, more extensive and on a greater scale than anything previously attempted in Greece.

The benefit arising from the building of the Metropolitan Railway is twofold. It provides breathing space for the residents of the city at the same time as it makes an invaluable contribution to our knowledge of the constant growth of Athens. The diverse movable and immovable finds complement the mosaic of the age-long history of Athens, uninterrupted from prehistoric times down to our own day.

Lasting features, ancient roadways, workshops and cemeteries, public and private buildings, water conduits, hundreds of works of art and thousands of artefacts compose a three-dimensional picture of everyday life in Athens over the course of many centuries. They throw light on the habits peculiar to the private and public life of Athenians, while certain finds illustrate ancient written sources in a striking way; they are the visible part of history.

The most representative products of the archaeological investigation, conducted in an exemplary manner, are displayed in the exhibition titled "The city beneath the city". In the rooms of the exhibition, mounted by the Ministry of Culture in collaboration with the Museum of Cycladic Art and generously sponsored by the Ministry of the Environment, Urban Planning and Public Works and Attiko Metro S.A., the visitor will discover a tangible record of the history of Athens.

Congratulations are due to all who have been engaged in this great archaeological project, to the 1st and 3rd Ephorates of Prehistoric and Classical Antiquities and in particular to the Ephor of Antiquities Mrs Liana Parlama, now in charge of the Directorate of Prehistoric and Classical Antiquities. In addition, all who supervised the setting-up of the exhibition at the Museum of Cycladic Art and the production of the catalogue which accompanies it, especially the Director of the Museum of Cycladic Art Professor Nikos Stampolidis, deserve felicitations. Finally, mention must be made of the outstanding collaboration enjoyed by the Archaeological Service and Attiko Metro S.A., a collaboration that succeeded in linking the past of the city of Athens with its creative present in furtherance of a better future.

ELISAVET PAPAZOI
Minister of Culture

The Metropolitan Railway of Athens, the "Attiko Metro", a twenty-first century project, highlights the science, art, technology and culture of our time.

A contemporary project executed in good taste, its function is to serve the citizens of Athens while its aesthetic merits aim to stimulate and inspire them.

Attiko Metro has converted its Stations into small museums whose displays of works by great artists and craftsmen of the period illustrate in the best possible manner an inimitable legacy accumulated over more than twenty-five centuries.

Attiko Metro has demonstrated that in acting with responsibility and sensitivity during the construction stage we have all shown respect for our cultural heritage, while in its operational stage it has made the history and fame of Athens part of its own identity.

There are some who have spoken of the incompatible and destructive relationship of the Metro with our cultural heritage.

I believe the time has come to reveal a suppressed truth of which few are aware. The most extensive single archaeological excavation and investigation, covering a surface area of 70,000 sq.m. and resulting in significant finds, has been carried out in conjunction with the construction of the Metro; it has revealed the continuity of Athens throughout every historical period spanning almost thirty centuries.

The exhibition titled "The city beneath the city", organised by the Ministry of Culture and the Museum of Cycladic Art and sponsored by the Ministry of the Environment, Urban Planning and Public Works and by Attiko Metro S.A., is a proof of the compatible and harmonious relationship of the Metro of Athens with cultural heritage.

This relationship has been translated into mutual confidence between the Ministry of the Environment, Urban Planning and Public Works and the Ministry of Culture, as it has between the engineers and the archaeologists once we had taken the salutary decision to change the alignment of the Metro and to route it at a distance from the bounds of the Kerameikos archaeological site. We may be certain that this reconcilable and harmonious relationship, this relationship of mutual confidence, will persist undisturbed in the coming years as the Metro network is extended.

As sponsors of this important exhibition, we are fully conscious of the need to thank most warmly all those archaeologists who laboured on the excavations and worked to bring about the exhibition.

We are conscious too of the need to thank the Museum of Cycladic Art which undertook to present to the Greek public and its very many foreign visitors the exhibition "The city beneath the city", which contains 500 or so artefacts out of the 30,000 and more which the archaeologist's spade and the construction of the Metropolitan Railway of Athens have together brought to light.

The Metropolitan Railway of Athens, a project marking the 21st century, and the exhibition itself so aptly called "The city beneath the city" give us all reason to feel pride in our past and pride and optimism in our future.

KOSTAS LALIOTIS
Minister of the Environment,
Urban Planning and Public Works

EXCAVATIONS IN ATHENS
FOR THE METROPOLITAN RAILWAY PROJECT
1992-1997

- The statues are in the Museum.
- They're not, they're chasing you; can't you see they are?
I mean, on their broken limbs,
in their former shape which you never knew,
though you're aware of it.

George Seferis, *The Thrush II*

Early in 1992 when we were still in the planning stage of the excavation project for the great endeavour named the Metropolitan Railway of Athens, it was being said that the convergence of such a project and the city's antiquities could result in a catastrophic contest or else a creative alliance. The excavations were a difficult undertaking, a fascinating challenge, and at the same time a confrontation both with ourselves and with the others, an undertaking which would for the first time present an opportunity for the relationship between antiquities and a modern-day project to be tested on so large a scale in conditions of an urban environment. At the same time the archaeological factor raised a reasonable question in the public mind, one which arose out of the natural reluctance ordinary people always feel about large projects that disturb the smooth tenor of their lives. Already, our ancient city has revealed an aspect of its character unknown till recently, and the present-day city has won some respite as a result of a procedure which neither was easy nor did it leave much scope for concessions by either side. However, the hard work of the archaeologists, their knowledge, and their composure in the face of difficult situations and, on the other hand, the generous, unstinting financing of every requisite archaeological investigation or task and the faultless technical support they received led to a synthesis of opposites. The Ephorates for the Antiquities of Athens and Attiko Metro S.A., together with the contracting company Olympiako Metro, proved that a high quality of excavation work, such as that which by common consent characterised the excavations carried out in Athens, can be reconciled with the pace demanded by its technical counterpart. It proved, too, that scholarly research in the sensitive realm of knowledge about life in antiquity can succeed even in the conditions of a construction site. Following an initial period of trial explorations, there emerged from the pits dug for the first twenty stations and the intermediate shafts a collaboration that rested upon recognition by all parties of the indispensability of the project and upon the obligation we all felt towards this city, which, since we have not let it develop according to the principles that history, the monuments, and its natural beauty should have dictated, we are bound at least to assist in its survival.

When the technical design for the Metropolitan Railway was finalised early in the 1990s, it incorporated some of the suggestions that had been made by archaeological authorities, in particular that any sort of digging should be kept distant from the perimeter of the fortification walls of ancient Athens and that the tunnels should be at a depth considerably below archaeological levels. It was clear from the siting of the stations and shafts that archaeological involvement would be inevitable in most instances and that the 3rd Ephorate of Antiquities of Athens would be the one which would have to carry out the burdensome archaeological work almost in its entirety since seventeen of the twenty stations and associated shafts lay within its jurisdiction and only the outlying Stations of DAPHNE on Line 2 (Sepolia to Daphne) and KATECHAKI and ETHNIKI AMYNA on Line 3 (Ethniki Amyna to Kerameikos) were in the area of the 2nd Ephorate[1]. For this reason help was sought from the other Athens Ephorates, and the lst Ephorate of the Acropolis undertook the investigation of the OLYMPIEION Station (later renamed the ACROPOLIS Station) located on Makryianni municipal land and the adjoining Makryianni and Athanassiou Diakou Streets. There an extensive and important excavation conducted by the Ephor Petros Kalligas and his colleagues revealed – uniquely among all the Metropolitan Railway Excavations – continuous occupation from the 3rd millennium B.C. down to our own day (see below, p. 28ff.). The lst Ephorate of Byzantine Antiquities, being particularly concerned with the monuments there that are under its control, undertook the investigation of MONASTIRAKI Station, where archaeological work is continuing on account of the unusual difficulties presented by the site, and the MITROPOLEOS and AGION ASOMATON Shafts, where it has completed its work. Nonetheless, the obligations placed on the 3rd Ephorate remained heavy given that, apart from the main sites around the Stations and Shafts, it had to contend with a host of preparatory trials and the auxiliary and peripheral trenches dug for the path of pipes and cables being laid by public utilities while, of course, it also had to keep an eye on all the tunnels that were being opened (a section of Line 3 in the Makryianni district was overseen by the lst Ephorate). For all these reasons it was a great achievement on the part of the 3rd Ephorate that it managed in the period between the summer of 1992, when the first excavation was begun in Syntagma Square, and 1997 to release free of any archaeological encumberment all the sites on which it had conducted archaeological research, namely, eleven Stations (there were no archaeological hitches at OMONOIA and AMPELOKIPI Stations, while ANALATOS was investigated but no antiquities were found) and seven Shafts, almost all of them the sites of large-scale excavations[2]. It is to the Ephor Theodora Karagiorga-Stathakopoulou who, besides other insights, had had great experience of field work in the midst of public works projects in Athens during the '80s[3], to whom are owed the faultless organisation and scholarly direction of this vast undertaking, the foundations upon which collaboration with Attiko and Olympiako Metro has rested, and the attempt to find the solutions that have led to the rescue of such ancient structures as have been conserved either in situ or by removal to another site.

Knowledge that had been acquired from systematic archaeological supervision of Athens building sites during the previous thirty-five years, was put to use initially in the clearing of "highly dangerous" Stations and Shafts (where the danger lay in the anticipated antiquities) and in suitably organising the work sites in such a way as to facilitate the work of excavation with all the necessary technical support. Even then, things were not all that easy. It required many hours of exhausting meetings and open minds to thrash out matters that were self-explanatory for one side or the other but not for both. The flow sheets, essential to the progress of the technical phases, were unintelligible to us just as the engineers in charge could not understand how it was we were unable to tell them once we started an excavation *when* we would finish it. The archaeologists attached to the Ephorate were responsible for the excavations simultaneously conducted on four or five sites in the two-year period 1993-95; they had also to conduct the daily discussions and settle a variety of large and small problems which happened to arise through the pressure of time and the need not to allow such pressure to disturb the progress of the excavations. They had a group of twenty-two outstanding young archaeologists working alongside them who were infected by the enthusiasm of their superiors and frequently worked at a furious pace, as in the case of Amalias Avenue, while also working night shifts in trenches they were unable to open up in daytime. A total of almost two hundred labourers were engaged, most of them at the large SYNTAGMA and KERAMEIKOS Stations. The overseers of ephorate excavations were in charge of these excavation teams; they worked altruistically in often harsh circumstances, directing, co-ordinating and in effect instructing the workers. We owe it to Lambros Nikolakopoulos, Haralambos Fameliaris, Haralambos Perdikkas, Stavros Dourekas and Ioannis Papadopoulos, to mention only these names, for their exceptional service. The contribution made by the ephorate conservators in the pits and especially in the laboratories was, and continues to be, of the greatest importance; they have to cope with an enormous quantity of material, the number of movable finds now belonging to the Ephorate having doubled through previous excavation activity extended over very many years.

The basic conclusions that may be drawn from the study of the material made so far are set out, in the catalogue pages which follow, by those in charge of the excavations at all the pits from which the finds come. These finds testify to the importance of the excavations of the Metropolitan Railway to the study of matters concerning Athenian archaeology, especially matters concerning the topography of districts of which we already have considerable knowledge, but of others, too, such as the eastern sector of the ancient city from Syntagma to the Evangelismos Hospital, of which our knowledge was fragmentary, and such conclusions as were reached rested on many assumptions[4].

A particularly valuable characteristic of these excavations should be noted here, namely, the opportunity presented by the extensive sites of the stations (each of between 0.25 and 0.70 ha.) and of the shafts (between 500 and 1,000 sq.m.), for large areas of ancient remains to be excavated and our understanding and interpretation of them to be made that much easier. From time to time we had dug sites of limited extent in Syntagma Square, particularly when trenches were being opened in connection with small-scale works, but without making any headway towards a proper investigation of topographical problems, whereas now, following excavation of the adjacent avenue, the most extensive investigation made in the area – it covered more than 0.70 ha. – we have a full picture of continuous use, borne out by an abundance of data, from the 5th c. B.C. down to our own day. The discovery of a stretch of the bed of the Heridanos River, with its drainage conduit, and of the adjacent ancient road to the Mesogeia plain, with cemeteries on each side of it dating from the 4th c. B.C. to the 3rd c. A.D.; the unearthing of sections of a long length of the early Classical Peisistratean aqueduct; extensive networks of conduits, wells and reservoirs of all periods; the remains of workshops, outstanding among them for their importance being seven foundry pits of the Classical era; the Late Roman balneum erected after the sack of Athens by Herulians in A.D. 267 and rebuilt in the 5th century; the remains of Byzantine habitations to the south of the river; and last, the reservoirs and conduits constructed during Ottoman occupation, Haseke's wall thrown up in 1778, and more recent additions, down to the Othonian stone-paved Amalias Avenue – all these are reference points in the centuries-long history of the city. This district, lying to the east of the ancient walls, incorporated into the Roman city when the fortifications were enlarged, is now under study in conjunction with the HERODOU ATTIKOU and ZAPPEION Shafts and EVANGELISMOS Station. It was the latter which afforded the greatest surprise in these excavations because it was in this area, previously unknown archaeologically, where important information was obtained concerning the thoroughfare leading to the Mesogeia which passes through it. Two other important digs during the 1990s, a notable decade for archaeology in Athens, were the excavations first of the Rigillis Street building plot leading to the discovery and identification of the Palaestra of the Gymnasium of the Lyceum and second of the precincts of the Greek Parliament, virtually the continuation of the Amalias Avenue excavation; they bring to a close the latest chapter in the investigation of the urban development of this general area, opened by the excavations of the Metropolitan Railway.

The area to the south of the Acropolis was already fairly well known from numerous excavations of building plots that have produced many finds which testify to it having been inhabited in very early times and utilised intensively as a burial ground from the Late Mycenaean to the end of the Geometric period, to its inclusion within the city boundaries after the walls were erected, chiefly from the 4th c. B.C. onwards, and to its densely populated character during the years of Roman occupation and the succeeding centuries of the Early Christian era. The successive uses and changes to which it was subjected became clearer especially after the thorough excavation of the Makryianni plot intended for the Museum of the Acropolis which gave rise to the discovery of impressive remains, in particular from the late years of antiquity and the Early Byzantine period. Further south, in the same district but outside the walls, the PETMEZA Shaft, with its sixty-four graves of various types and burial enclosures, belonging to a section of an organised cemetery dating from Archaic to Early Christian times, provided us with yet more information about the roadside burial grounds beside the very ancient road to Phaleron which traversed this area, while the roadside installations and a part of a Classical cemetery beside another very ancient road, the one that went to Sounion (following the route taken nowadays by Vouliagmenis Avenue), was found at AGIOS IOANNIS Station, also on Line 2, lying in the ancient deme of Alopeke.

The graves of Athenian cemeteries are the most frequent of all finds made in excavations of the city. The East cemetery, as we call the most dense concentration of graves stretching from the north side of Syntagma Square to Korai Street between Panepistimiou and Stadiou Streets, has been investigated at two points during excavations of the Metropolitan Railway: at AMERIKIS Shaft and AKADIMIA Station (now renamed PANEPISTIMIO - "University"); 209 mainly Classical graves were found in the former and only 24 – Classical to late Classical and Roman – in the latter. The Station, which was dug out largely from Korai Street and from in front of the University building, provided a surprise that contrasted sharply with the one at EVANGELISMOS Station; but it did reveal to us, if negatively, the northernmost extent of this huge cemetery, for it showed that the lay of the land around Korai Street and the low hill clearly delineate this boundary.

Excavation of KERAMEIKOS Station at the junction of Pireos Street and the Iera Odos unearthed, over an area of 0.25 ha., 1,191 graves of various types dating from the 7th to the 3rd c. B.C. and disclosed invaluable information about the configuration of this district, through which flowed the Heridanos River. This was the Station that was for a long while at the centre of our concern since the tunnel of Line 3 from Monastiraki could approach the Station only from below the archaeological site of the Kerameikos and moreover at only a shallow depth, the distance between them being very short. The anxiety and opposition of the archaeological world and many others and the risks that the sacred monuments were facing – confirmed by trial geophysical tests – persuaded the civil authorities to take the courageous decision to do away with the Station at this point and divert the tunnel away from the site. As a result, the last and a particularly interesting sector of the excavation, the so-called northern entrance beside the present-day Iera Odos, was unaffected, and its transformation into an archaeological site, the rest of the excavation being put to appropriate use, is the happy outcome of this rather trying time.

There is no doubt that the Metropolitan Railway project gave us the opportunity and the means to excavate crucial sites of the ancient city and to obtain important data for scholarly research. It also enabled us to conserve entire in situ the exceptionally well-preserved section of the Roman balneum, discovered in the ZAPPEION Shaft at the junction of Amalias and Olgas Avenues, a site which will also be made accessible to the public. Finally, in a costly undertaking unprecedented in Greek experience, a large part of the balneum on Amalias Avenue was removed, including its main rooms, together with important sections of all the other discoveries in this excavation. It will shortly be reconstructed at the University Campus in Zographou, where it will serve as a training site for students of archaeology. Responsibility for decisions concerning the fate of excavated antiquities was a heavy one for us all and was not lessened by our awareness of how important and necessary it was that the great project itself be constructed. In order to vindicate the endeavours we have all made and in particular so that antiquities do not continue to be the obvious victims of progress, the experience gained from the creative conflicts of interest in Athens and which continues to be gained from large arterial roadworks being undertaken throughout the country must lead to the development and embodiment in law of another perception of public works, the archaeological side participating in their planning and the securing of the rights of monuments.

The exhibition of movable finds made by the 3rd and 1st Ephorates in their excavations for the Metropolitan Railway, an exhibition documented by this catalogue, began with a gracious proposal by the President of the Nicholas P. Goulandris Foundation, Mrs Dolly Goulandris, and her careful nurturing of it and was consummated through the invaluable assistance of the Director of the Museum of Cycladic and Ancient Greek Art, Professor Nikos Stampolidis, and his colleagues. No doubt all the exhibits, sensitively displayed by the experienced architect Bessie Drounga, from humble objects illustrating everyday life to the stele from the Public War Memorial (the Demosion Sema) and the masterpiece of a bronze head in the Severe style, will both move and instruct the public, which has already expressed its interest by flocking to view the displays in the Stations. In addition, they will encourage the public to seek out and recognise a city that will not be lost beneath the other city so long as we all persist in our struggle for its survival.

Dr LIANA PARLAMA
Director of Prehistoric and Classical Antiquities

NOTES

1. Παρλαμά 1990-91, 231ff.; *eadem* 1992-98, 521ff.
2. The excavations conducted by the Ephorate for the Metropolitan Railway are continuing at the stations and shafts on the extension of Line 3 to Aigaleo, where already important finds have been made, in particular at the Station in Estavromenou Square, where a uniquely well-preserved section of the Sacred Way (Iera Odos) and the rock cuttings of roadside graves have been exposed.
3. Καράγιωργα-Σταθακοπούλου 1988, 87ff.
4. Despite the short time since the completion of the major excavations, this excavation work has already become the subject of scholarly review and has been presented in the annual reports on the work of the 1st Ephorate and in the 1996 and 1999 Meetings of the 1st Ephorate (Proceedings in press), *ADelt* 47 (1992) Chronika, 21-24; 48 (1993) Chronika, 31-35; 49 (1994) Chronika, 27-38. See also Παρλαμά 1992-98.

THE EXHIBITION "THE CITY BENEATH THE CITY"

The mounting of an exhibition whose purpose is to display even a small sample of the antiquities that came to light during the construction of the Metropolitan Railway of Athens resembles a journey conditioned by three factors.

To start with, there is the project itself that gave rise to the archaeological discoveries in which the two unities of time and place necessarily impinge on one another. Then, from the archaeological aspect, the time was of long duration, the opposite, that is, of what applies to the transportation project of our day, in which the place or area is conversely related to time, whereas the area was relatively small – at least the area occupied by ancient Athens. In this case the distance measured in kilometres is great, while the time taken to cover it is very short.

The third factor is the people of this city: those born in it, those raised in it, those who are transient, and those foreign to it, both then and now. The people of the present are ourselves: the excavators and labourers, the architects and mechanical and electrical engineers, the draughtsmen, the contractors and machine operators, the quarrymen and painters, the public service employees, both permanent and temporary, the artists, in short, all who work with their heads and their hands.

This picture of present-day creative activity in the city readily brings to mind the picture of Athens in the days of Perikles, as Plutarch describes it: "So he boldly laid before the people proposals for immense public works and plans for buildings which would involve many different arts and industries and require long periods to complete, his object being that those who stayed at home, no less than those serving in the fleet or the army or on garrison duty, should be able to enjoy a share of the national wealth. The materials to be used were stone, bronze, ivory, gold, ebony, and cypress-wood, while the arts or trades which wrought or fashioned them were those of carpenter, modeller, coppersmith, stone-mason, dyer, worker in gold and ivory, painter, embroiderer, and engraver, and besides these the carriers and suppliers of the materials, such as merchants, sailors, and pilots for the seaborne traffic, and wagon-makers, trainers of draught animals, and drivers for everything that came by land. There were also ropemakers, weavers, leatherworkers, roadbuilders and miners. Each individual craft, like a general with an army under his separate command, had its own corps and unskilled labourers at its disposal, and these worked in a subordinate capacity, as an instrument obeys the hand, or the body the soul, and so through these various demands the city's prosperity was extended far and wide and shared among every age and condition in Athens." (Plut., *Perikles*, 12.5-7, 13.1; tr. Ian Scott-Kilvert [from *The Rise and Fall of Athens*, Penguin Books, 1960]).

Archaeologists are the link between these two realities, outside place and in time. They are the ones who have toiled and borne the brunt, who have tackled the problems that arose and have laboured in the enclosed spaces, who have troubled the citizen in his daily routine, the ones whose penetrating eyes and painstaking work made them *the first to feel with their fingers* our ancient heritage *upon the stones* – like Seferis' King of Asine – and who swiftly handed it over intact so far as was humanly possible, *a possession forever*. For what else but an undertaking concerned with life and civilisation can this enterprise be considered, which effectively associates bygone Athens with present-day Athens and engages in projects affecting the future?

The stations of the Metropolitan Railway of Athens offer countless opportunities on the one hand for making the man in the street aware of his past and familiarising him with it and on the other for illustrating the workings and applications of modern technology. The result is to create that taut harmony of which Herakleitos wrote, contributing to the appeal of the technical work itself. Even when the novel and the spectacular have given way to the familiar and customary and an individual's anxiety about his survival and his urge to hurry hear and there will have persuaded him in the midst of a humdrum daily round to choose the Metropolitan Railway as the means of serving his needs, his fleeting glances will take in his surroundings and will remind him of Man and his fate, giving him strength as he seeks betterment. For making human beings – particularly young people – accustomed to beauty and progress is a one-way track to the creation of a better society.

To this attempt to extend education and culture may now be added this exhibition, the product of collaboration between the Ministry of Culture and the Museum of Cycladic Art. It presents the public with a display of about 500 movable finds selected from the 30,000 and more that were unearthed during the excavation of seventeen sites by the 3rd Ephorate of Prehistoric and Classical Antiquities and of one by the 1st, over a total area exceeding 60,000 sq.m.

While the title of the exhibition "The city beneath the city" was inspired by another capital city of the ancient world, Roma sottoterranea, we did not call Athens "Subterranean" or "Underground" largely because we wished to avoid the derogatory connotation implicit in using the modern Greek epithet. Moreover, in this case the circumstances were rather different. Very often the distance separating the footsteps of contemporary man from the earlier city is not greater than the thickness of the street surface or the pavement stones. Occasionally, the depth at which archaeological material was found and the time interval were, of course, greater than that, and the intrusions made into past centuries were more or less numerous, but all led to the same conclusion: the city was and remains a living organism that has retained its freedom of growth and has changed, as have its occupants, at a pace which has varied throughout its existence. In addition, the proposal by the Museum of Cycladic Art to host such an exhibition, and with it to welcome in the third millennium, was in entire conformity with this image of change in the unities of time and place. Archaeological investigation revealed that the arterial road linking the demes of the Mesogeia with the centre of ancient Athens passed through EVANGELISMOS Station and proceeded towards the Acropolis via Vasilissis Sophias Avenue and Syntagma Square, a route almost coincident with the present-day avenue, an axial thoroughfare, and the notable "cultural" route that commences at the Athens Concert Hall and thence proceeds by way of the National Gallery, the Byzantine Museum, the Museum of Cycladic Art, the Benaki Museum, and Syntagma Square to the juncture of the archaeological sites in the centre of Athens. I believe the manner in which the city beneath the city developed is made quite clear at the Museum of Cycladic Art by the ancient finds it now displays.

The objects in the exhibition were selected on the criteria of their being representative as much of the place of their discovery and their provenance as of their quality, the material of which they are made, and, finally, their date. To avoid giving a misleading impression of the excavation finds to the average visitor, the number of exhibits is directly proportionate to the number of finds consistent with the criteria mentioned.

Contrary to other archaeological exhibitions, we have avoided displaying objects according to their material and kind so as to give prominence to the place of their discovery. In this exhibition movable stratified finds do not reflect only their chronological, qualitative, and artistic values and their applications; they are exhibited as inseparable from the history of the site where they were discovered. In other words, they function as indicators of the use of the buildings, areas, or burial sites they come from since the latter, being fixed remains, on the one hand could not easily be moved and on the other may have served various functions in the course of their existence. Nonetheless, it was possible to make a few exceptions. For instance, the constructed grave of a dog was transferred to the exhibition in its entirety, as was the stone receptacle of a bronze urn containing the ashes of a deceased person and a larnax (a terracotta coffin). Photographs of excavations, drawings, projections and reconstructions (for example, of a pedimented stele on a two-stepped pedestal on which authentic white-ground lekythoi were stood in accordance with ancient custom), wall-mounted texts with explanatory notes, etc. help the average visitor to gain a better understanding of the finds and make it easier for him or her to obtain an intelligible impression of the whole.

Bearing in mind the difficulties and the limitations imposed by the internal arrangement of the Stathatos Mansion – where almost all the exhibits are on display – two planes of presentation evolved. On the first, the horizontal plane, are included on the one hand public and private life – at least such manifestations of it as archaeological excavation had the good fortune to come across during the conduct of research in the capital –, while on the other the cemeteries or individual graves. On the second, the vertical plane, each station has been presented separately as a topographically distinct site. The ACROPOLIS, AGIOS IOANNIS, SYNTAGMA, AKADIMIA, EVANGELISMOS and KERAMEIKOS Stations and the PETMEZA, ZAPPEION, HERODOU ATTIKOU, AMERIKIS, ERMOU-ARIONOS, IAKHOU and PALAIOLOGOU ventilation Shafts form topographical entities in both the exhibition and the catalogue that accompanies it. Thus the picture is more explicit for the scholar who wishes to trace the topography of ancient Athens, but also more intelligible to the viewer of the exhibition, whether he or she be an Athenian resident or a foreign visitor. An effort has been made to present the finds as complete entities in order that the visitor may acquire a rounded notion of the various categories. However, for economy of space, in very few instances identical objects have been excluded from a single category, while in others they are shown singly when this is dictated by the need to highlight a particular work or by the uncertainty of its provenance. For example, there are unstratified finds discovered in earth deposits in excavated areas whose interpretation and origin can only be conjectured or guessed at. Similarly, it is difficult to establish the provenance of reused, sometimes twice reused, stratified sculptures, relief carvings and architectural members found embedded in house walls or sections of the city walls. Rarely, and then almost always with the aid of ancient texts, are we able to reconstruct how it came about that materials were reused and the occasion when such an emergency structure was erected, as, for instance, the reinforced walls of Athens in 338 B.C.: "...the land itself offered its trees, whereas the dead offered their own coffins ... as for the living, they all worked, some in charge of the fortification, others constructing moats, others digging ditches; in short, no one was idle in the city" (Lykourgos, *Against Leokrates*, 44). In most cases – particularly where private or public buildings, especially of the Roman period, are concerned – reused material of earlier date may have been removed a considerable distance from its place of origin, and whatever interpretation is given to it may be insufficient to establish its topographical provenance with any certainty.

The finds displayed in the present exhibition offer the contemporary public a representative glimpse of the art and technical achievements of ancient Athens beginning in the Mycenaean period and ending in the Byzantine. They are an accessible part of the continuous history of the city as it emerges from the necessarily partial portrayal of the excavations. However, our knowledge of Athens, capital city of the ancient world, Ἑλλάδος παίδευσις (the school of Greece), is greatly extended by recent research that has revealed some of its well-kept secrets and in so doing has given us a fuller idea of it. Drawing upon ancient sources, a creative imagination can contrive to recompose scenes of everyday life in antiquity which often resembles life as we experience it nowadays. For example, successive surfaces of ancient roads and the materials they were made of are not all that unlike modern ones. Furthermore, contemporary main roads coincide partly or wholly with ancient thoroughfares. Obstructing public roads in antiquity – whether a temporary or permanent action – and the siting of the thresholds of exterior doors, which leaves no doubt that some doors opened outwards, are astonishingly similar to what is customary tresspass upon roads and pavements in our day. Nor are we pioneers in setting out a legal framework for the imposition of charges. Aristotle wrote about this subject in *On Economics* (II, 2.3): ."Hippias of Athens offered for sale upper floors that projected over public streets, all staircases, railings, even doors opening onto the street. These were bought by the owners of the properties themselves, thus providing a stable income to the state." I think there is nothing to choose between that practice and the exaction of fines for the illegal occupation of land by our Special Fund for the Enforcement of Prescriptive, Land Use and Urban Planning administered by the Ministry of the Environment, Urban Planning, and Public Works.

In the diverse and numerically large display of objects in this exhibition it is virtually impossible to give due emphasis to certain items, especially when one bears in mind the criteria for their selection referred to above. Moreover, so far as the information provided by each one of them is concerned, they are all of equal importance.

As for the visible part of the history of this city, particularly in its golden age, a special place is held by the grave stele (no. 452) erected to those who fell in battles related by Thucydides in his account of the Peloponnesian War. The solution to the problems arising from the texts inscribed upon the greater part of the stele's surface is not only the object of archaeological research but also a significant palpable part of the history of Athens. In contrast, the scant terracotta offerings (nos. 383-390) which accompany the 150 or so deceased – men, women and children – haphazardly interred in a large pit in the area of KERAMEIKOS Station, dating to the decade 430-420 B.C., are at once reminiscent of the graphic description by Thucydides of the burial of victims of the pestilence that afflicted Athens in the opening years of the Peloponnesian War: "...though no pestilence of such extent nor any scourge so destructive of human lives is on record anywhere ... for the calamity which weighed upon them was so overpowering that men, not knowing what was to become of them, became careless of all law, sacred as well as profane. And the customs which they had hitherto observed regarding burial were all thrown into confusion, and they buried their dead each one as he could." (Thuc. II, 47.3-54; tr. Charles Forster Smith).

The assumptions made regarding the reused and immured bronze head (no. 181) found in the HERODOU ATTIKOU Shaft and the interpretation placed upon it may add to the fascination of the work. Be that as it may, it is itself one of the masterpieces of bronze sculpture dating to around 480 B.C. and makes its own contribution in turn to the customary element of spirituality in all works of a predominantly aesthetic nature. The discovery of the marble torso of Apollo Lykeios (no. 70), a copy of the now lost original, attributed by many scholars to Praxiteles, might well be held to be of comparable significance in the history of Greek sculpture.

However, viewed from another angle, the perfume flasks found in graves and the strigils with which athletes scraped the grime from their naked bodies, the bronze bodkin (no. 166), the lamps that lit the dark hours, the cups and goblets from which the ancients drank water or wine, the children's toys made of clay – everything that expressed the heightened aesthetic sensitivity of the average individual of the time are all equally important for the information they supply about everyday life in antiquity. Finally, one cannot but be moved by the affection shown for domestic pets, illustrated by a carefully constructed dog's grave and the offerings found in it: two perfume flasks (nos. 162-163) and the animal's collar (no. 164).

It cannot be doubted that the compiling of an inventory of the material on display, the materials' conservation, the photographic record, and the study made of it in so very short a time amount, at least in the reckoning of those familiar with these matters, to a truly notable feat. It is not enough to say "Well done!" to the individuals who worked from the first stages that led to the discovery of the material to the material's publication. Our thanks extended to all those collaborators whose names are recorded in fine print on the first pages of the catalogue, pages we may often overlook in our haste to admire the beautifully illustrated objects or the book production by the Kapon team, are inadequate, even if they know they are heartfelt. May they be consoled by their knowledge of the service they have rendered to the Greeks and foreigners who will visit the exhibition or by the gratitude of specialists for their presentation of the material in this scholarly catalogue. Above all, though, may they be consoled by this creative part of the time we have spent together as associates and colleagues, despite its stresses and struggles and anxieties, and also by the outcome we have jointly achieved, this slice of life that we have gained for ourselves.

NICHOLAS CHR. STAMPOLIDIS
Professor of Classical Archaeology, University of Crete
Director, Museum of Cycladic Art

MAKRYIANNI STREET

ATHANASSIOU DIAKOU STREET

ACROPOLIS Station

MAKRYIANNI STREET

The area to the south and east of the sacred rock of the Acropolis was already of importance to the settlement of Athens in prehistoric times (Thuc. II, 15), but investigation of it by excavation in modern times was piecemeal and haphazard, being restricted by recent building activity. The present-day Dionysiou Areopagitou Avenue now marks the boundary between the archaeological site of the Theatre and Sanctuary of Dionysos and the district of Makryianni. The decision to construct one of the stations on the new Metro line in the district of Makryianni presented an opportunity to conduct a thorough investigation of an important site lying within the present-day builtup area of the city in the course of the excavations that had to precede construction.

The excavation site is adjacent to the site on which it had already been decided to erect the new Acropolis Museum. The new station would serve not only the residents of the district but also the very numerous visitors to the Museum; for this reason the Archaeological Service determined that the station should be named ACROPOLIS and not OLYMPIEION, the name originally chosen.

The excavations were an opportunity to establish the character of the area in antiquity and the relationship of the area to the nearby sacred places mentioned in literary tradition and in inscriptions, such as the Dionyseion of the Marshes (en Limnais) and the Sanctuary of Kodros.

Excavation work began in May 1993 and lasted until November 1996, and covered a total area of about 2,500 sq.m. It included the excavation of a site within the publicly owned part of Makryianni and in the adjacent Makryianni and Athanassiou Diakou Streets to the east of it, as well as a detailed investigation of the building remains revealed following the decisions taken by the Central Archaeological Council not to retain them on account of their overall dilapidated state.

The excavations were directed throughout their duration by myself with the 1 creative assistance of Mrs Stamatia Eleftheratou, an archaeologist attached to the 1st

CENTRE FOR THE STUDY
OF THE ACROPOLIS

STREET

CEMETERY OF THE
MID-BYZANTINE PERIOD

STREET II

STREET VI

MAKRYIANNI STREET

STREET IV

STREET V

ATHANASSIOU DIAKOU STREET

MYCENAEAN

GEOMETRIC

ARCHAIC

CLASSICAL

HELLENISTIC

ROMAN

EARLY CHRISTIAN

BYZANTINE

NEO-CLASSICAL

MODERN

DATE UNCERTAIN

0   2.5   5   10   20m

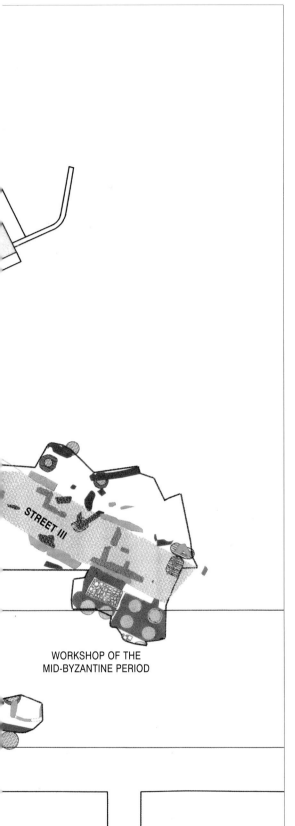

STREET III

WORKSHOP OF THE
MID-BYZANTINE PERIOD

2. Plan of the excavated site. The main building
phases are marked by different colours.

Ephorate of Antiquities, and, for part of the time, the archaeologist Mrs Melpo Po-loyiorghi. The detailed overview of the excavations, the writing-up of the day reports, the compilation of index-cards and inventories, and the photographic documentation were successfully undertaken by the young graduate archaeologists Takis Marinakis, Ioanna Papaloi, Elena Kassotaki, Makis Mavroeidopoulos, Maria Mougnai, Stella Ghika, Christos Kontochristos, Rena Poupaki, Mahi Katopodi and Hara Harami. Haris Stoupa and Vasso Christopoulou, who later joined the permanent staff of the Archaeological Service, also participated. Their contribution to compiling the entries in this catalogue is proof of our long and effective collaboration. Dimitris Koukoulas, a competent architect, working with a team of surveyors undertook to assemble the architectural records of the excavations. Conservation of the movable antiquities found during the excavations was undertaken by the conservators Thanassis Kangiouzis and Christos Laskaridis (pottery), Anthi Hatzipapa (metalware) and Mrs Marina Lykiardopoulou (coinage). Finds were classified and stored in a metal store-room constructed, after some delay, by Attiko Metro S.A. on the Makryianni building site. Human skeletal material was studied and conserved by Theodoros Pitsios, assistant professor at the Anthropological Museum of Athens.

The excavations were extended to the east and south of the listed building erected by the German W. Weiler in 1835 – and now occupied by the Centre for the Study of the Acropolis – into an area in which it was ascertained that the ancient levels had been disturbed by subsequent activities connected with the construction and utilisation of the main building as a military hospital and gendarmerie headquarters (cesspits, graves, concrete foundations, etc.). The bedrock slopes downwards and occurs at a depth of 1.25 m. below the present ground level to the north of the dig, while at the southern edge of the excavation it drops to 2.15 m. The bedrock to the east shows a similar inclination.

Ancient graves, floors, walls, wells, streets, drainage channels and other building remains of different periods were found to extend confusedly over the whole area, making investigation difficult and complex, for the inter-relationship and chronological sequence of successive finds had constantly to be sought (fig. 1 and 2). A typical instance are the massive solid walls of the Roman era whose foundations were laid deep down on the bedrock, cutting through and destroying all previous structures.

The site under investigation was first used probably at the end of the 3rd millennium B.C., in the late EH period as evidenced by related pottery finds, but more frequent human occupation is apparent in the transitional years between the MH and the LH period in the 16th c. B.C. (end of MH/LH I). A few isolated graves with a small number mainly of terracotta offerings (nos. 1-7) to the north of the excavated area (cf. tombs 81, 76, 88) reveal the existence of a nearby settlement, probably in the area of the Sanctuary of Dionysos or on the slopes above or even at the Olympieion to the east. That the neighbouring habitation persisted throughout the 14th c. B.C. (LH IIB/LH IIIA period) appears to be the case from the discovery in the excavation of a number of graves of that period and of a dump of fragments of undecorated ceramic tableware (nos. 26-28) and food remains (animal bones, sea-shells).

The site suggests there followed a lengthy period of abandonment, human occupation being next attested only during the years of transition from the LH to the PG period, that is, at the end of the 11th c. B.C. Graves, chiefly in the northern part of the excavation and found intact with funeral gifts to the dead, are attributable to the whole of the PG period (the 10th and 9th c. B.C.) and provide evidence of the burial customs of the time in Attica, such as isolated graves, cremation of the dead and the covering of graves with small mounds (see tombs 57 and 84).

The excavation revealed that from prehistoric times down to the Geometric period the site was used from time to time as a burial ground, though there was no evidence that in any period it was a regular cemetery (fig. 2). But at the end of the LG period (after the mid 8th c. B.C.) it evidently underwent an important change, for the site was to a large extent settled. Graves were no longer dug in the area and the barren resting-place of the dead seems to have made way for creative living. Subsequent building activity has in this instance, too, unfortunately disturbed the coherence of the remains of earlier dwellings though house floors, sections of walling, a small pottery kiln and some Late Geometric wells were discovered scattered over the whole area of the excavations (see wells 20 and 23).

Investigation of the site showed that there was continuous, uninterrupted occupation of it down to the end of the ancient world, and burial of the dead was therefore prohibited in the locality, in accordance with the invariable practice of the ancient world. At first the settlement was probably not a dense one and was interspersed with gardens and cultivated plots; no trace was found of any sanctuary or place of worship. Scattered housing remains and a quantity of pottery testify to the occupation of the excavated site during also the 7th and 6th c. B.C., though it is not possible, because of the poor preservation of the remains, to derive a coherent picture.

The 5th century B.C. is a crucial period for the general area, since thenceforward it was enclosed within the fortified part of the ancient city. The construction in 479 B.C. of the stout Themistoclean wall to the south of the area was a decisive event, for on the one hand it permitted the unfettered and safe development of the area but on the other it restricted the thoroughfares to such gateways as there were in the walls. The important gateway, the Alade Pyles, from which the road leading down to the sea at Phaleron Bay set out, must have been located in this area.

The parts within the walls were traversed by well-defined thoroughfares or streets which followed the natural lie of the land. Such a thoroughfare has been identified commencing on the south side of the Acropolis – where the then newly built Sanctuary of Dionysos Eleuthereus and adjacent area of the Theatre stood – and crossing the excavation from north to south (Street I). The carefully constructed cylindrical terracotta conduit for drinking water, which followed the course of the road and of which a 37-m. stretch (no. 30) was found in a rock-cut channel, formed a bend at the southernmost edge of the excavation and turned in a south-westerly direction (fig. 3). At this point were found the remains of the foundation of a small rectangular building of porous limestone, perhaps a wayside shrine like the one discovered some years ago higher up at the south-eastern corner of the enclosure wall

3. ACROPOLIS Station. Ancient Street I with its water-pipe network after the removal of the street layers. The 5th c. B.C. water-supply pipe is visible to the right.

of the Sanctuary of Dionysos. These little sanctuaries in the form of small shrines erected at the intersection of roads may have been dedicated to appropriate divinities such as Apollo Agyieus, Hermes or Hekate, but so far no inscription or other sort of confirmation has come to light. Lengths of polygonal walling, black-glazed pottery of the period and sherds of vases with notable red-figure decoration, collected from the lower levels and in rock cuttings, as well as a number of fine scattered Athenian silver tetradrachms prove the site was quite densely populated throughout the 5th c. B.C. The holding of a particularly Athenian ceremony, probably for the consecration of building plots (pyres or altars for burnt sacrifices), even at the end of that century and during the whole of the 4th and 3rd c. B.C., was attested at various places on the site. The ceremony included the burning of small animal or bird sacrifices and the offering of miniature terracotta vases (see pyres 7 and 2).

Again, the generally fragmentary nature of the finds unfortunately does not allow their reconstruction into an intelligible structured whole. By contrast, the period following the middle of the 4th c. B.C., a creative period for the wider area as it was for the city of Athens in general, left more tangible building remains on the site. It seems that the city's thoroughfares, facilitating the population's comings and goings to and from public spaces (the Agora, theatre, etc.), were laid down and defined in that period, being connected with the exits from the city, namely, the gates in the walls.

3

Within the area under excavation (below present-day Makryianni Street) a 6-m. wide main roadway was discovered (Street IV) leading from the centre of the city to the north towards the Alade Pyles in the south, close to the Ilissos river. On the southern edge of the excavated area this wide road intersected with another but narrower one 4 m. in width (Street I) which descended from the Sanctuary of Dionysos (fig. 1). Street I was investigated for about 40 m. of its length and it was ascertained that at the point where it met the larger Street IV it was joined at right angles by a third road (Street II) which approached from the west and was also 4 m. wide. In the place where these three roads met was a small paved area. Further to the north yet another road (Street III) came to light, which linked Street I with Street IV.

The roads are bordered on each side by a row of mostly conglomerate stone blocks and are paved with tightly compacted earth rutted by the wheels of vehicles, carriages and chariots. From time to time wear and tear necessitated the resurfacing of the road with the result that by and by the successive earth surfaces accumulated in a chronological sequence. A total of sixteen layers were identified on

Street I, with an average of thirteen, reaching to an overall height of 1.25 m. and stretching from the 2nd half of the 4th c. B.C. to its abandonment in about the middle of the 7th c. A.D., amounting to almost a thousand years of continuous use.

Repeated repairs are evidence of very frequent use of this arterial roadway and that there was state provision for its upkeep. As the road rose in height so was the height of the retaining walls raised on either side, these walls marking the boundary of adjacent dwellings. In fact the variations in the manner of constructing the walling of the road embankments define the boundaries of individual properties.

Effluents from the dwellings and workshops flanking the roads were channelled to the roadways. Street I is typical in that into the large central effluent conduit which ran down it lengthways flowed lesser discharges through smaller conduits, either of stone or terracotta, laid as circumstances required in the road surfaces (fig. 3). The large channel of Street I was very likely connected with the Theatre of Dionysos with the drainage system carrying the rainwater from the orchestra through a built conduit found to have traversed the stage and the portico of the Sanctuary of Dionysos in the direction of the gateway to the east and the beginning of Street I.

The excavations revealed that the eventual alignment and definition of the boundaries of the roads made possible in Hellenistic times the most effective form of occupation of the area, which was devoted exclusively to dwellings and workshops. The absence of any religious site or public building has been noted, and is confirmed by the absence also of any relevant inscriptions.

The fragmentary character of the building remains precludes any reconstruction of the houses. But the pottery recovered from the site, the terracotta lamps, the excavated wells dug in small open-air courtyards and the many pear-shaped cisterns lined with hydraulic mortar for the collection of rain-water testify to the continuous dense occupation of the site.

The existence of workshops is indicated by workplaces, deep circular or rectangular pits cut into the rock, the small built kiln for the processing of red earths to produce red pigment used in building (fig. 4) (the kiln was removed by a specialised team of conservators), the small open tanks with their drains, moulds for the making of terracotta figurines, and so on. There was no evidence of potteries and bronze foundries, but it is well known that these noxious work-places were sited outside the fortified part of the city. The same goes for graves, and it is significant that no grave dating to historical times was discovered in the excavation area.

Life persisted there in early Roman times. When Sulla devastated Athens in 86 B.C. the Alade Pyles and the walls were destroyed but the roads continued to be used by the inhabitants of the city, a fact borne out by the successive resurfacing. Perhaps the large embankment which was found to extend on the east side of the central Street

4. ACROPOLIS Station. The kiln for the production of red pigment (2nd half of 2nd c. B.C.).

4

5

5

5. ACROPOLIS Station. One of the two
hypocaust rooms of the small bath house.
The remains of the posts supporting the floor
are still visible, as well as the hot-air vent.

IV and to contain a great quantity of pottery dating between the lst c. B.C. and the lst c. A.D. had its origin in the widespread destruction of nearby residential areas and the subsequent burial of the rubble.

Some houses built on the east and west sides of Street I belong to the Imperial age. Two hypocausts carved out of the natural rock were excavated in the south part of the site; some of the circular columns made of baked clay tiles that supported the floor were still in situ (fig. 5). The site of the praefurnium, the heating chamber, was particulalry well-preserved in the basement; the house faced south on to Street II. This road also had a central conduit, flowing eastwards, with lateral channels.

Another house of the same date on the east side, whose boundaries are not clearly preserved, was supplied with water through a complicated system of wells, underground cisterns and tunnels which re-used some elements of Hellenistic installations. The wells were lined with hydraulic mortar and, by means of underground tunnels carved deep into the natural rock, were connected to subterranean reservoirs faced with fine brickwork.

These luxury homes, which as we know from other examples would have had internal courtyards and gardens, would have been furnished with marble statuary like that of the lst and 2nd c. A.D. found in more recent earth embankments at various points of the excavation, but which undoubtedly came from these buildings. A double-faced Herm with the heads of Hermes and Dionysos (no. 92) and a variety of small sculptures, such as Cupids from a composition featuring Aphrodite, and a small head of Athena are all noteworthy finds. So, too, is the marble head of a representation of Plato, a copy of an earlier famous statue of the seated philosopher, a work by the 4th c. B.C. sculptor Silanion.

Some remarkable pieces of pottery found at various points of the excavation, particularly inside wells, were once among the household utensils of these dwellings dating to the first centuries of our era. Items of interest include an oenochoe (wine pitcher) with an inscription making a glib reference to "good cheer" (no. 54) and some well-moulded terracotta lamps, one in the form of a phallus and another of a child divinity, Telesphoros (no. 47). An interesting small bronze shovel with a long cylindrical handle (no. 64), used in the burning of aromatic substances associated with the worship of certain divinities, particularly those of eastern origin, belongs to the same period. A series of bronze coins struck by the imperial mints are evidence of brisk commercial transactions.

It is not certain, but it seems likely, that the devastation wrought upon the city of Athens by Herulian raids in A.D. 267 also affected the area of excavation. No level of destruction is apparent, but the house with the hypocaust may have been aban-

6. ACROPOLIS Station. South view of the excavated site.

doned then. In any event, life went on unimpeded: the interesting ceramic objects found largely in wells date to the 3rd and 4th c. A.D. and are distinguished by their dark-coloured glaze with painted spirals of white slip. Another characteristic item discovered on the site are the amphorae with pointed ends and a cylindrical foot; they belong to a type widely distributed over the whole of the eastern Mediterranean and the Black Sea (no. 50).

There is also an interesting anthropomorphic vase with the head of a young boy (no. 52) which was cast in moulds and had perhaps a ceremonial function; it dates to the late 3rd or early 4th c. A.D. Some interesting clay figurines, designed as toys for small children, belong to the same period: a clay horse on wheels which can be pulled along (no. 53) and clay rattles with boldly painted details (no. 62). These toys were produced from moulds and are covered with a white slip.

The Late Roman-Early Christian period, which covers the years from the recognition of Christianity and the transfer of the capital of the Empire to Constantinople down to the decades preceding the reign of Justinian (4th, 5th and 6th c. A.D.), is marked by much building activity in the neighbourhood of the excavation (fig. 6). The extensive solid foundations of massive walling that were exposed indicate the existence of imposing, perhaps two-storey, villas. The frontage of one of these buildings was on the west side of Street I where the entrance

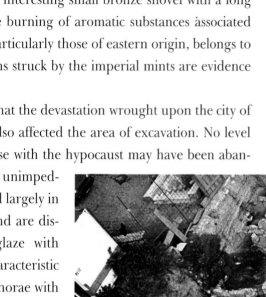

threshold to a large rectangular room (3.50 × 3.50 m.) with a mosaic floor of black and white tesserae was uncovered. Judging from the surviving portions of it, the mosaic was decorated with intersecting circles and a border of ivy leaves (no. 65). It seems that the centre of the building was taken up by a large circular space 6.50 m. in diameter, perhaps a courtyard open to the sky, of which the floor was not found. On the south and west sides of this probable courtyard lay other rectangular rooms; they too had mosaic floors, of which unfortunately again only fragments survived. More than one building phase was identified for this structure, indicating successive alterations and additions effected with used building materials. A number of fragments of older sculptures and architectural members were found built into the foundation walls. Of these it is worth mentioning architectural fragments (such as of capitals, cornices, etc.) of "Pergamon" marble which have been recognised as belonging to the now ruined Portico of Eumenes (no. 29) which lay higher up, west of the Theatre of Dionysos.

6

A large quantity of pottery ware of the same period, especially intact large vases in wells, was found in the course of the excavation, among them transport and other types of amphorae, oenochoae (wine pitchers) and askoi (flasks). Their decoration is no longer painted and is restricted to shallow oblique flutings or grooves intersecting horizontal ones ("gouged type") and to patterns of combed technique (nos. 55, 57, 58).

The production of pottery lamps was also flourishing; Athenian workshops belonging to Eutyches (nos. 42, 51), Soteria (no. 61) and Chione were particularly well known, as borne out by the seal-stamped examples that were found. Christian themes (Christograms, phoenixes) gradually replaced older pagan ones (Pan, Cupids, etc.) as the decoration on lamps.

Among miniature artefacts worth mentioning is an ivory plaque with a representation in high relief of a naked Dioskouros with his horse (no. 43). The plaque, probably accompanied by another similar one depicting the other Dioskouros, would have been part of the ornamental veneer of a 5th- or 6th-c. A.D. wooden casket.

The building remains of this period which were examined during the excavation were undoubtedly connected with those found earlier in the basement of the old Military Hospital building and to the north of either side of the extension to Street I in the more recent excavations conducted by the Department of Archaeology of the University of Athens.

Similarly related are the analogous recent finds in excavations made by the 1st Ephorate of Antiquities in the rest of the southern and western sections of the Makryianni building plot. The remains were once part of a number of large building complexes (villas, schools of philosophy) that belonged to members of leading Athenian families of the time, as we know from contemporary establishments in other parts of the city. Judging from all the related finds made in the area, most probably an entire quarter comprising similar outstanding buildings extended in these years from a low point on the south slope of the Acropolis to the boundaries of the sanctuaries of Dionysos and Asklepios until the function of these last ceased altogether.

Alterations and additions made to buildings in the 6th c. A.D., observed in the structures unearthed during excavations, show that the area was still densely inhabited at the time. Indeed, a small hoard of bronze coins dating to the 6th c. A.D. was found on the floor of a house in the south-eastern sector of the excavation area.

One of the many alterations, perhaps the last, to the central drainage conduit of Street I occurred at this time. Marble grave stelai of an earlier age, plinths of statues and votive offerings carved in relief taken from neighbouring sites, such as cemeteries, the Theatre of Dionysos and the Asklepieion once they had been abandoned at the end of the 5th c. A.D., were used to accomplish the repairs and to build the conduits.

It appears that the site was abandoned in the 7th c. A.D., occupation ceased and the ancient roads were no longer used. However, no particular level of destruction (perhaps by fire) was identified and abandonment must be attributed to the general shrinkage of ancient cities which is observed during the reign of the emperor

Herakleios (A.D. 610-644) and is connected with the crises provoked by Slav raids.

An artisan workshop (a tannery?) of the middle Byzantine age and an orderly cemetery of vaulted tombs (ossuaries), in addition to large corn-storage structures of late Byzantine and more recent times, were brought to light in the excavations; they prove the continuing use of the site after the end of the ancient world, but they occasioned the destruction of the underlying ancient remains.

In conclusion, it is a fact that, despite the fragmentary nature of the building remains of various chronological phases, the excavations provided generally speaking a large amount of archaeological information as well as a vast number of noteworthy movable finds. The excavation revealed a panorama of the long history of a part of the ancient city of Athens lying in the shadow of the Acropolis from its use as a burial ground in the prehistoric age to its planned residential function in historical times together with the road network, the houses and workshops down to the great private dwellings of the Late Roman era. It is to be hoped that the research involved in the excavation will shortly be complemented by the publication of the finds and the appropriate display of the most noteworthy of them.

BIBLIOGRAPHY: Τραυλός 1960 (Plates); Travlos 1971, 322-324 (Sanctuary of Kodros). For details and the bibliography of earlier investigations in the Makryianni district see Καλλιγάς 1994-95, 40-41.

PETROS G. KALLIGAS
Director emeritus of the Acropolis Museum

GRAVES OF THE PREHISTORIC PERIOD

The earliest finds from the Makryianni plot are prehistoric in date and are chiefly funerary, although there is some material which can certainly be described as settlement. The tombs from the site mainly date to the transition from the late MH to early Mycenaean periods, from the 17th to mid 14th c. B.C. (end of MH to LH IIB/IIIA1), while some scattered earlier and later finds indicate that the area was inhabited or used for burial purposes before as much as after this period, but less frequently.

The prehistoric material selected for the exhibition comes from this transitional period and includes as much Middle Helladic as Late Helladic (Mycenaean) funerary examples.

To the MH period or Middle Helladic tradition belong burial pit 81 and cist grave 76, while burial pit 88 is definitely Mycenaean in date. There follows a summary description of these three burials and a brief account of the skeletal material they contained, while the description of the grave gifts – mostly vases – which accompanied the dead is more detailed. It is characteristic of all the burials that they belong exclusively to small children or the newly born (even those which are not included in the catalogue of this exhibition).

M.M.

Pit grave 81

This was a child burial inside an elliptical pit cut into the bedrock. The tomb had an appropriately shaped recess at the height of its entrance to support cover slabs which were found in situ. The only grave good in the tomb, a vase (no. 1), was found near one of the four "corners" of the pit, in front of the face of the child (infant under 2 years old), which had been placed in a contracted position lying on its right side. Three other fragments of bone not associated with the skeleton of the "last burial" probably belonged to another child of an even younger age, the same tomb having been used at an earlier date for its burial (information on the osteological material from the tomb from Professor Th. Pitsios).

Tomb 81 provides a good example of an undisturbed primary burial of late MH or early LH date. For pit graves of the MH and LH period see Cavanagh - Mee 1998, 26, 43, 62.

M.M.

1 MINYAN GOBLET (KYLIX)
17th-16th c. B.C.

INV. NO. M 2441.
H. 0.076, B.D. 0.052, M.D. 0.081 M.

Complete. A few small chips on the rim and at other points. Grey clay. Hemispherical body. Two vertical strap handles have been attached on the exterior surface of the rim; they reach down to the point of the maximum belly diameter. The rim is slanting, slightly curved and everted. High pedestal, with concave walls. The discoid base is deeply hollowed. The relative asymmetry of the body, which is off the vertical axis, is due to a mistake in firing.

Heavy burnishing inside and outside the vase gives a "metallic" sheen. Other elements which enhance the metallic feel are the deep rings on the pedestal and the upper part of the base.

COMMENTARY - BIBLIOGRAPHY: Unpublished.

This double-handled cup is not an isolated example of Grey Minyan pottery from the Makryianni plot, but can be linked, in terms of the ceramic groups to which it belongs, with the vases from another burial found disturbed a little further away, also in the M.R.A. excavations.

1

For the LH I date of a similar shape of Grey Minyan pottery see Dietz 1991, 199, no. BB-3, fig. 61 bottom, middle (larger form, which comes from Tomb A of Grave Circle B at Mycenae). For this vase from Tomb A see also Μυλωνάς 1973, A, 23, B, pl. 13α, 214 (top left). For a similar shape from the West Cemetery at Eleusis, also of larger dimensions, see Μυλωνάς 1975, B, 106, no. Iπ1 - 770 (dated to late MH), Γ, pl. 143β.

M.M.

Cist grave 76

Tomb 76 was a cist grave and is a typical example of this burial type. Upright slabs had been used as walling for the tomb which in turn were covered by slabs and had been built into a pit cut in the bedrock. Two vases, one jug (prochous) with cutaway neck and one kantharos, the only grave gifts accompanying the burial, were found very close to one another, placed in the southern part, in front of one narrow side. The position of the vases and also the condition of the bones, which had been disturbed, indicate that this was not a primary but a secondary burial, probably removed, which belonged to a small child about 6 years old. Apart from the sweeping aside of the vases and disturbance of the bones, the absence of the pelvis gives the impression of removal, that is part of the body which, for a child of such an age, one would not expect to have been damaged and lost (information on the osteological material given by Professor Th. Pitsios).

This shaft-shaped type of tomb is Middle Helladic in origin which carried on into early Mycenaean times. Burial in cist graves was widely used in the MH period, continued to be practised relatively frequently in early LH, while it is only noted sporadically in the latest Mycenaean period. For cist graves of the MH and LH periods see Cavanagh - Mee 1998, 26, 43, 62.

M.M.

2 PROCHOUS WITH CUTAWAY NECK

17th-16th c. B.C.

INV. NO. M 2442.
H. 0.102, MAX.D. 0.102, B.D. 0.045 M.

Complete. Pale rosy clay. Bi-conical body. The handle, a strap handle although rather narrow and thick so as to be almost elliptical in section, has a central groove. The lip of the cutaway mouth is differentiated from the concave walling of the jug as it is thicker lower down, oblique and everted. The base is not separated from the body and bulges in the middle with the result that the underside is not absolutely flat and the vase does not sit well. The rosy-yellow surface of the vase, as with kantharos no. 3, has been burnished so as to give it a slight "metallic" look. Here again, the final result is lessened by large areas with encrustations, chiefly that close to the handle, around the area of the greatest belly diameter.

3, 2

COMMENTARY - BIBLIOGRAPHY: Unpublished.
For the date of this shape of jug from the end of MH to LH I see Dietz 1991, 172, fig. 53-54. For the shape and date of this type of jug in a building at ancient Nemea see Wright 1982, 375, pl. 91.

M.M.

3 KANTHAROS

17th-16th c. B.C.

INV. NO. M 2443.
H. (EXCL. HANDLES) 0.086, B.D. 0.059, M.D. 0.106 M.

Complete. Pale rosy clay. The deep, hemispherical body has pronounced bevelling. The two vertical, raised, strap handles begin from the edge of the rim and end on the belly, at the point of maximum diameter. They are grooved, more pronounced on their curved part. The rim is slanting and everted. The foot is low, marked by a coarsely formed ring. The discoid base is hollowed. The marked asymmetry of the body, which departs markedly from the vertical axis and inclines sharply towards the side of one handle, is due to a mistake during firing. The rosy-yellow surface of the vase has been burnished with the result that it has acquired a relative "metallic" look. The final result is lessened by large areas with marked encrustations, a feature also of prochous no. 2. To the metallic features can be added the grooving of the handles, the bevelling of the body and the ring of the foot.

COMMENTARY - BIBLIOGRAPHY: Unpublished.
The group of pottery comprising this kantharos, as well as the prochous no. 2, lies within the tradition of Yellow Minyan pottery, of late Middle Helladic origin, which continued into early Mycenaean times. For the date of

this shape of kantharos, but with a lower foot, at the end of the MH period to LH I, see Dietz 1991, 149-152, nos. AA-4 (1), AA-4 (2), AA-4 (3), fig. 47 (150). For the shape and date of this type of kantharos in a building from ancient Nemea see Wright 1982, 375, pl. 91-92. For similar kantharoi see also Μυλωνάς 1973, A, 55-56, B, pl. 43β, 1, 2, 3 (from Tomb Γ of Grave Circle B at Mycenae).

M.M.

7. ACROPOLIS Station. Tomb 88 during excavation.

Tomb 88 (fig. 7) was a pit cut into the bedrock and covered probably with two slabs, only one of which was preserved. The slabs were set on a ledge cut at the height of the entrance to the tomb, specially made for that purpose. Chalk had accumulated above the slabs filling a wider pit which followed the dimensions of the ledge. The tomb contained a child burial, apparently an infant less than one year old (according to Professor Th. Pitsios). Three vases (nos. 4-6) accompanied the burial, having been placed at three of the corners of the burial pit, and on the hand of the child would have been jewellery of faience and glass-paste beads found in the vicinity of the wrist. The double-handled kylix no. 5 was found near the head of the small child, and the single-handled kylix no. 6 towards that side of the tomb where the feet of the deceased lay. The double vase no. 4 was found in front in the other corner of the same narrow side where kylix no. 5 was discovered. From the bad state of preservation of the skeleton, we must observe that this double vase had been placed on the other side of the head and assume that the small child was accompanied by two vases placed on either side of the skull, immediately above shoulder height.

Tomb 88 is an isolated example of an early Mycenaean burial on the Makryianni plot. It can be linked chronologically with another Mycenaean tomb also found during the M.R.A. excavations at the same site (right on Makryianni Street outside the plot) and which can be dated securely from its content to the first part of the same period, namely LH IIB. Normally the two parts of the period, either LH IIB or LH IIIA1 cannot be separated satisfactorily, since they are considered continuous, although some division can be achieved in the case of the decorated pottery (see also no. 27). One or two burials from the same site, found in the same excavations, belong to later Mycenaean times.

M.M.

---

4 DOUBLE VASE

2nd half of 15th - 1st half of 14th c. B.C.

INV. NO. M 2444.
H. (EXCL. THE HANDLE) 0.048, L. 0.104, MAX.D. OF EACH VESSEL 0.051-0.052 M.

Complete. Pale yellow clay. This double vase is made up of two smaller spherical vases, which are completed by added, high, everted rims with curved walls and are joined in the area of the belly. They share a vertical, high-swung, basket-shaped strap handle. The bases are not fully shaped, resulting in a certain amount of instability. For reinforcement at the point of contact it seems that clay had been added, which in turn had been suitably moulded to follow the shape of the two small vases which were connected by an irregular rounded perforation, discernible on their interior.

The decoration is composed of brown-red to orange-red paint, thin and missing in places, on top of a yellowish slip. The rims are fully painted on the outside, apart from small parts where the handle projects. A narrower band decorates their interiors. Seven, almost horizontal, thick lines decorated the outside of the handle. Two successive, very wavy, narrow bands run around the body of the double vase, at the point of maximum belly diameter. Another band outlines the base, forming a "figure-of-eight" decoration which is bisected by a straight band, precisely at the point where the vase rests.

COMMENTARY - BIBLIOGRAPHY: Unpublished.

This vase belongs to a rather uncommon type. Its dating in the LH IIB-IIIA1 period was based on comparison with two other vases from the same tomb; these can be securely dated to this Mycenaean phase. For the occurrence of wavy-line decoration as much in LH IIB as the LH IIIA1 period see Mountjoy 1986, fig. 38, no. 14 (LH IIB) and fig. 57, no. 11 (LH IIIA1).

M.M.

5 DOUBLE-HANDLED KYLIX
2nd half of 15th - 1st half of 14th c. B.C.

INV. NO. M 2445.
H. 0.083, B.D. 0.048, M.D. 0.107 M.

Complete. Small part of rim missing. Pale yellow clay. Deep, hemispherical body. The two vertical strap handles sprout from the sloping, everted rim and end at the body on the lower part of the belly. The stem is low. The discoid base is hollowed.

The decoration of the vase is in orange-red to brown-red paint, missing in places, on a yellow slip. The interior is also coated. A band highlights the rim inside and out. The lower part of the body, stem, base and external part of the handles are solid painted. Four horizontal narrow bands on the lower part of the belly mark the end of the main decorative zone. On each side, between the handles, a palm with simple stem and, on

5, 4, 7, 6

either side of it, two ivy leaves with triple stems sprout from a rock-like landscape. The ivy leaves have long, wavy stems.

COMMENTARY - BIBLIOGRAPHY: Unpublished.
See Mountjoy 1986, fig. 53 (for the form and decoration in LH IIB) and fig. 75 (for the form and decoration in LH IIIA1). Also see Αηδόνια 1996, 39, cat. no. 2 (for similar decoration, but with double stemmed ivy leaf, on a LH IIB single-handled cup. For LH IIB and LH IIIA1 in Attica see recently Mountjoy 1999, I, 509ff.

M.M.

6 SINGLE-HANDLED KYLIX
2nd half of 15th - 1st half of 14th c. B.C.

INV. NO. M 2446.
H. (EXCL. HANDLE) 0.066, B.D. 0.048, M.D. 0.086 M.

Complete, with crack on body. Off-white clay. Deep, hemispherical upper body, conical below, a feature more obvious on the interior of the vase. One very high, vertical strap handle sprouts from the slanting, everted rim and, forming a normal curve, ends on the body at the point of the maximum diameter of the belly. The low stem has a slight swelling. The discoid base is hollowed underneath and wavy in outline above.

The decoration is in brown paint, thin and missing in places, on an off-white slip. The interior is also solid painted. A band highlights the rim inside and out. The stem is also solid painted. The paint spread onto the lower part of the base forming a narrow surrounding band, though rather thin and flaking. Four thick oblique bands embellish the exterior of the handle. A continuous wavy band hangs from the rim band forming semicircles, perhaps a variation of "rock-work" decoration. The larger of these surrounds the whole handle. Four horizontal bands of almost equal thickness, two by two and placed in pairs, complete the decoration, two on the lower part of the belly and the others at the point where the belly and handle project. The latter are cut by the large semicircle which surrounds the handle.

COMMENTARY - BIBLIOGRAPHY: Unpublished.
For the LH IIB-IIIA1 date see the commentary on no. 5. Likewise see Mountjoy 1986, fig. 53 (2) (for the same shape and similar decoration, with solid "rock-work" decoration and not pendent semicircles, in the LH IIB period).

M.M.

7 FAIENCE BEADS
2nd half of 15th - 1st half of 14th c. B.C.

INV. NO. M 2447.
MAX.D. 0.009, MAX.TH. 0.007 M.

These small, similar beads of blue faience are preserved complete. They are spherical in shape, lightly compressed at the points of perforation for the small piercing holes. Their walls are grooved, lengthwise.

COMMENTARY - BIBLIOGRAPHY: Unpublished.
The two beads of faience were found together with others of white glass-paste, their state of preservation preventing their exhibition. Two are nearly whole and two-three others just scraps. For the jewellery of which they would have been a part see the commentary on tomb 88. The accompanying pottery of the tomb was used to date the beads to the LH IIB-IIIA1 period.

M.M.

EARLY PROTO-GEOMETRIC BURIAL

From tomb 57

Pit grave 57 was found almost in the middle of the excavation area in the east part of the Makryianni plot and was investigated in January 1995 by archaeologist Vasso Christopoulou (area w, Excavation Notebook 18/1/1995).

Excavated in the soft bedrock, the *kimilia*, the main tomb (l. 1.20, w. 0.27 m.) had a NW-SE orientation and paid great attention to the cutting of the vertical interior walls. It was found undisturbed, covered with well-fitting schist slabs which are supported on a ledge cut around the interior, width 0.10 m. The deceased, a small child about 5 years old judging from the remaining bones (according to Professor Th. Pitsios), was placed directly on the floor of the tomb with head pointing north, while four small clay perfume vases were found at the bottom end of the tomb, in the area of the feet. The two gold earrings were in the region of the deceased's skull, while the rest of the jewellery, rings and fibulae, were found around the middle of the tomb. Fibulae are considered characteristic of a female burial and are normally found in pairs, although not in the case of this burial.

Owing to its fragmentary state of preservation, a small bronze fibula (M 2458) from the same grave is not included in the exhibition.

The relative wealth of the grave goods allows one to suppose that the deceased would have been the off-spring of a distinguished Athenian family of the time. This particular single tomb is a typical example of the early PG period (beginning of 10th c. B.C.) in Attica both in terms of form and grave gifts, clay vases and jewellery. It is worth noting in the decoration of the vases the transition from free-hand painting which characterises early periods, to the use of the compass with the multiple brush observed in later periods. Two further lekythoi were found in tomb 57 (M 2453 and M 2454), decorated free hand. The parallel use of bronze and iron for the jewellery is characteristic. Similar tombs with similar finds have been found in the Kerameikos, on the south side of the Acropolis and at other sites in Athens. The lekythos, at any rate, despite its distribution of the type in Thessaly, Euboea, the Cyclades and elsewhere, is considered an Athenian creation.

BIBLIOGRAPHY: Desborough 1952, 1ff., pl. 1; Kurtz - Boardman 1994, 34ff.; Σημαντώνη-Μπουρνιά 1997, 25ff. For contexts containing Attic vases of different styles see *Kerameikos* I, pl. 13, tomb 84. S. Slope of the Acropolis (Heidelberg): *Lefkandi* I, 401, n. 223.

P.G.K.

8 LEKYTHOS
Beginning of 10th c. B.C.

INV. NO. M 2451.
H. 0.131, B.D. 0.049, MAX.D. 0.098 M.

Complete. Relatively fine yellow clay. The vase has a spherical body, ring base and bell-shaped neck, from which springs a strap handle ending on the shoulder. Above the shoulder and beside the handle, a small perforation, an air hole, has been opened, essential for the free flow of the liquid due to the narrowness of the neck. The lekythos is embellished with linear decoration in brown paint on the light coloured clay. The rim, root of the neck and the base of the handle are defined by brown bands, while the shoulder zone is painted with a system of three concentric semicircles, with solid painted interior and dots on the periphery. The semicircles have been drawn free hand, without a compass. The belly, the lower part of the vase and the base are solid painted, apart from a zone of three thin parallel bands on the lower part of the shoulder and one band on the lower part of the belly.

COMMENTARY - BIBLIOGRAPHY: Unpublished.
In the PG period, the lekythos, in terms of use, succeeded the stirrup jar of Mycenaean times and was probably used to preserve aromatic oils. It comes from an Athenian ceramic workshop. – Burial on the SW Slope of the Acropolis (n. Heidelberg G. 82a): Desborough 1952, 2, pl. 1. For Euboean parallels (from Lefkandi) see *Lefkandi* I, 313-316

P.G.K.

9 LEKYTHOS
Beginning of 10th c. B.C.

INV. NO. M 2452.
H. 0.146, B.D. 0.046, MAX.D. 0.097 M.

Complete. Reddish clay, rather fine with some mica. The vase, in terms of shape,

8

9

is rather elongated compared with no. 8, marked by its tall neck and its emphatically pronounced rim.

The painted decoration is similar to no. 8, but heavily flaked. The tall neck is decorated with parallel bands. The shoulder zone is painted with a system of three concentric semicircles, with solid painted interior. As suggested by a nip in their centre, the semicircles have been drawn by means of a compass, with a multiple brush attached to it. Thus, greater speed and uniform execution was achieved.

The belly of the vase, the base and inside rim are solid painted, with the exception of bands along the belly.

No. 9 is the product of an Attic workshop introducing new techniques in pottery decoration (use of the compass).

COMMENTARY - BIBLIOGRAPHY: Unpublished.
See no. 8.

P.G.K.

10   PAIR OF GOLD EARRINGS
Beginning of 10th c. B.C.

INV. NO. M 2455A-B.
MAX.D. 0.02, MIN.D. 0.013 M.

(a) complete, (b) joined from fragments. Gold.

Pair of small earrings, elliptical in shape, made of gold wire. The wire is thicker at the girth and thins at the ends where it is twisted.

COMMENTARY - BIBLIOGRAPHY: Unpublished.
Both gold objects were found in the region of the skull and the small diameter precludes their use as rings for fastening hair. For the general scarcity of gold in early PG times see Desborough 1972, 313. For the gold finds (jewellery) from tombs at Lefkandi, Euboea, see *Lefkandi* I, 217ff.

P.G.K.

11-12   TWO IRON FINGER RINGS
Beginning of 10th c. B.C.

INV. NOS. (A): M 2456, (B): M 2457.
D. (A) 0.02, (B) 0.02 M.

(a) complete, (b) joined from fragments. Iron.

Two iron rings, small in section, made of a strip of sheet metal.

COMMENTARY - BIBLIOGRAPHY: Unpublished.
During the SubM and PG periods, the parallel use of iron is expanded to the manufacture of jewellery and articles of personal use such as finger rings, fibulae, brooches etc., which previously were manufactured chiefly from bronze. In Athens, in female tombs, a number of rings is found both of bronze and iron, even if the bronze examples occur more rarely. See *Kerameikos* I, 85, fig. 3; see also Lefkandi, Euboea, *Lefkandi* I, 247-248. For the use of metals see Snodgrass 1971, 213ff.

P.G.K.

13-14   TWO BRONZE FINGER RINGS
Beginning of 10th c. B.C.

INV. NOS. (A): M 2460, (B): M 2461.
D. (A): 0.02 M.

(a) almost complete, (b) preserved in non-joining pieces. Bronze.

Two small bronze rings of thin sheet metal. Undecorated.

COMMENTARY - BIBLIOGRAPHY: Unpublished.
Bronze finger rings are not encountered very frequently in Athens in the PG period, even if this observation is based on the small number of the published examples to date. See *Kerameikos* I, 85 and Styrenius 1967, 109.

P.G.K.

15   IRON PIN
Beginning of 10th c. B.C.

INV. NO. M 2459.
PRES.L. 0.071 M.

Incomplete, preserved in three non-joining parts. Iron.

Small, thin iron pin with widened head in the shape of a nail. Traces of a globule or swelling are not preserved, in order to determine the precise form of the shank.

COMMENTARY - BIBLIOGRAPHY: Unpublished.
This type of fibulae is appropriate for early periods, but also survived into a later period and is chiefly found in Attica (Athens) as well as Euboea (Lefkandi), and elsewhere. For Athens (Kerameikos) see Styrenius 1967, 70 (tombs S 113, PG 22 and PG 23). For Euboea (Lefkandi) see *Lefkandi* I, 246, pl. 242:G. and pl. 250:7 (9th c. B.C.).

P.G.K.

LATE PROTO-GEOMETRIC BURIAL

8. ACROPOLIS Station. Tomb 84, with the ash-urn, during excavation.

Tomb 84/Pyre 8

The burial, which constituted a four-sided pit and the ash-urn, was found at the northern edge of the excavation of the Makryianni plot and was investigated by archaeologist Elena Kassotaki in October 1995 (Trench Δ 22, date of excavation (a) 12-13/10/95 and (b) 31/10 and 1/11/95).

The pit, opened in the soft bedrock (l. 0.80, w. 0.60 m.), was found full of burnt earth, scorched stones and charcoal, which testified that the pyre was lit in the pit itself, probably, however, not for the body of the deceased, but for the grave offerings: found scattered in the earth of the pyre were a trefoil-mouthed oenochoe, a spherical pyxis, a handmade jug, a bell-shaped jointed toy, a clay spindle whorl and a bronze ring. The ash-urn, an amphora with horizontal belly handles, had been placed vertically at the southeastern edge of the pit, inside a circular receptacle dug in the floor. A double-handled skyphos with conical foot had been used as a lid for the vase, while two slab-like stones protected the two

vases. Similarly, stones held the ash-urn in place, which apart from the ash contained a pair of iron fibulae. Study of the preserved bones by Professor Th. Pitsios, allowed their attribution to an adult woman over 30 years of age, and this is in accordance with the finds from the pyre and the use of the belly-handled amphora as an ash-urn.

The important number of similar examples of tombs from the Kerameikos and other Athenian cemeteries strengthens the belief that, during the PG period in Athens, funeral customs and burial habits were uniform and very widely spread. The custom of cremating the dead and collecting the ashes inside a vase, which was also known even in prehistoric Greece, was particularly widespread during the Early Iron Age (PG and Geometric periods), at the same time as the habit of inhumation. Cremation was carried out on males and females, who probably belonged to distinguished families, to judge from the fact that it was an expensive custom which demanded elaborate preparation.

Tomb 84/pyre 8 was found north of tombs 90 and 91 and tomb 85/pyre 9. This concentration of tombs, which belong to the same advanced PG period, allows one to assume that a common earth mound would have covered them, although this was not verified, probably due to repeated later disturbance of the area. Tomb 84, judging from the grave gifts, can be attributed chronologically to the end of the PG period and is a typical example for the time both in terms of funeral customs and the objects which accompanied the dead woman in life.

BIBLIOGRAPHY: Snodgrass 1971, 147ff.; Desborough 1972, 268ff.; Kurtz - Boardman 1994, 34ff.

P.G.K.

16 AMPHORA (ASH-URN)
End of 10th c. B.C.

INV. NO. M 2462.
H. 0.36, B.D. 0.105, MAX.D. 0.25, M.D. 0.17 M.

Complete. Limited damage on the shoulder and in the region of the belly. Fine pink clay. Decoration in fugitive dark paint. Horizontal bands on belly. The body, bi-conical in profile, stands on a small ring base and the vase is characterised by its wide, relatively low neck. The decoration of the amphora is simple since the vase is almost dark monochrome, apart from the ground-coloured belly zone, which is bounded by bands above and below, as well as three bands on the neck. The handles are painted black.

COMMENTARY - BIBLIOGRAPHY: Unpublished.
The small size of the amphora, the extensive amount of paint covering the body and the absolutely balanced structure of the vase are elements which allow the vessel to be classified as in the advanced Attic Proto-Geometric style. This shape of vase began in Attica and was widely used in female cremations, as the typical vessel for holding the ashes, during the entire PG period. The ash of the deceased and a pair of iron fibulae were found inside the vase. See Desborough 1952, 20ff. (esp. Class II).

P.G.K.

17 SKYPHOS (USED AS LID OF THE ASH-URN AMPHORA)
End of 10th c. B.C.

INV. NO. M 2463.
H. 0.146, B.D. 0.062, M.D. 0.165 M.

Complete. Fine, light brown clay. Decoration black, with flaking on the interior and on the outside of the foot. It has a hemispherical body and stands on a high conical foot which is joined with a moulded ring (one particularity not often met). The horizontal roll handles turn outwards as does the vertical rim slightly.
Inside, the vase was solid painted black, while outside it has decoration chiefly in the body zone: on both sides of the vase, a pair of nine concentric circles frame a schematic, cross-hatched quadrilateral which is bound by three thin vertical lines.

The rim has a black line while one clay-coloured line accentuates the foot. The handles are highlighted by a black line and the lower part of the vase and foot are monochrome. The concentric circles are compass drawn.

COMMENTARY - BIBLIOGRAPHY: Unpublished.
The shape and decoration are often met in Attica, as well as in other Greek regions although there they are considered Attic imports and characterise the advanced PG period. It is a typical drinking vessel and, in this instance, was used as a lid for the ash-urn. See Desborough 1952, 77ff. (esp. Class IIa, 82ff.).

P.G.K.

16, 17

18 TREFOIL-MOUTHED OENOCHOE
End of 10th c. B.C.

INV. NO. M 2464.
H. 0.195, B.D. 0.054, MAX.D. 0.109, M.D. 0.056 M.

Joined from many pieces with gaps on the shoulder and belly. Fine pinkish clay. Black, lustrous paint. The oenochoe has a high neck, trefoil spout and vertical strap handle. The body is almost spherical and stands on a low conical base.

The decoration is standard for the type, since the vase is solid painted with the exception of the zone in the middle of the vase where two narrow parallel bands surround a ground-coloured zone with a zigzag, scarcely visible today. The back of the handle is decorated with horizontal lines.

COMMENTARY - BIBLIOGRAPHY: Unpublished.
It was found in the pyre. The shape of the vase and its typical decoration with lustrous black paint is appropriate for the advanced Attic Proto-Geometric style. See Desborough 1952, 45ff. (esp. Class B.2, 48ff.).

P.G.K.

19 PYXIS WITH LID
End of 10th c. B.C.

INV. NO. M 2465A-B.
H. 0.108, B.D. 0.047, MAX.D. 0.105, M.D. 0.084 M.

Joined from fragments with small gaps in the lower part of the body. The lid is also mended. Rather fine, terracotta coloured clay. Brown-black paint. Spherical pyxis with lid, standing on a low conical base and with a sharply everted rim. The lid rests on the lip and has two small holes opposite each other for attaching it to the vase.

The pyxis is solid painted with black paint, apart from a zone on the belly where there is a ground coloured band decorated with a double zigzag, between narrow parallel lines. The lid is solid painted, apart from three thin concentric circles on the periphery and a cross and lines on the knob.

COMMENTARY - BIBLIOGRAPHY: Unpublished.
It was found in the pyre. The vase is a typical Attic product of the middle to late PG periods and was probably used to hold cosmetics or jewellery. See Desborough 1952, 106ff.

P.G.K.

20 HANDMADE JUG
End of 10th c. B.C

INV. NO. M 2466.
H. 0.145, B.D. 0.055, M.D. 0.095 M.

Mended and missing parts of the belly and lip. Coarse brown clay with inclusions and mica. It has traces of intense burning in the region of the belly. Spherical body and flat base. The mouth is broad and lip slightly everted. The vertical strap handle sprouts from the lip and ends at the start of the belly.

The vase is unpainted, with external burnishing and was found incomplete inside the pyre.

COMMENTARY - BIBLIOGRAPHY: Unpublished.
Handmade pottery is not inappropriate for the PG period, especially in its middle and late stages and is often found in female graves. It is not known, however, whether it was made in Attica, since a great diffusion of similar vases – cooking vessels – is observed in Thessaly, the Peloponnese, Euboea and elsewhere. For similar from the Kerameikos see *Kerameikos* V$_1$, pl. 154-155. From Lefkandi, Euboea see *Lefkandi* I, 342-343, fig. 20.

P.G.K.

18

19

20

21 BRONZE FINGER RING
End of 10th c. B.C.

INV. NO. M 2467.
D. 0.026 M.

Complete, restored. Bronze.
Bronze link-like ring.

COMMENTARY - BIBLIOGRAPHY: Unpublished.
It was found in the pyre. The rarity of rings and particularly bronze has been noted in Athenian Proto-Geometric tombs, in contrast to the preceding late Mycenaean and following Geometric times, a fact which can, perhaps, be due to local customs and not to a paucity of metal. For the rarity of rings see Desborough 1972, 139-140.

P.G.K.

22-23 PAIR OF PINS
End of 10th c. B.C.

INV. NOS. (A): M 2470, (B): M 2471.
(A) L. 0.325, D. OF GLOBE 0.018 M.
(B) L. 0.245, D. OF GLOBE 0.018 M.

Generally good state of preservation, but heavy corrosion does not allow probable engraved decoration to be discerned. Iron and bronze.
Two almost complete pins, though of unequal length. The thin shaft ends at the top with a small, decorative disc while the upper part has a globe of bronze.

COMMENTARY - BIBLIOGRAPHY: Unpublished.
Pins would have been used to fix the clothing of the deceased in place at shoulder height, before the cremation. They were found inside the ash-urn. The simultaneous use of two metals – iron and bronze – on the same object, which is found in quite a number of examples of pins from Athenian cemeteries of the PG period, must be attributed to a phenomenon of fashion, rather than any other reasons, just like the rarity of bronze. See Desborough 1972, 141, 296ff., fig. 33.

P.G.K.

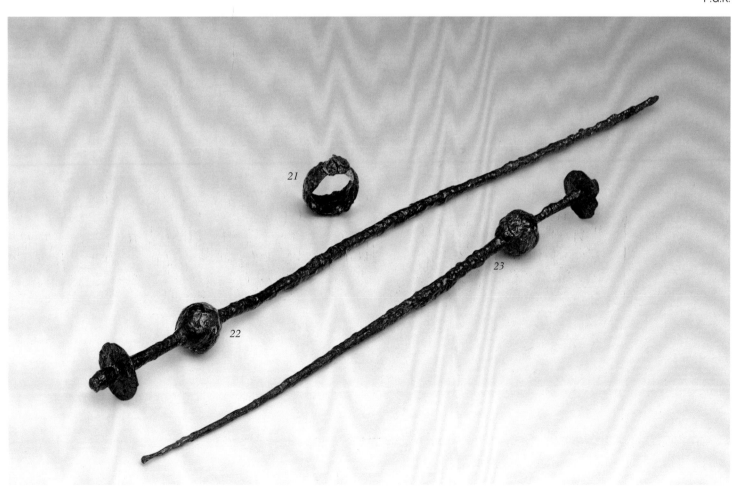

24 HANDMADE DOLL
End of 10th c. B.C.

INV. NO. M 2469.
H. 0.08, MAX.D. 0.06 M.

Complete. The body joined from fragments, the movable lower extremities are
missing and it is damaged. Fine clay, grey
on exterior and pink on interior.
Bell-shaped, handmade, small clay doll,
model of schematic female figure, as is
clear from the breasts. The features of the
bird-shaped head are incised, while the
decoration of the robe is imprinted (circles, parallel lines and rows of little lines).
Vertical piercing hole on inside of the
neck, for suspension, and small perforations on the sides of the body for attaching the movable lower bits, now missing.

COMMENTARY - BIBLIOGRAPHY: Unpublished.
It was found in the pyre. This type of jointed toy is
found in certain Proto-Geometric tombs in Attica, as
well as at Lefkandi, Euboea, chiefly in female infant
burials of the advanced PG period. In these two
examples, it is considered an imported form, although
the provenance is not yet known. For comparable
finds from the Kerameikos see *Kerameikos* IV, pl. 31
(from tombs 33 and 48). Also see Desborough 1972,
412ff., fig. 15. From Nea Ionia, Attica, see Smithson
1961, 172, pl. 30:54. From Lefkandi, Euboea, see
Lefkandi I, 334, pl. 137 (Tomb P. 22:30) and *Lefkandi* III,
pl. 72 and 107 (Tomb T. 74:11).

P.G.K.

25 CLAY SPINDLE WHORL
End of 10th c. B.C.

INV. NO. M 2468.
H. 0.025, MAX.D. 0.035 M.

Part of the circumference missing. Clay,
grey outside, pink on interior. Handmade
spherical spindle whorls with five excres-
cences and a big hole in the centre. The
spindle whorl is unpainted and is embellished with a series of impressed dots.

COMMENTARY - BIBLIOGRAPHY: Unpublished.
It was found in the pyre. Similar spindle whorls have
been found in female and infant graves in Attica and at
Lefkandi, Euboea, of advanced PG date, but as with the
handmade, jointed toy, the provenance is not known.
From Nea Ionia, Attica, see Smithson 1961, 170-173.
From Lefkandi, Euboea, see *Lefkandi* I, 83, pl. 125
(Tomb P. 3).

P.G.K.

25

24

26 PROCHOUS WITH CUTAWAY SPOUT
2nd half of 15th - 1st half of 14th c. B.C.

INV. NO. M 2450.
H. 0.278, MAX.D. 0.27, M.D. 0.094, B.D. 0.061 M.

Incomplete, joined from many fragments; a large part of neck and parts of the body are missing and have been restored. Red clay with grey core in places. The body is bi-conical. Vertical strap handle. The lip of the vase cut away. The neck, which broadens towards the top, has concave walling. The base is not differentiated from the body. The underside is very curved with the result that the vase is supported with difficulty and is unstable.

The intense burnishing of the surface gives the vase a metallic look. This impression is supplemented by the rings which have been formed on the base and walling of the neck. The jug appears "smoked" as large parts of its surface are blackened. A hollowing at the point of the maximum diameter is probably due to finger pressure before the vase was fired, or to contact with another vase during the firing in the pottery kiln. One other hollowing at another point of the maximum diameter is lost due to the fragmentary state of preservation of the vase.

COMMENTARY - BIBLIOGRAPHY: Unpublished.

Twelve vases from wells E and Z of the south slope of the Acropolis (see introductory text for the deposit) comprise the immediate parallels for this shape. Vase no. 26 belongs to the larger examples of the shape and may in fact be larger than the examples from the wells of the south slope since its height (0.278 m.) beats the tallest of these which reaches 0.268 m. It belongs to the type with a bi-conical body but also to the type with a ring at the base of the neck. It was a pouring vessel and belongs, with kylix no. 27, to undecorated, wheel-made, Mycenaean tableware, the surface of which is smeared and carefully burnished; for this see Mountjoy 1995, 25: Acropolis Burnished Ware. For a full treatment of this particular shape and its close parallels see Mountjoy 1981, 53, fig. 19, no. 217, pl. 17c, 18a.

M.M.

REFUSE DEPOSIT OF THE MYCENAEAN PERIOD

Apart from the funerary material found on the Makryianni plot, material of a settlement character comes from the same site, dating to various periods to which architectural remains – walls and structures – cannot be attributed. For the present exhibition, a closed group of the Mycenaean period has been selected which can be dated to LH IIB/IIIA1: it comprises pottery and certain other finds which made up the fill of a dump cut into the bedrock. Here is a comment on three vases of different shape which were found amongst others and are typical examples of this settlement group.

This dump had the shape of a rectangular pit, perhaps of an older abandoned tomb as is indicated by the small cuttings in its rim, probably to fit cross beams of a roof. The material which fills the pit is made up of a great amount of pottery (some almost complete vessels and sherds of others), but also small finds, animal bones and shells, a favourite kind of food for the Mycenaeans. The closest parallels for the pottery of the store come from four large well shafts found by Nikolaos Platon in 1963-64 on the south slope of the Acropolis, immediately behind the Portico of Eumenes. The difference with those wells is that the dump of the Makryianni plot is much smaller and was not used as a well. In common with those, however, no stratigraphical differences were able to be distinguished within the fill, whilst it is quite certain that the material from the five locations is domestic and comes from some clearance after the end of the LH IIB/IIIA1 period (LH IIB and LH IIIA1 are considered absolutely continuous and it has not yet proved possible to differentiate the two). For the discovery of pottery of this group in the region of the Acropolis see Πλάτων 1964, 30-32 and *idem* 1965, 28-32. For full publication of the material from the Acropolis wells see Mountjoy 1981. For reference to the same material see Mountjoy 1995, under the heading for the LH IIIA1 period, 22ff. and fig. 23, 27, 30 as well as p. 25 where another well is referred to which was also discovered behind the Portico of Eumenes and on the same line as the finds of N. Platon, that had also been used as a dump, likewise for LH IIIA1 material.

M.M.

27 KYLIX
2nd half of 15th - 1st half of 14th c. B.C.

INV. NO. M 2448.
H. 0.091, B.D. 0.049, M.D. 0.111 M.

Incomplete, joined from many fragments; missing small part of body and parts of the rim, which have been restored. Light brown-red clay. Deep, hemispherical body. One vertical strap handle, with central groove, starting from the edge of the rim and ending at the point of maximum diameter of the belly. The rim is sloping and everted. The stem is low with concave walling. The discoid base is flat underneath.

The surface of the vase has been burnished outside and in. Differentiation in colour from redder to a more pale indicates the existence of a slip which at certain points has probably disappeared.

COMMENTARY - BIBLIOGRAPHY: Unpublished.

Kylix no. 27 is a drinking vessel and has many parallels in the four Acropolis wells. It is part of the Mycenaean, undecorated tableware repertoire, which is wheelmade, given a light slip and then carefully burnished; see Mountjoy 1995, 25: Acropolis Burnished Ware. For a full treatment of this particular shape, single-handled or double-handled, and its close parallels, see Mountjoy 1981, 55, fig. 8 (no. 52), 10 (no. 85), 20 (nos. 232-239), 28 (nos. 378-379, 392), pl. 8b.

M.M.

28 HANDLELESS CUP
2nd half of 15th - 1st half of 14th c. B.C.

INV. NO. M 2449.
H. 0.073, MAX.D. 0.139, B.D. 0.041 M.

Mended; small part of lip missing. Pale pink clay. Deep, conical body. The mouth turns slightly inwards. The undeveloped ring base is differentiated. The underside of the base has grooving as well as marks indicating the use of string during manufacture to remove the vase from the wheel. The vase sits at an angle due the uneven underside of the base. Very rough (unburnished) external surface. Better finished inside.

COMMENTARY - BIBLIOGRAPHY: Unpublished.

This shape is a common one and finds its immediate parallels in all four wells of the south slope of the Acropolis, either as a whole shape or in the form of sherds. It belongs to a category of pottery characterised as rough and differs from Mycenaean tableware in the treatment of the surface which remains unburnished. Most vases of this category are similar handleless conical cups without an obvious rim and with an incurving mouth. For a full treatment of the particular shape and its close parallels see Mountjoy 1981, 57, fig. 10 (nos. 92, 94, 97), 21 (nos. 245-247), pl. 9b-c.

M.M.

28

26

27

29 FRAGMENT OF DORIC CORNICE FROM THE
ENTABLATURE OF THE PORTICO (STOA) OF EUMENES
200-150 B.C.

INV. NOS. M 1226 AND M 1212.
PRES.L. 0.84, W. 0.22, PRES.H. 0.12 M.

Fragmentarily preserved piece of Doric cornice from the entablature, joined from two pieces and made of white Pergamene marble. Part of the front side and of the decorated underside (soffit) is preserved. The front side is flat, slightly concave towards the bottom. The soffit preserves two channels and two mutules with twelve guttae arranged in two rows. It is difficult to find out the kind of tools which had been used due to the covering of this architectural limb with plaster.

ple of a portico next to a theatre, it was used as a hall for the spectators until the 3rd c. A.D. when it was destroyed by fire, probably during the Herulian invasion (A.D. 267). Its material, grey white marble and limestone, was used in the construction of the Valerian wall as well as in the broader region of the Acropolis. No-one can now see the arched buttress which was used as a support wall for the Portico. The great height to which it is preserved is due to the incorporation of the monument in the defensive system of the Late Roman walls which prevented the material from being stolen and continued to exist in the century which followed. In more recent years, the Turkish bastion, the "Serpentzes", sat above the arches of the Portico. It is worth noting that it is thought to have been a monument to a large extent, previously built in Pergamon, as the marble used, the construction details, the general conception and the shape of the masonry witness.

29

Marks from a claw chisel and a pointed chisel can be made out in the channels.

COMMENTARY - BIBLIOGRAPHY: Unpublished.
It comes from the Portico of Eumenes which the King of Pergamon, Eumenes II (197-159 B.C.), donated to Athens. An imposing, oblong, two-storied building, it is among the most important monuments on the south slope of the Acropolis, and mixes the Doric and Ionic styles, with rare capitals of Pergamene type. It is situated between the Theatre of Dionysos and the Odeion of Herodes Atticus, with which it communicated directly to the west when built in A.D. 165 at the latest. A typical exam-

For the Portico of Eumenes see Dörpfeld 1888, 100-102; Βερσάκης 1912, 173-182; Viale 192/22, 13-32; Polacco 1954, 719-724; Πλάτων 1965, 22-34; Travlos 1971, 523-526; Κορρές 1980, 18-20; *idem* 1984, 201-207; Μακρή - Τσάκος - Βαβυλοπούλου 1987-88, 329-363; Παπαχατζής 1974.

E.K.

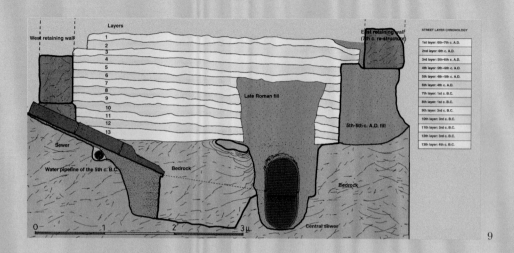

9

CITY ROAD NETWORK:
STREET I IN MAKRYIANNI SITE

The archaeological investigation of the Makryianni site produced some interesting facts about the ancient city's road network in the area south of the Acropolis. The information obtained is of particular significance because our knowledge of the ancient technique of building roads, of establishing their course and laying it out, and of vehicles and the harness of pack-animals, is far from complete. Research so far has mostly dealt with the Roman road network.

The lack of a co-ordinated effort on the part of city-states, the peculiarity of the terrain, and settlement in coastal areas did not favour the growth of a considerable road network similar to the Roman one, which was noted for its paved surfaces, road-metal and large technical works.

Special attention was paid in antiquity to roads serving the carriage of merchandise and affording access to sanctuaries (Sacred Ways). The Sacred Way was the main thoroughfare in the road plan of a city in Classical Greece. It started out from a gate – one of the city exits – and ended in the forecourt of a sanctuary. Divinities such as Hermes, Hekate, Apollo Agyieus and Artemis were considered protectors of roads. The roads themselves were held to be sacred, accounting for the custom of burying the dead either side of them. The carriage roads of Athens (*amaxitoi*, chariot or wagon roads; *leophoroi*, thoroughfares; *laophoroi*, highways; *eftheiai*, "straights", grid-roads), dirt roads without paving or lighting (as both Plutarch and Aristophanes point out), followed the natural lie of the land and were not everywhere the same width and seldom allowed two wagons to pass each other with ease. Though we know very little about the maintenance of roads, their systematic upkeep has been established as a result of excavating them. Also we learn from writers that among the duties of the *astynomoi*, the city magistrates, and later of the *agoranomoi*, the clerks of the market-place, was the obligation to see to it that roads were kept clean by the *koprologoi*, the "dung-collectors", and in good repair by the road-makers and state slaves. The minimum width was laid down by law and the law governed a person's freedom to display goods where in so doing he did not obstruct the traffic. The owners of roadside land were responsible for surfacing, or the cost of surfacing, that section of the road which was their frontage with it. The magistrates were obliged to exact the expenses and to fine offenders.

Street works were normally limited to surfacing or paving the route and in some instances to digging out the wheel tracks for the greater convenience of communication which was either on foot or with pack animals or wagons, usually two-wheeled. Wagons were pulled by oxen, horses, donkeys or mules, wearing not metal shoes but a kind of grass shoe. Wagon or chariot wheel ruts, a basic feature of ancient roads, were either natural, the result of use, or man-made, cut into the rock, particularly on difficult stretches. In such cases they served as tracks or ruts that guided the carts, mainly those whose front wheels were higher

than the frame itself. Using them prevented the animals from slipping. The depth of these ruts was greater on downhill slopes, possibly because of brake action on the wheels. They were usually only 5 to 7 cm. deep and from 10 to 15 cm. wide, while it is clear from the distance between them that the length of the vehicles' axis was 1.40 m. The initial depth and width cannot be ascertained on account of the wear and tear arising from use. The gradient is often in excess of 1:10, while in difficult places the transverse inclination (camber) of wheel-tracks is very great.

A road network calls for a strong centralised authority to undertake and implement its construction and maintenance. It is likely that one of the six roads discovered in the excavation for the M.R.A. on the Makryianni site, Street I, was the subject of such a state initiative. The road formed a junction with the main road artery in the area (Street IV) which, proceeding from the city, led to a gate in the fortification wall surrounding the city (Phaleron Gate). Street I linked Street IV to the Sanctuary of Dionysos to the north, while to the south it crossed another road (Street II). The finds suggest that Street I was in use from the middle of the 4th c. B.C. till the 7th c. A.D. The opening of it and its route are to be associated probably with the rebuilding of the Theatre of Dionysos, a project attributed to the orator Lycurgus which occurred in about 330 B.C. Research established that the road was constructed over an earlier one of unknown width and running in the same direction. Some lengths of a water conduit of circular section, connected with this earlier road and laid in a ditch dug in the bedrock inside the western retaining wall of Street I, have been preserved. The conduit (no. 30), dating to the 5th c. B.C., is an important find because it is proof of an activity in the public domain, related perhaps to a systematic attempt to plan the layout of the area.

The bed of Street I is 4 m. wide and lies in a NW-SE direction; it can be traced for about 40 m. on the ex-

9. ACROPOLIS Station. Section of the ancient Street I, noting the successive street layers, the embankments and the central sewer.

10. ACROPOLIS Station. View of Street I from the North. The excavation recorded a series of extended works on different parts of the street at various stages, for the maintenance of the central sewer.

cavation site, while other lengths of it have been discovered to the north in earlier excavations. In the course of its excavation, between thirteen and sixteen surface levels were identified and removed (fig. 9). These levels correspond with chronological phases of the use, maintenance and repair of the road. They were only partially preserved because they had been broken up by ditches dug for the laying of lateral drainage conduits, by foundation trenches of later retaining walls, natural deterioration and the large central drainage culvert running the full length of the road (fig. 10). The depth of these levels varied between 0.07 and 0.23 m. They consisted mainly of ground rock, clay,

11. ACROPOLIS Station. View of Street I from the North.
A number of side drains, leading to the central sewer, are visible.

12. ACROPOLIS Station. Ground plan of Street I and front views
of its embankments.

sand, shingle, small stones, cinders, finely ground tiles and pottery fragments. These last, together with the coins so often found on roads, help to date the several surface levels. The earliest such level of Street I (4th c. B.C.) was laid over a very solid substratum 0.20 m. in depth made of well-compacted earth, shingle and vase sherds. Most of the levels bore traces of wheel tracks which had been repeatedly repaired, a measure made necessary by the flow of rain-water or by domestic or workshop use causing wear and tear that endangered the passage of pedestrians and vehicles. Such recurrent repairs are evidence of a much frequented roadway.

Street I was bounded to the east and west by the retaining walls, only partially preserved, in which different building and chronological phases were recognised (fig. 12). The walls were constructed largely of conglomerate stone but also of hewn masonry and other, re-used, material. Their width varied between 0.60 and 0.80 m. and they were preserved to a height of about

11

0.70 m. Their rough-and-ready foundations consisted of irregular stones of different sizes. These walls simultaneously served as the sides of the structures that stood beside the road and marked the building line. Thus the variations in the materials and the manner of constructing the retaining walls allow one to reconstruct the boundaries of individual properties. The walls are penetrated every so often by vertical pipes, either stone-built or of terracotta, which carried waste waters from adjacent houses and workshops to the central drain (fig. 11).

The large central drain was found to run the entire length of the road passing across the Makryianni site. Its assumed extension to the north-west must connect it to the large drainage conduit of the Theatre of Dionysos, while its likely extension to the south-east connects it probably with the channel that is marked on the topographical drawing by Judeich. During the first stage of its construction the drain consisted of horseshoe-shaped "saddle" tiles placed upside down one on top of another. In the course of its long life it underwent many repairs for which a variety of material was used: walling constructed of baked clay bricks or stone shingles with a strong mortar for the lateral walls and re-used material for the capping, consisting mainly of portions of architectural members. In several instances large transport amphorae were placed over or next to the drain; acting as dampers they protected it from the high pressures to which it was subjected.

BIBLIOGRAPHY: For the road from the Theatre of Dionysos to the Phaleron Gate see Τσάκος 1986, 12; Judeich 1931, 178-179; Travlos 1971, 329-422. For road-making in general see Δεσποτόπουλος 1940, 5-30; Pritchett 1980, 143-195; Πίκουλας 1991, 23-25; Young 1956, 94-97. Sources: Arist., *Athenian Constitution*, 424; Pl., *Laws*, 6, 760B-763C; Plut., *Perikles*, 5, 2; Aristoph., *Wasps*, ll. 219, 248-257.

E.K.

12

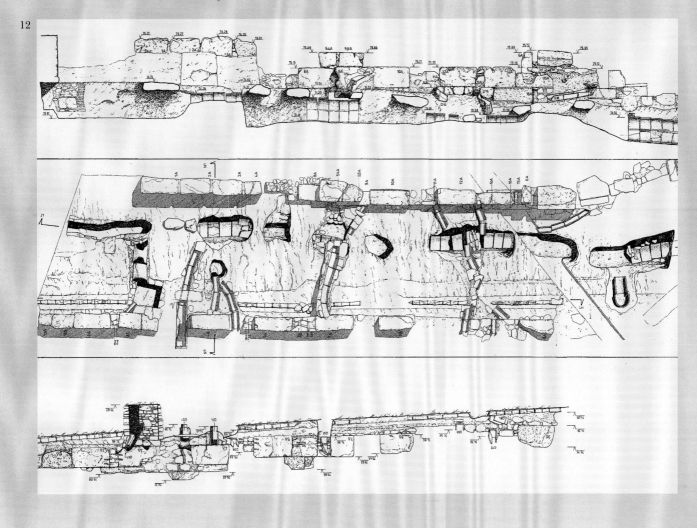

30 CLAY WATER-SUPPLY PIPES
5th c. B.C.

INV. NOS. M 2564A-Γ AND M 2565A-B.
L. 0.57, D. 0.108 M.

They are preserved whole but damaged; in two examples, parts of the attachment ring and rim are missing. Sediments testify to their use. Brownish red clay with inclusions. Unpainted. A brown-red band is painted around the middle and at the two ends of each pipe. Two have been joined together. The body is cylindrical with the greatest diameter roughly in the centre, where it begins to narrow bit by bit towards the point of attachment which is indicated by a narrower external cylinder. The ends of the body are fixed by a moulded ring. Most of the pipes have an ovoid hole for cleaning, shut by a lid; two have been detached, while three remain sealed.

COMMENTARY - BIBLIOGRAPHY: Unpublished.
These are, water-supply drainage pipes which were found in their original position, in a cutting in the bed-rock along the length of ancient Street I, which ran from the Theatre of Dionysos to the Phaleron Gate. For water-supply drainage see Tölle-Kastenbein 1994 and Lang 1968.

S.M.

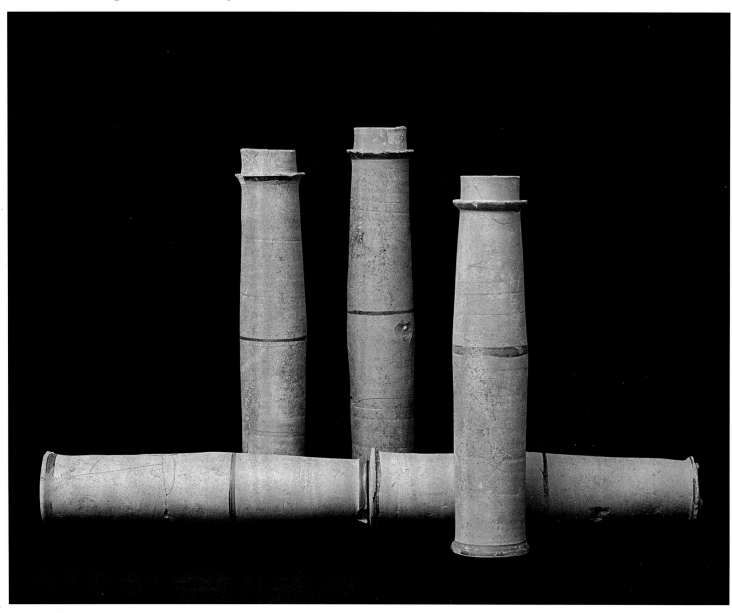

30

WELLS AND SYSTEM OF WATER CISTERNS

The particular geographic-topographic location of the site SE of the Acropolis, at the junction of at least two major arterial roads, draws attention to a powerful, if not comercial, at least residential presence in the area. An indication of this is a wide water-supply network consisting of a very large number of wells – no less than thirty wells cut into the bedrock, as well as the siting of five pear-shaped cisterns with linings of hydraulic cement, for collecting the rain-water. Moving away from the area of the Makryianni plot, following the passage of the underground digger, known among the Athenians as the "Metro-mole", a considerable number of wells cut into the bedrock were located with the same frequency as the ones on the plot, both in a northerly direction towards the SYNTAGMA Station and south towards the SYNGROU-FIX Station (fig. 14-15).

The cisterns, found in the basements of houses and buildings in general, collected water from the roofs sloping towards the interior courtyard, where the well of access for the cistern is also found. Usually, a second shaft acts as another access point, probably for drawing the contents (fig. 13).

The need to increase the capacity of the cisterns unifies other such systems with underground tunnels, likewise cut into the chalk, though normally without the cement lining. Such a complex is located in the excavation for the M.R.A.,

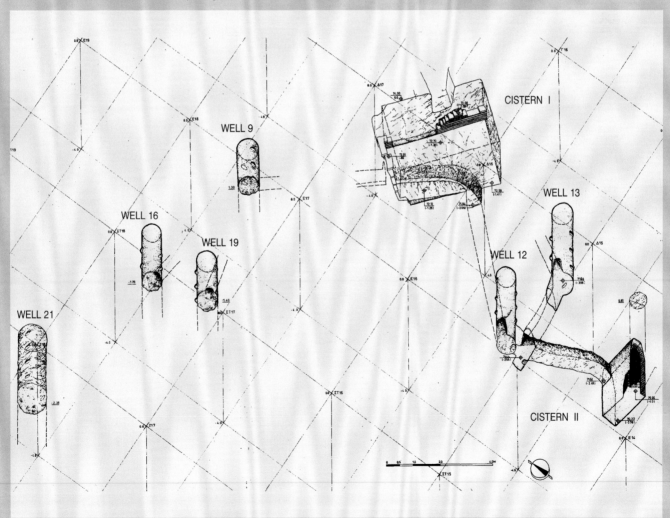

13. ACROPOLIS Station. A reconstruction of the cistern network when fully operational.

13

on the Makryianni plot, in the region that is bounded by ancient Streets I and IV.

It comprises three different, at first autonomous, systems of cisterns, most probably of Hellenistic date, which were joined up during the Late Roman - Early Christian period, by means of an underground tunnel, with one large built cistern shaped like a parallelogram. The connection probably happened in order to supply the built cistern with water, indicating that the cistern was still in use at that time.

Reference is made to the system which consists of pear-shaped cistern VII and well 9, to the system discovered in the south consisting of two shallow wells 12 and 13 which are joined by a tunnel and, finally, to the system of cistern II whose access well has not been found, probably due to its location outside the excavation area.

These three early autonomous systems worked throughout the Roman period, collecting rain-water in three different houses or, more likely, one settlement complex. The systems are reinforced with very strong hydraulic mortar, whilst the connecting tunnel is simply cut into the chalk, with a height of about 1 m., width of 0.70 m., and a total length of about 10 m. Of the built cistern, only the bottom with the cutting for the passage of the connecting tunnel and some of the side walls built of brick slabs were preserved. Very likely, the whole system was united in construction with a large paved hall located to the north, this also dating to the Late Roman - Early Christian period.

The levelling of the surface of the ground to create a Byzantine cemetery strengthens our information concerning the intended use of the system of cisterns and the identity of the owners of the land.

After studying the entire system, we observe the special need for water in the Late Roman and Early Christian periods in the area.

S.M.

14. ACROPOLIS Station. Pottery from well 68, subsequent to its collapse during the construction of a trial tunnel.

15. ACROPOLIS Station. The contents of the collapsed well 68, in the tunnel built for the installation of the "Metro-mole".

14

of the vessel is monochrome, apart from a zone with thin perimetric bands at the point where the handle projects. The back of the handle is decorated with successive horizontal lines. Broad band, applied carelessly, where the handle ends, outside and inside and on its uppermost inner part.

COMMENTARY - BIBLIOGRAPHY: Unpublished.
Trefoil-mouthed oenochoe no. 31 is placed in the category of Sub-Geometric oenochoae, which appear in the late 8th and span the whole of the 7th c. B.C. They comprise oenochoae of small size, carelessly made and painted compared with vases of the Geometric period. For Sub-Geometric oenochoae see *Agora* VIII, 37, no. 58, pl. 4, similar in decoration. For Sub-Geometric vases in general see Young 1939, 194-197.
The rather squat body of the oenochoe, the zone with bands where the handle projects, the careless application of the paint and the accompanying finds in well 20, allow the vase to be dated to the end of the 8th c. B.C. For parallels in terms of type see *Kerameikos* V₁, pl. 81, tomb 100 (late 8th c. B.C.); Brann 1961a, 126, no. M6, pl. 16; Young 1942, 25, 50, no. 47.5, fig. 1 (c. 700 B.C.), 40, no. 78.1, fig. 24 (3rd quarter of 7th c. B.C.).

M.-Ch.M.

32 HANDMADE TREFOIL-MOUTHED OENOCHOE
End of LG period

INV. NO. M 2480.
PRES.H. 0.113, MAX.D. 0.15 M.

Mended. Base missing as well as part of the body and mouth and the handle. Numerous gaps and chips and particularly many salts. Clay light pink at the core and pale yellow on the exterior. Pale yellow slip. The body of the oenochoe is spherical and slightly squat. The neck is short and cylindrical, slightly curved and ending in a trefoil lip.

COMMENTARY - BIBLIOGRAPHY: Unpublished.
The trefoil-mouthed oenochoe is of the Argive Monochrome ceramic group. This technique, which first occurs in Argos in about 800 B.C., spread out in stages to Corinth and Athens. To this Argive Monochrome ceramic group belong domestic vases of good quality with thin walls, such as oenochoae, aryballoi and kantharoi. Often, the surface of the vase is polished with a pointed tool. Some of the vases have incised decorative motifs. Vases of the Monochrome Argive ceramic group have been found in many parts of Greece and are dated to the 2nd half of the 8th c. and the 7th c. B.C. The finds from well 20 accompanying the oenochoe, which are dated to the late 8th c. B.C., allow the vase to be dated to the same period.
For Argive Monochrome pottery in general see Coldstream 1977, 111; Snodgrass 1971, 95-96, no. 51; Caskey - Amandry 1952, 202-205, pl. 57-58; Young 1939, 199; Pfuhl 1923, 82-83; *Perachora* II, 314-317, nos. 3299, 3303, pl. 125 (similar shape); Courbin 1966, 29ff., 467ff. For parallels of the late 8th c. B.C. see *Kerameikos* V₁, no. 297, pl. 156; Desborough 1954, 265, nos. 53-335, pl. 46; Pfuhl 1903, 28, 211, pl. XXXVIII, 1. For parallels in the 7th c. B.C. see *Agora* VIII, 28, 58, no. 235, pl. 13; Young 1942, 28, no. 27.6, fig. 3 and 30, no. 70.1, fig. 8; *Corinth* VII₁, 70, no. 301, pl. 37.

M.-Ch.M.

33 KOTYLE
End of LG period

INV. NO. M 2478.
H. 0.083, B.D. 0.042, M.D. 0.103 M.

Joined and restored; one handle is missing. Light pinkish brown clay, self slipped. Paint varying from black to brown, thin and fugitive in places. The base of the vase is flat with a slight ring. The body is deep and semi-ovoid and the lip undefined. A horizontal handle, circular in section, is stuck onto the upper part of the body.

Underside of base unpainted. The lower half of the vase outside is monochrome. A group of successive thin bands runs round the body up to the height of the handle. Between the handles and on both sides, two groups of vertical stripes frame a central panel with schematised birds which are turned to the right. The panel is delimited on either side by two zigzags of thicker paint, arranged antithetically. The decorative zone is crowned by two thin bands. The back of the handle is decorated with a series of vertical lines and the central part of its upper surface with a semicircular band. The interior of the vase is monochrome apart from a thin reserved zone around the lip.

Nos. 31-34 come from well 20 on the Makryianni plot, west of ancient Street I. The shaft, 1 m. in diameter, and depth about 5.15 m., was cut into the bedrock and was filled in a single chronological phase, as is clear from the sherds of the same pots in different levels. The pottery belongs mostly to the LG period, although a few prehistoric and Proto-Geometric sherds were found. The shaft chiefly contained finds of domestic use, probably coming from some nearby settlement complex.

M.-Ch.M.

31 TREFOIL-MOUTHED OENOCHOE
End of LG period

INV. NO. M 2479.
H. 0.124, B.D. 0.077, MAX.D. 0.106 M.

Mended and restored; missing part of the lip. Pale brown clay, self slipped. Worn paint, thin in places, varying from black to brown, due to careless application and uneven firing. The base of the vase is flat, rather broad and slightly concave, with an imperfectly formed ring. The body has a squat piriform profile, and ends in a trefoil lip. A strap, high-swung handle sprouts from the lip and ends at the middle of the body.

Underside of base unpainted. The body

COMMENTARY - BIBLIOGRAPHY: Unpublished.

The kotyle is a thin-walled drinking vessel that first appears in Corinth in the PC period and is a development of the MG II skyphos. At first, the body was hemispherical while later it became deeper. Kotyle no. 33 is a product of an Attic workshop as indicated by the reddish clay. The relatively deep body of the vase, its monochrome lower part, the succeeding zone with bands, and the row of schematic birds which decorates the panel, allow the kotyle to be dated to the 4th quarter of the 8th c. B.C.

For examples with an analogous row of birds from Athens, Corinth and the Heraion at Perachora, see Brann 1961a, 140, no. P17, pl. 20; Burr 1933b, 567, 569, no. 102, fig. 26; Young 1939, 146, no. C18, fig. 100; *Corinth* VII₁, 39-40, no. 123, pl. 17; *Perachora* II, 51-53, no. 377, pl. 19, 67-69, pl. 25, 27. In general for a decorative row of birds on a kotyle see Coldstream 1968, 105-107; *Corinth* VII₁, 39, 40; *Perachora* II, 67-69; Cook 1947, 147, fig. 6b, 152-153. For rows of birds on other shapes of vases see *Perachora* II, 69; *Agora* VIII, 43, no. 97, pl. 6; Weinberg 1949, 153, no. 159, pl. 9; *Kerameikos* V₁, no. 5498, pl. 132; Young 1939, 146, 147, no. C19, fig. 103. In general for the development of the kotyle and Attic imitations see *Agora* VIII, 49-50; Coldstream 1968, 87, 105-111; *idem* 1977, 178, 226-228, fig. 55d; Young 1939, 146.

M.-Ch.M.

34 PLATE (PINAKION)
End of LG period

INV. NO. M 2475.
H. 0.05, B.D. 0.073 M.

Mended, preserving 1/4 of the original. Chipped and damaged. Clay light orange-brown, self slipped. Paint worn in places, varying from black to brown and dark brown due to careless application and uneven firing. The base is flat. The profile of the vase, rather curved and gradually widening, ends at a flat everted rim. The decoration on the underside of the much worn base consists of a series of dots, flanked by groups of concentric circles. The motif at the centre of the base is indiscernible. A zone of leaves with triple outline and some with a central stem, decorates the body of the vase. The zone is surrounded on either side by two groups of successive bands running around the body. The two bands near the base are more thickly painted. The motif of running pseudo-spirals is depicted on the outside of the rim. A group of vertical lines on the upper surface of the rim is flanked by two narrow bands that highlight the edges of the rim. The interior of the vase is monochrome, apart from a wide reserved band roughly in the middle of the surface.

COMMENTARY - BIBLIOGRAPHY: Unpublished.

The plate in question is dated to the end of the 8th c. B.C., according to the study of its shape and decoration. Plates of the LG phase have a rather curved profile and the decoration covers the entire surface of the vase. The leaves in the central zone of the body, at first, were fine in outline, while later, at the end of the 8th c. B.C., they were carelessly rendered with a double or triple outline and central stem. For the development of the shape and decoration see Coldstream 1968, 49, 51, 87, pl. 15K; Young 1939, 205, 206, 215; Brann 1961a, 112, no. I 55; Σημαντώνη-Μπουρνιά 1997, 74; Καμπίτογλου 1991, 56. For parallels see *Agora* VIII, 45, 46, no. 114, pl. 42, no. 117, pl. 7; Brann 1961a, 135, no. O34, pl. 21; Young 1939, 30, no. VI 3, pl. 18, 162-163, no. C77, fig. 115; Thompson 1947, 209-210, pl. XLVI:4; Φιλαδελφεύς 1920-21, 135, fig. 4; *Kerameikos* V₁, no. 365, pl. 104.

M.-Ch.M.

31, 33, 32, 34

Towards the edge, thin bands are interrupted by a series of dots and a zigzag line.

COMMENTARY - BIBLIOGRAPHY: Unpublished.
The lid probably comes from a pyxis of the LG period, based on the study of the shape, size and decorative motif. Small sized pyxides of MG evolve into large sized pyxides in the LG I period with curved and vertical walls and rich decoration. Pyxides live on until the LG II period, before they are replaced by the skyphos-pyxis with high rim. In general, for the use and distribution of the pyxis in Geometric times see Bohen 1988, 5-10. For the development of pyxides see Coldstream 1968, 47, 48, 86; *idem* 1977, 153, 155; *Agora* VIII, 60; Young 1939, 200-201. For parallels see *Agora* VIII, 60, no. 253, pl. 15; Young 1939, 117, no. B27, fig. 84; *Kerameikos* V₁, no. 833, pl. 57, no. 338, pl. 59.

cessive oblique lines which cut across or form linear decoration (N's and M's). In the exterior zone of the rim a series of inverted triangles are framed by two pairs of wavy lines. Oblique intersecting lines embellish the inside of the triangles.

COMMENTARY - BIBLIOGRAPHY: Unpublished
Pithos no. 36 is a handmade, domestic vessel and is dated to the late 8th c. B.C. In this period, domestic vessels are handmade and often have incised decoration on the upper part of the body. Decoration is simple and the most common motifs are wavy lines, the swastika and the meander.
For examples of pithoi with incised decoration which contained burials from the Athenian Agora, the Dipylon cemetery and the Phaleron cemetery, see Brann 1960, 415, pl. 92, Tomb Q 17:6,1; Brückner - Pernice 1893, 119, 120, fig. 12; Πελεκίδης 1916, 18, 20, 26 fig. 8, 22, 25 fig. 7. In general, for the incised swastika motif see Coldstream 1977, 162; *Agora* VIII, 27. For the incised swastika on other vessel shapes see Brann 1916a, 124, no. L47, pl. 22, 142, no. Q10, pl. 22, p. 136, no. O39, pl. 23. For the pithos shape in general see *Agora* VIII, 27, 101, 102, nos. 607, 609, 612-617, pl. 40; *Kerameikos* VI₁, 139, 140, no. 1145, pl. 157; Young 1939, 189, 190, 199; Coldstream 1977, 162, see also 105; Burr 1933b, 597-599.

M.-Ch.M.

Nos. 35-37 belong, with others, to well 23. The well, which was situated on the Makriyianni plot, east of ancient Street I, had a diameter of 1.70 m. near its mouth and 1.30 m. near its bottom. It was cut into the bedrock and its depth is reckoned at 6 m. The majority of the finds belong to the Geometric period, whilst a few sherds were found which date from prehistoric to Roman times. Finds nos. 35-37 probably had a funerary use and perhaps came from a cemetery or isolated burials of the LG period which are found in the surrounding area.

M.-Ch.M.

35 LID OF A VASE
LG period

INV. NO. M 2472.
PRES.H. 0.039, D. 0.222 M.

Mended and restored. Its handle is missing. On the inside, traces of rust and considerable encrustation. Light pale brown clay with inclusions. Self slipped, partly flaking on the inside. Brownish black paint. The lid is slightly conical, with a concave interior surface.
Its decoration consists of zones, arranged in concentric circles. Its surface is decorated from the centre to the periphery with successive broad encircling bands, alternating with pairs of thinner bands.

35

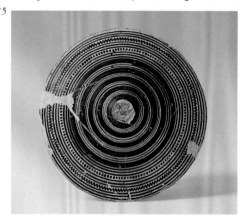

36 PART OF A PITHOS
LG period

INV. NO. M 2473.
PRES.H. 0.125, M.D. 0.275 M.

Mended. Part of the mouth is preserved. Encrustation and some traces of rust outside and in. Reddish coarse clay with many inclusions. Brown slip. The neck of the pithos is cylindrical and narrows slightly towards the flat everted rim. Incised motifs decorate the mouth of the vase. Swastikas on the neck, pointing towards the left. A double wavy line depicts the swastikas and their stems are highlighted on either side by vertical little lines, arranged asymmetrically. The vertical bands are defined on either side by a double wavy line and filled with suc-

36

37 PART OF A LARGE OPEN VESSEL
LG period

INV. NO. M 2474.
MAX.PRES.DIM. 0.24 × 0.257 M.

Mended. Part of the body, rim and one handle are preserved. Chips off and sediments. Brownish red clay with inclusions. Pale brown slip. Paint worn in places, varying from black to red on the outside and black to thin brown on the inside due to uneven firing. The body of the vessel has a slightly curved profile that gradually narrows towards the bottom and forms the biggest curvature at the height of the handle. The rim extends straight up. The horizontal strap handle below the rim has its two ends raised up from the surface of the body.

The decoration of the vase comprises horizontal adjoining zones. A decorative system of panels dominates at the height of the handle and rim. A zone of chequerboard decoration on the body beneath handle is bordered by two zones with outlined triangles, arranged antithetically with spots in the empty spaces. On the lower part of the body, a zone with a lozenge chain and a dot in the middle can be distinguished. The zones are separated by thin, successive horizontal bands. On either side of the handle, vertical bands are filled with lattice-work and chequer-board decoration. In part of the zone between the handles, a panel of an outlined swastika with hooked endings turned to the right (hooked swastika) is preserved. In the rim zone, a vertical outlined band and vertical lines separate two panels. In one panel, there is a quatrefoil outlined rosette and outlined triangles with cross-hatching in the spaces, while in the next, one can discern a network of lozenge stars. Vertical bands with a zigzag, outlined cross-hatching and chequer-board decoration embellish the rest of the rim zone. On the back of the handle, a crenel motif is depicted bordered by two successive bands. On the underside of the raised ends of the handle, three and four vertical bands respectively cover the unpainted part. The surface around and below the handle is unpainted. The vase is monochrome inside, apart from a thin reserved band on top of the chamfered inside of the rim. A black band highlights its edge.

COMMENTARY - BIBLIOGRAPHY: Unpublished.

The shape of the vase and the paint on its interior point to an open vessel of large size, probably a krater. More particularly, however, the vertical rim and horizontal strap handle are characteristics which mainly correspond to the type of skyphos-pyxis with high rim. It is worth noting that this type of skyphos-pyxis is normally smaller in size than find no. 37.

For the development of the skyphos-pyxis with high rim see Coldstream 1968, 86; Davidson 1961, 13, fig. A10, 11; *Kerameikos* V₁, pl. 119-127; McNally 1969, 459-461. For the shape of kraters in general in the Geometric period see Davison 1961, 12, fig. A2-3. For the development of the krater in the LG period see Coldstream 1968, 48, 86 and cf. 126, 142, 146, 147. For kraters of type IIb see Coldstream 1968, 48 and Pfuhl 1903, 164, no. C68, pl. XX:9, cf. 166 tomb 89 (109) 3, pl. XXI:2. For similar handles on kraters see *Agora* VIII, 63, no. 283, pl. 16. For kraters with horizontal strap handles see Benton 1953, 294-296, nos. 793, 796, pl. 48; *Corinth* VII₁, 26-27, no. 74, pl. 12 and 28, no. 79, pl. 13.

In the Geometric period, large vases – such as kraters, amphorae and pyxides – had a chiefly funerary use. The decoration of vases in LG is mainly composed of zones that cover the entire surface of the body. The division of the decorative zone into "metopes" and "triglyphs" reveals an advanced geometric sense. Amongst the most favoured motifs for panels are the swastika, quatrefoil rosette and lozenges in different forms. The motif of the swastika with hooked endings is mainly encountered in the "Hooked Swastika" workshop of LG IIa - early LG IIb; see Coldstream 1968, 66-67, pl. 12c. For a similar swastika on an amphora see Dennis 1994, 17-18, no. 6. Generally for the decoration of vases in the LG period see Coldstream 1968, 49-50; *idem*1977, 155; Σημαντώνη-Μπουρνιά 1997, 74.

M.- Ch.M.

37

ing hole, is surrounded by a slightly curved disc with a projecting exterior edge. The small but rather wide nozzle is flat on top and has a wide, nearly circular lighting hole that encroaches onto the edge of the disc. The vessel is wheel-made. The polished black paint is very worn and covers the inside of the lamp, the disc and the outside of the nozzle. Thin red paint has been spread on the outside of the walls and on the underside.

COMMENTARY - BIBLIOGRAPHY: Unpublished.

The type first appears in Corinth and became an export product to Athens in the 1st half of the 6th c. B.C. (type 16A). Rapidly, however, the Athenian craftsmen imitated its manufacture and, by the end of the 6th c. B.C., developed into major producers. From the Archaic to the Hellenistic periods, lamps, like other types of vessels, were wheel-made.

For similar lamps see *Agora* IV, 31-33, type 16B (525-c. 480 B.C.), pl. 4, 22, 32 - a somewhat similar lamp no. 98, pl. 4, 32; *Corinth* IV$_2$ (2nd half of 6th c. B.C.), 32, 35-38, section 12, fig. 14; *Isthmia* III, type II, 6-8, pl. 1, 14 (6th and early decades of 5th c. B.C.); *Kerameikos* XI, 16-17, DRL (520-480 B.C.), somewhat similar in section, lamp no. 13, pl. 6, 7 (490-480 B.C.); Bailey 1975, 31, Q13, pl. 6, 7 (4th quarter of 6th c. B.C.); Blondé 1983, Lamps with flat overhanging rims (late Archaic group - it appears that it continues even after 480 B.C.

until the 2nd quarter of the 5th c. B.C.), 61-68, analogous no. 47, fig. 6.

H.H.

39 SINGLE-SPOUTED LAMP
325-260 B.C.

INV. NO. M 2545.
H. 0.034, L. 0.098, D. 0.076, B.D. 0.044, D. OF FILLING HOLE 0.018 M.

Mended but complete. Pale rosy clay, Attic. Discoid base, high, slightly concave lower surface with central disc. Lenticular, wide body with small filling hole which is surrounded by a moulded ring and a reserved groove where the paint had been erased. A low moulded projection on the interior of the lamp. Small, perforated ear-handle to facilitate suspension. The nozzle, rather small and sloping upwards, has rounded edges and a small lighting hole. The traces of burning observed in the region of the nozzle attest its function. Wheel-made. The polished, slightly metallic black paint is very worn and covers the whole lamp.

COMMENTARY - BIBLIOGRAPHY: Unpublished.

The lamp comes from an Attic workshop as attested by its clay and shape. It is considered amongst the early examples of type 29A (325-250 B.C.; see *Agora* IV, 94-96, pl.14.41 - somewhat similar to example no. 406 (4th quarter of 4th c. B.C.). For an analogous example but with a solid ear-handle see *Isthmia* III, 20, 21, type IXA, no. 203 (early 3rd c. B.C.). Also see Δρούγου 1992, 49-53, lenticular lamp, no. 80, pl. 19 (c. 300 B.C.) and *Kerameikos* XI, 50-51, FSL (300-200 B.C.), no. 274, pl. 48, 49 (early 3rd c. B.C.). For a re-dating of type 29A of *Agora* IV, to 270-220 B.C., see *Agora* XXIX, Appendix III (no. 406; 325-260 B.C.).

H.H.

38, 39

| From well 4 |

38 SINGLE-SPOUTED LAMP
525-480 B.C.

INV. NO. M 2542.
H. 0.025, D. 0.074, D. OF FILLING HOLE 0.04, L. 0.093 M.

Almost complete, mended. Part of its periphery is missing. Orange clay. The underside is concave and thus its bottom is slightly curved. A very low, wide body with almost vertical walls and a large fill-

40 MARBLE STATUETTE OF A MALE FIGURE
HOLDING A CORNUCOPIA
Probably 1st c. B.C.

INV. NO. M 1942.
H. 0.307, MAX.W. 0.121 M.

The greater part of a clothed male figure
is preserved carrying a cornucopia. White,
fine-grained marble. Missing: the head
and neck, the forearm and hand, the
feet and plinth and the upper part of the
horn. Chipped in places. Eroded on the
naked part of the body, excoriations on
the clothing.

The figure – presumably youthful from
the length of the hair and the formation
of the musculature – supports the weight
of the body on the left leg. The relaxed
right leg bends at the knee and is turned
to the side and slightly back. The left
bent arm holds the cornucopia, supported obliquely between the upper arm and
the forearm. The right forearm was inserted as is indicated by the ellipsoidal
projection on the upper arm. The position of the latter so close to body allows
one to suggest that the right arm was bent
at the elbow and put forward holding
some object, probably a flask. The figure
wears a heavy himation which, doubled
at the top, runs obliquely around to the
back, covers the shoulder and left arm
and surrounds the lower part of the
body, leaving the chest and right arm
free. The folds of the garment, although

rather flat and more schematically rendered at the back, consequently follow the contours of the body. It is worth noting the long hair of the figure, apparent at the back, which is rendered as a uniform mass in the area of the nape of the neck and the upper part of the back. A slender plait is worn in front in the region of the right shoulder.

A deep cylindrical tenon on the lower left part of the figure's garment serves as the support for the sculpture. Its existence, joined with the fact that the end of the right legging is smooth and flat and not chipped, probably indicates a break followed by repair and renewal of the support of the statuette. The slender proportions with the long legs accentuate the vertical axis of the figure whose depiction in general displays influences from earlier models.

COMMENTARY - BIBLIOGRAPHY: Unpublished.

The cornucopia, a symbol of wealth and abundance, is associated in the Classical period with the iconography of chthonic deities, chiefly of Pluto and Meilichios or Zeus Philios. It is also met as a symbol in representations of Dionysos, Ploutos, Herakles and river gods. During the Hellenistic period, Sarapis, a deity of eastern origin who embodied elements of Pluto, Dionysos and Egyptian Osiris, is depicted with a horn. As early as the 4th c. B.C. and during the Hellenistic period, the cornucopia becomes a symbol characteristic of Agathe Tyche and its surrogate, Agathodaemon, deities with no mythological content, though exceptionally popular, in whose representations the horn functions as a more general symbol of good luck. The use of a similar iconographic type for many deities makes the identification of the figure depicted problematic. Nevertheless, its correlation with Agathodaemon, a benevolent deity, appears most probable, a deity which expressed the Agatho Pneuma (Good Grace) and endowed happiness.

Agathodaemon held an important position in private worship, although he was more frequently worshipped with Tyche or in conjunction with other deities primarily at the Asklepieia, as a god who fostered healing. Reliefs with representations of the Agathodaemon and Tyche as well as inscriptions which bear their names, have been found on the Acropolis slope and in the region of the Asklepieion. Apart from the philological tradition which refers to a statue of Agathodaemon and Tyche, the existence of a shrine and the worship of the two gods in Athens is witnessed in epigraphy from the 4th c. B.C. until the Roman period.

In general, for representations of figures with cornucopia see Bemmann 1994, where there is extensive reference to earlier bibliographies. For two similar statuettes of the 4th c. B.C., which are identified as Pluto or Agathodaemon, see Hermann 1900, 107, no. 3, fig. 3 and Themelis 1979, 245, fig. 45, 45a. Scholars look for their prototype in works of free-standing sculpture of the 5th or 4th c. B.C. Eschbach, 1986, 23ff., collected the information. For the Good Daemon see *LIMC* I, 277ff., s.v. Agathodaemon [Dunand]. Epigraphic evidence for shrines of Tyche in Attica is summarised by Tracy 1994. Meilichios or Zeus Philios are commonly presented sitting in reliefs of the Classical period, see Williams 1982, 175-181, pl. 30 for an archaistic relief with a representation of chthonic Zeus standing with horn and flask. A sanctuary of Zeus Philios existed in Athens, on the site immediately above the Odeion of Herodes Atticus; see Παπαχατζής 1974. With regard to the chthonic character of Dionysos and representations of him with a horn of plenty see Schauenburg 1953, 38-72. Of interest is the close relationship between Dionysos and Agathodaemon noted by Picard 1944/45, 248, n. 1. Sarapis generally follows the iconography of Pluto; usually, however, he also wears a chiton beneath the himation. For exceptions see Hornbostel 1973 and for its iconographic similarities with Pluto and Dionysos see Stambaugh 1972. For the depiction of Agathodaemon with a horn in shrines of eastern deities of the Roman period cf. Campbell 1968, pl. XXXI.

I.A.P.

41   MARBLE HEKATAION
1st c. B.C. - 1st c. A.D.

INV. NO. M 1189.
PRES.H. 0.188, MAX.W. 0.116 M.

Statuette of the three-figured goddess Hekate, of white fine-grained marble. It comprises a pillar of triangular section with concave sides, around which three archaising females figures are represented in relief. The upper part of the pillar with the heads of the figures is missing. The three figures are fragmentarily preserved. Extensive chips on the preserved parts and on the base of the object. Cracks, damage and flaking on the surfaces.

The figures are upright, rendered as panels, carved at rather large intervals around the pillar. They have a slender body, the weight of which is balanced on joined legs, without there being one for support and one relaxed. The figures are clothed in the archaising manner. They wear a peplos, high-girdled just below the breast, which forms a long fold with thin pleats ending in a curved outline. Two heavy side folds surround the lower part of the body and clearly define its profile. The rest of the garment is without folds. A single central fold at the back emphasises the vertical axis.

The first figure is depicted with its right arm parallel to the body and the left held bent in front of the breast. It may have held some object, a flower or fruit. The second figure holds a flask in its right hand which is parallel to and in contact with the torso. The modelling of the marble where the left arm is, indicates that this – positioned to the side and slightly bent – would have held an oblong object, probably a torch. On the lower right hand side, a row of angular carvings schematically depict the wavy fringe of the peplos which is open on one side according to the archaic manner. The third figure is half preserved. Its right arm, positioned vertically, follows the outline of the body. It may have held some object now indiscernible due to damage to the marble. A

slight swelling in the region of the right shoulder perhaps indicates a tress of the figure's hair which is worn forwards. The base of the object is flat, lavishly worked with a point on the lower part. Finishing touches using a point can be seen in places and on the surface of the pillar between the figures.

COMMENTARY - BIBLIOGRAPHY: Unpublished.

Hekate, a goddess with intensely mysterious and magical powers, is the personification of the lunar light. Already in Hesiod she is connected with justice and urban life. As a lady of the spirits, souls of the dead and forces of darkness, she has been connected with purification. After her propitiation, one could ward off invisible dark forces.

The worship of Hekate was widely known as early as the 5th c. B.C., as written sources and depictions in art

testify. They considered her guardian of entrances and propylaea (Hekate prothyraia or propylaia). As a deity of roads (Hekate Enodia), she was protectress of travellers and worshipped at cross-roads (Hekate Trioditis). Her representation as three figures is perhaps indebted to this characteristic allowing her image to be turned in the three directions of the cross-roads.

According to Pausanias (II, 30.2), the first to depict the three-figured Hekate was Alkamenes, the discilpe of Pheidias. The Hekate of Alkamenes (430-420 B.C.) was known as "Hekate on the Tower", because of its position above the tower of Athena Nike, near the entrance to the Acropolis of Athens. The statue, which depicted Hekate as a three-bodied figure like a goddess of the sky, earth and underworld, exercised a great influence on her iconography during later centuries.

It is very likely that the marble Hekataia of the kind represented here echoes the Hekate on the Tower (Hekate Epipyrgidia) by Alkamenes, which according most

scholars had archaising characteristics. Most examples, even if they differ in size, have a similar form: they depict three female figures in archaising dress around a column or pillar. On their head they wear a cylindrical cap (polos) and in their hands they hold the symbols characteristic of Hekate, torches, flasks, oenochoae and pomegranates.

Apart from Hekataia found in sanctuaries and the inscribed votive examples, most would have been set up at cross-roads, while some others must have been related to private worship. These would have been erected at the outer doors of houses in accordance with the custom of setting up shrines and representations of Hekate outside entrances (cf. Aristoph., *Wasps*, l. 804: Ἑκάταιον πανταχοῦ πρὸ θυρῶν.)

Harrison dates most of the marble Hekataia to the late Hellenistic and Roman periods (up to the 2nd-3rd c. A.D.). It seems that, in earlier centuries, the private Hekataia would have been of a perishable material, probably wood.

In general for Hekate see Kraus 1960. For the Hekate by Alkamenes see Willers 1975, 48-52 and Fullerton 1986, 669-675. For the worship of Hekate in Athens see Simon 1985b, 271-284, pl. 49-55. For parallels and the dating of Hekataia see *Agora* XI, 86-107. Simon, op.cit., attributes the increase in the number of Hekataia during the reign of Augustus to the particular interest of the emperor in the worship of the Roman deity Trivia who corresponds to Hekate. Fuchs identifies some buildings with a triangular plan, near cross-roads and gates as shrines of Hekate; for these probable shrines see Fuchs 1978. For the Thessalian deity Enodia, who had many attributes in common with Hekate and for the Hekataia of Thessaly and Macedonia see Χρυσοστόμου 1988b.

I.A.P.

42

42

42 TRIPLE-SPOUTED LAMP
1st half of 4th c. A.D.

INV. NO. M 2605.
MAX.H. 0.065, D. 0.092, B.D. 0.046, L. (INCL. ONE SPOUT) 0.128 M.

Complete. Pale rosy clay. Its underside is flat and circular, made of moulded rings between grooves. Rather high body, with curved outline. A circular, concave disc has a high, knob-shaped handle in the centre, with a hole for hanging the lamp and two for filling. The edge is slightly curved. The spouts, three in all, are elongated with a triangular end and a small lighting hole. The intense traces of burning on all three spouts testify to its use. Mould-made and unpainted.

The underside has an impressed inscription: EYT/YXH. The periphery is decorated with impressed herring-bone between moulded rings. The handle has three grooves on its back.

COMMENTARY - BIBLIOGRAPHY: Unpublished.
The Attic workshop of Eutyches flourished greatly from the middle of the 3rd to the early 5th c. A.D. Lamps with more than one spout, "chandeliers", make their appearance from the Classical up to the Late Roman period. Their greater size and the placing of many light-

spouts allowed a place to be better and more widely lit. The chandeliers were used either hanging up or secured on a high base.

For a similar example of comparable dimensions see *Corinth* IV₂, 116, 117, type XXX (with central handle), group 2, no. 1439, pl. XXI. For multiple-spouted lamps with a central handle and somewhat similar section etc. see *Agora* VII, 156-158, no. 1995, pl. 49 and no. 2001 (M244; early 4th c. A.D.). Likewise, see *Agora* V, no. M244, pl. 47, stratum VII (early 4th c. A.D.). For the workshop of Eutyches see Karivieri 1996, 95-104, signatures 1-9 (before the middle of 4th c. A.D.). For a multiple-spouted lamp in this workshop see Karivieri 1996, 240, no. 257, pl. 33 (with central handle; late 4th c. A.D.) and no. 277, pl. 27 (double-spouted, inscribed: [of] Eutyches; 1st half of 4th c. A.D.). For a comparable example see Thompson 1933, I, 209-210, no. L244, fig. 9.1, no. L129, fig. 9.2 (with analogous central handle, concave disc and herring-bone decoration).

H.H.

43 IVORY PLAQUE
5th-6th c. A.D.

INV. NO. M 2516.
H. 0.19, W. 0.088 (BOTTOM) - 0.083 (TOP), MAX. SWELLING OF RELIEF (TO THE NOSE OF THE DIOSKOUROS) 0.021 M.

The ivory plaque is completely preserved and its state of preservation is generally very good, with the exception of the attachment of the upper part of the spear on the far left, some few cracks and very slight chips and damage in places. The plaque is rectangular with a curved top and a narrow semicircular projection at the bottom. On the main polished side, one of the Dioskouroi with his horse is depicted in elaborate relief, without any particular framing of the scene. A shaving of gold preserved above the left knee of the figure may be evidence of some gilding. The circular heads and part of the shaft of three iron rivets are preserved above the mane of the horse, in contact with the forearm of the man and in between the feet of the latter. In the execution of the work, a gradual increase in the depth of the relief from bottom to top is confirmed, and at the highest point of the plaque the head of the male figure is nearly in full relief.

The horse-breaker god is depicted as a young man in idealised nudity, stand-ing up with a frontal view of the body and a three-quarter view of the head twisted to the right. He is wearing a pilos, the characteristic conical cap of the Dioskouroi, and a mantle fastened on the right shoulder and thrown back, reaching as far as the middle of the legs. He is holding the spear with his right hand with the point upwards, while with his left hand he clasps the bridle of the horse which is depicted in perspective behind the young god. The Dioskouros supports the weight of his body on the right leg, with the corresponding hip accentuated with a deep curvature, and he has the free left leg to one side in the direction his head is turned. The gaze of the viewer is attracted to the head of the young god with spirally ringlets which form the characteristic ending above the curved brow crowning the smooth rounded face. This is dominated by very expressive almond-shaped eyes with thick lashes, swollen eyeball and circular concave iris. The eyebrow follows the line above the lash and is deeply carved.

COMMENTARY - BIBLIOGRAPHY: Unpublished.

Gilding of ivory reliefs, like painting, has been verified in many instances. The preserved rivets, combined with the fact that the back of the plaque is nearly flat and unpolished, leads to the conclusion that this plaque, in all probability with the second of the deified twins facing the opposite direction, belonged to an ivory decorative covering probably of a wooden box which naturally would have been a luxury item.

The Dioskouros is portrayed with his characteristic, designated symbols, the cap, horse and spear. The method of depicting the youth is in accordance with a long classicising tradition. It is particularly worth noting that the pose of his body recalls as a distant echo the form of the Meleager of Skopas.

The rendering of the eyebrow with such deep carving is a much later characteristic in representational art. The work probably comes from a workshop in the east region of the Mediterranean. The worship of the Dioskouroi, which started in the pre-Doric period in Laconia and had a very wide distribution, also had deep roots in Attica. For the widespread introduction of the ivory plaque and the worship of the Dioskouroi in Athens see Πωλογιώργη forth.

M.I.P.

43

44 SINGLE-SPOUTED LAMP
Early Roman period

INV. NO. M 2547.
MAX.H. 0.054, MAX.L. 0.103, W. 0.066, B.D. 0.037 M.

Almost complete. Missing part of the spout. Brown-red clay, Attic. Small discoid base. Body has angular profile, almost bi-conical. The central filling hole is surrounded by a concave disc, a thin moulded ring and a channel. The small spout has an angular outline with a triangular ending and is accentuated on the upper part by a moulded band which extends as far as the disc. The vertical strap handle is high-swung and has a slightly curved back. The intense traces of burning in the region of the spout indicate its function. Mould-made. The paint, blurred and black, flaking in places and worn, appears to have covered the whole lamp. The upper part of the body is decorated with an olive spray relief of leaves and fruits.

COMMENTARY - BIBLIOGRAPHY: Unpublished.
The lamp is dated to the 1st c. A.D. and appears to be the development of a type which first occurs in Athens after the sack of the city by Sulla in 86 B.C. The olive wreath, for long a symbol of Athena as a goddess of peace, is now used by the Romans to allude to the new era of peace which had been imposed on Athens after the Roman conquest. During the Hellenistic period, a new craft appeared in ceramic workshops, namely the manufacture of objects using a mould. The old technique of making lamps on the potter's wheel draws to an end and is gradually abandoned. The use of moulds for making lamps is prevalent throughout the whole Roman period.

For somewhat similar examples see Agora IV, type 54B (late 1st c. B.C. - early 1st c. A.D.), no. 772, pl. 52 (20 B.C. - A.D. 15). See also Agora V, 86, no. M16, pl. 46 (mid 1st c. A.D.; stratum I). For similar see Kerameikos XI, 80-81, type SML/VI (70 B.C. - A.D. 20), no. 482, pl. 75 (with olive or myrtle wreath; 3rd quarter of 1st c. B.C.) For a re-dating of 54B (Agora IV) to the 1st c. A.D. see Agora XXIX, Appendix III.

H.H.

45 BONE SPOON
1st c. A.D.

INV. NO. M 2540.
PRES.L. 0.145 M.

Joined from two pieces at the handle; missing its tip. Fairly shallow concave body and correspondingly curved exterior surface. It has a long handle nearly rectangular in section, with vertical parallel carvings near the body on the upper and lower surfaces.

COMMENTARY - BIBLIOGRAPHY: Unpublished
The spoon is met throughout antiquity in different forms and with different decoration, bone or ivory, bronze, silver and frequently wood. Usually, the pointed end of the handle helped breaking an egg or removing the contents of an oyster. A similar one to ours is restricted to Corinth and dated to the 1st c. A.D.; see Corinth XII, 189, no. 1397, pl. 85. For parallels and for spoons in general see Délos XVIII, 228-230, pl. LXXV and 603 (with bibliography); Daremberg - Saglio, I, s.v. Cochlear, 1266.

S.M.

44

45

ens, they had an Alpha in relief on the base, the interpretation of which is problematic. It is probably connected with their place of manufacture, namely Athens, acting as a symbol of quality, a sign of the manufacturer or a signature. Lamps of this type, of low quality of manufacture, combine Hellenistic characteristics and elements of Roman lamps. Their origin is uncertain. They make their appearance in Attica in the 1st c. A.D. and dominate the Athenian market up to the end of the 2nd c. A.D. with some few exports to the Peloponnese.

For an attempt to interpret the relief Alpha on the base and for similar examples see *Agora* VII, alpha globule lamps, 15-17, 107, nos. 426-427 (2nd half of 1st - early 2nd c. A.D.). Likewise see *Corinth* IV$_2$, 70-73, type XX, no. 372, pl. VII. According to Karivieri 1996, 44, alpha globule lamps were manufactured in Attica from the middle of the 1st to the end of the 2nd c. A.D. Their mass production, however, appears to continue throughout the early 3rd c. A.D. (personal communication J. Binder).

H.H.

46

From well 12

46 SINGLE-SPOUTED LAMP
2nd half of 1st - early 2nd c. A.D.

INV. NO. M 2548.
MAX.L. 0.058, W. 0.055, MAX.H. 0.059, B.D. 0.033 M.

Complete. Its handle is joined together. Orangey clay with mica, Attic. Circular base formed from a moulded ring. A spherical body, with circular concave disc and nearly central filling hole, which is bounded on the exterior by two moulded rings. The spout has a curving end and small lighting hole. Vertical high-swung handle. Traces of burning on the spout indicate the function of the lamp. Mould-made. On the outside, it is covered with thin brown-red paint.

The underside has a relief letter A on its inside. The body is decorated with successive rows of relief spots, apart from the join of the two sections of the mould. The spout has a row of spots on its upper part, which is framed by double helixes in relief. A similar row of spots can be distinguished on its lower exterior side, while a curved moulded band separates it from the body. The back of the handle is embellished with a central groove.

COMMENTARY - BIBLIOGRAPHY: Unpublished.
Lamps of this type, made of Attic clay, are found in great quantities in Athens, and come from an Attic workshop. Throughout the long period they were produced in Ath-

the cloth in such a way as to create a fold just as it falls. Curved grooves on the back of the figure indicate the pleats formed by the garment as it hugs the body. The cloak closes in front at the waist with an accentuated vertical groove, while the hood is moulded. The facial features and hair are depicted in relief. The pupils of the eyes are accentuated by impressed dots. The long hair has tresses in relief above the forehead where the parting is. On the sides, groups of curved grooves. The ringlets on the back and sides of the head are arranged in three rows. The back of the handle is embellished with a groove.

COMMENTARY - BIBLIOGRAPHY: Unpublished.

The child god Telesphoros appears very late in the Greek and Roman pantheon. His worship penetrated Athens from Pergamon in the last years of the 2nd c.

A.D., perhaps as a result of the great plague which spread to Athens in A.D. 166, having come from the soldiers of Marcus Aurelius during the Parthian campaign. Then, it is mentioned that Telesphoros freed the land of the Kekropidae (i.e. Attica) from the plague. During the time of Hadrian, a great extension of his worship can be seen in many regions of the Graeco-Roman world. His depiction on lamps is common. Many have been found in Athens dating to the late 2nd and 1st half of the 3rd c. A.D.

The name Telesphoros means "he who accomplishes the purpose". As a god of healing, he constitutes a symbol of eternal life and occurs either by himself or with Asklepeios. His religious importance and his peculiar appearance is not clear, although he is certainly connected with the healing practices of Asklepeios. In an inscription of the 3rd c. A.D., from Athens, there is a hymn to Asklepeios, Hygieia and Telesphoros, where the latter is referred to as "phaesinbrotos", that is he who carries the light to mortals. He is connected with nocturnal rituals as well as with a vision of Aelian Aristeides where the brightness of Telesphoros was uncovered by him during the night. Lamps with the figure of Telesphoros strike terror into evil spirits or illness through his power. The common occurrence of the spout in the shape of a phallus is an indication of the vi-

47 SINGLE-SPOUTED LAMP MOULDED INTO THE FIGURE OF A CHILD DEITY (TELESPHOROS)
Late 2nd - early 3rd c. A.D.

INV. NO. M 2609.
MAX.H. 0.136, W. OF BODY 0.034, TH. OF BODY 0.025, D.B. 0.034 M.

Complete; unstable. Pale rosy to orangey clay with a little mica. The cylindrical base has a moulded ring in its middle and a second on its upper part, forming a pedestal for the figure. A semicircular spout sticks up and projects from this. The body has the figure of a standing boy facing the viewer and portrays the healing god, Telesphoros. On the back of the figure, a broad filling hole; vertical handle with suspension hole at mid-height. Traces of burning on the spout confirm its function. The lamp is mould-made. It is totally covered with vivid brown-red paint, flaking in places.

The figure is portrayed with a garment – a cloak, which lies heavily covering the whole body to the ankles, while the hood this god normally wears is thrown back leaving the head uncovered. The feet (with moulded toes indicated), part of the neck and the extremity below the garment are bare. The garment totally covers the arms which are stuck on the body at mid-height and bent forwards; the palms of the hands, turned inwards, lift

47

48

tal powers of the god, hence the reference to him in the hymn as Zoophoros (harbinger of life). Telesphoros is always represented standing and facing the viewer (often on top of a base) with a cloak which has a hood, leaving the face and always the legs free. The depiction of the figure is always static. Its representation with the arms slightly projecting beneath the cloak and lifting it up, constitutes a variation of the type, exactly as on lamp no. 47, a feature of the time of Hadrian. With the slightly projecting arms, the good healing god invites he who needs help to come close to him.

For the introduction of the worship of Telesphoros in Attica see *Agora* V, 52-53, n. 9-11. For a corresponding example of lamp see *Agora* V, 52, no. J14 (L2301), pl. 47 (comparable dimensions; late 2nd c. A.D.; the figure wears a hood thrown on the shoulders), no. L2503 (it has a spout in the shape of a phallus) and no. L3104 (2nd c. A.D.). For information regarding the worship of Telesphoros see *LIMC* VII.1, 870-878, s.v. Telesphoros and VII.2, 602-605. For the inscription which contains hymn and refers to φαεσίνβροτος and ζωοφόρος see op.cit., 870 (*IG* II-III²); for lamps with the figure of Telesphoros see op.cit., 871, 602.8 and 876-878. For approximations see *Agora* VI, 5, 35, 75, pl. 27, no. 954 (L2503) (with uncovered head and spout in the shape of a phallus; 1st half of 3rd c. A.D.), while for Telesphoros with a hood see nos. 943, 949, 951, 958.

H.H.

48 SINGLE-SPOUTED LAMP
Early 3rd c. A.D.

INV. NO. M 2610.
MAX.L. 0.096, MAX.W. 0.078, MAX.H. 0.043, B.D. 0.036 M.

Nearly complete. Fine, orangey clay, Attic. The underside is circular and formed from grooving. A broad and low body, has a central filling hole with a small circular concave disc formed around it. The spout is high and separated from the flat, broad surrounds by a groove on every side. It has a curved projecting end. Raised, vertical handle with suspension hole. Intense traces of burning on the spout demonstrate its use. Mould-made. Unpainted.

The underside has a fragmentarily preserved incised inscription: ΕΥΠΟ/ΡοΥ, (possibly Ευπόρου, [of] Euporos). The disc is decorated with impressed radial decoration. The surrounds have relief

vines, leaves alternating with grapes, with a shoot twisted between them. The back of the handle is decorated along its length with two grooves and ends in a moulded vine leaf near the base.

COMMENTARY - BIBLIOGRAPHY: Unpublished.

The lamp belongs to examples of 3rd c. A.D. Attic lamps that imitate the corresponding Corinthian lamps. The radial decoration of the disc and the motif around the edge is characteristic of Corinthian products. The moulded leaf, at the end of the handle is reminiscent of metalworking. One can recognise in this lamp an effort to imitate the light, elegant body of Corinthian lamps as well as the appropriate clay. The inscription on the base of the lamp refers to the workshop of Euporos who is known in Corinth but is not met amongst the Attic workshops of the period that were located in the Athenian Agora.

For a lamp imported from Corinth with similar decoration see *Agora* VII, pl. 8, no. 271 (from a much used mould of the late 2nd - early 3rd c. A.D.) and for similar Attic lamps of the 3rd-4th c. A.D. see nos. 1470 and 1472 (beginning of 3rd c. A.D.), no. 1474 (2nd half of 3rd c. A.D.), pl. 28. For corresponding lamps of the 2nd-3rd c. A.D. see Clement 1971, 101-111 (with an inscription of Euporos and similar decoration; 107, IRL 70-73, pl. 87a,b). For the imitation of Corinthian lamps in Athenian workshops in the 1st half of the 3rd c. A.D. see Karivieri 1996, 38. For reference to the workshop of Euporos as a large Corinthian workshop that exported lamps during the 3rd c. A.D. see Bruneau 1977, 285. For lamps with an analogous inscription see *Isthmia* III, 67, type XXVII, nos. 2796-2797, pl. 30 and *Corinth* IV₂, pl. XXXI, nos. 731-734.

H.H.

This is a water well about 18.50 m. deep, cut into the bedrock with a diameter of 1 m., apart from the upper section lined with stone which is 0.64 m. in diameter.

It was investigated in two stages: **a.** During the excavation, part of the stone lining was found, which rested on the bedrock. From there downwards, it was cut into the rock. The upper level of fill was taken off, a stratum 0.55 m. thick, which chiefly contained pottery of the late Byzantine period. **b.** During digging for the construction of the station basement, the lower section of the shaft was located down to its bottom at a depth of 19 m. from the surface. The fill collapsed in uniformly and for the most part contained pottery of Roman and Late Roman date. A good number of complete vessels were recovered amongst which were ten almost whole bucket-shaped vessels.

Ch.K.

49 BUCKET-SHAPED VESSEL (KADOS)
End of 2nd - beginning of 3rd c. A.D.

INV. NO. M 2536.
H. 0.323, MAX.D. 0.194, M.D. 0.111, B.D. 0.073 M.

Complete. It has small chips off the edge of the base and there are traces of wheelmarks on the body. Rosy-brown clay with inclusions. The vessel is covered in a whitish slip that in places differs radically in colour (brownish to dark brown hue) probably due to its proximity to an oxidising object. It has a ring base and ovoid body. The broad, cylindrical and rather high neck ends in a ring-shaped rim to which is attached a basket-handle with three grooves along its back.

COMMENTARY - BIBLIOGRAPHY: Unpublished.

The kados is a vessel for transporting and probably drawing water. The earlier examples have a ring base and a non-existent neck. Gradually, from the 1st c. A.D. onwards, the neck is developed while the vases become more slender and the bases are given a low foot. It appears that the shape occurs more rarely during the 3rd c. and is out of use before the beginning of the 4th c. A.D.

For similar kadoi see *Agora* V, 55, J45, pl. 10 (beginning of 3rd c. A.D.), 92, M88 and M89, pl. 22 (2nd half of 2nd c. A.D.), 102, M198, pl. 26 (similar vessel, smaller size, late 3rd c. A.D. after the Herulian invasion of A.D. 267). For kadoi, in general, see Buchholz 1966, 149, fig. 9 and Βόρδος - Τσαρδάκα - Χατζηδανιήλ 1997, 236, 239, pl. 156.

Ch.K.

49

50

From well 54

This was a shaft found very close to the excavation area, just outside the north-eastern corner of the Makryianni 2-4 plot. It is cut into the bedrock and has a diameter of about 1.20 m. It was located at a depth of 19.50 m. from the surface at the start of the construction of the pilot tunnel for the M.R.A. Its bottom was never found as the walling of the shaft continued deep. The rich fill material, small finds and pottery, which had fallen in all at the same time, was collected. Most of the pottery dates to Roman, Late Roman and Early Christian times.

Ch.K.

50 TRANSPORT AMPHORA
2nd half of 3rd - beginning of 4th c. A.D.

INV. NO. M 2534.
H. 0.635, MAX.D. 0.227, M.D. 0.059, B.D. 0.057 M.

Complete. There are chips, small manufacturing defects and various deposits at quite a number of points on the vessel's surface. Red to terracotta coloured clay with inclusions. Coated with same coloured clay. It has a high, conical neck. Immediately below the banded rim, a deep grooving is formed by an underdeveloped, horizontal, projecting collar for attaching a lid. The angular shoulder is clearly separated from the rest of the body which gradually narrows towards the bottom and ends in a concave, truncated conical foot with a button inside. The vertical handles curve round abruptly, a little above the height of the rim. They are elliptical in section and broaden where they join the rim. An obvious spine can be distinguished along the back of the handles. Shallow grooving runs around the inner surface of the neck and the foot.

COMMENTARY - BIBLIOGRAPHY: Unpublished.

Amphorae of this type were in all probability used for transporting wine. It is thought that they come from the Aegean region, but they spread out to the eastern Mediterranean, the Black Sea, some areas of the Italian peninsula and North Africa. Likewise, they have been found in Britain together with vases of the late 3rd - early 4th c. A.D. In Athens, they first appear from the 3rd c. A.D. (very rare before the Herulian invasion, A.D. 267), although they are more common in the 4th and 5th c. A.D. In Corinth, the same type is present mainly in the 2nd half of the 3rd c., although it is common during the 4th c. A.D.

For similar vessels which date to the early 4th c. A.D. see *Agora* V, 77, L33, pl. 16 and 106, M237, pl. 28. See also *Corinth* XVIII₂, 109, 116, 117, fig. 29, pl. 15, no. 254 (similar amphora of the 2nd half of the 3rd c. A.D.). In general for this type of amphora see Peacock - Williams 1986, 193-195, fig. 112-113, Class 47 and Keay 1984, 136, 137, 140, 393, fig. 52-53, type XII.

Ch.K.

51 SINGLE-SPOUTED LAMP
End of 3rd - beginning of 4th c. A.D.

INV. NO. M 2552.
MAX.L. 0.103, MAX.W. 0.077, H. OF BODY 0.032, B.D. 0.031 M.

Complete. Pale rosy clay, Attic. Circular underside formed from grooving. Broad body with curved lower outline with a circular concave disc. Slightly raised nozzle separated from the curved perimeter by a groove on each side. Vertical, raised handle with a piercing hole for hanging. The intense traces of burning on the spout and partly on the body give ample evidence for the use of the lamp. Mould-made. Unpainted.

The underside of the lamp has an impressed inscription: EY. The disc is decorated with a relief representation of Athena Promachos, side view facing left; One can distinguish the Corinthian helmet she is wearing and, faintly, her shield. The surrounds are decorated with two rows of relief globules that flank thin, moulded bands, and horizontal frames with an impressed branch. The handle has three grooves on the upper part of its back and two on the lower part ending in a point before the base.

COMMENTARY - BIBLIOGRAPHY: Unpublished.

The poor rendering of Athena's figure is due to multiple use of the mould for making the lamp. The representation of Athena Promachos is frequently encountered on Attic lamps of the 3rd and 4th c. A.D., while lamps with

51

this motif became export products of Athenian workshops to the entire Hellenic world, from Russia to Egypt, where they were copied. The lamp was made in the Attic workshop of Eutyches – as the abridged inscription indicates – which was active in the mid 3rd to roughly the mid 5th c. A.D., surviving the two great catastrophes for Athens, those of the Herulians and the Goths under Alaric. For the subject of Athena Promachos, which derives from similar representations on coins and in sculpture, see Karivieri 1996, 62. For a comparable representation on a lamp see Karivieri 1996, 154-155, no. 3, fig. 11 (late 4th c. A.D.). For the Attic workshop of Eutyches

see Karivieri 1996, 95-104. The inscription EY is very frequent, mainly before the middle of the 4th c. A.D. For the representation of Athena Promachos see *Agora* VII, 111-112. Our lamp belongs to Group 2. Somewhat similar are no. 660, pl. 15, of analogous dimensions, of the early 4th c. A.D. and no. 666 (inscribed EY). For the workshop of Eutyches see *Agora* VII, 34-35, part 1, signature 9, before the middle of the 4th c. B.C. For the depiction of Athena Promachos on metal vessels see *Agora* V, group L, stratum IV (early 5th c. A.D.).

For lamps which were either made in Athens in the 4th c. A.D. or are copies of Attic lamps see *Corinth* IV₂, no. 1102, fig. 174, no. 1103, fig. 175, no. 1104, pl. XXIX. See likewise, *Corinth* XVIII₂, no. 17, pl. I, fig. 1 (with Athena Promachos; 1st half of 2nd c. A.D.). For a somewhat similar example of a lamp with a bust of Athena see Miller 1979, 75, no. L42, pl. 20b (mid 3rd c. A.D.).

H.H.

heavy eyelashes. The pupils are rendered with impressed dots. The wings of the nose and the nostrils are depicted in the same way. The mouth is small with a imperceptible smile. The cheeks are depicted round and puffed up while the ears are placed low and forward. The boy wears an amulet on his neck, of simple design in the shape of a crescent. Traces of brown-black painted decoration are faintly preserved just about in the middle of his forehead, a little above the eyebrows; it is difficult to make out but is in the shape of a U. The hair, the outline and pupils of the eyes, the mouth and the amulet are highlighted by applied black-brown paint flaking at many points.

COMMENTARY - BIBLIOGRAPHY: Unpublished.
See *Agora* V, 52-53, n. 10. Such vessels are only known in Athens from the Kerameikos and Agora excavations and are thought to have been used for libations. For vessels of this type in general and their moulded rendering see Kübler 1952, 137-141, where he points out the simplified and linear elements which occur at the end of the 3rd - beginning of the 4th c. B.C. when the classicising features recede and 140, fig. 77-78 (similar vessel; 1st half of 4th c. A.D.). Also see Walker - Bierbrier 1997, 190, no. 257 (corresponding example, probably from Athens, of the 2nd or 3rd c. A.D.). For painted decoration on his forehead, which is probably related to the ceremonial or votive use of the object, see Shear 1938, 348-349, fig. 33 (corresponding vessel of the 3rd c. A.D.). For the jewellery in the shape of a crescent see Walker - Bierbrier 1997, 163-164, 190 and *Agora* VI, 19; it acts as a good-luck charm, which boys wore during the Roman period. It also occurs on female portraits of the late 1st - early 2nd c. A.D.

Ch.K.

52 MOULDED VASE IN THE SHAPE OF A BOY'S HEAD
3rd - 1st half of 4th c. A.D.

INV. NO. M 2532.
MAX.PRES.H. 0.192, B.D. 0.104 M.

Almost complete. Part of the neck is missing. Small chips and excoriations in places. Relatively fine, orange-coloured clay. The vessel is covered with a brownish slip, missing at various points.

The body and base of the vessel, that is the head and neck of the boy, comprise two mould-made parts. They are completed by the added wheel-made neck and vertical strap handle. The cylindrical neck, which broadens slightly towards the top, has two horizontal grooves, while a thin moulded ring surrounds its base. The handle sprouts from the neck and ends at the back of the head with four deep grooves along the length of its back. Flat base with a moulded ring formed around its edge.

The hair of the boy is thick, beautifully shaped and depicted in detail. Leaf-shaped clumps of hair fall carelessly on his forehead and temples while the back is formed from groups of wavy lines. The arches above the brows are faintly singled out and the curved eyebrows are rendered in brown-black paint. The eyes have an intense look and are almond-shaped, asymmetrically placed between

52

53 TOY HORSE
4th c. A.D.

INV. NO. M 2535.
H. 0.107, L. 0.188, MAX.W. 0.08 M.

Complete, carelessly made. It is mould-made in two parts, the joining seam of which can be made out. Flaking and deposition of substances in places. Rosy-brown clay with a little mica. On the sides of the body, at points where the limbs begin, there are piercing holes for fitting axles which supported wheels. There is also a piercing in the muzzle for pulling the toy. The anatomical and decorative elements are schematically rendered, combined with a relief and painted technique. The surfaces are covered with white slip and applied colour that for the most part has perished.

eyes, which are surrounded by a rectangular frame, the nostrils and the bridle are indicated by incision and highlighted with badly preserved black paint. The mane is indicated with a moulded swelling. The tail is also lavishly made, voluminous and raised up, and has traces of black and orange-brown paint. Oblique, black-coloured bands start from the side and neck, converging towards the back and filled with applied paint (traces of blue-grey and red paint are preserved). These features probably represented part of the harness.

COMMENTARY - BIBLIOGRAPHY: Unpublished.
Clay toys in the shape of a horse are larger in size than other zoomorphic figurines. Often, the horses are finished off with separate wheels, which are fitted to two, horizontal, probably wooden, axles and are dragged

tica. The zoomorphic clay figurines of the late 3rd and 4th c. A.D. comprise the best examples, from a technical point of view, which became less realistic with the passage of time. For comparable examples see *Agora* VI, 66, nos. 776-777, pl. 19 (heads of similar horses; 2nd half of 3rd - early 4th c. A.D.), no. 781 (similar little horse, more lavishly made; 4th c. A.D.), no. 784 (head of similar horse; 2nd half of 4th c. A.D.); Fitta 1997, 74, fig. 130 (comparable toy with wheels and rider incorporated on the back of the horse; Roman period); Shear 1930, 430, fig. 20 (similar, earlier example; 1st c. A.D., from a child's grave); *Corinth* XII, 62, no. 461, pl. 43 (head of similar horse; 3rd or 4th c. A.D.). In general for figurines-toys in the shape of a horse see *Agora* VI, 25, 28 and Fitta 1997, 69-72.

Ch.K.

53

The toy is roughly in the shape of a parallelogram and is depressed. The almost cylindrical neck is large compared to the body and the folds of the skin are plastically rendered on its sides. The head is lavishly made. The almond-shaped

by a rope. The relief elements and ostentatious colours, in which mainly the harness is rendered, lend an impressive look to the toy. These little horses were one of the more popular toys throughout the Roman period.
Two different types of horse occur: the earlier is a probable import from Corinth, while the later came from At-

It is located east of ancient Street I (Trench Στ 17). It is a shaft of a total depth of 19 m., cut into the bedrock, with a diameter of about 0.80 m. It is connected to a reservoir-collection tank of the Late Roman period. It reveals two different phases in construction and use: **a.** The upper part, depth 9.60 m., had walling lined with hydraulic cement, with ledges to facilitate descent, and served to collect water. **b.** The remaining part down to the bottom, which had been cut out in a later phase, had unlined walls and the well probably was used to collect water. Even though not all the pottery has been examined, it is considered that the shaft went out of use in a single phase.

The small finds and pottery from all levels are generally dated to Roman, Late Roman and Early Christian times. Apart from the huge volume of pottery sherds, the greater part of the fill comprised many vases and lamps. The homogeneity of the fill is indicated by the fact that many parts of vessels were made up from sherds found in different levels.

Ch.K.

54 OENOCHOE WITH PAINTED INSCRIPTION
3rd c. A.D.

INV. NO. M 2522.
H. 0.173, MAX.D. 0.151, M.D. 0.094, B.D. 0.061 M.

Complete. Small chips on edge of lip and base. It exhibits certain manufacturing defects and a piercing hole in the lower half. Substance deposits on the exterior and interior surface. Brownish clay with inclusions. A brown-red to brown-black slip covers the interior of the mouth and the outside of the vase, apart from a small part at the lowest point; dull, carelessly laid on and missing in places. Ring base, with concave underside. Spherical body slightly elongated towards the bottom. The neck is cylindrical, wide and short. Its exterior surface has an imperceptible hollowing and two horizontal grooves run around its base. Vertical strap handle slightly raised above the lip; it sprouts from the neck and ends at the height of the greatest diameter.

The painted inscription Ε Υ Φ Ρ Α C Ε Ι Α, which is bordered by two parallel, horizontal rows of spots, encompasses the body of the vase. It begins to the right of the handle and is spread out in the area between the base of the neck and the groove beneath the ending of the handle. The inscription and the spots are in applied white paint, of which, however, only slight traces are preserved. Inscriptions of this kind commonly convey a greeting to prosperity or a wish for longevity.

COMMENTARY - BIBLIOGRAPHY: Unpublished.
For comparable examples see *Agora* V, 97, M145, M146, M147, pl. 24, 57, 73 and 98, M148, pl. 57 (these are similar vases with comparable inscriptions that date to the middle of the 3rd c. A.D. up to the Herulian invasion of A.D. 267), 101, M190, pl. 26, 57 (similar vase of the late 3rd c. A.D., after A.D. 267); Shear 1938, 348, for these inscriptions in general, 348, fig. 32 (vase of this type of the 3rd c. A.D.; that is *Agora* V, M190); Hayes 1997, 68, 70, pl. 25 (comparable example with the inscription EYTYXIA, "good luck", which in all probability comes from Thrace). The type of oenochoe and the inscription copy vases which were manufactured in Athens after A.D. 200.
With regard to the inscription EYΦPACEIA: the word is met with the following spelling "εὐφρασία", see Liddell - Scott 1953, 737, s.v. Εὐφρασία, ἡ: good cheer, ἡ ἐν τῇ ψυχῇ εὖ; Κωνσταντινίδης 1902, 2, 574, s.v. εὐφρασία, ἡ: cheerfulness.

Ch.K.

55 OENOCHOE
End of 4th - beginning of 5th c. A.D.

INV. NO. M 2521.
H. 0.143, MAX.D. 0.112, M.D. 0.073, B.D. 0.044 M.

Complete. Chips off the edge of the base and handle. There are imperfections and careless marks from the wheel on the body. The vase has a brown-red to dark brown slip, dull, carelessly applied and destroyed at numerous points. It covers part of the inside of the neck and the outside of the vase, apart from the lowest part. Conical ring base. At the point where it is joined to the body, a shallow groove is formed around half of its circumference. Body almost bi-conical, with the walls of the upper half more sharply curved. The cylindrical neck, which broadens slightly towards the top, ends in a ring-shaped rim. Vertical strap handle with two grooves along the length of its back.

"Gouged" type decoration, according to the excavators of the Athenian Agora. Oblique successive grooves, carelessly executed, begin from the base of the neck and extend to the point of greatest diameter. They are intersected at the widest part of the belly by a row of horizontal, narrower grooves. The oblique grooves leave the triangular area beneath the handle free.

COMMENTARY - BIBLIOGRAPHY: Unpublished.
This is a vase for everyday use. In general, for this "gouged" type of decoration, which occurs only rarely before the Herulian invasion of Athens (A.D. 267), see *Agora* V, 6. For similar vases see *Agora* V, 78, L38, pl. 16 (late 4th c. A.D.), 111, M292-M293, pl. 30 (early 5th c. A.D.).

Ch.K.

56 OENOCHOE
End of 5th c. A.D.

INV. NO. M 2517.
H. 0.373, MAX.D. 0.221, M.D. 0.101, B.D. 0.11 M.

Complete. Traces of shallow grooves from the wheel can be distinguished in places, and there are chips off the base. Brown clay with inclusions. The surface of the oenochoe, apart from its lower part, is covered with dark brown slip, dull, carelessly applied and destroyed in many places. Ring base, ovoid body; cylindrical neck which broadens slightly towards the top and ends in a ring-shaped rim. The vertical strap handle sprouts from a little above the middle of the neck and ends on the shoulder, while there are two grooves along the length of its back.

A series of horizontal grooves run round the upper half of the body, whilst the point of greatest diameter is highlighted by a pair of horizontal grooves. Numerous traces of decoration in whitish, scattered, dull paint are preserved on the slip. This comprises two horizontal rows of running spirals, on the upper half of the body, twisting anticlockwise towards the centre and horizontal lines on the back of the handle.

COMMENTARY - BIBLIOGRAPHY: Unpublished.
See *Agora* V, 113, M311, pl. 31 (similar vase as far as size, shape and decoration are concerned; late 5th c. A.D.).

Ch.K.

57 OENOCHOE
End of 5th c. A.D.

INV. NO. M 2528.
H. 0.349, MAX.D. 0.229, M.D. 0.102, B.D. 0.102 M.

Part of the mouth and the handle restored. There are chips around the rim and base. Flaking in places. Rosy brown clay with inclusions. The oenochoe is covered in a brown-red paint, dull and carelessly applied on the inside of the mouth and on almost all the outer surface apart from its lowest part. Ring base, ovoid body. The cylindrical neck broadens slightly towards the top and ends in a ring-shaped rim which turns imperceptibly outwards. Two horizontal channels run around the base of the neck. Strap handle.
"Gouged" type decoration according to the excavators of the Athenian Agora. The upper part of the body to just below the point of greatest diameter is decorated with oblique grooves arranged antithetically, on either side of a vertical groove so as to form long leaves which are separated by vertical wavy lines. The lowest point of the decorative zone is bordered by horizontal grooves of which only one surrounds the whole of the body's circumference.

COMMENTARY - BIBLIOGRAPHY: Unpublished.
This is a vase of everyday use. In general for "gouged" type decoration see no. 55. See *Agora* V, 113, M312, pl. 31 (similar vase; late 5th c. A.D.).

Ch.K.

58 OENOCHOE WITH COMBED DECORATION
6th c. A.D.

INV. NO. M 2523.
H. 0.22, MAX.D. 0.166, M.D. 0.096, B.D. 0.104 M.

Complete, carelessly made. Small chips on the edge of the rim. Deposited substances. Pale brown to rosy brown clay at certain points, with many inclusions. Unpainted. Flat base; body, with very curved walls at the shoulder, narrows towards the bottom. The cylindrical neck narrows towards the top, where it turns into an everted rim with an almost flat upper surface. A small spout is shaped out of the rim by compressing the edges. The vertical strap handle sprouts from a little below the rim and ends on the shoulder. It has an imperceptible spine along the length of its back.
It is decorated with dense, horizontal grooves which run around the exterior of the neck and the upper half of the body. Reserved zone between the base of the neck and the sprouting of the handle on the shoulder.

COMMENTARY - BIBLIOGRAPHY: Unpublished.
This is a vase of everyday use. See *Agora* V, 6; certain vases of the 6th and 7th c. A.D. are decorated with parallel and horizontal wavy lines which are created by holding a comb as the vase is turned on the wheel. This technique, known in the Middle East from early antiquity, is used by Athenian potters even today. Also see *Agora* V, 114, M321-M322, pl. 31 (early 6th c. A.D.) and 118, M370, pl. 34 (similar vase; late 6th c. A.D.).

Ch.K.

59

INV. NO. M 2557.
MAX.L. 0.10, MAX.W. 0.074, MAX.H. 0.048, B.D. 0.045 M.

Complete. Orange clay, Attic. Circular underside formed from an asymmetrical moulded ring between grooves. The body has a concave, circular disc, with four holes for filling and ventilation. Handle not very high, vertical and thick. Intense traces of burning on the nozzle confirms its use. The vessel is mould-made. Unpainted.

The underside has two impressed lines perpendicular to one another forming a cross. Impressed dots are noted between their points and in other places. The disc is decorated with a representation of a relief Eros in three-quarter view. The figure is moving towards the right, turning his head backwards, and is holding a torch with one hand and a thyrsos in the other. The garment of the figure billows in the background on the left, and on the right one can distinguish a flaming altar. The facial characteristics are rendered in a very sketchy manner and in general the formulation of the subject is very care-

59   LID WITH RELIEF SCENE
4th-5th c. A.D.

INV. NO. M 2527.
MAX.D. 0.043, MAX.TH. 0.013 M.

Complete. Small, handmade, discoid lid. It has four holes on its circumference for attaching it to the vase. Small chips off the underside and a small incision through carelessness to the left of the head. Brownish clay with inclusions. Unpainted.

On the upper side, a sketchy bust of a figure is depicted in profile facing left. The hair is rendered with curved lines arranged in groups whilst a row of little lines, probably meant to represent a garland, surround the head. The eye is almond-shaped and the ear is shown by two small incisions. The attire of the figure comprises heavy folds depicted by wavy lines and straight-lined incisions. Two impressed knobs at the height of the shoulder probably indicate the heads of pins or buttons.

COMMENTARY - BIBLIOGRAPHY: Unpublished.
Similar representations of busts, in profile facing left, occur on lamp discs of the 4th c. A.D. There, however, the figures hold a double axe and are identified with Mithras, Athena or other deities. For specific similarities in the technical execution of the details of the relief representation see Karivieri 1996, 63, 159-160, pl. 31, no. 10 (lamp disc; late 4th c. A.D.) and *Agora* VII, 117-118, pl. 17, no. 752 (lamp disc; early 4th c. A.D.).
The material from the level in the well, from which the lid came, ranges from Late Roman to Early Christian periods. However, finds of the Late Roman period are in the majority (amongst them, there are a good number datable lamps and vases of the 4th and 5th c. A.D.). Based on the above, the period to which we can assign the find with relative safety is the 4th and 5th c. A.D.

Ch.K.

60

less. Herring-bone decoration and horizontal frames with an impressed branch around the border of the disc. The handle has two grooves on the upper part of its back and one on the lower part, while it is bounded by an impressed curved line at its end.

COMMENTARY - BIBLIOGRAPHY: Unpublished.
The representation of Eros with thyrsos and torch was very popular on lamps in Athens from the 1st quarter of the 4th to the 2nd half of the 5th c. A.D. The Attic workshops exported the type to Corinth, Lindos, Olympia, Tarsus etc. Mythological representations on lamps continued to be found in use in the 2nd half of the 5th c. A.D., an indication that idolatry had not lost its strength in this period. It is uncertain as to whether the impressed cross on the base of the lamp is accidental decoration or if it is linked with the symbol of Christianity. For the depiction of Eros on lamps see Karivieri 1996, 65-66 and for comparanda see Karivieri 1996, 158, no. 8, pl. 1 (Perlzweig 740; 1st half of 5th c. B.C.). For parallels see *Agora* VII, pl. 16, 17, no. 725 (Eros with torch and thyrsos; 1st half of 3rd c. A.D.) and no. 726 (late 3rd c. A.D.), no. 730 (Eros with torch and patera; 2nd half of 3rd c. A.D.); somewhat similar are no. 733 (1st half of 4th c. A.D.) and no. 740 (2nd half of 4th c. A.D.). Also see Bovon 1966, 72, nos. 500-501, pl. 12-13 (3rd-4th c. A.D.); *Corinth* IV₂, nos. 1115, 1120, pl. XV. For a comparable subject see Kübler 1952, 127, fig. 11 and 48. For much later representations of Eros on Roman sarcophagi see Toynbee 1934, pl. LI:4 and LIV:5.

H.H.

61 SINGLE-SPOUTED LAMP
After A.D. 450

INV. NO. M 2558.
L. 0.093, W. 0.065, MAX.H. 0.043, DIM. OF BASE 0.058 × 0.044 M.

Complete. Orange clay, Attic. Flat underside, almond-shaped. The body has nearly vertical walls and a circular concave disc with a central filling hole and three air holes. Solid, vertical handle. Intense traces of burning on the nozzle and body verify its use. Mould-made. Unpainted. The underside has an impressed inscription: ΣΩ/ΤΗΡΙ/ΑΣ. The disc is decorated with an impressed spoked rosette, and its lightly curved surround with im-

61

pressed herring-bone. Two impressed dots frame a ventilation hole in the region of the nozzle. The handle is embellished with two grooves on its back and broadens at its end near the base.

COMMENTARY - BIBLIOGRAPHY: Unpublished.
The lamp comes from the second largest workshop of the late 5th c. A.D., which belonged to Soteria (it worked almost parallel to the workshop of Chione, both female names). The precise site of the workshop has not yet been located. During the 5th c. A.D., the ceramic kilns may have been moved outside the city walls. This change in the centre of production can be attributed to the Vandal invasion of A.D. 467 or to a later invasion in A.D. 474.
For the workshop of Soteria see Karavieri 1996, 56-58 and 135-137, as well as no. 166, pl. 34 (comparable decoration of the disc and its surround; 1st half of 5th c. A.D.), no. 36, pl. 45 (comparable inscription; 2nd half of 5th c. A.D.). For the workshop of Soteria flourishing in the 1st half of the 5th c. A.D. see *Agora* VII, 52, as well as no. 2755, pl. 43 (for comparable spoked decoration), no. 2757, pl. 50 (comparable in profile and inscription ΣΩ (Σωτηρίας); 1st half of 5th c. A.D.). For the inscription ΣΩ (Σωτηρίας) see *Kenchreai* V, no. 340a-b, pl. 15 (1st half of 5th c. A.D.) and *Corinth* IV₂, pl. XXXII, no. 942.

H.H.

61

62 RATTLE
2nd half of 3rd - 4th c. A.D.

INV. NO. M 2524.
H. 0.144, MAX.W. 0.069, MAX.W. OF BASE 0.053 M.

Complete, carelessly made. The nozzle is slightly chipped. Reddish clay. It is a figurine in the shape of a child's bust on a cylindrical base, which was used as a rattle. It is in two mould-made parts, of which the back of the join is visible from the side view. There is a suspension hole pierced behind the head-dress and on the underside is a small air hole. It contains one or more solid objects, probably clay balls, to produce sound. The schematic anatomical and dress characteristics are finished off with painted elements on top of a white slip covering the whole figurine. The colours, although fugitive, are preserved on a great part of the surface whilst in other places they are completely destroyed.

The figure wears a tall head-dress, painted an orange-yellow colour on which linear, black painted decoration is spread. The ringlets of hair are indicated by a row of successive pendent semicircles and are finished off with red paint. The arched eyebrows are painted in black which also highlights the almond-shaped eyes and the pupils, whilst the mouth and dimple on the chin are highlighted in red. The body broadens noticeably where the arms would have been, as indicated by two vertical red lines. The oblique grooves, which depict the folds of the dress and the horizontal ring base, are strengthened by linear decorative elements in orange-yellow, black, red and blue-grey.

COMMENTARY - BIBLIOGRAPHY: Unpublished.

Figurines of this type in the form of schematised busts, are a characteristically Roman creation which is imported to Athens during the 3rd c. A.D. Frequently, and mainly in Athens, they are used as rattles by putting solid objects inside them so as to produce a rattling noise when shaken. Clay busts from the Athenian Agora are stuck on to cylindrical bases. Usually they depict children or men (priests or philosophers), whilst comparable female figurines are absent until the Late Roman period. In certain instances, children's busts take on the characteristics of Genius Cucullatus, namely a Good Daemon who wears a head-dress. However, his identification as Telesphoros is doubtful since the head-dress is the only element which would support this view. The linearity in the rendering of some of the features, painted or in relief, are characteristic of the 4th c. A.D.

For comparable examples see *Agora* VI, 51, no. 282, pl. 7 (somewhat similar; 2nd half of 3rd c. A.D.), no. 288, pl. 7 (head from similar figurine, mainly corresponding in colours; 4th c. A.D.), 52, no. 310, pl. 7 (head from similar boy's bust, with very close similarity in colouring; mid 4th c. A.D.), 57, no. 458, pl. 10 (similar example; late 4th c. A.D.), 18-20 (generally for the figurines-busts). For comparable figurines see Burr 1933a, 191-193, fig. 7. In connection with the hooded Daemon see Howatson 1996, 863, s.v. Genius. For Telesphoros see *LIMC* VII, 870-878, s.v. Telesphoros.

Ch.K.

62

5th-beginning of the 6th c. A.D., the importation of lamps from North Africa is observed. The local Attic workshops cease to produce unadulterated Attic types and begin to copy lamps which come from North Africa and Asia Minor. Their workshop products are no longer copied and remain nameless. The predominance is perhaps due to the better quality of the imports and the equivalent Attic products coming to an end, perhaps due to the Vandal invasion at the end of the 5th c. A.D. On the new type, Christian symbols are often portrayed, such as the Christogram, indicating the consolidation of the new religion in Attica. This symbol occurs very late in Attic lamps, during the 5th c. A.D., whilst Christian religion had spread much earlier. For comparanda see Karivieri 1996, 190, no. 95, pl. 45 (the upper part is a copy of an African lamp; 1st half of 6th c. A.D.). For parallels see *Agora* VII, 65, 180, no. 2492, pl. 40, 50 (2nd half of 5th c. A.D.).

H.H.

63 SINGLE-SPOUTED LAMP
End of 5th - 1st half of 6th c. A.D.

INV. NO. M 2603.
MAX.L. 0.097, W. 0.058, H. 0.025, DIM. OF BASE 0.044 × 0.30 M.

Complete. Brown-red clay with mica. Nearly flat underside. Oblong, boat-shaped body, very low, with almost vertical walls. A small circular, concave disc is joined to the lighting hole by a broad channel and has three filling holes. Broad, concave periphery. Four-sided, elongated nozzle. Handle not very thick, button-shaped and solid. Intense traces of burning are noticeable on the nozzle. Mould-made. Unpainted.

The underside, leaf-shaped formed by two grooves, has an impressed branch on its interior flanked by two dots. The disc is decorated with a Christogram with an open P, pointing right, whilst herringbone embellishes the points of the cross, which have double curved endings. The surround is decorated with detailed geometric design in low relief, triangles alternating with a trefoil, a branch and a bunch of grapes. The handle is embellished with a groove along the lower part of its back ending at the base.

COMMENTARY - BIBLIOGRAPHY: Unpublished.

In terms of shape and the relief decoration of its surround, the lamp imitates lamps which come from North Africa, while its base is typically Attic. At the end of the

64 BRONZE SHOVEL
Roman period

INV. NO. M 2539.
L. 0.27, L. OF HANDLE 0.19, H. 0.052, DIM. OF PAN
0.085 × 0.075 M.

Complete with limited restoration of the pan. Joined from two pieces in the middle of the handle. Heavily oxidised bronze with light coloured green patina.
In plan it is a parallelogram with trapezoidal side edges. They are taller than the third side, and have a lip triangular in section sloping outwards, with acute endings on the upper back section. In front, they have denticulated endings. The handle is circular in section. It starts off in the shape of a Corinthian column, with the capital joining the handle to the pan. The decoration of the handle is continued, increasing in diameter, with zones of moulded rings and ends in the shape of a kneeling bull.

COMMENTARY - BIBLIOGRAPHY: Unpublished.
The shovel, used for cleaning the altar after the sacrifice, is present from Mycenaean times; see Walters 1899, 7-8, nos. 107-111 and Richter 1915, 235, no. 657. Some examples show us its use in the Hellenistic and Etruscan region; see Lévêque 1952, 102, pl. 39, no. G105 (also earlier bibliography and other examples); Ars Antiqua, Auktion V Luzern, 7 Nov. 1964, Antike Kunstwerke, 16, no. 56, pl. XIV (shovel of Ptolemaic period, 3rd c. B.C. with a votive dedication to Serapis); Haynes 1974, 25-26, pl. XIV (perhaps from Praeneste, around 300 B.C., with decorated handle). It is also well represented in the Roman Imperial period. In this period, large centres of production are located in the Syro-Palestinian region and more rarely in Campania, Italy; see Richter 1915, 235-236, nos. 658-660 (all from Hauran in Syria); see Yadin 1963, 48-58; Yadin 1972, 107-109; Faider-Feytmans 1952, 174, no. F.25, pl. 61; Museo Borbonico X, pl. LXIV (richly decorated parallel from Pompeii); see Reinach 1917, 280-282.
In Roman times, the shovel takes on the shape of a real sacred object for burning aromatic offerings in the worship of different deities of Eastern provenance in the whole of the eastern Mediterranean region; for this see Goodenough 1954, 5, 195-208; Daremberg - Saglio, 1, s.v. batillum, 682-683, fig. 806. In eastern worship, even the position of the bull refers us to a specific shovel; see Goodenough 1953-1968, 3-28, just as numerous eastern deities were already imported even to Athens in the Roman period.

S.M.

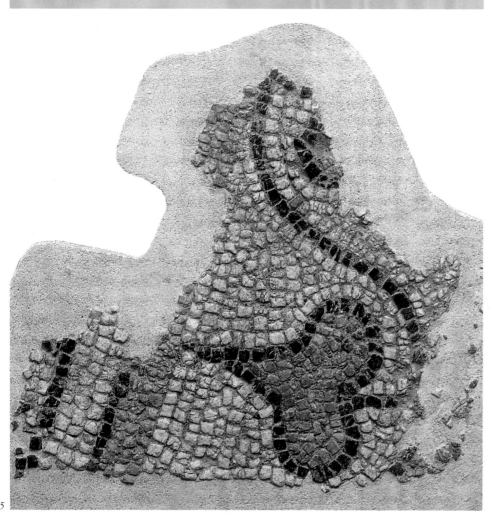

65

65 TWO FRAGMENTS FROM A SECTION
OF MOSAIC FLOOR
Early Christian period

INV. NO. M 2567A-B.
MAX.PRES.DIM. 1.345 × 1.232 AND 0.536 × 0.457,
SIZE OF TESSERAE 0.005-0.01 M.

Lifted and conserved. Traces of burn-ing on part of the surrounds of the cen-tral subject. Damaged in places. White, black, azure, rosy tesserae of hard cal-careous stone.
Main theme: tangential circles, arranged in a row, intersected by a parallel row of tangential circles, form quatrefoil deco-ration with varied lozenges in the centre. Intersected, divided in four, the circles form cruciform decoration with lozeng-es. The border is made up of a zone with schematic wavy vegetation and inverted, alternating ivy leaves. Two parallel bands are interposed between the main subject and this zone.

COMMENTARY - BIBLIOGRAPHY: Unpublished.

The exhibited mosaics comprise fragments of a de-stroyed mosaic floor, which was uncovered in an area of a room with its west boundary being the support wall of ancient Street I. Probable dimensions of the mosaic with preserved part of the bedding, 3.50 x 3.50 m. with a NW-SE orientation.

The mosaic is in the category of opus tesselatum with white and black tesserae, which is frequent from the 2nd c. until the 6th c. A.D.; for this see Becatti 1965, 112-118. The theme of tangential circles occurs in pre-Classical antiquity on pebble floors and is absent thereafter until the Imperial period, when it occurs once again up to the Byzantine period; see Bruneau 1969, 308-332. Tangential circles remain just that, whilst their decorative filling elements change; see Πελεκανίδης 1974, 32, n. 95-97, 99. Schematic vegetation with ivy leaves occurs at the end of the 4th c. A.D. and is prom-inent in the 6th; see Πελεκανίδης 1974, 27, n. 66-70. The decorative elements in our mosaic are met in divi-sions and panels of houses, public buildings, bath-houses and tombs. See Πελεκανίδης 1974, 103, pl. 72 (similar; 5th c. A.D.), 133-134, pl. 113β (comparable, chiefly for the arrangement of the circles; 6th c. A.D.), 91-92, pl. 60 (similar; 6th c. A.D.). Also see Ατζακά 1987, 173-175, pl. 293, 294β, 295β and γ, 299α (com-parable; end of 4th - beginning of 5th c. A.D.), 182-183, pl. 310-311α (comparable; 1st half of 5th c. A.D.), 228, pl. 106 (comparable; 2nd half of 4th c. A.D.), pl. 282 (similar; 4th c. A.D.); Ατζακά 1999, 257, pl. 177 (com-parable; probably 4th c. A.D.).

The floor in question is included in the first phase of the Athenian mosaic workshop which dates to the end of the 4th - 1st quarter of the 5th c. A.D., to which belong numerous floors uncovered near the Acropolis and the Olympieion with closely corresponding parallels in the Tetraconch of the Library of Hadrian and the Metröon of the Ancient Agora; for this see Ατζακά 1987, 9-13, 118-121, pl. 175β, δ and 118, pl. 172-173.

S.G.

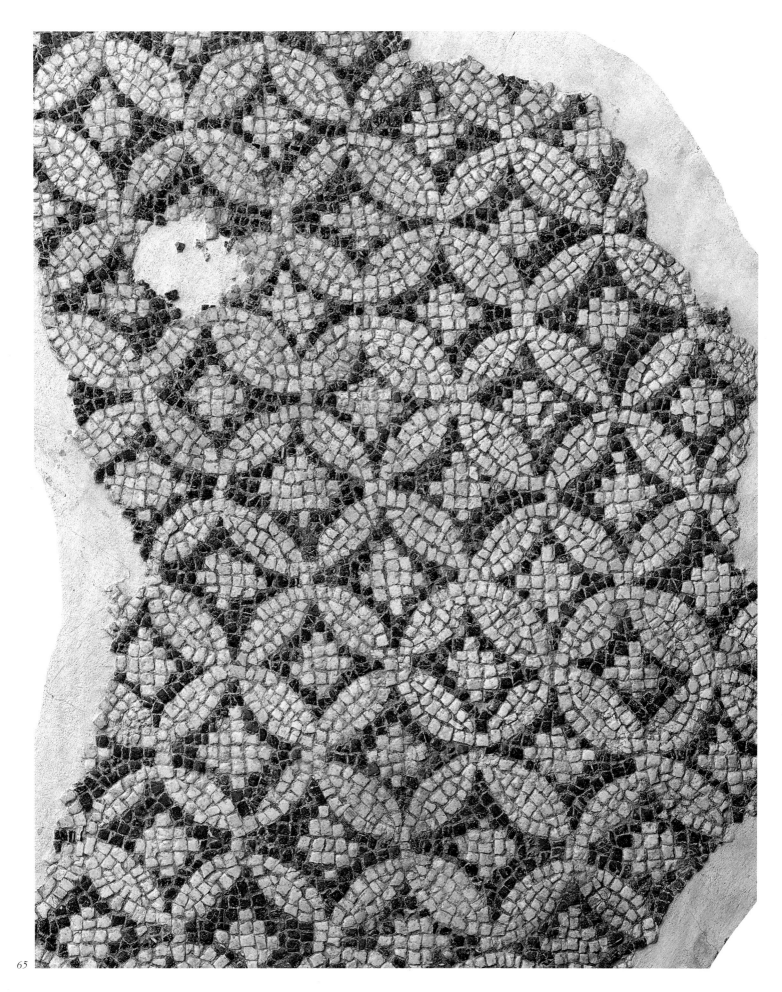

66 SECTION OF MOSAIC FLOOR
Early Christian period

INV. NO. M 2568A-Γ.
MAX.PRES.DIM. 1.20 × 1.90, SIZE OF TESSERAE 0.01-0.025 M.

Lifted and conserved in three divided sections. The greater part of M2568α is preserved and a section of 2568β. Damage to sections of the mosaic in places. White, black, rosy, blue tesserae of hard calcareous stone.

66

On the exterior section of the central theme, two tangential octagons encircle an octagon with an inscribed medallion of a clockwise eight-leafed rosette with right-turning tips in its interior. With the outline of the mosaic, the sides of the exterior octagons, which are not touching, form an isosceles triangle with a four-leafed clover. The panel consists of a broad band decorated by a zone of alternating right-angled borders which form swastikas at the point of contact. Thus, they delimit a parallelogram which encloses a zone of oblique bands. The exterior borders are indicated by double and single lines of black tesserae. The bands and decoration are rendered in alternating white, blue and rosy tesserae. The background is indicated with white tesserae.

COMMENTARY - BIBLIOGRAPHY: Unpublished.

The present find is part of a destroyed mosaic floor which was probably about 5.07 x 5.10 m. in size and with a N-S orientation in an area of a room west of ancient Street I. In the remaining section, the theme of octagons and the decoration are repeated, the only difference being that the non-touching sides of the octagons form a lozenge with a quatrefoil rosette. On the inner corner of the exterior section of the central theme, there is a right-angled triangle with a schematic ivy leaf.

The mosaic is in the category of opus tesselatum with polychrome decoration. The theme of tangential octagons is known from Roman Imperial times, from the 2nd half of the 2nd c. A.D. It is indicative of extensive areas of houses and public buildings. In the Greek area, it is chiefly met in the 2nd half of the 4th to the 5th c. A.D., where octagons are embellished with a combination of plant, zoomorphic or geometric motifs (for similar of the mid 5th c. A.D. see Πελεκανίδης 1974, 104, pl. 73; for a comparable example of the 5th - beginning of the 6th c. A.D. see Πελεκανίδης 1974, 131, 132, pl. 112; for a comparable example of the 1st half of the 6th c. A.D. see Ατζακά 1987, 80-83, pl. 107; for a comparable piece of probably the 1st half of the 6th c. A.D. see Ατζακά 1987, 190-191, pl. 326. For the meander pattern see Πελεκανίδης 1974, 34-35, n. 112-113).

The six-leafed or quatrefoil rosette is frequently used. The motif of the eight-leafed rosette "in motion" with the ends of the leaves bent is already known from the mosaics of Delos and is met in the Greek area and in other western and eastern regions of the Roman empire; see *Délos* XXIX, 256, 274-275, fig. 204-209, 229-231, pl. B4; Donderer 1986, 38, no. 54, pl. 13/3; Πετράκος 1969, 369, pl. 379α, 381β; Campbell 1979, 289, pl. 42, 3-5, 43-9; Borboudakis *et al.* 1983, 370, fig. 331, 371.

The floor in question, which belongs to the tradition of the Athenian workshop, can be paralleled by the mosaic floors in the National Gardens and Evripidou Street which are dated to the 2nd quarter - middle of 5th c. A.D. As far as the subject of rosettes and the varied colours are concerned, it is probably earlier than these; see Ατζακά 1987, 15-21, 129-133, pl. 200-210 and 134, pl. 212.

S.G.

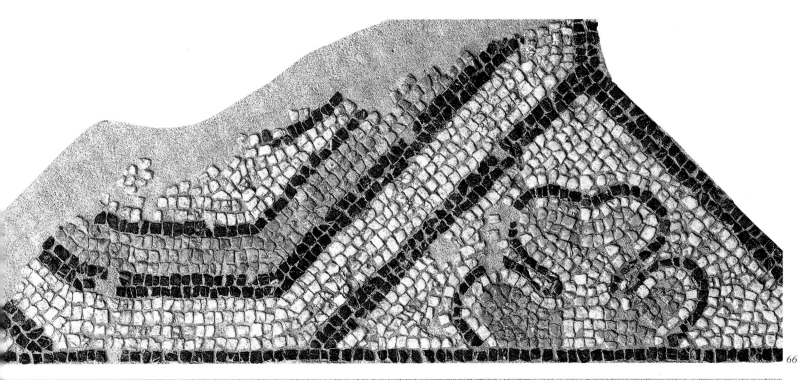

66

66

91

CEREMONIAL PYRES

One particular aspect of religious life for the inhabitants of ancient Athens was the "ceremonial pyres", as scholars call the relics of a category of religious practices known only from archaeological excavations. These were fires lit in small, shallow pits which are found in settlement sites, usually beneath the floors of houses, installations or workshops but absent from public areas. They are chiefly known from the large excavations of the Athenian Agora, the Areopagus, the Kerameikos and recently from the excavation for the ACROPOLIS station of the M.R.A., on the Makryianni plot.

The pits of pyres contain remains of burning (ash, charcoal), animal or bird bones as well as small or large groups of burnt and often smashed vases, of specific shapes. Thus, in the pyres we find drinking vessels (kantharoi, skyphoi), miniature versions of tablewares (bowls, basins and plates of different kinds), miniatures of kitchen utensils (saucepans, dishes), vases for oil or aromatics (lekythoi, alabastra, perfume bottles) and lamps. It is thought that many of these were specifically manufactured for religious use, since they are almost exclusively found at the sites of ceremonial pyres, in tombs and as burial offerings.

It is not absolutely certain if the presence of vases in pyres had only a symbolic meaning or if they – or most of them – were used for making libations and for deposits of fixed offerings. The absence of written sources makes it particularly difficult to review the ceremony and interpret the custom. However, from the character of the finds – very strong funerary elements – it follows that the character of the pyres was chthonic and consequently the recipients of the offerings would have belonged to the chthonic powers of Greek religion and particularly to those who, if appeased, could have protected against or warded off evil from private land. It has been stated that the ceremonial pyres were a kind of sacrificial foundation deposit and were related to the construction, renovation or re-use of a structure by new owners.

As far as the appearance and chronological span of the custom is concerned, our knowledge is not yet sufficient, for the time being at least. As far as we know, the custom goes back to the 5th c. B.C., although it is practised more frequently in the 4th and 1st half of the 3rd c. B.C. Until precisely when it survives is also unknown. Until recently, it was thought that it did not continue after the middle of the 3rd c. B.C., but excavation at the Makryianni plot has provided new evidence. Thus, after a first appraisal of the nine ceremonial pyres which have come to light, two date to the end of the 5th c. B.C., five to the end of the 4th or beginning of the 3rd c. B.C., one to the middle of the 2nd or a little later and the last, to the 1st quarter of the 1st c. B.C.

In the exhibition, pyre 7 was chosen for presentation since its content is typical of the kind of offerings which ceremonial pyres contained when the custom reached its peak, and pyre 2, since it bears witness to its survival even in times later than those in which it was until recently thought to have been practised.

COMMENTARY - BIBLIOGRAPHY: For ceremonial pyres in general see Thompson - Wycherley 1972, 16, pl. 26b; *Agora* XII, 45; Knigge - Kovascovics 1981, 388; Shear 1973, 151; Shear 1984, 45-47; Young 1951, 110-130; Knigge - von Freytag 1987, 488, fig. 14; Knigge 1993, 134, fig. 17-18; *Agora* XXIX, 212-214; Ελευθεράτου forth.; Jordan - Rotroff 1999, 147-154.

S.E.

Pyre 7

Pyre 7 was situated west of Street IV, in an area bordered by the west embankment of the road and the foundation of a wall at right angles to it (fig 16). We are certainly dealing with a room of some housing complex, the plan of which was not possible to reconstruct, owing to the limited excavation area at that point. Although the floor of the room was not preserved, it was nevertheless ascertained that the pit for the pyre had been opened in a thick, pebbly layer of earth that gave the impression of a floor bedding. The pit was an irregular ovoid shape (l. 0.67 m., w. 0.25 m. and depth 0.10 m.). Its sides and bottom were scorched and of the vases, some were found fragmented but in their original position and others shattered – most probably dug out – and mixed up with ash and bones. The pyre, apart from those vases included in the exhibition, also contained two small fragments of spindle-shaped perfume bottles as well as three rim fragments of utensils, probably dishes; these are not on display due to their very fragmentary condition. From all the finds, pyre 7 can be dated to the end of the 1st or beginning of the 2nd quarter of the 3rd c. B.C.

16. ACROPOLIS Station. The ritual pyre 7 during excavation. The wall of the room contemporary to it is visible to the left.
To the right, a large corn-storage structure of the mid-Byzantine period. Above, the street layers of the present-day Makryianni Street and the rails of the old tram.

16

67 BLACK-GLAZED KANTHAROS
WITH "WEST-SLOPE" DECORATION
300-275 B.C.

INV. NO. M 2495.
H. 0.11, M.D. 0.079, B.D. 0.044 M.

Mended. Part of the body and the end of the lobe of the handle are missing. Brown to greyish clay; brown-red to dark brown paint, lustrous, very fugitive. The base of the vase is stepped, in the shape of an inverted echinus with a ring base attached to it. On the steps as well as the underside, there is the characteristic scraped grooving of Attic Hellenistic vases, which is made by scraping away the paint with the help of a pointed implement. The base is joined to the body by a cylindrical stem. At the point where they meet, there is yet another scraped groove. The walls of the body are curving, adorned with relief oblong leaves. The neck is high, cylindrical with a light concave profile ending in a simple everted rim. The handles are vertical and crowned by horizontal, slightly raised, projections (lobes).

The vase is monochrome. On the neck and two sides, it has "West Slope" decoration: an olive branch with counterbal-

anced leaves is formed using diluted clay, applied on top of the dark paint.

COMMENTARY - BIBLIOGRAPHY: Unpublished.

Attic. The kantharos belongs to a particularly characteristic category of drinking vases of the Classical and Hellenistic periods. The shape was developed in the 2nd quarter of the 4th c. B.C., based on an older prototype and remained popular for more than a century. The oldest kantharoi of the Classical tradition had a moulded rim. Later, however – from the last quarter of the 4th c. B.C. – the rim was formed simply on the potter's wheel (plain rim). The present kantharos is of this last variation. The high body with its slender proportions and the raised backs of its lobes class it with later examples of the type and allow it to be dated to the end of the 1st quarter of the 3rd c. B.C. or a little later. For similar kantharoi see Young 1951, 122, Pyre 7:5, pl. 52a (turn of the 4th to 3rd c.); Vanderpool *et al.* 1962, 37, no. 37, pl. 20 (1st half of 3rd c. B.C.); Braun 1970, 142, no. 100, pl. 58,1 (beginning of 3rd c. B.C.); Miller 1974, 229, no. 7, pl. 30 (beginning of 3rd c. B.C.); Πατσιαδά 1983, 171, no. 94, pl. 63γ (mid 3rd c. B.C.); Rotroff 1983, 286, no. 27, pl. 53 (290-260 B.C.); Braun 1991, 29, no. 4:3, pl. 55b, 9c; *Agora* XXIX, 244, no. 26, pl. 3 (285-275 B.C.). For the origin and development of the shape see *Agora* XII, 11-124; Πατσιαδά 1983, 114-118; *Agora* XXIX, 83-104. For Attic pottery of "West Slope" type see Thompson 1934, 438-447; Rotroff 1991, 59-102; *Agora* XXIX, 38-71.

S.E.

68 BLACK-GLAZED KANTHAROS
WITH "WEST-SLOPE" DECORATION
275-250 B.C.

INV. NO. M 2494.
H. 0.076, M.D. 0.078, B.D. 0.04 M.

Mended; one handle restored. The clay is grey-brown, the paint black, lustrous, very fugitive on one side. It has a high ring base with shallow grooving where it is attached to the body. The body is broad with curved walls on the lower part, slightly concave above, and undeveloped joint in the region of its maximum diameter. Vertical strap handles crowned on top by rams' heads.

The vase is monochrome. On the neck and on both sides, it has "West Slope" decoration: an olive branch with counter-

balanced leaves without the stalks, rendered by applying thinned clay.

COMMENTARY - BIBLIOGRAPHY: Unpublished.

Attic. It belongs to the Hellenistic type of kantharos which is considered to draw on prototypes from the "Kabeirian" skyphos or kantharos made in Boeotia as early as the 5th c. B.C. The shape first turns up in Attica towards the end of the 4th c. B.C., is particularly popular in the 3rd and survives until the beginning of the 2nd c. B.C. The type is met in three basic variations: either with a uniform, angular or baggy profile to the body and nearly always with "West Slope" decoration. Smaller versions with the same characteristics are also produced. These small kantharoi, which become popular in the 2nd quarter of the 3rd c. B.C., are often found in ceremonial pyres. No. 68 belongs to a type of kantharos with angular profile and, on the basis of published parallels, can be dated to the 2nd quarter of the 3rd c. B.C.

For similar examples see Young 1951, 125, Pyre 9:2, pl. 52c, 129, Pyre 13:3-4, pl. 54a, 130, Pyre 14:2, pl. 54b; Thompson 1934, A31, fig. 5; Braun 1970, 139, no. 80, pl. 56; *Alt-Ägina* II.1, 73, no. 529, pl. 40; Rotroff 1984b, 32, no. 9, pl. 67e; *Agora* XXIX, 265, no. 221, drawing 6, pl. 21. For the origin and development of the shape see Thompson 1934, 444-445; *Corinth* VII3, 74, 86; Braun 1970, 167; *Agora* XXIX, 97-107. For the end of the sequence see Shear 1973, 155, pl. 335 (200-175 B.C.).

S.E.

69 BLACK-GLAZED SKYPHOS
300-250 B.C.

INV. NO. M 2496.
H. 0.069, M.D. 0.067, B.D. 0.034 M.

Mended, intense traces of burning. Brown to greyish brown clay, paint light to dark brown, thin and fugitive. The vase has a flat, discoid base and low foot. The outline of the body is a concave curve and the walls are fairly thick. Everted rim. The handles are horizontal, elliptical in section, placed high, near the rim with slightly raised ends. The vase is monochrome with the exception of the underside.

COMMENTARY - BIBLIOGRAPHY: Unpublished.

Skyphoi belong to one of the most widely dispersed

shape of drinking vases with a large life-span. Their production began in the 6th c. B.C. and was continued until roughly the middle of the 3rd c. B.C. Two basic types can be distinguished, the Corinthian and the Attic. The small skyphoi, which copied the larger ones in shape, are considered votives since they are very often found in funerary and ceremonial pyres as well as in assemblages from sanctuaries. The small skyphos no. 69 represents the Attic type and although the shape of the base differs slightly from that of known examples, nevertheless, its more general characteristics date it to the 1st half of the 3rd c. B.C.

For similar examples see Thompson 1934, 319, A26, fig. 5 (deposited before 260 B.C.); Young 1951, 121, Pyre 6:3-4, pl. 51c, 128, Pyre 12:3, pl. 53c (near the end of the 4th c. B.C.); Miller 1974, 231, no. 19, pl. 31 (around 260 B.C.); *Corinth* VII₃, 365, no. 71, pl. 50 (275 B.C.); *Kerameikos* IX, 44, Pyre 37, pl. 40:7; Rotroff 1984b, 347, no. 4, pl. 67 (315-285 B.C.); Braun 1991, 32, no. 9:2, pl. 4a; *Agora* XXIX, 207, no. 1397, pl. 107 (300-275 B.C.). For skyphoi in general see *Corinth* VII₃, 66-68; *Agora* XII, 84-85; *Agora* XXIX, 94. For dedicatory skyphoi see *Agora* XXIX, 207.

S.E.

70 BLACK-GLAZED HANDLELESS SKYPHOS
Beginning of 3rd c. B.C.

INV. NO. M 2499.
H. 0.04, MAX.D. 0.082, B.D. 0.045 M.

A little more than half the vase is preserved, mended and restored. Brown to grey-brown clay. Dark brown to black fugitive paint. Monochrome with traces of burning. Ring base with grooving on its underside. Deep body with curved outline and in-curving rim. The greatest diameter of the body is high up, near the rim.

COMMENTARY - BIBLIOGRAPHY: Unpublished.

The vase belongs to a category of skyphoi called "echinus bowls" because of their shape, which are counted as tableware. They are considered to occur first in the 4th c. B.C., probably based on older prototypes. They have a very wide distribution in the whole of the Mediterranean world and are common finds on excavations. The shape occurs in two basic types characterised by the depth of the body. The vase is categorised amongst the type of skyphoi with a deep body (deep echinus bowls), as a miniature variation thereof. The type is produced from the end of the 4th to the end of the 2nd c. B.C. or even a little later. In accordance with the typological development of the larger examples – where they are better traced – but also in tune with its own parallels, vase no. 70 can be dated to the beginning of the 3rd c. B.C.

For similar examples see Thompson 1934, 318, A20, fig. 4 and 117 (deposited before 260 B.C.); Young 1951, 116, Pyre 2:7, pl. 50b (3rd quarter of 4th c. B.C.); *Agora* XXIX, 343, no. 1027, pl. 77 (A.D. 300-290); Braun 1970, 143, no. 104, pl. 58:1; Metzger 1971, 50, no. 38, pl. 10 (end of 3rd - mid 2nd c. B.C.); Miller 1974, 234, no. 30, pl. 32; *Corinth* VII₃, 32, no. 32, pl. 2 and 44 (mid 3rd c. B.C.). In general, for the production and development of the shape see *Corinth* VII₃, 29-31; *Agora* XII, 131-132; Δρούγου - Τουράτσογλου 1980, 129-133; *Agora* XXIX, 162-163.

S.E.

68, 67, 69, 70

71 SMALL LEKANIS WITH LID
300-270 B.C.

INV. NO. M 2497.
BODY: H. 0.048, M.D. 0.06, B.D. 0.028 M.
LID: H. 0.033, D. 0.062 M.

Mended. Small parts of the body and rim are missing. Brown to grey-brown clay, dark brown to black paint, opaque. The base is broad, flat but very slightly concave while the underside has marks from string which helped to remove the vase from the wheel. The body is deep with walls which thicken towards the top. The rim is crowned with a projecting groove for receiving the lid, above which the top of the rim is slightly elevated. The lid is shallow with walls which turn downwards near their edge creating an angular join. On top it has a solid button-shaped handle.

COMMENTARY - BIBLIOGRAPHY: Unpublished.

The lekanides are vases with a long history in Attic pottery. As simple household pots, they were used to serve food and preserve spices. However, the black-painted lekanides or those with painted decoration, turn up among objects used for women's toiletries, contained unguents, cosmetics and different personal small objects, while they were most probably useful for looking after pigments and pharmaceutical substances. They were common as a wedding present and funeral offering. The small "pyre lekanides", of which no. 71 is one, are known from the beginning of the 4th c. B.C. and it is thought that they drew their origin from the so-called "Lycinic" lekanides of the 5th c. B.C. In the older examples, they were given a ring base and a mould-made handle. The shape developed during the 4th c. B.C. and acquired its final characteristics in the 3rd c. B.C. It is believed that its production continued until the 2nd quarter of that century, perhaps not much after 260 B.C. Lekanides are met in ceremonial pyres with particular frequency. No. 71, which represents a fairly late development of the type, is dated to the 1st quarter of the 3rd c. B.C.

For similar examples see Young 1951, 118, Pyre 4:7, pl. 51a (4th quarter of 4th c. B.C.) and 123, Pyre 7:8, pl. 52a (turn of the 4th to 3rd c. B.C.); Knigge - Kovacsovics 1981, 388, fig. 10; *Kerameikos* IX, 43, no. 35:2, pl. 39:9 (4th c. B.C.); *Kerameikos* XIV, 126, no. 159:28-30, pl. 54, 5 (3rd c. B.C.); Braun 1991, 29, no. 5:3, pl. 7d; *Agora* XXIX, 384, no. 1452, pl. 110 (300-270 B.C.). For the shape in general see Young 1951, 112; *Agora* XII, 173 (where there is reference to the name "λυκινικές"; *Agora* XXIX, 214.

S.E.

72

72 PLATE (PINAKION) WITH LOOP HANDLES
300-275 B.C.

INV. NO. M 2487.
H. 0.02, M.D. 0.128, B.D. 0.07 M.

Mended. Small parts of the body and rim have been restored. Rosy to grey-brown clay, fine-grained with a little mica and occasional white inclusions. Brown paint on rim near handles. Flat base, slightly concave with traces of string marks on the underside. The body has oblique walls. The matching strap handles are small and horizontal, pressed onto the edge of the rim.

COMMENTARY - BIBLIOGRAPHY:
Unpublished.
Similar to M 2488 from the same pyre. Small saucers with horizontal strap handles are very often met in funerary and ceremonial pyres and it is conjectured that they were made specifically for that purpose. They are known from the 5th c. B.C. and the older examples have painted decoration on the bottom, sometimes black figure, more often, however, wide, concentric bands. Towards the end of the 4th c. B.C., the bands are abandoned and the paint is confined to the region of the handles or does not exist at all. The two saucers from pyre 7 are considered amongst the latest of the type and date to the 1st third of the 3rd c. B.C.

For similar examples see Young 1951, 129, Pyre 13:10-11, pl. 54a (beginning of 3rd c. B.C.) and 128, Pyre 12:6-7, pl. 53c (end of 4th c. B.C.); *Kerameikos* XIV, 72, no. 79:8-9, pl. 48,2 (3rd c. B.C.) and 127, no. 159:64-67, pl. 65,5; Braun 1991, 30, no. 6:5, pl. 8b; *Agora* XXIX, 384, no. 1452 (300-270 B.C.). For the shape in general see *Agora* XII, 149, pl. 37 and 199, pl. 69 as well as *Agora* XXIX, 214-215.

S.E.

73 SHALLOW HANDLELESS PLATE (PINAKION)
300-275 B.C.

INV. NO. M 2486.
H. 0.015, M.D. 0.095 M.

About half the vase is preserved, mended and restored. Brown-red to grey clay, fine-grained with a little mica and occasional inclusions. Unpainted with traces of burning. Flat base with string marks where the vase was removed from the wheel. Broad body with thin, sloping walls, slightly concave above the base. The rim is imperfectly formed.

COMMENTARY - BIBLIOGRAPHY: Unpublished.
The vase is in the group of "Shallow Pyre Saucers", vases which were produced exclusively for ceremonial purposes. The shape is known from the end of the 5th c. B.C. and the older examples are painted. Unpainted saucers are common from the last quarter of the 4th c. B.C. and remain in use at least until the 1st quarter of the next century. No. 73, like its parallels, can be dated to the 1st quarter of the 3rd c. B.C.

For similar examples see Young 1951, 129, Pyre 12:9, pl. 53c (close to the end of the 4th c. B.C.); *Agora* XXIX, 385-386, no. 1467 (325-275 B.C.), no. 1468 (290-250 B.C.), pl. 111. For the shape in general see *Agora* XXIX, 215.

S.E.

74 MINIATURE PLATE (PINAKION)
300-275 B.C.

INV. NO. M 2482.
H. 0.016, M.D. 0.064 M.

Mended with a few chips in the rim. Brown-red to brown clay. Unpainted with traces of burning. Flat base, slightly concave with string impressions where the vase was removed from the wheel. Crudely made.

COMMENTARY - BIBLIOGRAPHY: Unpublished.
Similar examples (M 2483, M 2484 and M 2485) from the same pyre. Miniature saucers of the "Small Pyre Saucer" type are the most simple and common find in pyres and it is thought that they were exclusively produced for ceremonial use. Rarely do they occur alone, frequently forming small or large groups. They are known from the end of the 5th c. B.C. and were originally painted. After 325 B.C., paint occurs more rarely

71

73

75

74

and at the turn of the century, it is left off. There is no substantial development in shape, even if it has been noted that in the latest examples the body is shallower. For similar examples see Young 1951, 123, Pyre 7:22-36, 125, Pyre 8:13, pl. 52b, 129, Pyre 12:10-12; Schlörb-Vierneisel 1966, 92, no. 160:21-30, pl. 58,4; *Kerameikos* XIV, 72, no. 79:20-26, pl. 47,9, 127, no. 159:70-95, pl. 55,4; *Agora* XXIX, 386, no. 1471, pl. 111 (325-275 B.C.), 386, no. 1472, pl. 111 (300-259 B.C.). For miniature saucers in general see *Agora* XII, 199 and *Agora* XXIX, 215.

S.E.

75 DISH WITH LID
300-275 B.C.

INV. NO. M 2491.
BODY: H. 0.031, M.D. 0.093, B.D. 0.051 M. LID: H. 0.025, M.D. 0.083 M.

Complete apart from small part of rim. Rosy to brown clay, fine with a little mica. Traces of burning. The base is flat with a trace of the string with which the vase was removed from the wheel. The body is deep with curved walls. The rim is turned obliquely upwards and on its interior edge, an inner groove is formed to receive the lid. The strap handle is in the form of a loop, pressed on top of the rim. The lid has thin, slanting walls and on top has a solid, button-shaped handle. String marks are also preserved on the upper surface of the handle.

COMMENTARY - BIBLIOGRAPHY: Unpublished.
These small bowls are simply the miniatures of normal bowls, shallow pots for cooking and frying food. They were produced from the end of the 5th c. B.C. and, as indicated by the examples known to date, survived at least until the 2nd quarter of the 3rd c. B.C. During the Hellenistic period, their use was almost exclusively votive. They are found in the context of funerary offerings and ceremonial pyres, where their occurrence is particularly frequent. The earliest small bowls – as with the larger bowls – are made of the coarse, impure, fire-proof clay of cooking wares. Thereafter, a purer, fine-grained clay was used, although dishes made of both types of clay existed sometimes in the same group indicating that the material of manufacture does not constitute an adequately secure chronological criterion. The form of the base gives more evidence for their dat-

ing since on the older examples, it is rounded, whilst on later examples – after 300 B.C. – it is flat. Based on this criterion, no. 75 and the similar M 2492 from the same pyre, can be dated to the 1st quarter of the 3rd c. B.C. For similar examples see Young 1951, 125, Pyre 8:11, 12, pl. 52b (turn of the 4th to 3rd c. B.C.); Schlörb-Vierneisel 1966, 92, no. 160:31-33, pl. 58:3; *Agora* XII, 346, no. 1564, pl. 69 (1st quarter of 3rd c. B.C.); *Kerameikos* XIV, 72, no. 79:27-30, pl. 47,9 (3rd c. B.C.), no. 159:54-63, 127, pl. 54,3-4 (3rd c. B.C.); Braun 1991, 29, Brandgrab QO IX, pl. 8b; *Agora* XXIX, 388, no. 1489, pl. 112 (300-250 B.C.). For bowls in general see *Agora* XII, 227. For small bowls see *Agora* XII, 198 and *Agora* XXIX, 216.

S.E.

76 SMALL COOKING-POT (OR LADLE)
300-270 B.C.

INV. NO. M 2489.
H. 0.066, M.D. 0.062 M.

Mended. Rosy brown to grey clay, fine-grained with a little mica. Traces of burn-

ing in the region of the handle. Unpainted. Spherical body with uniform outline, flat base with string marks where the vase was removed from the wheel. Slightly everted rim. Strap handle, which begins at the rim, is raised a little and ends at the middle of the belly. A small lump of clay remains stuck onto one side of the pot.

COMMENTARY - BIBLIOGRAPHY: Unpublished.
This small vase, no. 76 (as well as a similar one, M 2490, from the same pyre), belongs to a category of pots on which views differ with regard to their nomenclature and use. Greek scholars normally call them "αρυτή-ρες", dippers, that is vases for scooping water. In the publications of the Athenian Agora, they are characterised as cooking-pots and are included amongst cooking equipment. However, the fact that they are made of coarse, unrefined clay, capable, as it seems, of withstanding high temperatures, may favour their use in cooking, without of course, excluding other uses. The shape is widely distributed, whilst the morphological changes to which it was susceptible in its long lifespan, were few. Small sauce-pots are simply miniature versions of the large ones. In this size, they are known as early as the 6th c. B.C. and were initially handmade

76

of the same unrefined clay as the larger versions. However, from the end of the 4th c. B.C., they were made on the potter's wheel with small-grained, fairly fine clay. They are very often found in tombs and ceremonial pyres and it is thought that they were produced specifically for these. In contrast, their presence in settlement complexes is considered pure chance. The flat base of vase no. 76 and M 2490, one of the few morphological developments of the type, points to a fairly late date and in agreement with their parallels, they can be placed chronologically in the 1st third of the 3rd c. B.C. For similar examples see Young 1951, 115, Pyre 1:7, pl. 50a, 125, Pyre 8:9-10, pl. 52b; Metzger 1971, 53-54, nos. 55-60, pl. 10; Agora XII, 372, nos. 1939-1940, pl. 10; Kerameikos XIV, 126, no. 159:19-27, pl. 54:5 and 55:1; Agora XXIX, 387, no. 1480, pl. 111 (300-270 B.C.). For cooking-pots in general see Agora XII, 224-225. For small cooking-pots of the Hellenistic period see Agora XXIX, 215-216. For the term "αρυτήρας" or "ladle" see Ανδρόνικος 1955, 45, n. 1; Δρούγου - Τουράτσογλου 1980, 120-122; Καλτσάς 1983, 31.

S.E.

profile of its body and the shaping of the rim, allows it to be dated to the 1st quarter of the 3rd c. B.C. For similar lamps see Agora IV, type 25B, particularly no. 305, 73, pl. 10, 38 (350-250 B.C. or according to Rotroff's dating in Agora XXIX – about 340-275 B.C.); Kerameikos XI, type RSL4, 26ff.; Davidson 1934, type VII, 1st group, 54, no. 52, fig. 22; Isthmia III, 17, type VIID, no. 126, pl. 3 and 17; Miller 1974, 239, no. 74, pl. 34; Rotroff 1983, 291, no. 61, pl. 56 (350-290 B.C.).

S.E.

77 SINGLE-SPOUTED LAMP
300-275 B.C.

INV. NO. M 2493.
H. 0.04, D. 0.065, B.D. 0.038 M.

Mended from four fragments. Brown to grey clay, black burnished paint, fugitive in places. Monochrome interior and exterior with the exception of the underside and the grooving around the rim. The base is raised up with a concave underside, which has a moulded disc in the centre. The profile of the body is curved. The rim is horizontal with a raised ring around the filling hole. The spout is long with a flat upper surface and curved end. There are no traces of fire distinguishing the hole for the wick, and consequently the lamp was left in the pyre unused. On its right side is a perforated projection (ear).

COMMENTARY - BIBLIOGRAPHY: Unpublished.
The lamp is Attic and is included in type 25B of the Athenian Agora. The type, amongst the most widely spread for the period, was in use from the middle of the 4th to the 1st quarter of the 3rd c. B.C. The particular characteristics of lamp no. 77, such as its size, the

Pyre 2 was discovered near the west embankment of Street I. Its pit had been opened in an earth floor of an area which belonged to a building that, during the excavation at least, was characterised as a workshop or installation. The pit was of an irregular ovoid shape (l. 0.65 m., w. 0.50 m. and depth 0.10-0.12 m.) and orientated E-W. Its sides were scorched and its contents were overflowing somewhat beyond its borders. After the burning had been completed and the offerings deposited, the pit was covered with earth and then sealed with the next earth floor. Most of the vases were found shattered or destroyed in their original position. The burning in the pyre caused strong fluctuations in the colours of the clay and paint of the vases. The animal bones were mainly ovicaprid, as shown by the osteological study of the material in the Anthropological Museum of Athens University. From all the finds of pyre 2, it turns out that it took place in the beginning or middle of the 3rd quarter of the 2nd c. B.C. (150-140 B.C.).

78 BOWL WITH RELIEF DECORATION
End of 3rd - 1st quarter of 2nd c. B.C.

INV. NO. M 2429.
H. 0.089, M.D. 0.137 M.

Mended and a good many parts of the body and rim restored. Brown-red to greyish clay. Black paint with a metallic sheen, destroyed in places. Hemispherical body with everted rim.

On the medallion base, a double rosette with four interior petals and eight on the exterior with flower buds sprouting from them. The medallion is divided from the calyx by a double, scraped, deep groove, in which traces of red paint can be distinguished (red ochre). A row of miniature leaves sprouts from the exterior groove and thick rows of fern leaves spread out. The body is decorated with scenes from the Dionysiac circle: a pair of standing antithetic goats are depicted with a krater between them and they alternate with pairs of Eros's who carry comic masks of bearded men and of slaves, figures known in New Comedy. Amongst the masks, a little lower down, birds carry garlands. Beneath the rim is a double decorative zone: in the lower, an Ionic wave unfolds, in the upper, pairs of double spirals with fern leaves sprouting from them, framed by dolphins. Beneath the top of the rim is a scraped groove with a trace of red ochre. The indiscernible figures on the rim and body indicate the use of a damaged mould or old seals.

COMMENTARY - BIBLIOGRAPHY

The bowl is a product of Athenian workshop A. The hemispherical handleless bowls with relief decoration of plants motifs and narrative representations, the so-called "Megarian bowls", comprise one of the most characteristic groups of Hellenistic pottery, with a considerable distribution throughout the Hellenistic world and provide a substitute for earlier shapes of drinking vessels. In Athens, which is considered their place of origin, they first occur in the last quarter of the 3rd c. B.C., become particularly popular in the 2nd whilst their production stops decisively at the end of the 1st c. B.C. Relief bowls do not develop from an earlier ceramic type, as do most clay vessels, but rather constitute a direct imitation of metal prototypes. Their manufacture was achieved through use of clay moulds. The finest quality bowls, with plant decoration or narrative representations, come from the period 225 until 175 B.C. From that time on, their quality diminishes and around 140 B.C. they are replaced by bowls with relief decoration of long petals, when their production was reduced to a few. See Ελευθεράτου forth.

For similar examples see Thompson 1934, 379, D35, fig. 66a-b (before the mid 2nd c. B.C.); Braun 1970, 150, no. 148, pl. 65.5; *Agora* XXII, 57, no. 108, pl. 19 (225-200 B.C.); *Agora* XXVII, 190, no. 169, pl. 44 (for body motifs). For bowls with relief decoration in general see Courby 1922, 277-437; Schwabacher 1941, 203; *Délos* XXXI; Siebert 1978; *Agora* XXII; Ακαμάτης 1993. For Attic workshop A see *Agora* XXII, 28-29.

S.E.

78

79 BOWL WITH RELIEF DECORATION
End of 3rd - 1st half of 2nd c. B.C.

INV. NO. M 2430.
H. 0.082, M.D. 0.145 M.

Mended and restored at a few points. Brown clay, brown to black paint, metallic, missing in places. It has intense traces of burning. Hemispherical body with everted rim.

A rosette is visible on the medallion and around it, elongated, pointed leaves with double veining. A broad, scraped groove divides the medallion from the body. Decoration on the body of the vase is of long, veined lotus leaves that alternate with acanthus leaves. Goat masks are interspersed among them. The decorative zone is a dense row of slaves' masks. Below the edge of the rim, there is yet another scraped groove. The bowl is made from an old, damaged mould.

COMMENTARY - BIBLIOGRAPHY

See Ελευθεράτου forth. It was not possible to locate a bowl identical with no. 79 amongst known and published examples of the type. However, on one level, characteristics of its decoration are traced in other parallels: for similar goat masks on relief bowls see *Agora* XXII, 57, 59, 63, 71, 72, 78, nos. 110, 123, 161, 223, 224, 273, 408, pl. 19, 23, 30, 43, 44, 54 and Braun 1970, 157, no. 185, pl. 73. For masks of slaves but alternating with bearded masks see *Agora* XXII, 68, no. 195, pl. 37 and *Corinth* VII₃, 172, no. 874, pl. 76 (146 B.C.).

S.E.

80 PLATE (PINAKION) WITH GROOVED RIM
175-150 B.C.

INV. NO. M 2431.
H. 0.036, M.D. 0.132, B.D. 0.06 M.

Mended. Brown-red to black paint. Ring base, broad rim which turns out and down. On the upper surface of the rim, two deep grooves form three steps. Inside, this paint covers the bottom, whilst the rim and exterior surface remain unpainted. The manufacture is not particularly careful.

COMMENTARY - BIBLIOGRAPHY

Small saucers with grooved rims, of careless manufacture and with paint which is confined to the bottom, were mass produced and exclusively made in Attica. They are of a dedicatory character and are closely linked with ceremonial pyres, although they are not absent from the household assemblage, where they are included amongst tablewares. Their production is considered to have begun around 375 B.C. and does not appear to have continued beyond 86 B.C. During that time, there were numerous morphological changes in the type, which, however, are not particularly linked with the dating of their development. However, on the basis of certain general criteria such as the shape of the rim, the height, the proportion of the height with regard to the base and the rim, saucer no. 80 can be dated with reasonable certainty to the 2nd quarter of the 2nd c. B.C. or a little later. See Ελευθεράτου forth.

For similar examples see Thompson 1934, 3, 9, 5, E 27, fig. 83, drawing 117 (before 110 B.C.); Braun 1970, 159, no. 196, pl. 741 (after 200 B.C.); Vogeikoff 1993, 96, no.

79

81

80

82

C20, fig. 52 (1st half of 2nd c. B.C.). For the origin, development and typological classification of saucers, see Thompson 1934, 435 and *Agora* XXIX, 151-152.

S.E.

81 MINIATURE CUP
c. 150 B.C.

INV. NO. M 2432.
H. 0.015, M.D. 0.025, B.D. 0.025 M.

Almost completely preserved, one handle missing and a small part of the rim and base. Unpainted. Pale brown clay. Body in the shape of a ring depressed in the middle, with a flat base, solid handles, placed vertically and adjacent on the body.

COMMENTARY - BIBLIOGRAPHY
Miniature vases, of differing shapes, are frequently found in sacred sites and cemeteries. Despite the fact that their character and precise use is unknown, they are considered miniature votives, probably containing – at least in some cases – some small offerings. Attic miniature vases are known from the 6th c. B.C., but become more popular in the 2nd half of the 4th c. B.C. Our vase belongs to a type of double-handled cup of the Athenian Agora despite the absence of a precise parallel. Despite this, its small size, the profile of the body and the type of handles suggest a later dating, probably around the middle of the 2nd c. B.C. See Ελευθεράτου forth. For a near example see *Agora* XXIX, 380, no. 1415, pl. 108. For miniature vases in general see Miller 1974, 207-208, pl. 34 and *Agora* XXIX, 208-210.

S.E.

82 SPINDLE-SHAPED PERFUME BOTTLE
c. 150 B.C.

INV. NO. M 2438.
H. 0.151, M.D. 0.025, B.D. 0.021 M.

Mended. Part of the neck and base missing. Dark brown to greyish clay, with inclusions. The discoid base is divided from the foot by a groove, the belly is elongated, the neck high, the rim with a suspension attachment.
Traces of three thin whitish bands on the belly, shoulder and neck. Impressions of wicker matting can be distinguished on the body, remains of the material with which the vase was wrapped.

COMMENTARY - BIBLIOGRAPHY: Unpublished.
A further five similar perfume bottles were found together with no. 82 in the same pyre (M 2435, M 2436, M 2437, M 2439 and M 2440). Of these, M 2439 also preserves traces of wicker netting.
Spindle-shaped perfume bottles belong to the most common type of Hellenistic and early Roman vases. They first appeared in the 4th c. B.C. or the beginning of the 3rd and were widely distributed throughout the Mediterranean world. They are a common grave gift, but are also found in domestic assemblages replacing in use the lekythoi of the Classical period. They contained perfumes and aromatic oils, essential ingredients in ceremonial proceedings. Perfume bottles first occur in a variety of types and with regional variations, often without important chronological differences. During the 3rd and 2nd c. B.C., the earlier spherical forms without foot are replaced by more slender forms with a higher neck and a shaped, higher foot. In the 2nd half of the 2nd c. B.C. and the 1st c., the profile becomes more elongated, almost tubular and the manufacture less careful. For protection, their safe transport and for hanging up, they were often made in a wrapping of wicker, matting which, as a perishable material, is preserved in exceptionally rare instances. See Ελευθεράτου forth.
For similar examples see Thompson 1934, 392, D77-D78, fig. 78 (after the mid 2nd c. B.C.) and 119, E137-E138, fig. 104 (until 110 B.C.); Braun 1970, 449, 451, no. 185.19, fig. 165, no. 185.22, fig. 168, no. 185.25, fig. 171 (from tomb of the middle or beginning of the 2nd half of the 2nd c. B.C.); *Alt-Ägina* II.1, 189, no. 719, pl. 56; *Kerameikos* IX, 164, no. 387:6-7, pl. 69 (2nd c. B.C.); Schlörb-Vierneisel 1966, 109, no. 199, pl. 61.8 (1st half to middle of 2nd c. B.C.); *Délos* XXVII, 254, D154, pl. 46; Λιλιμπάκη-Ακαμάτη 1994, 134, no. 58, pl. 7 (from tomb of the middle of the 2nd c. B.C.). For perfume bottles in general see Thompson 1934, 472-474; *Labraunda* II.1, 23-27 as well as more recent works by Rotroff 1984a, 258ff. and Anderson-Stojanović 1987, 105ff. including an extensive bibliography. For traces of wicker matting on perfume bottles see Λιλιμπάκη-Ακαμάτη 1989-91, 140, nos. 42-43, pl. 53ε-στ, as well as Λιλιμπάκη-Ακαμάτη 1994, 247, no. 178, 181, 251. Also Walker - Bierbrier 1977, 202, no. 281 (where a clay perfume bottle is portrayed with superbly preserved wrapping of palm leaves).

S.E.

83 SINGLE-SPOUTED LAMP
4th quarter of 3rd - 3rd quarter of 2nd c. B.C.
(225-150 B.C.)

INV. NO. M 2433.
H. 0.055, L. 0.124, D. OF BODY 0.087, B.D. 0.053 M.

Mended with intense traces of burning on half of the upper part. Brown-red to grey clay, dark brown to black paint. Imperfectly formed base, very slightly concave; body has curved profile. The upper part of the body is short with a flat upper surface and most probably a curved ending of which the right angular projection is preserved. On the left, a solid little handle. The inside of the lamp is monochrome but the paint has disappeared for the most part. On the outside there is a rough coating around the filling hole and the end of the spout.

COMMENTARY - BIBLIOGRAPHY: Unpublished.
Attic. Shape very close to type 33A of the Athenian Agora, but differs from that in terms of decoration of the

1.2. (after 200 B.C.); *Délos* XXVI, 22, no. 47, pl. 2; *Kerameikos* XI, 54-55, SSL2, 299-302, pl. 53 (200-150 B.C.).

S.E.

84 SINGLE-SPOUTED LAMP OF "KNIDIAN" TYPE
c. 150 B.C.

INV. NO. M 2434.
H. 0.029, D. OF BODY 0.056, B.D. 0.041 M.

Almost completely preserved, only the handle is missing. The clay is grey and coarse, the paint thin, black and rather fugitive. Discoid base, very slightly concave. The body has an angular profile. Small filling hole, deeply set disc forming a peak at the top. Long spout with a broad, curved ending and angular projection. On the left, a solid little handle. The lamp is wheel-made, monochrome inside and out, apart from the underside and the lower part of the body and spout.

and in other regions, they are not encountered before the middle of that century. See Ελευθεράτου forth. For similar examples see Bailey 1975, 137-138, Q277, Q278, pl. 46 (1st half of 2nd c. B.C. or a little earlier); *Agora* IV, type 40A (2nd half of 2nd - beginning of 1st c. B.C.); Φιλήμονος-Τσοποτού 1980, 83, pl. 25β.

S.E.

83, 84

exterior, which – in contrast to the monochrome lamps of the Agora – by comparison is unpainted, apart from the area around the filling hole and the end of the spout. In other ways, the similarities with type 33A are such that they allow the vase to be considered related to it and dated accordingly. See Ελευθεράτου forth. For similar examples see *Agora* IV, type 33A, "poor relations" (220-150 B.C.); Braun 1970, 162, no. 212, pl. 77,

COMMENTARY - BIBLIOGRAPHY: Unpublished.
Imported. No. 84 belongs to the so-called "Knidian" type, a nomenclature which stuck after the recovery of a large number of similar lamps at Knidos. They are considered products of Asia Minor origin and their shape reflects metallic prototypes. It is recognised that wheel-made lamps of this type were produced as early as the 1st half of the 2nd c. B.C., although in Attica

85 QUERN
Geometric - Archaic period

INV. NO. M 532+M 860.
L. 0.40, MAX.W. 0.16, MIN.W. 0.075, TH. 0.05-0.055 M.

It is joined together from two broken parts. Part of one of its ends is missing. Dark brown volcanic stone without pores (andesite).
The underside is narrow and flat, whilst the rubbing surface is wider and has engravings which form a herring-bone motif. The rubbing surface does not have curvature and the engravings are preserved, a fact which indicates limited use.

COMMENTARY - BIBLIOGRAPHY: Unpublished.
This is a millstone of alternating motion, shaped like a boat, for grinding cereals. In order to crush the grains on top of such a millstone, they used a rubber, of a size such as to fit into a man's hand, e.g. no. 86. The millstone remained stationary and the crushing worked with the backward and forward motion of the rubber on top of the broad surface of the former. Servants or slaves usually carried out this labour, who, on their knees and with the weight of their body falling on their arms, would hold the rubber and move it backwards and forwards on top of the millstone (see drawing). This shape of millstone is a development of prehistoric

86

85

examples and was established in the Geometric period. It rarely survived into the Hellenistic period, when it was replaced by more developed forms of hand-mills (e.g. the "Olynthian" millstones).

This particular millstone dates to the Geometric period, without excluding the beginning of its use even in the Archaic period, on the basis of the dating of other finds in the foundation trench of the west embankment of ancient Street I, where it was found. For millstones in general see Bennett - Elton 1898; Storck - Teague 1952; Moritz 1958; Πουπάκη 1998, 132-174. For backward and forward movement mills, boat-shaped with carinated section, without engravings, see White 1963, 201, pl. 47.3-4 (Archaic, from Morgantina); Amouretti 1986, pl. 21a (7th c. B.C., from Athens); Kardulias - Runnels 1995, I, 116-118, 430, fig. 95 (Archaic - Hellenistic, from the Argolid); Warden 1990, 58, nos. 447-449, pl. 45 (Archaic, from Cyrene). For millstones of the boat-shaped type, with straight parallel engravings, see *Olynthus* II, 69-71.1 (Classical?); *Délos* XVIII, 126, pl. 372; *Délos* VIII, 228-229, fig. 107.

I.P.

86 RUBBER
Archaic - Classical period

INV. NO. M 1717.
H. 0.055, D. OF RUBBING SURFACE 0.065-0.06 M.

Complete. Dark brown, volcanic stone. It is in the shape of an irregular truncated cone. The circular surface of the rubber is abraded, probably due to lengthy use.

COMMENTARY - BIBLIOGRAPHY: Unpublished.
The size of grinder no. 86 allows it to be held in a man's hand. It could have been used in conjunction with a stone mortar, as a pestle, even if pestles were usually longer. Similar rubbers were used in grinding corn, in conjunction with a millstone, such as no. 85 (see drawing). This shape of stone rubber is common from the prehistoric period to Late Roman times. Many similar rubbers were first used in the prehistoric period, but, due to the toughness of the material and their given use, survived into historic times. This particular example dates to the Archaic period and probably continued to be used in the Classical period, based on the dating of the pottery from the level in which it was found.

For similar truncated cone rubbers see *Délos* XVIII, 116, pl. 333 (prehistoric); Mylonas 1959, 38, 145, no. 60, pl. 168.60 (from Agios Kosmas, Attica; Early Bronze Age); Τζαβέλλα-Evjen 1984, fig. 26ε, pl. 96β (from Lithares; EH period); Sackett - Cocking 1992, 393, no. 13a, pl.

324.6, 326.13a (from Knossos; Geometric period); Cummer - Schöfield 1984, 120, no. 1462, pl. 44.1462 (from Agia Irini, Kea; historical era).

I.P.

87 PESTLE
Late Classical - Hellenistic period

INV. NO. M 412.
H. 0.065, D. OF RUBBING SURFACE 0.055-0.05 M.

Complete with scattered chips. Dark, volcanic stone. It is shaped like an irregular, truncated cone. The top end is lightly curved. The circular rubbing surface has been abraded due to lengthy use.

COMMENTARY - BIBLIOGRAPHY: Unpublished.
The size of pestle no. 87 allowed it to be held in a man's hand. Pestles were used for crushing fruits, either for preparing juice, or for producing flour, and grinding pigments, cosmetics or pharmaceutical substances. They were also made of wood, clay or metal. Sometimes, the stone pestles or the larger sized version, "hyperoi", had a deep central perforation for stabilising it on a wooden or metal handle. See *Délos* XVIII, 107, fig. 133 and Πουπάκη 1998, 137-138; see also Amyx 1958, 238-239. This type of stone pestle is common from prehistoric times through to late antiquity.

87

88

For similar pestles see *Délos* XVIII, 116, pl. 333 (prehistoric); Τζαβέλλα-Evjen 1984, fig. 26ε, pl. 96β (from Lithares; EH period); Sackett - Cocking 1992, 393, 395, nos. 13b, 55a, pl. 325.10, 326.13b, 55a (from Knossos; Geometric and Roman respectively); Chavane 1975, 21, nos. 31, 34, pl. 5-6, 58 (from Salamis, Cyprus; historic times); *Corinth* XII, 193, no. 1439, pl. 86 (from Corinth; Byzantine times). The pestle in question is securely dated to the interval between the 4th and 3rd c. B.C., on the basis of the pottery from the road level of ancient Street I, where it was found.

I.P.

88 MORTAR
Hellenistic period

INV. NO. M 1685.
H. 0.05, M.D. 0.24, B.D. 0.15, DIM. OF HANDLE 0.05 × 0.03 × 0.015, DIM. OF SPOUT 0.05 × 0.025 × 0.03 M.

Complete with small chips off rim, handle, centre of bottom and lower part of it. Dark, volcanic stone. One-handled, shallow mortar with spout.
Low, flat, circular base, slightly off-centre. Very high, broad, flat rim. Spout and handle cut out of the continuation of the rim and set opposite one another. Horizontal, rectangular, flat handle. Rectangular spout with internal grooving, which slopes downwards to facilitate flow of the vessel's liquid content. This grooving is found at a slightly higher level in relation to the bottom of the vessel so that the heavier, solid constituents sink into it and the liquid produced flows out. The exterior of the spout is slightly curved. The damage in the centre of the bottom is due to the rubber and the impact of the pestle.

COMMENTARY - BIBLIOGRAPHY: Unpublished.
Spouted mortars were most probably used for preparing juices with the help of a pestle, such as no. 87. This type of stone vase is common as early as the prehistoric period, e.g. the mortars of the "Agios Kosmas" type, belonging to the Early Bronze Age, have an almost similar shape, are made from the same hard volcanic stone, but have characteristic bobbin-shaped handles and are sometimes without a handle. See Mylonas 1959, 92-94, 145, pl. 169; Caskey 1960, 285-303; Τζαβέλλα-Evjen 1984, 172, pl. 86α, 87α; Runnels 1988, 257-272. This type of utensil lives on until the Hellenis-

tic period owing to its practical form and becomes made with more care and attention: its base has relief decoration and the spout is rendered more smoothly. The Hellenistic examples of such utensils are, of course, marble; in this regard see *Délos* XVIII, 110-114, pl. 319-326; Wiegand - Schrader 1904, 375ff., nos. 1541, 1559; *Corinth* XII, 122-123, 125, nos. 816-820, 827-829, fig. 19, pl. 61; Hiesel 1967, 105-106, nos. 179-184, pl. 19; Chavane 1975, 14-15, nos. 4-8, pl. 1-2, 57. Similar, four- and three-handled, spouted mortars, of the Hellenistic period, have been found on Délos and some are made of volcanic stone as with this particular mortar; see *Délos* XVIII, pl. 317 and *Délos* XXVII, 221, no. C26, pl. 33. It follows that a date in the Hellenistic period can be considered satisfactory.

I.P.

89 MARBLE PESTLE
Hellenistic - Roman period

INV. NO. M 1850.
L. OF PHALANGES 0.06 AND 0.08, TH. OF PHALANGES 0.035-0.03 M.

Complete with sporadic chips off. It has the shape of a bent human finger. White, fine-grained, Pentelic marble. It is most probably the middle or "ring" finger. Its anatomical details are rendered naturally, but concisely; one can distinguish the nail, the phalanges and the joints. Its rubbing surface is the circular and sloping surface at the point where the larger phalange projects onto the palm. This is rather abraded, due to lengthy use of the implement.

COMMENTARY - BIBLIOGRAPHY: Unpublished.
Similar pestles were used for grinding pigments, cosmetics and pharmaceutical substances. They were frequently dedicated at shrines (e.g. an inscribed pestle - dedication to Lindian Athena on Rhodes, see *Lindos* I, 748, no. 3229, pl. 152). Pestles of this shape have been found on Delos (*Délos* XVIII, 117-120), at Corinth (*Corinth* XII, 189-190, 192-193, nos. 1430-1436), at Olynthus (*Olynthus* II, 252-253), at Priene (Wiegand - Schrader 1904, 393), on Samos (Hiesel 1967, 106-107, nos. 185-188), at Delphi (*Fouilles de Delphes* V, 208, no. 701), at Knossos (Sackett - Cocking 1992, 395, no. 41, pl. 325.4, 326.D), at Cyrene (Warden 1990, 59, no. 451, pl. 45) etc.
As indicated by the finds from Corinth, these pestles first occur in the middle of the 5th c. B.C. and live on

until Roman times, a period from which most examples have been rescued. Of course, some Roman pestles have a shape of a man's bent leg; see *Délos* XVIII, 121, pl. 361. For similar pestles see *Délos* XXVII, 222, no. C44, pl. 33; *Délos* XVIII, no. B1759, pl. 356, 358 (Hellenistic); Chavane 1975, 25, no. 50, pl. 7, 59 (from Salamis in Cyprus; Roman Imperial period).
This particular pestle belongs to the Roman period, as the pottery of well 52 where it was found, shows. Well 52 was located outside the boundaries of the excavation area, east of the Centre for the Study of the Acropolis, at the opening of the north tunnel of the ACROPOLIS Station.

I.P.

90 MARBLE MORTAR
Roman - Early Christian period

INV. NO. M 621.
H. 0.06, M.D. (EXCL. HANDLES) 018, B.D. 0.115, DIM. OF HANDLES 0.037-0.043 (W.) × 0.028 (TH.) × 0.025-0.035 M. (L.).

Almost complete with sporadic chips off the two little handles and rim. One handle is missing. White Pentelic marble with dark veins. Flat base, hemispherical body and flat, broad rim. Horizontal little handles, shaped like quarter of a sphere, asymmetrically placed but arranged opposite each other – in twos – and carved as a continuation of the rim. Interior curvature carelessly polished. Exterior surface abounds with traces of working with a rasp.

COMMENTARY - BIBLIOGRAPHY: Unpublished.
Owing to their handy shape, stone vases such as mortar no. 90 can have a variety of uses: mortars for squeezing fruits, grinding cereals and pigments, cosmetics or pharmaceutical substances, or as religious equipment in shrines. The type of well-made utensil with four or three handles and a spout is frequent in the Hellenistic period. Nevertheless, similar four- and two-handled utensils with handles, which were decorated with different engraved linear or plant motifs, lived on into the Early Christian period and were probably used in Early Christian worship. In connection with this see Brondsted 1928, fig. 93; Dyggve 1939, 48-49, fig. 62-63; *Corinth* XII, 122-123, 125, nos. 816-820, 827-829, fig. 19, pl. 61; Hiesel 1967, 105-106, nos. 179-184, pl. 19; *Lindos* III₂, 312-313, fig. VII, 43, 46; Bliss - McAlister 1902, 202, pl. 90. Similar undecorated marble vessels, of the Roman period, have been found at Miletus

(handleless): Voigtländer 1982, 172, no. 445, fig. 63, at Corinth (with handles): *Corinth* XII, 123, no. 821, fig. 20, and at Sparta (half-finished, four-handled vessel of grey marble, no. 1167α; unpublished). Fragments of undecorated handles and a bottom of similar marble vessels, of the Early Christian period, have also been found at Salona in Dalmatia; see Dyggve 1939, 49, fig. 62. 6, 8, 10.

The utensil in question can be dated to the Late Roman or Early Christian period, given that the pottery of well 31, in which it was found, dates to between the 3rd and 8th c. A.D. Well 31 was located east of the system of wells 12 and 13 and cut into the rock of cistern I.

I.P.

89

90

91 HEAD OF THE STATUE OF A CHILD
350-300 B.C.

INV. NO. M 413.
H. 0.19, W. 0.155 M.

Head of figure of a child from white, fine-grained marble. It belonged to a life-sized statue. Part of the neck is preserved. The front part of the nose chipped. Small chips off lip, chin and cheeks. Excoriations and flaking at many points on the surface.

The face is round, with softly moulded flesh, particularly in the area of the cheeks. The eyes are large and almond-shaped, with discreetly indicated corners of the eyes and strongly formed eyelashes. A slight smile is traced on the lips, which faintly brightens up the soft facial features. The hair-style is of its own kind: two long plaits are distinguished that are twisted around the head, leaving the eyes uncovered, while another small braid is plaited above the forehead where the parting is. The hair on top of the head is lavishly rendered.

COMMENTARY - BIBLIOGRAPHY: Unpublished.

The small plait above the forehead is characteristic of a young age and is usual in representations of girls and boys, particularly in the 2nd half of the 4th c. B.C. More rare is the combination of plaits around the head with a parting in the middle. It is found on young female figures, on statues of Artemis and on representations of girls and boys in dedicatory reliefs of the 2nd half of the 4th c. B.C. The fact that the hair-style of the statue is as common on girls as on boys does not allow us to come to a safe conclusion as to the sex of the child portrayed.

Child statues, chiefly of the late Classical and Hellenistic eras, have been found in shrines of deities such as Artemis, Apollo, Eileithyia, Asklepeios and Amphiaraos, which have the title "kourotrophoi" and are connected with the birth, upbringing and protection of children. Some of these statues probably depict children who took part in the religious ceremonies (such as the young Arktoi at the shrine of Artemis at Brauron), while most are considered dedications by parents to deities, with a supplicatory or thanks-giving character. Girls and boys are usually depicted standing up and facing forward, and they often hold a small animal, a bird or some toy in their arms.

91

Our statue would have been iconographically similar. A likely place of dedication would have been one of the sanctuaries found in the vicinity, perhaps the Sanctuary of Brauronian Artemis on top of the Acropolis or the Asklepieion on the south slope of the sacred rock. For parallels see Vorster 1983. For representations of children in general see Rühfel 1984a and 1984b. For the hair-style see Despinis 1994, 173-198, pl. 31-45.

I.A.P.

92 DOUBLE-HEADED CAPPING OF A HERM
1st-2nd c. A.D.

INV. NO. M 35.
H. 0.227, W. 0.159, TOTAL TH. 0.23 M.

The two heads are preserved up to the beginning of the neck. One bearded figure with fierce chipping of the right eye and the corresponding part of the hair, as well as obliquely to the left part of the beard. The other, unbearded figure, is chipped on the nose. Lighter chipping in places all over the sculpture. White, crystalline marble.

The bearded head depicts Hermes at a ripe age as a Hermes Propylaios type, a work probably by Alkamenes. The face is framed by lightly rendered hair, of archaising type, which covers the greater part of the forehead. It is composed of three successive rows of button-shaped curls combed forwards, which are held by a thin relief band on the upper part of the scalp. Two thin curls spring from the whole hair-do on the sides thus framing the neck. The forehead is small and trapezoidal. Almond-shaped eyes with broad, heavy eyelashes and eyebrows in the shape of a closed arc. The nose is depicted with emphasis, while the lips are fleshy. The cheeks are covered with a well-kept, long beard, which is shown with wavy curls and is plaited with the moustache which lavishly projects above the edge of the upper lip.

The unbearded head depicts the figure of a young Dionysos and has idealised features. The hair, stiff and without structure, covers the ears and resembles a wig. There is a garland on its front part, of

double ivy leaves, whilst two spirally curls sprout from the side framing the neck. The face has an ovoid shape and hard expression. The eyes are almond-shaped, with heavy eyelashes projecting slightly, and arched eyebrows. The tear duct is indicated. The mouth is small with fleshy lips. The cheeks are delicate, whilst the chin projects slightly.

COMMENTARY - BIBLIOGRAPHY: Unpublished.

Hermaic columns or "Herms" were four-sided stone columns, which were initially crowned with the head of a bearded Hermes and supported on a cubic base. Usually, they had an erect phallic relief in front, and two rectangular slots on the sides for inserting arms. Some were clothed others not, and some bore inscriptions. They were a singular type of monument which was mainly erected in outdoor places. Their use was wide in the Classical and later periods in Athens and elsewhere.

They were probably first designed for worship. From the Archaic period, they acquired a dedicatory character. In these times, it seems that Herms were used for practical purposes, e.g. road measuring, the division of agricultural properties, of the cities' boundaries etc. There are many theories as to their origin and importance, which is related with different peculiarities of the god of the same name. According to one view, this kind of monument came from the piles of stones on roads which were signs for burials and signals for road directions. They are connected, in the first instance, with Hermes psychopompos and in the second, with the attribute of Hermes as guide and protector of travellers. They were placed at cross-roads and on town roads as sign-posts, indicating distances and direction. They are met in Attica from the 6th c. B.C. Many were put in place by Hipparchos with moral commandments inscribed on their front surfaces. It is also maintained that, as borders, that is landmark sign-posts, they educated in a moral way, with the explicit and symbolic phrases which they bore, e.g. "don't cheat a friend", "follow the path of the righteous" etc. It is likely that they were connected with the attribute of Hermes as protector of the city (Hermes Propylaios) and therefore stood on the gates of the city for protection. On analogy, they were placed at the frontages of private houses, at shrines, at public buildings etc. A lot of Herms were found in the Athenian Agora and it has also been proposed that they were dedications to Hermes Agoraios, just as Hermes was worshipped with the attribute of protector of commerce and the market-place. Some believe that the beginnings of the

monument must be sought in the worship of the rustic Dionysos and in the clothed wooden effigies with his mask, just as – figuratively speaking – Hermes is referred to as a rural-bucolic god.

At any rate, Herms were considered sacred, and that is why the Athenians felt outraged when, a little before the departure of their army to the Sicilian campaign in 415 B.C., the mutilation of the city's Herms was discovered. Alcibiades and his friends were charged as the hermokopidai ("herm-bashers").

The development of Herms gradually led, from the 4th c. B.C., to the representation of other gods apart from Hermes, such as Apollo, Dionysos, Pan, Aphrodite or mythical personalities such as Kekrops and Theseus. Two- and three-headed Herms have been preserved in which more than one deity is combined. The type of Herms, with a capping of two heads looking in opposite directions, initially had been created for Hermes psychopompos in the last quarter of the 6th c. B.C., whilst the combination of the young Dionysos and mature Hermes appears to allude to the contradiction between youth and old age. The present Herm is classified in this type. From the 2nd c. B.C., we have double-headed Herms of philosophers, historians and poets.

For similar examples see double-headed Herm in the Glencairn Museum, Academy of the New Church, Bryn Athyn, Pennsylvania, in the *J. Paul Getty Trust, Bulletin* 8, no. 3, 1994, which is dated to the 1st-2nd c. A.D. For Herms in general see Curtius 1903; Lullies 1931; *Agora* XI, 108-176; Willers 1967, 37ff.; Τριάντη 1977, 116-122; Wrede 1985.

V.Ch.

93 SINGLE-SPOUTED LAMP
Late Archaic period

INV. NO. M 2541.
MAX.H. 0.042, MAX.L. 0.123, W. 0.062, B.D. 0.05 M.

Almost complete, mended. Fine-grained, pale, rosy clay. Broad, circular underside, slightly concave. Open body, elongated and low, with curved profile. The shapeless, almost non-existent rim turns inwards and reaches its edge at the upper part of the body. It develops into an elongated, unbridged spout, widening at its end and with curved edges. High, vertical strap handle. Traces of burning on the spout prove its use. The vessel is probably handmade. It is totally covered with bright, metallic, black paint.

COMMENTARY - BIBLIOGRAPHY: Unpublished.

The lamp combines Archaic (mainly) and later elements and must be dated to the last years of the 6th to the beginning of the 5th c. B.C. Note that in the same trench, three lamps of a different type were found (M 2625, M 2628, M 2629), which date to the 4th quarter of the 6th c. and up to about 480 B.C. Lamp no. 93 is a type of its own as no corresponding example is found in the Athenian Agora. For examples with a similar section see *Agora* IV, type 15, pl. 4, 32, nos. 86, 89, 90 (with bridgeless spouts; end of 6th c. - 480 B.C.). For a somewhat similar example in terms of section and shape, more generally see *Isthmia* III, no. 5, pl. 1, 14 (end of 6th - beginning of 5th c. B.C.).

H.H.

94 DOUBLE-SPOUTED LAMP
c. 350 B.C.

INV. NO. M 2543.
MAX.PRES.H. 0.106, MAX.L. 0.166, D. OF BODY 0.09, B.D. 0.07 M.

Almost complete, mended. Orangey clay, Attic. The base is raised in the shape of an inverted echinus and is perforated in its centre. The profile of the body is curved and slightly depressed, and it forms a marked edge with the narrow, concave rim which surrounds the filling hole. The lamp has two diametrically opposed spouts, one of which is elongated, nearly flat on its upper part, with a curved ending and large wick hole. A high, vertical, cylindrical stem projects from the centre of the bottom and probably ended in an arched handle for hanging it up. The stem, on the interior, is pierced and conical. It had been used because traces of burning can be seen on one spout. The vessel is wheelmade. The paint, burnished, black and rather fugitive, entirely covers the lamp. The underside has been damaged.

COMMENTARY - BIBLIOGRAPHY: Unpublished.

The lamp comes from an Attic workshop. Its relatively big dimensions, its large capacity and the two spouts, presuppose the location of a large quantity of burning material, namely oil. Damage to the base which is seen on the inside of the stem is probably due to sit-

ting the lamp on a columned lamp stand, to keep it raised up and to carry it.

For an example comparable in dimensions-section see Deneauve 1969, 49, no. 118, pl. VI, XXVII (around the 2nd quarter of 4th c. B.C.; it is paralleled by type 23A, 23C of *Agora* IV). Also see *Kerameikos* XI, 45, no. 245, pl. 42-43 (similar, where the spouts are more elongated; mid 4th c. B.C.) as well as *Agora* IV, type 26A, 82-84, no. 367, pl. 13, 40 (somewhat similar lamp; late 2nd quarter of 4th - beginning of 3rd c. B.C.), no. 212, type 23A (similar in terms of section; late 3rd quarter of 5th - 1st quarter of 4th c. B.C.). For a re-dating of type 26A (of *Agora* IV), to 350-275 B.C., see *Agora* XXIX, Appendix III. For analogies for the arched ending of the handle see *Olynthus* XVI, 378-381, no. 127 and no. 131, pl. 157 (where the arched handle is preserved, Group VII; early 4th c. B.C.).

H.H.

COINS

95 Obv.

95 Rev.

95 ATHENIAN BRONZE COIN
c. 330 to 322-317 B.C.

INV. NO. M 2602.
D. 0.01 M., WT. 1.6 GR.

Bronze. Badly preserved. Damage around the edge.

Obv.: Head of Athena with Attic helmet, to r.

Rev.: Two-bodied owl en face. Eleusinian ring beneath. Inscription damaged: [AΘE].

COMMENTARY - BIBLIOGRAPHY: Unpublished.

For the specific coin cf. *Agora* XXVI, 41-42, pl. 4, no. 43a-m. The ring on the reverse is a symbol related to the Eleusinian Mysteries: on the fifth day of the Great Mysteries and during the procession from Athens to Eleusis, the initiates carried garlands of myrtle and held mystic staff or "bacchus", both symbols of Eleusinian worship. The "bacchus" was a thick staff, made from branches of myrtle. Rings of woollen thread carried the branches between them. For the ring see Mylonas 1961, 224-258; Seltman 1955, 258; *Agora* XXVI, 28.

The kind of two-bodied owl above the Eleusinian ring is met on bronze coins of the last quarter of the 4th c. B.C. and is directly related to the festivals of the Eleusinian Mysteries. The obverse of these coins portray the head of Athena more naturally, such as that depicted on silver coins of the type (pi style). For the type with a two-bodied owl see *Agora* XXVI, 31-32.

A.K.

96 ATHENIAN BRONZE COIN
c. 270-261 B.C.

INV. NO. M 2600.
D. 0.013 M., WT. 2.3 GR.

Bronze. Rather poorly preserved. Damage around the edge.

Obv.: Head of Athena with Corinthian helmet, to r.

Rev.: Standing owl to r., the head en face. Cornucopia in the zone, lower right. Inscription: A Θ E.

COMMENTARY - BIBLIOGRAPHY: Unpublished.

For the specific coin cf. *Agora* XXVI, 47, pl. 6, no. 59a-e. After the defeat of the Athenians in the Chremonideian War (268-261 B.C.), Athens was seized by Antigonos Gonatas, who was the winner of this war. In 255 B.C., Antigonos Gonatas, having relaxed his control over the region, transferred formal control to the Athenians.

96 Obv.

96 Rev.

Initially, the type of owl to the right with inscription A Θ E and with symbol (cornucopia) was dated to after 255 B.C., a time when it was thought Athenian coinage showed a backward move due to the autonomy conferred by Antigonos Gonatas. However, after detailed study, it is concluded that the type dates to before 261 B.C. For the dating of this type see *Agora* XXVI, 10-13, 34-37 and Kroll 1979, 143-144.

According to mythology, the nymph Amaltheia, assuming the form of a goat, nursed the infant Zeus on Mount Dikte in Crete. Her horns was used in Greek art as a symbol of plenty and prosperity, hence its depiction filled with fruits and ears of wheat. The cornucopia was the characteristic emblem of many personifications, particularly during the Roman period. For the cornucopia see Melville-Jones 1986, 11, 57-58 and 1990, 72-73.

A.K.

falls down freely on the neck at the back. Dotted circle.

Rev.: PVDICITIA (Modesty). Personification of Modesty. Seated female figure to l. on throne with raised back. She wears a chiton and himation, which covers her head and right arm. With her left arm, she holds the end of her himation.

COMMENTARY - BIBLIOGRAPHY: Unpublished.
For the type cf. Robertson 1971, 174, no. 32.

A.K.

97 Rev.

97 Obv.

Area of clay floor (from the disturbed fill)

97 BRONZE SESTERTIUS OF SABINA (CONSORT OF HADRIAN)
A.D. 128-138
Mint: Rome

INV. NO. M 2594.
D. 0.032 M., WT. 28.8 GR.

Bronze. Poorly preserved. Damage to reverse.

Obv.: SABINAAVGVSTA - HADRIANI-AVGPP. Bust of Sabina to l. with diadem. The hair is raised up in front and held in place by the diadem. It

Area of clay floor ("intrusion")

98 ATHENIAN BRONZE COIN
c. mid-80's - mid-70's B.C.

INV. NO. M 2601.
D. 0.01 M., WT. 1.7 GR.

Bronze. Rather poorly preserved. Damage around the edge.

Obv.: Head of Apollo to r. Wears laurel garland. Dotted circle.

Rev.: Two ears of wheat. Inscription: A - [Θ] E . Dotted circle.

COMMENTARY - BIBLIOGRAPHY: Unpublished.
For the specific coin cf. *Agora* XXVI, 100, pl. 12, no. 135a-g. The wheat is a symbol related to the worship of Demeter and to the Eleusinian Mysteries. For wheat as a symbol see Mylonas 1961, 158, 159, 275.

After 86 B.C. (destruction of Athens by Sulla) bronze Athenian coinage is altered. It issued a new large bronze subdivision, which as far as types are concerned copied those bearing a wreath of the 2nd and 1st c. B.C. (silver coins of the new style). For the new style see Οικονομίδου 1996, 36 and Τουράτσογλου 1996, 111. Apart from this large subdivision and during the same period 86-42 B.C., smaller bronze subdivisions were issued, which introduced a variety in terms of types. On the obverse, the head of Athena was replaced by the head of Apollo, Demeter, Kore and Triptolemos, while on the reverse Eleusinian symbols were used. For Athenian coinage (86-42 B.C.) see *Agora* XXVI, 80-84 and Kleiner 1975.

This specific coin, along with coins nos. 99-104 belong to a total of 69 bronze coins found in an "intrusion", beneath a clay floor and were at first considered to be a hoard. The coins, however, date from the 1st c. B.C. to the beginning of the 5th c. A.D. The dispersion of the

98 Obv.

98 Rev.

coins in the area and the great date range amongst them raises doubts as to whether it is really a question of a uniform hoard.

A.K.

99 ATHENIAN BRONZE COIN OF THE IMPERIAL PERIOD

c. A.D. 264-267

INV. NO. M 2581.
D. 0.017 M., WT. 4.3 GR.

Bronze. Poorly preserved. Damage around the edge.

Obv.: Head of Athena with Corinthian helmet, to r.

Rev.: Competition table with four legs. Amphora beneath. Above the table: owl to right, with head en face, bust of Athena to l. with Corinthian helmet, garland. In the zone right, palm-tree branch. Inscription: AΘH - N - AI [ΩN]. Dotted circle.

COMMENTARY - BIBLIOGRAPHY: Unpublished.
For the type cf. *Agora* XXVI, 161, pl. 21, no. 392b. For the coins found in the same region see no. 98. The competition table was popular on the reverse in the coinage of Athens and other Greek cities during the 2nd and 3rd c. A.D. (Roman period). This type refers to the great festivals: Hadrianic, Eleusinian, Olympian, Panathenaic, Panhellenic. Depicted as trophies on top of the table were: the garland, image of an owl, image of the bust of Athena. For the competition table see *Agora* XXVI, 123, n. 53. During the Roman period, Athens retained the prerogative to depict the head of Athena on the obverse of its bronze coins, as opposed to the imperial portrait. The minting of Athenian coins, as with many other cities was stopped by Gallienus (A.D. 260-268). For the Athenian coinage of the Roman period see *Agora* XXVI, 113; Kleiner 1975 (Roman Athens); Οικονομίδου 1996, 38.

A.K.

100 BRONZE COIN (AE 3) OF CONSTANTINE II

A.D. 324-330
Mint: Siskia (in modern Croatia)

INV. NO. M 2589.
D. 0.018 M., WT. 3 GR.

Bronze. Poorly preserved. Damage around the edge.

Obv.: CO[N]STANTINVSI [VN] NOBC. Crowned bust of Constantine II to r. Dotted circle.

Rev.: PRO[VI]DEN - TIA[ECA]ESS. Gate of fortified army camp with two raised towers, a star above. On the exergue: Ⅽ SIS.
Where Ⅽ is the letter indicating the mint, a symbolic crescent (half-moon). Dotted circle.

COMMENTARY - BIBLIOGRAPHY: Unpublished.
For the type cf. *LRBC* I, 19, no. 739. For the coins found in the same area see no. 99.

100 Obv.

99 Rev.

99 Obv.

One of the most important mints of the central provinces (region of Illyrium) of the Roman empire functioned in Siskia (modern Sisak in Croatia). It began working in the era of the monarchy of Gallienus (A.D. 260-268). Initially, the coins of Siskia are of lower quality than those of other mints, but gradually during the reign of Probus (A.D. 276-282) their quality improved. Due to the fact that Siskia existed as a military centre for the defence of the northern borders of the empire, the production of coinage was often great.

During the period of the first tetrarchy (A.D. 294-305) Siskia acquired great military and strategic significance for the defence of the empire. In this period, the mint of Siskia reached a great peak. A rather large production of gold and silver coins is observed whilst its bronze coinage appears as a model (a great variety of types, signs of issue and generally high standards of execution). In the second tetrarchy (A.D. 305-307), the coinage of Siskia, due to different internal disturbances, becomes weak and reduced. After a temporary gap of the mint and during the third tetrarchy (A.D. 308-311), the control of Siskia was claimed by Licinius, who established it as one of the most important bases on his western borders, particularly during the period of the fourth tetrarchy (A.D. 311-313).

The coinage of Siskia is the first important mint to pass from the kingdom of Licinius into the hands of Constantine the Great, the latter having seized the city already in the first days of the First Civil War (A.D. 314/316). Siskia, from A.D. 324 to 340, was one of the most important mints of Europe, mainly for minting bronze coins, and preserved this role until the period which is overshadowed by the mint of Sirmion (A.D. 357/359). The mint of Siskia worked until the first years of reign of Arcadius (A.D. 383-408) and closed around A.D. 387.

100 Rev.

For the mint of Siskia see Robertson 1978, X; *LRBC* I, 18; *LRBC* II, 69; *RIC* V.1, 15-23; *RIC* V.2, 7-13, 214-215; *RIC* VI, 436-454; *RIC* VII, 411-421; *RIC* VIII, 339-347; *RIC* IX, 137-140; *RIC* X, 35; Grierson - Mays 1992, 48-56, 67.

A.K.

101 BRONZE COIN (AE 3) OF CONSTANS
A.D. 348-350
Mint: Thessaloniki

INV. NO. M 2586.
D. 0.017 M., WT. 2 GR.

Bronze. Rather badly preserved. Damage around the edge.

Obv.: DNCONSTA - NSPFAVG. Bust of the emperor to r. He wears a diadem with a double row of pearls.

Rev.: FELTEMP - [R]EPARATIO. The emperor, in military dress, to r., in a boat. He holds a palm above a sphere in his raised right hand, while with his left, a standard (labarum). Right, Nike (Victory) seated to l. holding a rudder. On the exergue: TESB. Where B is the letter indicating the mint.

COMMENTARY - BIBLIOGRAPHY: Unpublished.
For the type cf. Robertson 1982, 297, no. 55. For the coins found in the same area see no. 99.

The mint of Thessaloniki, like most mints of the Greek cities of the East under Roman sovereignty and particularly in the period A.D. 32/1 to the period of the monarchy of Gallienus (A.D. 260-268), only cut bronze coins that were designed for the everyday uses of the citizens. The works of the mint throughout the whole of this period were particularly important, despite some gaps occurred in production, which were not, however, of great duration. The bronze coins of Thessaloniki copied and imitated the corresponding imperial examples chiefly as far as concerned the depiction of the images of the Caesars, and that because there was direct dependence on the mint of Rome.

The mint of Thessaloniki began to work once more in A.D. 298/9, after a decision of Diocletian and Galerius. During the period of the first tetrarchy (A.D. 298/299-

303), the coinage of Thessaloniki comprised gold, silver and bronze coins. As early as the second tetrarchy (A.D. 308-310), Thessaloniki had become the most important mint in the southern Balkan region and its bronze coinage acquired its particular characteristics which it maintained during the next two periods, the third (A.D. 310-311) and fourth (A.D. 311-312) tetrarchies whilst some gaps in the production of gold and silver coins has been observed.

After the First Civil War (A.D. 314/316) and after the defeat of Licinius, Thessaloniki passed to the control of Constantine the Great (A.D. 317). As early as the beginning of A.D. 317, the gold coinage of Thessaloniki is clearly influenced by the West, whilst the bronze appears totally different due to the residence of the emperor and his court in the city. Apart from the old types, new ones were now made and new symbols used. Some of these types, with only small changes, were to continue to be used even after the death of Constantine the Great (A.D. 337), by his three sons who had already been proclaimed Augusti. During the period of the co-regency of the three emperors Constantine II (A.D. 337-340), Constans (A.D. 337-350) and Constantius II (A.D. 337-361), the coinage of Thessaloniki was particularly extensive. The most popular type of this period was the FEL TEMP REPARATIO. Thessaloniki held a peculiar position. It belonged to the most western empire but had great contact with the East.

The influence of the East was clear for a long time even in the use of its mint. In the 4th and 5th c. A.D., it was the seat of the military province of Illyricum, at first with sovereignty over the administrative regions of Illyricum, Dacia and Macedonia. In A.D. 388, Theodosius I recaptured the region of Illyricum (including Thessaloniki) and annexed it to the eastern empire, an arrangement which did not change thereafter. The mint of Thessaloniki throughout the whole of the 4th and 5th c. A.D. minted gold, silver and bronze coins, often with a freedom in the choice of types and symbols. The bronze

101 Obv.

101 Rev.

coinage of Thessaloniki, in the 4th c. A.D., exhibits a variety in terms of types and symbols. In the period A.D. 392-408, a gap in the bronze series of the city's mint is observed and a decline in the number of mint workshops. The bronze mints of Thessaloniki, in the 2nd half of the 5th c. A.D., is greatly curtailed and appears once more in the 1st half of the 6th c. A.D.

The silver coinage of Thessaloniki in this period was curtailed in contrast to the gold which, after the monetary reform of Valentinianus I in A.D. 368, exhibits great growth. After the reform of A.D. 368, Siskia and Thessaloniki continued to mint gold coins, emphasising the demand for continuing to use the mint of gold coins in the Illyricum region. Apart from the use of local symbols on the solidi of this period (4th-5th c. A.D.), it also used a variety of symbols which reflect the influence which the mint of Thessaloniki received from the West and the East. The mint of Thessaloniki continued to work even in the next Byzantine centuries.

For the Thessaloniki mint see Touratsoglou 1988, 5-24; *RIC* VI, 500-508; *RIC* VII, 481-497; *RIC* VIII, 395-400; *RIC* XI, 163-167; *RIC* X, 36-38; *LRBC* I, 20; *LRBC* II, 77; Grierson - Mays 1992, 48-56, 67-8.

A.K.

102 BRONZE COIN (AE 3) OF ARCADIUS
A.D. 383-392
Mint: Thessaloniki

INV. NO. M 2655.
D. 0.018 M., WT. 1.7 GR.

Bronze. Rather badly preserved. Damage around the edge.

Obv.: [D]NARC[ADI]IVSPFAVG. Bust of the emperor to l. He wears a diadem with a double row of pearls. He holds a mappa in his right hand and a sceptre in his left.

Rev.: [GLORIA REI] - PVBLICE. Gate of an army camp. On the exergue: TES.

COMMENTARY - BIBLIOGRAPHY: Unpublished. For the type cf. *LRBC* II, 82, nos. 1856-60. For the coins found in the same area see no. 99. For coins from the same mint see no. 101.

A.K.

103 BRONZE COIN (AE 3) OF VALENTINIANUS II
A.D. 383-392
Mint: Thessaloniki

INV. NO. M 2656.
D. 0.017 M., WT. 2.2 GR.

Bronze. Rather badly preserved. Damage around the edge.

Obv.: DNVA[LEN]TIN [I] - [A]NV[SPF] AVG. Bust of the emperor to r. He wears a diadem with a double row of pearls.

Rev.: [VIRTVS] - AVGGG. The emperor to l., in a boat. He tramples a prisoner. He holds a palm above a sphere in his raised right hand, whilst with his left a double axe. Right, a seated Nike (victory) holds a rudder. On the exergue: T[ES]

COMMENTARY - BIBLIOGRAPHY: Unpublished. For the type cf. *LRBC* II, 81, nos. 1848-49. For the coins found in the same area see no. 99. For the coins of the same mint see no. 101.

A.K.

103 Obv.

103 Rev.

102 Obv.

102 Rev.

104 BRONZE COIN (AE 3) OF THEODOSIUS I
A.D. 383-392
Mint: Thessaloniki

INV. NO. M 2654.
D. 0.018 M., WT. 2.2 GR.

Bronze. Rather badly preserved. Damage around the edge.

Obv.: DNTHEODO - SIVSPFAVG. Bust of the emperor to r. He wears a diadem with a double row of pearls. Dotted circle.

Rev.: VIRTVS - [AV]GGG. The emperor to l., in a boat. He tramples a prisoner. He holds a palm above a sphere in his raised right hand. Right, a seated Nike (Victory) holds a rudder. On the exergue: TES. Dotted circle.

COMMENTARY - BIBLIOGRAPHY: Unpublished.
For the type cf. *LRBC* II, 81, nos. 1848-49. For the coins found in the same area see no. 99. For coins from the same mint see no. 101.

A.K.

105 MARBLE WEIGHT
Roman period

INV. NO. M 674.
H. 0.075, PLINTH: 0.15 × 0.08 M., WT. 1740 GR. OR 5.313 LBS.

Complete, chipped. The integral suspension handle is missing. White, rather grainy marble, probably from an island. It is in the shape of a rectangular parallel-piped brick with two mastoid projections on one of its broad sides. The mastoids are slightly pointed and still have the remains of the suspension handle on the insides and their sides diametrically arranged. The carving of the mastoids on the base is asymmetrical. The initial weight of the weight may have been as much as 5.5 lbs (1 lb. = 327.45 gr.) or 4 mnas (1 soloneian mna = 436.6 gr.).

COMMENTARY - BIBLIOGRAPHY: Unpublished.
The shape of weight no. 105 presents a problem in that some weights of the same type do not have a handle. The idea had originally been put forward that they had been used as dedications due to the depiction of the female breasts on top of the brick, following the example of other dedicatory objects with depictions of

104 Obv.

104 Rev.

human parts. However, this is not a strong argument since the inscriptions on some weights ratify their specific measurement.

Stone weights were normally made of island marble and weighed between 5 and 10 pounds. Aside from stone examples, there were also, in antiquity, metal weights of bronze and lead usually in the shape of slabs or coins, spheres or cubes. Unlike their metal counterparts, stone weights have the advantage of being able, with a little further working, to conform to the legal market standard, i.e. with a little more abrading they attained the required weight. However, this property of theirs, to be quickly worn down, rapidly rendered them useless. Anyway, it is now generally accepted that weighing standards and other forms of measurement in antiquity (length, volume etc.) rarely conformed to one standard of measurement (e.g. 1 Corinthian mna = 412.5 gr., 1 common mna = 654.9 gr., 1 trade mna = 602.6 gr. etc.).

Generally, for weights and measures in antiquity see Pernice 1894; Hültsch 1882; Daremberg - Saglio, s.v. Pondus; *RE* Suppl. III, s.v. Gewichte. The most important Hellenistic weights come chiefly from Delos (*Délos* XVIII, 144-145, pl. 413ff.). Roman weights of this type are more frequent and come mainly from Corinth (*Corinth* XII, 213, nos. 1646-1653) and the Athenian Agora (*Agora* X, 37, no. 18). For similar weights see *Corinth* XII, 213-214, nos. 1647, 1649, pl. 97 (without handle; Roman period); Hiesel 1967, 113-114, nos. 213, 219, pl. 24-25 (from Samos; Roman period); *Agora* X, 36-37, nos. 8-10, 12, pl. 11-12 (Roman period). The dating of our weight to the Roman period is supported by its discovery amongst the stonework for a Late Roman wall belonging to an industrial area south of the paint kiln.

I.P.

105

PHALIROU STREET

PETMEZA Shaft

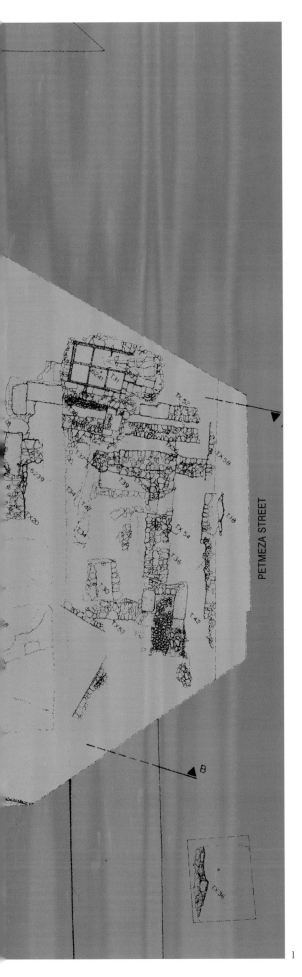

PETMEZA STREET

The M.R.A. shaft at the junction of Petmeza and Phalirou Streets in Koukaki was investigated in the course of excavations that began on 16 April 1996 and ceased in May 1997. An area of 515 sq.m. was examined, part of which was occupied by a house built at the beginning of the 20th century (fig. 1-2).

The excavation concerned a section of an ancient cemetery which appeared to have developed on the south side of the very ancient road leading down to Phaleron and contained burial enclosures and graves dating from the Archaic period to the Early Christian era. There were no burials of the Hellenistic age. In addition, the greater part of the foundations of a large rectangular, pillared building of Late Roman or very Early Christian times was uncovered.

In total sixty-four graves of different types and burial enclosures were excavated at depths ranging from 0.50 to 1.86 m. below ground level on Petmeza Street. They belonged to the following periods:

One cremation and three pit-burials found in the north-western sector of the site date to the Archaic period. Dating to the same period and discovered in levels disturbed by later burials are finds, chiefly black-figure and red-figure pottery, of the late 6th and early 5th c. B.C. An offering ditch which had been disturbed by subsequent burials and the foundations of the modern-day building must have been part of these levels. In it were found vase fragments decorated by great vase-painters of the early 5th c. B.C. Sections of walling destroyed in the same process also date to this period. They are constructed of clay bricks and a mud mortar, and must have belonged to a complex of unknown function and use.

Cremations, burial pits, four terracotta tubs for children burials (larnakes), a cist grave, and one tile-covered and one bronze ash-urn for ashes are all of Classical date. It is interesting to note that the cremations were located in the north-western

2

sector of the site in successive levels and often muddled up together. The children's urns were discovered in the same area in small pits dug out of the natural earth deposit and formed a cluster of graves containing a considerable number of red-figure vases dating to the 3rd quarter of the 5th c. B.C. Tomb 41, a child larnax (clay burial tub) was found containing a number of offerings, along with the few remains of the small child (fig. 3). Most offerings from this grave have been included in the exhibition.

A burial enclosure was found lying in an E-W direction at the northern extremity of the excavation. It consists of rectangular conglomerate blocks of stone laid lengthwise and survives to the height of three courses. A corner-block at its eastern end clearly defines the south side of the enclosure which continued in a westerly direction, sections of it covering a distance of 19.50 m. The style of construction dates it to the beginning of the 4th c. B.C. It seems that the burial enclosure stood at that time on the northern boundary of the cemetery. Smaller stone structures unearthed in the northern sector of the excavation must have belonged to older enclosures, probably of early 5th c. date.

2. PETMEZA Shaft. General view of the excavation from the West.

3. PETMEZA Shaft. Tomb 41. Clay-tub burial of a child.

3

Eleven tile-covered and four built graves found in the northern and eastern sectors of the site date to the Roman period. They are simple shallow cuts in the bedrock covered over with terracotta slabs. Most of them were disturbed by the foundations of the overlying modern-day house.

Five built tombs discovered in the northern and north-eastern sectors of the site are or Early Christian date (fig. 4). They are vaulted tombs approached by three built steps. The vaulted roofs had been destroyed by the modern dwelling erected above them and by networks of public services. The length of the tombs varies from 3.40 to 3.60 m., the width from 1.72 to 1.95 m. and the height from 1 to 2 m. Their interior surfaces had been plastered with mortar. One of the graves preserves a cross incised on its side walls, and signs of fish on the floor. The floor of two of these graves is paved with square plaques, while the floor of the third was covered with mortar (fig. 5).

The south-western sector of the site was occupied by the foundations of a large rectangular building (its preserved l. 15.25 m., w. 6.57 to 8.45 m.). Its orientation lies in an E-W direction. Discovered 1.50 m. below the surface, the foundations were at a depth of 2.43 m. A section of its south-eastern corner and the greater part of its western side had been disturbed during construction of the modern building.

The bases of the entrance portico, 1.45 m. in width, were found on the narrow west side. The east wall curves outwards, forming a kind of small apse, while the wall on the long north side does not follow a straight line. The walls of all three surviving sides are built of clay bricks with mortar joints. The bedrock had been hewn out to receive the foundations of the building and earlier graves, and the walls of grave surrounds had been disturbed. The bedding of the floor, which consisted of clay bricks and mortar, is preserved in the interior, while an area of the floor itself, laid with rectangular terracotta tiles, survives in the western part. Three rows of stone bases, probably for timber uprights supporting the roof, were found in the interior. The northern and southern colonnades each comprised five uprights, but the bases of only three are preserved in the central one. It is particularly difficult to date the structure on account of the earth embankments piled up during the construction of the modern-day building, but it must belong to the Late Roman age or Early Christian period. Its erection or function may possibly have to do with the Early Christian tombs found in the same area.

It is particularly interesting that Early Christian tombs of vaulted type and stepped entrance should have been discovered in this area which is outside the walls, that is, outside the Themistoclean fortifications and the Late Roman enclosure wall built by Valerian. These tombs are of added interest for the topography of Athens but also for Greece as a whole because they are associated with the remnant of a pillared building held by scholars of the period to be one of the first devotional buildings in which Christians assembled for worship.

In view of the importance of these finds, it was decided to lift the three best preserved examples among the Early Christian graves of the site, and transport them to the Byzantine Museum in Athens, where they are going to be exhibited once their restoration is completed. The colonnade building on the other hand, once the works for the construction of the Shaft are completed, it is going to be re-modelled on its original place.

EUTYCHIA LYGOURI-TOLIA

4-5. PETMEZA Shaft. Early Christian vaulted tombs.

106 BLACK-GLAZED LEKYTHOS
450-425 B.C.

INV. NO. A 15524.
H. 0.099, M.D. 0.025, B.D. 0.027 M.

Intact. The neck and the handle have been restored. A small part beneath the handle is missing. It has chips and flakes. Red-brown clay. Uneven firing. Discoid base, cylindrical body. The shoulder is slightly sloping. Thin, rather tall neck. Echinus mouth. Vertical handle.

The upper part of the base, the body, the mouth and the outer side of the handle are covered in black glaze. On the lowest and the upper part of the body, there are two reserved bands with clockwise meander. Ray pattern on the shoulder with a row of dots over it.

COMMENTARY - BIBLIOGRAPHY: Unpublished.
This lekythos belongs to type BL (or the type VI in the Kerameikos); see *Kerameikos* XII, 37. For typological parallels, mainly concerning the shape, see *Corinth* XIII, 253, pl. 58, 6:363. Regarding the decoration see Μυλωνάς 1975, 170, pl. 272-240 and Schlörb-Vierneisel 1966, pl. 30.1 67 (hs 192) 1.

E.L.-T.

107 WHITE-GROUND LEKYTHOS
440-430 B.C.

INV. NO. A 15525
H. 0.117, M.D. 0.029, B.D. 0.032 M.

Complete. Mouth mended from four sherds. It is flaking and chipped. Brown-red clay. Discoid base, cylindrical body narrowing towards the base, vertical strap handle, calyx-shaped mouth.

A black coating covers the interior and exterior of the rim, the outside of the handle, the lower part of the body and upper part of the base. Off-white slip covers the main body, which is decorated with a horizontal shoot made up of antithetic pairs of alternating ivy leaves. The decorative zone is bordered by a line above and three lines below. Radial decoration with a string of rays and row of dots above on the shoulder.

COMMENTARY - BIBLIOGRAPHY: Unpublished.
It belongs to type BL (or type VI at the Kerameikos); see *Kerameikos* XII, 37. For typological parallels see *Kerameikos* XII, 295, 3, pl. 41 and 301, 1, pl. 66.

E.L.-T.

108 RED-FIGURE LEKYTHOS (SECONDARY TYPE)
450-425 B.C.

INV. NO. A 15522.
H. 0.101, M.D. 0.026, B.D. 0.03 M.

Red-brown clay. The mouth is mended and restored. Handle mended. Many chips and flakes. On the body a Nike is depicted flying to the right. She wears a long chiton and himation. Her hair is caught up in a sakos. In her right hand she is holding a mirror.

COMMENTARY - BIBLIOGRAPHY: Unpublished.
Nikes, chthonic spirits, are depicted in wedding scenes, offering presents to the new couple, indicating the gifts of abundance and fertility for their new life; see Roberts 1978, 183. It also seems that in these scenes they are the embodiment of the triumphant female beauty; see Kenner 1939, 82. At the same time, due to their chthonic substance, they also have a close relationship to death and are depicted in vases, found in graves as in our lekythos.

For parallels with flying Nikes on lekythoi see *Corinth* XIII, 232-233, no. 306.4, pl. 26 and for flying Nikes on squat lekythoi see *Agora* XXX, no. 929 and *CVA* Berlin 8, pl. 41, fig. 9-10. Generally for Nike see *LIMC* VI.1, s.v. Nike, 850-904 [Goulaki-Voutira].

E.L.-T.

106 *107* *108*

109 RED-FIGURE CHOUS
450-425 B.C.

INV. NO. A 15526.
H. 0.086, B.D. 0.05 M.

Intact. The handle is mended from two pieces. It has chips and flakes. Red-brown clay. Traces of red ochre (miltos) on the base.

On the figural panel, a nude boy is depicted wearing a wreath. He stands frontally, with his head turned to the right. His legs are apart, the right one stretched backwards, the left one bent. With his right arm, bent on the waist, he is holding the long stem of a cart. At the same time, he is extending his left arm, holding two ivy branches. The figural panel is crowned with egg-pattern.

COMMENTARY - BIBLIOGRAPHY: Unpublished.

The choes which gave their name to the second day of the Anthesteria are small, trefoil-mouthed oenochoae and their largest production is dated in the last quarter of the 5th c. B.C. This chous belongs to Oenochoe type 3, see *Agora* XII, 60-63. This type of vase has rarely been found outside Attica. They come in many variations, according to their use. Their iconography has been given various interpretations: they are mainly connected with representations of children playing. According to Boardman (*ARV*², 170), these vases were possibly toys for children, or presents offered to them during the festival of the Anthesteria. It was also a common burial offering in graves of young children, commemorating their first participation and initiation during the festival of Dionysos; he was the god of vegetation, also related to the world of the dead. This festival was connected to the worship and the invocation of the souls. Choes are also found as burial offerings in children's graves, victims of the plague during the Peloponnesian War.

On this particular example, the small boy is depicted with a cart. For a similar vase, as far as the scene and the shape are concerned, see Van Hoorn 1951, no. 73, fig. 509. The cart was probably a present offered to children during the Anthesteria; see Van Hoorn 1951, 44 and Hamilton 1992, 117. Generally for choes see Van Hoorn 1951; Bažant 1975, 72-78; Rühfel 1984b; Hamilton 1992; Τζάχου-Αλεξανδρή 1997a, 473-490 (depictions of the Anthesteria and the chous from Pireos Street, by the Eretria P.).

E.L.-T.

111

109

112

110 CHOUS
450-425 B.C.

INV. NO. A 15527.
H. 0.086, B.D. 0.043 M.

Intact with chips and flakes. Added colour faded in places. Red-brown clay. Irregular firing. Traces of red ochre (miltos). The decoration is rendered with added cream colour (Six technique).

On the figural panel which is defined by simple, thin bands of added colour, a nude young man is depicted, running to the right. His right arm is bent on the waist, while his left hand is extended in front of him, with his palm open, playing with a small ball. His right leg is bent and stands firmly on the ground which is de-

110

fined with a line; his left leg – also bent – is stretched backwards. In front of the figure, there is a huge ivy leaf which stems from an elevation on the ground.

COMMENTARY - BIBLIOGRAPHY: Unpublished.

In this particular scene, the nude young man is playing with a ball. For a vase with a similar scene see Van Hoorn 1951, no. 276. The ivy leaf on the scene symbolises the fertility and vegetation abundant in the first days of spring. At the same time, it alludes to the netherworld, since it springs from the earth. This oversized ivy leaf may be perceived as a symbol of the god Dionysos himself, whose cult was worshipped in the Anthesteria. For similar scenes, where figures run toward an over life-sized ivy leaf, see *KdA* 277 (Perseus) and Van Hoorn 1951, no. 947, pl. 421, pl. 37 (female figure). This vase belongs to a special group of choes, where the depiction is rendered with a variant of the Six technique, that is without the use of incisions. For choes of the same technique see Van Hoorn 1951, 167, nos. 811-812, pl. 426-427 and *KdA* 277. Over the black glaze, cream colour was added, and the details were rendered with deep red colour. For this technique see Green 1970, 475 and also for the Six technique in general see Kurtz 1975, 116ff. For the cult of Dionysos see *LIMC*, s.v. Dionysos. Also see commentary on no. 109.

E.L.-T.

111 RED-FIGURE CHOUS
450-425 B.C.

INV. NO. A 15528.
H. 0.082, B.D. 0.044 M.

Intact. Chips and flakes. Red-brown clay. Uneven firing. On the ring base there are traces of red ochre (miltos).

On the inside of the mouth, a relief mask of a bearded and balding man, probably a Silen, is formed as an extension to the handle. On the figural panel, defined above and below by a band of egg-pattern, a small child is depicted walking to the right. His hair is long, reaching to his nape. His body is wrapped in an himation, which is fastened on the area of his belly with his left hand. In his hand he is holding a skyphos. Behind him, there are myrtle branches which the child is most probably holding with his left hand.

COMMENTARY - BIBLIOGRAPHY: Unpublished.

On this chous, the small boy appears to be dressed for a special occasion, probably to participate in the Anthesteria and in particular in one of the many athletic contests that took place during this festival. This probably concerned one's ability to run, carrying a vessel at the same time, in this case a skyphos, full of wine. See Van Hoorn 1951, 34 and Hamilton 1992, 114-115. The relief mask of the Silen was probably indicative of the god Dionysos's spirit as a drinker who first enjoys his own gift to humans, wine. For a chous with a relief mask of Silen see Van Hoorn 1951, pl. 405a-b. Also see commentary on no. 109.

E.L.-T.

112 CHOUS
450-425 B.C.

INV. NO. A 15529.
H. 0.072, B.D. 0.037 M.

Intact. Mended handle. Chipped. The added colour is partially flaked. Very few traces of red ochre (miltos) on the underside of the base. Red-brown clay. Uneven firing. The decoration is rendered with added, cream colour (Six technique).

On the figural panel framed by simple, thin bands of added colour, a female dancer is depicted facing right. She wears a short chiton. Her hair is brought up in a kekryphalos. Her right arm is bent to the waist, while with her left one raising forward, she is holding rattles (krotala). With her right foot firmly on the ground, she raises her left one and stretches it backwards. She is wearing bracelets around her ankles and thighs. In front of her, an oversized ivy leaf grows from the ground.

COMMENTARY - BIBLIOGRAPHY: Unpublished.

This chous is exactly the same in shape and technique as no. 110. Only in this case, a female figure is depicted, dancing in front of an ivy leaf. It is a work from the same workshop and most probably by the same painter. An element they both share is the presence in front of the two figures of the oversized ivy leaf, the symbol of Dionysos, the god of the Anthesteria. The dance is an indispensable part of the cult of Dionysos, and scenes with various dance styles are depicted on such small choes; see Van Hoorn 1951, 38-39. Also see commentary on no. 109.

E.L.-T.

113 BLACK-GLAZED LEKANIS WITH LID
450-420 B.C.

INV. NO. A 15517.
H. 0.02, H. (INCL. LID) 0.105, M.D. 0.116 M.

Intact with chips and flakes mainly on the handles. Red-brown clay. All over the body and the lid are covered with good quality glaze. The flat, resting surface of the base is reserved as well as the underside where there is a round black band with a dot in the centre. Ring base with concave walls. Hemispherical body. Deep, in-curving rim. Horizontal handles of cylindrical section, raised sharply over the rim. On the surface of the vase, in the middle part and below the handles a thin incised line in band.

lekanis contained the black-glazed salt-cellar no. 115. For the shape and its typological parallels see *Agora* XII, 164-170, pl. 42:1242. Especially for the lid see *Agora* XII, 172, pl. 42:1261.

E.L.-T.

114 BLACK-GLAZED SKYPHOS OF CORINTHIAN TYPE
425-400 B.C.

INV. NO. A 15519.
H. 0.05, B.D. 0.039, M.D. 0.068 M.

Intact and covered unevenly in black glaze. It has small chips and flakes. Ring base, deep body with thin walls and mouth, horizontal handles of cylindrical section.

115 BLACK-GLAZED SALT-CELLAR
450-425 B.C.

INV. NO. A 15518.
H. 0.032, B.D. 0.036, M.D. 0.057 M.

Intact with chips on the rim and flakes on the body. Red-brown clay. Glazed all over apart from the reserved base and the edge of the rim. Echinus body. Flat base. On the bottom of the vase, residue of some material.

COMMENTARY - BIBLIOGRAPHY: Unpublished.
It was found inside the lekanis no. 113. A small vase which is used only during the Classical period domestically and for storing various spices and mainly salt. This shape occurred at the beginning of the 5th and remained in use until the 4th c. B.C. For the shape's history and its typological parallels see *Agora* XII, 132-136, pl. 34:912.

E.L.-T.

COMMENTARY - BIBLIOGRAPHY: Unpublished.
It is a product of an Attic workshop. The lekanides were vases used for storage of many objects, of everyday domestic use. Especially the black-glazed ones were toilet articles and were a quite usual wedding gift as well as a burial offering in graves. This particular lekanis belongs to the Lycinic type, a term suggested by Beazley. It is one of the rare example of lekanis which preserves its lid. The shape occurs from the mid 5th c. B.C. and is abandoned in the mid 4th c. B.C., in a period when the red-figure lekanis becomes popular. Our

COMMENTARY - BIBLIOGRAPHY: Unpublished.
The skyphos is the most popular drinking vessel in Athens from the 6th until the 4th c. B.C. This particular vase is an Attic product and according to its characteristics, it belongs to one of the categories of skyphoi, the so-called Corinthian skyphos, which has been modelled after a similar vase of the Corinthian workshop with small variations. For the shape and the typological parallels see *Agora* XII, 81-83, pl. 15:321.

E.L.-T.

116 TERRACOTTA FIGURINE OF A KNEELING
CHILD
475-450 B.C.

INV. NO. E 1045.
H. 0.072, L. 0.061 M.

The right hand is missing. Restored from
many fragments with extensive chipping
and damage on the surface. Brown-red
clay, traces of black paint on the whole
figure, traces of white and red on the
knee and red on the left eye.

The figure, naked, in a frontal kneeling
position, is half-seated on the ground,
which has been rendered as a low pedestal. The legs, bent at the knees, touch
the ground; the right with the front of
the shin, the left with the outside shin
and thigh. It is supported on the ground
with the left hand. The head is slightly
turned to the right, the face much damaged with the features difficult to discern.

COMMENTARY - BIBLIOGRAPHY: Unpublished.
The type is common, known also as Temple boy.
Rhodes and Attica have been proposed as a place of
origin in the Greek world. In cemeteries it is found
exclusively in graves of small children and is interpreted
as a depiction of a common child. It appears at the end
of the 6th c. and continues to be produced until the end
of the 5th c. B.C. For latest discussion of the type
including extensive bibliography see *Kerameikos* XV,
58-62, nos. 183-184, pl. 34-35 and Μπόνιας 1998, 85-
86, pl. 55. The basic study remains that of Hadzisteliou-
Price 1969, 95-111, pl. 21-23. For typological parallels
see Winter 1903, II, 268, 3; *BMC* I, 93, no. 257, pl. 45
(mid 5th c. B.C); *Olynthus* VII, no. 283, pl. 36;
Hadzisteliou-Price 1969, 99, type II, pl. 21, 7-13.

Th.K.

117 TERRACOTTA FIGURINE OF A LIONESS
450-400 B.C.

INV. NO. E 1046.
H. 0.058, L. 0.15 M.

Whole. Mended from many fragments
with chips and flaking on the surface.
Brown clay. Traces of white and red slip.
The animal, seated on a rectangular base
to the right, has its head turned to the
front and its tail is wrapped around its
buttocks. The face is worn. The front is
made in a mould while the back is handmade. Under the base there is an air hole.

COMMENTARY - BIBLIOGRAPHY: Unpublished.
See *BMC* I, 76, no. 172, pl. 32; Nicholson 1968, 17, no.
28, pl. 5; *Olynthus* XIV, no. 305, pl. 99 (end of 5th -
beginning of 4th c. B.C); *CIRh* III, 99, no. XXV, 15, fig.
85 and 147, no. LIV, 6, fig. 143; Sinn 1977, 45, no. 96,
pl. 29.

Th.K.

117, 116

CHURCH
OF AGIOS IOANNIS

AGIOS IOANNIS Station

AGIOS IOANNIS Station on Line 2 (Sepolia-Daphne) of the M.R.A. occupies the space taken up by the square of the church of St John the Hunter (Agios Ioannis Kynegos) on Vouliagmenis Avenue. This district lies within the ancient deme of Alopeke, intimately connected, according to ancient sources, with Kynosarges, and 11 or 12 ancient stades (about 2 kilometres) distant from the Wall of Athens. The ancient road to Sounion, which lay along the axis of present-day Vouliagmenis Avenue, commenced at the Diomeiae Gates.

Because of the topographical importance of the location and of excavation finds formerly made in the area, the Ephorate of Antiquities conducted excavations in 1994 and 1995 which extended over 3,700 sq.m. and resulted in the following (fig. 1):

1. The discovery of a torrent-bed which ran almost the entire length of the excavation site from SE to NW and followed the slopes of the hill. The width of the bed varied according to periodic rainfall and drought; at the south end it could have reached 20 m., while in the north-western corner it was down to 5 m.

2. On the north-eastern side of the dig, the site of the entrance to the Station, a section of a pottery kiln, 2.50 m. in length overall and initially on two levels, was uncovered together with part of its associated workshop. The complex dates to the 2nd half of the 5th c. B.C.

3. Also twelve graves were discovered. There was one isolated stone cist grave – tomb 1 – at the centre of the site; the remaining eleven were clustered together on the north-western side, almost at the edge of the Station (fig. 2). While they are distant from tomb 1, they lie on the same bank of the torrent-bed. Seven are pit-burials, two tile-covered, one an urn burial, and one a cremation pit. They are not all similarly oriented. All were unrifled, assuming some never contained grave goods. The offerings were Beldam-type lekythoi (oil-flasks), white-ground lekythoi (no. 118), red-figure lekythoi (no. 119), small lekythoi, skyphoi (beakers) and stemless kylikes (drinking-cups); all date to the mid 5th c.

1

The excavation at AGIOS IOANNIS produced fresh details concerning the topography of the locality, complemented the relief map of the area as a result of the study of the torrent-bed and the relationship it bore to the uses to which the site was put by the inhabitants, and confirmed it was a burial-ground since the new finds complement the old. The explanation of the discovery of a pottery workshop lies in its having served the needs of the cemetery or alternatively in the workshop workers being local residents and the group of eleven graves forming part of their own burial-place. Furthermore, we must not overlook the existence at this point of the ancient road leading to Sounion which, while no traces of it were found in the excavation, is certainly to be connected with the activity that developed there.

ELISSAVET HATZIPOULIOU

2

2. *AGIOS IOANNIS Station. Tomb 11 with grave offerings.*

118 WHITE-GROUND LEKYTHOS (SECONDARY TYPE - ATL)
c. 460 B.C.

INV. NO. A 15531.
H. 0.20, B.D. 0.047, D. AT SHOULDER LEVEL 0.064, M.D. 0.039 M.

Complete. The white slip on the main body of the vase has mostly flaked off. A simple rectangular, plank-shaped funeral stele resting on a two-stepped pedestal takes up the centre of the scene. With difficulty, one can make out its stippled cornice. Left, a bearded man is depicted sitting cross-legged on a rock, supporting his head with his left arm, meditating, and leaning on his right thigh. The shoulder, which is left clay-coloured, is decorated with radial and schematic tongue-ornament. The outlines have been drawn with a glistening, smooth line.

COMMENTARY - BIBLIOGRAPHY: Unpublished.

For the "plank-shaped" funerary stelai, the Workshop of the Tymbos P. and for lekythoi of the ATL type, see the commentary on no. 231. Lekythos no. 118 is probably by the same hand as that which also decorated a white-ground lekythos in a private collection in Münster; see Stupperich 1979, 209-211, pl. 29.1-3. The stele belongs to type A-II of Nakayama 1982, 60-69. The rocky landscape is probably meant to depict the shore of lake Acherousia, presumably following its depiction in the Nekyia by Polygnotus. Figures sitting on rocks are not unknown on white-ground lekythoi, see Olmos 1980, 93-94, as also crouching figures, see the slightly earlier lekythos by the Inscription P. in Athens, NM, no. 1959 (*ARV*[2] 748,3 and *Addenda*[2] 284) and another, broadly contemporary, by the Bosanquet P. in London, British Museum, no. 1905.7-10.10 (*ARV*[2] 1227, 10; *Addenda*[2] 350; *Pandora*, 145-146), where the deceased is sitting on the steps of the tomb. The posture is reminiscent of that of the grieving Hector, as Pausanias relates in his description of the Nekyia at the Club (Lesche) of the Knidians at Delphi, see Φωκικά 10.31.5 [Παπαχατζής]. For this subject see Neumann 1965, 136-140; Laurent 1898. See Simon 1963, 44. Also, see

Τιβέριος 1985, 24, n. 32 and Stansbury-O'Donnel 1990. The rendering of the peaceful rocky landscape, the outpouring of grief and also the thoughtful confrontation of death by the deceased refers to the figure of Demokleides on the homonymous stele in Athens, NM, no. 752.

Workshop of the Tymbos P.

G.K.

118

From tomb 1

119 RED-FIGURE LEKYTHOS (SECONDARY TYPE) 440-430 B.C.

INV. NO. A 15530.
H. 0.345, H. OF NECK 0.103, B.D. 0.068, MAX.D. 0.091, M.D. 0.062 M.

Complete. Brown-red clay, flaking in different parts. Exceptionally slender body, with a neck to body ratio of 1:3.

A young male figure is depicted turned to the right. He has a petasos behind his head and wears a mantle. His right arm slightly bent at the level of his waist, while he is supported by his left arm on his spear. A peplos-clothed female figure

119

opposite holds a small box above her left shoulder.

COMMENTARY - BIBLIOGRAPHY: Unpublished.
This is a scene of farewell in a household setting. The lekythos is a product of an Attic workshop and may be attributed to the Klügmann P. For painters of red-figure lekythoi of the 2nd half of the 5th c. B.C. see *ARV²* 1198-1200. For the shape of the vase see *Agora* XXX, 45-47.

E.H.

From the fill

120

120 GOLD DANAKE 140-90 B.C.

INV. NO. Θ 348.
D. 0.01 M.

Gold, single-stamp "coin" with representation of female head to r. A crescent in the field to the right. Dotted circle surrounds the representation.

COMMENTARY - BIBLIOGRAPHY: Unpublished.
For the type cf. bronze Athenian coin, *Agora* XXVI, no. 106b.

I.T.

AMALIAS AVENUE

NATIONAL GARDENS

0 1 2 3 4 5   10m

ZAPPEION Shaft

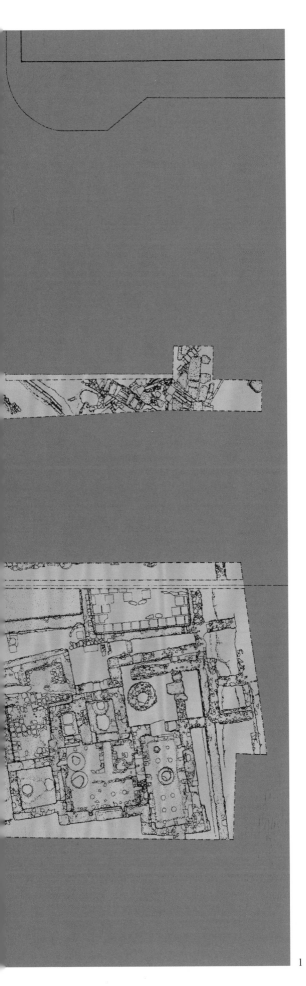

An area of 670 sq.m. on the south-western edge of the Zappeion Gardens close to the junction of Amalias and Olgas Avenues, where a ventilation shaft for the M.R.A. was to be sunk, was excavated and investigated with important results[1] (fig. 1-2). The district which, until its extension under Hadrian, lay outside the fortified city, the nearest surviving part of which is at the Olympieion, has been of importance ever since antiquity. We know from what is recorded in ancient sources – and confirmed by earlier research in excavations[2] – that this idyllic spot with the abundant water of the nearby Ilissos river and heavy vegetation was a place in which many divinities were worshipped. It was here that the sanctuaries of Olympian Zeus, Apollo Delphinios, Panhellenic Zeus, Olympian Gaia, and Artemis Agrotera were all established. It had been a human settlement from prehistoric times and became a burial-ground in the Geometric period.

Once Athens had begun to expand during the reign of the emperor Hadrian, the temple of Olympian Zeus had been completed and the triumphal arch built in honour of the emperor had been erected, the district was incorporated into the inner city and acquired a character of its own, for new sanctuaries, public and private buildings and luxurious baths were constructed in it.

A large trapezoidal building, 16.80 m. on its longest side and 8.60-10.60 m. wide and divided by a lateral wall, was the oldest archaeological evidence obtained from the excavation of the shaft (fig. 3). It is built of large conglomerate blocks of stone laid lengthwise and is preserved to a greatest height of four courses. It rests on bedrock, previously cut to receive it. Unfortunately finds from the excavation were few for the exterior of the building had been entirely swallowed up by embankments when the National Gardens were laid out. It can be dated to late Classical times from the style of its construction and from the scant pottery acquired in carefully sifting the soil at foundation level.

To the north of this site a rectangular structure measuring 3.72 × 2.70 m. and standing to the height of two courses was uncovered. In the Roman era a rectangu-

1

lar well-shaft, in which a large terracotta conduit ended, was opened at its centre point. A similar structure was found during the excavation of the baths in the Zappeion Gardens and was identified as an altar.

It should be noted that walls constructed of large blocks of stone were revealed when the large complex with the mosaics opposite the entrance to the Olympieion, identified as a Gymnasium of Hadrian's time, was being excavated. From a careful study and comparison of the plans it was evident that the excavation of the ZAPPEION Shaft had again brought to light the walls and rectangular structure discovered in the old excavation of 1889[3].

The irregularly shaped structure is not easy to identify as archaeological finds are lacking. The fact that it was left open to the south, taken in conjunction with its asymmetry, tends to preclude its identification as a building. It is not unlikely it was the enclosure of an open-air sanctuary and the rectangular structure a pedestal or altar. Sanctuaries and altars close to the Ilissos are mentioned in ancient sources[4] as being in the general area, such as the altar of Boreas, the altar of the Ilissian Muses, the sanctuary of the Nymphs and Acheloos, and the sanctuary of Pan.

The northern sector of the excavation includes a very well preserved baths complex (balneum). It stands on a levelled site 21 m. wide between two long and particularly high walls of fine construction in which many re-used architectural members have been incorporated.

2. ZAPPEION Shaft. General view from the South.

3. ZAPPEION Shaft. The trapezoidal building and the rectangular structure.

3

The baths continue both eastwards, inside the National Gardens, and westwards along Amalias Avenue and probably are somehow connected with bath-house J mentioned by I. Travlos[5] as being at this point. In a later excavation on the pedestrian division of Amalias Avenue, opposite to where the shaft was being dug, the baths were found to continue in a westerly direction. The baths complex contains two hypocaust rooms, two praefurnia (heating spaces) and nine cisterns (fig. 4). They were established after the Herulian raids at the end of the 3rd or early in the 4th c. A.D. and were later destroyed, but repaired and enlarged during the 5th-6th c. A.D.

The two hypocaust rooms, the two praefurnia and four of the cisterns belong to the first building phase. The larger of the hypocausts has fifteen hypocaust column supports, some of them cylindrical, some square, and dividing walls which provide openings for underfloor access to the praefurnia. Clearly this hypocaust served the room with the hot baths (caldarium). Immediately to the north lies another oblong hypocaust, the floor of which was supported on seventeen re-used marble grave columns instead of hypocausts. This is the room with the warm baths (tepidarium). The two furnaces are connected with the caldarium by underground vaulted passages built of bricks and mortar. The hot air was circulated by means of three small chambers which were heated, the heat then being channelled to the two hypocaust rooms. Vertical openings in the walls of the chambers provided ventilation and the heating of the walls themselves. To this phase belongs a large well-built rectangular tank, with a thick coat of hydraulic plaster inside and marble slabs outside, which supplied water through two openings to two marble basins found in situ. Many oil-lamps were discovered inside the tank (nos. 121-122).

In the second phase, occurring in the 5th-6th c. A.D., the hypocaust rooms were repaired and brought back into use. Openings were inserted into the floors of the three small chambers and their outlets plastered. Four new chambers were built with tiled floors. One of these was constructed underground with a vaulted roof[6]; in it a well was dug for drawing up water. The interior is nicely finished with a tile and mortar floor; on its north wall are traces of a rather clumsy scene with human figures, fish, herons and crosses (fig. 5). These rough wall-paintings point to its later use as a refuge or martyr's memorial.

To the south of the baths a section 12 m. long of a Roman road running in an E-W direction and 5.38 m. wide was examined. Four or five surface levels survive with Roman and Late Roman pottery. The road probably served the needs of the baths.

The site of the baths and the land lying to the south of them was occupied in Byzantine times by large constructed corn-bins and storage jars. Nine clay storage chambers were sunk into the floors of the rooms of the bath-houses while throughout the excavation area twenty-nine corn storage-bins had been placed in a row (fig. 2). It seems that some of these – such as had survived previous disturbances to the site – were visible at the end of the 19th century[7], but these were buried when the National Gardens were laid out.

4. ZAPPEION Shaft. The bath complex (balneum).

5. ZAPPEION Shaft. Sketches in the interior of the cistern.

Two late Byzantine kilns furnish evidence of the final use made of the site before it was converted into part of the Royal Gardens in King Otto's reign (1833-1862).

Among the movable finds from the excavation are a stele inscribed on its back with an account of the Athenian Amphictyons of Delos (no. 123) and a small marble head of Asklepios (no. 124).

By decision of the Central Archaeological Council, the well-preserved baths complex has been declared a protected site. It will be an archaeological site open to visitors and incorporated into the programme for the unification of the archaeological sites of Athens.

In a pilot trench dug a few metres to the south of the ZAPPEION Shaft wells serving also as rubbish tips were found at a depth of about 20 m. In one of these wells (well 3) many late 2nd - early lst c. B.C. transport amphorae were found (see no. 125), while in another (well 4) bronze sculptures such as the figurine of a youth (no. 126) and the foot of a statue (no. 127), were found.

OLGA ZACHARIADOU

5

NOTES

1. The first presentation of the excavation results were made by the then Head of the 3rd Ephorate, Dr Liana Parlama, in an article of hers titled "The Metropolitan Railway and the antiquities of Athens", in a paper she delivered on "Finds to-date in excavations for the Metro" at a seminar held by the School for Guides on 8.2.95, and in another article she wrote on "Athens 1993-95, from excavations for the Metro" (all in Greek).

The excavation of the ZAPPEION Shaft was the subject of a detailed paper presented (in Greek) by the undersigned on "New topographical facts concerning the Eastern sector of Athens" during the 1st Scientific Meeting of the 3rd Ephorate in March 1996 and included in her talk "The Eastern district of the ancient city of Athens. Composite data" delivered at the 2nd Scientific Meeting of the 3rd Ephorate in February 1999 (proceedings, forth.).

2. Θρεψιάδης - Τραυλός 1961/62, 9-14.

3. Κουμανούδης 1889, 12.

4. Paus., Αττικά I, 19, 5; Παπαχατζής 1974, 285-286, n. 3.

5. Travlos 1971, 181.

6. Similar water tanks have been found during many excavations in Athens: in the area around the Olympieion, in Neos Kosmos, in Koukaki, in the city centre, etc.

7. Κουμανούδης 1889, 11.

157, pl. 32, no. 2007 (mid 4th c. A.D.). The incised branch on the base, often combined with an initial, is a characteristic of many examples. In Athens it is usually found combined with one or two signatures from the 3rd until the early 6th c. A.D. and often with the signature omitted from the 4th until the 6th c. A.D. This emblem is used by the Athenian potters when they start to incise on the archetypes or the moulds their signatures instead of stamping them. This emblem is not identified with a specific workshop. According to Perlzweig (*Agora* VII, 28) it is possibly a sign of good luck for the lamp's user. For similar emblems on lamp bases cf. *Agora* VII, 14, nos. 1353-1355 and Karivieri 1996, 77, pl. 27, no. 278.

O.Z.

On the base, two concentric circles. On the disc, a lion seated to the right is depicted, ready to attack. The scene's ground is a band of short vertical lines. On the rim of the disc, two panels with herring-bone pattern. The nozzle is framed by two incised lines. On the handle there are deep grooves.

COMMENTARY - BIBLIOGRAPHY: Unpublished.
The Attic lamps of this type do not appear until the end of the 3rd c. A.D. A similar decoration appears in Attic sarcophagi. For parallels see *Agora* VII, 130, pl. 21, no. 974 (1st half of 4th c. A.D.); Karivieri 1996, pl. 31, no. 46 (2nd half of 4th c. A.D.); *Corinth* IV$_2$, 259, pl. XVIII, nos. 1216-1218, type XXVIII; *Isthmia* III, 76, nos. 2987-2988, type XXVIII C.

O.Z.

BALNEUM

121 DOUBLE-SPOUTED RED-GLAZED LAMP
c. A.D. 350

INV. NO. Δ 7190.
H. 0.043-0.065, B.D. 0.032, MAX.W. 0.088 M.

Intact. Chips on one of the spouts and in other parts of the vase. Flakes on the surface. Red-brown clay. Flat base, hemispherical squat body, slightly concave disc, conical nozzles. In the centre of the disc, a solid conical handle with suspension hole. Air holes on both sides of the handle, and on the base of the nozzles. The lamp is mould-made.
Thin red glaze on the vase. On the base an incised branch within two concentric circles. Around the disc, a band with herring bone and on the rim two small oblique panels with the same pattern and small circles on both sides. On the nozzles, alternate striped triangles and circles with dots. On the handle deep grooves.

COMMENTARY - BIBLIOGRAPHY: Unpublished.
It belongs to the multi-spouted type with central handle. For the shape and decoration see *Agora* VII, 156-

121, 122

122 SINGLE-SPOUTED RED-GLAZED LAMP
c. A.D. 350

INV. NO. Δ 7191.
L. 0.103, H. 0.038, B.D. 0.027, MAX.W. 0.078 M.

Intact. Red clay. Traces of black colour on the nozzle and in other parts. Flat base, hemispherical squat body, slightly concave disc, short conical nozzle, solid conical handle. Filling hole on the disc and small air hole at the junction of the nozzle with the disc. The lamp is mould-made. Thin, red-brown glaze on the disc and the lower part of the body. Traces of fire on the nozzle.

123 MARBLE DOUBLE-SIDED STELE WITH A FINANCIAL REPORT OF THE ATHENIAN AMPHICTYONS OF DELOS
c. 345-343 B.C.

INV. NO. M 5585.
H. 0.21, W. 0.184, TH. 0.087 M.

Part of one narrow side is preserved while all the other sides are broken. Text on both sides is arranged in lines, slightly inconsistent where numbers are included. There are 21 lines preserved on side A and 18 on side B. Height of the letters on side A: 0.004-0.005 m. The space between the lines is 0.005 m. Height of the letters on side B: 0.004-0.005 m. Some letters (Φ, Β, Τ) are as tall as 0.007 m. The space between the letters is 0.004 m. There is considerable damage to the inscribed surface, as well as three parallel lines which were cut at a later date. The letters on side B are similar but somehow more carelessly executed than the letters on side A. On side A, there is a left margin 0.022 m. wide while the upper margin of side B is 0.02 m. Lastly, between lines 13 and 14 of side B there is space of 0.012 m.

COMMENTARY - BIBLIOGRAPHY: Unpublished.

The inscription contains extracts from a financial report of the Athenian Amphictyons of the sanctuary at Delos. It is known that the sacred island of Delos, famous for the Sanctuary of Apollo and place of pilgrimage for the Ionians everywhere, was the seat of the first Athenian League, which was founded in 478 B.C., immediately after the end of the Persian Wars. The city of Delos kept its autonomy (despite the occasional banishment or cleansing imposed by the Athenians), but the administration of the temple and the management of the enormous revenues were undertaken by the body of Amphictyons, with a secretary and an assistant secretary. Apart from the Athenians, the people of Andros belonged to the original body of Amphictyons, and the term was for five years. After about 367 B.C., the rule of the temple was renewed annually, but remained exclusively Attic. This was continued until the year 314 B.C. when Delos gained its independence, which lasted with small breaks from 404 B.C. (defeat of Athens during the Peloponnesian War) until 394 B.C. and for a short period a little after 386 B.C. (King's Peace).

According to the prevailing practice, and for other comparable bodies, the Amphictyons had to present a financial report at the end of their period of rule. These reports were written on stelai with two copies, one for Delos and one for Athens. Equivalent reports have been published in the series *Inscriptions de Délos*, 89 to 104-33 and *Inscriptiones Graecae* II² 1633-1653.

Apart from the names of the Amphictyons who relinquished and those who took up their posts, and the eponymous archons during whose term they performed their duties which they discharged, these financial reports usually contained: a record of various revenues according to source (alliance tax of various cities, return of capital and interest from lending sanctuary money, fines, income from renting sanctuary land and buildings, income from other exploitations, like the right of passage for a ship, fishing, export of purple dye, cutting wood etc., as well as income from selling various animals or items). Then followed the expenditure report, which was usually the expenditure on construction of different works in the sanctuary, building or restoration-conservation of the buildings of the sanctuary, staff salaries, among which salaries of the Amphictyons themselves, expenses for worship and the different games that were part of the festivals.

A large part of the report is occupied with various inventories of offerings and generally of the property of the sanctuary, which includes detailed catalogues of the various offerings, old and new, with the names of the donors as well as their present state of preservation. For precious objects, quantity or weight is recorded. They are arranged in categories according to place of keeping and material (gold, silver, bronze, iron, wood). Finally, there is a brief report of the court cases that the Amphictyons dealt with, the judgement of which was carried out by the Athenian courts. The hieropoioi continued the practice of writing financial reports during Independence (314-166 B.C.); they succeeded the Amphictyons. The same practice continued during the period of Athenian domination (after

123 a

166 B.C.) until the Roman conquest, with the last preserved report in the year 140/139 B.C.

In this specific fragmentary stele, the following extracts of the report are preserved:

On side A, in lines 1-11, there is an extract from an inventory of sacred objects, with an indication of their weight or number, which is written in the acrophonic numerical system, like all the numerals on the stele. The objects were probably kept in the House of the Naxians, in the Temple and probably in the Thesmophorion. Among the other objects mentioned are a "gastroptis" (kind of a cooking utensil), lebetes (cauldrons) and other pots, probably of bronze, some of which are not in good condition. Also wooden couches, probably used for ceremonial symposia, most of which are completely broken.

The remainder of the lines of side A (12-21) contain recordings of income from renting to various private tenants pieces of land and houses. It is known that the sanctuary owned large agricultural areas mainly on Rheneia, Delos and Mykonos, which it leased to farmers usually for a decade, on the basis of the conditions of a sacred contract. It should be remembered that the whole of Rheneia was dedicated to Apollo of Delos in 523 B.C. by Polycrates, the tyrant of Samos. There were ten agricultural areas in Rheneia and as many in Delos. Similarly, the sacred houses, other properties or workshops, which were also leased to private citizens, came from compulsory dedications of the properties of various people who had clashed with the Athenian lords of the Sanctuary. We know for instance that in 376/5 B.C. some Delians were convicted to life banishment and their property confiscated for impiety, because they tried to regain the management of the Sanctuary by throwing out and beating up the Amphictyons.

Our inscription refers to income from leasing land in the agricultural areas of Phoinikes (Delos), Panormos, Limnai (Rheneia), and from some port. The two last lines refer to income from renting sacred houses. The rents collected range from 50 to 326 drachmae a year. From the two names of the tenants preserved (Apatourios and Tharsagoras), the second one is unknown from other sources.

Side B is damaged and it is difficult to decipher the texts. In lines 1-13, court cases are mentioned with which the Amphictyons and their secretary are dealing. The verdicts are in summary form.

One of the cases seems to have been particularly serious. It was taken to the Athens court known as the Trigonon. This is the first mention of this court, which was known to us only from literary evidence. The death penalty was imposed on the guilty party. This verdict can be taken as more evidence of the harsh attitude of the Athenians around 345 B.C. to the Delians who never stopped seeking independence. We know that in 343 B.C. the Delians turned to the "international court" of Delphi asking for the condemnation and the expulsion of the Athenians from Delos. The Athenians sent as their advocate the orator Hyperides who was helped by Demosthenes. Eventually the Amphictyonic court of Delphi (which was influenced by Philip) acquitted the Athenians.

However, before the trial at Delphi, it seems that there was tension on Delos and one of the leaders of the pro-Athenian side, one Peisitheides son of Peisitheides of Delos was threatened and in order to save his life, he escaped to Athens where the Athenians honoured him and offered him citizenship and free meals (*IG* II², 222). From our inscription we learn that a case relating to this person was taken to Athens, to the court known as the *Meson ton kainon*. The information in our inscription comprises new precious evidence for the tension of the relationship between the Athenians and the Delians during the period before the trial in 343 B.C.

For the inscriptions with reports of the period of the Athenian Amphictyony on Delos see *IG* II², 1633-1653 and *ID*, 89 to 104-33. On the temeni of the Sanctuary of Delos see mainly Kent 1948, 243-338. For the sacred houses see mainly Molinier 1914. For the courts of Athens see mainly *Agora* XXVIII.

Ch.B.K.

123 β

124 MARBLE HEAD OF ASKLEPIOS
Roman period (possibly 2nd c. A.D.)

INV. NO. M 5272.
H. 0.047 M.

The neck is cut at the base of the nape. Chipped on the lower part of the forehead, the eyes, nose and the right cheek. White, fine-grained marble.

The god here is rendered with a tall forehead, with rather prominent cheekbones and thick lower lip. The beard has plasticity. The hair is parted to two above the forehead and falls in three rows of waves, at first gently, down to the ears which it covers completely. Here on the locks of hair traces of a drill are discernible. He wears a wreath-shaped strophion (corona torsilis) on the head. At the back of the skull, the unworked hair is divided vertically in two.

COMMENTARY - BIBLIOGRAPHY: Unpublished.

The head was identified on the basis of the strophion adorning the head of Asklepios especially during the Roman period; see Krug 1968, 46, type 12. The worship of this rather Peloponnesian deity starts in Athens in 420 B.C. In sculpture, it first appears in reliefs where the iconography is not constant. On statues, however, he is shown leaning on a stick with a snake wrapped round it. In free-standing sculpture, the closest example with strophion and similar hair-style is the statue in the Museum of Naples; see Neugebauer 1921, 42, pl. 3,1 and de Franciscis 1963, fig. 32.

P.Z.

124

123

From well 3

125 TRANSPORT AMPHORA
End of 2nd - beginning of 1st c. B.C.

INV. NO. A 15551.
H. 0.818, MAX.D. 0.369, M.D. 0.17 M.

Almost intact, with small chips on the mouth and the toe. Signs of corruption and incisions on the surface. Buff clay with yellowish slip. Ovoid body tapering at bottom to blunt toe. Cylindrical neck, collar mouth, handles oval in section. On the mouth there is the stamped inscription MAH.

COMMENTARY - BIBLIOGRAPHY: Unpublished.
It comes from a total of fifty amphorae found in an ancient well in the present-day National Gardens. The amphorae belong to an Italian group, classified between the types of Dressel 6 and Lamboglia 2. These amphorae are dated at the end of the 2nd and the beginning of the 1st c. B.C. Their origin is considered to have been Apulia or Istria and they were used to export olive oil or wine mainly to the Adriatic Sea and the western Mediterranean. Smaller quantities were also found in the Aegean, while very few of them reached the Black Sea. The three-lettered inscriptions on the rim or the handles are usually the initials of the three-partite Roman name (prenomen, nomen, cognomen) of the producer or the potter. The inscription MAH is rather unusual but, according to information provided by J.Y. Empereur, it has been impressed on similar amphorae found on Delos. For this group of amphorae see Peacock - Williams 1986, 98-101; Scalliano - Sibella 1994, 23; Empereur - Hesnard 1987, 9-71, esp. 33-34, pl. 8. For examples from the Athenian Agora see Grace 1961, fig. 36 (right) and from the Kerameikos see Böttger 1992, 315-381, esp. 323-333.

E.B-V.

125

126

126 BRONZE STATUETTE OF A NAKED YOUTH
1st c. B.C.

INV. NO. Δ 7156.
H. 0.275 M.

Bronze with dark green patina and incrustations in places. The left shin is joined at the height of the knee. The index and little fingers of the right hand are broken. Snub-nosed as a result of pressure on most of it.

Naked, young standing figure with the right leg standing firmly and the relaxed left leg, slightly bent at the knee and projecting forward. The body weighs almost evenly on both legs which are firmly placed on the ground. Both arms are down, bent forward slightly at the elbows. The head is turned slightly to the right.

The hair is carefully made with the parting in the middle and creates a crown round the forehead and the temples and ends at the back in a low bun, almost at the base of the neck. Small, shallow hook-like locks project onto the forehead and right temple, as well as onto the upper part of the neck, behind the ears.

COMMENTARY - BIBLIOGRAPHY: Unpublished.

The posture of the figure with the hands free, the large almond-shaped eyes and the dreamy, hazy look suggests athletes (or deities) at rest. A number of stylistic and technical details make a clear impression of an exceptional classicising creation of the late Hellenistic period, contemporary with the creations of Pasiteles, namely: the proportion of the lower to the upper torso; the shaping of the muscles as much on the legs as the stomach, chest, back and arms; the quiet and flowing form of the surface of the face, the eyes and full lips; and, generally, the saddened character of the face as well as, lastly, the detailed rendering of the hair with the protruding locks.

For this type see Kozloff - Mitten 1988, 95-98 (statuette of a young man of 450-425 B.C., probably from Locri or Taranto); likewise, cf. Kozloff - Mitten 1988, 317, no. 59 (bronze statuette of an athlete; A.D. 1-40). See also Vermeule - Comstock 1972, 103, no. 109 (statuette of Hermes).

N.S.

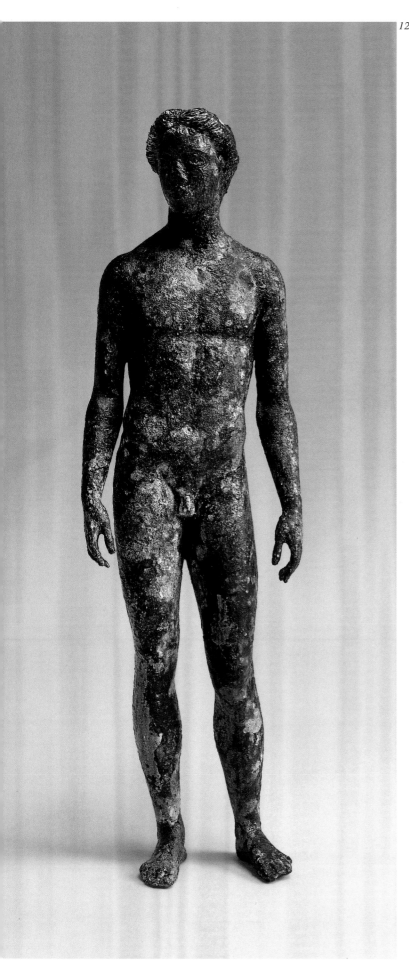

127 BRONZE FOOT WITH SANDAL
Late Hellenistic period (?)

INV. NO. Δ 7157.
L. 0.26, H. 0.145, W. 0.10, TH. OF BRONZE SHEET 0.003 M.

Manufactured from a thick sheet of bronze, now with a dark green patina. In places, especially the toes, the original bright surface is preserved. Parts of the right tarsus and just below the ankles are missing. The sole (kattyma) is empty in the whole region of the sole. Irregular break just above the ankles.

Right foot wearing a sandal with thick sole. The two main straps of the sandal cross on the tarsus and the base of the toes. At the back, the central strap comes to the middle of the heel from which other straps begin left and right, which pass elliptically beneath the ankle-bones towards the arch of the sole. In between, cross-straps and smaller elements make up its formation. The shoe laces pass through two holes on top of the straps of the tarsus.

COMMENTARY - BIBLIOGRAPHY: Unpublished.
For the shape – Hellenistic or later – cf. Morrow 1985,

155, fig. j. The method of tying occurs as early as the Archaic period for men and women (cf. Morrow 1985, 164, fig. 10b-c) but continues in the Hellenistic and Roman periods, in conjunction with the shape of the sandal and the decorative motifs on the horizontal strap; see Morrow 1985, 96. Likewise cf. Morrow 1985, 100, fig. 78 (acrolithic statue of Apollo from Bassae) and 129, fig. 106 (clay askos in the shape of a foot); Kozloff - Mitten 1988, 119-123, no. 18 (sandal of bronze statue of Asklepios; 150-50 B.C.).

N.S.

SYNTAGMA Station

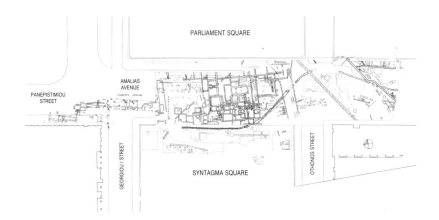

This was one of the most extensive excavations ever made in Athens[1], for the total area investigated, along the length of Amalias Avenue and throughout the eastern sector of Syntagma Square, covered 7,500 sq.m. (fig. 1-4). Apart from the excavated area of SYNTAGMA Station itself, the ground examined included the shafts dug for the Station's three entrances and a quantity of small openings made to by-pass or replace public utility networks.

The excavation occurred on the west slope of the low hill known as Agios Athanasios or Agios Thomas. The top of the hill was levelled in 1836 when King Otto's palace was erected, now housing the Greek Parliament.

This district lay outside the walls of the city of Athens in antiquity, that is, outside the eastern part of the ancient fortification which lay close to the present-day Ministry of Education. In the time of Emperor Hadrian it was included in the extension of the city's limits to the eastern edge of the National Gardens.

It was a privileged locality, for it possessed abundant water from two considerable rivers, the Ilissos to the south and the Heridanos that was smaller but had an ample flow. One branch of the Heridanos descended Lycabettus Hill, crossed under the square of the Unknown Soldier, traversed obliquely Amalias Avenue and progressed down Othonos, Mitropoleos and Adrianou Streets to the Kerameikos.

Notwithstanding repeated intrusions throughout the centuries, the finds that were made were both numerous and important and confirmed the site had been continuously occupied from SubM times down to the reign of King Otto.

The oldest archaeological evidence brought to light in the extensive excavation on Amalias Avenue was provided by two 11th c. B.C. Sub-Mycenaean graves (tombs 55 and 126). They are shallow cuts in the Athenian schist bedrock covered over by irregular slabs of schist such as were used in burials. The grave offerings were plentiful (vases, beads and bronze jewellery; see nos. 128-136).

1

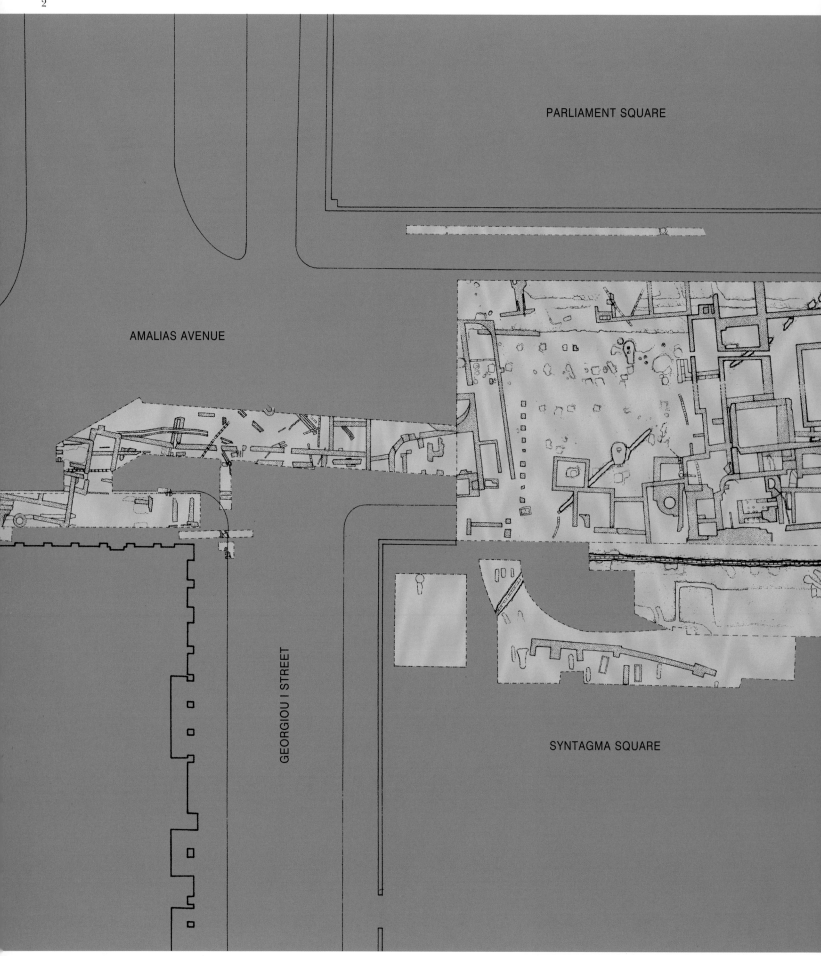

PARLIAMENT SQUARE

AMALIAS AVENUE

GEORGIOU I STREET

SYNTAGMA SQUARE

OTHONOS STREET

0   5   10   15   20   25   30   35   40m

3

4

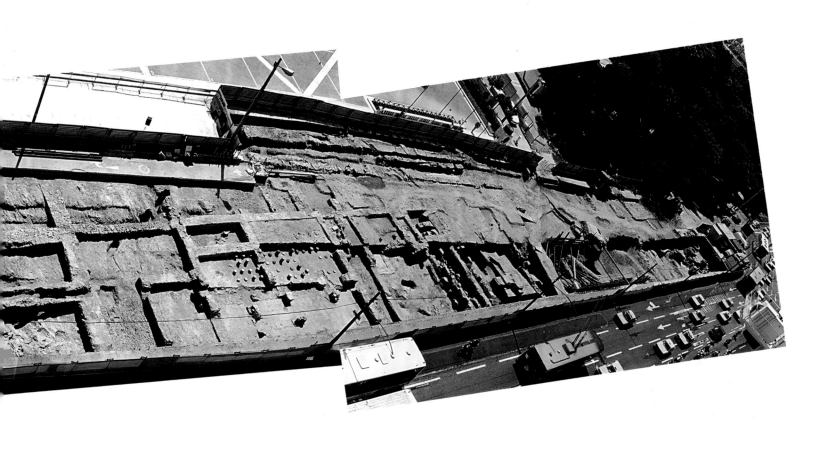

5

6

The discovery of three more graves during the excavation of the precincts of the Parliament Building and the earlier investigation of a regular cemetery of the same period in the building of the Presidential Guard in the National Gardens have shown that from the SubM-PG period groups of graves were placed beside a very ancient main roadway leading from Athens to the Mesogeia plain.

Basic layout considerations which in large measure determined the use and disposition of the district over a long period of about 3,000 years were the river bed, identified as that of the Heridanos[2], and the ancient road that set out from the Diochares Gates in the city wall to the demes of the Mesogeia.

The river bed was found at the level of Othonos Street to lie obliquely beneath Amalias Avenue and to have a width of more than 50 m. including its banks. Apart from the deepest point along the axis of the main bed, elongated hollows, often crossing each other were observed throughout, a feature suggestive of the turbulent flow of the river and bearing out descriptions of it by ancient authors. The presence at frequent intervals of circular cuts in the rock may point to attempts to bridge the river at the time it flowed through the district. Recent excavation and examination of the ramped approach from Amalias Avenue to Parliament Hill revealed that after descending the Lycabettus foothills and before reaching the Avenue the river bed passed under the square of the Unknown Soldier.

Sections of the so-called Peisistratean aqueduct were uncovered in Syntagma Square and on Amalias Avenue and were examined (fig. 7-8).

The first section, about 50 m. in length and lying in a NW-SE direction, includes cylindrical terracotta components with painted black bands placed in a deep channel carved out of the schist bedrock. These objects, thicker at mid point than at the ends, fit inside each other, their joints sealed with lead to make them waterproof. To facilitate cleaning they are provided with openings blocked with stones and the ma-

3. SYNTAGMA Station. Amalias Avenue. Phases 0, 1, 2. General view of the excavation site.

4. SYNTAGMA Station. Amalias Avenue. Phase 3. General view of the excavation site.

5. SYNTAGMA Station. Amalias Avenue. The street leading to the Mesogeia.

6. SYNTAGMA Station. Amalias Avenue. Phase 3. The north part of the excavation site with the foundries and the colonnade courtyard.

7. SYNTAGMA Station. Amalias Avenue. The "Peisistratean" pipeline from the 1st half of the 5th c. B.C.

7

terial cut from them. There are incisions in the channel to receive schist cover-slabs, some of which were found in situ. This section runs diagonally below the ancient road, at the centre of the excavation; it seems that some time in the 4th c. B.C. the terracotta components were removed and the cutting was used as a drainage conduit carrying rainwater to the river bed.

The second section, about 70 m. long and with the same lie as the first, was found in the northern part of the excavation and in Syntagma Square. A short run of these terracotta components has been preserved; they are of similar make and decoration, but more slender in shape (longer and as delicate; three are on display). Only the deep rock cutting survives over the greater part of this section which was penetrated by a foundry pit in the 2nd half of the 5th c. B.C.

A third section was examined where an entrance to the SYNTAGMA Square station was being constructed. It was 43 m. in length and lay in a N-S direction; the continuation of the first section, it appeared to be linked with the second. The terracotta components, identical in form and decoration, are preserved over the entire length of the cutting. Finally, in the southern part of the excavation, in the river bed and close to the south bank, there was discovered a deep cutting whose embankments contained fragments of identical components.

The well-known aqueduct which brought drinking water from a spring in the Hymettus foothills to Athens was located also in the HERODOU ATTIKOU Shaft and at the EVANGELISMOS Station. A short section of it was uncovered in the west forecourt of the Parliament Building.

The shape and design of the components[3] and stratigraphical examination of the conduit cutting suggest that the Syntagma Square aqueduct may be dated to the 1st half of the 5th c. B.C.; in other words, it is a later extension and branch of the original late 6th c. B.C. network which was discovered at the EVANGELISMOS Station and in the HERODOU ATTIKOU Shaft.

During the 2nd half of the 5th c. B.C. the area was occupied by bronze foundries. It should be noted that the location lent itself to such an activity for it lay only a short distance outside the walls, on an elevation, and close to water sources and a thoroughfare essential for the carriage of materials. Seven foundry pits[4] (fig. 6, 9) carved from the bedrock were discovered and examined; in most cases they preserved remains of the clay foundry moulds (a clay mould from Foundry no. 7 is on display). In some instances two moulds were found in the same pit but at different levels, re-

8. SYNTAGMA Station. Part of the "Peisistratean" pipeline.

*9. SYNTAGMA Station. Amalias Avenue.
Foundry 4 with the clay mould.*

*10. SYNTAGMA Station. Amalias Avenue.
Tomb 82 containing the remains of a dog
and grave offerings.*

vealing the foundries were engaged in the making of more than one product. An impressive quantity of fragments of moulds and ventilation pipes, bronze slag and other foundry material was unearthed, frequently scattered about the surrounding area. Remnants of twenty rooms encircling the pits can be associated with the activities of the workshops and the storage of materials. In one of them were found neatly stored clay slabs which were used to pave the foundry pits.

To the south of the workshop installations and below the paving levels of the later central thoroughfare a 4.50 m. wide road was located lying in an E-W direction, of which a few surfaces survive on top of the rock. Of the two retaining banks the southern one was noticeably reinforced and thick, evidently to afford greater protection to the road from the nearby fast-flowing river.

The business of bronze foundries increased during the 2nd half of the 5th c. B.C. At the beginning of the 4th c. B.C. the foundry pits were filled in with earth. A quantity of vases (kantharoi, small dishes, drinking-bowls, and lamps) and statuettes have been assembled from the pottery fragments found in the pits. On top of the workshop levels in the northern part of the excavation a colonnaded courtyard was erected; remnants of its plinths were found at regular intervals on the rock (fig. 6).

The area was re-planned and its use changed in the 2nd half of the 4th c. B.C., a time of intense building activity in Athens with the repair of its fortifications, the digging of a protective dike and a realignment of the thoroughfares. The main roadway to the demes of Mesogeia, starting from the Diochares Gates located at the junction of Voulis and Apollonos Streets[5], was widened in this period.

The north embankment of the road was reinforced with large conglomerate stone blocks, while the south one was constructed from the outset 2.50 m. further south than the old so that the road could be made about 7 m. wide. Again, care was taken to protect the road from the river waters, the south embankment being buttressed externally.

The road (fig. 5) was investigated over a length of 35 m., that is, for the width of the Amalias Avenue excavation. At its easternmost point, towards the square of the Unknown Soldier, the south embankment bends and the road forks. One branch of the forked road was examined in the west forecourt of the Greek Parliament Building; the presence of many graves and potteries in the north forecourt indicates the existence in this area of the other branch. This main thoroughfare was constantly repaired and was in uninterrupted use until the 2nd c. A.D.[6], as shown by the thirty or so successive road surfaces that were encountered, many with clear traces of wheel ruts. A section of the road's impressive stratigraphy was removed with a view to exhibiting it, together with other finds, in a specially designed space.

An extensive roadside cemetery, in continuous use from the 4th c. B.C. to the early 3rd c. A.D., developed during that period alongside the northern verges of the road. In late Classical times the cemetery was rearranged into grave enclosures, groups of graves and individual graves and spread out over a distance of 45 m. from the north side of the road. A tomb plinth of conglomerate stone blocks was erected against the north embankment, while three grave enclosures containing clusters of graves were built·in the area. In the Hellenistic period graves again occupied the same site, being placed on top of the older ones and following the northern verges of the road. By contrast, in Roman times one observes that, apart from occupying the initial site, the cemetery expanded, being arranged in compact groups on the north side along the axis of Amalias Avenue as far as its junction with Panepistimiou Street.

A total of three hundred graves was examined. They belonged to all known types: rock-cut, sarcophagi, clay tubs, burial in amphorae and terracotta cases, cist graves paved with stone slabs or tiles, graves roofed with tiles, primary cremations, or secondary cremations contained in cinerary urns. There was a considerable number of new-born babies and infants (more than thirty) buried in vases or family graves, while quite often earlier burials had been set aside to make room for new ones in the same grave. Mention should be made of three graves of animals, two of dogs and one of a horse and a dog together. In one case the grave of a dog (tomb 82, fig. 10) was particularly well constructed of terracotta sides and with a tile floor. The dead animal was accompanied by grave gifts of two glass perfume bottles of the lst-2nd c. A.D. (nos. 162-163), while the copper studs of its collar were preserved in situ (no. 164).

10

Offerings in late Classical graves were usually bottles, kantharoi, askoi, kotylae (small beakers), lekythoi, strigils (scrapers) and mirrors (see tomb 196); in Hellenistic graves they were spindle-shaped perfume flasks, oenochoae, lamps, mirrors, combs, strigils, coins (no. 175) and some gold jewellery (nos. 145-146); and in Roman graves there were usually glass and terracotta perfume bottles (see tomb 68), lamps, strigils, coins, beads and jewellery (nos. 147-149). A bronze allotment tablet of 370-360 B.C. (no. 137) that had belonged to the judge Chairestratos was found to have been buried with him as a grave offering in tomb 148.

This cemetery, which advanced along the length of the road and was in use as long as was the road itself, has been encountered in many excavations conducted by the 3rd Ephorate: in the precincts of the Parliament Building, in digging up Vasilissis Sophias Avenue for public utilities, in the HERODOU ATTIKOU Shaft, in the grounds of the Presidential Guard barracks, in various excavations in the area of Rigillis Square and neighbouring streets and at EVANGELISMOS Station.

The river bed was filled up with earth in the early Roman period once its waters had been diverted to the south and a large stone conduit had been constructed in the river bed in a NE-SW direction. This conduit was investigated over a length of 47 m. It had constructed walls and a massive vaulted roof. The fill contained pottery and lamps chiefly of the late 3rd and early 4th c. A.D., at which time it was abandoned. Similar conduits have been discovered in many excavations in Athens[7]: in Neos Kosmos, Koukaki and in the neighbourhood of Rigillis Street, Psyrri and the Olympieion. They would seem to be sections of a central drainage system of early Roman date and often lead into adjacent rivers or the fortification ditch.

Following the Herulian raids of A.D. 267 and the extensive destruction inflicted upon the city, the use of this space changed once again. The entire area to the north of the river was taken over by an enormous bath-house (balneum) built over the cemetery and the surface of the road which was henceforth abandoned. Taking into account the space it occupies on Amalias Avenue up to the Grande Bretagne Hotel, the bath-house covered an area about 140 m. in length and 35-40 m. in width. It should be noted here that only its southern limit, facing the river, has been established. We do not know if it extended northwards beyond the entrance to the Grande Bretagne and how far[8]. An old excavation by G. Mylonas[9] provided clear evidence that it continued eastwards in the square of the Unknown Soldier. The picture towards the west in Syntagma Square is unclear as a result of the numerous intrusions the area has suffered, but many of the walls unearthed point in the direction of the square. Given the above facts, on the most conservative estimate the complex would seem to have covered a ground area in excess of 5,500 sq.m.

It is worth remarking that the growth of the city during Emperor Hadrian's reign, especially of its western part as far as the Olympieion, was accompanied by an astonishing accumulation of bath-houses, all of them in close proximity to a thoroughfare. Some previously existed, others were erected as the city expanded and yet others were built after the Herulian raids, when the city was laid out anew.

The bath-house complex of Amalias Avenue was built in the late 3rd and the early 4th c. A.D. (after the Herulian raids). The first building phase is distinguished by thick walls constructed of irregular stones and hard red clay with gravel as a binding agent. It was then that its central block with hypocaust rooms and hearths generating the heat was erected. Towards the end of the 4th c. A.D. it suffered appalling destruction, which may have been connected with the well-known raid by Alaric in A.D. 396; during the 5th c. A.D. it was rebuilt. The hypocaust rooms were repaired and added to, some were filled with rubble from the destruction and new rooms and apsidal spaces were constructed. The room walls were reinforced with the hardest white lime plaster, and the floors of the chambers were laid with marble slabs.

The hub of the complex (fig. 11), which was wholly detached, consisted of two hearths (praefurnia), four hypocaust rooms comprising the caldaria (hot baths) and the tepidaria (tepid baths), and a room with a tiled floor. A second, lesser focal point was discovered close to the retaining wall of Syntagma Square. Around each of these centres were clustered a number of rooms serving various functions for visitors (waiting-rooms, changing rooms, lodgings, etc.). The area occupied by the complex, taken in conjunction with the large number of rooms around the main bath installations, leads one to conclude this may have been a huge state or public welfare building.

In the northernmost sector of the excavation beyond a large uncovered area, perhaps an open-air courtyard, another part of the complex with two apsidal structures came to light, one above the other and belonging to the two apparent building phases of the baths. During excavation of the Grande Bretagne pavement, beneath which the complex stretched, a section of a mosaic floor was discovered with vegetal and geometric decoration (rhomboids, circles containing anthemia, crosses and eight-pointed stars, and plaited ribbons). Another floor was decorated with grey and white marble tiles. The rest of the rooms excavated lacked decoration on their walls and floors or, rather, none had survived, whereas countless fragments of wall-paintings with plant and geometric patterns were picked up in their interiors. Among other objects, many lamps (see no. 165) were found in the earth fills of the bath-house rooms.

A congested system of water conduits, of which some were water supply and others waste water pipes, was spread throughout the bath-house. For the most part they were terracotta pipes with pi-shaped protuberances (open-topped conduits of square section) which formed branch lines either to supply the tanks or to carry off the waste water.

11. SYNTAGMA Station. Amalias Avenue.
The hypocaust room.

In the same period an aqueduct, of which seven piers constructed of conglomerate stone blocks and mortar have survived, was erected on the south bank of the river. The area around the piers is a dense network of pipes and shafts. That these installations gathered and distributed a large quantity of water in a southerly direction is apparent from the heavy encrustation of salts in their interior.

A few levels of a Roman road lying in a N-S direction were found in the same area; the road probably afforded access to the bath-house. A Late Roman lamp imported from North Africa (no. 167) was found in one of the levels. Sections of a road running in the same direction were excavated in small trial trenches opened on Amalias Avenue a little further to the south.

During the 5th and 6th c. A.D. a group of seventeen Early Christian graves was introduced into the earth fill of the river bed. Most of these graves, often in twos or threes with built walls, vaulted roof and interior plastering, contained the bones of many dead and few offerings, generally bronze jewellery, crosses and coins. The coins found there suggest the graves were very likely used as ossuaries until the 11th or 12th c. A.D. A large number of similar graves have been investigated in the past in the districts of Neos Kosmos, Metaxourgeion and central Athens, Koukaki, etc.[10].

A part of the Byzantine city came to light in the southern sector of the excavation where rooms and thirteen storage bins[11] were found (fig. 12). An important discovery made in one of the earth fills in this area was a gold solidus issued in A.D. 705 in the reign of Justinian II (no. 178). The area continued to be used in late Byzantine times and during the years of Ottoman occupation for the construction of large reservoirs and a compact water supply network of terracotta cylindrical pipes.

Sections of a long wall, of slipshod workmanship and built of stones and a great quantity of re-used marble material, may be ascribed to the famous wall erected by Haseke, the Governor of Athens in 1778[12] which passed through the area. One of its main gates, the Mesogeia gateway known as Boubounistra, was hereabouts.

The historical survey of the excavation area ends with mention of sections of a stone-paved road that was examined over a considerable distance at the eastern end of the Avenue and may be identified as the surface of Amalias Street in the time of King Otto.

Examination of the earth fills produced some notable sculptures (nos. 168-173), the inscribed plinth of a bronze torch (no. 174) and numerous coins of different periods (nos. 176-178).

The excavation of Amalias Avenue was carried out in intensely pressing circumstances but with all requisite care and with the overriding objective of extracting all available archaeological information. The fourteen archaeologists, the chief technicians of the 3rd Ephorate in charge of a team of one hundred experienced workers, the architects, surveyors, draughtsmen and foremen all gave of their best in this demanding project. On the decision of the Central Archaeological Council, the most outstanding and representative architectural members were removed with a view to their eventual display. The exhibition space is now under construction at the University Campus at Zographou. When it is complete it will bear witness to a highly important excavation that has enabled us to gain a better understanding of the historical growth of ancient Athens.

OLGA ZACHARIADOU

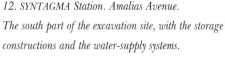

12. SYNTAGMA Station. Amalias Avenue.
The south part of the excavation site, with the storage constructions and the water-supply systems.

NOTES

1. See p. 137, n. 1.
2. Judeich 1931, 47-49 and 138; Τραυλός 1960, 6 and 120; Παπαχατζής 1974, 285 n. 4; Θρεψιάδης 1960, 26.
3. Of similar shape are sections of the conduits found in previous excavations in the National Gardens, the ancient Agora, at the junction of 5 Adrianou and Theseiou Streets, in Dionysiou Areopagitou north-west of the enclosure of the shrine of the Nymph, at the corner of Megalou Alexandrou and Plataeon Streets in Metaxourgeion, and in Kerameikos where U. Knigge has observed that the section found there belongs to a later extension dating to the 1st half of the 5th c. B.C., as does the section uncovered at 24 Aktaiou Street by the Theseion.
4. Identical foundry pits have been found around the Agora, at Kerameikos and in two earlier excavations of the 3rd Ephorate in Vassilis Street, Theseion.
5. Θρεψιάδης 1960, 25-27; Τραυλός 1960, 53; Travlos 1971, 159-160.
6. Threpsiadis (Θρεψιάδης 1973, 69) unearthed a section of the Roman phase of the road in Othonos Street.
7. Annals of excavations by the 3rd Ephorate in *ADelt* 22-43 covering the years 1967-1988.
8. It is not possible to say if it may be related with the sections of the bath-house which were found at the junction of Panepistimiou and Voukourestiou Streets (Θρεψιάδης 1960, 28-29).
9. Μυλωνάς 1931-32, 46-48.
10. Annals of excavations by the 3rd Ephorate in *ADelt* 21-35 covering the years 1966-1980.
11. A large quantity of bins and storage jars has been discovered in all the Metro excavations on Amalias Avenue in the vicinity of Xenophontos Street, as well as during previous excavations in side-streets off Amalias as far as the Olympieion. This concentration is not a chance occurrence; it presents a picture of the configuration and utilisation of the land in the eastern district of Athens during the Byzantine period.
12. Τραυλός 1960, 195-200; Καμπούρογλου 1931, 58-60.

SUB-MYCENAEAN TOMBS

The Sub-Mycenaean tombs 126 and 55 from the excavation in Amalias Avenue (see Παρλαμά 1992-98, 525, n. 12) were the oldest remains from this region and, since they are about 50 m. apart from each other on a N-S axis, they certainly indicate the existence of another Athenian cemetery of the earliest historical period. This must be a continuation of that of the Presidential Guard in the HERODOU ATTIKOU Shaft, just as the cemeteries had spread to the north-northeast foot of the low hill which existed before the construction of the building on the site of the present-day Parliament Building (see Παρλαμά op.cit.; *eadem* 1990-91, 233 as well as *ADelt* 38 (1983) Chronika, 23-25).

Tomb 126, a little earlier than tomb 55, was a rectangular cutting in the bedrock, dim. 1×0.50×0.45 m., covered by three schist slabs and containing a few decayed bones and vases nos. 128 and 129; of these, oenochoe no. 129 is reported to have contained scraps of bone. These two vases date the tomb to the early SubM phase. Oenochoe 129 is very close to the LH IIIC type, like the oenochoe of tomb 6 at Asine (see Mountjoy 1988, fig. 18) and still preserves the spherical body, but the interesting spiral-formed decoration on the shoulder with the peculiar different rendering of the two stalks – where one is a normal spiral and the other has been made into concentric circles – suggests a SubM date. Cup no. 128 has the typical features of a Sub-Mycenaean cup with the base formed into a conical foot, the deep body disproportionately narrow for the body shape and the sharply widening lip (see *Lefkandi* I.1, 294).

Tomb 55 was also a rectangular cutting in the bedrock, dim. 1.30 × 0.50 × 0.40 m., with a cover of three schist slabs and contained the skeleton of a young person in a supine position, furnished with vases nos. 130-135 and the fibulae no. 136a-b; these grave goods were centred on the chest and around the head of the deceased. Tomb 55 is a little later than tomb 126 and should be dated to the transition to the PG period, since – apart from the small cup no. 134, which is clearly Sub-Mycenaean (cf.

tomb 19 of the Pompeion, *Kerameikos* I, no. 437, pl. 23 and Styrenius 1967, fig. 5, which however has been dated by Mountjoy 1988, 15 to late LH IIIC – the oenochoe no. 131 (cf. *Kerameikos* I, tomb 94, no. 501, pl. 24; Mountjoy 1988, 12 fig. 11), two lekythoi nos. 132-133 (cf. *Kerameikos* I, pl. 13; *Kerameikos* IV, pl. 4; Styrenius 1967, fig. 17-18) and amphoriskos no. 130 (cf. *Lefkandi* I.1, 307-308, fig. 11b) have all the elements of the transitional phase to the PG period, whilst cup no. 135 – where the formation of the lip is like the cup from the Agora no. 7693 from tomb V dated by Styrenius to a transitional SubM/PG phase – must be dated to the PG period based on the reserved band below the lip on the inside (see also *Lefkandi* I.1, 294). The arched bronze fibula no. 136a and fragments of another, no. 136b, are typically Sub-Mycenaean (cf. *Kerameikos* I, 28, from tomb 108, particularly the second from the left in the first row).

These two tombs of the SYNTAGMA Station confirm the dating of Athenian Sub-Mycenaean pottery to a very short period, very close to the end of the 11th c. BC, between late LH IIIC and the PG period. In addition, with the interesting coexistence of elements of both periods, they also support the theory that the SubM period is a last dying phase of the Mycenaean culture, which assimilates new elements: for this see Mountjoy 1988, esp. 29ff.

L.P.

BIBLIOGRAPHY: *Kerameikos* I; *Lefkandi* I; Mountjoy 1988; Παρλαμά 1990-91; *eadem* 1992-98; Styrenius 1967.

128 SINGLE-HANDLED CUP
End of 11th c. B.C.

INV. NO. A 15147.
H. 0.096, M.D. 0.116, B.D. 0.0415 M.

Complete. Conical base, rather high. Yellow-red clay, brown-red decoration, fugitive in places.
Monochrome interior with reserved circle at the bottom and monochrome exterior surface of the base. Immediately beneath the rim, a band and two more below the projection of the narrow handle – the back of which is covered with horizontal stripes – border the main decorative field, where there is a wavy band.

COMMENTARY - BIBLIOGRAPHY: Unpublished.
Cf. the comments on p. 162.

L.P.

128, 129

129 TREFOIL-MOUTHED OENOCHOE
End of 11th c. B.C.

INV. NO. A 15146.
H. 0.163, MAX.D. 0.127, B.D. 0.056 M.

Complete after mending a small part of the lip; small chips on the edge of the base. Spherical body, discoid base and strap handle. Yellow-red clay, brown decoration, fugitive in places.
The lip is painted inside, while outside it is surrounded by a broad band, the two ends of which end in the verticals which frame another wavy band along the length of the back of the handle; the intrusion of the latter onto the shoulder is outlined with a ring. A ring also outlines the base of the neck from which hang two groups of respectively eight and six tongue-like lines. Between them, a double spiral with one of its stems forming concentric circles with a painted core. The shoulder zone is bordered below by three parallel bands, whilst lower down, near the unpainted base, there are two more identical bands to complete the decoration of the vase.

COMMENTARY - BIBLIOGRAPHY: Unpublished.
Cf. the comments on p. 162.

L.P.

130 AMPHORISKOS
End of 11th c. B.C.

INV. NO. A 15838.
H. 0.113, MAX.D. 0.092 (INCL. THE HANDLES 0.134), B.D. 0.042 M.

Complete. Conical base, spherical body with broad funnel-like mouth and cylindrical handles at the height of maximum diameter. Yellow-red clay, brown-red decoration.
The mouth is painted outside, but only on the lip inside; immediately beneath the mouth, on the shoulder, are a row of dots and three parallel bands. The field between the handles, which is bordered by another band below, is decorated with two freely painted wavy lines on each side; the lowest part of the body is monochrome apart from the base. The backs of the handles are outlined with a band which drops down low until the monochrome part, where it is met by curves which surround the outside only of the handles projections.

COMMENTARY - BIBLIOGRAPHY: Unpublished.
Cf. the comments on p. 162.

L.P.

131 TREFOIL-MOUTHED OENOCHOE
End of 11th c. B.C.

INV. NO. A 15833.
H. 0.157, MAX.D. 0.117, B.D. 0.043 M.

Complete. Discoid base, ovoid body with short, broad neck, handle almost cylindrical in section. Yellow-red clay, brownish decoration, fugitive in places.

The lip is painted inside, and outside it is encircled by a broad band, the ends of which are continued on the back of the handle forming an X; the projection onto the shoulder is surrounded by a ring. A double wavy band on the neck and at the base of the ring from which hang four groups of clumsily drawn vertical tongue-like lines, which run onto the first of three parallel bands closing off the decorative field of the shoulder. Two more bands surround the lower part of the belly, a little higher than the unpainted base.

COMMENTARY - BIBLIOGRAPHY: Unpublished.
Cf. the comments on p. 162.

L.P.

132 LEKYTHOS
End of 11th c. B.C.

INV. NO. A 15834.
H. 0.114, MAX.D. 0.083, M.D. 0.036, B.D. 0.0385 M.

Complete with small amount of flaking on the surface. Low, conical base, ovoid body with small perforation on the shoulder, handle cylindrical in section, broad lip. Yellow-red clay, brown-red decoration. The lip painted inside and out; ring bands at the base of the neck and around the projection of the handle on the shoulder, while the back of the handle has horizontal stripes. Three groups of concentric semicircles with dotted outline take up the whole of the shoulder zone. The rest of the body down to the unpainted base is monochrome, with a reserved zone of two parallel bands.

COMMENTARY - BIBLIOGRAPHY: Unpublished.
Cf. the comments on p. 162.

L.P.

133 LEKYTHOS
End of 11th c. B.C.

INV. NO. A 15835.
H. 0.13, MAX.D. 0.09, M.D. 0.042, B.D. 0.045 M.

Complete with a limited amount of chipping on the surface; of similar type, shape and system of decoration as lekythos no. 132, although here the body is taller and the groups of semicircles with dots have a painted core and take up less space in the shoulder zone, which is bordered below by two bands. The coating, which covers the body and the exterior walling of the base, leaves a narrower reserved zone low down with one band.

COMMENTARY - BIBLIOGRAPHY: Unpublished.
Cf. the comments on p. 162.

L.P.

134 SMALL CUP
End of 11th c. B.C.

INV. NO. A 15837.
H. 0.039, M.D. 0.043, B.D. 0.025 M.

Small break on edge of lip. Conical base, strap handle. Yellow-red clay with brown-red decoration.

On the inside of the vase, the coating is virtually black and covers all the surface up to the edge of the rim, leaving a small reserved circle in the centre of the bottom. Outside, three bands of which the one in the middle is almost wavy-like. Horizontal stripes on the back of the handle.

COMMENTARY - BIBLIOGRAPHY: Unpublished.
Cf. the comments on p. 162.

L.P.

130, 131

135 CUP
End of 11th - beginning of 10th c. B.C.

INV. NO. A 15836.
H. 0.094, M.D. 0.108, B.D. 0.043 M.

Complete with small chips and flaking. Conical base, double handle of two stems cylindrical in section, high lip. Yellow-red clay. Brown-red coating covers the whole of the interior surface except for a reserved circle at the bottom and a band immediately beneath the edge of the rim. The coating also covers most of the exterior, only the lowest part of the body including the foot left unpainted. To one side of the handle, on the raised lip, one can distinguish an incision in the shape of a cross with unequal bars.

COMMENTARY - BIBLIOGRAPHY: Unpublished.
Cf. the comments on p. 162.

L.P.

136 BRONZE FIBULAE
End of 11th c. B.C.

INV. NO. Δ 7171A-B.

Bronze, oxidised with dark green patina. The first arched fibula is completely

136 a-b

preserved, while the second is in two joining pieces.

COMMENTARY - BIBLIOGRAPHY: Unpublished.
Cf. the comments on p. 162.

L.P.

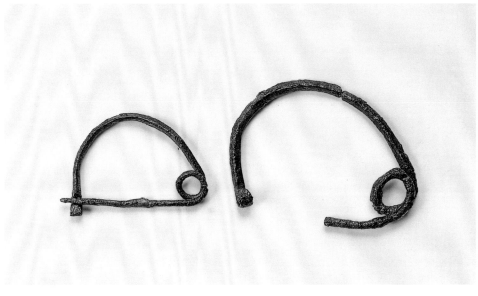

hand side (diameter 0.012 m.), with a representation of an owl. It must have borne the letters AΘE [Ἀθη(ναίων)], as well as an olive branch, which, nevertheless, is indiscernible because of the corrosion. Similar seals, which imitate the reverse of the Athenian triobols, comprise the main seals on tablets, which are stamped by the appropriate state authority, and ensure the validity of the tablet. Between the last letter of the second line and the main circular seal, there is a relief secondary square stamp (0.008×0.008 m.) which has been impressed upside down and a little slanting, with a representation of a smaller owl. That must also have borne the letters AΘE and olive branch, which are indiscernible. The secondary seals are stamped, as an additional certification, on tablets which were already in use.

made of box-wood (πυξάρι), while their use was interrupted in 322/1 B.C. when democracy was abolished. On the basis of other known examples, which are better preserved, we can conclude with relative certainty that the plate under discussion went through two stages of use. Originally, there must have been a man's name accompanied by his municipal name, written in one line between the stamped A and the main circular seal (category I of Kroll's typology). Next, after the end of the tenure of its first owner, his name was erased by hammering to give the tablet to the new judge Chairestratos, who engraved his details on two further lines (category II of Kroll's typology).

Chairestratos must have died during his tenure as judge and taken the tablet with him to the grave, as an indication of the rank he exercised within the framework of the democratic system of Athens.

For comparable examples see Kroll 1972, particularly nos. 1-5 (category I) and 6-19 (category II).

Ch.B.K.

From tomb 148

137 INSCRIBED BRONZE ALLOTMENT PLATE
c. 370-360 B.C.

INV. NO. Δ 7105.
L. 0.112, W. 0.022, TH. (AT UNCORRODED PART) 0.003, H. OF LETTERS 0.005 (THE Os) - 0.007, DISTANCE BETWEEN LINES ABOUT 0.002 M.

Mended from many fragments, with cracks and intense corrosion.

The plate bears an engraved inscription in two lines, which is completed as follows:

Χαι[ρ]έστρατος Λα-
μ(πτρεὺς) Φορυσκίδο

(Chairestratos, son of Phoryskides from the Attic deme of Lamptrai, of the Erectheid tribe).

Both names are also found on other inscriptions, but the specific citizen is unknown from other sources.

In the middle of the left hand side of the tablet is the letter A, stamped inside a hollow square, about 0.008×0.008 m. This is the so-called "serial letter", which determined one of the ten sub-groups to which the candidate belonged and which were characterised by the letters A to K. There is a corresponding relief circular stamp in the middle on the right

137

COMMENTARY - BIBLIOGRAPHY: Unpublished (forth. in *Τιμαί Ιω. Τριανταφυλλοπούλου*).

Bronze plates of this type, on which the names of candidates are mentioned, were placed in special slots of the marble allotment machines (κανονίδες) for the election every year of judges and other officials, drawn by lots. They first make an appearance around 378/7 B.C. In the time of Aristotle (*c.* 350 B.C.) they were

138 BLACK-GLAZED KANTHAROS
WITH "WEST-SLOPE" DECORATION
End of 4th - beginning of 3rd c. B.C.

INV. NO. A 15167.
H. 0.103-0.11, B.D. 0.043, M.D. 0.089 M.

Mended from many pieces. A small part of
the neck is missing. Red-brown clay. Discoid base with plastic rings. High stem
with plastic ring approximately in the
middle. Calyx-shaped body, broad, bi-
concave neck, flaring echinus rim. Double
rounded handles which rise a little above
the rim. Shiny black glaze all over the vase.
Thin, reserved bands at the edge of the
base, the stem and the lower part of the
body. Two reserved, concentric circles
in the interior. On the vase, plastic ribs
creating spear-like leaves. On the neck
floral decoration of antithetic flowers with
clay wash.

COMMENTARY - BIBLIOGRAPHY: Unpublished.
This type of kantharos, which resembles metal ware,
has been studied by Pfrommer 1987, 9-29, pl. 40, KP 88
(c. 300 B.C.). For similar examples in metal see also
Θέμελης - Τουράτσογλου 1997, 103, pl. 113, nos. Δ8-
Δ9 (beginning of 3rd c. B.C.), with bibliography. Gradually, the production of this shape was expanded to
clay. In Attic pottery, it appeared around the end of the
4th c. B.C. An early example from Dresden, with low
foot, dates to the last quarter of the 4th c. B.C., see
Barr-Sharrar - Borza 1982, 125, fig. 4, no. 1417. For an
almost identical example from Amphipolis see Ρωμιοπούλου 1964, 102, fig. 9α, no. 447, while for examples
with similar decoration from the Kerameikos see Zimmermann 1998, 155, KT 28, pl. 11, 1-2, fig. 5-2, 3 no.
10271; all early 3rd c. B.C. For similar types see also
The Glories of the Past 1990, 185, no. 132 (New York,
Metropolitan Museum) and *CVA* Belgique 3, Brussels
3, 138, pl. 3, nos. 7 and 11.

O.Z.

139 BLACK-GLAZED RIBBED SQUAT LEKYTHOS
325-300 B.C.

INV. NO. A 15169.
H. 0.08, MAX.D. 0.036, B.D. 0.075, M.D. 0.088 M.

Mended. Part of the mouth missing.
Chips and flakes on the surface. Red-
brown clay. Flat base, squat, piriform
body. Narrow neck, flaring rim, vertical
strap handle. Black fading glaze on the
vase, with base unglazed. The body is
decorated with fine, vertical, plastic ribs.

COMMENTARY - BIBLIOGRAPHY: Unpublished.
It is an Attic version of the last Corinthian squat lekythoi
of the characteristic Blister Ware variety. This handmade Corinthian pottery, which spreads from the early
5th till the 3rd c. B.C., is mainly used for jugs with a flat
base, small or large, used as perfume bottles. The
name of the pottery derives from the blisters that appeared unevenly on the exterior of the vases, owing to
imperfections in their manufacture and they remained
as a decoration pattern with a more regular form even

138

when the process of fabrication and firing improved. Gradually, the blisters became grooves or ribs which by the 4th c. B.C. became regular and at the end of that century were replaced by diagonal grooves. For parallels from Corinth see *Corinth* VII₃, 146-147, pl. 64, no. 768 (2nd quarter of 4th c. B.C.); Broneer 1962, 24-25, pl. 12f, nos. 20-21. Most of the examples from the Athenian Agora are of small size. For parallels in shape and decoration see *Agora* XII, 206-208, pl. 77, no. 1681 (2nd quarter of 4th c. B.C.) and *Agora* XXIX, 421, pl. 138, no. 1749 (300-250 B.C.).

O.Z.

140   BLACK-GLAZED LEKANIS WITH LID
325-300 B.C.

INV. NO. A 15172.
H. 0.049-0.053, B.D. 0.045, M.D. 0.094, H. OF LID 0.04,
D. OF LID 0.103, D. OF HANDLE 0.046 M.

Small pieces from the body and the lid are missing. Chips and flakes on the surface. Red-brown clay. Ring base, hemispherical body, flaring rim with groove for fitting the lid. Conical lid with steep walls and ring-shaped handle.
On the body, there is black glaze and a reserved fine line over the base, which preserves the underside unglazed. The lid is also black glazed, with fine red bands on the edge and round the handle which has the upper top of its lip unglazed.

COMMENTARY - BIBLIOGRAPHY: Unpublished.
This shape belongs to the type of the small covered bowl, which first appeared in the 4th c. B.C. for exclusive use in votive pyres. For the type see *Agora* XII, 173, pl. 42, no. 1280 (1st half of 4th c. B.C.) and *Agora* XXIX, 192, 364, pl. 93, fig. 78, nos. 1254-1255 (300-250 B.C.) (for the vase) and 192, 364, fig. 78, nos. 1263-1264 (300-275 B.C.) (for the lid).

O.Z.

141   LOPAS WITH LID
350-300 B.C.

INV. NO. A 15177.
H. 0.048-0.052, H. (INCL. HANDLE) 0.06-0.068, M.D. 0.158,
H. OF LID 0.04, D. OF LID 0.142 M.

Mended from many pieces. Brown-red clay. Convex resting surface, hemispherical body with an angular contour. Flaring rim with groove for the lid, loop handles that are upraised, in comparison to

141

139

143

the rim. Traces of fire all over. Domed lid with roughly made round knob.

COMMENTARY - BIBLIOGRAPHY: Unpublished.
This shape was popular in Attica in the late 5th and early 4th c. B.C. For the vase see *Agora* XII, 227-228, 373, pl. 95, no. 1965 (350-325 B.C.). For the lid see *Agora* XII, pl. 95, no. 1980 (350-300 B.C.). In Corinth, it appeared *c.* 460 B.C., and persisted until the 3rd quarter of the 4th c. B.C.; see *Corinth* VII₃, 124, pl. 29 and 62, nos. 667, 679 (for the vase) and 129-130, pl. 62, nos. 692-695 (for the lid).

O.Z.

142 PLATE WITH STRAP HANDLES
325-300 B.C.

INV. NO. A 15171.
H. 0.04-0.043, B.D. 0.066, M.D. 0.177 M.

Mended from many pieces. Chips and flakes on the surface. Brown clay. Low, discoid base, short conical body, flaring rim, horizontal strap handles.
Traces of brown-black glaze on the vase. Traces of fire on the edge and on one handle.

COMMENTARY - BIBLIOGRAPHY: Unpublished.
These small plates, which are used as pyre offerings, are a cheap substitute for the larger, glazed, decorated and often black-figure plates. The earlier examples retain the traditional decoration of glaze bands while the later are plain. For similar examples see *Agora* XII, 199, pl. 69, nos. 1569-1571 (end of 4th c. B.C.); *Agora* XXIV, 214-215, pl. 110, fig. 87, nos. 1455-1456 (325-300 B.C.); Schlörb-Vierneisel 1966, 91-92, pl. 58, no. 160 (HS 83), 5-6 (early 4th quarter of 4th c. B.C.).

O.Z.

143 BLACK-GLAZED HANDLELESS SMALL BOWL
325-300 B.C.

INV. NO. A 15180.
H. 0.027, B.D. 0.06, M.D. 0.082 M.

Mended from many pieces. Small part of the body missing. Partially chipped. Red-brown clay. Low ring base with a nipple-knob on the resting surface. Shallow, hemispherical body, in-curving rim.
The vase is covered in black glaze, which in parts changes to red-brown due to uneven firing. Thin, reserved band above the base which has its underside also re-

uted from the end of the 4th and the beginning of the 3rd c. B.C. For a typological and technical analysis of the jewel with bibliography see Παπαποστόλου 1990, 121-122, fig. 27-28. Also Higgins 1961, 161-162, fig. 47H (an identical earring) and Deppert-Lippitz 1985, 18, pl. 16 (38) (a similar earring but of later date; 3rd-2nd c. B.C.).

M.D.Th.

served. On the bottom, four roughly impressed palmettes.

COMMENTARY - BIBLIOGRAPHY: Unpublished.

This type appeared from the late 5th c. B.C. onwards, expanded during the 4th c. B.C., and lasts through the early Hellenistic period. For the shape see Θέμελης - Τουράτσογλου 1997, 38-39, pl. 47, no. A35, A36 and 124, pl. 137, nos. Z25-26; *Agora* XII, 135, pl. 33, no. 889, group D16:1 (300-250 B.C.); *Agora* XXIX, 165, pl. 78, fig. 65, nos. 1055, 1057, 1059 (300-250 B.C.). The rather common decoration with impressed palmettes at the centre of the base was abandoned by the end of the 4th c. B.C. For decoration see *Agora* XXIX, pl. 146, nos. 968 (325-300 B.C.) or 970 (300 B.C.).

O.Z.

144 BLACK-GLAZED SALT-CELLAR
325-300 B.C.

INV. NO. A 15170.
H. 0.038, B.D. 0.05, M.D. 0.064 M.

Mended from many pieces. The base is partly missing. Chips and flakes on the surface. Red-brown clay. Tall, ring base with a central nipple-knob and groove on the resting surface. Deep, hemispherical body with in-curving rim. The vase is covered with black glaze which, in parts, becomes red-brown due to uneven firing.

COMMENTARY - BIBLIOGRAPHY: Unpublished.

This type of salt-cellar appears in the early 5th c. B.C. and lasts until the Hellenistic period. Two groups can be distinguished, the earlier with a discoid base (5th c. B.C.) and the latter with a ring base, which is widespread during the 2nd and 3rd quarter of the 4th c. B.C. Cf. *Agora* XXIX, 167, pl. 79, fig. 65, nos. 1075-1078 (325-300 B.C.) and *Agora* XII, 137, 303, pl. 34, no. 948 (350-325 B.C.).

O.Z.

From the removal of bones near tomb 3

145

145 GOLD EARRING
3rd c. B.C.

INV. NO. Θ 319.
DIM. 0.024 × 0.019, HEAD OF ANIMAL 0.009 × 0.009, TH. OF BUCKLE 0.001-0.0024 M., WT. 2 GR.

Loop-shaped earring of twisted gold wire and ending in a bull's head; it is made of hammered gold with anatomical details in repoussé and engraved. The head is fastened into the tube-shaped sheet which terminated in six triangles with edges decorated with dot wire; the rest of the surface of the sheet is decorated with a double wire spiral framed in three rows of plain and dot wire, which forms three concentric arches on the upper surface of the bull's head. The cylindrical earring hoop ends in a hook and is fastened to a strap loop on the chin of the bull.

COMMENTARY - BIBLIOGRAPHY: Unpublished.

The type of this earring is very common, especially that terminating in a lion's head, and is widely distrib-

From tomb 3

146

146 GOLD LEAVES
2nd-1st c. B.C.

INV. NO. Θ 318.
MAX.L. 0.052, MAX.W. 0.024 M., WT. 2 GR.

Nine complete and two incomplete trilobed plant leaves from fine sheet of gold with incised veins along the long axis of each leaf and pointed ends for attachment.

COMMENTARY - BIBLIOGRAPHY: Unpublished.

The leaves are dated by the other finds in the tomb, which comprised seventy-two spindle-shaped perfume bottles from the turn of the 2nd to the 1st c. B.C. Cf. similar in Τσάκος 1977, 358, 360, pl. 122 and 127; Παπαποστόλου 1983, 6-7, pl. 4β; Ρήγινος 1994, pl. 75β. On the burial leaves, which are common grave offerings during the Hellenistic and Roman periods, see Higgins 1961, 158; Παπαποστόλου 1977, 291; *idem* 1983, 7 (with thorough account on technique, use and symbolism).

M.D.Th.

147 PAIR OF GOLD EARRINGS
1st c. B.C. - 1st c. A.D.

INV. NO. Θ 329A, B.
D. 0.015 M., WT. 1 GR.

Gold earrings of cylindrical wire which narrows at the ends and, with twisting, terminate in a hook and loop. At the junction of the thinner to the thicker part of the wire are a small gold ring and a transparent spherical emerald, which are the decorative accessories of the earrings.

COMMENTARY - BIBLIOGRAPHY: Unpublished.
The pair of earrings, which come from a cremation urn, were together with a piriform perfume bottle of the 1st c. A.D. See similar from the Taranto tomb of 1st c. B.C., De Juliis 1984, 192, no. 133a-b. On the loop and buckle type see Davidson - Oliver 1984, 136, no. 188 (1st-2nd c. A.D.). Also Greifenhagen 1976, pl. 49, 4a-b and Hackens 1976, 100, no. 40.

M.D.Th.

148 GOLD FINGER RING
1st c. B.C. - 1st c. A.D.

INV. NO. Θ 539.
D. 0.017-0.02, D. OF HOOP 0.01 M.

Ring with elliptical hoop of gold sheet, the outer piece semicircular in section and the inner, flat. The two pieces are joined rather roughly creating an obvious fold at the circumference of the hoop. The fine circular bezel forms the case for a now worn off-white glass inlay which is held in place by the turned-in edge of the bezel.

COMMENTARY - BIBLIOGRAPHY: Unpublished.
The ring accompanied by a glass perfume bottle of the 1st c. B.C. - 1st c. A.D. and a bronze coin of the beginning of the 2nd c. B.C. were the only finds of the grave. For parallels cf. the ring M 933 of the 2nd c. B.C. from a grave in Veria, Δρούγου - Τουράτσογλου 1980, 40, pl. 15.

M.D.Th.

149 GOLD EARRING
1st-2nd c. A.D.

INV. NO. Θ 335.
D. 0.007-0.011 M., WT. 1 GR.

Ring-shaped earring decorated with granulation. The hoop/ring is made of beaten wire of cylindrical section and ends in a hook and a loop for fastening and is decorated with 51 granules arranged in triads except the two single ones at one end; at the other a larger lentil-shaped granule covers the joint of the loop and the ring.

COMMENTARY - BIBLIOGRAPHY: Unpublished.
The earring was found in a pithos-burial. For general similarities of fastener, granule and the row of granules though in a different arrangement, see Higgins 1961, 183, fig. 54A (dated to the 1st-2nd c. A.D.). For parallels cf. also Greifenhagen 1975, 66, pl. 51, 5-7 (2nd c. A.D.) and Hackens 1976, 160, fig. 41a-b. Cf. also earring no. 193.

M.D.Th.

147

148

149

150 PIRIFORM (BULBOUS) PERFUME BOTTLE
1st c. B.C. - 1st c. A.D.

INV. NO. A 15113.
H. 0.087, MAX.D. 0.039, B.D. 0.019, M.D. 0.024 M.

Intact. Slight chips on the vase. Orange clay. Small, flat base, bulbous body, tall cylindrical neck, flaring rim.
At the lower part of the body, two incised circles. Light grooves on the body and the neck, where there are also light, black bands.

COMMENTARY - BIBLIOGRAPHY: Unpublished.
Lekythoi were replaced by perfume bottles in their various uses from the 4th c. B.C. onwards. The latter became a very popular and much used vessel in the Hellenistic period. They are often found in excavations of habitation areas, and very often in cemeteries. The category of the bulbous perfume bottle appears after the mid 1st c. B.C. and lasts until the late 1st c. A.D. It is also often met in graves of the 1st c. A.D., where it is found in the company of glass unguentaria, as in this particular case. While the glass unguentaria become increasingly popular, this type is gradually becoming obsolete, only surviving in Thrace and Cyprus in a variation of the original shape. For parallels see Anderson-Stojanović 1987, 107, form d; *Agora* V, 15, pl. 2, no. F50, 31, pl. 5, no. G97; *Kerameikos* IX, pl. 98, E112 (1st c. B.C - 1st c. A.D.) and E117 (1st c. A.D.); Ανδρόνικος 1955, 36, 1-3, fig. 23-2; Τσάκος 1977, 344ff. and esp. 413. In Corinth, the type appears in graves after A.D. 44. See *Corinth* XIII, 167, nos. 505.3, 506.5 (4th quarter of 1st c. B.C.).

O.Z.

151 PIRIFORM (BULBOUS) PERFUME BOTTLE
1st c. B.C. - 1st c. A.D.

INV. NO. A 15114.
H. 0.085, MAX.D. 0.042, B.D. 0.019, M.D. 0.026 M.

Intact. Orange clay, misfired. Small, flat base, bulbous body, tall cylindrical neck, flaring rim.

COMMENTARY - BIBLIOGRAPHY: Unpublished.
For parallels and bibliography see no. 150.

O.Z.

152 MINIATURE GLASS BOTTLE
A.D. 1-50

INV. NO. Δ 7047.
H. 0.064, MAX.D. 0.039, M.D. 0.017 M.

Complete. Intense oxidisation on rim. Blown, clear glass. Flat base, spherical body, tall cylindrical neck narrowing towards the top, everted ring-shaped rim. Shallow ribbing on the upper part of the body and neck.

COMMENTARY - BIBLIOGRAPHY: Unpublished.
The technique of glass blowing occurs first in the 2nd half of the 1st c. B.C., probably in the eastern Mediterranean. Blown-glass vases were not initially easy to acquire; soon, however, owing to their potential for mass production, they were established as vases of everyday use, just like clay vessels. At the beginning of the 1st c. A.D., they were widespread in all areas of the Mediterranean. For parallels see Grose 1989, 341, Family VI, no. 616 (A.D. 1-50); Isings 1957, 40, type 28a; Dusenbery 1967, 41-42, fig. 23, no. 26 (from Samothrace; 2nd quarter of 1st c. A.D.).

O.Z.

153 MINIATURE GLASS BOTTLE
A.D. 1-50

INV. NO. Δ 7048.
H. 0.039, MAX.D. 0.021, M.D. 0.014 M.

Part of rim missing. Fugitive corrosion. Blown blue glass. Flat base, piriform body, tall cylindrical neck, ring-shaped rim.

150, 151

COMMENTARY - BIBLIOGRAPHY: Unpublished.
See no. 152. Cf. also Isings 1957, 40, type 28a; Dusenbery 1967, 41-42, fig. 19-20; Biagio-Simona 1991, I, pl. 17, nos. 000.1.049 and 176.1.061.

O.Z.

154   MINIATURE GLASS BOTTLE
A.D. 1-50

INV. NO. Δ 7051.
H. 0.081, MAX.D. 0.036, M.D. 0.019 M.

Complete. Crack at the rim and neck. Corroded on the upper part of the neck and the mouth. Blown green glass. Flat base, piriform body, short, irregular neck, rim opening outwards. Shallow channel at the base of the neck.

COMMENTARY - BIBLIOGRAPHY: Unpublished.
See no. 152. Cf. also Isings 1957, 40-42, type 28a; Vanderhoeven n.p.d., 25, pl. 24, no. 1 and 28, no. 24; Corinth XII, 104-105, fig. 669 (1st c. A.D.); Biagio-Simona 1991, I, pl. 18, nos. 176.1.191 and 176.1.194, pl. 23, no. 176.1.016; Platz-Horster 1976, nos. 121-122 (1st c. A.D.).

O.Z.

155   MINIATURE GLASS BOTTLE
1-50 A.D.

INV. NO. Δ 7052.
PRES.H. 0.068, MAX.D. 0.038 M.

Recomposed of many fragments. Neck and rim missing. Corrosion on the body. Blown turquoise-green glass. Slightly concave base, piriform body.

COMMENTARY - BIBLIOGRAPHY: Unpublished.
See no. 152. Cf. also Grose 1989, 340, Family VI, no. 613 (A.D. 1-50); Corinth XII, 104-105, fig. 669 (1st c. A.D.); Isings 1957, 40, type 28a; Biagio-Simona 1991, I, pl. 23, no. 76.2.194.

O.Z.

156   MINIATURE GLASS BOTTLE
A.D. 1-50

INV. NO. Δ 7053.
H. 0.063, MAX.D. 0.033, B.D. 0.033, M.D. 0.017 M.

Complete. Corroded. Blown greenish glass. Flat base, conical body, cylindrical neck, ring-shaped opening outwards rim. Shallow channel at the joint of neck and body.

COMMENTARY - BIBLIOGRAPHY: Unpublished.
See no. 152. Cf. also Grose 1989, 340, Family VI, no. 610 (A.D. 1-50); Davidson-Weinberg - McClellan 1992, 35-36, 116, pl. 79, nos. 2926, 2928 (1st c. A.D.); Corinth XII, 104-105, fig. 669 (1st c. A.D.); Isings 1957, 40, type 28a; Biagio-Simona 1991, I, pl. 17, no. 163.2.035, pl. 18, no. 176.2.239.

O.Z.

157   MINIATURE GLASS BOTTLE
A.D. 1-50

INV. NO. Δ 7054.
H. 0.059, MAX.D. 0.028, M.D. 0.017 M.

Complete. Transparent greenish glass. Flat base, conical body, cylindrical neck, opening outwards rim. Shallow channel at the base of the neck.

COMMENTARY - BIBLIOGRAPHY: Unpublished.
See no. 152. Cf. also Corinth XII, 104-105, fig. 669 (1st c. A.D.); Grose 1989, 340, Family VI, no. 610 (A.D. 1-50); Isings 1957, 40, type 28a; Biagio-Simona 1991, I, pl. 17, no. 176.1.061, pl. 18, no. 176.4.041.

O.Z.

158   MINIATURE GLASS BOTTLE
A.D. 1-50

INV. NO. Δ 7055.
H. 0.04, MAX.D. 0.038, M.D. 0.017 M.

Complete. Blown greenish glass. Convex base, spherical body, short cylindrical neck, opening outwards flattened rim.

COMMENTARY - BIBLIOGRAPHY: Unpublished.
See no. 152. Cf. Biagio-Simona 1991, I, pl. 17, no. 176.2.237.

O.Z.

159   MINIATURE GLASS BOTTLE
A.D. 1-50

INV. NO. Δ 7056.
PRES.H. 0.044, MAX.D. 0.028 M.

Mouth missing. Blown turquoise glass. Convex base, spherical body, cylindrical neck.

COMMENTARY - BIBLIOGRAPHY: Unpublished.
See no. 152. Cf. also Biagio-Simona 1991, I, pl. 17, no. 000.1.049 and Μυλωνάς 1975, A, 131, Γ, pl. 195α, no. Γ29-209.

O.Z.

160   MINIATURE GLASS BOTTLE
A.D. 1-50

INV. NO. Δ 7057.
H. 0.065, MAX.D. 0.043, M.D. 0.018 M.

Complete. Blown colourless glass. Slightly broken rim. Cracked and corroded body. Convex base, spherical body, short cylindrical neck becoming narrower near flattened rim.

COMMENTARY - BIBLIOGRAPHY: Unpublished.
See no. 152. Cf. also Isings 1957, 34ff., type 16 (flask; 2nd quarter of 1st c. A.D.) and Biagio-Simona 1991, I, pl. 16, no. 163.2.024.

O.Z.

161   MINIATURE GLASS BOTTLE
A.D. 1-50

INV. NO. Δ 7058.
H. 0.066, MAX.D. 0.04, M.D. 0.021 M.

Recomposed from many fragments. Body and neck corroded. Blown yellow-brown glass. Small flat base, spherical body, tall cylindrical neck, rim opening outwards.

COMMENTARY - BIBLIOGRAPHY: Unpublished.
See no. 152. Cf. also Biagio-Simona 1991, I, pl. 17, nos. 176.2.107 and 163.2.031 and Μυλωνάς 1975, A, 131, Γ, pl. 195α, no. Γ29-209.

O.Z.

160

158

155

154

156

152

157

153

159

161

162 GLASS PERFUME BOTTLE
1st-2nd c. A.D.

INV. NO. Δ 7064.
H. 0.151, MAX.D. 0.072, B.D. 0.072, M.D. 0.04 M.

Complete but joined from fragments. Blown green glass. Slightly convex base, piriform flattened body, tall cylindrical neck, opening outwards ring-shaped flat rim.

COMMENTARY - BIBLIOGRAPHY: Unpublished.
See no. 152. Cf. also *Corinth* XII, 107, fig. 11, no. 670 (1st-2nd c. A.D.); Harden 1936, nos. 797, 805 (2nd c. A.D.); Platz-Horster 1976, no. 128 (1st-2nd c. A.D.); Isings 1957, 97ff., type 82A (2nd c. A.D.); Dusenbery 1967, 44, no. 30 (from Samothrace; 2nd c. A.D.); Biagio-Simona 1991, I, pl. 26, fig. 70, nos. 000.1.075 and 134.2.077.

O.Z.

163 GLASS PERFUME BOTTLE
1st-2nd c. A.D.

INV. NO. Δ 7065.
PRES.H. 0.18, MAX.D. 0.074, B.D. 0.074, M.D. 0.036 M.

Incomplete and joined from fragments. Body and largest part of neck preserved, also the rim which cannot be joined with the body. Blown green glass. Slightly convex base, piriform flattened body, tall cylindrical neck, opening outwards ring-shaped flat rim.

COMMENTARY - BIBLIOGRAPHY: Unpublished.
See no. 152. Cf. also no. 162.

O.Z.

162, 163

164 BRONZE STUDS FROM THE COLLAR OF A DOG
1st-2nd c. A.D.

INV. NO. Δ 7066A-Z.
D. OF DISCS 0.0235-0.025, TH. 0.0015-0.003, H. OF STUD
SHANK 0.005, EXT. D. OF LOOP 0.0245, INT. D. OF LOOP
0.0185, D. OF BUTTON 0.022 (INCL. KNOBS), 0.0185 (EXCL.
KNOBS), H. 0.0165 (INCL. BASE) 0.011 (EXCL. BASE).

Bronze with dark green patina.
On all nine disc-studs, three concentric circles are rendered, slightly elevated circles, which create two zones of equal width and one central division, inside which is placed dull yellow and blue-green or blue glass paste in divisions (4-5 in the outer zone, 3-4 in the inner). On six disc-studs the nail is preserved complete on the reverse, the other three being broken half or a third of the length

up. All are roughly rectangular in section, while three of the complete ones preserve a very slight widening on the upper part. Thus, the thickness of the leather collar into which they were fitted appears clear (0.004-0.005 m.).

There is a circular ring with a small corroded lump of iron attached, probably a plate for adjusting the leather collar. The button belonging to it comprises a discoid base with seven knobs on the exterior surface, while underneath, it has two diametrically opposed supports of upside down Ts. A flattened cone with eight divisions, in the shape of a truncated pyramid, rests on the base; four divisions are filled with red and four with blue glass paste. Above, a central circular division which appears to have corroded iron inside it which goes through to the interior of the button and ends at the tip of the T-shaped support.

COMMENTARY - BIBLIOGRAPHY: Unpublished.
As anyone can clearly see even from the excavation picture (see above p. 157), the disc-studs must have been fitted to a leather collar in a row. After careful

measurements and maintaining in general terms the distances between them at the time of excavation, the collar can be reconstructed with a length of approximately 0.45-0.50, width 0.025 and thickness 0.005 m. Leather dog-collars with metal studs as well as representations of collars are known to us as early as tombs of the 18th Dynasty in Egypt; see Janssen 1989, 9ff., fig. 3-4. In Greek art, we know of representations of dogs with collars of leather, rope or something similar; cf. Γιαλούρης 1994, 237-238, no. 62, fig. p. 96 (base in NM; end of 6th c. B.C.). Likewise, cf. the collar of the Maltese dog in the representation of the Douris aryballos (see below, no. 311). For comparable decorative discs cf. *Corinth* XII, 305, no. 2641, fig. 71 (inset geometric decoration) and no. 2642, pl. 125 (decoration not preserved).

For the ancients' love for their dogs and the depiction of these animals on funerary reliefs, although it is not certain that the latter belong to the tombs of dogs, see Koch 1984, 59-72, with relevant bibliography.

N.S.

164

BALNEUM

165 SINGLE-SPOUTED LAMP
Late 1st c. B.C.

INV. NO. Δ 7194.
L. 0.09, H. 0.029, B.D. 0.034-0.035, MAX.W. 0.068 M.

Incomplete. The handle is missing, chipped and flaked all over. Grey clay. Slightly concave base, hemispherical squat body, slightly concave disc with two solid rectangular panels at the edge. Concave nozzle, rectangular at its end. Wheel-made. Dilute black glaze covers the vase. Around the base two concentric incised rings. In the centre, rough grooves, perhaps an unsuccessful effort of incising a signature. On the disc an erotic scene. A man is depicted half-lying on the bed, leaning his left arm on a cushion with decorative grooves and raising his right arm.

165

On top of him, there is a nude woman seated with her back turned (position of κελητίζειν - riding position). Incised patterns on the solid lugs of the disc.

COMMENTARY - BIBLIOGRAPHY: Unpublished. Imported from the eastern Aegean, probably produced by the workshops that produced the so-called Ephesos lamps. For parallels in the shape see *Agora* VII, 72 pl. 1, no. 5 (late 1st c. B.C.); *Corinth* IV$_2$, 64, 79, types XVIII and XIX; *Délos* XXVI, 122, pl. 28, no. 4570 (1st c. B.C.). The depiction of erotic scenes had been quite popular since the Archaic period and became a standard iconographical theme in painted and relief pottery, in minor arts and sculpture. Erotic scenes are a popular subject in relief wares of the late Hellenistic and early Roman period. The lamps of this period often bear erotic complexes, a habit that was carried through to later years. The workshop of Peirithos, which flourished during the 3rd c. A.D., specialised in such scenes, reproduced on its own lamps as well as by moulds lent to other workshops. In the 4th c. A.D. the depiction of such scenes on lamps was limited drastically, while only few examples may be dated to the 5th c. A.D.
For erotic scenes on vases see Ακαμάτης 1993, 292-299, pl. 302, 304 and p. 296-297 with bibliography. For similar scenes see *Agora* VII, 72; Bailey 1975, III, 131, no. Q3396 (copy); Waldhauer 1914, 182, pl. XVII.

O.Z.

166 BRONZE NEEDLE
Roman period

INV. NO. M 7166.
L. 0.124, MAX.D. 0.04, L. OF EYE 0.0095, W. OF EYE 0.002 M.

Bronze with slight traces of oxidisation. Needle, circular in section, with rectangular eye and the upper part of the stem flattened.

COMMENTARY - BIBLIOGRAPHY: Unpublished.
Corinth XII, 173-178, nos. 1234-1247, pl. 78 (bronze needles, 0.09-0.11 long); *Olynthus* X, 362-363, nos. 1750-1754, pl. 115 (bronze needles, 0.13-0.19 long); *Kerameikos* XIV, 39-40, no. 27.4, pl. 37.5 (2nd quarter of 4th c. B.C.).

N.S.

167 SINGLE-SPOUTED LAMP
Late 5th - early 6th c. A.D.

INV. NO. Δ 7201.
L. 0.11, H. 0.03, B.D. 0.038, MAX.W. 0.068 M.

Incomplete. Parts of the handle and nozzle are missing. Orange clay.

A mould-made lamp. Plain, traces of fire on the nozzle. Low ring base, hemispherical squat body, slightly concave disc with a channel to an ovoid nozzle. On the disc, two filling holes.

On the underside, two concentric, incised circles. On the disc a female bust is depicted, of a woman richly dressed wearing a necklace and facing left. Round the figure a band with alternating concentric circles with crosses and concentric circles inside squares as decoration.

COMMENTARY - BIBLIOGRAPHY: Unpublished.

This type has been imported from North Africa. North African lamps, possibly produced by Tunisian workshops, appeared during the 4th c. A.D. and gradually spread all over the Mediterranean. In Greece they appeared for the first time in Corinth, Kenchreai and on Delos. In Athens, they are not imported before the end of the 5th c. A.D., since the city itself exported its own production. During the 6th c. A.D., and mainly after the invasion of the Vandals when several workshops were destroyed, lamps of this type became extremely popular in Greece. From the end of the 5th c. A.D. Corinthian workshops start to produce imitations, since local production was receding, see Σκιάς 1918, 17, fig. 10,4. The female bust represented has caused some debate. Delbrück 1933, 167-168 identifies the woman with Fausta. On a lamp from Tunisia, the same figure is taken to be male, see Bailey 1975, III, 42-43 pl. 24, no. Q1804 (MLA; A.D. 400-500). For similar representations see *Agora* VIII, 99, pl. 10, no. 323 (5th c. A.D.; from Cyrene); Karivieri 1996, pl. 5, no. 306 (late 5th - early 6th c. A.D.; with relevant bibliography); Lyon-Caen 1986, 103, no. 54 (cat. no. 6474); Αλεξανδρή 1976, 27, pl. 32β (excavated at 5 Aristeidou Street, in Athens); *Fouilles de Delphes* V, 540, fig. 829. For the subsidiary pattern and its provenance see Πάντος 1992, 419, pl. 91δ.

O.Z.

166

167

168 MARBLE FEMALE HEAD
4th c. B.C. (?)

INV. NO. M 4347.
H. 0.067, H. OF HEAD 0.054 M.

The neck is broken obliquely towards the back. Chips on the nose and the hair just above the left eye. Incrustations on the right side of the neck and head. White marble, fine-grained, sparkling.

On the somewhat rounded, full face with the firm chin, the eyes are gazing into the distance. The hair above the low forehead is parted in two and with snake-like locks, runs to the back where it forms an unsophisticated knot. The hair is not well worked between the bands and the back. The head has a double band at the front; probably the same band holds the knot at the back and continues obliquely to the upper part of the skull. Just above the forehead it joins a shorter band.

168

COMMENTARY - BIBLIOGRAPHY: Unpublished.
This powerful head – with the unusual multiple ribbon, which perhaps protected most of the hair when the head moved abruptly – would better suit a huntress or an athlete. A similar powerful face, with a related hair-style with a double ribbon around the head is seen in a bronze statuette in Vienna; cf. Von Schneider 1892, 51, no. 78 and *LIMC*, s.v. Atalante, 99.

P.Z.

169 MARBLE ACROLITH
Early 3rd c. B.C.

INV. NO. M 4154.
MAX.H. 0.60, H. OF NECK 0.135, MAX.H. OF INSERTION 0.15, W. (AT THE LEVEL OF THE EYES) 0.185, H. (FROM CHIN TO TOP OF HAIR) 0.28 M.

White marble with heavily weathered surface. The head, larger than life size, was intended to be inserted. Nose chipped and mended. Shallow chips on the right eyebrow and under the eye.

It has not been finely polished in the neck area, the chin and the lower parts of the cheeks. The back of the head, almost vertically chiselled, bears a shallow depression on the top right. The whole surface is roughly worked until half way down the back of the head, where a semi-circle can be distinguished (an attempt to depict a knot). There is noted to be a turning of the head and the gaze upward to the right. The base of the acrolith, wider on the right side, follows and stresses the movement of the head.

COMMENTARY - BIBLIOGRAPHY: Unpublished.
Elements inherited from the Classical period are the hair-style (an obvious, if somewhat indifferent attempt of the sculptor to carve the mass of hair into strips "melon coiffure"), the small closed mouth, the calm modelling of the surface of the face, the upward turning gaze of the eyes set deeply in their sockets, recall the sculptures by Skopas, from Tegea; see Stewart 1990, fig. 500 (Leconfield Aphrodite), fig. 542 (head of Telephos).
The long neck, almost the same length as the face, the deep cutting below the eyebrow, which is not rendered plastically, the long, narrow face with the abrupt transition from the cheek-bones to the almost vertical cheeks, are elements found in early baroque. A similar cutting under the eyebrow is already seen in the portraits of Menander (a copy) and of Alexander on the

Acropolis, for which see Stewart 1990, fig. 613 and 560 respectively. The modelling, however, is more powerful than that of the Amazon from Ephesus of the 5th c. B.C., which displays the same combination of a long, narrow face and semicircular forehead and hair (see Boardman 1993, 103, fig. 94b) or Themis from Rhamnous (see Stewart 1990, fig. 602-603). Conversely, there does not exist the deep carving on the hair and the intense fluctuations on the surface of the so-called Pergamene baroque or the head of Helios from Rhodes. For this see Stewart 1990, fig. 696 (Alkyoneus); Boardman 1993, 190, fig. 187; Merker 1973, 12; Kabus-Preisshofen 1989, nos. 92-93.

It may be the work by a sculptor of the early Hellenistic period (beginning of 3rd c. B.C.) or somewhat later, an artist influenced by the art of Rhodes - Cos or Alexandria; cf. Lawrence 1925, 179-190 and Kyrieleis 1975, 108, C.N.L5 (Arsinoe III from the Serapeion of Alexandria). Facial similarities and similar study problems are seen in the head no. 1027 in the Thessaloniki Archaeological Museum; see Despinis *et al.* 1997, 47-48, fig. 50-53.

The back of the head is interesting. It is roughly worked and the cuttings do not follow a definite direction. On the basis of this side, only hypotheses can be formed. It is either unfinished, like other fragments of sculpture, or this side was not meant to be visible. Or perhaps the sculptor intended to "scoop out" the back part like, for instance, on a head from Larisa or on the larger than normal head of Herakles from Rome, even if in this case we would expect it to be cut more obliquely. See Hager-Weigel 1997, 244-252; Bieber 1961b, 158-159; Δεσπίνης 1975, 34-35; Smith 1991, fig. 299-302. Another suggestion would be the finishing off of the back of the head with plaster, a practice found in the Hellenistic period and mainly at Alexandria in Egypt; see Lawrence 1925, 179-190 and Kyrieleis 1975, 108, C.N.L5 (Arsinoe III from the Serapeion of Alexandria).

Akrolith no. 169 was intended to be inserted either into a cult statue or into a statue of a member of the royal family of the period; cf. Palagia - Coulson 1998, 83-91.

M.N.

170 MARBLE STATUE OF A NAKED YOUTH
1st c. A.D.

INV. NO. M 4509.
MAX.PRES.H. 0.525 M.

White fine-grained marble. Traces of patina and incrustations in places. Almost horizontal break roughly in the middle of the neck. The head, most of the right arm, all the left forearm from the elbow as well as the legs, with an oblique break immediately beneath the knees, are missing. The male member, once inserted, is now missing.

Naked young male figure standing frontal. The right leg is fixed and the left relaxed, appearing to have been bent at the knee and borne slightly backwards.

The direction of the lowered left arm, the curvature of the elbow and the small, cylindrical sectioned hole, which helped the insertion of the forearm, reveal that the latter would have been put forward and, perhaps, the figure would have held some object in that hand. The small chamfered rhomboid prop (puntello), part of which is preserved on the side of the left buttock, was probably used to support the left arm or the object which it held or was possibly joined with some support in this position.

The right arm was raised up and slightly towards the front. At the level of the left shoulder-blade, there is a deep, elliptical but uneven hole (max. depth 0.037, w. 0.021, h. 0.038 m.) and a small roughly worked shallow channel (0.023×0.018 m.) at the continuation of the periphery on the upper part of the hole.

The navel is indicated by a shallow oval depression. Body musculature is well-defined, by means of successive rises, deepenings, and even transitions. Muscle delineation intensifies in the belly and groin regions, on the shoulders, the back, the spine, the loins and the buttocks. The surface is smooth and well worked all around.

COMMENTARY - BIBLIOGRAPHY: Unpublished.

On the left shoulder-blade, at the left of the spinal channel and in part of the well-worked channel, another small protrusion is preserved, apparently not connect-

ed with the rendering of muscles at that point. It may have been connected with an additional object e.g. a quiver, which would have come obliquely to that point. The large hole and the depression accompanying it (perhaps a channel for pouring in molten lead) are most probably related to a later suspension or propping up of the statue on some wall or something similar.

The type of the statue, judging from the position of the legs and arms, from the hair which seems either to have been short or not to have reached the lower part of the neck and the shoulders, from the athletic (and not delicate) modelling of the muscles in combination with the observations made above, is suited more to the Apollo Lykeios; see Milleker 1988. Even though sometimes the same, approximately, type is used to depict Dionysos (see Schröder 1989), I do not think that this is so in our instance for reasons referred to above. Judging by technical details (e.g. absence of traces of drilling), the superlative quality of workmanship etc., the Syntagma copy probably dates to the 1st c. A.D. For a nearly precise parallel see Picard 1954, 338-339, fig. 142 (torso of marble statue in Kassel). Likewise, cf. *LIMC* II, 193-194, pl. 184-185, esp. no. 39q (bronze from Patras; NM, no. 15234) and 39r (from the Athenian Agora, no. B1236) [Palagia]. For a Hellenistic variation of the type see Marcadé 1996, 98, no. 39 (A 4124).

N.S.

171 MARBLE STATUETTE OF ATHENA
2nd c. A.D.

INV. NO. M 4507.
MAX.PRES.H. 0.38 M.

White fine-grained marble. Head thoroughly cut off from the base of the neck, as is the right arm from the middle of the forearm; the left arm is missing. The right leg chipped off at the lower part of the shin and also the left foot. Small chips mainly at the edges of the folds of the dress and traces of incrustations mainly at the back. Intense traces of a drill can be discerned in between the folds. Standing female figure in full stride with the right leg forward and the left one back. The upper part of the body is turned sharply to the right. The right arm is held down at her side; the left arm was inserted, as it can be seen from the rectangular dowel hole at shoulder level. The figure is wearing a peplos, fastened

high just below the breast and with long folds. Over the left breast the bust of a Medusa - Gorgo can be distinguished. The lower part of the face is slightly worn, but one can clearly discern the eyes and the nose, the modelling of the cheeks and the hair, the snakes under the neck as well as the large wings flanking the head.

The strap, in relief, for fastening the boot (riding-boot?) the figure would have worn, is discernible on the lower part of the left leg.

The rich folds of the dress are formed by oblique, vertical and spiral furrows; the dress seems to cling to the belly of the figure, especially above the advanced right leg, emphasising her firm stride and twisting.

COMMENTARY - BIBLIOGRAPHY: Unpublished.

Her firm stride and twisting, combined with the Gorgoneion (oblique aegis?) and the position of the arms, indicate that we are dealing with Athena in battle. In this way, we can better explain the inserted left arm (for holding her shield, see Δεσπίνης 1975, 27ff.), as it would have been heavier and more complex to render together with the shield. She would probably hold a spear in her right hand. This is a small, succinct creation sculpted in the round, which is inspired by Hellenistic prototypes, such as the Pallas of the great artist of the altar at Pergamon (see Bieber 1961b, 116, fig. 460), which in its turn is based on Classical sculptural and ceramic creations, or on classicising originals, like e.g. the statuette from Delos (see Marcadé 1969, 290, 510, pl. LV, no. A1621). Likewise, for Roman parallels see *LIMC* II, s.v. Athena, 996-997, nos. 453, 456, while for later examples see 989, no. 373 and 1089, no. 204, pl. 802. It is probably a work of the Antonine period.

N.S.

172 MARBLE HEAD OF SARAPIS
Late Hellenistic (?)

INV. NO. M 4305.
H. 0.075, W. 0.06 M.

Chipped on the nose and upper part of the kalathos. Incrustations on the left side. Surfaces generally weathered. Fine-grained, white island marble.

The simple, combed down beard gives the face an oblong look. The lower lip is fleshy. The details of the eyes are not picked out. The hair is parted just above the low forehead and the slightly curly locks are pulled back into a roughly made knot or bun. He wears a cylindrical kalathos with ring-base on his head. On the right, the upper part of a cornucopia (horn of Amalthia) is preserved. On the rear, its grooves can be discerned while on the front there is a bunch of grapes.

COMMENTARY - BIBLIOGRAPHY: Unpublished.
Private worship of Sarapis started in Athens in 215/4 B.C., but became more widespread mainly from the beginning of the 2nd c. A.D.; see Hornbostel 1973, 323. The kalathos head-gear, an element perhaps borrowed from Sabazios, is a symbol of agricultural fertility, whereas the horn he held presumably symbolised the abundance of the earth. In a relief from Lycia – now in London – he is depicted standing besides Isis holding the grooved cornucopia, topped with a bunch of grapes. Perhaps it was intended for private cult; see Kater-Stibbes 1973, no. 417 and Tinth 1983, 151, pl. 93.

P.Z.

173 MARBLE MALE HEAD
Middle of 1st c. B.C.

INV. NO. M 4092.
H. 0.25, H. (CHIN TO FOREHEAD) 0.205, D. (AT THE LEVEL OF THE EARS) 0.19 M.

Pure white marble, fine-grained and crystalline. Life-size marble head of a man. It may have come from a large relief, part of which is preserved and protrudes at the back, on the right-hand chipped part of the head. The head is chipped at the level of the beginning of the neck, at the back part of the ears. The left part of the nose is missing.

The crescent-shaped locks of hair are in low relief, pulled back at the temples, combed down on the forehead above the middle of which they join like two antithetic crescent-shaped locks.

COMMENTARY - BIBLIOGRAPHY: Unpublished.
It is interesting to compare this specific portrait with two others found at Delos (A 4186 and A 4187), which give a secure base for dating them at around 100-60 B.C.; see Stewart 1979, 66-69. Similarities are evident in the way specific characteristics are portrayed, the length of the hair at the back of the head and the way it is pulled at the temples, the reserved and serious expression of the face. The comparison with the portraits in NM, nos. 320 and 321, which were found in Athens (see *Agora* I, 11-12 and Stewart 1979, 81, fig. 25b), stresses even more the contrast between the more "Greek" realistic features and artistic style of the latter, and the image of the male head under examination which is closer to the Roman prototypes of the portraits from Delos.

Portraits of private citizens and priests found in Athens and dated to the reign of Augustus, like NM, nos. 353 and 356 (see *Agora* I, 17-19 and Ντάτσουλη-Σταυρίδη 1985, 26-27, pl. 12-13α), display similarities in the affected way the hair is shown in low relief and without much volume. The portrait of Diodoros Pasparos from Pergamon, which dates to *c.* 80-60 B.C., presents the same accuracy and technical perfection in the rendering of the features, without particularly intense and harsh realism, as head no. 173 under discussion; see Stewart 1990, 232-323, fig. 872 and Smith 1991, 257, fig. 324.

The hair-style above the forehead is already seen in portraits of the early Hellenistic period, on a male head from the Kerameikos as well as in portraits of Drusus the Younger. See Pryce 1928, 78-79, fig. 125, 127; Stewart 1979, fig. 23a-b; Rose 1997, fig. 162, 172; Kiss 1975, pl. 312-313, 341-342.

The stylistic relationship of the above portrait with the art of Delos in the 1st half of the 1st c. B.C. and with the art of the Augustan era permits a date – on the basis of stylistic similarities – around the middle of the 1st c. B.C. The sculptor produced a portrait which is distinct for its artistic and technical perfection and, perhaps, depicts one of the Roman aristocrats of the time; see Smith 1981, 24-38.

M.N.

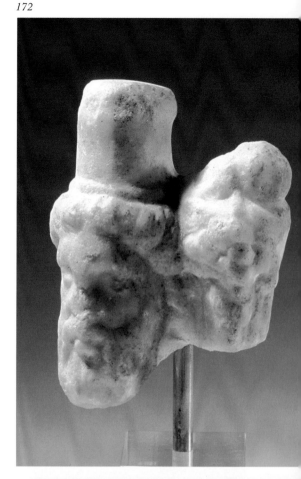

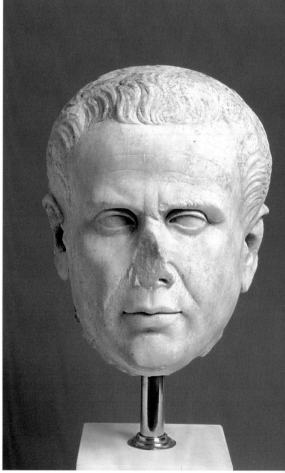

173

174 INSCRIBED MARBLE VOTIVE BASE FOR A BRONZE TORCH
2nd half of 1st c. B.C.

INV. NO. M 4135.
MAX.PRES.H. 0.145, W. OF INSCRIBED SIDE 0.18,
W. OF LOWER PART OF BASE (INCL. MOULDING) 0.21,
W. OF BACK SIDE 0.23, L. 0.415 M.

Base made of white veined, Hymettus marble, for a votive bronze torch. The inscribed front, the two sides, the back and the lower sides are preserved. The upper surface is broken, but it preserves the bottom of a round dowel 0.065 m. in diameter to support the torch. There are chips off the upper inscribed left corner.

The front part of the base, up to 0.26 m. in depth, is perfectly polished and is surrounded by carved band and wave projection, which separate it from the back which is roughly carved and was obviously fitted into a wall of some building. The base gave thus the impression of a flange, which protruded from the wall. On the front, it has an incomplete votive inscription which consists of seven lines (of the first only traces are preserved). It is thought that there must not have been other lines, and that the missing upper part was occupied by the wave projection and the carved band which surrounded the whole front part of the base.

The inscription, which is carefully inscribed, can be completed thus (h. of letters 0.009 [the Os] - 0.01 m.; line spacing 0.003 m.):

> [Name]
> [deme's name τ]ὴν λαμπάδα
> [ἀνέθηκε;]ν ἐκ τῶν περε[υ]-
> [τάκτων] νικήσας Ἀπόλλω-
> 5 [νι, γυμν]ασιαρχοῦντος Ἀ-
> [πολ]ήξιδος τοῦ Ἀπελλι-
> [κ]ῶντος ἐξ Οἴου.

COMMENTARY - BIBLIOGRAPHY: Unpublished.
The dedicator, from whose municipal-name (demotikon) one can deduce the tribe (phyle) to which he belonged, dedicated to the god Apollo a bronze torch commemorating his victory at a torch-race (lampadedromia), the year when Apolexis, son of Apellikon from the deme of Oios was gymnasiarch (head of gymnasium), also known from another inscription of 20/19 B.C. (*SEG* XXX, 93, ll. 20-21).

Lampadedromiai were performed in Athens during the festivals of the Panathenaia, Hephesteia, Prometheia, Paneia, Theseia, Epitapheia, Anthesteria, Hermaia, Aianteia and later the Diogeneia and Ptolemaia were added. Lampadedromiai on horseback took also place during the Bendideia, in honour of the Thracian goddess, Bendis. Originally it was a team game with teams (according to age) from every tribe. During the Imperial period, as related by Pausanias, there were lampadedromiai with individual participation. Every participant in the game could commemorate his victory by making a dedication, which was usually a bronze torch, a small Hermaic column or some statue. Often, however, the victor-devotee was the "coach" or the head of the victorious team (sophronistes, lampadarches, who was sometimes also gymnasiarch too), whom the tribe appointed each time.

In our case it seems that the dedication was made by the lampadarches of the winning team of the pareutaktoi, young men who had just completed the first stage of their training (ephebes), but continued to participate in gymnasium exercises and they had not yet entered the group of adult men. The games in which the team of the pareutaktoi of the unknown dedicator won, are not recorded in the preserved part of the inscription. It is also unknown into which building this dedication was incorporated, which must have been a building of some shrine or gymnasium. Apollo, like Hermes and Herakles, were the main deities to whom dedications were made by victors.

On lampadedromiai in antiquity see Daremberg - Saglio, s.v. Lampadédromia [J. Toutain]; *RE* XII.1, s.v. Lampadedromia, 569ff.; Tréheux 1952, 585ff.; Πάντος 1973, 176-180, no. 2; Θέμελης 1989, 23-29. Concerning the shape of lamps see Plassart 1912, 390, n. 1 and Πετράκος 1991, 44-46, 50-52. About representations of lampadedromiai see Giglioli 1922, 315-335.

Ch.B.K.

COINS

175 GOLD DANAKE
284-270 B.C.

INV. NO. Θ 330.
D. 0.01 M.

Gold "coin" stamped on the one side with a representation of an owl surrounded by a laurel wreath. ΔΟΥ ΑΚ

COMMENTARY - BIBLIOGRAPHY: Unpublished.
For this type cf. a bronze Athenian coin, *Agora* XXVI, no. 54.

I.T.

175

176 Obv.   *177 Obv.*

From the fill

176 BRONZE COIN OF MESSENE
After 280 B.C.

INV. NO. N 1532.
D. 0.02 M., WT. 5 GR.

Obv.: Head of Demeter to r.
Rev.: Zeus Ithomatas. A tripod on the right; left ΔΙΩΝ/ΜΕ on a wreath.

COMMENTARY - BIBLIOGRAPHY: Unpublished.
Cf. *SNG* Cop., no. 511.

I.T.

177 ATHENIAN BRONZE COIN
Early 70s B.C.

INV. NO. N 1531.
D. 0.02 M., WT. 8 GR.

Obv.: Head of Athena wearing a helmet, to r.
Rev.: Owl in a wreath. Inscription: Α ΘΕ.

COMMENTARY - BIBLIOGRAPHY: Unpublished.
Cf. *Agora* XXVI, no. 118.

I.T.

176 Rev.   *177 Rev.*

178 SOLIDUS OF JUSTINIAN II (SECOND REIGN: 705-711)

A.D. 705

Mint: Constantinople

INV. NO. Θ 321.

D. 0.019 M., WT. 4.4 GR.

Obv.: ƆNIhSChSREXREGNANTIЧM (*Dominus Noster Ihsous Christos Rex Regnantium* = Our Lord Jesus Christ, king of kings). Bust of Jesus en face with the head projected onto a free cross. Christ is shown with a short beard and curly hair. He is blessing with his right hand and holds a closed Gospel decorated with precious stones in his left.

Rev.: DNIЧS TINIA NVSMЧLTЧSA (*Domino Nostri Iustiniani Multos Annos* = Our Lord Justinian, may he live for many years). Bust en face of Justinian II with a short beard. The emperor is wearing a diadem which ends in cross shaped ending and a band. He is holding a cross on a stepped base in his right hand and an orb crowned with a patriarchal cross in his left. Inside the orb, the word PAX (= Peace) is written.

COMMENTARY - BIBLIOGRAPHY:

Unpublished.

The youthful figure of Jesus with curly and short hair, known works of Syrian origin, belongs to the so-called miraculous acheiropoietes icons, which were reputedly of divine, not human making. The choice of type, which is characterised by the Byzantine texts as that which renders the most true and familiar form of the Saviour, moves more within the framework of the human background of Jesus Christ and contrasts with the picture of Christ Pantokrator on the solidi of the first reign of the Emperor (685-695). There Christ's figure, with the long hair and beard, shows austerity and emphasises his divine and authoritative character. This iconographical differentiation is, without doubt, an artistic answer to the dogmatic religious search which has not yet been crystallised, and it expresses the orthodox dogma, the unity of the two natures of Jesus, the divine and the human.

The iconography of the back of the coin shows a strong symbolism with the epicentre now being the emperor himself. There is a characteristic lack of realism in his portrayal which, despite the careful tracing, remains unsubstantial and conventional, far from human things. The earthly king borrows from the heavenly lord, the "king of kings", power, protection and a long life. At the same time, he develops into a guardian of Christian peace on earth, according to the prophesy: "Almighty God, ruler, Lord of peace, Father of the age which is about to come, I shall bring peace to the lords, peace and health on them". However, apart from the confirmation of the imperial existence, the symbolism of the reverse inscription hints at dynastic stability. The patriarchal cross, which crowns the sphere, is identified with the True Cross, the cross of Martyrdom, which the founder of the dynasty, this king's great-grandfather Herakleios, managed to recover from the hands of the "infidels". The True Cross – which as early as the last quarter of the 7th c. had been carried to Constantinople – becomes the symbol of glory of the dynasty and in this way, ratifies the return to the throne of the exiled Justinian, who had in the previous years suffered the severance of his nose. The lawful emperor as "lord of Peace", under the protection of the Jesus Christ, promises his subjects peace and stability, at a moment when the empire is threatened by external dangers, internal political and religious disputes.

The recovery of this rare solidus in an excavation has come to strengthen the numismatic evidence from the city of Athens during the so-called "dark ages", and, in combination with the bronze coins of the period found earlier during the excavations of the American School at the Athenian Agora, demands a reassessment of the historical development of the town during the 1st half of the 8th c. A.D.

For the type see *DOC* II₂, 644-645 and 648, Class I and *BNP* I, 396-397 and 429 no. 03; for the iconography see Breckenridge 1959, 59-62; for the numismatic testimonia see Thompson 1940, 358-380 and Πέννα 1996, 202 n. 23.

V.P.

178 Obv.

178 Rev.

AQUEDUCT

GREENHOUSE

T 13

T 11
T 10
T 9
T 3
T 8
T 6
T 5
T 4
T 2
T 1

T 23
T 15
T 77
T 52
A 8
T 25
T 24
T 153
T 154
T 21
T 18
T 20
T 17
T 16
T 19

0   1   5   10

HERODOU ATTIKOU STREET

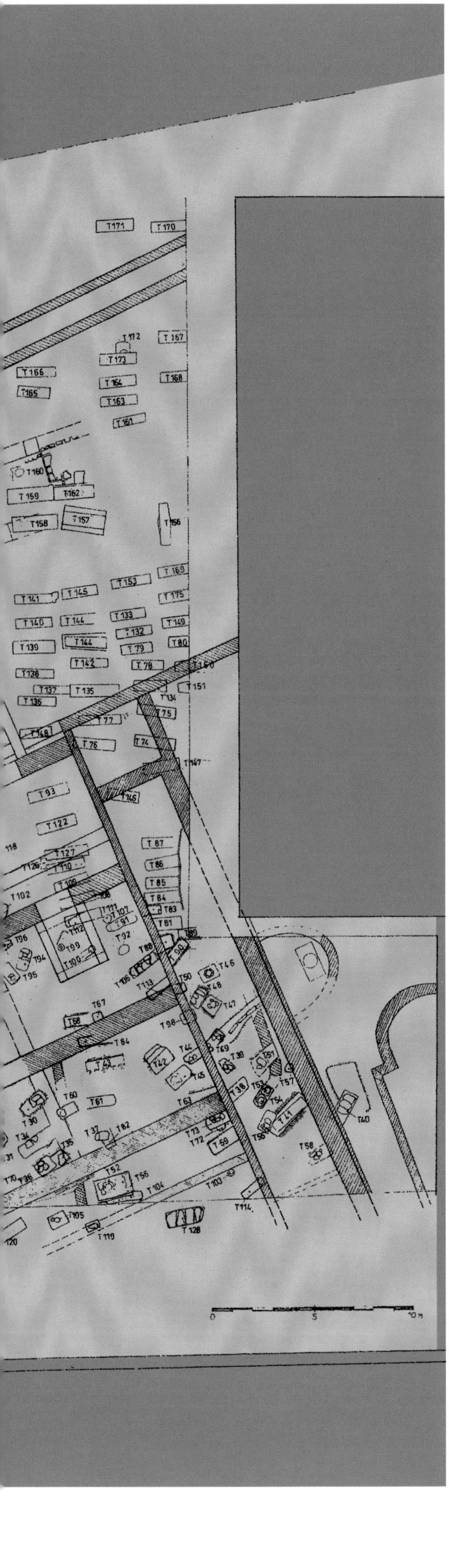

HERODOU ATTIKOU Shaft

Excavation and investigation[1] of an area covering 510 sq.m. at the north-eastern edge of the National Gardens close to Herodou Attikou Street brought to light the continuation of the extensive building complex, the cemetery and the large drainage conduit that had been discovered in an adjacent excavation carried out in 1982-83 by the 3rd Ephorate in the course of the construction of a new building for the Presidential Guard[2] (fig. 1).

Discoveries made while excavating the shaft and the site of the Presidential Guard barracks as well as neighbouring sites provide a good picture of the area which until the city was extended under Hadrian, lay outside the city walls and near the thoroughfare leading to the Mesogeia.

The earliest archaeological evidence on the site is provided by a section of the so-called Peisistratean aqueduct which was located beneath the floors of the Roman building (fig. 2) and below the graves. Two sections of it were examined. In the first, 15 m. long, are preserved seven cylindrical terracotta components with painted red bands laid in a cutting hewn from the rock. In the second only the hewn-out cutting, disturbed by the introduction of later graves, had been preserved. A painstaking study of the form of the components and a stratigraphic examination revealed that the aqueduct dates to the late 6th c. B.C. and is therefore part of the original network.

In late Classical, Hellenistic and early Roman times the site was used for the burial of the dead. A stretch of the Mesogeia road, a branch of it and the cemetery situated close to a side-street to the east of it, which dates back to the SubM-PG period, was re-developed in the 4th c. B.C. and continued in use till the 2nd c. A.D., were discovered in the excavation of the nearby Presidential Guard building.

Thirty-five graves of the eastern cemetery[3] were examined in the shaft opened in the National Gardens; they belonged to well-known types: rock-cut, urns for cremated remains, and built cist graves, and graves with terracotta covers. Most of them had been plundered or disturbed by the rooms of the overlying Roman building.

191

The manner of their construction and the few grave offerings preserved in some of them (terracotta and glass perfume bottles, mirrors and coins) date them largely to between the lst c. B.C. and the lst c. A.D. Very few of the graves belonged to the late Classical or early Hellenistic period; proof, however, that there was a regular cemetery in the area during this period is provided by the use of numerous late Classical and Hellenistic grave-stones in the wall structures of later tombs (no. 179).

A large building complex was erected on the cemetery site in the 2nd c. A.D.; the first phase of construction was discovered in the course of our excavation, as occurred also in the excavation of the barracks for the Presidential Guard.

Two main building phases were identified, the earlier of the late 3rd-early 4th c. A.D. and the later of the 5th-6th c. A.D., as well as several intermediate repairs to the fifteen rooms (fig. 3) and destruction levels of their floors that were constantly being raised. The walls of four of the rooms were decorated in the final building phase with ribands, spirals, rhomboids and rectangular frames in imitation of marble panelling (fig. 4-5). By decision of the Central Archaeological Council these mural paint-

2. HERODOU ATTIKOU Shaft. The "Peisistratean" aqueduct underneath the rooms of the building complex.

3. HERODOU ATTIKOU Shaft. The rooms of the building complex.

2

ings were removed and transferred to the Byzantine Museum with a view to their eventually being put on display there. The room interiors produced a quantity of Roman and Late Roman pottery. A typical find inside one of the rooms was a collection of about one hundred oil lamps (fig. 6), mostly of the 4th-6th c. A.D. (see no. 180). Very many coins of different periods were found in the earth fills of the building's rooms (see nos. 184-189).

In the north-western and central section of the excavation a compact network of twenty-seven conduits, five sumps and two wells presents a picture of a site supplied with an efficient system of water supply and discharge. Among the various conduits, one distinguished by its size and construction is the large early Roman stone conduit 26 m. long with a solid vaulted cover and built walls, identical to the one found in Amalias Avenue and in many parts of Athens; that it used to be a section of the central drainage network is apparent from the fact that six terracotta open-topped conduits terminate in its interior.

Among the portable finds made in the excavation, particularly the sculptures (see

3

no. 182), mainly grave memorials (see no. 183) of the late Classical, Hellenistic and Roman periods, there stands out a late Archaic bronze head (no. 181) which on reuse was set in a large roughly worked block of stone and secured in lead. The block with this important find was discovered in a deeply chiselled cutting full of water.

Initially, the large building complex incorporating luxurious rooms, marble reservoirs, mosaic flooring and mural paintings and built on the eastern edge of the Roman city of Athens, a few metres east of the new fortification[4], was recognised as a private villa. But its ground area is large considering that only its southern boundary was established by our excavation. It seems that it extends further north than the Presidential Guard barracks, if it is associated with the still visible 5th c. A.D. mosaic in the north-eastern corner of the National Gardens[5].

The excavation has shown that it continues in a westerly direction in the Gardens, but also towards the east where it may be connected with the bath-house (valaneion) investigated in 1953 at the intersection of Mourouzi and Herodou Attikou Streets[6]. Its great extent, taken in conjunction with the high quality construction and the important portable finds, supports the view that here we have a complex serving a public function.

OLGA ZACHARIADOU

4-5. HERODOU ATTIKOU Shaft. The wall paintings in the rooms of the building complex.

6. HERODOU ATTIKOU Shaft. The lamps from room 1.

NOTES

1. See p. 137, n. 1.

2. Σπαθάρη - Χατζιώτη 1983, 23-25.

3. Apart from the substantial cemetery in the grounds of the Presidential Guard, graves have been examined at various points in the area such as in Sekeri Street, Vasilissis Sophias Avenue, at the junction of Herodou Attikou and Mourouzi Streets, and in Rigillis Square.

4. Sections of the Roman fortification have been uncovered in the district, in Vasilissis Sophias Avenue (Θρεψιάδης 1971, 31) and in the National Gardens at a distance of 65 m. from Herodou Attikou Street. A part of the same wall was found, in an unfavourable situation, a few metres to the west of our excavation, during the opening of the Metro tunnel; it collapsed on account of the unstable character of the subsoil.

5. Τραυλός 1960, pl. VI-VII; Travlos 1971, fig. 221, 379.

6. Spyros Iakovidis excavated the bath-house in 1953, but his findings were not published. It is referred to by I. Travlos (Travlos 1971, 181) by the key letter P.

6

179 MARBLE PEDIMENTAL GRAVE STELE
c. A.D. 150

INV. NO. M 4609.
H. 1.06, W. 0.55, TH. 0.08-0.10 M.

Pentelic marble. Complete except for the central akroterion; restored from two large fragments. The surface is very corroded, while the sides are smooth. In the central akroterion, now missing, there are traces of lead for fastening it. Two perforations can be distinguished just under the epistyle.

A standing figure is depicted, en face, with the head slightly inclined to the right. The face, idealistically rendered, is ovoid in shape with expansive surfaces and is framed by long plain locks of hair. The figure is supported on the right leg, while the relaxed left leg is slightly turned back and to the side. She is holding a sistrum with her right hand, the arm bent and raised, and a situla with the left. She is dressed in a chiton and a tasseled himation, which is tied at the breasts with the Isis knot, while part of it is brought back to the side. A diagonal strap is hanging

179

from the left shoulder, decorated with rosettes and adorning the torso.

On the epistyle is the inscription ΜΟΥΣΑ ΔΙΟΝΥΣΙΟΥ ΕΣ ΑΛΕΩΝ.

COMMENTARY - BIBLIOGRAPHY: Unpublished.

The temple-shaped stele belongs to type B of Von Moock 1998. From the iconographic elements – the sistrum the figure is raising so ostentatiously, the situla, the Isis knot and the festoon – we assume that a priestess of the Egyptian goddess Isis is represented. From epigraphic evidence, we know that the worship of Isis was introduced to Piraeus in the 3rd c. B.C. and continued into the Roman period; see Eingartner 1991. Isis had many attributes in Egypt and gained more when her worship spread to the whole Greek and Roman world; see Dunand 1973, 148-150. The female figures in the dress of Isis and the sacred objects accompanying her belong to the lowest level of clergy, like the class of the hymn-singers or songsters; see Dunand 1973, 162-188. On Isis see *LIMC* V.2, s.v. Isis [Tran Tam Tinh]; Dunand 1973, 148-153; El Shahat 1983, 1-75. For representations of priestesses of Isis see Walters 1988, 1-82; Von Moock 1998, 135, 266, 41b, 162, no. 409, 57a, 169, no. 446, 58d; Μποσνάκης 1998, 43-74; Κατάκης 1997. For typological parallels see Witt 1971, 168, fig. 31; Merkelbach 1995, 626, fig. 157; Conze 1911-22, IV, no. 1995. The depiction of priestesses of Isis usually includes the iconographic attributes of the goddess, such as the sistrum and the situla; for the sistrum see Von Bissing 1936-37, 211-224. For the use of the situla in the worship of Isis see Baudain *et al.* 1994, 61-87. On the Greek stelai, the iconography is enriched with a festoon, which covers the breast diagonally; see Walters 1979, 218; Malaise 1992, 329-346; Von Moock 1998, 147, no. 324, 49c.

For the name Mousa see Osborne - Byrne 1994, 124. For the patronym Dionysus see Eliot 1862; *IG* II², 2086; *SEG* XXXVI; Osborne - Byrne 1994, 124. In Attica, there are two municipalities with the name Halai: Halai Araphenidai (modern Rafina) and Halai Aixonidai (modern Voula); see Eliot 1962, 6ff., 34, 370-373; Whitehead 1986, 370, 410, 435; Traill 1975, 40, 50, XXXVI.

T.K.

ROMAN BUILDING COMPLEX

From room 1

180 SINGLE-SPOUTED LAMP
Late 2nd - early 3rd c. A.D.

INV. NO. Δ 7197.
L. 0.10, H. 0.032, B.D. 0.033, MAX.W. 0.078 M.

Intact. Buff clay. Flat base, hemispherical squat body, slightly concave disc, small triangular nozzle, solid triangular handle with suspension hole. Small air hole on the disc. Mould-made. Plain. Traces of fire at the end of the nozzle.

On the base within two concentric circles is the signature ONHCIMOY. On the disc, a scene of two winged Erotes playing. The ground of the scene is rendered with a relief on band. At the rim of the disc a band of leaves, interrupted by the handle and the nozzle as well as by two horizontal panels on the rim. Deeply grooved handle.

180

COMMENTARY - BIBLIOGRAPHY: Unpublished.

The signature ONHCIMOY recalls a Corinthian workshop known from many examples. For parallels see *Agora* VII, 97, pl. 9, no. 308 (late 2nd - early 3rd c. A.D.); *Corinth* IV₂, 210, pl. XXXII, no. 754, type XXVIII; *Kenchreai* V, 46, no. 215 (2nd half of 2nd c. A.D.); *Délos* XXVI, 136, pl. 32, no. 4666 (3rd c. A.D.). The scenes of small Erotes are very popular decorative subjects on the discs of Roman lamps, as well as in the Attic sarcophagi of the Late Roman period. More usual are those with an Eros playing the lyre, the syrinx or the double-flute, Erotes with torches, thyrsoi, kantharoi, turtles, Erotes riding dolphins etc. This repertory is used until the end of the 5th c. A.D. A lamp with identical shape and decoration came from an excavation on Vasilissis Olgas Avenue, in Athens; see Αλεξανδρή 1976, 107, pl. 68γ. For the panelled rim see *Corinth* IV₂, fig. 48, no. 9, 10 and *Agora* VII, 118, pl. 16, no. 711 and pl. 51, no. 17 (early 3rd c. A.D.).

O.Z.

181 HEAD OF A BRONZE STATUE
c. 480 B.C.

INV. NO. M 4608.
PRES.H. 0.22, H. OF FACE 0.117 M.

Severed unevenly from about half-way up the nape of the neck to the base of the throat. Some small and rather corroded fragments survive, a few of them stuck together and obviously once part of the head. On the surface of some of them are grooves or incisions that are probably features of the still missing remainder of the sculpture. The lower eyelash of the right eye was found attached to the right ear, but its corroded state made it impossible to restore it to its proper place. Cracks both small and large are apparent, most of them on the face (in the middle of the forehead, above the left eyebrow, on the bridge of the nose, at the corner of the white of the left eye, on the cheeks and on the lobes of the left ear) but also on the back and upper parts of the skull. There are some breakages, chiefly the mid sections of the extremities of the curls forming the triple-tiered fringe of hair.

The entire surface of the head is badly corroded. A dark chestnut-green patina overlies the greater part of the front of the face and the central part of the triple-tiered fringe of hair. There are small areas and spots of chestnut-russet colour at the side of the cracks, on the front of the throat and over the fringe of hair. A large area of the skull covered with hair is dappled a deep blue patina caused by the azurite content of the metal. Corrosion has produced small swellings or eruptions on the face, neck and head.

The condition of the bronze head gives rise to a number of observations regarding the technique used in its production. It is apparent that the head was cast separately from the body to which it was subsequently joined. Indications of the horizontal joint are to be seen in the jagged points on the throat where the walls are particularly thick. The front and back were cast in two parts. The seams of the joints are clearly visible on the inner surface, whereas on the outer they have been completely eliminated and so present a thoroughly agreeable aesthetic impression. It is obvious that the ears were attached afterwards; their upper part protrudes quite noticeably, a result of later-day damage rather than of a deliberate attempt to portray a particular feature. The fringe of curls above the forehead was also an addition and was cast in three successive tiers. The eyes are inset and made of different materials: white for the eyeball (usually of a white paste of bone), grey-green for the pupil (a polished and worked stone) and black for the iris and the outline of the pupil. The eyelashes of both the upper and lower lids are also inset, their invisible inner surface forming a cavity to receive the eyeball. The lips are similarly inset.

The outline of the skull is spherical and follows an almost constant curve from the top of the forehead to the nape of the neck. The face is oval and displays several large flat surfaces.

The hair is rendered in low relief with a rounded contour on the upper part of the forehead and tends to a crest at the mid point of the nape of the neck. A covering of curls in low relief, the waves shallowly chased, begins at the crown of the skull and spreads out to the front, back and sides. Above the forehead this covering ends in a virtual arch formed by a three-tiered fringe of duplicated curls resembling tiny tongues of flame in which the details of the wavy hair can barely be made out. Close to the left ear, where the fringe ends, and in the space between the first and second tiers of curls, is a small opening which may be assumed to be matched on the right side; it cannot be seen because of the degree of corrosion. The two openings were probably attachment points for an appliqué fillet or diadem. The shape of the ears, left exposed by the cut of the hair, is defined by the outer edge of the helix or rim which starts from the top of the tragus and ends at the thick lobule and by the inner edge which follows the outer and defines the central cavity.

The arched eyebrows are placed at the juncture of the sloping forehead and the sockets of the eyes. These sockets are not deep; they consist of the broad curved surface immediately under the arched brow, the narrow concavity directly below it and the inset eye itself. The latter is almond-shaped, the inner tear-duct distinctly curved and with a slanting outer extremity.

The long nose commences at the inner end of each eyebrow and ends close to the upper lip with which it is organically connected. On both sides the lobes are bounded externally by a shallow furrow, while the nostrils are rendered by small elliptical hollows. What seems to be a curvature at the tip of the nose is a consequence of corrosion and not an attempt to portray a characteristic feature. The upper lip is clearly separated from the lower by a narrow gap which suggests a barely perceptible inhaling of breath. The chin is broad and powerful, the flesh slightly curved and raised on its left and right sides; in the vertical plane it juts out a little in front of the lips.

The head is supported by a sturdy neck denoting strength and firmness; it is modelled with broad and rippling surfaces on which the ligaments to the left and right of the throat and towards the nape of the neck stand out.

Despite its uneven impairment the work preserves every detail of the art and technique it represents, thus facilitating an overall appreciation of it. At first sight the impression it conveys is of a frontal pose, but on taking a closer look this impression changes, for the head is very slightly inclined to the left. This is quite apparent when one notes the distance of the centre of the cheek-bones from the sides of the nose: the distance is clearly less on the left side. This observation is consistent with the shape of the hair at the nape of the neck, the hair falling on the left side and rising on the right. This impression is reinforced by the modelling of the back and base of the head, the depression on the right of the head gradually being transformed into a bulge on the left.

The obviously different expression of the eyes, presumably the deliberate choice of the creator of the work, is now accentuated by the distinct sideways and downwards cast of the left eyeball and by the inherent impossibility of restoring it to its original position because of the corrosion. It might be posited that the curvaceous sweep of the upper eyelash of the right eye was indeed intended by the sculptor, contrasting it with the almost straight eyelashes of the left. The sculptor thus differentiated between the darting glance of each of the statue's eyes and so conveyed the impression that the man is winking in a leftwards and inclined direction.

COMMENTARY - BIBLIOGRAPHY: Unpublished.
The bronze head no. 181 was found inset in a rectangular, roughly worked block of stone, the dimensions of which are l. 0.93-0.935, w. 0.556-0.63 and th. 0.30-0.325 m. The head was secured with lead poured around it in layers, leaving only the face visible.

The block was not discovered in stratified levels, in an archaeological context, but had been placed in the interior of a rectangular rock cutting measuring l. 1.10-1.14, w. 0.82-0.90 and depth 0.90 m.; water stood at the bottom of the cutting. One can only guess at when the head was inset into the stone. The reason why it was so inset cannot be firmly ascertained. However, some conjectures may be advanced on the basis of similar examples.

In Αττικά (I, 2. 4) Pausanias recorded that in the fabric of the residence of one Poulytion on the dromos (track) leading from the Dipylon Gate to the Agora was immured the face of Akratos, a demonic follower of Dionysos. The immuring of his visage in the building was of the nature of a talisman warding off misfortune since the place was dedicated to Dionysos Melpomenos (Musician) (Παπαχατζής 1974, 156-161).

Similarly, the block of stone with its bronze head may have been set up or immured, for the same talismanic and averting purpose, in the large building at the eastern edge of the National Gardens in the vicinity of which it was found. Moreover, it seems probable that this important building used to be connected with religious beliefs or doctrines, for small statues and reliefs dedicated to the gods (Cybele, Asklepios, Hygieia) were found in one of its rooms in the adjacent excavation of the grounds of the Presidential Guard, where indeed a sanctuary was discovered (Σπαθάρη - Χατζιώτη 1983, 25). The rough treatment of the stone block also points to this conclusion. The countenances of demonic figures on the fronts of workshops and pottery kilns are of an apotropaic and talismanic nature and intended to keep likely danger at arm's length (Scheibler 1992, 122).

The same conception seems to have survived on traditional houses in various parts of Greece where other symbols with talismanic and apotropaic properties carved in relief in stone have been placed above entrances. For instance, in Karytaina, Arcadia, a talismanic mask was placed on the tip of the archway over the threshold of a traditional house (Πετρονώτης 1986, 37, fig. 55). At Vatheia in the Mani there is a talismanic-apotropaic relief on a cornerstone of a tower-house and at nearby Koita an apotropaic fertility symbol (Σαΐτας 1992, 125, fig. 276-277).

Another conception dominates the stone grave stelai of the Late Hellenistic period (Jemen 1998/99, 344-345, fig. 316. 318, 318). In this instance alabaster heads embedded in hot lead or some other material are set in grave stelai. These are finely executed in limestone and gypsum, and are inscribed. The absence of any remains of a bonding material on the sides and back of the block with the bronze head, taken in conjunction

with the slight reduction in the width of the upper part, might lead one to a comparison of it with grave tokens from the Yemen. This interpretation finds support in the fact that the place where it was discovered is adjacent to a cemetery of the late Hellenistic - early Roman age. The bronze head no. 181 is imbued with an air of severity, gravitas and restraint, both in itself and in the features of its several parts, features which clrealy distinguish it from the suggestive characteristics of ancient figures and place it among other works in the Severe style. It displays all the essential hallmarks, such as the spherical structure and unbroken outline of the

skull, the arched eyebrows which patently delineate the fleshy part of the eye socket, the wide open and clearly defined eyes, the pronounced eyelashes that circumscribe them, the modelling of the mouth, the upper lip, the corners of which curve downwards conveying a sullen expression, the strong chin and the firm neck. The close-cropped style of hair, represented by an incised pattern of short wavy curls spreading out from the crown of the head, and the stylised curls of the forehead that terminate in points are all common to other works of the Severe style.

Despite the latent movement of the head, the static out-

lines of the face and the relative immobility of the lips are reminders of Archaic inertness. The head seems therefore to be a transitional work in both time and space as well as in the manner of its execution.

As to the place of its production, a comparison of both its structural and stylistic characteristics leads one to contemporary products of north-eastern Peloponnesian workshops (see Langlotz 1967, 30-85; Ridgway 1970, 56-70; Rolley 1983, 86-89; Rolley 1994, 273-276). It may be compared more closely still with the head of a bronze statuette, NM, no. 6590, from the Acropolis (see Langlotz 1967, fig. 43b and Rolley 1983, 232, fig. 239), a work attributed to a Corinthian workshop and dated to c. 470 B.C. Moreover, a comparison of the two heads establishes both their similarities and their dissimilarities.

In each of these works the profile is identical. The sturdy, prominent chin and the hollow formed between it and the lower lip, the slight parting of the lips, the organic unity of the outline of the upper lip and of the lower part and sides of the nose are characteristics shared by both. The sense of firmness conveyed by the powerful neck that holds erect the head with its broad expanses and plastic undulations, which are at once noticeable and evident in the sinews, is shared by both heads. To these similarities must be added also the slight inclination of the two heads towards the left. On more careful examination the apparent resemblance of the shape of the ear lobes is vitiated by the more fluent outline and undulation of the helix of the ears on the head from the Acropolis. Though the modelling of the eyebrows is not all that different, the more curvaceous shape of the head no. 181 compared with the less arched, straighter brows of the NM head is less spherical, having a more fluid profile irrespective of the variations introduced by the fillet and different cut of hair. But also on the face the broad oval moulding of the work under consideration seems less developed than the more mobile surfaces of the triangular face of the Acropolis head which gradually die away towards the temples and at the back of the cheeks. The lips of the NM head are more mobile, as are the subtle undulations of the cheeks as regards both the cheek-bones and the more functional transition of the plastic masses from their frontal positions to lateral ones. The modelling of the eyes is similarly varied, perhaps because of the artist's likely intention to portray the two subjects as distinct persons (the eyes of the Acropolis head are more horizontal and wider than those of no. 181, which are rounder and almond-shaped).

These distinctions do not indicate a different stylistic concept but, in our view, represent stages in the development of one and the same workshop. In other words, if the Acropolis head dates to 470 B.C. then ours must be dated to c. 480 B.C.

The general features of the Acropolis head are to be found in eight male statues which Furtwängler classified as a common type (see Langlotz 1967, 81-82, nos. 18, 19, 22-28, fig. 42b-d), but differentiated by their date. Among these works is the kithara-player (Apollo) from Naples (see Langlotz 1967, 81, no. 28, pl. 43a) whose "fraternal" relationship with the Acropolis head was identified long ago. Another series, this time of female figures on mirror handles, belongs to the Corinthian school, such as NM, no. 6197 (see Langlotz 1967, 80, 83, no. 3, pl. 40b); a second is in the Louvre (see Rolley 1983, 96, fig. 73); and a third in a private collection in Switzerland (see Rolley 1983, 97, fig. 75). These have the same face and hair, but display figural variations attributable to the difference in their dates. Similarly identical are the figures of athletes from Olympia (see Mallwitz - Hermann 1980, 156, pl. 107,1 and 157, pl. 107,2), and the statuette NM, no. 6615+6930 from the Acropolis (see De Ridder 1896, 281, no. 757, fig. 265-266); but the head of a warrior in NM, no. 6446, also from the Acropolis (see Walter-Karydi 1987, 20, fig. 15, 16), a work of 490-480 B.C., is attributed to a workshop on Aegina on the grounds of its typological affinity to the figures of warriors on the east pediment of the temple of Aphaia.

Another work with which the bronze head no. 181 might be compared is the marble head BE 35 from Corinth (see Κρυστάλλη-Βότση 1976, 182-193 and Rolley 1994, 324, fig. 331) sculpted between 480-470 B.C. on a scale three-quarters of natural size, as is the head under review and many others of the same period. It has been suggested that this head belongs to the same type as the "blond youth" and the "Kritios boy", a type to which many other Corinthian works belong as do clay figurines of various sizes and the figure of Ganymede from an akroterion at Olympia (see Walter-Karydi 1987, 89, fig. 126). This type of male head with shared characteristics, such as the general style of hair and the structure of the face, made its appearance in the decade 490-480 B.C. and seems to have persisted till 460 B.C.; it was widespread not only in the Greek world but also outside it. Representative examples are the grave statue found at Kerameikos dating to 480-470 B.C. or a little later (see Rolley 1994, 324, fig. 332), the head of unknown provenance now in the Metropolitan Museum in New York and dating to probably 470 B.C. (see Rolley 1994, 325, fig. 333), the head no. 532 in Volos Museum, produced between 480 and 470 B.C. (see Rolley 1994, 325, fig. 334 and Ridgway 1970, 58, fig. 76-77), the heads from Aegina post-dating 480 or about 470 B.C. (see Walter-Karydi 1987, 77, no. 40,

pl. 30-31), from Metapontum (see Rolley 1994, 326, fig. 418), from Cyrene (see Ridgway 1970, 58, fig. 80-83) and from Cyprus (op.cit., 58, fig. 84-87) and the heads in the Capitoline Museum (op.cit., 58, fig. 78-79) and in Cleveland (op.cit., 59, fig. 88-91).

This type is held to be Corinthian because of the affinity of the "blond youth" to the Apollo from Olympia. Indeed, its widespread distribution makes is difficult to attribute works to particular workshops as local or individual features occur in every case. Perhaps for this reason the bronze head from the Acropolis, with which the above comparison is made, has been attributed to a workshop in north-eastern Peloponnese (see Rolley 1983, 232, fig. 239), but also to an Attic workshop (see Καλλιγάς 1989, 176-177, fig. 67).

Viewed in this light it would perhaps not be too far fetched to compare head no. 181 with another important work of the same period, the head of Harmodios from the well-known bronze group of the Tyrannicides made in 477/6 B.C. by the sculptors Kritios and Nesiotes and reproduced in a marble Roman copy from Hadrian's villa at Tivoli (see Rolley 1994, 332, fig. 338, Archaeological Museum of Naples, no. G 103-104) and in other copies preserved at the Thermae National Museum in Rome (see Brunnsåker 1971, pl. 20) and in the Metropolitan Museum, New York (see Richter 1950, 200, fig. 565-566). In this case there is a general similarity apparent in the structure of the head, in the arrangement of the hair with its successive rows of curls above the forehead, in the modelling of the broad cheeks, in the shape of the lips, and in the strong chin and firm neck.

However, perhaps this general impression of similarity, along with all the qualifications which must be constantly borne in mind when making comparisons with a Roman copy, may rest on nothing other than its likely provenance from a common type to which belong works of different origin such as the head from Corinth, the "Kritios boy", and the "blond youth", of which two have been attributed to Kritios, joint creator of the bronze group of the Tyrannicides.

Similarities found in works considered to be the products of different workshops during the period of the Severe style are not to be wondered at, for in that age artists were itinerant, local workshops were making replicas of popular works and commercial exchanges ensured artistic communication and influence.

O.Z. - N.S.

203

182 MARBLE STATUETTE OF A BOY (EROS ?)
Roman period

INV. NO. Δ 5614.
MAX.PRES.H. 0.119 M.

White fine-grained marble. An oblique break has removed the upper part of the chest, the neck and head. The left arm is broken off from the height of the beginning of the forearm and there are chips on the shoulder, forearm and elbow of the right arm. The legs from the level of the knees are missing. The end of the himation and the support (?) under the left arm pit are broken off. Heavy patina and encrustations at the back of the statue. Traces of the flat chisel and drill.
Standing, young, naked figure rendered en face; the right leg is static while the left – slightly bent at the knee – is brought backwards. The right hand comes downward and, bent at the elbow, is brought obliquely back behind the lumbar region with open palm, which is roughly worked. Under the left arm pit projects a swelling, cylindrical in section, on which the figure carries its weight. A small himation or mantle covers the chest of the figure leaving uncovered part of the right breast, while it falls at the back at least to the level of the hips. The folds of the clothing on the chest are indicated with rather shallow curved incisions, while on the back they are rendered with wide, roughly worked planes. Two incisions highlight the groin area. The naval is indicated with a deep perforation on the soft, swollen stomach which, together with the slightly extended right breast, point to the young age of the figure.

COMMENTARY - BIBLIOGRAPHY: Unpublished.
The figure is reminiscent of youths, naked or mantled, who hold an animal or some object in their left hand; see Vorster 1983, 159ff., pl. 7,8.1-2. Unfortunately, the state of preservation does not allow one to identify the broken object in the left hand with a torch or some other object and to make reference with more accuracy to figures of Eros, for which see Στεφανίδου-Τιβερίου 1985, 88-89 (with bibliography).

N.S.

182

183

183 SMALL, MARBLE INSCRIBED FUNERARY PILLAR WITH RELIEF REPRESENTATION
1st c. B.C. - 1st c. A.D.

INV. NO. M 4662.
H. 1.258, D. 0.44 M.

Complete but chipped. White Pentelic marble. Topped by a round, plain moulding. On one side, representation of a youth, standing en face, in a deep niche with an arched top. The head, with short hair, is turned slightly to the left. He is naked, wearing only a mantle which covers the left part of the torso together with the left shoulder and arm. Part of the mantle projects behind the right hand. The right arm is relaxed, while the left holds a shield. The left leg steps firmly on the ground, while the right is brought slightly to the right.

Directly under the relief representation of the youth there is an engraved loutrophoros. It is sitting on a rectangular base and is decorated with grooves on the body, while at the level of the shoulders, the decoration is foliate. Above the relief representation, an inscription is preserved with four lines:

ΕΠΙΓΟΝΟΣΣ
ΙΣΙΔΩΡΟΣ
ΕΠΙΓΟΝΟΥ
ΜΕΙΛΗΣΙΟΣ

The letters of the first line are smaller than those of the other three and were probably added at a later date. Also it should be noted that the names of the first two lines are in the nominative while the name in the first line in two Σs, clearly by mistake.

At the back of the column, a representation of a Hermaic column is preserved. Only its outline is shown, without any details. It is possibly an exercise of a pupil of the master who decorated the column.

COMMENTARY - BIBLIOGRAPHY: Unpublished.

The column is an Attic grave monument widely distributed in the Hellenistic period after the law passed by Demetrios of Phaleron in 317 B.C. which forbade the use of luxury and costly funerary monuments. The example under discussion is different from the usual type

183 a

in that it is decorated with a relief representation. It is evident that after the conquest of Athens by Sulla in 86 B.C., as is shown by the monuments themselves and later, by the continuous increase in the flow of immigrants from foreign cities, Miletus for instance, the production of funerary reliefs begins anew in Athens; see Muehsam 1953, 58-59.

Small columns were used even after the re-introduction of relief stelai, but now a relief representation is adapted to the surfaces, comparable to that on a stele or carved in secondary use. The figure of the youth on this small column recalls older funerary reliefs, as it follows Classical originals and not those of the Roman period. For small columns with relief decoration see Conze 1911-22, nos.1819, 1820, 1822-25. Cf. Budde - Nickols 1964, 82, no. 132, pl. 43. Generally for short pillars of the Roman period see Von Moock 1998, 53ff.

From the letter type (the Ω with the raised tails, the H with the horizontal bar not joining the two verticals) combined with the rendering of the relief, that is the stationary pose of the figure and the folds of the mantle, not so carefully worked and with shallow grooves, we can conclude that the small column must date from the end of the 1st c. B.C. to the beginning of the 1st c. A.D. For the letter type see Kirchner 1948, pl. 44, no. 120 and pl. 45, no. 122.

The incised loutrophoros immediately under the relief is probably contemporary with it to show at the same time that the youth was unmarried; see Kokula 1984, 143ff. For parallel examples on funerary reliefs, where a loutrophoros is depicted under a male figure see Kokula 1984, 80, pl. 27,1. From an ephebe catalogue of A.D. 116 (IG II², 2026.61) we know the name of a Milesian: Επίγονος Ισιδώρου; see Osborne - Byrne 1996, 209, no. 4933. Perhaps the Isidoros Epigonou of our small column is an ancestor of the youth of A.D. 116.

E.L.-T.

COINS

184 BRONZE COIN OF MEGARA
2nd half of 4th - beginning of 3rd c. B.C.

INV. NO. N 1525.
D. 0.016 M., W. 2 GR.

Obv.: Ship prow with tripod.
Rev.: Two dolphins encircle the inscription ΜΕΓ. Representation inside a dotted circle.

COMMENTARY - BIBLIOGRAPHY: Unpublished.
Cf. *Agora* XXVI, no. 643.

I.T.

184 Obv.

184 Rev.

185 BRONZE SESTERTIUS OF TRAJAN
A.D. 115(?)-116
Mint: Rome

INV. NO. N 1528.
D. 0.036 M., W. 24 GR.

Obv.: Bust of Trajan crowned with a laurel wreath, to r. Inscription: IMP.CAES. NERVAE.TRAIANO.AVG. GER.DAC.P.M.TR.P.COS.V P.P.
Rev.: Fortune (FORTUNA) seated to l. holds a helm in the right hand and the cornucopia in the left. Inscription: SENATUS POPULUSQUE ROMANUS.
On the exergue: FORT RED S.C.

COMMENTARY - BIBLIOGRAPHY: Unpublished.
Cf. *BMC* III, 219, no. 1026.

I.T.

186 ATHENIAN BRONZE COIN
120s - 140s A.D.

INV. NO. N 1530.
D. 0.012 M., W. 4 GR.

Obv.: Head of Athena wearing helmet, to r.
Rev.: Persephone (Kore) standing to r. and holding two torches. Representation inside dotted circle.

COMMENTARY - BIBLIOGRAPHY: Unpublished.
Cf. *Agora* XXVI, no. 187.

I.T.

185 Obv.

185 Rev.

186 Obv.

188 Obv.

188 BRONZE "ASSARIUM" OF CONSTANTINE I
AND HIS SUCCESSORS
A.D. 330-335
Mint: Siskia

INV. NO. N 1529.
D. 0.017 M., W. 1.5 GR.

Obv.: Helmeted bust of Constantinople
to l.
Inscription: CONSTANTINOPOLIS
Rev.: Nike with spear and shield to l., on a
prow. On the exergue: .ASIS.

COMMENTARY - BIBLIOGRAPHY: Unpublished.

Cf. *LRBC* I, no. 751.

I.T.

186 Rev.

188 Rev.

187 Obv.

189 Rev.

189 BRONZE "ASSARIUM" OF CONSTANTINE II
A.D. 346-350
Mint: Constantinople

INV. NO. N 1524.
D. 0.018 M., W. 2 GR.

Obv.: Bust of crowned Constantine to r.
Inscription: DNCONSTANTIUS
PFAVG.
Rev.: Virtus with spear and shield de-
feating a fallen horseman.
Inscription: FEL. TEMP. REPARATIO.
On the exergue: CONSA

COMMENTARY - BIBLIOGRAPHY: Unpublished.

Cf. *LRBC* II, no. 2010.

I.T.

187 Rev.

189 Obv.

187 ATHENIAN BRONZE COIN
End of period A.D. 120-140

INV. NO. N 1527.
D. 0.018 M., W. 4.5 GR.

Obv.: Bust of Athena wearing helmet, to r.
Rev.: Amphora with a sceptre right and
palm branch on left. Representation
inside a dotted circle. Inscription:
AΘH-N-AI.

COMMENTARY - BIBLIOGRAPHY: Unpublished.

Cf. *Agora* XXVI, no. 212.

I.T.

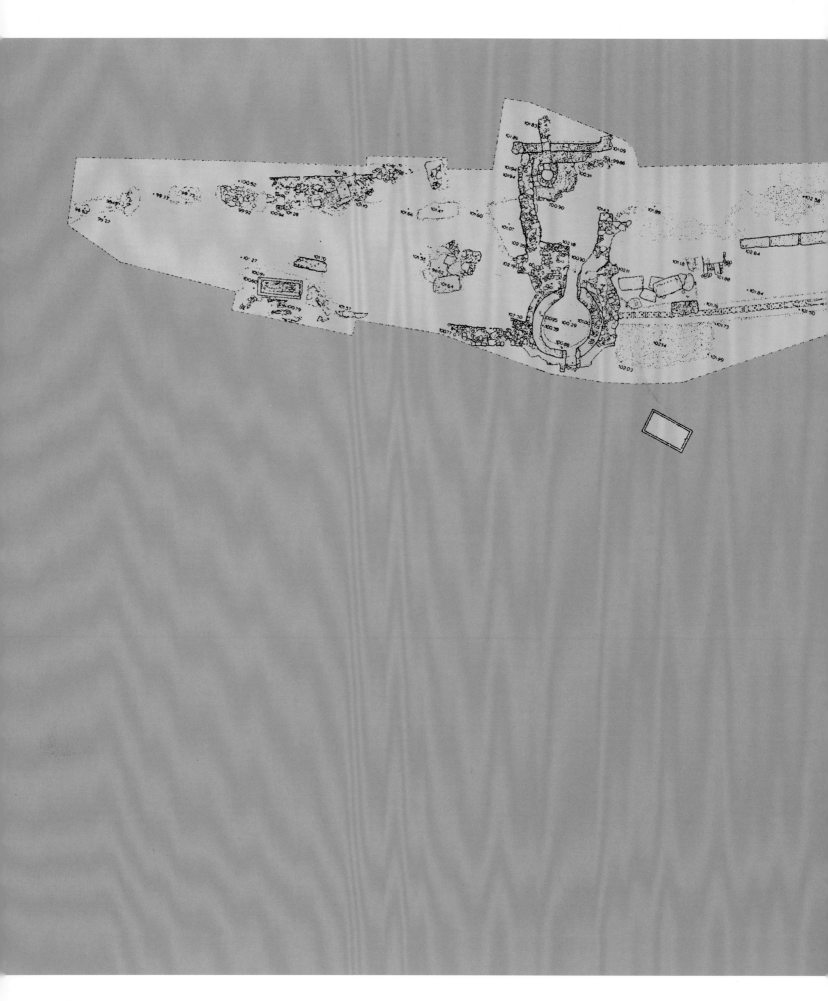

EVANGELISMOS Station

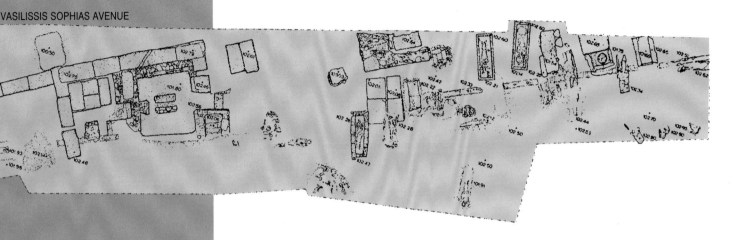

VASILISSIS SOPHIAS AVENUE

1

During excavation of the site of the EVANGELISMOS Station on the M.R.A. antiquities were unearthed in a long narrow strip of land (60 × 6 m.) north of Rizari Park and south of Vasilissis Sophias Avenue (fig. 1-2). The excavation began on 8 June 1995 and was completed within one month[1].

Remains of various kinds were found at a depth of less than one metre below the present level of Vasilissis Sophias Avenue; they included a water conduit, a tomb enclosure, pottery works and a cemetery, all of which are connected with the existence in the area of one of the main arterial roads of the ancient city of Athens, namely, the road leading to the Mesogeia.

A cylindrical terracotta pipeline running in an E-W direction for almost the entire length of the excavation (62 m.) was the most ancient of the finds. A large section of it lay in a cutting made in the bedrock (fig. 5). A four-piece section from the pipe is included in the exhibition (no. 197).

This type of conduit is held to have been part of the large-scale water supply network initiated in the time of the Peisistratids, a time when the city lacked the water it needed, that is, in the period 527 to 510 B.C. Though many sections of the network have been found in earlier excavations at various points of the city, it has not been possible to identify this conduit as unmistakably part of what was at the time a colossal undertaking. A telling factor in dating the find is the presence of painted symbols on the components. The letter type belongs to a pre-Euclid script and so must date to the late 6th c. B.C. Consequently the Evangelismos conduit is the earliest indisputable evidence of the main pipeline carrying water to Athens from the sources on Hymettus of the Ilissos river lying to the east.

A large tomb enclosure oriented in an E-W direction was discovered on the north side of the conduit (fig. 5). Built of conglomerate pink ashlar masonry, its western section is preserved to the height of one course but has been displaced by later building structures while the eastern, including one end of the enclosure, stands three courses high. A rectangular tomb pedestal lay within it. To the east and only a short distance outside the enclosure there were two more tomb pedestals of identical stone blocks laid along the same axis. The enclosure and associated contemporary tomb pedestals must be dated to the 4th c. B.C. The absence of tombs observed in its interior must be accounted for by their destruction, for fragments of marble tomb monuments found in later structures confirm they once existed there. To the south of the enclosure and at some distance from it was a burial in a broken marble larnax of the Classical period. A red-figure pyxis and a bronze mirror found with it date it to the last quarter of the 5th c. B.C. To the north of the enclosure and almost adjacent to it were three thin but compact road surfaces laid on the bedrock, the two latest of which belong to the Hellenistic period.

Following the destruction of the enclosure the area became a pottery workshop. The eastern end of it was divided by a stone block taken from the tomb pedestal into two parts occupied by pottery kilns. Their side walls were composed of rough stones and successive courses of bricks held together by copious applications of mortar. Of the two kilns only the firing chambers remained (fig. 5). Their interiors, full of dark red clay and a thick layer of ash, produced a large number of supports used in the baking of pots. A section of a kiln grid and carbonised olive pits, the remains of the fuel employed, were collected from a deep rectangular trench to the north of the pottery kilns which had been filled with workshop debris.

A third kiln was discovered in the western part of the excavation (fig. 4). It was of the twin-level circular type and of impressive dimensions. The exterior diameter was 3.30 m., while the interior one at the level of the grid was 2.70 m.; at the bottom it was 2.20 m. It was preserved to a height of 2.20 m. The underground firing chamber was carved out of the bedrock. A ledge for the support of the grid, of which no trace was found, ran round the interior walls of the kiln. There were two openings into the kiln from the chamber providing the heat. The original opening was in the north-eastern walls and was formed as an arch made of tiles arranged in a radial manner. At a later stage this opening was blocked up. A rectangular pit had been dug in front of the opening, evidently as a sort of antechamber used in preparing for the firing; there were steps at the east end to provide easy access.

The northern opening which had been destroyed and a similar sunken chamber extending northwards were constructed later. In the north-west corner of the chamber was a wall with a high contemporaneous well-head. This chamber must have functioned as a lime-pit in the final phase of the kiln's use, around the middle of the 3rd c. A.D.

A channel cut into the bedrock was found north-east of the kiln. The north-eastern end of it, where the cutting is superficial, was covered over with semicircular tiles cemented with mortar; rectangular holes have been left in them, apparently as inspection openings. At its south-western end the cutting abruptly disappears into the bedrock and

2. EVANGELISMOS Station. The east part of the excavation site.

continues as a simple underground channel. It must have been incorporated into the workshop complex and have supplied the workshop with the water it required. Its orientation indicates it carried water from nearby Lycabettus Hill.

We may conclude from the pottery collected from inside the kilns and from the pits in their vicinity that the kilns were first used in the 2nd half of the 2nd c. B.C. It is quite likely that the two rectangular kilns were of earlier date but that the large circular one was built only a little while later. A considerable quantity of pottery, chiefly coarse ware, was assembled from the debris of the three kilns. Platters, flagons and earthenware pots predominated. There was also an impressive number of cylindrical terracotta beehives.

The eastern sector of the excavation was once a cemetery, the burials continuing beyond the boundaries of the excavation and beneath Vasilissis Sophias Avenue. In all, thirty-five graves were found. Twenty-three of these were plain makeshift graves covered with tiles, often re-used material taken from the kilns themselves. Most of them were found to be without offerings. The remainder were three marble sarcophagi, two sarcophagi of a shelly marble, three cist graves, one built out of large tiles, one marble urn, one urn with built walls and an infant burial in a pan. It is to be noted that secondary burials were quite common, especially using the sarcophagi. Similarly urns with cremated bones were located.

The oldest graves were those with tile covers dating from the late 2nd c. B.C. to the 2nd c. A.D. The offerings they contained were mostly perfume bottles, spindle-shaped bottles of the end of the 2nd c. B.C., perfume bottles of the 1st c. B.C. and 1st c. A.D., glass perfume bottles of the 1st-2nd c. A.D. Of the remaining graves, one marble sarcophagus was outstanding for the finds made in it: the skeleton was accompanied by a large quantity of trefoil gold leaves (see no. 196) (fig. 3). Close to the skull were two gold rings with precious stones (see nos. 194-195). Glass bottles of the 1st or 2nd c. A.D. were placed at the deceased's feet.

According to the finds, the cemetery which developed eastwards of the pottery workshops must have been in use between the end of the 2nd c. B.C. and the middle of the 2nd c. A.D., that is, contemporaneously with the functioning of the pottery kilns. The discovery of these antiquities in a part of the EVANGELISMOS Station site is of particular importance in establishing the topography of the eastern district of the ancient city of Athens.

The unearthing of a length of the cylindrical conduit which supplied Athens with water from an eastern source in late Ar-

3. EVANGELISMOS Station. The interior of a marble sarcophagus. The glass perfume bottles are visible.

4. EVANGELISMOS Station. Large circular pottery kiln. The north stocking channel.

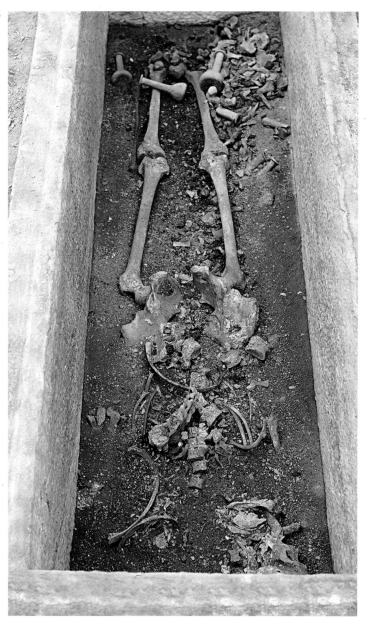

3

chaic times is of considerable interest. Data provided by the excavation suggest that the operation of the Archaic network must have been interrupted in the late Hellenistic age when it was encroached upon by the pottery workshops and the graves dug in the same period. This confirms Strabo's statement that the sources of the Ilissos temporarily ran dry during this period[2].

For the first time it has been established that there was a pottery workshop far from the city walls on the east side of Athens, given that the Valerian wall had not yet been erected. This workshop must have supplied its products to the inhabitants of the district thereabouts. According to what is known to-day, pottery workshops sprang up outside the gates in the walls, particularly on the north-west side of the city in the general area of the Kerameikos and in the direction of the Academy and Hippios Kolonos.

The discovery opposite our excavation site of three destroyed graves of the Classical period in the corner of Marasli Street and Vasilissis Sophias Avenue in the course of excavation in the periphery of the Station is a strong indication of the existence of an arterial road on each side of which cemeteries were established. This road must have started at the Diochares Gates situated at the junction of Mitropoleos and Pentelis Streets, have ascended hence to Amalias Avenue where a section of it was uncovered in the excavation of the M.R.A. Station in Syntagma Square and thence have proceeded to Vasilissis Sophias Avenue, following it to Mesogeion Avenue. In 1965 a burial enclosure and pedestal and grave monuments of the 2nd half of the 4th c. B.C.[3] were found at the junction of Mesogeion Avenue and Ipatis Street.

Another strong indication that there was a very ancient arterial road in the district is the course of the late Archaic water conduit, for it is known that conduits were constructed alongside or below roads. The existence of this assumed thoroughfare is further supported by the discovery of marble grave monuments during the excavation of the M.R.A. tunnel at a depth of about 15 m. at the level of the War Museum below Vasilissis Sophias Avenue and in an ancient quarried tunnel. These grave monuments had evidently been covered by the overlying roadside cemeteries. The marble loutrophoros no. 198 has been included in the exhibition. As the excavation revealed, the road must have been re-routed in the late Hellenistic age but not to positions far distant from its original course. In addition the potters, like other members of their craft, selected a site very close to a major arterial road. This is the road that leads to the fertile lands of the Mesogeia[4].

The discovery of these antiquities in a part of the site of the EVANGELISMOS Station, in an area where previous archaeological evidence was sparse, was the prelude to the discovery which proved decisive in respect of the eastern region of Athens. During the rescue excavation carried out in 1996 on the Rigillis Street plot, where the Palaestra of the famous Lykeion (Lyceum) Gymnnasium[5] was found, the boundaries of the extensive area occupied by the Lykeion in antiquity, in particular the eastern ones defined by the Gymnasium itself, were established for the first time ever. Thus the antiquities found at the EVANGELISMOS Station may now be placed outside the area of the Lykeion.

EUTYCHIA LYGOURI-TOLIA

NOTES

1. The results of the excavation at EVANGELISMOS Station were first presented by the author at the lst Scientific Meeting of the 3rd Ephorate in March 1996. For a summary of the results of the excavations of the M.R.A. see Παρλαμά 1992-98, 521-544.
2. Strabo IX 1, 24.
3. *ADelt* 21 (1966) Chronika, 64-66, plan 9, fig. 77α-δ.
4. Τραυλός 1960, 53.
5. E. Λυγκούρη-Τόλια, *Archaeological Reports for 1996-1997*, 8-10, fig. 8.

190   RED-FIGURE PYXIS WITH LID
430 B.C.

INV. NO. A 15532.
H. (EXCL. LID) 0.027, H. (INCL. LID) 0.047,
M.D. 0.106, D. OF LID 0.133, B.D. 0.071 M.

Intact. It has chips mainly in its bottom and flakes. Red-brown clay. All the reserved parts, including figures, are covered with thin red ochre (miltos). Low body with oblique, concave walls ending in broad ring base. The lid rests on a projecting convex mouth above the vase's walls. On top of the lid, a suspension hole for the metallic handle. Around the handle of the lid and its edge, there are relief fine rings. The body is covered in black glaze, apart from the reserved resting surface, which has been decorated with concentric circles and dot in the centre.

190

The decoration is limited only in the upper part of the lid. A women's quarters (gynaikonites) scene is presented. The scene consists of two female figures and two Erotes. The figure dominating the scene appears to be the woman seated on a chair. She wears a long chiton and himation. Her hair is pulled back and she wears a wreath that is rendered with added white colour. She is facing to the right, while at the same time she turns the upper part of her body and her head to the left, pointing with her stretched right hand backwards, where there is an object that resembles an incense burner or a lamp stand. Towards the female figure, on both sides, two Erotes are flying. The one on the left is flying putting his arms on a rock. Beneath his body there is a stalk of curving tendrils, while in front of him stands the incense burner/lamp stand. He has long hair and a fillet which is rendered in added white colour. The second, on the left, is tip-toeing with spread wings, as if ready to fly away. He, too, wears a fillet with added white colour. In the space between the two Erotes, a female figure is depicted, which stands smaller in size than the first. She is turning left, while with her right hand she is pointing to the ground, where she looks. She is wearing a peplos and her hair is loose. On her head, she has a wreath of added white colour, now faded. Around the hole, at the centre of the lid, there is a band decorated with drops and dots. On the edge of the lid there is an oblique laurel band. The resting surface of the vase preserves a graffito which seems to have been made before the firing of the vase.

COMMENTARY - BIBLIOGRAPHY: Unpublished.

Product of an Attic workshop. The pyxides were containers of toiletries but they were also used as burial offerings in graves. This particular one belongs to the type C of the Attic pyxides, which appears in the mid 5th c., was widely spread from the last quarter of the 5th c. until the 1st half of the 4th c. and was abandoned in the mid 4th c. B.C. For this type see *Agora* XII, nos. 1292-1302, pl. 43, fig. 11; Roberts 1978, 147, pl. 86.3, 87.3, fig. 16a; *Agora* XXX, 53, nos. 1039-1054, pl. 100-101. A characteristic of these pyxides is that the decoration appears only on the lid. The scenes depicted on them are mainly about the women's everyday life or the wedding festivities. See Boardman 1985, 193. Especially from the mid 5th c. B.C., the wedding scenes increase considerably. In this particular scene, the dominant female figure that is surrounded by Erotes is probably the bride-to-be, while the second female figure, depicted in smaller scale than the former, must be her maid. Since 440 B.C., Erotes became important figures in wedding scenes and in scenes that are rather abstract – as is the case for the pyxis no. 190 – they are the bride's only attendants. Generally for wedding iconography see Oakley - Sinos 1993, 45 (especially for the depiction of Erotes).

The object between the bride and the Eros is an incense burner or a lamp stand. Both are found in wedding scenes between the groom and the bride; see Rutkowski 1979, 211ff. For incense burners and lamp stands see Testa 1989, 83, no. 31 (incense burner) and 78, no. 28 (lamp stand). In the scene, this object must be a lamp stand indicating the interior where the scene is placed.

E.L.-T.

191 BRONZE MIRROR
425-400 B.C.

INV. NO. Δ 7158.
D. 0.175, MAX.PRES.H. (INCL. HANDLE) 0.205 M.

Bronze heavily corroded and encrusted. Dark green patina.

Around the periphery of the disc on one side is a marked rim. On the same side the handle attached to the lower part of the disc has a triangular termination, while towards the front, smooth surface, the periphery is decorated with a fine, slightly shallow rope-shaped border. The handle is embellished with spirals like an "Aeolian" capital on the upper part of which sprout volute palmettes. A band can be made out between the spirals, while in the middle outside the spirals, a small relief like a flower blossom can be discerned. Finally, in the middle of the lower end of the capital there is a very small part of a terminal, almost square in section, from the rod that was inserted into the handle made of wood or some other material.

COMMENTARY - BIBLIOGRAPHY: Unpublished. Cf. Oberländer 1967, nos. 157-165; Boulter 1963, 117-118, pl. 38.A12 (from a burial in Lenorman street, with a handle ending in the shape of an Ionic capital); Karouzou 1951, 566-567, fig. 1, pl. 45 (= Oberländer 1967, no. 157; 450-440 B.C.). Also Cameron 1979, nos. 35-36, pl. 76-77 (Greek mirrors from graves at Locri in southern Italy; end of 5th c. B.C.). For representations of mirrors in vase-painting see *CVA* Copenhagen III.1, pl. 134, 1a (red-figure stamnos by the Eucharides P.); *ARV²* 1516.81 (red-figure hydria; 375 B.C.). For a mirror suspended on a wall see Zimmer 1987, no. F2376, fig. 4 (red-figure hydria from Aegina; *c.* 460/50 B.C.).

N.S.

192 BRONZE MIRROR
1st c. A.D.

INV. NO. Δ 7159.
D. 0.09, TH. OF DISC 0.002, D. OF PERFORATIONS 0.002-0.003 M.

The metal is corroded, with small chips on the periphery of the disc. Golden brown patina.

On one (exterior) side, there are two concentric circles defined by a slightly raised edge. At the centre of the circle, there is a shallow depression. Shallow incision defines the outer part of the disc, where a zone with perforations of different size unfolds. Today thirty-seven are preserved; originally, there may have been as many as fifty. The zone with the perforations is interrupted only at one point of the periphery, most probably because the handle was attached there.

192

COMMENTARY - BIBLIOGRAPHY: Unpublished. See *Délos* XVIII, 274, no. 716, pl. 84; Lloyd-Morgan 1975, 107-116; *idem* 1981, 49-56, Group K (the earliest examples come from Italy; 1st half of 1st c. A.D.), esp. 55, no. 1, fig. 11a-b; Vierneisel 1978, 173, fig. 220.

N.S.

191

193 GOLD EARRING
1st-2nd c. A.D.

INV. NO. Θ 361.
D. OF LOOP 0.012 × 0.015, L. OF STONE 0.005 M., WT. 2 GR.

Loop-shaped earring with an emerald stone. The gold band-shaped piece is decorated on the edges with granulation and eight globules stuck on eight arches formed by folding the sheet metal in two. Two more single globules have been stuck on the hammered cylindrical wire which curves and ends in a hook and a loop. The grey-green emerald stone is fixed between the dotted sheet metal and the wire buckle of the loop.

COMMENTARY - BIBLIOGRAPHY: Unpublished.
The technique of the earring can be seen very well in

193

that of earring no. 149. For the decoration and the manner of fastening see Higgins 1961, 183, pl. 54 (1st c. B.C. - 3rd c. A.D.).

M.D.Th.

194 GOLD FINGER RING
1st c. A.D.

INV. NO. Θ 357.
D. 0.02, TH. 0.005, D. OF BEZEL 0.014, D. OF STONE 0.013 M., WT. 3 GR.

Gold ring with inset ring-stone, which has an incised representation, on its curved upper surface, of a head from the Dionysiac circle in profile facing left. The circular ring is made of sheet metal, curved on the outside, flat on the inside. The joining of the two is visible at one point of the periphery. The bezel holds a curved ovoid sealstone of transparent, red-brown garnet, which is framed by the doubled edge of a separate band of sheet metal and which has been stuck onto the interior of the bezel.

The figure depicted has marked facial features: large eyes with relief eyelashes and long eyebrow arch, half-open full lips and a serious face. The hair, divided horizontally in two by a band of antithetic ivy leaves, is pulled tight on the forehead in a ring. On the temple it is more loose, while at the nape it is gathered again in a kind of ring. On the side, two tight curls are formed, which fall onto the neck and nape.

COMMENTARY - BIBLIOGRAPHY: Unpublished.
The ivy-wreathed head belongs to a member of the Dionysiac entourage (Dionysos, Bacchus, Maenads, Bacchids), a particularly loved theme in Hellenistic art and iconography, especially in the court of the Ptolemies, where the worship of Dionysos and the related representations reached their peak from the 2nd c. B.C. In coin and gemstone representations of late Ptolemaic iconography, the Dionysiac circle was a major theme. The type was developed in the 3rd c. B.C., became widespread mainly on these objects and was popular again with variations in the Augustan era. The

elements of the type, which are the full face with marked facial features and particularly the schematic rendering of the hair and the technique of engraving, are recognised on the Athens ring, an exceptional accomplishment.

The depiction of the head on this ring can be paralleled with intaglios nos. 124, 127 and 128 of the Karapanos Collection in the Numismatic Museum in Athens (see Σβορώνος 1913, 154-155, pl. 2). The head no. 127, identified as a Maenad head (see Plantzos 1999, 86-97, pl. 61:410), has a comparable hair-style and facial characteristics with our own head, which also can be identified as a Maenad. Similar is the type of ring of garnet from Piraeus in the Benaki Museum, from the Augustan era, which bears an engraved representation of a head interpreted as a young Dionysos "in der mannweiblichen Form"; see Segall 1938, 84, pl. 25, no. 96. Cf. also gem intaglios of the 1st c. B.C. - 1st c. A.D., such as the head of a youthful, ivy-crowned Dionysos/Bacchus in profile; see *AGDS* IV, 115, no. 1370, pl. 67:496 (1st c. B.C.) and 383, pl. 263, no. 66, where the

194

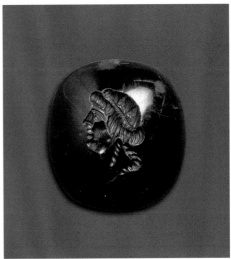

representation is interpreted as a Bacchid and the ring dated to the 1st half of the 1st c. A.D. Likewise, see Vollenweider 1984, 80, no. 124 (1st c. B.C.). Apart from coins and gems, similar types are also recognised on the seal impressions from Delos of the 2nd-1st c. B.C.; see Σταμπολίδης 1992. Lastly, for the type of ring see Hackens 1976, no. 66 (1st-3rd c. A.D.); Deppert-Lippitz 1985, pl. 38, nos. 89-90 (1st-2nd c. A.D.).

M.D.Th.

195 GOLD FINGER RING
1st-2nd c. A.D.

INV. NO. Θ 358.
D. OF HOOP 0.018 × 0.015, W. OF HOOP 0.003-0.005, DIM.
OF BEZEL 0.009 × 0.012, DIM. OF SIGNET 0.008 × 0.01 M.,
WT. 2 GR.

Ring inlaid with glass paste. The hoop consists of two joined gold pieces, the joint of which is barely discernible. The outside is semicircular in section and the empty space is covered with a separate layer of sheet. The oval-shaped bezel holds a curved glass, grey-white in colour on its upper curved surface, which has an engraved lion attacking a stag. The lion is portrayed proud and strong with his tufted tail raised and his forelegs on the back of the deer which is on its knees under the lion's weight, with its head still up and its hind right leg stretched to an almost horizontal position.

COMMENTARY - BIBLIOGRAPHY: Unpublished.
The theme of a group of animals was known and popular from Mycenaean seal engraving. There is a long series of seals, sealings and coins from the 5th c. B.C. and it continues into the Roman period. Especially for the representation on Roman gems see Richter 1971, 77, no. 368 and *AGDS* III, 161, pl. 83, no. 615 (2nd c. A.D.). On the type of ring see Deppert-Lippitz 1985, 31, pl. 49, no. 133 (1st-2nd c. A.D.).

M.D.Th.

196 GOLD TRILOBED LEAVES
1st-2nd c. A.D.

INV. NO. Θ 356.
L. 0.025-0.048, W. 0.015-0.035 M., TOTAL WT. 10 GR.

Sixty-nine trilobe shaped leaves in two sizes, fourty-six large and twenty-three small ones made of thin gold sheet with incised veins along the length and pointed ends.

COMMENTARY - BIBLIOGRAPHY: Unpublished.
The stone sarcophagus contained the skeleton of a male on which the leaves were found scattered, presumably having been attached onto the shroud as decoration. See Παπαποστόλου 1983, 6-7, on the use of such leaves and the relevant bibliography. See also the commentary on no. 146.

M.D.Th.

196

195   *194*

WATER-SUPPLY WORKS

197 COMPONENTS OF A TERRACOTTA PIPELINE
525-500 B.C.

TOTAL L. 2.041, L. OF STEM 0.605, EXT.D. 0.305 M.

Yellowish clay.
Part of a cylindrical terracotta pipeline, consisting of four components. It is chipped. Each part has a projection at one end and a dowel at the other in order to fit one into the next. The joints are strengthened by a wide and strong ring which opens outwards like a collar. Each section has three painted red bands one at either end and one in the middle. On the upper surface, on the right half of each component, there is a semicircular opening which was covered with a piece of tile of the appropriate shape judging from the one preserved on the section second from the right. On the left half, painted symbols have been preserved – letters of the alphabet accompanied by dots. Another painted symbol – the letter ⊕ – has been preserved on the tile/lid fragment that has been preserved. It is observed that the two letters are not accompanied by the same number of dots. (⊕ is accompanied by three dots when it is on the drain section and by one, when on the tile/lid).

COMMENTARY - BIBLIOGRAPHY: Unpublished.
This type of pipe has been thought to belong to the great water-supply network which began to be constructed during the Peisistratid era in Athens, i.e. between 527 and 510 B.C. The construction of such large works during the Archaic period seems to have been undertaken by the tyrants of independent cities like Megara, Corinth and Samos. It seems that it had become necessary then to provide the city with a stable supply of water. On the Archaic water-supply system see McKesson-Camp 1979, 62ff. and Tölle-Kastenbein 1994, 5ff. In particular, the water-supply network of Athens has been thought to have imitated the aqueduct built by Eupalinos on Samos, see Tölle-Kastenbein 1994, 102. The river Ilissos and its abounding springs on the north-eastern slopes of Hymettus were considered the starting point for this water-supply network during this period. The pipeline then continued and crossed the Ilissos valley following the right-hand river bed, a point which has been confirmed by the discovery of a large part of the pipeline orientated E-W at the EVANGELISMOS Station. About the starting point and course of the Archaic water-supply network see Ziller 1877, 107-131, fig. 6-9 and Tölle-Kastenbein 1994, 5ff. This system, on reaching the city, branched off in different directions in order to supply fountains and water tanks. About the relationship of this type of drain to the Enneakrounos Fountain ("fountain of nine faucets"), also a Peisistratid work, see Camp 1986, 42-44.
Judging from the fact that pipes of this type have been found at various points in the city, it seems that the system was expanded and repaired from time to time even after the late Archaic period. Concerning the construction phases of the system see Tölle-Kastenbein 1994, 103. This particular pipeline, typologically and chronologically, must belong to type 1 of Tölle-Kastenbein, as far as the Athenian water-supply network is concerned, which was considered the earliest and is dated to the last quarter of the 6th c. B.C.; see Tölle-Kastenbein 1994, 101. For typological parallels see op.cit., 48, no. 1, fig. 61-63 and 59, no. 21, fig. 90-92 (with a painted bust of a man), 62, no. 26, fig. 99.
A crucial element in the dating of the pipe is the presence of specific painted signs on its sections. For examples of pipe components with inscriptions see Tölle-Kastenbein 1994, 50, no. 4, fig. 68, with abstract sym-

197

bols 51, nos. 5 and 7, fig. 70 and 72 and with a painted bust of a man 59, no. 21, fig. 90-92; for the same see Knigge 1972, 612, 615, 621, fig. 46.1, 47.1, 48. These letters of the alphabet which are accompanied by dots may be interpreted as numerals, which played the role of guides to help fit the parts into their correct place, as the construction of a lengthy work requires. The type of letters belongs to the pre-Euclid script and so these letters should be dated to the end of the 6th c. B.C. The dating of the letters in combination with the clay quality and the careful manufacture of the sections and the comparison with examples from the Athenian Agora, on which painted symbols have also been preserved (see Lang 1968, no. 11, fig. 16) lead to the conclusion that the pipe which was found at the EVANGELIS-MOS Station belongs to the first construction phase of the water-supply system and must be dated to the last quarter of the 6th c. B.C. Consequently, this is part of the basic artery of the late Archaic aqueduct, which brought water to the city from the east and more specifically from the springs of Ilissos on the mount Hymettus.

E.L.T.

From the fill

198 FUNERARY MARBLE LOUTROPHOROS
360-350 B.C.

INV. NO. M 4634.
PRES.H. 0.41 M.

White Pentelic marble. The whole body, a small part of the neck and traces of the twisted handles on the shoulders are preserved. It is chipped. The body of the loutrophoros is decorated with petal-shaped stripes in relief which are crowned with a simple plaited band. Similar stripes on the shoulders.

COMMENTARY - BIBLIOGRAPHY: Unpublished.

Carved marble loutrophoroi were Attic burial monuments which appeared for the first time at the end of the 5th and beginning of the 4th c. B.C. (see Kokula 1984, 127) and flourished in the middle of the 4th c. B.C. Their production was discontinued in 317 B.C. when Demetrios of Phaleron passed a law against the use of luxurious grave monuments. They usually stood on rectangular bases or on marble tables, on which the name of the deceased was written. The type derives from the vase with the same name, the use of which was originally connected with the wedding ceremony and later it gained a symbolic character as a sign for the graves of unmarried people. On the connection between the loutrophoros-amphora with men and the loutrophoros-hydria with women see Kokula 1984, 116ff.; Boardman 1988, 171-179; Sabetai 1993, 145-146 and 159-161.

This specific example with the slender body and the simple decoration – especially that of the plaited band – and, in agreement with the typological parallels, must be dated to the peak in the production of these funerary vases, that is 360-350 B.C. For the marble loutrophoroi in general see Kokula 1984, and especially for a typological parallel see 198, no. 0.17, fig. 37,1.

E.L.T.

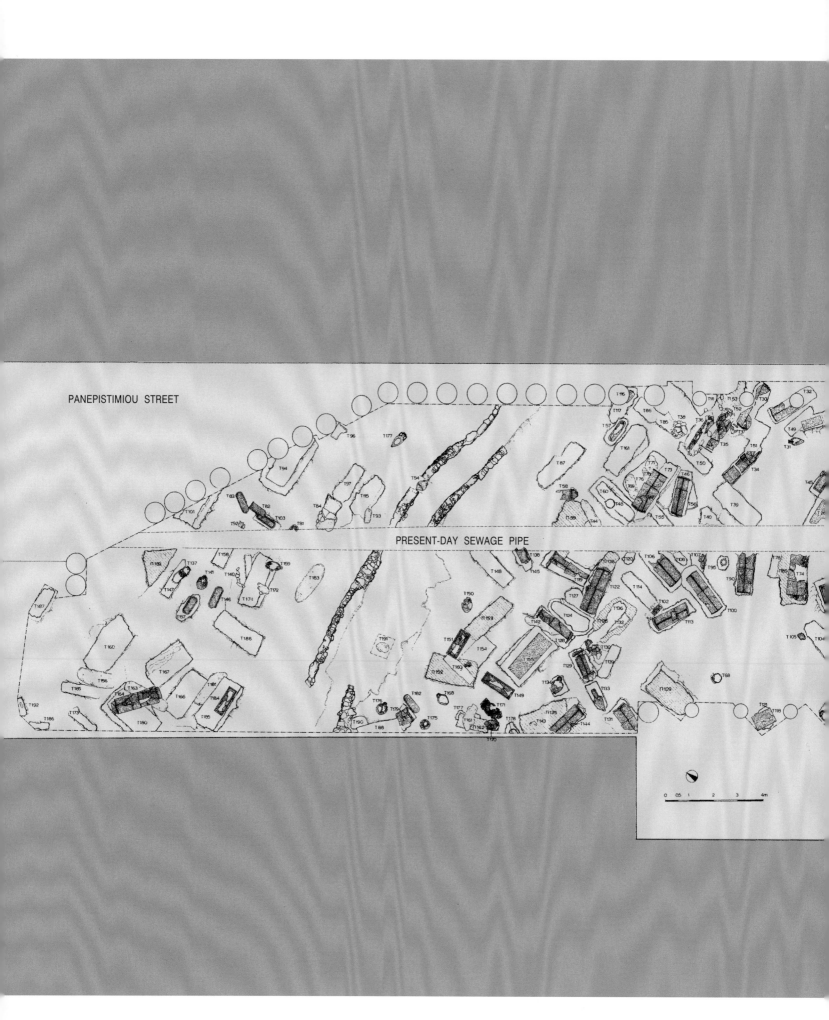

PANEPISTIMIOU STREET

PRESENT-DAY SEWAGE PIPE

0 0.5 1   2   3   4m

AMERIKIS Shaft

2. AMERIKIS Shaft. Tomb 155.

3. AMERIKIS Shaft. General view
of the excavation site.

The ventilation and inspection shaft of the M.R.A. at the junction of 11-13 Panepistimiou and 5 Amerikis Streets was excavated in 1995 and 1996. A total of 209 graves were found at depths ranging from 1.04 m. to 6.22 m. (fig. 1). The graves are part of the great cemetery of the ancient city of Athens which was first discovered under Karageorgi Servias Street in 1958. It has been excavated also at several points on Stadiou Street, but chiefly along the length of Panepistimiou and Amerikis Streets, its western boundary lying on Gregoriou V Street.

The graves uncovered in the AMERIKIS Shaft are for the most part pit burials, tile covered graves, children's clay tubs (larnakes), burials in pots, and cremations (fig. 2). Adult burials numbered 146, child burials 42. Most of the graves (148) contained offerings. A few graves had been plundered or had been disturbed by modern construction works. By far the greater number of graves dated to the Classical period (5th and 4th c. B.C.). There were also ten graves of the Roman period. A few, at the lowest levels, may be ascribed to the transitional years between the Archaic and Classical periods. The grave offerings were very numerous and of an exceptionally high quality; all were the products of Attic workshops. They included lekythoi, white-ground lekythoi (nos. 213-214, 220), squat lekythoi (nos. 215-219 and 221-223), skyphoi (no. 200), phialae, pitchers, kylikes (no. 211), feeders (no. 210), lekanides (nos. 201, 212), terracotta and glass jugs (nos. 199, 209, 202), pyxides (nos. 206, 226), askoi (no. 204), oil-flasks (no. 205), alabastra (nos. 224, 228), terracottas (no. 229) and metal objects (nos. 207, 225, 227).

At the north-western edge of the shaft the bedrock was found to have undergone a small man-made alteration with the addition of an embankment wall built in an E-W direction in order to retain a small torrent bed causing widespread flooding, given that at certain points in the area which borders on the Heridanos river there are steep declivities. Traces were identified of a workshop area (perhaps a foundry), commonly built close to cemeteries.

ELISSAVET HATZIPOULIOU

199 BLACK-FIGURE TREFOIL-MOUTHED OENOCHOE (CHOUS)
500-475 B.C.

INV. NO. A 15487.
H. 0.119, H. (INCL. HANDLE) 0.12, MAX.D. 0.09, B.D. 0.07, M.D. 0.053-0.066 M.

Complete, restored. Small part of the rim missing. Chips and flakes on the surface. Pink-brown clay. Ring base, ovoid body with a sigmoid section, broad neck, trefoil-mouth, vertical strap handle. Black glaze covers the vase. The resting surface is reserved, along with the lower part of the base.

On the main surface, there is a black-figure scene in a panel, framed by thin, black line. A donkey is depicted moving to the right. Behind the animal there is a thyrsos and below its lifted front leg there is the cornucopia. The scene is rendered rather schematically, with no additional details.

COMMENTARY - BIBLIOGRAPHY: Unpublished. These black-figure vases are manufactured in the period of the red-figure style, which is imitated in their own technique. The scenes are usually Dionysiac and the figures are rendered as silhouettes in lively movement. For the shape see Boardman 1974, 187, Class III (for oenochoae of sigmoid cross-section eventually becoming choes). *ABV* 439, Class of Vatican G.50; Van Hoorn 1951, 53-54, 162, fig. 419, no. 781, 166, fig. 807, 179, fig. 46, no. 899, 186, fig. 421, no. 947; Βοκοτοπούλου 1986, Α', 17, Β', pl. 14α and drawing 77ζ, no. 2008/Τ 5α (500-480 B.C.); Θρεψιάδης 1960, 28, pl. 28β, no. 164 (exactly the same shape from an excavation at 59 Panepistimiou Street); *CVA* Italia 48, Ferrara 2, pl. 8, nos. 1, 2, 3 and pl. 33, nos. 1, 2 (490 B.C.). The scene is rare. It indicates, however, a Dionysiac connotation, as attested by its three iconographic elements, the thyrsos, the horn and the donkey, the usual beast of Satyrs (see Lissarague 1987, 335-348). Donkeys also appear in similar red-figure vases, indicating the presence of Satyrs or Silens. For additional iconographical parallels see *Agora* XXIII, 42, pl. 72, nos. 754-772; Van Hoorn 1951, 143, fig. 98, no. 633; Hamilton 1992, 200 (no. 704), 201, no. 8619; Αλεξανδρή 1973, 149, pl. 110δ.

O.Z.

200 SKYPHOS ("ONE-HANDLER")
500-475 B.C.

INV. NO. A 15488.
H. 0.043, H. (INCL. HANDLE) 0.05, B.D. 0.074, M.D. 0.116 M.

Complete, mended. Chips and flakes mainly on the handle area. Pink-brown clay. Ring base, hemispherical body, horizontal, cylindrical handle rising slightly above the level of the rim. Shiny black glaze all over the vase.

On the bottom and the resting surface, reserved discs with dot within two concentric circles. On the body, two broad, reserved bands. Black-glazed band over the foot and a thin line around the resting surface.

COMMENTARY - BIBLIOGRAPHY: Unpublished. Banded single-handled skyphoi are a common Attic drinking vessel. This type appeared during the late Archaic period and remained in use well into the Classical period, covering a time-span of approximately 70 years (since 520-450 B.C.). During the 4th c. B.C., this shape survived in its black-glazed variation, while its use was interrupted during the Hellenistic period, at which time it was replaced by the handleless bowl. For parallels see *Agora* XII, 124-126, pl. 30, nos. 734-737 (500-480 B.C.) and *Kerameikos* IX, 107, pl. 26,6, no. 78, HW 39a, (480 B.C.) and 138, pl. 81, no. 215,9 (475-450 B.C.).

O.Z.

199

200

201 BLACK-GLAZED SINGLE-HANDLED LEKANIS
480-450 B.C.

INV. NO. A 15490.
H. 0.067, B.D. 0.058, M.D. 0.117 M.

Complete, flaked on the handle. Red-brown clay. It has one handle and a lid with knob-handle and a thin reserved band around it.

COMMENTARY - BIBLIOGRAPHY: Unpublished.
A product of an Attic workshop. For typological parallels see *Agora* XII, pl. 40-42 and *Kerameikos* IX, pl. 52, 94:2, 93:E65:2.

E.H.

202 SMALL GLASS-PASTE TREFOIL-MOUTHED OENOCHOE
500-450 B.C.

INV. NO. Δ 7339.
H. 0.072, H. (INCL. HANDLE) 0.08, MAX.D. 0.044, B.D. 0.024 M.

Mended. A small part of the base is missing. Glass in a deep blue colour. Discoid base, piriform body, short neck, trefoil mouth, vertical strap handle which rises a little above the rim. At the lower part of the base, a thin yellow line. On the body, a decoration with a continuous, zigzag line of blue colour, among bands of yellow colour. On the rim a thin blue band.

COMMENTARY - BIBLIOGRAPHY: Unpublished.
The technique used on these vases is attributed to the coastal cities of Phoenicia, but since the 6th c. B.C., they spread all over the ancient world. Their production began in Greece soon after, with the most important workshops settling in Rhodes and other islands of the Dodecanese. The shapes imitate their contemporary smaller clay vases (alabastra, amphoriskoi, aryballoi, oenochoae, etc.). Many of these vases are used as perfume pots or unguentaria and are usually placed in graves as burial offerings. The oenochoe was established as a widely accepted shape during the 5th c. B.C., decorated in various ways. The vases with this particular decoration (blue and yellow zigzag lines over a deep blue ground), spread in the Mediterranean countries from the late 6th c. and mostly during the first three quarters of the 5th c. B.C. For parallels see Davidson-Weinberg - McClellan 1992, 19, 20, 88, nos. 22-23 (500-450 B.C.); Harden 1981, 59-60, type 2a, nos. 258, 259-262; Grose 1989, 112-113, 149-150, fig. 114-116, type I B (late 6th-5th c. B.C.); *Αρχαία Μακεδονία* 1988, 220, no. 161 (480-470 B.C.); Ιγνατιάδου 1990-95, 226-227, fig. 23-3, no. Θε532 (500-450 B.C.).

O.Z.

201

202

203 BONE DICE
500-450 B.C.

INV. NO. Δ 7169.
DIM. 0.017 × 0.0185 × 0.018 M.

Complete. Severe damage to surface. The numbers on the six surfaces of the cubic die are indicated with small holes, sometimes pierced.

203

COMMENTARY - BIBLIOGRAPHY: Unpublished.
Dice of different materials, size and periods have been found from the Levantine coast to Etruria but also in mainland Greece and elsewhere. Together with astragaloi (knuckle-bones) they are evidence of table games of aristocratic society in the Archaic period, which we know from representations on black-figure vase-painting. Naturally, they continue in the Classical period. Cf. Laser 1987.
For numerous examples from all periods see *Corinth* XII 221-222, nos. 1739-1752, pl. 100; likewise, Dawkins 1929, 237, pl. 166; Μπόνιας 1998, 207, no. 520, pl. 61 (of ivory; 7th-6th c. B.C.). For clay examples see Σταμπολίδης 1994, 128; *idem*, 1996, 158-159, fig. 201-202.

N.S.

204 BLACK-GLAZED ASKOS
475-450 B.C.

INV. NO. A 15371.
H. 0.078, M.D. 0.032 M.

Complete. The handle is partially mended. On few parts chips and flakes. Red-brown clay. The body is covered in good quality black glaze, apart from the reserved underside of the base. The body is deep and broad. It has a vertical spout.

COMMENTARY - BIBLIOGRAPHY: Unpublished.
Askoi were produced in a variety of shapes. This particular example is among the earliest. It is mostly found after 480 B.C. and was not produced widely before the end of the century. On rare occasions, black-glazed askoi are decorated. Product of an Attic workshop. For the shape and typological parallels see *Agora* XII, 157ff., fig. 11, pl. 39:1166.

E.H.

204

205 BLACK-GLAZED OLPE
450 B.C.

INV. NO. A 15502.
H. 0.085, B.D. 0.03, M.D. 0.041 M.

Complete. Small chips all over the body which is covered with shiny glaze. Red-brown clay.

COMMENTARY - BIBLIOGRAPHY: Unpublished.
Tomb 176 is a burial contained in a pot. The vase is a product of an Attic workshop. It is a variant of the footless olpe, a popular shape in the 5th and 4th c. B.C. For the shape and for typological parallels see *Agora* XII, 78-79, fig. 3, pl. 13:265, 268.

E.H.

206 BLACK-GLAZED PYXIS
500-475 B.C.

INV. NO. A 15501.
H. (INCL. LID) 0.097, B.D. 0.086, M.D. 0.096, D. OF LID 0.076 M.

Complete. A few small chips and flakes mainly in the interior. Light brown clay. It is covered with black glaze, except for the underside and two thin bands on the shoulder and the lid. Ring base, bi-conical body. The lid bears a knob-handle with pointed tip.

COMMENTARY - BIBLIOGRAPHY: Unpublished.
The vase is a product of an Attic workshop. Pyxides, a name meaning "box", were very popular as women's articles. They were used as containers to store toiletries, perfumes and trinkets. Many of them were decorated. They have been mainly found in graves, as burial offerings. For the shape's history and for typological parallels see *Agora* XII, 173-178, fig. 11 and *Kerameikos* IX, pl. 44, 9:3, pl. 50, 88:1.

E.H.

207 BRONZE LADLE
c. 450 B.C.

INV. NO. Δ 7162.
H. 0.25, H. OF BOWL 0.027, D. OF BOWL 0.044 M.

Heavily oxidised bronze with encrustations and deep green patina.
The virtually vertical handle, rectangular in section, the upper part of which curves sharply ending in a schematic head of a water bird, widens towards its juncture with the bowl of the ladle. The latter is nearly hemispherical in shape with a lipless rim.

COMMENTARY - BIBLIOGRAPHY: Unpublished.
For the history and development of the shape see Strong 1966, 91-92, 115-116. For parallels see *Olynthus* X, 194-198, nos. 613 and 614-622 (shallow body and handle ending in swan's head), as well as 195, n. 25 (with extensive bibliography and examples); Τουράτσογλου 1986, 643, nos. M 1012-1013 (with plastic projection and swan's or duck's head on the handle); Ρωμιοπούλου 1989, 214, no. 16 (from tomb in Oraiokastrou Street, Thessaloniki); Μοσχονησιώτη 1992,

353, fig. 6 (from tomb 3 at Agios Mamas, Potidaia); Vermeule - Comstock 1972, 418, no. 605 (early Hellenistic). For more sumptuous examples see Θέμελης - Τουράτσογλου 1997, 104, no. Δ10 (bronze with handle ending in a lynx head), 70, no. B2 (silver with handle ending in a goose's head) and no. B26 (bronze with handle ending in swan's head). Likewise see Γιαννικουρή 1999, 65, no. M298, pl. 17β (inscribed ladle from the Sanctuary of Demeter on Rhodes; 4th c. B.C.).

N.S.

206

205

207

208 CLAY LARNAX WITH LID
450-425 B.C.

INV. NO. Δ 7337A-B.
L. 0.835, W. 0.346, INT.L. 0.73, INT. W. 0.26, H. 0.14 M.

Two identical rectangular larnakes, mended. The second is used as the lid of the first, which contained the deceased. Light red clay; there is an evenly coloured slip in a few places.

COMMENTARY - BIBLIOGRAPHY: Unpublished. It contained a child's burial. Vases nos. 209-212 belong to it. Clay larnakes are thought to imitate stone sarcophagi, which contained adult burials, but of smaller size and of cheaper quality of construction for burials of children, which comprise the overwhelming majority mainly during the 5th and 4th c. B.C. For this type of burial see Kurtz - Boardman 1971, 97-98. For contemporary parallels see *Kerameikos* IX, pl. 42:289.

E.H.

209 BLACK-GLAZED TREFOIL-MOUTHED OENOCHOISKE
420 B.C.

INV. NO. A 15482.
H. 0.08, B.D. 0.045, MAX.D. 0.067 M.

Complete with some chips and flakes. At the centre of the front part of the vase, opposite the handle, a relief Hermes stele is depicted. The Hermes head is bearded and the face is framed by locks. From both sides of the stele, there are lugs with suspension holes. The vase has a filling decoration of impressed palmettes and vertical ribs.

COMMENTARY - BIBLIOGRAPHY: Unpublished. The vase, product of an Attic workshop, was an offering in a child's burial in the clay tub (larnax) no. 208. The relief representation is unusual for black-glazed pottery, obviously deriving from metal-ware prototypes, possibly Macedonian; see Barr-Sharrar - Borza 1982. For Herms see Lullies 1931 and Wrede 1985.

E.H.

208

210 BLACK-GLAZED FEEDER
430-420 B.C.

INV. NO. A 15484.
H. 0.058, B.D. 0.036 M.

Intact. Hemispherical body with horizontal spout.

COMMENTARY - BIBLIOGRAPHY: Unpublished.
This type of vase is considered a feeder, since the few surviving examples bear traces of use and small teeth marks, which lead us to the conclusion that they were used by small children or adults who were physically impaired and could not eat properly. Another interpretation is that they were used for fluids (e.g. oil) for domestic use or for filling lamps. Since these vases were found mainly in graves, it is possible that they are grave offerings. The vase is a product of an Attic workshop. For the shape's history and for typological parallels see *Agora* XII, 161-162, pl. 39:1197-99 and Χαριτωνίδης 1958, 61, fig. 104.

E.H.

211 BLACK-GLAZED "BOLSAL" CUP
420 B.C.

INV. NO. A 15481.
H. 0.05, B.D. 0.066, M.D. 0.102 M.

Complete, with large chip on the rim. Ring foot. The entire body is covered with shiny black glaze.
On the inside, it has an impressed decoration of four palmettes set on a cross, enclosed in double circle framed by six more upright palmettes.

COMMENTARY - BIBLIOGRAPHY: Unpublished.
The type's conventional name (from BOL-ogna and SAL-onica) indicates the provenance of red-figure examples. This type, however, was created for black-glazed vases, its production continued until the 4th c. B.C., with its peak in the end of the 5th c. B.C. The vase is a product of an Attic workshop. For the shape's history and for typological parallels see *Agora* XII, 107-108, pl. 24:542.

E.H.

212 BLACK-GLAZED LEKANIS
450-420 B.C.

INV. NO. A 15483.
H. 0.055, B.D. 0.067, M.D. 0.112 M.

Part of the handle missing. Red-brown clay. The vase is covered all over with a good quality glaze.

COMMENTARY - BIBLIOGRAPHY: Unpublished.
The vase is a product of an Attic workshop. The lekanides were containers of everyday articles. The black-glazed lekanides especially belonged to the toilet articles and were a usual wedding gift and also a grave offering, since many of these were found in graves. They fall into many categories. This particular example is a Lycinic-type lekanis, a shape owing its name to Beazley. Usually, these lekanides are lidless. The particular shape occurs in the mid 5th c. and was abandoned in the mid 4th c. B.C. For the shape's history and for typological parallels see *Agora* XII, 167-170, fig. 11, pl. 42:1242.

E.H.

212

211

210

209

213 WHITE-GROUND LEKYTHOS
(MAIN TYPE)
c. 420 B.C.

INV. NO. A 15373.
H. 0.253, B.D. 0.05, D. OF RESTING RING 0.043,
D. AT SHOULDER LEVEL 0.069, M.D. 0.047 M.

Intact. Small chips and flakes partially, especially on the depiction of the young man.

In the centre of the scene a broad three-stepped stele, ending in dotted cornice. Three large acanthus leaves form the culmination of the stele, which is adorned with red bands. On the left, a young man in profile, facing right, is walking slowly towards the stele. On the right, a kneeling mourner is seen lamenting. The figures' garments, the himation of the young man and the long chiton of the woman, are rendered in a dark red colour, now faded. The scene's outline is also dark red. The band of simple clockwise meander which frames the scene is rendered in a deep-black colour. The shoulder is decorated with multi-leaved palmettes with alternate dark-red and black leaves.

COMMENTARY - BIBLIOGRAPHY: Unpublished.
For the iconographical theme of the "visitation to the tomb" see no. 237. For the kneeling mourner see no. 232. For the shoulder palmette see Kurtz 1975, fig. 23c (type II A, P. of the Woman). For the stele see Nakayama 1982, 126-129, pl. 23 (type E-V-4). For the bands decorating the stele see no. 377.
This lekythos was produced by the same hand that painted the white-ground lekythos in Tübingen, Sammlung des Archäologischen Institut des Universität, no. 5608, see *CVA* Tübingen 5, 70-71, fig. 32, pl. 31.5-7 [Burow]. The lekythos at Tübingen is in turn connected with the Group of Berlin 2459 (*ARV²* 1374), which follows the style of the P. of the Woman. Cf. also the white-ground lekythos attributed to the Style of the P. of the Woman [Buschor] in Berlin, Staatliche Museen, no. V.I. 3369 (*ARV²* 1373,2; *CVA* Berlin 8, 40-41, pl. 26,4-5. 7-9, pl. 31,3, Beil. 12.2) [Wehgartner] and the white-ground lekythos by the P. of the Woman in San Antonio, Museum of Art, no. 86.134.170, see Shapiro - Picón - Scott 1995, 196-197, cat. no. 99. For the P. of the Woman and the Groups following his style see

ARV² 1371-1376, 1692; *Para* 485; Stupperich 1979, 212-215.
Style of the P. of the Woman. Group of Berlin 2459.

G.K.

214 WHITE-GROUND LEKYTHOS (MAIN TYPE)
c. 420 B.C.

INV. NO. A 15372.
H. 0.282-0.298, B.D. 0.056, D. AT SHOULDER LEVEL 0.08,
M.D. 0.056 M.

Complete. The neck and the handle are mended.

At the centre of the scene, a large pedimental grave stele (the central and the right akroterion are red, the left akroterion is light blue). The stele is decorated with red and azure bands which are tied around it. On the left, a woman is shown in profile to the left holding a basket. On the right, a second woman is shown in profile to the left. On her extended arm she was probably once holding a band. Her hair is pulled back, over the nape, in a knot (λαμπάδιον). Both women wear purple chitons, their folds rendered in black strokes. The outlines are grey-black. The meander framing the scene is rendered in black, mostly faded today. The palmettes decorating the shoulder are also faded, with alternate leaves of black and red.

COMMENTARY - BIBLIOGRAPHY: Unpublished.
For the iconographical theme of the "visitation to the tomb" see no. 237. The shoulder's palmette belongs to the type II-A of Kurtz 1975, fig. 23c (P. of the Woman). For the stele, often found in scenes by the Reed P. and Group R., see Nakayama 1982, 77-78, pl. 14-16 (type B-V). The decoration of the shoulder connects this lekythos with the Workshop of the P. of the Woman, while the use of colours, especially of the azure, along with the type of the stele, connects it with Group R. For the Workshop of the P. of the Woman see no. 213. For the λαμπάδιον see no. 220. This lekythos is possibly the work of the same painter who decorated the unattributed lekythos in Paris, Petit Palais, no. 339, see *CVA* Petit Palais, 34, pl. 35.7-9 [Plautine].

G.K.

213

213, 214

215 BLACK-GLAZED RIBBED SQUAT LEKYTHOS
425-400 B.C.

INV. NO. A 15375.
H. 0.074, MAX.D. 0.048, B.D. 0.042, M.D. 0.027 M.

Complete with chips and flakes. Pink-brown clay. Ring base, globular body, short neck, echinus mouth with flat rim, vertical strap handle.
Shiny black glaze covers the vase. The resting surface and the lower part of the base are reserved. The body is decorated with plastic, vertical ribs that converge under the handle.

COMMENTARY - BIBLIOGRAPHY: Unpublished.
This shape appeared in the late Archaic period, but its use expands into the 2nd half of the 5th c. and the beginning of the 6th c. B.C. Basic study tool for its typology is Rudolph 1971. The group of ribbed lekythoi appeared in the 3rd quarter of the 5th c. B.C. and remained in use until its end. The grooves, made before the vase was glazed, are lighter in the earlier types and became deeper towards the end of the century. For parallels see *Agora* XII, 154, pl. 38, nos. 1129-1131 (420-400 B.C.); Χαριτωνίδης 1958, pl. 20β; Knigge 1966, 127, pl. 70,1, no. 4 (400 B.C.).

O.Z.

216 BLACK-GLAZED RIBBED SQUAT LEKYTHOS
425-400 B.C.

INV. NO. A 15376.
H. 0.075, MAX.D. 0.052, B.D. 0.044, M.D. 0.026 M.

COMMENTARY - BIBLIOGRAPHY: Unpublished.
For the shape, decoration and comments on the vase, see no. 215.

O.Z

217 BLACK-GLAZED SQUAT LEKYTHOS
End of 5th c. B.C.

INV. NO. A 15374.
H. 0.112, MAX.D. 0.068, B.D. 0.055, M.D. 0.036 M.

Intact. Chips and flakes on surface. Pink-brown clay. Ring base, globular body, short neck, echinus mouth with flat rim, vertical strap handle. Black dots all over. Black shiny glaze all over the vase. The

resting surface and the lower part of the foot are reserved. On the upper part of the body reserved band with S-pattern between black lines.

COMMENTARY - BIBLIOGRAPHY: Unpublished.
This shape appeared in the late Archaic period, but its use was extended in the 2nd half of the 5th c. and the beginning of the 4th c. B.C. Basic study tool for its typology is Rudolph 1971. The group of squat lekythoi with a patterned band below the shoulder is especially popular in the late 5th c. B.C. The band's decoration varies with the running volute being the most usual, the S- or Z-patterns, the dots and rarely the running tooth-pattern and the schematised ivy leaves. For parallels see *Agora* XII, 153-154, pl. 38, no. 1124 (425 B.C.); Schlörb-Vierneisel 1966, 37, pl. 38, no. 69 (HS 152; 3rd quarter of 5th c. B.C.) and 49, pl. 40, no. 100 (HS 163; end of 5th c. B.C. from the Kerameikos); Χαριτωνίδης 1958, 7, fig. 6, 29, fig. 48, 88, fig. 150 and pl. 18β; Μυλωνάς 1975, B, 289-290, Γ, pl. 429, nos. B27-B28; Γραμμένος - Τιβέριος 1984, 8, pl. 1β (420 B.C.).

O.Z

217

218

218 BLACK-GLAZED SQUAT LEKYTHOS
End of 5th c. B.C.

INV. NO. A 15377.
H. 0.106, MAX.D. 0.067, B.D. 0.051, M.D. 0.035 M.

Cf. no. 217. In no. 218, nevertheless, the reserved band on the upper part of the body is decorated with schematised ivy leaves between black bands.

COMMENTARY - BIBLIOGRAPHY: Unpublished. See no. 217.

O.Z.

219 RED-FIGURE SQUAT LEKYTHOS
End of 5th c. B.C.

INV. NO. A 15378.
H. 0.109, MAX.D. 0.065, B.D. 0.048, M.D. 0.03 M.

Intact. Parts of the body and the handle mended. Chips and flakes on the surface, especially on the area of the scene. Pink-brown clay. Ring base, globular body, short, thin neck, echinus mouth with flat rim, vertical strap handle. Shiny black glaze covers the vase. The resting surface and the lower part of the foot are reserved.

A female figure is depicted walking right, clad in long chiton and himation and holding an object (probably a ciste), with a ribbon hanging. In front of the figure there was an object, which is not detectable due to the vase's damage on this part. The ground in the scene is depicted by a wide red band.

COMMENTARY - BIBLIOGRAPHY: Unpublished.
This Attic type was widely spread during the 2nd half of the 5th and during the early 4th c. B.C. Basic study tool for its typology is Rudolph 1971. The scenes with female figures on these small vases are very common. They are either depicted seated, slightly bending or standing up, in motion, with their extended hands holding various objects. On this particular vase, the scene with the figure holding the ciste refers to figures of the wedding festivities (ἐπαύλια), who are often depicted on lids of lekanides and lebetes gamikoi at the end of the 5th and during the 4th c. B.C. For the themes standard in these scenes see *Agora* XXX, 47-48. On similar scenes see *Agora* XXX, 267-268, pl. 93, nos. 939-954 (end of 5th c. B.C.); Χαριτωνίδης 1958, 24, fig. 37, 82, fig. 140, 106, fig. 180 (end of 5th c. B.C.); Langlotz 1968, 116, pl. 209, no. 581 (430 B.C.); Μυλωνάς 1975, Β, 289-290, Γ, pl. 430, E24-336 and 337.

O.Z.

219

216

215

220 WHITE-GROUND LEKYTHOS (MAIN TYPE)
c. 420 B.C.

INV. NO. A 15533.
PRES.H. 0.35, D. AT SHOULDER LEVEL 0.132, M.D. 0.095 M.

Only the upper half of the lekythos is preserved, mended from many fragments. Flakes on the added colours. The matt outline on the shoulder decoration and the meander crowning the depiction is faded. The upper surface of the lip is covered with red ochre (miltos).

At the centre of the scene, a large funerary stele, ending in a double cornice and crowned with acanthus leaves. A red ribbon, which can be seen behind the seated woman, decorates the middle of the stele. Behind the stele, another broad tomb monument can be seen, with an Ionic cornice, probably a sarcophagus as the scrolls running on the side indicate. A woman, in profile on the right, is seated on the steps of the stele, in a melancholic mood, as one can understand from the slightly lowered head. She is wearing a chiton, part of which is rendered with added yellow colour (ochre). A head-cloth covers the back of her head and falls onto her shoulders. On the left, a woman in profile to the right is depicted, standing and wearing a chiton with purple border and cloak on her back. Her hair is gathered up over the neck in a knot. In her extended arms, she holds a red ribbon, of which only a small part is preserved. On the right, the scene is balanced by a young man in profile to the left, slightly bending and leaning with both hands on his staff. He wears an himation that leaves his torso uncovered. The outlines are matt red. Added yellow colour (ochre) was used for the chiton of the seated woman, while strokes of yellow enhance the women's hair. The palmettes (with red petals) decorating the shoulder, along with the meander crowning the scene, are quite flaked off. On the stele's cornice, as well as on the lekythos no. 237, one finds the, difficult to interpret, rectangular "notches". In addition, a shallow indentation on the white ground of the scene, perhaps for colour application, follows the outline of the seated woman's head-cloth.

COMMENTARY - BIBLIOGRAPHY. Unpublished.
For the Reed P., one of the most prolific lekythos painters of the end of the 5th c. B.C. and his workshop, see *ARV*² 1376-1382, 1692, 1704; *Para* 485, 524; *Addenda*² 370; Kurtz 1975, 58-68; Παπασπυρίδη 1923. Lately for the Reed P. see *CVA* Japan 2, 22, pl. 9 [Misuta]; *CVA* J.P. Getty 7, 63, pl. 384.3-4 and 385 [Neeft]; *APP* 1995, 55-56 [Oakley]. For the iconography of the "visitation to the tomb" and the youth leaning on his staff see commentary on no. 237. The pensiveness, the restrained sadness characterising the figures of this scene, is expressed with the slightly lowered head, see Plut., *Moralia* 528E [Lay-Einarson]: "ὡς γὰρ τὴν κατήφειαν ὁρίζονται λύπην κάτω βλέπειν ποιοῦσαν". See also Olmos 1980, 110-111. For the hair-knot (λαμπάδιον) see Olmos 1980, 121; Poll., *Onomastikon* 4.154; *CVA* Oxford, text on pl. 46.1 [Beazley]; cf. the Reed P. lekythos in Athens, NM, no. 1848 (*ARV*² 1379, 74). The stele belongs to the type E-V-12 and E-V-16 of Nakayama 1980, 126-129 and pl. 24. See also Παπασπυρίδη 1923, 122, fig. 2δ.
Closer parallels in style are the lekythos at Edinburgh, Hunterian Museum, no. 1908.388 (*ARV*² 1379,55 and *CVA* Edinburgh, 30, pl. 30.4-6 [Moignard]), on the sherds at Giessen, Antikensammlung der Justus-Liebig Universität, no. S-445 (*CVA* Giessen 1, 67, pl. 45.3 [Sipsie-Eschbach]) and in Tübingen, Sammlung des Archälogisches Institut des Universität, no. 5494 and no. S./10 1714 (*CVA* Tübingen 5,72, pl. 32.2-3 [Burow]) as well as on the lekythos in Madrid, Museo Arqueologico Nacional, no. 19499, see Olmos 1980, 99-102. Very close to this is another lekythos by the Reed P. from the north cemetery of Pydna, see Μπέσιος - Παππά n.p.d., pl. 57 (left), pl. 58 (top left) and pl. 59. For the traces of ochre and for bibliography on the use of various pigments see Θέμελης - Τουράτσογλου 1997, 59.
Reed P.

G.K.

220

220

221 RED-FIGURE SQUAT LEKYTHOS
End of 5th c. B.C.

INV. NO. A 15496.
H. 0.08, B.D. 0.037, MAX.D. 0.047, M.D. 0.026 M.

Complete. Mended from two pieces. Chips and flakes on the surface. Pink-brown clay. Ring base, globular body, short neck, echinus mouth with flat rim, vertical strap handle. Black glaze, which changes in parts into brown, all over the base. The resting surface is reserved.
On side A, a bird is depicted (swan or duck) in front of a schematised bird. The body's details are rendered with thin lines and dots. The ground is depicted by a red band.

COMMENTARY - BIBLIOGRAPHY: Unpublished.
For the shape of these vases, which are widely spread at the end of the 5th c. B.C., see Rudolph 1971, type XIII M (E687 in London and 231 in Göttingen), 65 no. 1, 66 nos. 6-7, 63 no. 2, pl. 30, nos. 3, 5. Depictions of birds are rather common. Painters of such vases depicting a single figure, human or animal, are listed by Beazley, *ARV²* 1353-1354, 1363-1364, 1366-1368 and 858, no. 9. Especially birds (swans, ducks, geese) are painted by the Al Mina P. and the Goose P. (Gans Maler). For similar scenes see also Wooley 1938, 23, fig. 8, no. 3; Langlotz 1968, 117, pl. 209, no. 589 (swan); *Olynthus* V, pl. 117, nos. 258-259 and esp. no. 260; *Olynthus* XII, pl. 101, no. 92 (swan or goose); *Corinth* VII₄, 4, pl. 29, no. 187Q; *Corinth* XIII, 72, fig. 23, pl. 70, no. 10 (swan); Σίνδος 1985, 210-211, pl. 331 (415-405 B.C.; goose); *CVA* USA 1, Hoppin and Gallatin Collection, pl. 26, no. 10 (goose); *CVA* Germany 26, Stuttgart 1, pl. 31, no. 3 (KAS139; swan).

O.Z.

222 RED-FIGURE SQUAT LEKYTHOS
End of 5th c. B.C.

INV. NO. A 15497.
H. 0.084, B.D. 0.037, MAX.D. 0.05, M.D. 0.03 M.

Intact. Chips and flakes on the surface. Pink-brown clay. Ring base, globular body, short neck, echinus mouth with flat rim, vertical strap handle. Black glaze covers the vase all over. The resting surface is reserved.
On side A, the head of a young man is depicted, in right profile, among volutes. The coiffure is characteristic, with locks of hair visible along the man's left cheek. The ground line is denoted by means of a band with running volutes and dots.

COMMENTARY - BIBLIOGRAPHY: Unpublished.
For the shape of these vases, whose use was widespread at the end of the 5th c. B.C., see Rudolph 1971, type XIIID, pl. 28, nos. 1-2. This particular iconographical type is quite common. Scenes of male busts (Hermes, youth) are depicted by the Al Mina P. and the Straggly P. (*ARV²* 1366-1368). For similar scenes see also Wooley 1938, 23, no. 1; Χαριτωνίδης 1958, 42-43, fig. 76, no. 4; *CVA* Great Britain 3, Oxford 1, pl. 40, no. 8 (1910, 71).

O.Z.

223 RED-FIGURE SQUAT LEKYTHOS
End of 5th c. B.C.

INV. NO. A 15498.
H. 0.077, B.D. 0.037, MAX.D. 0.048, M.D. 0.027 M.

Intact. Chips mainly on the left side of the scene. Pink-brown clay. Ring base, globular body, short neck, echinus mouth with flat base, vertical strap handle. Black glaze all over the vase. The resting surface reserved.
On side A, a female head with a sakos is depicted facing right in front of a volute; the details of the sakos rendered with thin bands and dots. On the woman's right cheek locks of hair. The ground of the scene is a reserved band.

COMMENTARY - BIBLIOGRAPHY: Unpublished.
For the shape of these vases, whose use was widespread at the end of the 5th c. B.C., see Rudolph 1971, type XIIID, pl. 28, nos. 1-2. This particular iconographi-

cal type is quite common. Scenes with women's busts are depicted by the Al Mina P. and the Straggly P. (*ARV²*, 1366-1368). For similar scenes see also Wooley 1938, 23, nos. 2 and 4-9; *Agora* XXX, 47-48, 269, pl. 94, nos. 969-971 (late 5th c. B.C.); *Olynthus* V, 47, pl. 116, no. 251 (4th c. B.C.); *CIRh* III, 77, fig. 166, 181, fig. 170; Langlotz 1968, 116, pl. 209, no. 582 (420 B.C.); Χαριτωνίδης 1958, 80, fig. 138, no. 4 (similar figures on a lekanis lid); *CVA* USA 1, Hoppin and Gallatin Collection, pl. 26, no. 2; *CVA* Germany 46, Würzburg 2, pl. 28, nos. 5-6 (with bibliography).

O.Z.

224 BLACK-GLAZED BULAS-TYPE ALABASTRON
End of 5th c. B.C.

INV. NO. A 15499.
H. 0.094, MAX.D. 0.028, M.D. 0.029 M.

Complete, mended. Chip on the rim. Flakes on the surface. Pink-brown clay. Fusiform body, short neck, disc-shaped mouth with flat rim.
The lower part of the vase is covered with black glaze and bears a reserved band with a white line. On the vase's upper part, between two broad black bands, a net-pattern with roughly added white dots. On the brim a black band.

COMMENTARY - BIBLIOGRAPHY: Unpublished.
The unusual shape of this alabastron indicates glass vases of Phoenician type. Alabastra with net-pattern appeared already in the 1st half of the 5th c. B.C.; see Kurtz 1975, 77, pl. 72, nos. 5-6 (1st half and 2nd-3rd quarter of the 5th c., respectively) and *CVA* Spain 3, Barcelona Museum 1, pl. 15, nos. 2-5 and 7-9. For the alabastra decorated in the Bulas type see Bulas 1932, 388-398, pl. XXI, nos. 5-9 and Beazley 1940-45, 15-17, pl. 4, nos. 13-14.

O.Z.

225 BRONZE STRIGIL
End of 5th c. B.C.

INV. NO. Δ 7163.
L. 0.143, W. OF HANDLE 0.005-0.011, W. OF STRIGIL 0.022 M.

Bronze with heavy oxidisation; at certain points, one can distinguish the original shiny brown surface. The tip of the main body of the strigil is broken.

A strap handle is curved in the middle of its length at a sharp corner and comes back parallel with the rear half, clearly narrower and ends in an ellipse which is fixed onto the exterior surface of the body of the strigil. The main part of the strigil is rather broad, curved on the interior, forming the curving angle roughly in the middle of its length.

COMMENTARY - BIBLIOGRAPHY: Unpublished.
Generally for strigils and their accessories see Πωλογιώργη 1988, 123-129 and Marwitz 1979. For typological parallels see Vermeule - Comstock 1972, 426, nos. 612-619, esp. no. 614 (5th c. B.C.); *Corinth* XII, 183, no. 1311, pl. 82 and no. 1315, pl. 82 (2nd quarter of 5th c. B.C.); Θέμελης - Τουράτσογλου 1997, 49, no. A125, pl. 54 (iron strigil); likewise A68 (bronze) and A76-79, Δ 56-59 (fragment of iron strigil), pl. 120; Δρούγου - Τουράτσογλου 1980, 179, drawing 47, esp. M 972, pl. 54 (2nd c. B.C.); Τουράτσογλου 1986, 645, no. M 1009, 1014 (iron strigils); Λιλιμπάκη-Ακαμάτη 1994, 161, no. 187, pl. 24 and 171, no. 248, pl. 27 (iron strigils; 2nd c. B.C.), as well as 196, no. 350, pl. 41 (iron strigils; 3rd-2nd c. B.C.); Πωλογιώργη 1998, 33, no. MΩ 384, pl. 7γ (iron strigil; late Hellenistic). Likewise, see *Kerameikos* XIV, 35, no. 23.4, pl. 33.11 (2nd quarter of 4th c. B.C.) and 113, no. 107.3, pl. 49.2 (350/40 B.C.); *Olynthus* X, 172-180, nos. 517-562 (bronze strigils) and 563-569 (iron), esp. nos. 542, 546, 549, 550 and 172 n. 49 (with bibliography). Likewise, cf. Kurtz - Boardman 1994, pl. 30 (grave stele of 430 B.C., where the deceased Eupheros holds a comparable strigil).

N.S.

223

222

221

224

225

226 RED-FIGURE PYXIS
c. 400 B.C.

INV. NO. A 15504.
H. 0.065, H. OF LID 0.061, M.D. 0.088, D. OF LID 0.099 M.

The body and lid are mended from many pieces, with various pieces restored mainly on the foot and the lid's flange. Chips and flakes on the scene. Tall ring base, cylindrical body, lid with tall, vertical wall and a slightly convex upper part.

The decoration appears on the vase's lid and presents a scene from a woman's life. On its vertical side, there are six figures, arranged in pairs facing each other. A woman is seated on a rock facing left, with a mirror in her extended right arm, looking at her maid who is walking towards her holding a box with ribbons. Behind the seated figure, an Eros is gathering fruit from a tree and putting it in a sack. Opposite him, another female figure is seated to the right, holding a mirror. Between the two figures stands a tree with fruit rendered in relief. Further to the right, the same tree is repeated, its fruit being gathered by a female figure and an Eros. The woman is placing the fruit in a basket; the Eros has both his arms extended, his himation hanging over his left arm.

The upper surface of the lid is decorated with two female figures, a male figure and an Eros. The central figure is the woman seated on a chair, putting her left hand on the back of the chair, while her right hand is bent behind her head. She is facing left but at the same time she turns her body backwards, looking at her maid who is standing, holding in her left hand a box with ribbons. The Eros is crouching, turning towards the female figure and looking carefully at an object in his left hand. Behind the Eros, a pigeon is shown with its wings open. The young man, with his left leg bent, is extending his right arm in an effort to pick fruit from a tree in front of him. The scene is framed beneath a reserved circle that outlines the

226

226

242

edge of the lid and over a concentric circle with dot in the centre.

Added white colour is used for the body of the Eros, and added azure for the back wing and for the pigeon. The tree, fruit and ornaments, are in relief. The front wing of the Eros is also rendered in relief and was probably once gilded.

COMMENTARY - BIBLIOGRAPHY: Unpublished.

This is a scene depicting women's life. It is a well-known theme in Attic pottery: richly-dressed women, with beautiful coiffures and jewellery, seated comfortably holding mirrors or other toiletries, accompanied by their maids who are holding boxes with ribbons. The ever present Eros, who appears repeatedly, creates a pleasant atmosphere. Beazley referred to the scenes as "the mistress and the maid", or "women, seated with Eros and women". Many of these scenes take place in a garden, a pleasant setting which inspires love and is connected with Aphrodite. The gardens, the Erotes, the beautiful women, all create an idyllic environment which was a theme presumably popular with Athenian women, allowing them to dream of escaping reality.

The pyxides, cosmetics containers, attracted men, who painted or bought them for their wives, and also women, who used them in their everyday life and took them to their grave. For these see Burn 1987, 82ff., pl. 51a-b (for similar scenes) and pl. 49a-b (for the relief ornaments, decoration of the wings of the Erotes and the relief fruit).

The depiction of the pigeon is unusual for scenes of such type. For a bird that looks like a pigeon see Nicole 1908, pl. 8-6 and Becatti 1974, pl. 14, 1-2. For an Eros gathering fruit see *CVA* Louvre 25 (France 38), pl. 49 and *CVA* Tübingen, pl. 42, 14. For the use of the pyxis in general see no. 272.

I.T.-D.

From tomb 5

227

227 BRONZE IMPLEMENT (SPATULA)
400-350 B.C.

INV. NO. Δ 7164.
L. 0.0845, D. OF HANDLE 0.0025, W. OF BODY 0.006 M.

Bronze with oxidisation and dark green patina.
Handle cylindrical in section which flattens out slightly as it approaches the body, which stretches out in a strip of uneven thickness with a curved tip.

COMMENTARY - BIBLIOGRAPHY: Unpublished.
For numerous examples see *Délos* XVIII, 222-223, fig. 249 and pl. 74, 599-601; *Olynthus* X, 352-354, no. 1689-1704, esp. no. 1689, pl. 112; Πωλογιώργη 1998, 29, no. ΜΩ 451, pl. 6β (1st c. B.C.).

N.S.

mouth. Lugs below the neck. On the body thin black lines and fading grooves.

COMMENTARY - BIBLIOGRAPHY: Unpublished.
It is a usual burial offering of the 4th and 3rd c. B.C. For this type of vase see Θέμελης - Τουράτσογλου 1997, 43 (with bibliography); Λιλιμπάκη-Ακαμάτη 1989-91, 87; Zaphiropoulou 1973, 615, fig. 18, nos. 22-29, 616, fig. 19, nos. 30-31 and 633; *Αρχαία Μακεδονία* 1988, 313, no. 269.

O.Z.

Tomb 72

228 ALABASTRON
350-300 B.C.

INV. NO. Δ 7154.
H. 0.124, MAX.D. 0.037, M.D. 0.053 M.

Complete. It has two parts. The neck and the rim are inlaid. Slightly convex foot, cylindrical body that is tapering to the upper part, short neck, broad disc-shaped

228

229 TERRACOTTA FIGURINE OF A DANCING
FEMALE FIGURE
350-300 B.C.

INV. NO. E 1038.
H. 0.21 M.

Complete, apart from a small chunk of the hair above the forehead. Rosy clay. Applied white paint on the main side, traces of blue on the clothing.

The figure, firmly frontal, is standing up on the points of her feet on top of a low four-sided base, in a dancing pose. She wears a chiton and himation which falls from the shoulders, covering the arms and body down to the ankles leaving the feet uncovered. The right arm, bent on the breast, is holding on to the himation, while the left is supported at the middle on the hips. The left leg is crossed over the right and is outlined beneath the clothing. The hem of the himation follows the movement of the legs with small waves below, whilst its end blows slightly at the sides to the left at the height of the thighs.

The neck is tall, the face ovoid with firm physiognomy which is rendered plastically, e.g. the eyeballs and eyelashes, the tightened lips, the small chin. The hair is covered at the back by a sakos, while divided in the middle at the front, it falls in waves onto the forehead and temples. She is wearing discoid earrings. The statuette is hollow inside with a large rectangular opening in the rear.

COMMENTARY - BIBLIOGRAPHY: Unpublished.
See a similar statuette, apart from the head, from Eleusis, Μυλωνάς 1975, B 91, no. Θ ειδ. 53, Γ, pl. 371β.
See also *Olynthus* VII, 53, nos. 185-186, pl. 23 (beginning of 4th c. B.C.); *Lindos* I, 698-699, pl. 138, no. 2971 (after 400 B.C.). For the head see *Kerameikos* XV, nos. 133-134, pl. 26.7,4. For the position of the legs and the hands see the statuettes of dancers covered with himation from the Boeotian workshop of the mid 4th c. B.C.: *BMC* I, 237, no. 886, pl. 128; *Fouilles de Delphes* V, pl. XXII:1; Bol - Kotera 1986, 117, no. 59; Winter 1903, II, 143ff.

Ih.K.

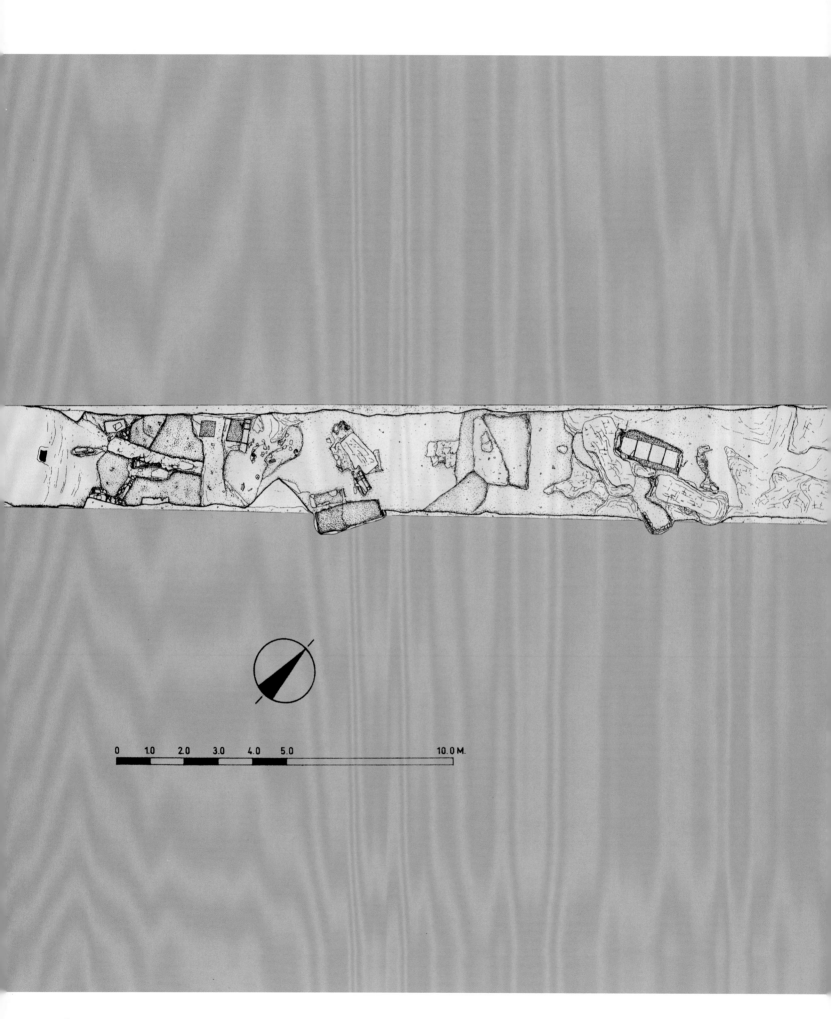

AKADIMIA Station

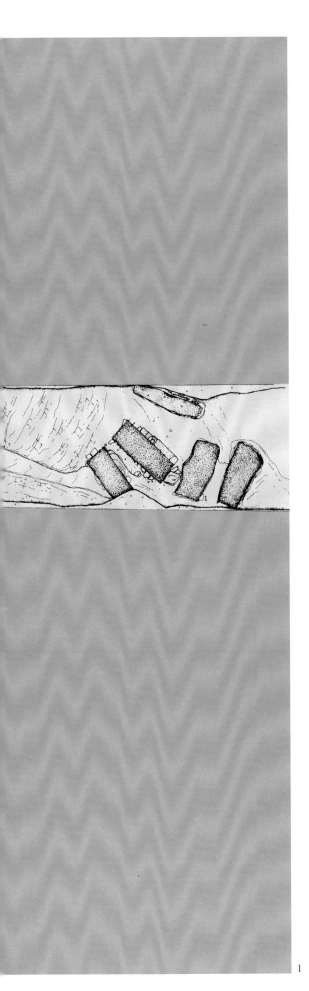

I nvestigation of a pit with a surface area of 1,104 sq.m. which was excavated on the Korai Street pedestrian way (fig. 1, 3) and comprises part of the AKADIMIA Station (today PANEPISTIMIO) of the M.R.A. produced a number of surprises. Previous excavations conducted by the 3rd Ephorate along the length of Panepistimiou and Stadiou Streets as far as Syntagma Square had revealed the most crowded cemetery on the north-eastern fringes of the city that had been in use from the 5th c. B.C. down to the 3rd or 4th c. A.D. Despite every indication of there having been a cemetery on the site, no grave had been found below the pavement of Korai Street or even in nearby excavations.

The discovery of the Athenian schistose bedrock directly beneath the paving-stones and bed of the pavement, together with the picture of the district conveyed by old maps of Athens, indicates that the area in which Korai Street lies was once a hill top, one of several that dominated the north-eastern part of the city. It would seem that the nature of the terrain discouraged the creation of a cemetery in this locality.

The only archaeological remains that had been discovered and investigated were two wells and a bell-shaped cistern, all quarried from the Athenian bedrock. The two circular wells, each 1 m. in diameter, were examined to a depth of about 3.50 m.; pottery collected from the fills were of Classical, Hellenistic and Roman date. The bell-shaped cistern, 1 m. wide at the top and 2.33 m. wide at the bottom, was accessed down a ramp and connected with an underground tunnel (fig. 2). A large quantity of household terracotta utensils of the 5th and 4th c. B.C. was gathered from the fills. Similar bell-shaped cisterns have been excavated in many parts of Athens: in the town centre, in the Theseion and Metaxourgeion districts, at Akadimia Platonos ("Plato's Academy") and elsewhere. An identical cistern and two more wells were examined in pits dug for the diversion of the public utilities network around the excavation of the Station.

During works connected with the Metro for the replacement of a large sewage pipe, part of a Classical and Roman cemetery was uncovered and an area of 92 sq.m. was examined. It lay at the western edge of the extensive congested cemetery previously excavated along the entire length of Panepistimiou and Stadiou Streets[1] to the point at which it abuts on Syntagma Square, where S. Haritonidis carried out noteworthy excavations in 1960[2].

Thirty-eight graves were examined on this site, many of them disturbed by earlier public utilities networks. The graves were crowded together and variously oriented. They were of familiar types: three were chamber tombs cut out of the natural rock with built entrances, six were rectangular quarried pits, six cist graves with stone, brick or marble walls, seven cremations in pits, twelve graves with pitched tile coverings, two burials of infants in pots and two infant burials in clay tubs (larnakes). There were eight instances of communal burials or the translation of several remains to a single grave, the original graves being re-used at a later time.

Six of the graves belonged to the Classical period, mainly the 2nd half of the 5th c. B.C., nine to the late Classical period, mainly the late 5th and early 4th c. B.C., six to the early Roman period, mainly the 1st c. B.C. to the 1st c. A.D., and four to Late Roman times, that is, to the end of the 3rd - beginning of the 4th c. A.D. The remaining thirteen graves, some destroyed, others rifled, provided insufficient evidence for them to be dated with certainty.

The offerings found in Classical and late Classical graves were lekythoi with black-figure decoration on a white ground (nos. 230-237), small aryballoid lekythoi, olpai, salt-cellars, kantharoi, skyphoi, bowls, alabastra, mirrors and pins. Roman and Late Roman graves contained miniature amphorae, pitchers (nos. 241-244), terracotta and glass perfume flasks, lamps (nos. 245-246), strigils (no. 238) and coins. In the child's tomb 4 there was a pair of children's gold earrings and a gold finger ring (nos. 240, 239).

Examination of the excavation made at the junction of Gregoriou V and Panepistimiou Streets was of importance from a topographical point of view, for it was here that the western boundary of the large cemetery was located. A little later, in an excavation conducted by the 3rd Ephorate at 33 Panepistimiou Street, exactly opposite, a section of the same cemetery was exposed which established its boundary on that side. The north-eastern cemetery serving this district is usually identified with the extensive burial ground lying beside the street and stretching from the Diochares Gates towards the Mesogeia; it was first opened at the beginning of the 4th c. B.C.

2. AKADIMIA Station (now PANEPISTIMIO).
The bell-shaped cistern.

3. AKADIMIA Station (now PANEPISTIMIO).
General view of the excavation site.

2

On the other hand the north-eastern cemetery was already in use in the 5th c. B.C. and was unusually congested, largely in its Classical phase, in the block defined by Panepistimiou, Amerikis, Stadiou and Voukourestiou Streets. This was demonstrated by many excavations made by the 3rd Ephorate, the latest being those in the AMERIKIS Shaft and at 3 Amerikis Street. The greatest congestion of graves in Athenian cemeteries is generally found close to roadways and the city's fortifications. This fact, taken in conjunction with the opening passage in Plato's dialogue *Lysis*[3] and a 19th-century examination made in the angle formed by Stadiou and Kolokotroni Streets[4], where evidence was found of the existence of a gateway, leads to the conclusion that the north-eastern cemetery was a roadside burial-ground beside a so far unknown road which set out from another gate or doorway in the city wall. Thus, it is now certain that in the greater district of eastern Athens there were once two distinct burial-grounds which may well, as time passed and in response to the constantly growing demand for burial space, have been amalgamated, as happened elsewhere in Athens.

OLGA ZACHARIADOU

3

NOTES

1. The cemetery was discovered on a large building site in the block bordered by Panepistimiou, Amerikis, Stadiou and Voukourestiou Streets (see Κυπαρίσσης 1924/25, 68-72) and during numerous excavations made by the 3rd Ephorate (see *ADelt* 15-36 (1960-1981)).
2. Χαριτωνίδης 1958, 1-152.
3. Pl., *Lysis*, 203A: "I was walking straight from the Academy to the Lyceum, by the road which skirts the outside of the walls, and had reached the little gate where is the source of the Panops, when I fell in with Hippothales, the son of Hieronymos, Ktesippos the Paeanian, and some more young men, standing together in a group. There, he replied, pointing out to me an enclosure facing the wall, with a door open." (Tr. by J. Wright, *Plato - The Collected Dialogues*, Bollingen Series LXXI, Pantheon Books, New York 1963).
4. Χαριτωνίδης 1958, 125, n. 3.

230   WHITE-GROUND LEKYTHOS (SECONDARY TYPE - ATL)
470-460 B.C.

INV. NO. A 15069.
H. 0.131, D. AT SHOULDER LEVEL 0.06 M.

Mended from many pieces and restored. The base, the handle and the neck are missing. Chips and flakes in the main body of the vase. The shoulder is reserved, decorated with a black ray pattern, while the junction with the neck is emphasised by a schematised tongue-pattern.

Nike is depicted standing in right profile. She wears a chiton and an himation rendered in thick violet colour. She holds in her two hands a band or flower wreath and raises it ritually over a low, cubic altar decorated on its side with a horizontal band or a branch (thallos).

On the altar's surface, one can see the flames of fire. The scene is rendered with quick strokes of shiny, gilded glaze, which is also detectable underneath the added violet colour of her himation. In the same glaze is also rendered the simple meander band, capping the scene, while the same band that represents the ground in the scene is black.

COMMENTARY - BIBLIOGRAPHY: Unpublished.
For the shape of the ATL lekythos and the Workshop of the Tymbos P. see no. 231. Vases depicting Nike raising a band over an altar are rather rare. Cf. an alabastron by the Villa Giulia P. (*ARV*² 625, 90, now lost). In one lekythos by the Providence P., once in the Antiquities market at Lugano, Nike is shown bending over the altar to place a band on it, see Παπουτσάκη-Σερμπέτη 1983, 121, no. 84. For the use of added colour in early Classical white-ground lekythoi see Wehgartner 1983, 16-29.
Workshop of the Tymbos P.

G.K.

230

231 WHITE-GROUND LEKYTHOS (SECONDARY TYPE - ATL)

c. 460 B.C.

INV. NO. A 15016.
H. 0.187, B.D. 0.049, D. OF RESTING SURFACE 0.04,
D. AT SHOULDER LEVEL 0.06, M.D. 0.042 M.

Complete. Mended and restored. The handle and part of the vase missing. Small chips on the vase. Flakes of black glaze mainly on the rim and the lower part of the vase.

A woman in a long chiton and himation, hair gathered over her neck in a bun tied with a band, is moving to the right, looking back, toward the small plank-shaped, three-stepped stele. In her open arms she appears to be holding a ribbon, now faded. The band of the meander crowning the scene is also faded. The shoulder and neck are reserved. The shoulder, reserved, is decorated with a black ray pattern while the transition to the neck is enhanced by a schematised tongue-pattern. The painter renders the scene with quick but firm strokes of shiny, golden glaze.

COMMENTARY - BIBLIOGRAPHY: Unpublished.
According to shape, no. 231 belongs to the category of lekythoi of the secondary type ATL, which were produced by the prolific workshop of the Tymbos P. and that of the Aeschines P. The lekythoi of this type are usually white-ground with reserved shoulder, while their pattern-work consists of black-figure palmettes or rays. See *ARV²* 675, 709; Kurtz 1975, 82-83, pl. 22-23; Stupperich 1979, 209-222 (esp. 209-211). For the Workshop of the Tymbos P. and the ATL lekythoi see recently Pülz 1991, 367-370. The position of the female figure resembles work by the Workshop of the Tymbos P. and that of the Aeschines P., cf. the white-ground lekythoi in Athens, NM, nos. 17923 and 18867 (Tymbos P.) and the red-figure lekythos in Athens, Ancient Agora Museum, no. P 10324, see Boulter 1963, 119, no. B7, pl. 37 (Aeschines P.). For the rendering of the characteristics of the face cf. the similar figures on the white-ground lekythoi at the NM, no. 12744 (*ARV²* 845, 166 and Καββαδίας 2000, cat. no. 173) and at the Staatliche Antikensammlugen und Glyptothek in Munich (ex. Schoen no. 77) (*ARV²* 845, 179 and Καββαδίας 2000, cat. no. 186). For a similar rendering of the breast by means of a semicircle, cf. the figures on the lebes gamikos at the Staatliche Museen, Berlin, no. F 2404 (*ARV²* 841, 70) and Καββαδίας 2000, cat. no. 74) as well as the Nolan-type amphora at the Graz, Universität, no. G21 (Καββαδίας 2000, cat. no. 130). On the Sabouroff P. see *ARV²* 837ff. Recently, see Oakley 1997, 105-106 and Καββαδίας 2000. For the type of the simple, oblong stele, see Nakayama 1982, 60-69 (type A-II). For the existence of small, wooden "plank" grave stelai, which bridged the gap between the prohibition of the construction of luxurious grave monuments at the end of the 6th or beginning of the 5th c. B.C., and their re-emergence around 430 B.C., see Scholl 1996, 204-205 with earlier bibliography. For the decoration of stelai with ribbons see no. 377. An overview of all views on the subject may be found in Τζάχου-Αλεξανδρή 1998, 82-83.

Sabouroff P.

G.K.

231

232 WHITE-GROUND LEKYTHOS (MAIN TYPE)

440-430 B.C.

INV. NO. A 15039.
H. 0.33, B.D. 0.073, D. OF RESTING SURFACE 0.065,
D. AT SHOULDER LEVEL 0.104, M.D. 0.065 M.

Complete. Mended from many fragments and restored.

At the centre of the depiction, a tall, pedimental stele on a two-stepped base, and decorated with many red ribbons. On the left, a young man standing frontally, a peripolos who is inclining his head gloomily to the right towards the stele. He is only wearing a deep-purple chlamys and a petasos on his shoulder. In his bent left hand, he holds up two spears, while the right hand is lowered to the waist. On his feet he wears tall boots. On the right, a lamenting mourner, kneeling in a position that probably depicts the position of worship. She holds up her left arm to her forehead, while extending her right one. Of her garment, only a few traces are left. The outlines are rendered with a thin matt red line, apart from the straps of the boots. The meander band crowning the scene is rendered with matt red glaze. The palmettes' leaves, decorating the shoulder, are rendered with alternate matt red and matt black glaze.

COMMENTARY - BIBLIOGRAPHY: Unpublished.
The P. of Munich 2335 was one of the last white-ground lekythoi painters who also worked with the red-figure technique. His career covers the 3rd quarter of

232

233

the 5th c. B.C. (*c.* 440-420 B.C.) and connects the Achilles P. Workshop in which he had initially worked with the Bird P. Workshop and other later lekythoi painters like, e.g., the Woman P. For the P. of Munich 2335 see *ARV*[2] 1161-1170, 1685, 1703, 1707; *Para* 458-459; *Addenda*[2] 337-338. See also Kurtz 1975, 55-56; Oakley 1990, 65 and Oakley 1997, 106. For the red-figure side of his work see Τιβέριος 1989.

Peripoloi were the young, lightly armed men who, before they were to return to the citizenry of Athèns, had to complete their military service in remote parts of Attica. See Pélékides 1962, 35-49; Hollein 1988, 165-175, esp. 162; Vidal-Naquet 1983, 31 and 162. The mourner was not the dead man's relative, but a professional mourner. Pl., *Laws* 800e [Burnet], tells us that in ancient Athens, there were professional mourners from Karia; "δέον ἂν εἴη μᾶλλον χορούς τινας ἔξωθεν μεμισθωμένους ᾠδούς, οἷον οἱ περὶ τοὺς τελευτήσαντας μισθούμενοι Καρικῇ τινι μούσῃ προπέμπουσι τοὺς τελευτήσαντας". On a lekythos by the Phiale P. in Athens, NM, no. 19335 (*ARV*[2] 1022, 139bis) a Thracian mourner is depicted; see Oakley 1990, 43, n. 300-301. The attitude of worship (προσκύνημα or προσκύνησις) pays homage to the dead, according to Plato; see *Republic* 469b [Burnet]: "τε καὶ προσκυνήσωμεν αὐτῶν τὰς θήκας;". Contrary to the wail (γόος) which helps in expressing the restrained grief of the deceased's relatives, the lament over the tomb was not spontaneous, but part of the funerary ceremony. For the iconographic theme and a list of similar scenes see Athusaki 1970, 45-53. Shapiro 1991, 651-652, connects these scenes with contemporary literary references from Tragedy; cf. Aeschylus, *Choephoroi*, 334-335 [Murray]: "δίπαις τοί σ' ἐπιτύμβιος θρῆνος ἀναστενάζει"; and 424-428: "ἔκοψα κομμὸν Ἄριον ἔν τε Κισσίας νόμοις ἰηλεμιστρίας, ἀπρικτόπληκτα πολυπάλακτα δ' ἦν ἰδεῖν ἐπασσυτεροτριβῆ τὰ χερὸς ὀρέγματα, ἄνωθεν ἀνέκαθεν, κτύπῳ δ' ἐπιρροθεῖ κροτητὸν ἀμὸν καὶ πανάθλιον κάρα". For the figures cf. the lekythoi in Athens, NM, no. 19354 (from Anavyssos Tomb, *ARV*[2] 1168, 131bis), no. 1947 (*ARV*[2] 1168,133; *Addenda*[2] 338), no. 14856 (*ARV*[2] 1168, 134), no. 12793 (*ARV*[2] 1168, 136) and in Cracow, Czartoryski Museum, no. 1251 (*ARV*[2] 1168, 127; *Addenda*[2] 338). For the pedimental stele with small field, with no akroteria, see Nakayama 1982, 75-77 and 216-219, pl. 12-13 (type B-IV). For the stele decoration with fillets and wreaths see no. 377. For the palmette pattern-work on the shoulder of the vase see Kurtz 1975, 32 and 160-161, fig. 22-24 (type II-A). For subject-matter of the "visitation to the tomb", see no. 237.

P. of Munich 2335.

G.K.

232

233 WHITE-GROUND LEKYTHOS (MAIN TYPE)
440-430 B.C.

INV. NO. A 15041.
H. 0.335, B.D. 0.075, D. OF RESTING SURFACE 0.061 M.

Mended from many pieces and restored. Large parts of the vase, the shoulder (almost entirely) with the neck and the mouth missing. Chips in parts. Flakes and signs of wear on the scene. The colours in many parts are faded. At the centre of the scene, a large, oblong stele, on a two-stepped base. It is decorated with violet ribbons ending in a red epikranon, crowned by a squatting hare to the left. On the left a young man is depicted frontally, who is turning and slightly inclining his head to the stele. He is standing relaxed with his right hand on the waist. In his bent left hand, he holds a spear. He is only wearing an himation, which leaves three quarters of his torso uncovered. The folds of the red himation are rendered with strokes of black glaze.

On the right a woman in profile to the left, approaching the stele and holding in her right, bent arm a globular aryballos, obviously an offering to the dead youth. She is wearing a chiton, barely detectable over her right arm and a red himation, with its folds rendered with black glaze. The slightly tilted head and the lowered gaze, not fixed on anyone, convey with sensitivity the restrained sadness of the scene. The scene and the meander band above it are rendered with matt violet outlines. On the part of the shoulder that is preserved, one can see a palmette with matt black colour.

COMMENTARY - BIBLIOGRAPHY: Unpublished.
For the "visitation to the tomb" see commentary on no. 237. For the P. of Munich 2335 see no. 232. The rendering of the figures, especially of the woman, is indicative of the strong influence of the Achilles P. and parallels are found in other lekythoi by of the P. of Munich 2335, like those in Athens, NM, no. 19354 (*ARV²* 1168, 131bis) and NM, no. 19358 (*Para* 467, unattributed, between the P. of Munich 2335 and the Bird P. They come from a tomb in Anavyssos, where two white-ground lekythoi by the Bird P., one of the Phiale P. and one of the Achilles P. were found together; see Kurtz 1975, 53-54). Cf. also the lekythos in Athens, NM, no. 1947 (*ARV²* 1168, 133) and the hydria bearer on the lekythos in New York, Metropolitan Museum, no. 34.32.2 (*ARV²* 1168, 131). For the form of the stele see Nakayama 1982, 64-65, type A-IV-25/31 (P. of Munich 2335 and Bird P.), 208, pl. 9. Hare on a frieze of a stele is also depicted on a lekythos connected with the Achilles P. in New York, Metropolitan Museum, no.

233

06.1075, see Kurtz 1975, 51, 216, pl. 39,1; Nakayama 1982, 64, pl. 9, type A-IV-24; Oakley 1997, 168, no. L60, pl. 175A. Hare hunt is depicted in two white lekythoi by the Thanatos P., in London, British Museum, no. D60 (*ARV²* 1230, 37) and in Bonn, Akademisches Museum, no. 1011 (*ARV²* 1230, 38).
P. of Munich 2335.

G.K.

234

236

235

234 WHITE-GROUND LEKYTHOS (MAIN TYPE)
440-430 B.C.

INV. NO. A 15040.
H. 0.275, B.D. 0.062, D. OF RESTING SURFACE 0.055,
D. AT SHOULDER LEVEL 0.084, M.D. 0.052 M.

Complete. Mended from many fragments and restored. Chips on the shoulder and the neck. Flakes and signs of deterioration on the scene.
At the centre of the depiction, a funerary stele with a palmetted frieze, on a broad base. Around the stele and its base five red ribbons are bound with terminal strings. On the left, a young warrior on the right in profile, slowly approaches the stele. He is wearing a deep-purple chlamys and a petasos behind his back. In his bent, right hand he is holding diagonally, two large spears. On his feet he wears boots rendered with red colour. The paint on the youth's head is flaked. On the right, a mourner in a frontal position is turning her head left towards the stele and the young man. She has both hands bent on the chest, as a sign of grief and mourning. Of her red multi-folded garment, only a few folds are saved; the rest is flaked. The outlines are matt black. Matt black colour on the meander band crowning the scene along with the palmettes and the Ionic moulding.

COMMENTARY - BIBLIOGRAPHY: Unpublished.
For the iconography, the peripolos and the mourner see no. 232. The palmette decorating the shoulder of the vase belongs to the type II-A of Kurtz. The palmette adapted to the cornice of the stele without intermediate tendrils is close to the type D-II of Nakayama 1982, 93, 101-103, pl. 18-19. For the rendering of the figures cf. a white lekythos of the Bird P. style in New York, Metropolitan Museum, no. 22.139.10; see *ARV²* 1236 (a) and Kurtz 1975, 55, pl. 41.2-3.
Style of the Bird P.

G.K.

235 WHITE-GROUND LEKYTHOS (MAIN TYPE)
440-430 B.C.

INV. NO. A 15046.
H. 0.23, B.D. 0.053, D. OF RESTING SURFACE 0.048,
D. AT SHOULDER LEVEL 0.072, M.D. 0.045 M.

Complete. Mended from many fragments and restored, mainly on the shoulder and the upper part of the vase's main body.
At the centre of the scene, a tall pedimental stele on a two-stepped base. It is decorated with red ribbons, bound around it, now faded. On the left, a woman in right profile is walking towards the stele holding in her extended hands a ribbon, now faded. Her red garment is also faded, with very few traces found, mainly between the hands and the feet. On the right, a young warrior is standing in frontal position, turning his head to the left towards the stele. He is wearing deep-purple chlamys and a petasos behind his back. In his feet he wears boots with black straps. The young man is extending his right hand to the woman. The outlines, the meander crowning the scene, the palmettes and the Ionic moulding on the shoulder are all rendered with matt black colour.

COMMENTARY - BIBLIOGRAPHY: Unpublished.
For the "visitation to the tomb" see no. 237. For the peripolos see commentary on no. 232. For the ribbons see the commentary on no. 377. For the shoulder palmette see Kurtz 1975, fig. 23 (type II-A). For the type of stele see Nakayama 1982, 64-65, 203, pl. 7 (type A III-12). For the Sabouroff P. see commentary on no. 236.
Style of the Sabouroff P.

G.K.

236 WHITE-GROUND LEKYTHOS (MAIN TYPE)
440-430 B.C.

INV. NO. A 15042.
PRES.H. 0.25, B.D. 0.072, D. OF RESTING SURFACE 0.064,
D. AT SHOULDER LEVEL 0.096 M.

Mended and restored. Handle, neck, and mouth missing. Large chips and flakes in parts. The colours are faded in many parts.
At the centre of the scene, an oblong pedimental stele on a three-stepped base. The stele's cornice is rendered with a hor-

izontal dotted band. The stele is decorated with red ribbons bound around it and on the steps. On the left, a woman in right profile, is approaching to decorate the stele with a red ribbon, now faded, that she is holding in her extended hands. She is wearing a long chiton, now faded from the knees down. On the right, a man is standing frontally, turning his head left towards the stele. He is wearing a long, red himation, with its folds rendered with matt black colour. The himation covers his body, except for the half right part of his torso and the right hand, placed on the waist. The scene's outlines and the crowning meander, are in a matt black colour. The shoulder is decorated with palmettes with alternate leaves of matt black and red colour. Also with matt black colour, the Ionic moulding at the join of the shoulder to the neck.

COMMENTARY - BIBLIOGRAPHY: Unpublished.
For the "visitation to the tomb" see commentary on no. 237. For the Sabouroff P. see Oakley 1997, 105-106 and Καββαδίας 2000. Closer parallels: NM, no. 17324, see Καββαδίας 2000, cat. no. 221 (*ARV²* 847, 211) and NM, no. 17314, see Καββαδίας 2000, cat. no. 247 (*ARV²* 849, 247), of the Acropolis Museum (no inv. no.), see Καββαδίας 2000, cat. no. 231 (*ARV²* 848, 221) and of New York, Metropolitan Museum, no. 06.1021.132, Καββαδίας 2000, cat. no. 255 (*ARV²* 849, 245). For the pedimental stele see Nakayama 1982, 78-85, 213 and pl. 11 (type B-II-1 and B-II-2). Cf. the lekythos at Oxford, Ashmolean Museum, no. 1966.771, see Καββαδίας 2000, cat. no. 273 (*ARV²* 850, 264). For the ribbons see commentary on no. 377.
Style of the Sabouroff P. (late period).

G.K.

From tomb 33

237 WHITE-GROUND LEKYTHOS (MAIN TYPE)
420-410 B.C.

INV. NO. A 15037.
H. 0.343, B.D. 0.082, D. OF RESTING SURFACE 0.078,
D. AT SHOULDER LEVEL 0.192 M.

Mended from many fragments. Large part of the shoulder, the handle and the mouth missing.
In the centre of the scene, a large funeral monument is depicted. It consists of a

stele with cornice and a lyre-shaped palmette, which is framed by a pair of two large acanthus leaves. A large, oblong monument is in front of the stele, or forms its base and is possibly identified with an offering table. Two lekythoi on the table frame the stele. The stele and the lekythoi, perhaps made of stone, are decorated with ribbons. The front side of the table is covered with a heavily ornamented cloth, the hem of which is rendered with dots. The ribbons and the cloth are rendered with violet colour, almost completely faded now. On the cornice, two rows of, difficult to identify, irregular lozenge-shaped notches of the white ground of the scene, nine up and six down, as if the painter wanted to either scrape off the decoration or the inscription that existed in this area, or on the contrary, to prepare the surface in order to apply colour.

On the left, a young man with himation, holding a ribbon and leaning on his staff. The himation's violet colour has almost

completely faded apart from the lower hem. On it, five irregular violet dots are depicted. On the right, the scene is balanced by a woman in left profile. In her right bent hand she is holding a large basket, while with her left one, she is raising her chiton's hem, according to the "ἡραῖον σχῆμα". The colour of the chiton is faded. The meander band above the scene and the palmettes decorating the shoulder of the vase are also faded.

COMMENTARY - BIBLIOGRAPHY: Unpublished.
The figures of the Triglyph P., who was the last of the lekythoi painters, are statuesque and are characterised by monumentality. For the Triglyph P. see *ARV*[2] 1835, *Addenda*[2] 372. See also Kurtz 1975, 66-69 and *Agora* XXX, 46. The grave monument with the large base probably combines the oblong stele with palmette finial and the table. For the tables see Δεσπίνης 1963, 47-48 and Nakayama 1982, 43-59 "Blockförmiges Grabmonument-Grabbau" and 248-250 (type E-V-19) - (E-V-30). The "visitation to the tomb" is the most common theme of the white-ground lekythoi, see Garland 1985, 104-120; Kurtz-Boardman 1985, 169-187; Lissa-

rague 1991, 159-251, esp. 189-190; lately see Oakley 1997, 66-69 and Τζάχου-Αλεξανδρή 1998, 81-86. In Athenian iconography, the young man leaning on his staff represents the model young Athenian citizen, see Hollein 1988 and Wehgartner 1989, 223-231. For the "ἡραῖον σχῆμα" and female revealing gestures see *Pandora* 126-128. The "ἡραῖον σχῆμα" is well known from another lekythos by the Triglyph P. in Madrid, Museo Arquelogico Nacional, no. 11192, see Olmos 1980, 12-124, cat. no. 31.

In the basket (kanistron or kanoun), women carried all the necessary articles for the worship at the tomb, like perfume pots, wreaths, ribbons etc., see Schelp 1975 and Reilly 1989, 417ff. For the ribbons decorating the grave see commentary on no. 377. There is no satisfactory explanation for the characteristic violet dots that fill the ground of the depiction in the white-ground lekythoi by the Triglyph P. They have been identified with leaves, buds, olive or myrtle fruit, etc., see Olmos 1980, 117-120 and *CVA* Berlin 8, 51 [Wehgartner]. For the acanthus see Meurer 1909, 133ff. and Richards-Ματζουλίνου 1981. The notches on the stele indicate a painted inscription, which was erased for some unknown reason. Inscriptions on stele depicted on white lekythoi are rare. Cf. the Akrisios white-ground lekythos in Bern, see Wehgartner 1989, 223-231.
Triglyph P.

G.K.

From tomb 22

238 BRONZE STRIGIL
1st-2nd c. A.D.

INV. NO. Δ 7167.
L. 0.208, L. OF HANDLE 0.08, W. OF BODY 0.007-0.016 M.

Complete. Mended from four joining fragments. Bronze with dark green patina. The handle, almost rectangular in section, has a rectangular perforation on its upper part. The slender, strap-shaped lamina of the main body of the scraper, of uneven width and convex on the inner side, curves sharply in roughly the middle of its length and outwards at its tip.

COMMENTARY - BIBLIOGRAPHY: Unpublished.
A cloth band or leather strap passed through the perforation to facilitate suspension. Cf. Kulov 1999, 64-66, pl. 3 (2nd-3rd c. A.D.). For the type see Vagalinski 1992, 435-445.

N.S.

237

239

238

From tomb 4

239   GOLD FINGER RING
2nd-3rd c. A.D.

INV. NO. Θ 323.
D. 0.015, W. OF LOOP 0.005-0.001 M., WT. 3 GR.

Child's finger ring inlaid with a gem-stone. Its solid loop comprises a curved exterior and flat interior hammered lam-ina and the transition to the raised, ovoid bezel is achieved by pressing its walls to-gether, which are swollen, concave at the base of the two sides. It holds the red-brown cornelian, which has an engraved symbolic representation of a palm with fingers extended, apart from the middle and index, which is curved and converg-es towards the thumb.

COMMENTARY - BIBLIOGRAPHY: Unpublished.
The position of the fingers suggests that there was something between them which is not shown. It is a question of the symbolic representation of an ear known from other engraved ring stones, the lobe of which is held or touched by the fingers of a right hand as a reminder or an expression of feelings of love or friendship to the owner of the ring, the meaning of which is often stressed with the addition of a remind-

ing inscription such as e.g. MNHMONEYE or MEMENTO. Similar representations of a hand on gems in the Kara-panos Collection at the Numismatic Museum of Ath-ens, see Σβορώνος 1913, 171, pl. VIII, nos. 602-604. In relation to the representation of a hand, as it appears from the 2nd c. B.C. and the corresponding interpreta-tions, see *AGDS* II, 198, pl. 96, no. 562 (2nd c. A.D.); *AGDS* IV, pl. 219, no. 1652 (2nd c. A.D.). Likewise, see Vollenweider 1979, II, 499-500, pl. 140, 2-3 (1st c. B.C.). On the same subject from the 1st c. B.C. to the 3rd c. A.D., with full bibliography, see *AGDS* Nürnberg, 158-159ff., esp. pl. 61:48 (1st c. A.D.).

M.D.Th.

240   PAIR OF GOLD EARRINGS
2nd-3rd c. A.D.

INV. NO. Θ 324A, B.
D. 0.011-0.015 M., TOTAL WT. 1 GR.

Earrings of a child consisting of a ring of gold wire, the ends of which form a hook and loop for fastening. The cylindrical holder has been attached to the side of the loop, with a wire edging for the stones that are now missing and a wire loop stuck onto its side, perhaps for hanging another ornament.

239

COMMENTARY - BIBLIOGRAPHY: Unpublished.
See in relation to this type of earring Davidson - Oliver 1984, 119, nos. 133, 134 (2nd-3rd c. A.D.); Deppert-Lippitz 1985, 20, pl. 19, 47 (2nd c. A.D.). Likewise cf. the somewhat similar earrings with their holders, Athens, Byzantine Museum, no. 4067, *Ελληνικό Κόσμημα* 1997, 177, no. 188 (which, however, have been dated to the 4th-6th c. A.D.).

M.D.Th.

241 AMPHORA
Late 3rd - early 4th c. A.D.

INV. NO. A 15000.
H. 0.211, B.D. 0.088, MAX.D. 0.16 M.

Part of the mouth missing. Chips on the base and the handles. Orange clay. Ring base, ovoid body, short neck, flaring rim, vertical strap handles on the shoulder. The larger part of the vase is covered with thin, runny red glaze. Group of grooves on the shoulder, at the base of the neck and below the rim.

COMMENTARY - BIBLIOGRAPHY: Unpublished.
For parallels see *Agora* V, 65, 74, pl. 16, no. L3 (2nd half of 3rd c. A.D.) and pl. 13, no. K68 (mid 3rd c. A.D.).

O.Z.

242 AMPHORA
Late 3rd - early 4th c. A.D.

INV. NO. A 15003.
H. 0.196, B.D. 0.062, MAX.D. 0.12, M.D. 0.046 M.

Mended from many pieces. Parts of the body, the lip and base missing. Flakes on the vase. Orange clay. Ring base, piriform body, short neck, flaring ring-shaped lip, strap handles.
Grooves on the neck, body and handles. Incised lines on the base of the neck, on shoulder and handles. The larger part of the vase is covered with red, runny glaze. The base and the lower part of the body are unglazed.

COMMENTARY - BIBLIOGRAPHY: Unpublished.
For parallels see *Agora* V, 74, 77, pl. 16, nos. L3 and L28 (2nd half of 3rd c. A.D.).

O.Z.

243 AMPHORA
Late 3rd - early 4th c. A.D.

INV. NO. A 15001.
H. 0.21, B.D. 0.056, MAX.D. 0.125, M.D. 0.05 M.

Mended from many pieces. One handle and fragments of the body and rim missing. Pure, red clay. Ring base, ovoid body, low neck tapering on the upper part, everted ring rim, vertical strap handles on the shoulder. Grooves on the body and the handles, incisions on the shoulder and below the rim.

COMMENTARY - BIBLIOGRAPHY: Unpublished.
For parallels see *Agora* V, 77, no. L30, pl. 16 (beginning of 4th c. B.C.).

O.Z.

244 UNGLAZED PROCHOUS
Late 3rd - early 4th c. A.D.

INV. NO. A 15002.
H. 0.21-0.215, B.D. 0.105, MAX.D. 0.165, M.D. 0.058 M.

Intact with slight chips on the foot. Brown clay. Flat base, pear-shaped body, very low neck, thick ring rim, vertical strap handle on the shoulder.
Shallow incised circles on the resting surface. Comb pattern on the body, thin incision on the shoulder. Vertical groove on the handle.

COMMENTARY - BIBLIOGRAPHY: Unpublished.
For parallels see *Agora* V, 77, pl. 16, no. L27 (early 4th c. A.D.).

O.Z.

241

245

246

24

245 SINGLE-SPOUTED LAMP
Late 3rd - early 4th c. A.D.

INV. NO. Δ 7000.
L. 0.115, H. 0.032, B.D. 0.037, MAX.W. 0.089 M.

Almost intact. Small part of the disc missing. Slight chips on the base. Buff clay. Low ring base, hemispherical squat body, concave disc, short conical nozzle. Solid, semicircular handle with suspension hole. The lamp is mould-made. Unglazed. On the resting surface, a double ring. On the disc, around the filling hole, ray-pattern among incised rings. On the disc's edge, alternate vine leaves and grapes. Deep grooves on the handle and a relief ivy leaf on its edge.

COMMENTARY - BIBLIOGRAPHY: Unpublished.
The relief leaf is the emblem of a large Athenian workshop, known as the "Leaf Workshop", which blooms from the early 3rd until the late 4th c. A.D. For this emblem see *Agora* VII, 163, pl. 34, no. 2076 and Karivieri 1996, 146-148, pl. 29, no. 300. The decoration with vine leaves and grapes is along with rosettes the most popular themes of the workshop and this decoration type was being constantly reproduced from the 3rd till the 5th c. A.D. For parallels see *Agora* VII, 21, 146, fig. 28, no. 1544 (mid 3rd c. A.D.) or no. 1522 (late 3rd - early 4th c. A.D.).

O.Z.

246 SINGLE-SPOUTED LAMP
Late 3rd - early 4th c. A.D.

INV. NO. Δ 7001.
L. 0.11, H. 0.034, B.D. 0.034, MAX.W. 0.082 M.

Mended. Part of the nozzle missing. Cracks on the disc. Pale brown clay. Flat base, hemispherical squat body, slightly concave disc, short conical nozzle. Solid, semicircular handle with suspension hole. On the disc, apart from the filling hole, small air hole. The vase is mould-made. Unglazed. Traces of fire on the nozzle. On the base, relief outline of ivy leaf, defined by two concentric, plastic rings, relief scene. A seated figure is depicted in front of a tripod. On the disc's edge, groups of dot-rosettes and two small undecorated panels. Deep grooves on the handle.

COMMENTARY - BIBLIOGRAPHY: Unpublished.
For the shape see *Agora* VII, 124, pl.19, nos. 844, 839, 883, 888 (2nd half and mainly late 3rd c. A.D.); *Délos* XXVI, 136, pl. 32, no. 4666 (3rd c. A.D.). The relief outline of the ivy leaf on the base is the emblem of the great Leaf Workshop, which flourished in Athens from the early 3rd until the late 4th c. A.D. Cf. also *Agora* VII, 57-58, pl. 37, no. 1178 (early 3rd c. A.D.) and 163, pl. 34, no. 2076 and Karivieri 1996, 146-148, pl. 29, no. 300. The depiction of the seated figure in front of a tripod is one of the usual subjects of the Leaf P. and the scholars interpret it as either a slave heating up water or a salesman of a liquid; see *Agora* VI, 80, nos. 1053-1056. For figures in front of tripods see *Agora* VII, 126, pl. 19, nos. 883, 888 (2nd half of 3rd c. A.D.).

O.Z.

244

243

ARIONOS STREET

ERMOU - ARIONOS Shaft

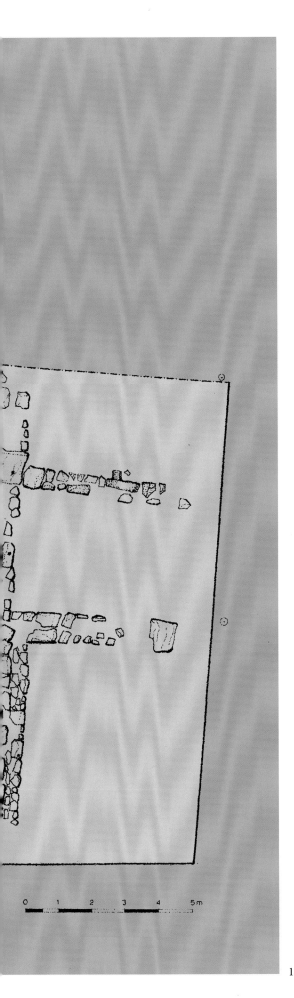

onstruction work for the ventilation shaft on the junction of Ermou and Arionos Streets on Line 3 of the M.R.A. was preceded by examination. Because of technical difficulties investigation of the 220 sq.m. site ceased before it could be completed; nevertheless, the greater part of the site was examined. Removal of recent earth fills beneath the structure that previously stood there revealed the remains of buildings in the dilapidated state to which they had been reduced by later successive disturbances. In all, twenty-two remnants of walls, seven wells and three conduits were discovered (fig. 1).

The roughly built walls, most of them of short length and low height, were in many cases a single course of small uncut stones and earth mortar; they belonged to buildings erected between the Classical and Late Roman periods. It was not possible to complete their ground plan because of the fragmentary state of their preservation (fig. 2). The most recognisable part of the site examined lies around its centre. It is a stone-built Roman rectangular structure defined by walls constructed of rubble masonry, tiles, small fragments of marble and a hard mortar. A small area of a tiled floor, lacking walls that might have defined its edges, was discovered to the north-east. Another characteristic feature is the wall along the north side of the excavation; it is about 1 m. wide, lies in an E-W direction and was built of large uncut stones, with its foundations laid on the limestone bedrock at a depth of 3.20 m.

Of the seven conduits discovered, some with built sides and others quarried out of the rock, most are more recent and at some time had been used for drainage. The remains of three terracotta conduits were also found, but were too fragmentary to establish either their orientation or their purpose.

Only a single pot burial was unearthed in the entire excavation area; it contained a few bones and some sherds of Classical date.

1

The site has been in continuous use. The pottery collected from the disturbed fills is of various periods, stretching from Classical times to the Byzantine era and even to the centuries of Ottoman occupation. In contrast with the remains of buildings which were in a poor state as a result of repeated intrusions, the pottery collected from all over the site and from a small depository comprises a large number of sherds, mainly from red-figure vases. Though only very few whole vases survived (no. 247) the sherds, mostly of Classical date, are particularly representative of their time. Apart from the pottery, various marble fragments of architectural members, marble figurines and small columns, as well as more recent remains from neo-classical buildings, were gathered on the site.

Examination of the excavated area is continuing in the remaining section, now that the technical difficulties have been resolved.

2. ERMOU-ARIONOS Shaft. General view

of the excavation site.

IOANNA TSIRIGOTI-DRAKOTOU

2

247 ASKOS
325-300 B.C.

INV. NO. A 15512.
PRES.H. 0.097, B.D. 0.077, MAX.D. 0.107, M.D. 0.032 M.

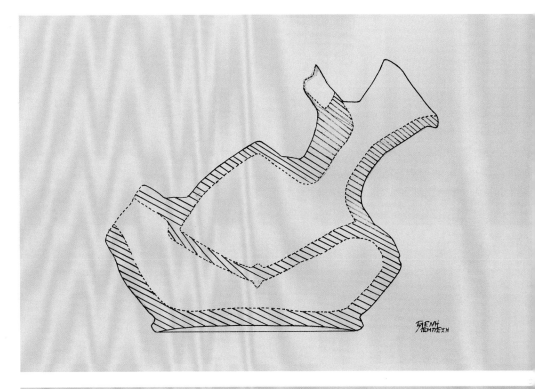

The handle and the side spout missing. Several chips and flakes, mainly on the lower part of the vase and the spout. Short, ring base, bi-conical body, cut-away spout (on the preserved spout). A strap handle joined the two spouts. On both sides two hemispherical ribs.

The decoration is limited to the upper half of the vase, above an incised ring, which separates the body from the shoulder. On the shoulder, a band of laurel leaves. The transition from the shoulder to the ridge is rendered with a plastic ring. The conical ridge of the vase is decorated with a group of four volutes, surrounding a small one at its pointed ending. On the empty space between the volutes, black schematised petals.

COMMENTARY - BIBLIOGRAPHY: Unpublished.

The interior of the vase is divided with an intermediate base into two chambers communicating with the two spouts respectively (see drawing). In similar vases, these spouts are usually formed each in a different shape (e.g. one trefoil, the other round), thus enabling the user to identify the contents of each chamber.

These askoi were tableware used to mix food condiments like oil and vinegar during meals. For the possible uses of the double-spouted askos see the essential study by Bovon - Bruneau 1966, 140ff.

This original and very functional shape is found from the 5th c. B.C., spread during the 4th c. B.C., and used until the end of the 2nd c. and the beginning of the 1st c. B.C.; see also Πατσιαδά 1983,126. Also see *Agora* XII, 157-160, n. 1, pl. 39. For the shape see *Agora* XXIX, no. 1176, pl. 86 and for the decoration, nos. 1173-1175, pl. 86.

V.O.

247

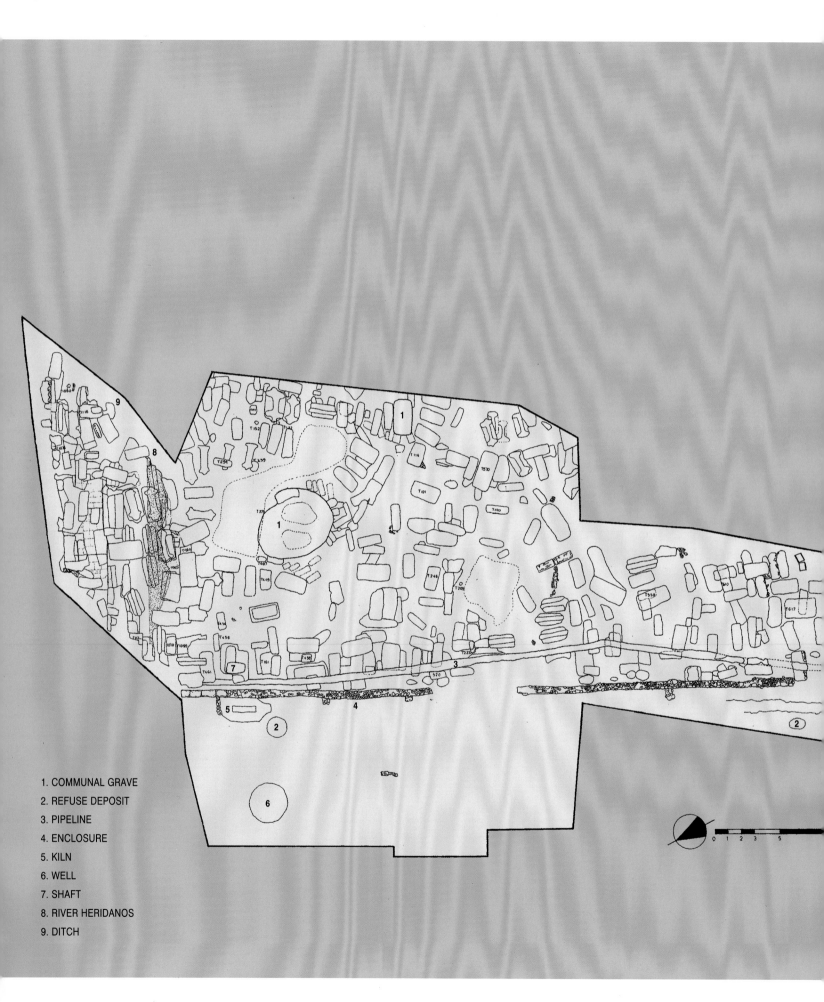

1. COMMUNAL GRAVE

2. REFUSE DEPOSIT

3. PIPELINE

4. ENCLOSURE

5. KILN

6. WELL

7. SHAFT

8. RIVER HERIDANOS

9. DITCH

KERAMEIKOS Station

1

THE DEME OF POTTERS

According to Thucydides (II, 34), Kerameikos was the "most beautiful suburb" of the ancient city of Athens; it was so named "from the ceramic craft, and from the habit of making sacrifices to a certain hero named Keramos" (Harp., s.v. Κεραμεῖς).

The aptness of this name was borne out by the discovery in the course of rescue excavations carried out in recent years of pottery workshops of Archaic and Classical date situated outside the north-west walls of the city and as distant as Plato's Academy[1]. The myth about the hero Keramos, son of Dionysos and Ariadne, was a later fabrication, evidently to provide an explanation of the deme's name.

The boundaries of the deme of Kerameikos are no clearer than those of other city demes. From information provided by ancient writers we know that the deme was already in existence in the Archaic period. The construction of the Themistoclean walls in 479/8 B.C. split it into inner and outer Kerameikos (Thuc. VI, 57), while it seems that in the period of Roman occupation it expanded considerably towards the inner part of the city, absorbing the area of the Ancient Agora (Paus. I 3.1, 2.4, 20.6 and 14.6).

Findings made during excavations, chiefly of the archaeological site of Kerameikos, have added considerably to the information concerning outer Kerameikos given in ancient writings. The road to the Academy set out from a point immediately outside the city walls; the official city cemetery, the State War Memorial, developed either side of it. The Iera Odos (Sacred Way) traverses the same area, a few metres further away from the Iera Pyle (Sacred Gateway), and intersects the Street of the Tombs, forming an acute angle with it. Cemeteries, where notable families as well as nameless citizens were buried, sprang up beside both these thoroughfares. The waters of the river Heridanos flowing through the peaceful grounds of the cemetery and close to the most important gateways of Athens, the Dipylon and Iera Gates, would have emphasised the natural beauty of the landscape of this much frequented district[2].

This picture of antiquity is in complete contrast with the one of the 19th c. A.D. described by Ludwig Ross and in accounts of the excavations made by the first Greek archaeologists who worked in the area. Ross, who was one of the pioneer archaeologists in the newly formed modern state of Greece, described the view from the hill of Agia Triada in 1832: "This is not the brilliant violet-crowned Athens! It is a heap of rubble, a shapeless, dreary grey-green mass of ash and dust"[3]. Towards the end of the 19th century the district was smothered beneath sand which in places reached a height of 9 m. above the level of the antiquities. There were vineyards as well as the Gas Works, small factories – such as the soap works with its lye store – kilns, sand quarries and an open sewage channel. For the most part the land was publicly owned, though private individuals often laid claim to it.

In 1861, confronted by the works in which Daniel, the government engineer, was engaged in constructing the new Pireos Street, the Archaeological Society took it upon itself to conduct excavations and to oversee the expropriation of land and secure the site. When the first grave stelai were found in about 1863 A. Roussopoulos, Professor of Archaeology, suspected that Kerameikos lay where the archaeological site known by the same name is located today. Excavations were carried out by the Archaeological Society until 1913 when the German Archaeological Institute undertook to continue and complete the archaeological investigations (fig. 2-4)[4].

This 19th century picture applies, of course, not only to the archaeological site but also to the district in general. It seems that intensive quarrying for sand per-

2. KERAMEIKOS Station. The excavation of the Pompeion in the beginning of the 20th century.

3. Kerameikos archaeological site. Some of the earliest monuments excavated on the site, 19th century.

4. Kerameikos archaeological site. The Street of the Tombs. The Vegetable Market building may be seen in the background.

sisted up to the end of that century; it was used not only for building but also for earth fills such as, for instance, in the construction of a section of the electric railway in 1879. Thus, these sand quarries but particularly the landfills, were the first finds that were discovered stratigraphically in excavating the station.

The area of the eastern section of the excavation was covered in the late 19th century by earth fill dumped from the side of the Iera Odos. These earth fills were dated by the discovery of the inscribed foundation stone laid during the mayoralty of Lambros Kalliphronas in 1899. Evidence of a large water reservoir in the north-east

corner of the site was recorded on the map of Athens compiled by Judeich[5]. Further disturbances to the site were occasioned by lime-pits sunk in connection perhaps with the erection in this location of the Athens Vegetable Market in 1902.

Only scant information about antiquities was available before the middle of the 20th century; simple graves and fragments of grave stelai are recorded as having been found on Pireos Street under the pavement of what is now the archaeological site and near the entrance to the Gas Works. A rescue excavation conducted in 1984 in a ditch beside the south pavement of the present-day route of the Iera Odos and close to its junction with Pireos Street revealed a section of a very congested cemetery in use from the 5th c. B.C. down to Roman times[6].

THE EXCAVATION

The 1984 rescue excavation and the neighbouring archaeological site indicated that a cemetery crowded with graves was likely to be found in the course of excavating the site of KERAMEIKOS Station (fig. 1, 5-7). However, the disturbed earth fill, 3-4.50 m. deep, which once covered the site did not initially confirm our expectations. Nonetheless investigation of the undisturbed levels brought to light a great number of graves which are the continuation in a westerly direction of the graves of Archaic-Classical date in the Kerameikos archaeological site. Thus, the Kerameikos cemetery expanded chiefly within the triangle formed by the Iera Odos to the north, the street of graves to the south and a small low enclosure to the west, situated at a distance of about 200 m. from the city wall. No large sumptuous monuments were found, nor fragments of architectural members or monumental grave reliefs. Their absence, explained only in part by subsequent disturbances to the earth fill, is further accounted for by the distance at which the cemetery lies from its hub close to the walls. Notwithstanding the absence of monumental structures and rich finds, this excavation provided us with important data about the topography of Kerameikos and the products of its workshops; at the same time it yielded finds that relate to historical events.

During investigation of the 0.25 ha. site set aside for the construction of the KERAMEIKOS Station antiquities were found in the eastern sector covering about 0.15 ha. and lying closest to the ancient walls. 1,191 graves, scattered over almost the entire site and dating from the early 7th c. B.C. down to Roman times, were examined. Graves of the 6th and 5th c. B.C. were found here and there in the largest sector excavated; they lay under levels 2.50 m. below the surface. In the northernmost sector, where the disturbance was shallow and less destructive, a few 4th c. B.C. graves and even fewer Hellenistic ones were found[7]. Here the congestion in the cemetery was considerable, not only because of the limited interference occurring at a later date, but also because of the proximity of the Iera Odos close to which burials were more numerous (fig. 6)[8].

THE RIVER HERIDANOS

It was here, beneath graves of the 5th and 6th and probably of the 7th c. B.C., that the south bank and bed of the river Heridanos in pre-Geometric and Geometric times were situated. The absence of Geometric graves at this point in our excavations may be accounted for by the unobstructed flow of the river prior to its diversion in the 5th c., at the time the Themistoclean walls were being built. Examination of the Heridanos was not completed because of the overlying Archaic and Classical cemetery and also because the need to continue the excavation ceased once the decision had finally been reached not to build the KERAMEIKOS Station in this location. Abandonment of the station proved beneficial since not only the archaeological site but also the north-western sector, close to the Iera Odos, of the Kerameikos cemetery were thus preserved. We hope that the eventual continuation and completion of the investigation of the site, with a view to conserving the antiquities, will not again necessitate a rescue excavation.

5. KERAMEIKOS Station. The central part

of the excavated site. The enclosure may be seen on the left.

5

THE CEMETERY

Almost every form of burial was found in the cemetery examined on the site of the KERAMEIKOS Station[9]. The following were identified: 262 graves with pitched tile coverings, 548 pit burials, 74 tile graves, 230 cremations, 38 clay burial tubs (larnakes), 74 burials in pots, 2 sarcophagi, 7 cist graves, 4 cinerary urns, 2 communal graves and 2 offering ditches. In addition the bones of nine dogs, covered with a layer of pebbles that suggested the animals had been tossed in there rather than buried, were discovered in disturbed fills. Some of the graves had been only partially preserved on account on the one hand of the intensely congested use made of the burial site and on the other of various later encroachments. This explains the fact that many of the graves were bare of offerings. As regards the typology and the variety of the graves, the picture was the same as the one we came across in the cemetery in the neighbouring Kerameikos archaeological site.

Finds from forty-two of the 1,191 graves and from one of the two pits with offerings were selected for display in the present exhibition. So far as was possible selection was made on the grounds that the objects most accurately reflected the character of the cemetery, rather than on the importance of each individual object.

Five of the burials were cremations of the usual kind, an abundance of incinerated material lying on the floor. Five pot burials were found in large household vases, mostly amphorae, containing secondary burials or child interments with associated offerings placed either inside the burial vessel or outside it. Two larnakes (clay tubs) containing child burials and one kalpis (cinerary urn) round off the picture. Other selected objects include seven tile-covered graves with vase offerings typical of such burials and three cist graves faced with tiles. However, plain rectangular pits quarried from the natural rock comprise the most numerous category of graves. Nineteen of these are exhibited with representative offerings from all periods in which the cemetery was in use. It should be noted that though no graves of a date later than the 3rd c. B.C. were found, there are indications that the cemetery was in use down to Roman times. This is confirmed by two Roman graves found almost on the surface in an undisturbed level and in immediate proximity to the 1984 rescue excavation mentioned above.

Despite the simple construction of the graves, the offerings in them vary greatly in quantity and quality. Terracotta objects outnumber all others, while jewellery is almost entirely lacking (the bone beads, no. 411, are an exception).

There are three graves dating to the 7th c. B.C., the offerings in them belonging to the "Phaleron Group". Two of them (tombs 152 and 239) are child pot burials in which amphorae of Geometric date were used as burial vessels. A small schist slab covered the mouth of these vessels, thus sealing the burial, while the offerings were placed around them as is usual with pot burials of the period. The third (tomb 191) was likewise a pot burial, destroyed by a later pit burial. Nonetheless, its offerings were discovered under the few sherds of the burial vessel.

Only a few offerings (nos. 276-279) were selected from the plain rectangular cutting in the bedrock of tomb 461. Of these the lekythos of Deianeira type (no. 276)

6. KERAMEIKOS Station. The north part of the site, which has been preserved and remains visible.

7. KERAMEIKOS Station. The south part of the excavation. The pipe shaft is visible in the centre.

6

is especially interesting because of its decoration depicting a subject which probably relates to an erotic conversation between males. The fragment of a loutrophoros hydria (no. 410) had probably been used as an urn for the ashes from a rifled grave.

An example of the early 5th c. B.C. graves is cist grave no. 1099 close to the northern sector of the excavation containing the grave of a young man with offerings of vases and knuckle-bones (no. 313). Prominent among the grave vases is a small red-figure aryballos (no. 311) of unconventional shape decorated with a palaestra (wrestling school) scene, the work of Douris, one of the outstanding vasepainters of the late Archaic period. The rest of the vases are attributed to the Workshops of the Diosphos and Haimon Painters. Comparison with the find in the grave on Stadiou Street (from the excavation at the Royal Stables in 1928) is only to be expected for it contained similar offerings that were of fundamental importance to the study of the workshops which produced black-figure Attic pottery in the early 5th c. B.C.[10]. The illustration on the aryballos and on a blackpainted alabastron (no. 312) reveal the tender age of the dead man and his "gymnasium" upbringing.

The pit grave 1010 was found close to the one just mentioned and dates to the same period. It contained a child burial accompanied by numerous vase offerings, a usual burial practice in late Archaic - early Classical graves, as may be seen also in corresponding burials in neighbouring Kerameikos. Vase no. 289, painted with an erotic scene, clearly had nothing to do with the age of the deceased.

Finally, the offering ditch, a rectangular rock-cutting 2.50 m. in length, contained in two layers numerous vases and figurines that showed traces of fire. The most representative of these figurines have been selected for the present exhibition. The types of pottery and the figurines, the majority of which are of females, denote that the trench contained grave offerings to a woman.

COMMUNAL GRAVES

The two communal graves discovered at the mid point of our excavation occupy a significant position in the cemetery.

The first was uncovered in a simple pit 6.50 m. in diameter[11] (fig. 8-9). Excavation of the pit proved particularly difficult on account of the disturbed overlying fills as well as of the five intrusions into the pit in antiquity. These

7

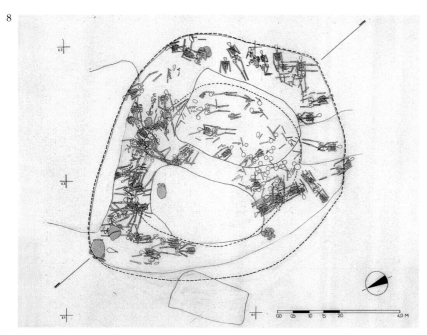

8. KERAMEIKOS Station. A sketch of the first communal grave.

9. KERAMEIKOS Station. The north part of the first communal grave. A shaft dug into it at a later date may be seen.

10. KERAMEIKOS Station. The second communal grave.

made it virtually impossible to identify the edges of the pit. Such information as we were able to extract came by and large from isolated heaps of soil that had remained undisturbed[12].

The first graves appeared at a depth of 4.30 m. in the eastern sector of the pit, but there must have been others at shallower levels destroyed by the disturbance of the upper soil during the past two centuries. The excavation revealed successive burial levels of eighty-nine corpses, buried in disorderly fashion and in most cases in outstretched positions, but also in other positions dictated by the shape and size of the pit (fig. 8). At the lower levels there was a modicum of space left between the dead, but it grew less towards the upper ones. Some pot burials of infants were found between the interments. The grave offerings were scattered among the dead and were very few considering the number interred there.

There are indications that this burial place was even more extensive and that there were other layers of dead; it could be argued that the communal burial comprised at least 150 dead. The number of dead and the hasty manner of their burial, which suggest a state of panic, and the dating of the offerings to around 430 B.C. can be attributed only to the mass burial of victims of the plagues which struck Athens in 430/29 and in 427/6 B.C. Thucydides' account (II, 47.3-54) presents the most graphic description of the burial: «... Οὐ μέντοι τοσοῦτος γε λοιμὸς οὐδὲ φθορὰ οὕτως ἀνθρώπων οὐδαμοῦ ἐμνημονεύετο γενέσθαι ... ὑπερβιαζομένου γὰρ τοῦ κακοῦ οἱ ἄνθρωποι οὐκ ἔχοντες ὅ,τι γένωνται ἐς ὀλιγωρίαν ἐτράποντο καὶ ἱερῶν καὶ ὁσίων ὁμοίως ... νόμοι τε πάντες ξυνεταράχθησαν οἷς ἐχρῶντο πρότερον περὶ τὰς ταφάς, ἔθαπτον δὲ ὡς ἕκαστος ἐδύνατο»[13]. It would seem that the city authorities gathered up the dead lying in the streets and buried them in a common grave to one side of the cemetery at Kerameikos, being concerned for the survival of the living and the health of the city.

The grave offerings date to around 430-426 B.C. The most representative of them have been chosen for exhibition. Among them is the white-ground lekythos by the Reed P. (no. 385) whose work is generally ascribed, on the basis of a study of stylistic criteria, to the last quarter or last decades of the 5th c. B.C.[14]. However, the existence of vases painted by him in the context of this find supports the view that the Reed P. was already at work in the opening years of the 430s B.C.[15].

The second communal grave, near Pireos Street, was both undisturbed and bare of offerings (fig. 10). A large rectangular pit (2.80 × 1.50 m.) had been dug into a

10

level of Classical date; it contained the burials of twenty-nine adults. Scattered bones covered with an earth fill about 30 cm. deep were found on the floor of the pit. There followed three successive layers of burials in which the dead lay full length and in some kind of order. The pottery in the fill that covered the lowest layer of bones gives the years around 430 B.C. as *terminus post quem* for the burial. Dating the communal grave to the last third of the 5th c. B.C. relates it to some event or other that occurred in the course of the Peloponnesian War[16].

ENCLOSURE - MARSH

It has already been mentioned that the cemetery was bounded on the west by an unobtrusive embanked enclosure (pres. h. 0.60 m., w. 0.50 m.), built of rough stones and mud mortar. This low 4th c. B.C. wall was uncovered for a distance of 50 m. At regular intervals along its exterior face it was supported by similarly constructed buttresses which, however, were not bonded with the wall itself. Immured in one of the buttresses was the tombstone Siren no. 445 whose date provides the *terminus post quem* for the construction at least of the buttresses. No graves were found to the west of the enclosure. On the other hand a few Archaic graves of which the latest dates to the 1st quarter of the 5th c. B.C. were discovered under its foundations and to the east of it, that is, in the direction of the cemetery. Underneath and for two metres to the east of the wall and over a large area to the west of it was a layer of marshy soil full of numerous small holes, all that was left of the reeds and other aquatic plants which once grew in it. This attests to the former existence of a swamp which stretched westwards of the enclosure for at least 60 m. and followed its length for about 50 m.; thus the swamp covered an area of some 3,000 sq.m. Its stratigraphy indicates that the water level rose or fell according to the season. The few graves found in the mud of its eastern bank suggests that in the 6th and 5th c. B.C. the marsh formed a natural barrier to the further extension of the cemetery in a westerly direction. The enclosure was built when the marsh shrank in size in the 4th c. B.C.; the boundary of the cemetery with the adjacent land formed by the receding waters was then clearly defined.

POTTERY WORKSHOP

One or more potteries were established here at that time; their remains were found outside and 65 m. distant from the enclosure. The floor of the firing chamber of a kiln with an opening on its south side, a circular depository with pieces of 4th c. B.C. unpainted household pots, a well with traces of the remains of a workshop at the bottom, together with four shallow pits close to the southernmost part of the excavation, two of which contained black-glaze pottery of the same period, were discovered on this site. Noteworthy features were the extensive deposits of waste pottery material and a stone-paved area of 80 sq.m., the forecourt of the workshop. These deposits acted as sumps that drained off any water penetrating the forecourt from the adjacent marsh. The kernoi (small ritual vessels) nos. 439-442 were found among the material in these deposits.

11. KERAMEIKOS Station. A view of the interior of the drainage tunnel.

11

DRAINAGE TUNNELS

The partial drainage of the swamp which allowed the workshops to be set up was probably connected with the monumental drainage tunnel constructed within the cemetery and very close to the enclosure wall (fig. 11). In the process of its excavation through the stable ground in the form of a tunnel 1.70 m. high and 0.50 m. wide it destroyed the 6th and 5th c. B.C. graves it met with. Its visible extent is 65 m. with a slight slope from north to south, as determined by altitude measurements taken all along its length. This slope betrays the purpose of the tunnel which was to collect and carry off water southwards from the northern sector (in which lay the swamp, several wells, and the old river bed). A technical hitch or destructive event or simply the inadequacy of the tunnel gave rise to the necessity of opening another tunnel parallel to the first, one similarly constructed but at least 1.50 m. deeper in the ground. The most impressive feature of this tunnel which it was impossible to examine, largely because of the abundance of water welling up into it, was a rectangular shaft 1.70 × 0.90 m. which descended to a depth in excess of 7.50 m. from the surface. This shaft was discovered in the northern sector where the water is most plentiful. The two drainage tunnels were urban land reclamation works and display a profound understanding of hydraulics. They were intended to draw off the waters and to drain the whole area. We do not know if their construction was effective and if they drained the swamp or merely reduced its extent.

Before the drainage of these waters it is unlikely that the landscape underwent any dramatic change. Away from the noise and bustle of the Sacred Way, the silence of the cemetery and the calm immobility of the marshland were a scene familiar to the potters. One of them, who seems to have worked in such a setting, expressed his fondness for the reeds by painting them into the sepulchral scenes decorating his white-ground lekythoi. The Reed P. depicts, with the freedom and simplicity of his line, the images with which he is familiar, portraying both the landscape and the loss of human life in the calm sorrow of his figures. Some of his white vases returned, as grave offerings, to the Kerameikos cemetery, once more beside the reed-girt marsh.

EFFIE BAZIOTOPOULOU-VALAVANI
IOANNA TSIRIGOTI-DRAKOTOU

NOTES

1. Μπαζιωτοπούλου-Βαλαβάνη 1994, 44-54.

2. Knigge 1990, with the relevant bibliography.

3. Ρος 1832-33, 281 (tr. L. Spilios).

4. Πετράκος 1998.

5. Judeich 1931.

6. Πλάτωνος - Χατζηπούλιου 1984, 11-14.

7. Μπαζιωτοπούλου - Δρακωτού 1994 , 34-36.

8. For the route of the ancient Sacred Way see Τσιριγώτη-Δρακωτού 1992, 28-32 and *eadem* 1987, 521-544.

9. For initial details of the excavation see Καράγιωργα-Σταθακοπούλου 1988, 90-93; Παρλαμά 1990-91, 238-239 and *eadem* 1992-98, 521-544.

10. Παπασπυρίδη - Κυπαρίσσης 1927-28, 91-110.

11. A communication on the communal grave and the finds from it was given by E. Baziotopoulou-Valavani to the 1st Scientific Conference of the 3rd Ephorate in March 1996.

12. The two main disturbances had already by the 4th c. B.C. almost destroyed the core of the burial to its full depth of 6.10 m.

13. "... no pestilence of such magnitude nor any scourge so destructive of human lives is anywhere on record ... for the calamity which weighed upon them was so overwhelming that men, not knowing what was to become of them, became careless of all law, both sacred and profane ... And the customs which they had hitherto observed regarding burial were all thrown into confusion, and they buried their dead each one as he could" (tr. Charles F. Smith, Heinemann / Harvard, London 1919).

14. Kurtz 1975, 58.

15. The poor quality of the grave offerings, the fragmentary nature of the bones on account of later intrusions, the irregular, haphazard character of the pit preserved only at floor level, deny the communal burial any sense of monumentality or even burial typology. Its significance rests on its attribution to an important historical incident recorded by Thucydides.

16. We know of communal burials from the first excavations carried out by the Archaeological Society in the sand fills of the Kerameikos archaeological site to the south of the very ancient church of Agia Triada (Holy Trinity). This burial is attributed to the Athenians executed by Sulla in 86 B.C. (Πιττάκης 1860, 2102 n.). However, the lack of excavation data makes it difficult today to accept this proposition without reservation.

ever, more developed with differences in the framing of the face and in the hair-style of the "Daedalic wig". The head belongs to the early Daedalic period, although it cannot be attributed with certainty to an Attic workshop. For the plastic arts of the LG period see Kunze 1930, 141-162, esp. 155ff., pl. XLII:2, XLIII:2. For the early Daedalic style see Jenkins 1978, 24-27, pl. I and Vierneisel 1961, 41-45, pl. 16-21.

Th.K.

lighted by inverted radial decoration. Two zones, divided by triple lines, decorate the neck area. In the upper, there is a system of vertical wavy lines and in the lower, upright, back-to-front "S" motifs. The trefoil mouth is decorated with irregular, vertical little lines which sit on top of a broad black band. The upper half of the back of the handle is decorated with a pair of vertical S-shaped motifs and the lower, with thin horizontal bands. Similar bands decorate the projection of the handle to the rim.

COMMENTARY - BIBLIOGRAPHY: Unpublished.
The slender shape, the high conical neck and the elongated body places it in a characteristic group of the early Proto-Attic oenochoae, known as the Phaleron

248

From tomb 101

248 HEAD OF A TERRACOTTA FIGURINE
Beginning of 7th c. B.C.

INV. NO. E 1039.
MAX.H. 0.034 M.

Broken at the neck. Pale brown clay, brown-black slip.
The head is solid and handmade, flat on top. The moulded hair is pulled back. It is held together with a band depicted in paint and the details of the curls are also indicated with vertical brush strokes. The elongated face has an intensely natural look. Large almond-shaped eyes with eyeballs bulging outwards and looking down. The nose is triangular, the chin pointed. The eyelids, the pupils, the nose and small mouth are all highlighted with a brown-black coating.

COMMENTARY - BIBLIOGRAPHY: Unpublished.
The depiction of the figure is somewhat primitive but detailed. As far as the characteristics are concerned, they exhibit similarities with clay figurine heads from the Heraion of Samos, which are dated to the LG and Early Daedalic periods, see *Samos* XVIII, 39, no. 896, (710-700 B.C.), no. 1000 (700 B.C.), pl. 46, no. 969, pl. 47 or the female-bust rhyton no. 1126, pl. 58 (660 B.C.) and the head from a terracotta figurine from Lindos, *Lindos* I, 459, no 1861, pl. 80. Cf. also Wallenstein 1971, 15-18, 96, I/B1, pl. 2,1.2, and the small head by a Corinthian workshop from Perachora, which is, how-

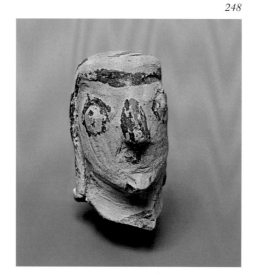

From tomb 191

249 TREFOIL-MOUTHED OENOCHOE
700-675 B.C.

INV. NO. A 15345.
H. 0.22, B.D. 0.059 M.

Complete. The handle is mended. Small chips particularly off the mouth. The paint is fugitive at many points particularly on the back of the vase.
The decoration is organised into zones which run around the body of the vase. Large painted leaves decorate most of the lower half of the body. The upper half is covered with thin, encircling bands which contain a zone with a row of compact squares of alternating black and light paint. The shoulder zone is high-

249

Group, cf. *Agora* VIII, 36-37, no. 52, pl. 4. The Phaleron Group, so named from the place where most vases have been found, includes small vases, chiefly trefoil-mouthed oenochoae and single-handled cups. A similar oenochoe was found in the Kerameikos, no. 1154, see *Kerameikos* VI₂, 173 and 422, no. 8, pl. 8 (from the "Opferplatz a/IV"; 700-690 B.C.). This type of oenochoe from the Kerameikos with tall neck belongs to the first type of Young 1942, 49 and 53-55 (for the dating of the Phaleron Group). For the shape see *APP* 1995, 19-20, no. 8 [Dennis] and Petrocheilos 1996, 45-46, n. 1. For the band with squares of black and light paint see *Kerameikos* VI₂, 111, fig. 4; Kunisch 1998, 4, fig. 1 i. For the vertical S-shaped motifs see *Kerameikos* VI₂), 115, fig. 5. In general for Proto-Attic pottery see Morris 1982 and Walter-Karydi, *APP* 1997, 385-394. Also, Whitley 1994, 51-70. For the transition from Late Geometric pottery (Workshop of Athens 894) to Proto-Attic (Analatos P.) see Sheedy 1992, 26-28 and Denoyelle 1996, 71-87. For the "offering ditches", where they have found great quantities of Proto-Attic pottery, see Kistler 1998.

G.K.

250 BLACK-GLAZED OENOCHOISKE
700-675 B.C.

INV. NO. A 15348.
H. 0.072 (EXCL. HANDLE), H. 0.076 (INCL. HANDLE), B.D. 0.047, M.D. 0.038 M.

Complete. The handle is mended. Small part of the mouth restored. The black paint is either flaking or fugitive on a large part of the body and handle.

One reserved zone, with four thin encircling bands, covers the main body of the vase at the point of maximum diameter. The back of the handle is decorated with long diagonal lines, largely fugitive today. The interior of the rim is covered with fugitive black paint. A shallow incision divides the flat base from the main body of the vase.

COMMENTARY - BIBLIOGRAPHY: Unpublished.
It belongs to the Phaleron Group. It is placed amongst the second of Young's groups, which include the small Proto-Attic oenochoae with low neck. For the shape and decoration see Young 1942, 50 and 25, fig. 1, 47.5 (oenochoe from Tomb 47 at Phaleron). For a Sub-Geometric precursor of the shape see Brann 1961b, 322, no. E3, pl. 75 and 377, no. S15, pl. 87.

G.K.

251 *250*

251 BLACK-GLAZED ARYBALLOS
700-675 B.C.

INV. NO. A 15349.
H. 0.046, B.D. 0.03, EXT. M.D. 0.028, INT.M.D. 0.008 M.

Complete, apart from a small part of the rim.

The centre of the figured zone is indicated with a mastoid projection, which is highlighted by a central dot and a pair of concentric circles which are linked to one another by small lines. Two trios of birds flank the mastoid projection, walking to the right. The zone between the birds is filled with carelessly executed decoration of alternating angles in rows, circles and lozenges. The main figurative zone is framed by bands of Z-shaped motifs. In the base zone, radial decoration. The upper half of the mouth is highlighted by a pair of broad black bands. The upper surface of the rim is embellished with a band of Z-shaped motifs and the edge is highlighted by small spots. Three vertical bands on the cylindrical handle. The centre of the flat base, which is distinguished from the main body by a thin, shallow incision, is indicated by black paint.

COMMENTARY - BIBLIOGRAPHY: Unpublished.
The shape refers to a category of aryballoi of the end of the 8th c. B.C. and the beginning of the 7th, which is decorated with the "spaghetti" motif, see Σταμπολίδης - Καρέτσου 1998, 184-186, nos. 193-197 [Σταμπολίδης, Γιαννικουρή, Γκαλανάκη]. For the Z-shaped motifs see *Kerameikos* VI₂, 337, fig. 27.

G.K.

252

252 BLACK-GLAZED FEEDER WITH STRAINER
700-675 B.C.

INV. NO. A 15346.
H. 0.057, B.D. 0.038, M.D. 0.062 M.

Complete. The handle and spout have been mended. Small part of the rim restored. Small cracks on the strainer.

The decoration of the main body is organised in two zones. On the handle zone, a long, thin wavy line ends in a snake's head. Clusters of small irregular wavy lines fill the zone. A four-leafed decoration is painted in the panel created between the spout and handle with a small reserved circle at its centre. A cross divides the quadrants between the leaves. In the lower body zone there are eleven, left-turned, upside down hooks. The transition to the high ring base is emphasised by a row of black spots and a broad black band. The edge of the ring base is highlighted by an encircling black line.

The back of the handle is decorated with an "hour-glass" motif. The lower half of the handle is decorated with a simple strand. The exterior of the sloping rim and the spout are painted black. Concentric circles on the disc of the strainer. The zone between the circles is filled with the perforations of the strainer, apart from the exterior circle near the rim, which is decorated with large carelessly executed spots. Finally, the edge of the rim is highlighted with irregular small spots.

COMMENTARY - BIBLIOGRAPHY: Unpublished.

For the shape see *Agora* XII, 161. Proto-Attic feeders (thelastra) in Athens: Kerameikos Museum, no. 63, see *Kerameikos* VI$_2$, 170 and 551, no. 230, pl. 107 and in the NM, no. 14890. For the wavy line ending in a snake's head see the commentary on no. 261. For the "hour-glass" motif see Kunisch 1998, 138.

G.K.

253

253 BLACK-GLAZED LEKANIS WITH LID
700-675 B.C.

INV. NO. A 15353.
H. 0.062 (EXCL. LID), 0.117 (INCL. LID), B.D. 0.044, M.D.
0.09, D. OF LID 0.109 M.

Complete. Joined from several sherds. The paint flaked off a large part of the body. Chips off the main body of the vase.

The decoration is organised on the main body of the vase into three zones. Large radial decoration takes up the base zone. There is an encircling zone of upright left-turned hooks on the middle of the body. Pendent hooks decorate one side of the handle zone, and the other, a band of vertical broken lines which are framed by panels with a pair of antithetic concentric semicircles, now fugitive. The rim is highlighted by spots and a black band. The handles are horizontal, cylindrical, with a projection on either side and are decorated with black bands. Three broad bands can be distinguished on the interior at the bottom, middle and upper part of the body of the vase.

The decoration of the lid is organised into four zones which are divided by a thin, double band. A row of spots decorates the outer zone near the edge. Zones with pendent right-facing hooks and "drops" follow. Around the knob is a second zone of right-facing hooks. The stem of the knob is monochrome, apart from a thin band on the lower part and a broader one on the upper. A flowering rosette inside pairs of concentric circles adorns the flat upper side of the knob.

COMMENTARY - BIBLIOGRAPHY: Unpublished.
For the shape see *Kerameikos* VI₂, 159. For typological parallels of the rosette on the knob see *Kerameikos* VI₂, 119, fig. 8.

G.K.

254 BLACK-GLAZED PHIALE MESOMPHALOS
700-675 B.C.

INV. NO. A 15344.
H. 0.057, B.D. 0.033, M.D. 0.132 M.

Complete. Joined from many sherds and restored. Extensive chipping on the rim and flaking, especially on the exterior surface of the vase. Differential firing on the interior where traces of two horizontal black bands can be distinguished. In the middle of the bottom, a conical omphalos is surrounded by a concentric ring, pointed in section. The upper half of the interior of the conical area of the low base is unpainted.

COMMENTARY - BIBLIOGRAPHY: Unpublished.
Phialae presumably derive from metallic prototypes; cf. a bronze phiale mesomphalos of Phrygian type in Rethymnon Museum, no. M 1664, see Σταμπολίδης - Καρέτσου 1998, 240-241, nos. 292-293 [Σταμπολίδης, Μαρινάτου].

G.K.

255 BLACK-GLAZED KOTYLE
700-675 B.C.

INV. NO. A 15347.
H. 0.058, B.D. 0.029, M.D. 0.073 M.

Complete. The handles are mended. The black paint on the inside of the vase and handles has flaked off. Small chips off rim.

The decoration is organised into five zones which run around the body of the vase and are divided by triple horizontal bands. There is a radial decoration in the lower zone towards the base, followed by one with "drops". In the middle zone, irregular vertical Z-shaped motifs form panels. A black lozenge divided by a reserved X decorates the centre of each panel. A zone of upside down hooks follows this. On each side in the zone between the two handles, triple vertical lines form three panels. The two smaller side panels contain a black lozenge divided by an X and flank the larger central one which, on one side, includes a band of vertical broken lines and on the other, a chain of spirals. The centre of its flat base is highlighted by a large spot which is surrounded by three concentric circles.

COMMENTARY - BIBLIOGRAPHY: Unpublished.

For the shape see *Agora* VIII, 49-50. Both the shape of the kotyle and the panel arrangement in the handle zones is reminiscent of Corinthian prototypes; see Σταμπολίδης - Καρέτσου 1998, 145-146, nos. 94-96 [Τασούλας]. Besides the similarity of shape, the decoration of Proto-Corinthian type of successive thin encircling bands has been replaced by zones of black-glazed Proto-Attic decoration. For the upside down hooks see *Kerameikos* VI₂, 136, fig. 18.

G.K.

256 SINGLE-HANDLED CUP
700-675 B.C.

INV. NO. A 15360.
H. 0.074, B.D. 0.066, M.D. 0.105 M.

Complete. Joined together from many sherds. The black paint is fugitive to a great extent on the handle and to its right on the main body. Small chips off the rim. The decoration is organised into four zones which encircle the body of the vase. The lower half is arranged in two zones The first, to the base, comprises radial decoration and that above, upright, left-turned hooks. The zone at handle height is decorated in six panels divided by double vertical lines.

A now fugitive water bird is depicted in the first panel next to the handle. In the second, a pair of antithetic protomes of standing horses are depicted putting their bent front legs forward. Their mane is rendered by a row of small solid arcs. There is a black lozenge divided by an X between the horses. A plant ornament hangs down from the upper defining line of the panel and two alternating triangles are suspended from the right. A seated sphinx is depicted in the third panel, in profile and facing right. The face and sickle-shaped wings are rendered in outline. There is a lozenge between its legs. Alternating triangles are suspended from the vertical border lines of the panel. The fourth panel contains a large plant ornament consisting of upright antithetic S-shaped spirals ending in a flower. The heart of the decoration consists of a double lozenge divided by an X. A pair of horses' protomes like that in the second panel is depicted in the fifth. The gap between the animals is filled by a simple vertical chain. A small plant ornament is hanging from the upper border of the panel. There is a small solid lozenge behind the right hand horse. The sixth panel is divided by a vertical chain. A deer is depicted in the left half, grazing to the left. An irregular horizontal band of S-shaped little lines is above the deer, and a vertical U-shaped ornament is accommodated in the space between the hind legs. A triangle with a solid core is attached to the left vertical border line. A water bird in silhouette facing left is depicted in the right half of the panel. The space between bird's legs is filled with a hatched triangle. A pair of alternate triangles is attached to the right hand border line. The main figurative zone is surmounted by a band of radial decoration. The interior of the vase is monochrome, apart from the rim zone which is decorated with a double series of "buttons" and a zone of upside down hooks. The exterior surface of the handle on its projection towards the rim is decorated with a combination of vertical antithetic spirals. Two horizontal bands with upside down hooks and a horizontal broken line follow. The rest of the handle is filled with a vertical system of three circles with a large spot in the middle of each, now fugitive. All the representations in the figured fields are rendered in silhouette with the exception of the eyes of the deer and of the two birds as well as the face, chest and wings of the sphinx, all of which are in outline. The flat base is decorated with a black four-spoked wheel. In the four spaces between the spokes of the wheel are black lozenges divided by a cross.

COMMENTARY - BIBLIOGRAPHY: Unpublished.

For the shape of cup see the commentary on no. 257. The sphinx first appears in the Late Geometric Workshop of Athens 894 (skyphos in Athens, NM, no. 784) but became established with the arrival of the Proto-Attic period, see Rombos 1988, 244-254 (esp. 253-254), pl. 36 and Sheedy 1992, 18. For the sphinx see *Agora* VIII, 78, no. 419, pl. 26 (Mesogeia P.). For antithetic sphinxes see Borell - Rittig 1998, 120-125.

The grazing deer as an iconographic motif already occurs in the LG IA period in the Dipylon P.; see Rombos 1988, 53-64. Cf. the trefoil-mouthed oenochoe of Athens, Ancient Agora Museum, no. P 15122 (c. 740 B.C.), see *Agora* VIII, 60, pl. 14. According to Brann 1961b, 310-311 and 347-348, no. G4, pl. 68-69, the heraldic horse protomes occur in Proto-Attic iconography around 630-620 B.C. (cf. the amphora in Athens, Ancient Agora Museum, no. P 22551). However, it appears that here we have an earlier occurrence of this theme in Proto-Attic pottery. It exists, of course, in early Proto-Corinthian pottery, cf. the oenochoe of Athens, Kerameikos Museum, no. P 1267 from the "Opferplatz a/IV", see *Kerameikos* VI₂, 14-15, pl. 58 and 126, 152. For horse protomes generally cf. Μαραγκού 1995, 54-57 [Μαραγκού]. Brann, *Agora* VIII, 96-97, no. 573, pl. 36, maintains that heraldic horse protomes have Cycladic prototypes, cf. *Délos* XVII, pl. XV, b and *Délos* XV, pl. XXIV, 11b-c (hydria of Group Ad), see Ζαφειροπούλου 1981, 43-45. For the eastern provenance of antithetic winged horses see Kunze 1950, 60-61, n. 1 and Sheedy 1992, 20-25 (for the eastern origin of heraldic representations). For the view that the theme is indigenous see Benson 1970, 67. See likewise, *Kerameikos* VI₂, 222 and 44-46, esp. 46 n. 80, and 39 n. 56, where the existence of horse protomes from the Geometric period is noted.

For the four-spoked wheel see *Agora* VIII, 67, cat. no. 320, pl. 18 and Kunisch 1988, 217-218, fig. 83. For technical terms related to the wheel see Μανακίδου 1994, 298-299. For an interpretative approach to the frequent occurrence of the wheel on Proto-Attic vases and its connection with the upper classes, chiefly the Alkmaionids, see Benson 1970, 67-68. For the plant motif of the second panel (pendent anthemion) see *Kerameikos* VI₂, 133-134, fig. 16 and 349, fig. 32 and for the vertical strand, 138, fig. 19. For the big plant ornament of the fourth panel, cf. plant ornaments of similar concept in *Kerameikos* VI₂, 127, fig. 13.

G.K.

257 SINGLE-HANDLED CUP
700-675 B.C.

INV. NO. A 15350.
H. 0.041, B.D. 0.043, M.D. 0.058 M.

Complete, apart from a large part of the base and a small part of the rim. Slightly chipped in places.

Vertical bands of Z-shaped motifs creates five pictorial panels. The first from the left and next to the handle contains a black lozenge divided by an X. A water bird facing left is depicted in the second panel. The larger third and central panel contains a water bird facing left, which is framed by black lozenges divided by an X. The fourth also contains a water bird facing left. Lastly, the fifth contains two circles, one above the other, with spots

COMMENTARY - BIBLIOGRAPHY: Unpublished.
For single-handled cups with curved walls see *Agora* VIII, 52-54, no. 193, pl. 10. See also *Kerameikos* VI₂, 169-170 and 452, no. 42, pl. 31.

G.K.

258 SINGLE-HANDLED CUP
700-675 B.C.

INV. NO. A 15359.
H. 0.048, B.D. 0.028, M.D. 0.064 M.

Complete. Mended and restored. Small chips off rim.

Six pictorial panels are formed in the handle zone out of vertical double rows of lines, concentric circles, strands and Z-shaped motifs. In the panel first from

birds are rendered in a combination of silhouette and outline. The eyes are rendered in outline, whilst the necks of the birds of prey are spotted.

The lower half of the main body towards the base is taken up with a row of upside down left-turning hooks. The back of the handle is divided in two parts. On the upper there is a careless decoration which comprises a "St. Andrew's cross" formed by concentric semicircles. The lower part is decorated with a row of circles with black spots in their centre. The interior surface of the slanting rim is embellished with "drops". Inside, the vase is monochrome, apart from the rim zone, which is decorated with radial lines above a group of encircling bands. The centre of the flat base is indicated by a

259

258

257

in their centre. The pictorial zone stands above a band of radial decoration, which is divided from the flat base by a shallow incision. Three thin bands run around the rim zone. The back of the handle is decorated on its upper half with a schematic black lozenge divided by an X and on the lower half, with thin horizontal bands. The interior of the vessel is monochrome, except for the rim zone which is left clay-coloured and contains carelessly rendered Z-shaped motifs. The base is decorated with five concentric circles.

the left next to the handle, a bird of prey pointing right but turning its head backwards. A black rosette with an X inside decorates the second panel. A water bird roaming towards the left is depicted in the third. A carelessly executed cross-shaped decoration is above the bird's head. Two small lines hang from the line which is the upper border of the panel. A black rosette with an X inside decorates the fourth panel. A water bird, as in the third panel, decorates the fifth. A large bird of prey, pointing left and balancing the corresponding bird in the second panel, is portrayed in the sixth, its head turned backwards. All the

black spot surrounded by two concentric circles.

COMMENTARY - BIBLIOGRAPHY: Unpublished.
For the shape see the commentary on no. 262.

G.K.

259 BLACK-GLAZED SINGLE-HANDLED CUP
700-675 B.C.

INV. NO. A 15356.
H. 0.044, B.D. 0.024, M.D. 0.055 M.

Complete, apart from a small part of the rim. Mended and restored. Small chips off rim. The black paint on the interior, the rim and the upper half of the handle has mostly flaked off.

A series of fourteen circles runs around the body in the handle zone. Thin encircling bands surround the lower half of the vase. The transition from the main body is highlighted by a black encircling band. Two "St. Andrew's crosses" decorate the handle, the uppermost now being fugitive. The edge of the flat base is highlighted by a black band. The inter-

260 BLACK-GLAZED SINGLE-HANDLED CUP
700-675 B.C.

INV. NO. A 15354.
H. 0.043, B.D. 0.026, M.D. 0.053 M.

Complete. The handle is mended. Small chips off rim.

Seven circles, inside panels, with black blobs in the centre, decorate the zone on a level with the handle. There is a row of upside down hooks in the base zone, which is framed by a triple encircling band. The transition from the main body to the oblique rim is highlighted by a thin encircling band. The exterior of the rim is embellished with an irregular wavy band and the interior with radial decoration. The edge of the rim is highlighted by a thin encircling band. A horizontal

261 BLACK-GLAZED SINGLE-HANDLED CUP
700-675 B.C.

INV. NO. A 15358.
H. 0.037, B.D. 0.025, M.D. 0.043 M.

Complete. Small chips off rim.
The main handle zone is decorated with a wavy line and ends on the left in a snake's head. The field is filled with groups of triple, vertical S-shaped lines. Radiate decoration occupies the zone of the ring base. The zone on the slanting rim on the outside is highlighted by a row of irregular spots. The interior of the vase is monochrome, apart from the rim zone, which is decorated with large irregular spots. There is a pair of antithetical concentric semicircles and a "hour-glass" motif on the upper part of the strap handle.

261   *260*   *262*

ior of the slanting rim is decorated with a row of thin encircling bands.

COMMENTARY - BIBLIOGRAPHY: Unpublished.
For the shape see the commentary on no. 262.
G.K.

band of spots divides the handle into two parts. There is a pair of antithetic solid triangles ("hour-glass" motifs) on the upper half, while on the lower, there are broad horizontal bands. The interior of the vase is monochrome. The ring base is highlighted with a black band.

COMMENTARY - BIBLIOGRAPHY: Unpublished.
For the shape see the commentary on no. 262.
G.K.

A "St. Andrew's cross", which is developed into a lozenge, decorates the lower part of the handle. There are carelessly rendered black spots between the bars of the cross. The centre of the inside of the base and the underside are highlighted by black circles.

COMMENTARY - BIBLIOGRAPHY: Unpublished.
For the shape see the commentary on no. 262. For the wavy line which ends in a snake's head see *Kerameikos* VI₂, 111, fig. 4, 113, 230-231 and Kunisch 1998, 19-21, fig. 8-9 and 243, fig. 94d-e. For the funerary symbolism of the snake see, recently, Grabow 1998, esp. 15-37.
G.K.

262 BLACK-GLAZED SINGLE-HANDLED CUP
700-675 B.C.

INV. NO. A 15357.
H. 0.058, B.D. 0.037, M.D. 0.073 M.

Complete. Extended gaps on the main body of the vessel and chips off the rim. Uneven firing, mainly on the rear. The vase is monochrome inside and out, apart from the interior surface of the slanting rim which has three thin black bands running around it. The edge of the rim is highlighted with a dense row of black spots. The back of the handle is decorated with a row of irregular horizontal lines. An irregular reserved circle is on the bottom. The flat base is also reserved, apart from two points where the black paint has covered it.

COMMENTARY - BIBLIOGRAPHY: Unpublished.

It belongs to the Phaleron Group. The shape first occurs in the LG period and was produced throughout the 7th c. B.C. With regard to the typological development of single-handled cups see *Agora* VIII, 37, pl. 4, as well as 52-53. See also Brann 1961b, 312. According to Young, the deep single-handled cups with the characteristic developed slanting rim belong to the 7th c. B.C. For the shape see Young 1942, 36-38 and 46-47 (single-handled cups from the Phaleron tomb no. 48 - 2A, 2B, 2C). See also *Kerameikos* VI₂, 511, no. 126 (no. 1369), pl. 3 (similar). On the predecessors of the 8th c. B.C., the rim is smaller; cf. Brann 1961b, 337, no. F37, pl. 79.

G.K.

263 TREFOIL-MOUTHED BLACK-GLAZED OENOCHOE
680-660 B.C.

INV. NO. A 15335.
H. 0.173, B.D. 0.043 M.

Complete. Mended on the handle and rim. Brown clay. High cylindrical neck, ovoid body, slightly angular handle cylindrical in section, flat base. The vase is surrounded by five decorative zones. Below the rim, zone of four birds facing right, with raised hatched wings. The bodies of two are hatched whilst the others are in silhouette. A great deal of filling ornament: dotted rosette, hook, herring-bone, circle with dot. The second zone, at the base of the neck, is decorated with left facing S-shaped motifs. A third zone on the shoulder with pendent hooks. A fourth zone on the body made up of oblique zigzags. Slender radial decoration takes up the rest of the vase. Careless little lines on the rim and handle, with a black line running up its sides.

COMMENTARY - BIBLIOGRAPHY: Unpublished.

Small trefoil-mouthed oenochoae of this type are classified in the Phaleron Group. Chronologically, they cover the period between LG and the mid 7th c. B.C. The neck – conical or cylindrical – and the body – globular or more slender – does not appear to reflect differences in date. A common characteristic is the panel on the neck with animal and bird decoration, while the rest of the body follows linear or a freer decoration, divided up into zones. The present vase is between oenochoae 262 of London and 319 of Munich, for which see *Kerameikos* VI₂, 173 (between 710 and 680 B.C.). For the closest parallel see *CVA* Berlin 1, 45, 2-4 (from a tomb at Acharnai). Other parallels come from the Athenian Agora (*Agora* III, 36-37, 52, pl. 4) and Tomb 34 from the Phaleron cemetery (see Πελεκίδης 1916, 13ff.) which is dated by Young 1942, 23ff., from the end of the 1st quarter of the 7th c. B.C. Closer chronological parallels, for an earlier type, see *CVA* Kiel 2, pl. 24, 5-7 (710-690 B.C.) and for later see *CVA* München 3, 31, pl. 134, 1-3. Cf. also Καλλιπολίτης 1963, 120ff., pl. 49 (from tomb at Anagyrous). For vases of this type see recently *APP* 1995 [Dennis], 19-20, no. 8 and Petrocheilos 1996, 45-65, with bibliography.

E.B.-V.

264 BLACK-GLAZED CYLINDRICAL PYXIS WITH LID
680-660 B.C.

INV. NO. A 15340.
H. (EXCL. LID) 0.04, H. (INCL. LID) 0.068, M.D. 0.071, B.D. 0.063, D. OF LID. 0.068 M.

Complete. Mended with some restoration. Brown clay. Broad cylindrical body. Small horizontal handles on rim. The lid almost flat with a handle in the shape of a stylised pomegranate. Three zones decorate the body: in the first, below the rim, a row of Z-shaped motifs with black dots in the intervals; on the other side of the vase, a chain of lozenges. In the central zone, a row of black dots and in the third, a row of solid black isosceles triangles. Four black bands run around the interior, whilst a circle divides the mastoid central projection of the bottom. Incised broken lines on the horizontal handles. The handle of the lid is decorated with solid triangles, which sprout from a black band. At the base of the handle, spread-out radial decoration supplement double lozenges. On the edge, semicircles with a dot, whilst the decoration is finished off with a zone of dots on the perimeter of the lid.

COMMENTARY - BIBLIOGRAPHY: Unpublished.

The pyxis belongs to the Phaleron Group with clear similarities in terms of shape, decoration and the dimension to vases from the Phaleron cemetery, such as pyxis no. 39 from Tomb 11,8 which Young 1942, 33, fig. 13, dates to the early 7th c. B.C.; also see Πελεκίδης 1916, 13ff. For the body there is a parallel in pyxis 13 from Phaleron; cf. Böhlau 1887, 55, fig. 19. Likewise, see Brann 1961b, 343, no. F70, pl. 85 (close in terms of shape from the Agora; early 3rd quarter of 7th c. B.C.). For the decoration of the lid see *CVA* München 3, pl. 134, 4, 6 (lekanis lid; 2nd quarter of 7th c. B.C.). Cylindrical pyxides are the earliest of the Phaleron Group and it appears that they start to rise in the 8th or beginning of the 7th c. B.C. Later in the 7th c., they become taller and with curved walls. The handle of the lid also has a Geometric origin and differs from the conical handles which dominate in the 7th c. B.C. For more on the development of the shape see *Kerameikos* VI₂, 183, no. 38, pl. 31. See also Young 1942, 40, fig. 22, 2A-B.

E.B.-V.

265 MINIATURE BLACK-GLAZED FEEDER WITH STRAINER

680-660 B.C.

INV. NO. A 15337.
H. 0.033, M.D. 0.051, B.D. 0.021 M.

Complete with a few pieces missing. Brown clay. Spherical body, projecting rim, small discoid base. The disc which covers the cup is slightly curved towards the centre and has two rows of perforations. The strap handle begins at the rim and ends on the belly. The cylindrical spout projects horizontally from the belly of the vase.

The disc is decorated with two concentric zones of "double axes" in outline between the perforations. In the interior zone, they alternate with solid triangles. Row of dots on the edge of the disc. The body is decorated with three zones: Solid triangles in the first around the rim. Lozenges in the second. Between the handle and spout, a "St. Andrew's cross" with solid triangles in three of the bar intervals and a double angle in the fourth next to the spout. Left turned hooks in the third zone above the base. A sprouting spiral ending in a flower occupies the upper part of the handle.

COMMENTARY - BIBLIOGRAPHY: Unpublished.
The vase belongs to the Phaleron Group and is considered rare. The body follows the type of single-handled cups of the category with high rim and belly; cf. *Agora* VIII, 54, no. 192, pl. 10 (cup of the early 7th c. B.C.). For a similar feeder, without strainer, from 700 B.C., see *Kerameikos* VI₂, 230, pl. 107 and p. 170 for date and commentary. For related Sub-Geometric shapes see *CVA* München 3, pl. 119, 3-5 (spouted kantharos) and 6-7 (kylix with strainer and spout). In general for the shape see *Agora* XII, 161, with bibliography.

E.B.-V.

263

264

266

265

266 BLACK-GLAZED HIGH-FOOTED CUP
680-660 B.C.

INV. NO. A 15343.
H. 0.13, M.D. 0.089, B.D. 0.071 M.

Complete. Mended from many sherds. Small amount of restoration on the rim, body as well as the lower part of the foot. Brown clay. Conical body with straight walls. A strap handle begins on the rim and, with an angle, ends on the lower part of the body. A second, horizontal handle on the other side sprouts from its lower part. The foot is cylindrical and high, and has two zones of fenestrations: the upper zone has six rectangular vertical fenestrations and the lower, twelve, in the shape of alternating triangles.

The body is crossed by two decorative zones. On the first zone, in the upper part, a row of six water birds towards the left with bent necks ending in outlined heads. Small supplementary decoration in the intervals. The second zone is decorated with right-turned pendent hooks. On the secondary side of the vase, in the upper zone, three deer facing left with necks lowered towards the ground. Beneath the body of each animal, supplementary decoration of a lozenge with two intersecting Xs. Careless zigzags in the lower zone.

Small zone of solid right-turned hooks above the horizontal handle. Groups of careless vertical zigzag on the stem in the intervals of the first zone. Scattered black dots between the zones. Trace of black on the dividing segments of the triangles. The edge of the rim and base as well as the handles are decorated with careless small lines. A group of lines runs round the interior of the rim, whilst the inside of the cup is black with a ground-coloured band on the bottom.

COMMENTARY - BIBLIOGRAPHY: Unpublished.

The shape of the conical cup follows one of the two categories of cups of the Phaleron Group; in general for vases of this type from Phaleron see Young 1942, 23ff. For the shape, the history of the conical cup as well as dating problems, see *Kerameikos* VI₂, 170. The adoption of triangular openings on the foot happens in the early 7th c. B.C. but similar cups from the Keramei-

kos are dated by Kübler to the 3rd quarter of the 7th c. B.C. Other close examples come from wells in the Athenian Agora of the 7th c. B.C.; for this see Young 1939, 139, no. XII.6, fig. 39 and XII.5 (from a pyre). For another close example in terms of the high-footed cup shape, but with different decoration, see Kübler 1934, 219, fig. 14 (from pot burial X of the Kerameikos; middle or 3rd quarter of the 7th c. B.C.). For a similar cup see Καλλιπολίτης 1963, 122, pl. 52α (from tomb at Anagyrous, of the middle Proto-Attic period). For the pose of the bird see Benson 1970, pl. XXV:21 (amphora from the Geometric cemetery at Eleusis). For the zone of birds, which are identified as waterfowls, see Karouzou 1979, 127ff. (oenochoe in Toulouse; 1st half of 7th c. B.C.). For the representation of the deer in a zone see *Agora* VIII, 72, no. 360 and 70, no. 342, pl. 21. For bibliography on the high-footed cup see *Kerameikos* VI₂, 168. Owing to the absence of decoration connected with the middle Proto-Attic period, as well as elements of colour, the vase can be dated to the 2nd quarter of the century.

E.B.-V.

267 MINIATURE BLACK-GLAZED SINGLE-HANDLED CUP
680-660 B.C.

INV. NO. A 15341.
H. 0.05, M.D. 0.067, B.D. 0.03 M.

Complete. Mended and restored on parts of the rim and body. Brown clay, red decoration. Spherical body. The raised rim forms a division with the curve of the body. Flat narrow base. Strap handle.

The rim is decorated with careless vertical little lines. A panel occupies half the vase between the encircling lines and three vertical ones on either side of the handle. Two boats facing left are represented in it. Six rowers and four oars are depicted on the first boat. Lines at an angle above the prow indicate the sail. Eight rowers and five oars on the second boat. Broken lines in a horizontal arrangement above the rowers. The lower part of the vase is covered by a zone with a double row of radial decoration in silhouette. Three encircling lines on the interior of the rim, a circle on the reserved bottom. The rest of the interior is brown. Traces of decoration on the lower part of the handle.

COMMENTARY - BIBLIOGRAPHY: Unpublished.

The cup belongs to the spherical cup category of the Phaleron Group. Its decoration is careless and the reddish colour is due to the uneven firing of the vessel. For the shape of the cup see *Kerameikos* VI₂, 169-170. For similar cups from the Phaleron cemetery see Πελεκίδης 1916, 13ff.; for their date in the 1st quarter of the 7th c. B.C. see Young 1942, 27, fig. 4 (19 IA-IB), whilst the shape is closer to 62 IA (fig. 20) and 32.1 (fig. 21), of the 2nd quarter of the 7th c. B.C.

Interest is centred upon the representation of the two boats. The fact that they are rendered backwards is not due to the depiction of a shipwreck, since the rowers are in their positions, but can, perhaps, be explained by the broader field which is created for depicting the boat in this position. On the other hand, the whole rendering is careless.

267

The subject of boats is a favourite in the Geometric period, whilst it is not known amongst the Phaleron Group. According to Brann, *Agora* VIII, 17-18, boats disappear from Attic vase-painting in the 7th c. B.C. The boat on a Proto-Corinthian skyphos from Eleusis is somewhat close, for which see Σκιάς 1898, 110, n. 2, pl. 5,3. A boat depiction, without rowers, on a krater sherd of this period, from a well in the Agora, is attributed by Brann 1961a, 139, fig. 14, to the Analatos P. For a representation of boats of this period see Hampe 1936, pl. 22; Cook 1934-35, pl. 40b; Τζάχου-Αλεξανδρή 1987, 333-361; Wedde

1999, 505-523. For boats in general see Kirk 1949, 93ff.; Williams 1958, 121ff.; Rombos 1988; Gray 1974, 57-61, fig. 18; Basch 1987, 156-201; Morrison - Williams 1968 with catalogue and bibliography. Finally, for the double radial decoration see *Kerameikos* VI₂, 376, fig. 44.

E.B.-V.

268 MINIATURE BLACK-GLAZED SINGLE-HANDLED CUP
680-660 B.C.

INV. NO. A 15342.
H. 0.05, M.D. 0.062, B.D. 0.028 M.

Almost complete. Mended, with a number of restorations. Brown clay. Spherical body, broad projecting rim, narrow flat base, strap handle.

Groups of three vertical lines on the rim form schematised triglyphs and panels. A double encircling band beneath the rim, as well as a system of lines on the lower part of the body border a zone which is decorated with a row of circles with a central dot. Group of encircling lines on the interior of the rim. Vase black-painted inside. Traces of three concentric circles on the base of the vase. Horizontal short lines on the handle.

COMMENTARY - BIBLIOGRAPHY: Unpublished.
This type of cup is widely known in the Phaleron Group. For the shape and its development see *Kerameikos* VI₂, 169-170. It is derived from Geometric prototypes of the last 30 years of the 8th c. B.C. with a development from more slender shapes (in the 8th c. B.C.) to more spherical ones towards the middle of the 7th c. B.C. For a closer parallel, more in terms of decoration than shape, see Young 1942, 38, no. 96, fig. 20 (Tomb 62, 1; 2nd quarter of 7th c. B.C.). In general, it appears that for these cups, a chronological development is followed based not so much on morphological criteria as on archaeological context. Their shape and decoration are clearly influenced by the LG period.

E.B.-V.

269 MINIATURE BLACK-GLAZED SINGLE-HANDLED CUP
680-660 B.C.

INV. NO. A 15339.
H. 0.041, M.D. 0.051, B.D. 0.037 M.

Complete, with rim mended. Brown clay. Broad mouth, concave walls, flat base, strap handle.
Six left-pointing S-shaped motifs decorate the main zone of the vase. Lozenges divided with an X are in the intervals; small solid triangles above and below each lozenge. Narrow zone with row of solid triangles runs around the vase above the base. Three encircling bands on interior of rim. Horizontal and vertical lines alternating on the handle. A circle with a dot in the centre of the base is surrounded by two concentric circles.

COMMENTARY - BIBLIOGRAPHY: Unpublished.
The cup is included in the conical cup category of the Phaleron Group, even if it has differences in shape. For the shape of conical cups see *Kerameikos* VI₂, 169-170 esp. no. 72, 83, pl. 75 as well as 452, no. 42, pl. 31 (similar motif on a vase of 690-680 B.C.). For similar S-shaped motifs see *CVA* Berlin I, pl. 6, 3-4 (krater A12) and Young 1942, fig. 18 (krater of the 1st quarter of the 7th c. B.C. from T. 18 at Phaleron). Likewise see *Agora* VIII, 52-54, no. 193, pl. 10 (cup of the early 7th c. B.C.).

E.B.-V.

270 CONICAL SINGLE-HANDLED CUP
680-660 B.C.

INV. NO. A 15336.
H. 0.04, M.D. 0.102, B.D. 0.035 M.

Almost complete, mended, with a few restorations. Brown clay. Conical body, with flat base and horizontal handle.
Wavy lines below the rim. The rest of the

vase is decorated with encircling lines in two groups. Black band separates the base. Zone of black dots on the interior of the rim, with two encircling lines a little lower down. The rest of the interior of the vase is black-painted.

COMMENTARY - BIBLIOGRAPHY: Unpublished.
It belongs to the Phaleron Group and is common in terms of shape and decoration, which reflects Late-Geometric prototypes. Young 1939, 205-206, classifies cups of this type starting from the deeper ones of the end of the 8th c. B.C., to the shallower examples (C81-82), up to the middle of the 7th c. B.C. The closest examples come from the Athenian Agora; for this see Young 1939, 157, no. C53, fig. 111; Burr 1933b, 624, no. 336, fig. 90; Young 1938, 414, no. D12, fig. 2. Close, but more developed, is that from Tomb 74,1 at Phaleron, no. 94 (Πελεκίδης 1916, 13ff.) which is dated by Young 1942, 23ff., to the 3rd quarter of the 7th c. B.C. on the basis of the archaeological context.

E.B.-V.

271

271   MINIATURE BLACK-GLAZED TREFOIL-MOUTHED OENOCHOE
675-650 B.C.

INV. NO. A 15379.
H. 0.068, MAX.D. 0.058, B.D. 0.04 M.

Restored on rim and beginning of handle. Chips on the mouth. Light brown clay. Flat base, depressed spherical body, high-swung strap handle, trefoil mouth. Black coating with traces of uneven firing covers the vase. The belly zone is left the colour of the clay, decorated with a pair of black lines. On the reserved back of the handle, vertical black band on top of a horizontal black zone at the point where the handle joins the body. Shallow incision divides the flat base from the body.

COMMENTARY - BIBLIOGRAPHY: Unpublished.
It belongs to the category of small oenochoae and is a

grave offering. It belongs to the Phaleron Group which took its name from the Phaleron excavation of the beginning of the 20th century at the delta of Palaion Phaleron; see Πελεκίδης 1916, 13-64. For parallels see Young 1942, 24 (78,2); *Agora* VIII, pl. 4,58; *Kerameikos* VI₂, pl. 81, no. 621. For further comments see no. 250.

I.T.-D.

272   PROTO-CORINTHIAN CYLINDRICAL PYXIS
675-650 B.C.

INV. NO. A 15382.
H. 0.076, M.D. 0.073, B.D. 0.068 M.

Mended from many pieces, and restored on part of the body. One handle missing. Many chips and flakings. Light yellow clay. Flat base, cylindrical body, cylindrical handle attached to the rim, surface of lid flat ending in a conical knob.
There are three decorative zones on the body. Radial decoration in black and red due to differential firing, in the base zone. There follows an encircling zone in the middle of the body with dotted rosettes, framed by two violet bands, which in turn are surrounded by a pair of lines. The handle zone is decorated with a row of spots. Black coated interior. The lid is decorated by two zones. An encircling zone with dotted rosettes, framed by two violet bands; radial decoration around the knob. Three black bands run around the conical-shaped knob.

COMMENTARY - BIBLIOGRAPHY: Unpublished.
The pyxis, a toiletries vase, was used for holding jewellery and cosmetics. This use, as well as its frequent presence as a grave offering, links it with female burials. The pyxis from the Kerameikos belongs to the Phaleron Group. For a closer parallel see Young 1942, 22 (71,2b) and 24 (78,2) and *CVA* France, no. 30, Musée des Beaux Arts à Jours, pl. 1,1. For further observations see other comments on the same group (Tombs 191 and 152).

I.T.-D.

273 BLACK-GLAZED LEKANIS WITH LID
675-650 B.C.

INV. NO. A 15380.
H. 0.087, M.D. 0.09, D. OF LID 0.097, B.D. 0.04 M.

Mended from many pieces and parts of the body and rim of the lid restored. A large part of the decoration is fugitive. Ring base, hemispherical body, slightly curved lid ending in conical knob. Light brown clay.

There are three decorative zones on the body: the zone near the base is decorated with vertical, left-turned hooks. Two encircling black bands in the middle of the body, framed by a pair of black lines above and one black band below. The zone at the level of the handles is decorated on one side with S-shaped patterns and on the other, with a row of circles with an X inside. A black band covers the rim. The horizontal cylindrical handles, with a projection on the side, are decked with a row of spots between black bands. Five concentric black bands run around the interior of the body.

Three decorative zones, each separated from the other by a pair of black bands, are spread out on the lid. A zone of left-turned hooks near the rim. A zone with a dentate motif follows, while the larger zone has radial decoration with dots between the spokes. The upper part of the knob is black-painted, the lower left the colour of the clay, decorated with a pair of black lines. The upper surface of the knob, on a white background, is decorated with a black circle and an inscribed cross as well as encircling spots some of which are linked radially with the circle. Two concentric circles on the concave base.

COMMENTARY - BIBLIOGRAPHY: Unpublished.
It belongs to the Phaleron Group; see Young 1942, 19 (40,7) and 21 (72,6). For the decoration on the lid see Young 1942, 24 (78,2) and 17 (18,3) while for the shape see *Kerameikos* VI$_2$, 159. For further observations see comments on the same group (Tombs 191 and 152).

I.T.-D.

273

274 BLACK-GLAZED LEKANIS
675-650 B.C.

INV. NO. A 15381.
H. 0.053, M.D. 0.088, B.D. 0.041 M.

Mended from many pieces and parts of the body and one handle slightly restored. Much chipped or flaking, mainly of the applied violet. Light brown clay. Flat base, hemispherical body, horizontal cylindrical handles with projections on the sides, in-turned rim to hold the lid. Successive black bands decorate the interior and exterior of the body. The intervals between the bands are covered with applied fugitive violet. Traces of white wavy lines in the handle zone and on the surface of the handles themselves.

COMMENTARY - BIBLIOGRAPHY: Unpublished.
It belongs to the Phaleron Group. For the shape see no. 273, whilst for the interior decoration see *Kerameikos* IX, pl. 15,3. For further observations see the comments on the same group (Tombs 191 and 152).

I.T.-D.

275 BLACK-GLAZED KOTYLE
675-650 B.C.

INV. NO. A 15383.
H. 0.05, M.D. 0.06, B.D. 0.026 M.

Mended and slightly restored. Small chips off rim and handles. Pale yellow clay. Low ring base, deep almost hemispherical body, shapeless rim.
Group of multiple successive lines in red run around the body. They are cut off a little above the base by a row of vertical left-turned hooks. The handle zone is decorated with vertical, asymmetrical S-shaped motifs which also continue onto the horizontal handles. Pair of parallel lines in red on the rim. The interior is painted red, apart from a zone near the rim which is reserved.

COMMENTARY - BIBLIOGRAPHY: Unpublished.
It belongs to the Phaleron Group; for a parallel see Young 1942, 29 (33,1). For the shape see *Agora* VIII, 49-50; for the reversed hooks see *Kerameikos* VI₂, 136, fig. 18. For Corinthian kotylae in general see no. 374.

I.T.-D.

276 BLACK-FIGURE LEKYTHOS (DEIANEIRA TYPE)
End of 6th c. B.C.

INV. NO. A 15245.
H. 0.155, M.D. 0.037, B.D. 0.053 M.

It is preserved complete with lower part of body and base mended. Much chipping and flaking mainly in the pictorial panel. Brown-red clay. Discoid base, ovoid body, short cylindrical neck, vertical strap handle with concave outer surface, calyx-shaped mouth. Polished black coating covers the vase, apart from the neck and the pictorial panel. The rim is covered with violet paint. A reserved band runs around the body below the representation.
The pictorial panel is bounded above by a destroyed tongue-like decoration with traces of violet and below by a pair of parallel bands. A mature man occupies the centre of the scene, with a trailing chiton and himation in profile facing left. He holds out a wreath with his right hand towards a young man who holds a spear diagonally in his right hand and the fringe of his himation in his left which is worn around his waist. The composition finishes off with a figure, on the right of which traces of the attire and the soles of his feet show that it is moving to the right. Details of clothing and the wreath are rendered in applied violet. The ground line of the scene is a red band.

COMMENTARY - BIBLIOGRAPHY: Unpublished.
The Deianeira type is the earliest of the lekythos category with a relatively small production span, placed in the whole of the 6th c. B.C. It is not a particularly widespread type, often met as a grave good. It belongs, according to Haspels, to the Sub-Deianeira shape category, see *ABL* 130, pl. 9,3. Also see Kurtz 1975, pl. 67,1; *Agora* XII, 151; Boardman 1978, 148. For the closest typological parallel see *CVA* Nantes Musée Dobrée (France 36) pl. 9, D947-2-4. Despite the fragmentary state of preservation of the scene, the pose of the figures as well as the wreath, a gift perhaps of the mature man to the young one, probably is meant to indicate an amorous exchange between the two men. For a comparable representation see Keuls 1993, 279, fig. 245

274, 275

(where a man holds a wreath in an erotic scene between men). For wreaths in general see Blech 1982; for amorous exchanges see Shapiro 1981, 133-143 and Kilmer 1993.

I.T.-D.

277 MINIATURE BLACK-GLAZED LEKANIS WITH LID
End of 6th c. B.C.

INV. NO. A 15244.
H. 0.07, M.D. 0.075, D. OF KNOB 0.04, B.D. 0.039 M.

Complete with restoration on one handle, slight chips mainly on the handles and flaking all over the body. Light brown clay. Conical base, hemispherical body, horizontal strap handles with projections on the sides. The lid with curved walling ends in a conical knob.

Black coating covers the vase. Reserved are: the underside of the base, the bottom on the inside, which has a conical projection with a black dot, and the lower part of the exterior surface. The inside of the handles, the rim of the vase and of the lid, the inside of the lid and the disc of the knob are also reserved. The interior of the vase is decorated with two pairs of red lines whilst the bottom has a circle with a black dot in its centre. On the disc of the knob there are two concentric red bands around a black-painted recess.

COMMENTARY - BIBLIOGRAPHY: Unpublished.
The lekanis is regarded mainly as a vase for toiletries and is usually found in tombs. This example belongs to the category of small lekanides; see *Kerameikos* IX, pl. 84, E2 (with bibliography).

I.T.-D.

276, 277

278 LYDION
End of 6th c. B.C.

INV. NO. A 15246.
H. 0.111, M.D. 0.051, B.D. 0.0365 M.

Complete, with slight chips off the rim and flaking of the black glaze. Brown-red clay. Discoid base with deepening at its bottom, spindle-shaped body, high cylindrical neck, flat everted rim.
Black coating, iridescent due to firing, covers the inside and outside of the neck, the low foot and the surface of the base. A black band runs around the shoulders. The rest of the body is reserved.

COMMENTARY - BIBLIOGRAPHY: Unpublished.
This is a perfume bottle which is met mainly in the 6th c. B.C. It is usually found in tombs of this period, without being so very widespread. It is one of the rare Athenian imitations of a Lydian perfume bottle, from which it also takes its name. For a very close parallel see Young 1951, 101, pl. 46,6. For lydia in general see Greenwalt 1920, 163, 170; Bottini 1966, 138-143; *Agora* XII, 157 (with bibliography). Most recently see Özgen - Öztürk 1996.

I.T.-D.

279 LYDION
End of 6th c. B.C.

INV. NO. A 15247.
H. 0.096, M.D. 0.036, B.D. 0.038 M.

Complete. Flaking mainly on the black glazing. Brown-red clay. Discoid base with concentric shallow grooves on its surface and deepening at its bottom, spindle-shaped body, high cylindrical neck, flat everted rim.
Black coating covers the interior and exterior of the neck, the low foot and the surface of the base. A black band runs around the shoulders. The rest of the body is reserved.

COMMENTARY - BIBLIOGRAPHY: Unpublished.
See no. 278.

I.T.-D.

280 LYDION
End of 6th c. B.C.

INV. NO. A 15253.
H. 0.112, M.D. 0.06, B.D. 0.034 M.

Complete. Limited restoration on rim and some flaking mainly on the neck. Red-brown clay. High conical base, spindle-shaped body, cylindrical neck, flat everted rim.
Black coating covers the base, neck and interior of the vase. On the underside, two concentric red coloured circles with black dot in the centre. Successive bands of black run around the body and shoulders. Pair of red concentric circles decorate the rim.

COMMENTARY - BIBLIOGRAPHY: Unpublished.
For a very close parallel see Sheer 1940, 302. For observations and relevant bibliography see no. 278.

I.T.-D.

281 LYDION
End of 6th c. B.C.

INV. NO. A 15254.
H. 0.12, M.D. 0.062, B.D. 0.039 M.

Complete with small chip off rim and much flaking mainly on the interior of the neck Reddish clay. High conical base, spindle-shaped body, cylindrical neck, flat everted rim.
Black coating covers the base, neck and interior of the vase. On the underside, a large black dot is surrounded by concentric circles in red. Successive bands of black run around the body and shoulders. Red concentric circles decorate the rim.

COMMENTARY - BIBLIOGRAPHY: Unpublished.
See nos. 280 and 278.

I.T.-D.

278, 279

280

281

282 BLACK-FIGURE LEKYTHOS (SECONDARY TYPE)
500-475 B.C.

INV. NO. A 15415.
H. 0.185, B.D. 0.052, M.D. 0.044, D. AT SHOULDER LEVEL
0.071 M.

Complete. Small chips off rim and shoulder. Extensive flaking on the lower black section of the body of the vase and the base.

Naked Theseus occupies the centre of the scene where he has felled the Marathon Bull and halted it with a rope. He is holding, though not using, a club in his right hand. On the left, bordering the scene, is a youth with an himation covering the upper part of the body and the extended left arm. He also holds a club in his right arm. On the right, another youth is distanced from the scene, though turning his head backwards to the central pair, Theseus and the Marathon Bull. Vines fill the background of the scene, with the clothes and weapons of Theseus deposited above them.

A double row of black spots, some highlighted with applied white, crown the scene. The clubs are also rendered in applied white, as well as the lower part of the Bull's tail, the clothes of Theseus above the vines and the scattered spots which border them. The bands which decorate the hair of the figures, details of the clothing and of the Bull's neck are rendered in applied violet. A black-painted radial motif embellishes the shoulder which is left clay-coloured, whilst the transition to the neck is highlighted by a schematic tongue-shaped decoration.

COMMENTARY - BIBLIOGRAPHY: Unpublished.

For the myth and the identity of the figures who felled the Marathon Bull see *LIMC* V, s.v. Herakles, 61-62 [Todisco]; *LIMC* VII, s.v. Theseus, 936 [Neils]; Καββαδίας 1997. Also for the iconographic mixing of two myths see a white-ground oenochoe of the Group of Vatican G47 in Naples, no. 86372 (R.C.203), *CVA* Museo Nazionale di Napoli V - Raccolta Cumana, 44, pl. 60 [Nazarena Valenza Mele]. For the contemporary red-figure version of the myth by Onesimos see Nachbaur 1998, 97-108 and by the Euergides P. on a kylix at the J.P. Getty Museum, no. 86.AE.305.1-2, see *CVA* J.P. Getty 8, 15-16, no. 20, pl. 399.1-3 [Moore]. For the identification of the supplementary figures with the imaginary exemplification of Athenian youth see *APP* 1995, 32-34, no. 21 [Nicgorski]. For the tree (olive?) above which the clothes of Theseus and Herakles are hanging see Κόρτη-Κόντη 1993-94, esp. 16-17 and 21-22.

The Class of Athens 581 comprises a very numerous group of small black-figure lekythoi of the 1st quarter of the 5th c. B.C. Beazley distinguished two variations: in the first, Athens Class 581, i, the shoulder is decorated with black-painted lotus calyxes and is of slightly better quality than the second Class of Athens 581, ii, where the shoulder bears schematic radial decoration. For Athens Class 581 see *ABL* 99ff.; *ARV²* 487ff.; *Para* 222ff.; Kurtz 1975, 8, 119, 147-149; *Agora* XXIII, 46-47. We have a similar scene on a lekythos of the Class of Athens 581, ii, Agora Group P 24486 in Athens, Ancient Agora Museum, no. P 24487; see *Para* 236 and *Agora* XXIII, 229, no. 1022, pl. 83. Cf. also a lekythos from the Kerameikos; *Kerameikos* IX, 94, no. 31.2, pl. 47.3-4 (c. 490 B.C.; from Tomb HW 210).

Class of Athens 581, ii.

G.K.

283 BLACK-FIGURE LEKYTHOS (SECONDARY TYPE)
500-475 B.C.

INV. NO. A 15423.
H. 0.11, B.D. 0.032, M.D. 0.028, D. AT SHOULDER
LEVEL 0.045 M.

Complete. Mouth mended but missing a small piece. Much chipping and flaking on the main body of the vase.

Theseus has bent down to tie the kneeling Marathon Bull with a rope of myrtle. Above the vines, which fill the background of the scene, the hero has laid down his clothes and weapons, because according to the myth, he took hold of the bull using only his hands. The band of Theseus's hair and the rope are rendered in applied white paint as also are details of his clothing and arms. A band with a double row of carelessly rendered white and black spots surmounts the scene. Black-painted radial motif embellishes the shoulder which is left the colour of the clay, whilst the transition to the neck is highlighted with a schematic tongue-shaped decoration.

COMMENTARY - BIBLIOGRAPHY: Unpublished.
See the commentary on no. 282. It is most probably by the same hand as a lekythos in Paris, the Rodin Museum, no. 145, *ABV* 499,28, *CVA* Rodin, pl. 17.6 [Plautine]. Also see *Kerameikos* IX, 93, no. 29.3 (Tomb HW 107), pl. 26.8 (3).
Class of Athens 581, ii.

G.K.

284 BLACK-FIGURE LEKYTHOS (SECONDARY TYPE)
500-475 B.C.

INV. NO. A 15424.
H. 0.15, B.D. 0.042, M.D. 0.038, D. AT SHOULDER LEVEL 0.06 M.

Complete. Mended and restored. Much chipping and flaking on the main body and deep cracks in the representation. Herakles defeats the Nemean Lion. Left, a male figure with a club on his bent right arm draws back, although turning backwards towards the hero struggling with the lion. The club is depicted in applied white as are the clothing and weapons of Herakles which have been placed above the vines which fill the background of the scene. The mane and belly of the lion are rendered in applied violet paint. A band with a double row of carelessly rendered white and black spots crowns the scene. Black-painted radial motif embellishes the shoulder which is left the colour of the clay, whilst the transition to the neck is highlighted with a schematic tongue-shaped decoration.

COMMENTARY - BIBLIOGRAPHY: Unpublished.
For Herakles's struggle with the Nemean Lion see *LIMC* V, 16-27, s.v. Herakles [Felten] and *APP* 1995, 32-34, no. 21. Also cf. a lekythos of the Class of Athens 581, i, in Athens, Ancient Agora Museum, no. P 24506, see *Agora* XXIII, 215-216, no. 897, pl. 80. Also see the commentary on no. 282.
Class of Athens 581, ii.

G.K.

283

282

284

285 BLACK-FIGURE LEKYTHOS (SECONDARY TYPE)
500-475 B.C.

INV. NO. A 15417.
H. 0.153, MAX.B.D. 0.042 D. OF RESTING SURFACE, 0.039,
M.D. 0.039, D. AT SHOULDER LEVEL 0.062 M.

Complete. Mended. Limited restoration on the neck. Chips and flaking mainly on the shoulder and the calyx-shaped mouth. Applied white paint is fugitive at many points.

The centre of the scene is occupied by a Maenad above an ithyphallic mule facing right. Another Maenad on foot and a dancing satyr follow her. Dionysos leads the company turning his head back and holding a horn in front of his chest. Vines with schematically rendered leaves fill the background of the scene. The face and naked limbs of the Maenads are covered with applied white paint, and details of the chiton of Dionysos are highlighted. Details of the folds, the beard of the Satyr and Dionysos as well as the mane of the mule are rendered in applied violet. A band of simple right-turned meander pattern crowns the scene. A black-painted radial motif embellishes the shoulder which is left clay coloured, whilst the transition to the neck is highlighted by a schematic tongue-shaped pattern.

COMMENTARY - BIBLIOGRAPHY: Unpublished.

For the Class of Athens 581, ii see the commentary on no. 282; cf. Athens, Ancient Agora Museum, nos. P 24434 and P 24358, see *Agora* XXIII, 221, nos. 948, 957, pl. 82 (for Group P). For the Dionysiac troupe see *LIMC* III, s.v. Dionysos, 451ff., pl. 327ff. [Gaspari] and Schöne 1987. For Dionysiac scenes in the 5th c. B.C. see Carpenter 1997. The slight bending and forward incline of the Satyr's body corresponds to the movement of "ἔμπροσθεν ἐπικύπτειν", whilst the moment when his left leg is ready to hit the ground corresponds to "σκέλος ῥίπτειν". For the names of body and arm movements in ancient dance terminology see Schreckenberg 1960, esp. 76-84. For the literary sources see Roos 1951. Also see Franzius 1973 and Μαραγκού 1995, 138. For Maenads in black-figure style vase-painting see most recently Moraw 1998.

G.K.

286 BLACK-FIGURE LEKYTHOS (SECONDARY TYPE)
500-475 B.C.

INV. NO. A 15420.
H. 0.142, B.D. 0.038, M.D. 0.073, D. AT SHOULDER LEVEL
0.062 M.

Complete. Small chips and gaps on the main body and the calyx-shaped mouth. Dionysos sitting cross-legged on a stool occupies the centre of the scene, in profile facing right. He wears a multi-folded chiton trailing at his feet, has a wreath in his hair and holds a large kantharos. Two women frame him, also sitting cross-legged on a stool. They hold unknown objects, probably vases (alabastra?). They wear multi-folded chitons and have wreaths in their hair. Vines with schematically rendered leaves fill the background of the scene between the two figures. Scattered spots are rendered in applied white paint in the field of the representation as well as details of the clothing. The wreath and beard of the male figure are rendered in applied violet paint, as are the wreaths of the women and details of their folds. A band with a double row of white and black carelessly executed spots crowns the scene. A black-painted radial decoration embellishes the clay-coloured shoulder, whilst the transition to the neck is highlighted with tongue-shaped decoration.

COMMENTARY - BIBLIOGRAPHY: Unpublished.

For the seated Dionysos between two seated figures see *CVA* Genève 2, 43-44, pl. 73. 9-10 [Dunant-Kahil]. For the Kalinderu Group, a sub-group of the Class of Athens 581, see *ABV* 503. Cf. the following lekythoi of the Kalinderu Group in Athens, Ancient Agora Museum, no. P 24438 (*Para* 244; *Agora* XXIII, 234, no. 1075, pl. 85), and Vienna, Universität, 739.5 (*ABV* 503,8; *CVA* Wien 1, 17, no. 10, pl. 6.10 [Kenner]). Cf. also a lekythos of the Class of Athens 581, ii in Naples, Museo Archeologico Nazionale, no. 86379 (R.C. 1361), see *CVA* Museo Nazionale di Napoli V - Raccolta Cumana, 43-44, pl. 59.3,6,9 [Nazarena Valenza Mele] and another in Athens, Kerameikos Museum, Tomb HW 211 (*Kerameikos* IX, 96, no. 35 and pl. 24.5). Class of Athens 581, ii. Kalinderu Group.

G.K.

287 BLACK-FIGURE LEKYTHOS (SECONDARY TYPE)
500-475 B.C.

INV. NO. A 15421.
H. 0.152, B.D. 0.044, M.D. 0.039, D. AT SHOULDER LEVEL
0.059 M.

Complete. The mouth and handle are mended. Chips and gaps particularly on the main body.

Right, a symposiast reclining on a cushion holds a kantharos in his raised right hand. Left, a naked courtesan, likewise reclining on cushion, turns her head towards the symposiast. Vines with schematically rendered leaves fill the background of the scene. Part of the body of the courtesan and the pillows are covered in fugitive applied white paint. The bands on the hair of the two figures is rendered in applied violet. A band of a double row of carelessly rendered white and black spots crowns the scene. A black-painted radial decoration embellishes the clay-coloured shoulder, whilst the transition to the neck is highlighted with tongue-shaped decoration.

COMMENTARY - BIBLIOGRAPHY: Unpublished.

For the Class of Athens 581, ii see the commentary on no. 282. For symposia see Μαραγκού 1995, 138, no. 19 (with earlier bibliography) and more recently, Schäfer 1997. For the subject cf. the lekythoi in Athens, Ancient Agora Museum, nos. P 24402, P 24376 and P 24375, see *Agora* XXIII, 227, nos. 1002, 1011 and 1015, pl. 83 (all belong to the Class of Athens 581, ii).

G.K.

286

287

285

296

288 BLACK-FIGURE LEKYTHOS (SECONDARY TYPE)
500-475 B.C.

INV. NO. A 15419.
H. 0.142, B.D. 0.04, M.D. 0.037, D. AT SHOULDER LEVEL
0.062 M.

Complete. Mended from many sherds. Chips and flaking particularly on the main body. The applied white paint is fugitive at many points in the representation.

Athena occupies the centre of the scene in the Promachos-posture, charging to her right and readying herself to beat a Giant who is identified as Engelados. The Giant totters and, while trying to flee, defends himself with his shield and puts up resistance with the javelin which he holds in his left hand. Another Giant cuts off the scene on the left, balancing the adversary of Pallas. Vines with schematically rendered leaves fill the background of the scene on both sides of Athena.

The face and details of the aegis, the helmet crest and the shield of the goddess are covered with fugitive applied white paint. There are also spots of applied white on the helmet of the left-hand Giant. Details of the chiton and helmet of Athena are rendered in applied violet paint, as are the loop of the shield of Engelados and the weapon strap and the folds of the chiton of the right-hand Giant. A band of a double row of carelessly executed spots crowns the scene. A black-painted radial motif embellishes the clay-coloured shoulder, whilst the transition to the neck is highlighted with tongue-shaped decoration.

COMMENTARY - BIBLIOGRAPHY: Unpublished.

For the Class of Athens 581, ii see the commentary on no. 282. Cf. two lekythoi with the same theme in Athens, Ancient Agora Museum, nos. P 24327 and P 24329, which belong to the Class of Athens 581, ii, Group P 24327, see *Agora* XXIII, 229, nos. 1027 and 1029 respectively, pl. 83 (for the Agora Group P 24327). For the Gigantomachy see *LIMC* IV, 191-270, s.v. Gigantes [F. Vian, M.B. Moore].

Class of Athens 581, ii. Agora Group P 24327.

G.K.

288

289 BLACK-FIGURE LEKYTHOS (SECONDARY TYPE)
500-475 B.C.

INV. NO. A 15418.
H. 0.119, B.D. 0.034, M.D. 0.032, D. AT SHOULDER
LEVEL 0.052 M.

Complete. The mouth is mended. Limited chipping and flaking, particularly of the applied white paint.
The neck, shoulder and upper part of the main body are covered with applied white paint. A black-painted radial decoration embellishes the shoulder, whilst the transition to the neck is highlighted by a schematic tongue-shaped decoration.
The scene, which occupies the entire body

of the vase, transports us to the interior of an ancient brothel (κασωρεῖον, καυσάριον, ἀγνεών, ἀσώτειον, ἀσωτεῖον), as the column on the left of the main side indicates. Two large couches occupy the centre of the scene, on top of which three pairs of entwined couples are found in differing poses of erotic embrace. On the left couch, the left group is engaged in intercourse (Aphrodite's schema) in the missionary position, the middle group in the "jockey" position (κελητίζειν or καθιππάζεσθαι), whilst the right-hand group is standing and is found at the stage of the "foreplay" (ἐρωτοπαίγνια) and fondling (ἐφάπτεσθαι, ψηλαφᾶν, ὀρχι-

πεδᾶν, ὀρχιπεδεῖν, ὀρχιπεδίζειν). On the right-hand couch, another three couples are depicted, which correspond to those on the left couch. In front of each couch a low table can be seen with food and cakes upon them.
Another three couples making love are depicted on the rear of the vase, entangled in the bedspreads, on the floor of the brothel. It seems that the three couples are engaged in sodomy. One of these can be made out behind the column. The other two are found entwined under the same blanket, below the handle of the vase. The vines which fill the background of the scene and the clothes which can be seen hanging above them increase the atmosphere of an orgy. The bodies of the women and details of the couches and vines are rendered in applied white paint, fugitive at many points.

COMMENTARY - BIBLIOGRAPHY: Unpublished.
The representation on the lekythos recalls the passage from the *Acharneans* by Aristophanes, ll. 1090-1093 [Hall-Geldart]:

> Couches, tables, headrests, blankets
> Garlands, myrrh, the lot; the nuts and raisins are out, so are the tarts,
> And sponge-cakes and flat-cakes and seed-cakes and honey-cakes
> And heaven knows what else - Oh yes, and lovely dancing-girls
>
> (tr. A.H. Sommertein)

For the shape cf. a lekythos of the secondary type DL at Columbia (Missouri) University of Art and Archaeology, no. 58.12, see Kurtz 1975, 199, pl. 6.4. For lekythoi of the Workshop of the Diosphos P. see Kurtz 1975, 96-102 and 149-150. For the Gela P. see *ABL* 78 and *Agora* XXIII, 46, 211-212, nos. 869 and 870, pl. 79. More recently for the Workshop of the Diosphos P. see Galinier 1996; *eadem* 1998; *eadem* 1999. For a selective bibliography on sex in ancient Greece see Stewart 1997, 255-259 and Simon *et al.* 1997, 48-50 [C. Weiss]. For the terminology of methods of intercourse see Vorberg 1988; Χαριτωνίδης 1935; Bain 1991. More recently see Ακαμάτης 193, 292-299; Papadopoulos 1995, 223-235, pl. 72-73; Lemos 1997. For erotic entanglements and couples in congress see also Veyne *et al.* 1998. For symposia and courtesans see *Kunst der Schale* 1990, 222-234. For terminology relating to prostitution and brothels see Licht 1942, 329-337. Workshop of the Diosphos P. (Sappho P. or Gela P.).

G.K.

289

290 BLACK-GLAZED PYXIS
500-475 B.C.

INV. NO. A 15413.
H. 0.054, B.D. 0.062, M.D. 0.065 M.

Complete. Small chips, particularly on the rim. Three concentric circles with a central spot and a black band at the edge of the underside, which is otherwise left the colour of the clay.

COMMENTARY - BIBLIOGRAPHY: Unpublished.
The pyxis is a variation of the later type D. For a closer typological parallel see *Agora* XII, 177, nos. 1306-1317, pl. 43. Also see *Kerameikos* IX, 124, no. 146(2), pl. 8.7, 40.4, 83.3 and *APP* 1995, 59-60 [Vogeikoff].

G.K.

291 BLACK-GLAZED LEKANIS LID
500-475 B.C.

INV. NO. A 15410.
H. 0.032, M.D. 0.096 M.

Complete. Mended. Some chipping and flaking. The discoid knob is left the colour of the clay.

COMMENTARY - BIBLIOGRAPHY: Unpublished.
See *Agora* XII, 167-168 and 322ff., no. 1231, pl. 41. Also see *KdA*, 322, no. 274. Recently, for the typological development of the shape of the lekanis, see Breitfeld-Von Eickstedt 1997, 55-61.

G.K.

292 BLACK-GLAZED PYXIS WITH LID
500-475 B.C.

INV. NO. A 15414.
H. (INCL. LID) 0.076, H. (EXCL. LID) 0.049, B.D. 0.047, M.D. 0.69, D. OF LID 0.077 M.

Complete. Chips on ring base and interior of the vase. On half of the vase the paint is red due to uneven firing. The edge of the interior surface of the base is highlighted by a spot surrounded by a circle.

COMMENTARY - BIBLIOGRAPHY: Unpublished.
For a close typological parallel see *Agora* XII, 172-173 (covered bowl) and 236, no. 1272, pl. 42. Also see *Kerameikos* IX, 128, no. 168(1), pl. 54.2 (with handle).

G.K.

293 BLACK-GLAZED "SALT-CELLAR"
500-475 B.C.

INV. NO. A 15412.
H. 0.046, B.D. 0.063, M.D. 0.061 M.

Complete. The paint has disappeared from the rim and one side of the vase. A band of thin applied white paint runs around the vase at the height of the handles. The walls are slightly concave. Black ring base. The interior surface of the base is left clay-coloured, apart from a small irregular black spot in the centre.

COMMENTARY - BIBLIOGRAPHY: Unpublished.
See *Agora* XII, 136-137 and 301, no. 924, pl. 34. Also see *Kerameikos* IX, 86, no. 9(3), pl. 44.1.

G.K.

290, 291, 292, 293

294 BLACK-GLAZED BOWL
500-475 B.C.

INV. NO. A 15408.
H. 0.046, B.D. 0.044, M.D. 0.093 (EXT.), 0.085 (INT.) M.

Complete. Many chips, particularly on base, and flaking. Reserved band at the join between the base and the main body. The underside of the ring base is

small knob at its centre. The vase is not painted outside, apart from an encircling black band roughly in the middle of the main body.

COMMENTARY - BIBLIOGRAPHY: Unpublished.
The vase may perhaps be identified with the ancient κάναστρον or κάνασθον or τρύβλιον, see *Agora* XII, 124-125 and 288-289, no. 737. Likewise, see *Keramei-*

reserved. Reserved circle inside at the bottom with a small mastoid protuberance highlighted by a black spot surrounded by a black circle.

COMMENTARY - BIBLIOGRAPHY: Unpublished.
For a very close typological parallel see *Agora* XII, 133 and 296, nos. 843-844, pl. 33.

G.K.

kos IX, no. 78, pl. 26.5 (Tomb HW 95) and *ADelt* 17 (1961/62) Chronika, pl. 26. For the knuckle-bones see the commentary on no. 297.

G.K.

296 BLACK-GLAZED CORINTHIAN-TYPE SKYPHOS
500-475 B.C.

INV. NO. A 15411.
H. 0.057, B.D. 0.043, M.D. 0.082, M.D. (INCL. HANDLES) 0.126 M.

Complete. Mended. Numerous gaps and chips, chiefly near the rim. A band of thin applied white paint runs around the vase at the height of the handles. The ring base is black. The interior surface of the base is reserved, apart from a small irregular black knob in its centre.

COMMENTARY - BIBLIOGRAPHY: Unpublished.
Cf. *Agora* XII, 81-83 and 257, no. 313, pl. 14.

G.K.

295 SKYPHOS (ONE-HANDLER)
500-475 B.C.

INV. NO. A 15409.
H. 0.038, B.D. 0.068, M.D. 0.119 M.

Complete. Many chips, particularly in the interior and flaking. Deep crack in the interior surface of the base. Small restoration next to the handle. It contained three knuckle-bones.
The interior of the vase is black glazed, apart from a small reserved circle at the bottom highlighted by a circle with a

297 SIXTY-NINE NATURAL KNUCKLE-BONES
500-475 B.C.

INV. NO. Δ 7185.

COMMENTARY - BIBLIOGRAPHY: Unpublished.

Knuckle-bones, whether natural or their imitations in another material (clay, ivory, glass), were used as much as a favourite children's game as a way of foreseeing the future and prophetic divination. They are usually found in children's tombs, although they do exist in those of adults. Tomb 1010 of the Kerameikos, where these knuckle-bones were found, was of a child. Most were concentrated near the left hand of the deceased and, perhaps, had been contained in a small pouch (ἀστρα-γαλοθήκη or φορμίσκος). The players (ἀστραγαλίζο-ντες) threw the knuckle-bones and, from the position in which they landed on the ground or the palm of the player, the winner or the divination was decided (the diviner was called the ἀστραγαλομάντις). The four sides of the knuckle-bone were called "one" (μονάς or εἷς, οἴνη, ἴση, κύων="dog", χῖος=Chian), "three" (τριάς), "four" (τετράς), "six" (ἑξάς or ἐξίτης, κῖος). The player who threw "one" four times won the game. Sometimes, the knuckle-bones had numbers on each side, in which case he who threw four different numbers won. If the knuckle-bones were numbered, then the highest total won. For knuckle-bones and their use see Πωλογιώργη 1995, 121, n. 18; Θέμελης - Τουράτσογλου 1997, 59 and 167-168; Gräpler 1997, 170, no. 194; Καλτσάς 1998, 302, n. 1152. For the use of knuckle-bones in divination, and their relation to metaphysical beliefs, chiefly of the Pythagoreans, see Hoffmann 1997, 107-112.

G.K.

298 TERRACOTTA GROUP OF SHEPHERD WITH FLOCK
500-475 B.C.

INV. NO. E 1048.
H. 0.04, W. 0.09 M.

The tails of the three animals are missing as well as the front right and rear left leg of the middle animal. The rear right leg of the first animal is mended. Small chips and flaking of the applied white paint. Light brown clay. Traces of a white slip are found on all the figures; traces of red paint on the three animals and on the base.

The group is handmade, in miniature and rendered succinctly. The bearded shepherd, with a bird-like face and conical hat, is seated on the ground which is rendered as a low rectangular base, holding a small sheep tenderly in his arms. Three other larger sheep stand in front of him, one next to the other, turning towards him. They have short legs – the front ones bent at the end, the rear ones slightly at the knees –, a small head with a conical muzzle. Deep incising on one sheep's muzzle indicates the mouth. The shepherd holds a spherical object in his right hand, perhaps a fruit intended for the animals.

COMMENTARY - BIBLIOGRAPHY: Unpublished.

No similar clay group is met in Attic-Boeotian or Corinthian terracotta production of the late Archaic or early Classical periods. Judging by the clay, it can be attributed to an Attic workshop. It probably symbolises the care and paternal love which binds the prematurely lost child to his life after death. For the symbolism and bibliography cf. no. 344 below and Bloesch 1974, no. 170, pl. 27. For the face of the shepherd cf. the type of rider with bird-like face, *Kerameikos* XV, 170, nos. 542-546, pl. 96-97 (1st half of 5th c. B.C.). For the representation of sheep cf. *Corinth* XV₂, 181-183, category XXVI (rams), pl. 39-41, and esp. XXVI, 8. For shepherds in general see Schmaltz 1974, 99-103, nos. 251-261, pl. 20-22.

Th.K.

298

299 SMALL TERRACOTTA FIGURINE OF A MAN LEADING A PAIR OF HORSES
500-475 B.C.

INV. NO. E 1049.
H. (INCL. B.) 0.05, H. OF THE MALE FIGURE 0.048 M.

Part of the base and the tail of one horse are missing. Two legs of one horse, front and hind left, as well as the human figure are mended from a few pieces. Brown clay. The group is handmade and rendered succinctly.

Two schematised ponies with extended legs and tails are supported on two separate bases for their front and hind legs. A miniature figure of a rider is supported on the rear base between the horses, plank-shaped with a bird-like face, arms extended in front and bent forwards.

COMMENTARY - BIBLIOGRAPHY: Unpublished.
Clay groups of horses, or four horses with riders, warrior charioteers, in different forms, are produced in Attic-Boeotian workshops from the 7th to the beginning of the 5th c. B.C. A comprehensive study of their classification and interpretation is attempted in the article by Szabo 1975, 7-20 and 125-131. Similar groups of horses or oxen are interpreted as ploughing scenes (Szabo, Nicholson). For the type see Winter 1903, I, 25 2. For typological parallels see Nicholson 1968, no. 69, pl. 12 (end of 6th c. B.C.). With four horses see Szabo 1975, 11, fig. 5 (from the Athenian Agora); Sinn 1977, 37, no. 58, pl. 21 (Boeotian); Nicholson 1968, 57, no. 61, pl. 12 (Boeotian); Schürmann 1989, 47, no. 105, pl. 23 (Boeotian).

Th.K.

300, 299

300 TERRACOTTA FIGURINE OF A DOG
500-475 B.C.

INV. NO. E 1047.
H. 0.048, PRES.L. 0.06 M.

The hind left leg and part of the tail are missing. Chipped surface. Brown clay. Solid, handmade, short-bodied figurine of a dog with rigid conical legs. The head is conical with traces of white colour, the ears conical, painted red. The eyes are painted. It may be holding a morsel of food in its teeth. A band of red paint encircling the neck indicates a collar. Traces of black paint on the body.

COMMENTARY - BIBLIOGRAPHY: Unpublished.
A toy, often met in children's tombs. For clay figurines of dogs in general see *Kerameikos* XV, 165, 174-175, nos. 575-579 and *Corinth* XV₂, 179-181, pl. 39-40 (Corinthian type XXV). For typological parallels see *Kerameikos* XV, 174, no. 579, pl. 100, 9; Μυλωνάς 1975, A, 87, no. Γ1-ειδ. 18, pl. 219 (490-470 B.C.); Mollard-Besques 1954, I, 22, no. B126 (with cake in the mouth).

Th.K.

301, 302

301 TERRACOTTA FIGURINE OF A BIRD
500-475 B.C.

INV. NO. E 1043.
H. 0.065, MAX.L. 0.076 M.

Complete. Chips and cracks on the surface. Light brown clay. Traces of black paint on the body.
The bird (hen or waterfowl) is standing upright with wings closed on a conical base. The head is bent forward, the neck thin and short, the tail pointing down.

The crest, bill and eyes are moulded. There is an air hole beneath the tail.

COMMENTARY - BIBLIOGRAPHY: Unpublished. See *Kerameikos* XV, 176-177, no. 593 and no. 596, pl. 102. See also no. 301.

Th.K.

302 TERRACOTTA FIGURINE OF A BIRD
500-475 B.C.

INV. NO. E 1044.
H. 0.066, MAX.L. 0.088 M.

Intact. The bill is broken, numerous chips on surface. Brown clay, traces of black paint. Similar to figurine no. 301, with bibliography.

Th.K.

303

303 SEA SHELL
500-475 B.C.

INV. NO. Δ 7186.

Intact.

COMMENTARY - BIBLIOGRAPHY: Unpublished.
Natural shells were used in antiquity for the preservation or mixing of cosmetics. For their use and their funerary symbolism see Θέμελης - Τουράτσογλου 1997, 119 and 168, n. 176 and Καλτσάς 1998, 302, n. 1153.

G.K.

304 BLACK-FIGURE WHITE-GROUND LEKYTHOS (SECONDARY TYPE)
500-475 B.C.

INV. NO. A 15538.
H. 0.175, B.D. 0.043, MAX.D. 0.056, M.D. 0.033 M.

Complete. Small chip off base. Red-brown clay, whitish background, black lustrous coating. Black glaze covers the calyx-shaped mouth, the outside of the strap handle, the lower part of the vase with two ground-coloured bands and the base, apart from the ground-coloured side. Radial decoration on its shoulder and a series of vertical dashes on the lower part of its neck. The scene is bordered at the top by a left-turned isolated meander pattern, and at the bottom, by a ground-coloured band. Four horses and rider are depicted, the latter holding the reins and the goad. Behind the chariot, a female figure with lyre and Dionysos holding a horn. A seated female figure, in a chariot with a flower in each hand, finishes the scene on the right. Two leafy branches on the white ground. Violet for details of the clothing, the hair-bands, Dionysos's beard, the reins and the horses' tails.

COMMENTARY - BIBLIOGRAPHY: Unpublished.
The theme of chariots framed by different figures is particularly widespread in the iconography of late Attic black figure. These scenes belong to a group of pseudo-narrative divine leave-takings and generally bring up the subject of divine appearance. The scene on lekythos no. 304 belongs to this group, since indications of its connection with a particular mythological or literary theme are absent; see Μανακίδου 1994, 135 and 154-155. For chariot scenes with an escort of different figures see *Kerameikos* IX, 41 and 122, no. 134.2 (for iconographic parallel from the Workshop of the Haimon P.). For a closer parallel in terms of typology and iconography see *Corinth* XIII, 220, no. 7, Tomb 272, pl. 94 (it is attributed to the Gela P.). For chariots and the figures accompanying them see Μανακίδου 1994. Our vase is probably to be placed in the late phase of the Workshop of the Diosphos P. For a lekythos of the same type and with a similar iconographic theme see *ABL* 100, pl. 38.2. For the Diosphos P. and his Workshop see no. 305.

E.B.-V.

304

305 BLACK-FIGURE WHITE-GROUND LEKYTHOS (SECONDARY TYPE)
500-475 B.C.

INV. NO. A 15537.
H. 0.17, B.D. 0.044, MAX.D. 0.057, M.D. 0.035 M.

Complete. Extensive flaking on the surface of the body, mainly on the representation. Black coating on calyx-shaped mouth, the strap handle, the cylindrical body and the two-stepped discoid base. Two double bands, on the lower part of the body and on the side of the upper disc of the base, are reserved. Radial decoration runs around the shoulder of the vase and a series of vertical dashes are on the lower part of the neck. A double row of spots above the pictorial zone. The theme of the struggle of Herakles with the Nemean Lion is depicted on a whitish background. The tangle of Herakles and the lion struggling occupies centre stage on the ground in the usual position according to which the hero overcomes the animal grasping it by the neck. Of the lion, one can only discern the hind quarter of the body with its long tail twisting into a loop, and of Herakles, only the lower part of his body. Left, the standing Athena, with chiton down to her feet and himation on her shoulder, stretches her left arm, which is concealed by the shield, in a gesture of help towards the hero. In her bent right arm, she holds a spear, while one can just make out the crest of her helmet, which reaches up to the shoulder of the vase. Iolaos in himation completes the scene on the right in a position arching to the left, holding the bow of Herakles and with a dagger on his midriff. Foliate branches in the background of the scene; the clothing of Herakles is left on one of these, a known iconographic feature in scenes where the hero is fighting.

COMMENTARY - BIBLIOGRAPHY: Unpublished.

The iconographic theme of Herakles struggling with the Nemean Lion, whether upright or on the ground, is one of the most loved of the late Attic black-figure style. For the subject see *LIMC* V, s.v. Herakles, 16-34 [Felten]; Bell 1977, 329-340; Brommer 1973, 109-143; Steiner 1989. Iolaos in this scene, despite being depicted holding a bow with his right arm extended, is not shooting. The myth, moreover, does not show the hero actively participating in this labour. Usually, in most scenes, he is in attendance simply holding Herakles's weapons; regarding this see *LIMC* V.2, 36-37, nos. 1793, 1800 and 1803. For a parallel in terms of the iconographic type see *Kerameikos* IX, 96, 36.1, pl. 47 (without the presence of Athena) and pl. 40 (for the motif on late black-figure lekythoi). Lekythos no. 305 belongs, most likely, to a late phase of the Workshop of the Diosphos P. For a lekythos from the same workshop with the same iconographic theme see *ABL*, pl. 39.1 (Louvre, no. MNB 909). For the Diosphos P. see *ABL*, 94-130 and 232-241; *ABV*, 508-511; *Para* 248-250; Kurtz 1975, 149-150; *Agora* XXIII, 95-96; lately Jubier in *Céramique* 1999, 181-184. Lastly, for the tree in scenes of the Labours of Herakles see Κόρτη-Κόντη 1993-94, 13-19.

E.B.-V.

306 BLACK-FIGURE WHITE-GROUND LEKYTHOS (SECONDARY TYPE)
500-475 B.C.

INV. NO. A 15539.
H. 0.027, B.D. 0.051, M.D. 0.043, MAX.D. 0.066 M.

Complete, restored from many sherds. Restored mainly on the representation zone. Black-glazed calyx-shaped mouth, outside of the strap handle, lower part of the vase – two reserved bands run round it – and the ring base, which has a ground-coloured section on its side.

Radial decoration on the shoulder and a series of vertical dashes on the lower neck. On a whitish background, a black-figure scene of the Battle of the Gods and Giants (Gigantomachy) is spread out, crowned by a zone of chequer-board pattern. From the left, Zeus striding out with a multi-folded chiton and himation brandishes his thunderbolt in his right hand ready to fell a Giant (Eurymedon?), who, with bent knees, is already staggering. In the centre of the scene, a commanding Poseidon, likewise striding out, dressed in a multi-folded chiton and himation, is holding a trident in his right hand, the tip of which is distinguished in the zone which tops the scene. The god of the sea is throwing a rock with his left arm against the Giant Polyvotes, who is depicted falling to the ground. A figure with a helmet, short chiton and leggings finishes off the scene from the left, and is attacking holding a spear and Boeotian shield. It is not impossible that this is Ares who often takes part in the Gigantomachy, on account of his particular weaponry and his contradictory course towards the gods. Foliate branches amongst the figures. Red for details of the figures (beards of gods, folds of clothing) as well as for the crests of the helmets, shield blazons and details of the rock.

COMMENTARY - BIBLIOGRAPHY: Unpublished.

The scene of the lekythos depicts excerpts of the Battle of the Gods and Giants. The Gigantomachy, a theme both mythical and heroic and as such placed in the universal theory of the Archaic period, particularly moved not only the great artists but also the vase painters of the epoch. Nevertheless, this particular excerpt, with the presence of Zeus and Poseidon, is relatively rare in the iconography of the myth. In late Attic black figure, the presence of Athena is more common. For the composition and the positions of the figures of Zeus with the first Giant see *ABL* 255, 13 (lekythos of the Athena P. where, however, Athena takes the place of Zeus); see also *LIMC* IV.2, 133, no. 258c. Poseidon, with trident and rock, does not occur often. More usual is the iconography of the god only with a rock, thus depicting the episode of the Gigantomachy known from written sources, in which Poseidon, throwing a rock at Polyvotes, creates the island of Nisyros. The same theme is depicted on an amphora in Copenhagen, National Museum, no. 3672; regarding this see *LIMC* VII.2, 368, no. 174. The blazons on the shields are difficult to discern due to damage of the paint with which they have been rendered. For the Gigantomachy see *LIMC* IV, 191-270 [Vian] and particularly the black-figure vases nos. 170-297. Also see Vian 1951. Our lekythos belongs to the Workshop of the Haimon P. and, perhaps, is a work by that very vase-painter. For the Workshop of the Haimon P. see *ABL* 130-141, 241-249; *ABV* 539-571; *Para* 269-287.

E.B.-V.

307 BLACK-FIGURE LEKYTHOS (SECONDARY TYPE)
500-475 B.C.

INV. NO. A 15544.
H. 0.175, B.D. 0.044, M.D. 0.036, MAX.D. 0.053 M.

Complete. Mended at the mouth. Black glazing on the calyx-shaped mouth, on the outside of the strap handle, on the lower part of the body – around which run a pair of reserved bands – and on the base with the top part of its side reserved. Radial decoration on the shoulder and a series of vertical dashes on the lower part of the neck. The body of the vase is decorated with three black-figure anthemia, interposed, amongst which are four schematic lotus flowers. The nucleus of the anthemia are highlighted in violet. Each anthemion is painted inside an arch which is embellished with schematic lotus "sepals". The anthemia are placed above a chain with a black dot in each link.

COMMENTARY - BIBLIOGRAPHY: Unpublished.

This type of lekythos is widespread in Attic pottery, as a grave offering of the 1st half of the 5th c. B.C. Of the many parallels from the Kerameikos, three are selected as closest: lekythoi 25.2, 71.1-2, pl. 28.4 and 96.8-10; see *Kerameikos* IX, 92, pl. 24.4, 106, pl. 28.4 and 112, pl. 27.2. For the category see *Kerameikos* IX, 35-36. Similar black-figure lekythoi in the National Archaeological Museum, Athens come from a tomb in Stadiou Street, where the well-known aryballos by Douris was also found, dated to 490 B.C.; see Παπασπυρίδη - Κυπαρίσσης 1927/28, 91, fig. 1 (top row, nos. 8-10).

309

306

308

311

305

These lekythoi were found with lekythoi from the Workshop of the Haimon P. (*ABL* 186). For a similar lekythos from the Workshop of the Megaira P. (Beldam P.) see Σίνδος 1985, 49, no. 68 [Τιβέριος] and bibliography. Lekythos no. 307 bears features of the Workshops of both the Haimon P. and the Beldam P. The shape of the vase refers to the Workshop of the Haimon P. while the upright anthemia and the white ground are usual for the Workshop of the Megaira P. (Beldam P.); regarding this see Kurtz 1975, 152-153, pl. 69, 2.5 and 151, n. 11.

E.B.-V.

308 BLACK-FIGURE LEKYTHOS (SECONDARY TYPE)
500-475 B.C.

INV. NO. A 15540.
H. 0.17, B.D. 0.043, M.D. 0.034, MAX.D. 0.053 M.

Complete. Mended at the neck and handle. Red-brown clay. Black glazing on the calyx-shaped mouth, outside of the handle, lower part of the vase – which is interrupted by a pair of reserved bands – and on the base, with its side reserved. Radial decoration on the shoulder and series of vertical dashes on the lower part of the neck. The representation is crowned by a zone with two rows of alternating black and white dots. The theme of the representation is a pair of harnessed horses (chariot with two horses) with a rider, who holds the horses' reins and the goad. Behind the chariot, a female figure gestures towards Dionysos, who occupies the centre of the scene holding a horn. Right, in front of the horses, another standing female figure. Foliate branches decorate the background of the scene. Fugitive, applied white paint, on the naked parts of the female figures, the tails of the horses and the details of the harness. Red on the beard of Dionysos, the bands of the hair, the details and decoration (rosettes) of the clothing, on the reins and the harness of the horses.

COMMENTARY - BIBLIOGRAPHY: Unpublished.
The subject is one particularly liked by vase-painters of the late black-figure style. The representation is similar to that on lekythos no. 304 (see for bibliography on the subject). The differences in the two representations in terms of iconography are few: the companion of Dionysos, here, does not hold a lyre and the female figure in front of the harnessed horses is not seated. For other iconographically closer examples see *Kerameikos* IX, 121, no. 132.1, pl. 53.1 and 77.3 (with bibliography) and no. 170.2, pl. 40.6 (part of lekythos).
Lekythos no. 308 is placed in the Workshop of the Haimon P. For the workshop see the bibliography for no. 306.

E.B.-V.

309 BLACK-FIGURE LEKYTHOS (SECONDARY TYPE)
500-475 B.C.

INV. NO. A 15542.
H. 0.026, B.D. 0.052, M.D. 0.04, MAX.D. 0.068 M.

Complete. Mended, chipped and flaking. Brown-red clay. Black glazing on calyx-shaped mouth, the handle, the lower part of the body – which is interrupted by a pair of reserved bands – and on the base with its side reserved. Radial decoration on the shoulder and a series of vertical dashes on the lower neck. A zone of two rows of black and white dots crowns the representation. A Dionysiac troupe is depicted. In the centre of the scene, Dionysos, to the fore, turns his head left. He holds a horn which can be distinguished with difficulty above his right shoulder. The god is framed by Maenads mounted on donkeys. Garlands hang on the phalluses of the animals. A dancing Silenus closes the scene from the right. Applied white paint is found on the chiton of Dionysos, on the naked flesh of the Maenads, on the bridles of the animals. Violet on the folds of the clothing, on the beards of the male figures and on the manes of the donkeys. Branches with schematic leaves in the background.

COMMENTARY - BIBLIOGRAPHY: Unpublished.
For the subject of the Dionysiac troupes and its iconography, a particular favourite of the late Archaic period, see *LIMC* III, s.v. Dionysos, 415-514 [Gasparri] and mainly headings IIID and E. For the closest typological-iconographic parallel see *Kerameikos* IX, 90, nos. 20-25, pl. 19.3,5; cf. also *Agora* XXIII, 250, no. 1228 (which is depicted in the manner of the Haimon P.). For Dionysos between two mounted Maenads on lekythoi of the same type (IV) see *Kerameikos* IX, 39, nos. 109.4, 117.8-10, 127.1, pl. 32.8, nos. 155.1, 215.5-6, pl. 58, 2-3 and no. 250.2, pl. 37.7. For an iconographic prototype of the scene on our vase see lekythos 86. AE134 in the Paul Getty Museum (*LIMC* VIII, Suppl., s.v. Maenades, 780-803 [Krauskopf - Simon] and mainly 789, no. 83), which belongs to the Leagros group. For Meanads in general on black-figure vase-painting see Moraw 1998, 73-82 and mainly 162-165 for their connection with donkeys.
Our lekythos is a work of the Haimon P. For the bibliography on the vase-painter and his workshop see no. 306.

E.B.-V.

310

310 BLACK-FIGURE LEKYTHOS (SECONDARY TYPE)
500-475 B.C.

INV. NO. A 15541.
H. 0.176, B.D. 0.05, M.D. 0.039, MAX.D. 0.057 M.

Complete, restored. Red-brown clay. Black, lustrous coating on the calyx-shaped mouth, the strap handle, the lower part of the body – where a pair of reserved bands are inserted – and on the base, with its side reserved.

Radial decoration on the shoulder and a series of vertical dashes on the lower neck. A careless, right-twisted meander borders the top of the representational zone above a double line. The abduction of Thetis by Peleus is depicted. The central pair is rendered in the well-known iconographic manner, with a small-bodied Peleus dressed in a short chiton bending to grab Thetis by the leg, his right arm almost fully extended. Nereids in flight frame the rape scene, two to the left and one to the right. In the background of the scene, large foliate branches with even bigger white fruit at intervals. Applied white paint can be made out on the naked parts of the female figures, as well as decorative rosettes on their clothing. The bands of the hair and the folds of the clothing have been rendered in violet.

COMMENTARY - BIBLIOGRAPHY: Unpublished.
The abduction theme is often met on vase-painting of the late black-figure style. The scene, albeit careless, portrays powerful motion, vividly depicting the fright of Thetis and the panic of the Nereids. Both iconographically and technically, lekythos no. 310 is very close to a lekythos from the Kerameikos cemetery, see *Kerameikos* IX, pl. 38, no. 68.7) which is attributed, as is this vase, to the Workshop of the Haimon P. For the subject see *Kerameikos* IX, 41-42 and esp. nos. 138, pl. 77 and 98.2, pl. 28. Also see *Agora* XXIII, 185, no. 653 (for the subject in general) and 246, no. 1185, pl. 87 (for a sherd of a lekythos with the same subject, perhaps by the Haimon P.). Cf. also *LIMC* II, s.v. Peleus, 251-269 [Vollkommer] and esp. 259, nos. 109-150 (particularly lekythos no. 137, which is placed in the Workshop of the Haimon P.). Also see *LIMC* VIII, s.v. Thetis, 6-14 [Vollkommer] and particularly no. 8. For the subject of Peleus and Thetis in Attic black figure see Brommer 1973, 321-326. For the subject in gener-

al see Schweitzer 1961, 13-19 and Krieger 1973. For bibliography on the Haimon P. see no. 306.

E.B.-V.

311 RED-FIGURE ARYBALLOS
490-480 B.C.

INV. NO. A 15535.
H. 0.0755, B.D. 0.04, MAX.D. 0.047, M.D. 0.027 M.

Complete. Ovoid body. Short neck, with concave walls, which is joined to the shoulder with a curved ridge. Echinus-shaped mouth, flat rim, handle rectangular in section which is slightly elongated where it joins the shoulder. The flat base is differentiated from the body by a reserved groove. Applied violet paint highlights the handle. The rim is reserved as is the base, the centre of which is marked by a black dot with a circle round it.

The scene stretches over the whole body

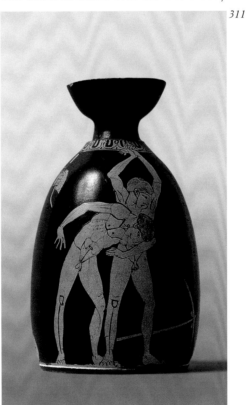

311

surface. Elements of a Lesbian and Ionic wave run around the shoulder above the decorative zone. The groove around the base is the ground for the scene while a vertical zone with cross-hatched decoration below the handle marks its edges. A palaestra scene is depicted, with two youths wrestling. The naked young men are rendered with their bodies en face

and heads to the right, in profile. They stand on their right leg, stretching their left sideways. Their hair is held in place by the caps peculiar to athletes, which are tied with a lace beneath the chin. The left-hand youth bends down and applies a waist hold with his left arm to his opponent. The latter, bending his head slightly and with half open mouth, perhaps to indicate he is speaking or shouting, raises his arms, the ends of which run onto the wave zone above. His fingers are spread, with right-hand thumb grasping left-hand wrist. The main muscle treatment of the figures is indicated with a thin black line, while secondary treatment is with continuous or stippled, as appropriate, thin brown paint. The caps of the athletes are rendered in the same colour but of a different quality.

Objects indicating the palaestra area sur-

round the central scene: from the left, two javelins are portrayed stuck in the ground forming an X, on one of which the ἀγκύλη is indicated (strap at roughly the centre of the javelin used for throwing). A bow is hanging next to them and a discus is lying on the ground. Hanging on either side of the young wrestlers are two sets of personal items needed in the palaestra, a strigil, a sponge and an aryballos bound together. All were used for cleaning the body after exercise. They scraped the dirt away with the strigil, washed themselves in the gymnasium bath with the sponge and took scented oil from the aryballos to smear on the body after the bath. Behind the wrestlers and pinned to the ground are the pickaxe which was used to loosen the earth of the palaestra. A μελιταῖον κυνάριον closes off the scene on the right, a small bodied Maltese dog facing left in a unique pose. The head is raised and twisted so that the neck and its muzzle show, and the rear left leg is lifted probably to scratch its body. Right and left of the young men, two "Kalos-names" are written: ΘΩΔΙΣ ΚΑΛΟΣ ✝ΑΙΡΙΠΠΟΣΚΑΛΟΣ. The details of the objects, the dog's collar and the letters of the inscription are all in applied violet paint.

COMMENTARY - BIBLIOGRAPHY: Unpublished.

The shape of the vessel is unique and it has proved impossible, at this stage of research, to provide a parallel. Nevertheless, a parallel is shown on the medallion of a kylix at the Vatican attributed to the Euaion P., a pupil of Douris. It is a combination of an aryballos, owing to its mouth and handle, and an alabastron of the "Columbus type" because of the shape of the main body. Thus, we characterise this hybrid shape as an aryballos of "Columbus type". Equally unique is the wrestling scene. It is certain from the pose of the figures that we do not have a contest going on here but a demonstration of the training rules taught in the palaestra. The one-armed waist hold is not so common as the waist hold performed with two arms. The defensive position in wrestling is rare

mainly in terms of the raised arms and the way in which they are entwined.

The subsidiary elements of the scene are also usual in depictions of athletic scenes of Attic red figure. The hanging bow, however, which indicates that archery was practised in the gymnasium, is rare in analogous scenes. The presence of Maltese dogs is usual in palaestrae and gymnasia, where it appears they are mainly associated with young men.

The inscriptions with "Kalos" names, often referring to male offspring of aristocratic Athenian families notorious for their beauty are quite popular in Attic red figure at this period and usually are closely linked to the subject of the scene. The inscriptions on this vase, however, are probably meant to indicate the names of the young people portrayed. This hypothesis is supported by the fact that the two specific names are not common, at least among the "kaloi" known to us. On the one hand, Chairippos occurs as "Kalos" on a further two vases of about the same period, while the same name is included in a stele of those fallen in battle of the 2nd quarter of the 5th c. B.C., and on the other, Thodis is an unattested name not only amongst the "kaloi" but, as afar as one can see, in the whole of ancient prosopography.

The entire scene and, in part, the technical characteristics lead one to attribute the aryballos to Douris, a great vase-painter of the early Archaic red-figure style. The rendering of the athletes, mainly of the one who is practising his waist hold, presents an uncertainty and a stiffness in his movement, characteristic of work of the early period of the vase-painter. However, the analogies of the bodies, the anatomical details, the writing of Δ as Λ in the name ΘΩΔΙΣ and the rather simple unfolding of the scene on the vase which is focused on describing the movement of the athletes, dates the work to the "early middle period" of Douris (according to Beazley) or to the "intermediate plain period" of the artist (according to Buitron), namely between 490 and 480 B.C.

Up to now, there are two aryballoi of this vase-painter known, both with peculiarities in terms of shape. One belongs to the early period of the painter and is kept at the 3rd Ephorate of Antiquities, no. T.E. 556. The second, known as "lekythos of Asopodoros" is a vase signed by Douris as a potter, dates to his middle career and is on display in the NM, no. 15375. The aryballos from the Kerameikos is the third aryballos by the painter and chronologically is the link between the other two. We can, therefore, maintain that this, likewise unique aryballos is the work by the skill of Douris, not only as a painter but also as a potter. The names of the two "kaloi", the athletic representation in question but also the shape of the vase, leads easily to the suggestion that the aryballos was a special commission. Moreover, the skeletal material of tomb 1099 of the KERAMEIKOS Station belongs to a youth. The tomb may have belonged to one of these two young men, Thodis or Chairippos. For the representation of the rare type of aryballos in vase-painting see the medallion of the kylix by the Euaion P., in Γιαλούρης 1982, fig. 18. For representations of scenes from the gymnasium on vase-painting see Beck 1975, pl. 26-41. For wrestling and its role in education see Pl., *Laws* 7,796a. For general bibliography regarding wrestling see Patrucco 1972, 308; Poliakoff 1987, 23-53; Βαλαβάνης 1991, 126-132. For athletes wearing caps see Eckstein 1956, 90-95; Patrucco 1972, fig. 80, 85-87; Poliakoff 1987, 15, n. 17. For the pick-axes see Jüthner 1965, pl. 6. For the strigil-sponge-aryballos set see Haspels 1927/28, 216-223. For bows see *RE* VI. A₂, s.v. τόξον, 1847-1853 [Miltner] and for the few archery scenes see Patrucco 1972, 365-370. For Maltese dogs see Zlotogorska 1997, 71-117. For Douris see Buitron-Oliver 1995, also with an extensive bibliography. Likewise, in general see Robertson 1992, 84-93 and Τιβέριος 1996, 15, 39, 306-308. Lastly, for the names of "kaloi" see *ARV²* II, 1559-1616; Robinson - Fluck 1937; Fuchs 1974.

E.B.-V.

312 WHITE-GROUND ALABASTRON
490-480 B.C.

INV. NO. A 15536.
H. 0.121, MAX.D. 0.056 M.

Mouth and a large part of the body missing. Much damage to the surface of the vase, chipped and flaking. Elongated, ovoid body. Solid pseudo-handle. Part of the scene is preserved bordered above by a zone of two rows of spots linked by dashes between a pair of bands. The ground of the scene is a black band with a zone of simple right-turned meander between bands below bordering the lower black part of the vase. A reserved band below the meander runs around the lower part of the vase.

An athletic scene in a gymnasium is depicted, the latter represented by the column in the middle of the scene. The capital of "Aeolian" type and richly decorated rests on a "base" decorated with vertical little lines and is crowned by a large abacus. Left of the column a youth is depicted striding towards the left, knees bent, and, with his right arm forward and left arm back, he holds dumbbells. The head of the figure is missing and the forearm of the right arm. Right of the column is preserved, very fragmentarily, the lower part of the body of a naked youth who is depicted from the rear, supported on his left leg and has the relaxed right leg slightly twisted. The lower part of two javelins can be made out below right, which he probably holds in his right hand. Above left, part of a curve is preserved. On either side of the column part of a retrograde inscription can be distinguished:]ΣΙΜΑ-ΧΟΣ and the word Κ]ΑΛΟΣ written left-to-right. Next to the javelins is preserved the last letter Σ of a male name or more likely the word "kalos".

COMMENTARY - BIBLIOGRAPHY: Unpublished.
White-ground alabastra with athletic scenes are common in the late Archaic period. The stance of the youth with dumbbells is interpreted either as the opening phase of a jump, or as "ἀλτηροβολία", that is an exercise during which "γυμνάζουσι δὲ οἱ μὲν μακροὶ τῶν ἀλτήρων ὤμους τε καὶ χεῖρας" (Philostratus, Γυμν., 56).

The depiction of another athlete from the rear is a favourite motif of vase-painters of this period and has its origin in the "pioneers" of the red-figure style. The curved line at the top of the body is probably the remains of a discus holder hanging in the background of the scene. The inscription]ΣΙΜΑΧΟΣ ΚΑΛΟΣ should probably be completed ΠΑΥΣΙΜΑΧΟΣ on analogy with an inscription on the now lost kylix from Vulci with a scene of a discus-thrower and javelin-thrower (ARV² II, 1605). Less likely is the conjecture ΙΑΣΙΜΑΧΟΣ ΚΑΛΟΣ on analogy with inscriptions on two lekythoi, with female representations, a little later than our vase (ARV² II, 1586, 1587).

For representations of athletic scenes in gymnasia and palaestrae as well as for the "kaloi" see bibliography on no. 311. For a similar iconographic motif see Karouzou 1962 and Vanhove 1992, 276-278, fig. 140. For the

312

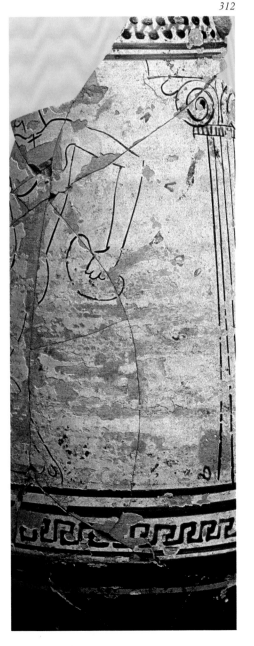

same athletic pose with dumbbells see Patrucco 1972, 90, fig. 23. For the long-jump contest see Jüthner 1968, 159-221 and Patrucco 1972, 61-91 and bibliography on p. 92. For dumbbells and the ἀλτηροβολία see Patrucco 1972, 83-89 and Jüthner 1968, pl. 44b and 54b. For the rendering of the body from the rear see Williams 1991, 292, fig. 8. For the representation of a column in vase-painting see Oliver-Smith 1981 and particularly for the way in which the Aeolian capital is rendered see Oliver-Smith 1964, 232ff. For discus holders hanging up see Vanhove 1992, 272, no. 135, 276-278, no. 140, 281, no. 145.

E.B.-V.

313 KNUCKLE-BONES
500-475 B.C.

INV. NO. Δ 7336.

A total of nine complete and eighteen fragmentary knuckle-bones found together by the right forearm of the deceased in tomb 1099. Surfaces rather damaged. Two knuckle-bones are pierced, while three have been worked so as to give flat surfaces. On the flat surface of one of the knuckle-bones an incised B can be made out.

COMMENTARY - BIBLIOGRAPHY: Unpublished.
Knuckle-bones, the central ossicles of the tarsus of a sheep, were in antiquity – as in recent times (κότσια) – one of the favourite children's games. Moreover, that is why it is frequently found as an offering in children's burials. Many were placed together in a tomb, usually in a cloth or leather pouch, there where the children kept them even during their lives. The pouches, of a perishable material, have, of course, not survived but they are known to us from clay copies and from their depiction in ancient vase-painting.

Many different games were played with knuckle-bones. The simplest was the ἀρτιάζειν, with two knuckle-bones, like today's "ones and twos". There were the πεντέλιθα (five-ball), with five knuckle-bones, during which they threw them with sudden force on top of the hand trying to balance as many as possible on the palm. They tried to catch as many as fell with the same hand while at the same time trying not to allow the first bones to fall. The most usual game, however, the main knuckle-bones contest, was throwing four knuckle-bones attempting to let them come to rest with a specific side up, because the different sides had particular importance in the game, as was also the case with the standard knuckle-bones game (e.g. "king", "vizier" etc.). The game was based on a combination of marbles and four knuckle-bones or on a total of the points given by the four sides, as today in dice. The incised B probably indicates a number or a term in the game. The perforations in some of the knuckle-bones which are exposed here perhaps indicate their use as beads of a necklace, while more shallow piercings perhaps held lead or another metal so that when they threw them they came to rest on a desired side. Apart from the game, knuckle-bones were used in a particular kind of divination, knuckle-bone prophecy. Likewise, some were dedicated as offerings at shrines, particularly those from sacrificed animals.

For games with knuckle-bones see *RE* II.2, s.v. Αστρά-γαλος, col. 1793 [Mau]; May 1991, 100ff.; Schädler 1996, 61-73, with all the details of the games. For clay pouches see lately Neils 1992, 225-235. For scenes of children playing with knuckle-bones see Schmidt 1971, 44-56 and Beck 1975, pl. 63.

E.B.-V.

From tomb 449

314 BLACK-FIGURE VOLUTE LEKYTHOS
480-470 B.C.

INV. NO. A 15222.
H. 0.18, B.D. 0.051, MAX.D. 0.056, M.D. 0.037 M.

Complete. Mended from many fragments, chipped and flaking on the rim, base and main body, partially restored. Brownish yellow clay. Discoid base widening towards the bottom with the upper surface covered with black coating and the lower left reserved, with conical cavity in the centre and peripheral incised ring, cylindrical body narrowing towards the base, strap handle, calyx-shaped mouth covered inside and out with black glaze, with reserved flat rim.

Row of little vertical lines at the base of the neck and schematic lotus calyxes on the slanting shoulder. On the body, representation of double volutes with schematic lotus calyxes in between, arranged above and below a chain with a black spot in the centre of the links. The leaves, the arches surrounding the kernel of the anthemia and the edge of the chain links are all indicated by incision. Applied white paint is used to indicate the arches surrounding the anthemia and for the spots, traces of which are preserved between the incisions of the kernel. Bands surrounding the rim and the centre of the kernels of the anthemia are depicted in applied violet. The transition from the shoulder to the body is indicated with a black line and the ground line, with a black band followed by reserved bands with a broad black band in between and the black lower part of the body. A black band runs around the lower part of the side of the base.

COMMENTARY - BIBLIOGRAPHY: Unpublished.
The vase is related to the late phase of the Workshop of the Diosphos P. but also with the Workshop of the Haimon P. For similar vases see *CVA* Palermo, Collezione Mormino (I) III H, pl. 20, nos. 11-12; *Kerameikos* IX, 112, 96 (SW 117), pl. 27, no. 17; *CVA* Bucarest II, Musée de la Ville, 20-21, pl. 22, no. 4. For the workshop

see *ABL* 93ff. and 186 and Kurtz 1975, 149, 150ff. This decoration has probably been influenced by earlier prototypes of which the most likely are those of the "Tyrrhenian" amphorae in combination with lotus calyxes of the middle of the 6th c. B.C. (see Heesen 1996, fig. 3) and of the Nikosthenic amphorae with an analogous type of decoration on the main body zone, dated to the last quarter of the 6th c. B.C. (see Tosto 1999, 50, 89, nos. 33-39, pl. 101-104).

H.S.

315 BLACK-FIGURE LEKYTHOS
500-475 B.C.

INV. NO. A 15228.
PRES.H. 0.15, B.D. 0.048, MAX.D. 0.0565 M.

Missing the mouth and part of the neck, with chips and many gaps particularly on the lower part of the main side. Brown clay. Double-tiered, discoid base the surface of which is covered with black glaze and a black band runs around its reserved side, slender cylindrical body narrowing towards the bottom, vertical strap handle.
Row of little lines where the neck starts and schematic lotus calyxes on the shoulder, rendered in black paint. Below the shoulder, black lines border a band, only extending round the main side, with a double row of dots of black and applied white paint.
Dionysiac scene opposite the handle. In the centre, the bearded Dionysos proceeds to the right with his head turned backwards. He is wearing a full-length chiton and himation and holds a horn. He is framed on the left and right by Maenads wearing himatia and riding mules or donkeys, the left one being ithyphallic with a garland hanging from the phallus. The details are partly rendered by incision, applied violet and white paint. A black ground line, followed by alternating reserved and black bands and the lower black part of the body.

COMMENTARY - BIBLIOGRAPHY: Unpublished.
The vase belongs, in terms of the representation, to the style of the Haimon P. For the painter and the workshop see *ABL* 93-94, 185-186; *ABV* 538; *Para* 269; *Addenda* 64; *Addenda²* 133. For similar representations on lekythoi see *ABV* 549, nos. 296-304; *Para* 278; *Addenda²* 135; Brownlee 1995, 356, no. 200, pl. 76; Giudice *et al.* 1992, 134, no. D178 and 135, no. D184. For a comparable scene, this on a lekythos of the late phase of the painter, see *CVA* Bruxelles, Musées Royaux d'Art et d'Histoire II, III He, 12, no. 22, pl. 21; Παπασπυρίδη - Κυπαρίσσης 1927/28, 91, fig. 1, middle row, no. 6, with, moreover, two satyrs, *ABL,* Appendix XIII, 244, no. 59. The motif of a garlanded phallus on a mule is often met on beasts of burden accompanying Dionysos; see e.g. *Münzen und Medaillen* 1964, 44, no. 77 (trefoil-mouthed oenochoe) as well as the type B amphora in the *J.P. Getty Museum* 2, fig. 13b, while there are also scenes with an oenochoe hanging from the phallus of the beast of burden – regarding this see Moon 1981, no. 56 – underlining the festive and joyous atmosphere of the scene.

H.S.

316 BLACK-FIGURE LEKYTHOS
c. 480 B.C.

INV. NO. A 15229.
H. 0.182, B.D. 0.0445, MAX.D. 0.059, M.D. 0.037 M.

Complete. Mended at the neck, handle and base, chipped and flaking. Brown-red clay with uneven firing. In terms of shape and the rest of the body's elements, it is similar to lekythos no. 315. Double-tiered discoid base widening towards the bottom with conical hollow in the centre of the reserved underside. Black mouth inside and out and flat reserved rim.
Below the shoulder but above the representation, a band with a double row of black and white dots. Dionysiac scene on the body. Bearded Dionysos in the centre, with white chiton and himation, sitting on a stool, in profile facing right, holds a kantharos. His hair, in a bun behind the nape of the neck, is decorated with a garland of schematic ivy leaves. Right and left of the god, two dancing Maenads play castanets and advance in opposite directions turning their heads and extending their hands towards the centre of the scene. They are wearing full-length chitons and himatia and headbands. Amongst the figures, on the red ground, branches with schematic dot-leaves and round white fruit. Applied vi-olet, purple and white paint and incisions partially indicate the details.

COMMENTARY - BIBLIOGRAPHY: Unpublished.
A work in the style of the Haimon P., it is one of the most studied works of the Group. Dionysiac scenes are well represented in the subject matter of the artists, as well as the dancing Maenads. The combination of the two is amongst his rarer subjects and the influence of the Diosphos P. appears strong here; for a comparable example on an amphora of the Diosphos P. see Schefold 1981, 29, fig. 20. For the Workshop of the Haimon P. see no. 315. For comparable representations of Maenads on lekythoi see *CVA* Prague Musée National (1), pl. 45, nos. 2-4; *CVA* Bologna II, III H e, pl. 40, no. 4; *CVA* Bruxelles - Musées Royaux d'Art et d'Histoire III He, 13, no. 26, pl. 21; *CVA* Genève, Musée d'Art et d'Histoire, 2, 47, pl. 75, nos. 16-18. For white paint in divine worship see Pekridou-Gorecki 1989, 166, n. 43.
The type of god seated facing right, dressed in a white chiton, is well represented in the late black-figure style and it is tempting to see its origin in prototypes of the 2nd half of the 6th c. B.C. For a comparable example see *CVA* Agrigento I, 33, pl. 81, nos. 3-4 (lekythos with seated Apollo; in the style of the Haimon P.; 2nd quarter of 5th c. B.C.).

H.S.

317 BLACK-FIGURE LEKYTHOS
480-470 B.C.

INV. NO. A 15232.
H. 0.177, B.D. 0.046, MAX.D. 0.058, M.D. 0.035 M.

Complete. Chipped, particularly on the rim, and flaking. Pale brown clay. Unevenly fired. Double-tiered discoid base, widening towards the bottom, its surface covered with black paint and a black band on its side below the step, while the underside is reserved, with a shallow cavity in the shape of a circular cone. Cylindrical body, strap handle, calyx-shaped mouth, covered with black lustrous paint, flat rim reserved.
Row of vertical little lines at the start of the neck and schematic lotus calyxes on the shoulder. Beneath the shoulder, a row of black dots and a pair of parallel black bands. Representation of three women on the body, seated on stools, in

a languid pose, with one arm supported on the back-rest and the other raised.
All three figures wear a chiton and himation. Branches with schematised leaves
dominate the field on the red background. Incisions are used to render the
folds of the himatia, fugitive applied white
for the naked flesh of the figures, according to the ancient convention, as well as
for the fruit on the branches, while applied violet renders the hairpins of the
central and left-hand figures and the decoration of the himatia.

COMMENTARY - BIBLIOGRAPHY: Unpublished.
The vase is related to the style of the Haimon P. and
betrays a strong influence by the Diosphos P. For the
workshop and parallel examples on lekythoi see *ABV*
554; *Para* 282; *ABL* 130ff., 244, Appendix XIII, no. 63;
Veder Greco 1988, 348, tomb 414; Brownlee 1995,
356, no. 201, pl. 77 (with relevant bibliography).

H.S.

Incisions, applied fugitive white and violet paint partially indicate the details.

COMMENTARY - BIBLIOGRAPHY: Unpublished.
In the style of the Haimon P. The theme of a goddess
boarding a chariot, followed by other deities, is widespread on small vases of the late black-figure style and
particularly common on this kind of vessel and in this
workshop; regarding this see *ABL* 130ff., Appendix XIII A;
ABV 539ff., nos. 1-120; *Para* 271ff.; *Addenda²* 134ff.
This composition of the scene is also the most widespread of the theme, that is with a female or male divinity holding a lyre or kithara. Iconographically, it follows
the tradition of vases of the 2nd half of the 6th c. B.C.,
but with a more abstract propensity which mass production and its small shape favoured. For comparable
examples of the theme see Jacquemin 1984, 107-108;
CVA Musée de Rennes, 26, nos. 4-6, pl. 20; *CVA*
Tübingen 3, nos. 7-9, pl. 50; Brownlee 1995, 355-356,
no. 198, pl. 76 (with relevant bibliography). For the same
theme cf. no. 321.

H.S.

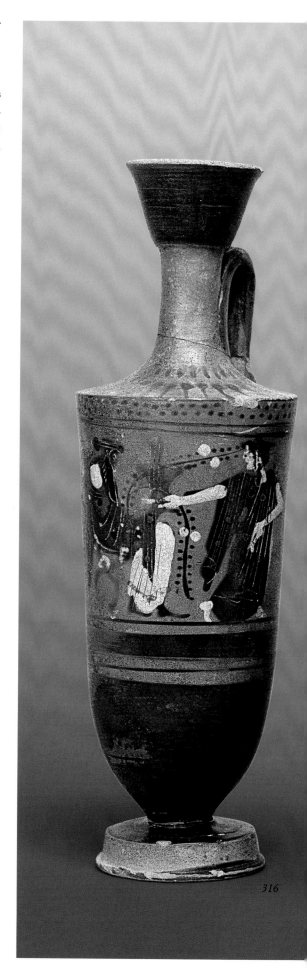

316

318 BLACK-FIGURE LEKYTHOS
480-470 B.C.

INV. NO. A 15328.
H. 0.211, B.D. 0.052, MAX.D. 0.067, M.D. 0.039 M.

Complete. Mended from many fragments with much chipping mainly on
the representation, flaking and uneven
firing. Brown-red clay. For the shape
and the other details of the body see lekythos no. 317. The reserved underside
of the base has a conical cavity surrounded by an incised ring.
Below the shoulder, a row of alternating black and white dots, framed above
and below by black lines. The departure of a goddess is depicted (Ariadne,
Semele or Leto), on a four-horse chariot.
Behind the chariot, two standing deities;
one woman in three-quarter view, in front
of the woman who is mounting, holds a
kithara. In front of her, a bearded male
figure – usually identified as Dionysos –
turns his head left towards the other figures brandishing a spear. To the right,
a woman seated on a chair defines the
border of the scene, in profile facing left.

318

315

317

319 BLACK-FIGURE TREFOIL-MOUTHED
OENOCHOE

490-480 B.C.

INV. NO. A 15233.
H. (INCL. HANDLE) 0.12, B.D. 0.036, MAX.D. 0.067 M.

Complete. Chip on the mouth and some flaking. Brown-red clay. Discoid base with a sloping upper surface and slightly curved underneath, depressed, spherical body, narrowing towards the base, curving shoulder, short neck, vertical strap handle, trefoil-shaped mouth. Black lustrous coating covers the larger part of the vase, the upper surface of the base and the upper part of its side, while a thin reserved band surrounds the lower part. There is a pictorial panel on a red background on the body opposite the handle, which, in the upper part, is decorated with a row of little lines and the represen-

tation, right and left, is framed by a double, vertical, black line. A youth (hunter?) is depicted moving forward to the right, with his head turned back. His hair is short and he wears a short sleeveless chiton. He holds a spear diagonally with his right hand while his raised left is covered by his himation. The field is decorated with two branches with white fruit and leaves which are rendered by black dots. The figure is depicted in silhouette, while incision is used to indicate the facial features, the fringes of the chiton and the folds of the himation. Dots of applied white paint decorate the himation and indicate the fruit on the branches.

COMMENTARY - BIBLIOGRAPHY: Unpublished.
The vase belongs to the Copenhagen category 68 which is included in the late black-figure style and probably comes from the Workshop of the Athena P. For a

comparable example in terms of shape and representation see *CVA* Copenhague 3, pl. 122, 5. For the position of the figure's feet, with the forward sole horizontal and the back raised on tiptoe, which indicates walking or running, see Prudhommeau 1965, 1, 31-32, par. 28 and 2, fig. 17-18. For the category see *ABV* 532, no. 8-9; *Para* 266; *Addenda* 63; *Addenda²* 132; *ABL* 160-161, Appendix XV bis, 260-261. For other examples of the category see *Kerameikos* IX, no. 196,5 (SW 2); *CVA* Ferrara II, pl. 19, nos. 1-6 and pl. 20, nos. 3-4; *CVA* Toronto 1, pl. 26, nos. 8-9. In general for the oenochoe shape see *Agora* XII, 58ff. and Noble 1988, 54-55.

H.S.

321

319

322

320 MINIATURE BLACK-FIGURE HYDRIA
500-475 B.C.

INV. NO. A 15240.
H. 0.057, B.D. 0.03, MAX.D. 0.054, M.D. 0.0335 M.

Complete. Chip on rim and extensive flaking. Brown-grey clay. Discoid base with curved upper surface and circular hollow in the middle of the underside, filled with a spherical swelling, spherical body, two horizontal, almost cylindrical handles on the sides and one vertical strap handle at the back, flat everted rim. Black coating covers the inside of the mouth, the back of the handle, the upper surface of the base and the lower part of the body, the top of the black here forming the ground line of the representation.

Opposite the vertical strap handle, against the ground-coloured background, representation of a ram, in section facing left,

320

with trace of applied white paint on the horns and body.

COMMENTARY - BIBLIOGRAPHY: Unpublished.

For miniature vases in general see *Agora* XII, 185-186. For comparable examples in terms of the representation see *Kerameikos* IX, 88, no. 16.2, pl. 44 (HW 167); *CIRh* VIII, 55ff., fig. 42, 44 (on a miniature amphoriskos). For the shape see *Agora* XII, 200-201. For earlier prototypes of the representation see *Veder Greco* 1988, 275, Tomb 200 (late Rhodian lekythos of the 2nd quarter of the 6th c. B.C.); *Münzen und Medaillen* 1964, 33, no. 59 (lip cup); Heesen 1996, no. 39, fig. 113-117 (band cup); both of the 3rd quarter of the 6th c. B.C. For a contemporary example on the tondo of a kylix see *CVA* Adria II, 49, pl. 46, no. 1.

H.S.

321 BLACK-FIGURE SKYPHOID KYLIX
500-475 B.C.

INV. NO. A 15235.
H. 0.053, B.D. 0.067, M.D. 0.105 M.

Complete with two large cracks. Brown-red clay. Ring base, hemispherical body, horizontal handles nearly circular in section. The interior of the vase, the back of the handles and the ring of the base are covered with a lustrous black glaze. A broad black band runs round the edge of the rim and a thinner one is the ground line for the representation.

On both sides of the vase, on a red-coloured background, a four-horse vehicle is depicted facing right which the charioteer, who holds the reins, has boarded. There are two upright figures behind the horses. The left figure, in front of the charioteer, is rendered in profile facing right and is holding a spear in his left hand and has the right raised in a gesture of farewell to the other one facing him. The right-hand figure is male and bearded with hair gathered into a bun; he turns his head back and is probably to be identified as Dionysos. Both figures have headbands. The scene on both sides of the vase is almost identical, with small differences in the rendering of the figures. While on one side the charioteer

appears to be a male figure, on the other the figure is female, usually in these circumstances thought to be Ariadne.

Applied violet paint is used for the rendering of the folds of the himation of the figures, the bands which crown the heads, the beard of Dionysos as well as for the manes, bridles and tails of the horses. The facial features of the figures are rendered by incision, as are the folds of their himatia, the chariot and the outline of the horses and their bridles. The representation is bordered right and left by an upright black-painted anthemion with a sprouting spiral which goes up to the handle.

COMMENTARY - BIBLIOGRAPHY: Unpublished.

The vase in terms of style belongs to that of the Haimon P. who is placed in the late black-figure style and is included in category K2 according to Ure 1927, 68ff. For comparable kylix scenes see *ABV* 568ff.; *Para* 286ff. For the same combination of representation but with the middle figure holding a lyre see Stähler 1983, 48, no. 26, pl. 29c; *Agora* XXIII, 282, no. 1504, pl. 102; Brownlee 1995, 369-370, pl. 87 (with relevant bibliography). In general, for the Workshop and the Haimon P. see the commentary on no. 315. For an example of a variation of the theme where the charioteer is a male figure see *Corinth* XIII, 241, no. 333-12, pl. 50. For the same theme cf. no. 318.

H.S.

322 BLACK-GLAZED CORINTHIAN-TYPE SKYPHOS
500-475 B.C.

INV. NO. A 15234.
H. 0.055, B.D. 0.046, M.D. 0.081 M.

Complete. Mended from many fragments, with small restorations, much chipped and flaking. Brown-yellow clay.

The body, widening towards the top with slightly curved sides, is covered inside and out with black glaze, as are the backs of the horizontal, cylindrical handles and the lower surface of the conical base. The parts between the handle stems, the band on the lower part of the body – with traces of applied red paint – and the base reserved. A red line runs around the vase below the handles. The underside of the base is decorated with a ring and, in the centre, a spot of red paint.

COMMENTARY - BIBLIOGRAPHY: Unpublished. For the use and technique see Noble 1988, 60. For parallel examples of skyphoi see *Agora* XII, pl. 45, no. 1377 and *Kerameikos* IX, 86, no. 7, 3 (SW 108), pl. 46.3. For the development of the shape see *Agora* XII, 81-84 and Oakley 1988, 168-170.

H.S.

324, 323

323 MINIATURE BLACK-FIGURE EXALEIPTRON
500-475 B.C.

INV. NO. A 15236.
H. 0.036, B.D. 0.032, MAX.D. 0.04, M.D. 0.017 M.

Intact with some flaking. Light brown clay. The inside of the vase, the lower part of the body, the foot and the upper surface of the discoid base are all covered with black lustrous glaze. The upper surface of the base is sloping, while the underside is flat, reserved and has a rather large conical hollow placed off-centre. Cylindrical stem which narrows towards the bottom and deviates from the vase centre. Bi-conical body with slightly curved shoulder.
A black band runs around the rim. On the upper part of the vase, on a red background, the decoration comprises three schematic birds, with a double row of black brush stroke spots placed between them.

COMMENTARY - BIBLIOGRAPHY: Unpublished. The use of miniature vases as offerings in sanctuaries and as grave goods in tombs is widespread; they were probably children's toys. The vase is related to the Swan Group. In general for the Swan Group cf. no. 324. For comparable examples see Ανδρειωμένου 1977, 277, fig. 6 (for older examples of the type); *Agora* XII, 186, pl. 45, no. 1413; for the same decoration on

a miniature amphoriskos see *Ashmolean Museum* 1967, 47, pl. XIV, no. 133. For the finds from the Agora relating to the group see *Agora* XXIII, 98, while for the shape see Scheibler 1964 and 1968.

H.S.

324 MINIATURE BLACK-FIGURE BELL
End of 6th - beginning of 5th c. B.C.

INV. NO. A 15237.
H. (INCL. HANDLE) 0.067, B.D. 0.065, M.D. 0.0135 M.

Intact, chipped and flaking. Brown-yellow clay, unevenly fired, brown-black coating. Vertical handle, cylindrical in section, widening towards the base, with decoration on the back of three schematic birds. A row of thick spots in the rim. Bell-shaped body.
Below the handle, two black bands, one wide and one narrower, run around the bell. A row of swans around the body, which are surrounded above and below by groups of vertical little lines. A narrow black band runs around the base.

COMMENTARY - BIBLIOGRAPHY: Unpublished. The vase belongs to the Swan Group. This is a series of miniature vases, roughly decorated with little lines and schematic swans, often rendered inversely. This group is dated to the 2nd half of the 6th and continues until the beginning of the 5th c. B.C. For the Swan Group in Attic vase-painting see *ABV* 655-658, 713-714; *Addenda* 69; *Addenda*[2] 146-147; *Para* 315; Boardman 1980, 204, 217, 221; Μαραγκού 1985, nos. 103-110; Πωλογιώργη 1995, 233, no. 6247, with bibliography. For comparable examples of the shape see *ABV* 658, no. 140; *Kerameikos* IX, 96, no. 36, 4, 5 (HW 45), pl. 47, with relevant bibliography.

H.S.

325 TERRACOTTA FIGURINE OF HORSE
AND RIDER
500-475 B.C.

INV. NO. E 1006.
H. 0.092, L. 0.10 M.

Complete. The left front and right hind legs of the horse and the rider are mended. Chipped and flaking all over the surface. Reddish clay, traces of white coating.

The group is handmade and has been rendered succinctly. The horse, narrow shouldered, has short straight legs, pointed oblong head, tail stretched backwards. The mane is rendered plastically, the rider, with bird-like face and beard, leans towards the neck of the animal, which he holds with his two hands. The legs of the rider at the back are not rendered from the back down.

COMMENTARY - BIBLIOGRAPHY: Unpublished.
The type of handmade horseman with bird-shaped face is met at the end of the 6th and the 1st half of the 5th c. B.C. in Attica and Boeotia, chiefly in tombs of small children. They are children's toys in everyday life which often accompanied the prematurely lost child in the grave and as such had a symbolic-apotropaic character. For the type and their interpretation see *Kerameikos* XV, 164, n. 295-297 with earlier bibliography; Szabo 1994, 90ff., n. 56-57, pl. 99; Schürmann 1989, 46, no. 100, pl. 21 (Boeotian). For typological parallels see *Kerameikos* XV, 170, no. 542 (500-480 B.C.), no. 544 (480-470 B.C.), no. 545 (1st half of 5th c. B.C.); Μυλωνάς 1975, Α, 86, Γ1-ειδ. 17, pl. 219α-β (490-470 B.C.), Β, 120, Τ I 17 no. 55, pl. 385α (490-480 B.C.).

Th.K.

326 TERRACOTTA FIGURINE OF HORSE AND RIDER
500-475 B.C.

INV. NO. E 1014.
MAX.H. 0.098, L. 0.115 M.

Missing the right hind leg of the horse and part of the head of the rider. The tail, the front right leg of the horse and the head of the rider are mended. Chipped and flaking on surface. Reddish clay.

COMMENTARY - BIBLIOGRAPHY: Unpublished.
Cf. no. 325 with bibliography.

Th.K.

327 TERRACOTTA PONY FIGURINE
500-475 B.C.

INV. NO. E 1010.
H. 0.045, MAX.L. 0.057 M.

Tail missing. The head is mended. Cracks and chips on surface. Reddish clay.
The animal has a long cylindrical body, high neck, pointed head and short legs which are rendered succinctly without being separated. The face and mane are depicted plastically.

COMMENTARY - BIBLIOGRAPHY: Unpublished.
It is a toy, a variation of the type of individual clay ponies, which are rendered in brief. For terracotta figurines of horses without rider see *Corinth* XV$_2$, 166-167, category XXIII (Corinthian).

Th.K.

328 TERRACOTTA PONY FIGURINE
500-475 B.C.

INV. NO. E 1011.
H. 0.038, MAX.L. 0.052 M.

Missing the front and rear left legs. The head is mended. Chipped on the muzzle and tail. Brown-red clay.
The animal has a long cylindrical body, short neck, conical head. The mane is plastically rendered with a separate piece of clay.

COMMENTARY - BIBLIOGRAPHY: Unpublished.
Cf. no. 327.

Th.K.

325, 326

327, 328

329 TERRACOTTA BOAR FIGURINE
500-475 B.C.

INV. NO. E 1013.
H. 0.053, L. 0.102 M.

Complete. The head is mended. Brown-red clay. A few traces of white paint on the surface. Completely mould-made. Air hole in belly. The back, tail, ears and eyes are plastically rendered.

COMMENTARY - BIBLIOGRAPHY: Unpublished.
The type is common, very widespread, particularly in Rhodes, Attica, Boeotia and at Olynthos, and is met without change throughout the whole of the 5th c. B.C. The Attic examples most probably copy Rhodian originals. For its provenance and origin see *Kerameikos* XV, 165, n. 299-301, with earlier bibliography. For its significance see *Lindos* I, 579, 583, no. 2410, pl. 113; *Olynthus* XIV, 244, no. 308, pl. 100 and 101; Schürmann 1989, 46-47, no. 104, pl. 22 (Boeotian). For typological parallels see *Kerameikos* XV, 173, nos. 565, 566 (from Rhodes?), nos. 567-569, pl. 99 (Attic); *BMC* I, 77, nos. 176-185, pl. 33 (Rhodian) and 184, no. 691, pl. 90 (Attic); Μυλωνάς 1975, A, 46, no. B17-ειδ. 9.10, B, pl. 204γ, and A, 65, no. Βρ.-ειδ. 14, B, pl. 215β; *Σίνδος* 1985, 38, fig. 45 (with bibliography). See also nos. 343 and 369.

Th.K.

329, 330

330 TERRACOTTA BOVINE FIGURINE
500-475 B.C.

INV. NO. E 1009.
H. 0.073, L. 0.095 M.

Tail missing. The head and the left leg are mended. Many cracks, chips and flaking over the whole body. Reddish clay, traces of white paint.
The animal has a long body, low stretched out legs and pointed head. The horns and neck are plastically rendered. The lower part of the neck is indicated plastically.

COMMENTARY - BIBLIOGRAPHY: Unpublished.
See Bloesch 1974, 30, no. 175, pl. 28.

Th.K.

331, 332

331 TERRACOTTA BIRD FIGURINE
500-475 B.C.

INV. NO. E 1005.
H. 0.096 M.

Intact. Small chip on beak and on base. Light brown clay. Traces of white paint all over the surface and of red on the beak and head.
The bird (waterfowl) stands motionless and upright with closed wings, pointed head, supple neck, tail turned down, with low cylindrical stalk on a projecting flat base. The beak, eyes and crest are plastically rendered.

COMMENTARY - BIBLIOGRAPHY: Unpublished.
See *Kerameikos* XV, 165, 176-177, no. 593 (end of 6th c. B.C.) and no. 596 (2nd quarter of 5th c. B.C.), pl. 102.

Th.K.

332 TERRACOTTA TORTOISE FIGURINE
500-475 B.C.

INV. NO. E 1015.
H. 0.041, L. 0.066 M.

Intact, chipped on surface. Brown-red clay, traces of white paint.
The small head and shell, divided on the upper surface into low relief parts, are mould-made. The feet and lower part of the body, with air hole, are handmade.

COMMENTARY - BIBLIOGRAPHY: Unpublished.
A common type, known from Rhodes but also Attica and Boeotia, it is found in children's tombs of the 5th c. B.C. and remains the same until the 3rd quarter of the century. See *Kerameikos* XV, 165, n. 306, with earlier bibliography and Dumoulin 1994, 139-144, nos. 49-51, pl. 22. For their interpretation as children's amulets or toys and their relationship with chthonic deities see Klein 1932, 10, pl. IXA and *Olynthus* XIV, 257ff., nos. 350,

352, 353, pl. 105. For typological parallels see *Kerameikos* XV, 178, nos. 609-610, pl. 104.1,2,3 (Rhodian?; 1st half of 5th c. B.C.), nos. 611, 612, pl. 104.4 (Attic; 430/20 B.C.; Bloesch 1974, 29, no. 172, pl. 28 (with bibliography); Bol - Kotera 1986, 63, no. 33, with bibliography (Corinthian?; 1st half of 5th c. B.C.).

Th.K.

333 TERRACOTTA RELIEF PLAQUE OF GORGON
500-475 B.C.

INV. NO. E 1012.
H. 0.075, MAX.W. 0.079 M.

Complete. Mended from four fragments. Chipped on surface. Grey-brown clay. The Gorgon is depicted in the standard running/flying pose of the ἐν γούνασι δρόμος (on knees). The head and body are rendered en face, while the legs are in profile towards the right. Her wings are open and her arms, bent at the elbows, are brought into the waist. She is wearing boots on her feet. Two suspension holes at the figure's shoulder height.

COMMENTARY - BIBLIOGRAPHY: Unpublished.
The relief plaque belongs to the category of Melian reliefs. For these reliefs and their use see Jacobsthal 1931, 121ff., who supports their Melian origin, highlighting the general island character. They were used, as the same scholar forcefully explains, for lining wooden boxes. For their place of origin see also Κώστογλου-Δεσποίνη 1979, 174. For the specific type with a Gorgon representation see Jacobsthal 1931, 89-90, pl. 2:XVIa and Higgins 1967, 83, pl. 36B. For typological parallels see Mollard-Besques 1954, I, 98, C89, pl. LXXI; Breitenstein 1941, no. 244, pl. 25; Παπασπυρίδη-Καρούζου 1933-35, 31, fig. 15; *Olynthus* XIV, 230, no. 291, pl. 98 (470-460 B.C.).

Th.K.

From tomb 530

334 BLACK-FIGURE LEKYTHOS
480-470 B.C.

INV. NO. A 15507.
H. 0.203, B.D. 0.055, MAX.D. 0.063, M.D. 0.042 M.

Complete, restored. Mended at the mouth, handle and the upper part of the body. Brown-red clay. The shape and the other details of the body as on no. 316. The underside of the base is reserved with a conical cavity and circular swelling in the centre, while the reserved side of the base has a violet band on the upper part and a black band below. Its shoulder, neck, flat rim and interior surface are covered with an off-white slip. The rim is framed inside by black and the outside of the mouth by a violet ring. Two violet bands run around the upper part of the black lower body of the vase. Below the shoulder, a double row of black dots is bordered by black lines. On the body, against a red background, a Battle of the Gods and Giants (Gigantomachy) is depicted. In the centre, Athena with a sleeveless chiton, himation, shield and Attic helmet with a high crest, in profile facing right. She is stabbing with her spear a Giant who has been felled. To the right, traces of a second upright battling Giant brandishing his spear are preserved, and to the left of Athena, a third Giant, in profile facing right, tries to wound the goddess with his spear, while holding in his left arm his doubled-up himation and shield. The Giants bear helmet, zoma, shield, spear and sword at their waist. The details are partly indicated with incision, such as the folds and fringes of the clothing and in part the outline of the body of the Giants who are otherwise in silhouette. Applied violet paint embellishes the periphery of the shields, the himatia and the crest of Athena's helmet. Applied white paint covers the naked limbs of Athena, according to the ancient convention, the crest of the left-hand Giant's helmet, the dotted distinguishing marks of the shields and the scabbards.

COMMENTARY - BIBLIOGRAPHY: Unpublished.
The vase is related to the late phase of the Workshop of the Diosphos P., who was one of the artists of the late black-figure style. His characteristics are the slenderness, grace and elegance of his figures, the use of incision to indicate the limbs of the figures and often to render outstretched arms. For the painter see *ABV* 508ff., 702-703; *Para* 248ff.; *Addenda* 60-61; *Addenda²* 127-128; *ABL* 94ff. and Appendix XII, 232ff.; Haspels 1972, 103-107. For comparisons in terms of the representation of the Giants see *CVA* Karlsruhe Badisches Landesmuseum I, pl. 13, nos. 5-6. For the subject see Vian 1951, 48ff. and esp. 59ff.; *LIMC* II.1, s.v. Athena, 990.992 and IV.1, s.v. Gigantes, 191-192, 222-226.

H.S.

335 BLACK-FIGURE LEKYTHOS
500-475 B.C.

INV. NO. A 15506.
H. 0.231, B.D. 0.058, MAX.D. 0.071, M.D. 0.047 M.

Complete. Mended neck, handle and mouth. The most extensive damage is on the mouth. The shapes and other details of the body, as on no. 334, apart from the reserved underside of the base, which has a circular cavity with a conical swelling in the centre. Neck and shoulder reserved. Beneath the shoulder, a double row of alternating black and white dots is bordered below by a double series of black lines. The representation is related to the Trojan Cycle. In the centre of the scene, Athena is depicted in profile facing right, with a sleeved chiton and himation, flanked by Achilles and Ajax who are playing dice, covered with their himatia. The heroes are turned towards the goddess, on low seats, with a table in the middle and carry helmets and a spear. The red background zone

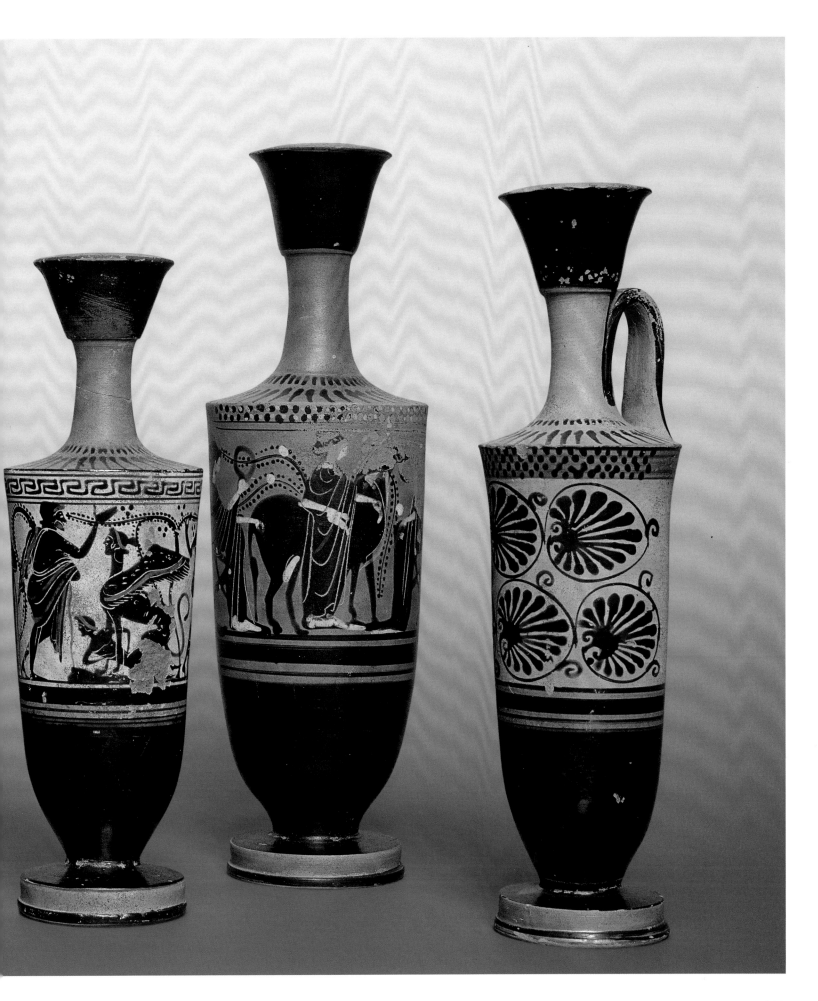

is embellished with branches which have schematic black dot-leaves and white fruit. Incision (for folds of the himatia, shins and helmets of the heroes), applied white and violet paint are used to render the partial details.

COMMENTARY - BIBLIOGRAPHY: Unpublished.

In the style of the Haimon P. The subject is met in Attic vase-painting a little after the middle of the 6th c. B.C. and is quite widespread in the late black-figure style. For the workshop and painter cf. no. 315. For the representation see *Para* 279; *CVA* Vibo Valentia, Museo Statale "Vito Capialbi" I, 24-25, nos. 3-4, pl. 15 (on a lekythos of Athens Category 581, ii, with extensive bibliography); *CVA* Agrigento, Museo Archeologico Nazionale I, 29, nos. 3-4, pl. 69; *CVA* Tübingen 3, pl. 49, 9-11. For the theme see *LIMC* I.1, s.v. Achilleus, 96ff.; Kemp-Lindemann 1975, 75-87 and generally for vases with this theme see Brommer 1973, 334-339. For a comparable representation on a kylix, but also more generally for the theme, see Shapiro - Picón - Scott 1995, 128-129, no. 64. For an immediately older prototype of the theme see *Veder Greco* 1988, 152, no. 34 (on a lekythos of Athens Category 581, i; *c.* 500 B.C.). For the symbolism and the connection of the scene with death see *Vases à mémoire* 1988, 119-120, no. 81, pl. p. 123. For the game of dice and generally for its depiction see Steinhart 1996, 80-81, no. 15, with bibliography.

H.S.

336 BLACK-FIGURE LEKYTHOS
c. 480-470 B.C.

INV. NO. A 15510.
H. 0.192, B.D. 0.051, MAX.D. 0.06, M.D. 0.042 M.

Complete. Neck and handle mended. Chipped and flaking. Brown-red clay. Mouth, handle, decoration of the shoulder, lower part of the body and base as on no. 334. The neck, the underside of the handle and the shoulder are reserved and the background of the scene is covered in an off-white slip.
Below the shoulder, a simple, black-painted, right-turned meander. The centre of the scene includes a sphinx, in profile facing left, which is felling its victim and is flanked by spectators, three male figures. Left, a standing figure in profile facing right and gesturing fiercely, who is

probably to be identified as Oedipus. Left and right, two other male figures are at a distance looking towards the centre, while all four male figures carry himatia and sticks. A dog borders the scene on the right. In the field, branches with schematic leaves and dotted fruit arranged in threes. Applied violet paint is used on the himatia, beards and headbands of the figures and on the wing of the Sphinx. Rendered by incision are the folds of the himatia, the facial features, the few anatomical details of the figures and the dog, as well as the lower extremities of the Sphinx, its victim and the left-hand standing figure which stand in the forefront.

COMMENTARY - BIBLIOGRAPHY: Unpublished.

Work of the Haimon P. The subject is related to the Theban Cycle, and is found on lekythoi by the painter who took his name from the last victim of the Sphinx, Haimon, son of Creon. The representation has its origin in Near Eastern prototypes and it first occurs in Attic pottery during the 3rd quarter of the 6th c. B.C. For comparable scenes on lekythoi see *ABL* 130-131, Appendix XIII, A, 241, nos. 7-10, pl. 41,4, which refer to lekythoi with the same subject; Σταυρόπουλλος 1958, Tomb 10, pl. 10β-γ; *ABV* 539, no. 12 and 551; *Para* 279; Boardman 1980, fig. 273. For its representation and origin, with comparable examples, see Moret 1984, 15ff., pl. 8-9; for the dog see 18 and n. 3. For the myth see Kerényi 1966, 344-347 and for the subject see *LIMC* VII.1, s.v. Oidipus, 6.

H.S.

337 BLACK-FIGURE LEKYTHOS
480-470 B.C.

INV. NO. A 15505.
H. 0.23, B.D. 0.058, MAX.D. 0.072, M.D. 0.046 M.

Complete. Flaking, mainly on the representation. Brown-red clay. The shape and other details of the body, as on no. 335, apart from the rim which has an off-white slip.

In the middle of the scene, an upright female figure is depicted in profile facing right and leading a mule by the reins, which is behind her. She is flanked by two figures seated on stools and cross-legged, turned towards the centre. The left figure holds a garland rendered in black paint, in his right hand. The figures are depicted with chiton, himation, hair gathered into a bun and a band on the head. In the decorative field, branches with schematic, black, dotted leaves and white fruit. Incision and fugitive applied white paint indicate some of the details.

COMMENTARY - BIBLIOGRAPHY: Unpublished.
Workshop of the Haimon P. The subject is met on a limited number of lekythoi towards the end of the 1st quarter of the 5th c. B.C. and with different variations. For comparable representations see Jacquemin 1984, 112, no. 459 (AC 19360); *CVA* Vibo Valentia, Museo Statale "Vito Capialbi" I, 30, no. 2.4 (C44) pl. 23; *Para* 282 (with oxen in place of the mule).

H.S.

338 BLACK-FIGURE VOLUTE LEKYTHOS
c. 480 B.C.

INV. NO. A 15508.
H. 0.209, B.D. 0.051, MAX.D. 0.058, M.D. 0.0435 M.

Complete, chipped and flaking. Light brown clay. The shape and the other details of the body as on no. 336. In the centre of the reserved underside of the base, a conical cavity with an incised ring. The neck, shoulder, interior surface of the handle and the background of the representation are covered with applied off-white slip.

Beneath the shoulder, chequer board pattern arranged in four successive rows. On the body, two rows of three, fifteen-leafed anthemia enclosed by the extension of their sprouts, in a horizontal arrangement with the upper part facing right. A sprout-spiral grows out of the top of the anthemia in the upper row, while two grow out of the top and bottom of those in the lower row, curling downwards. The kernel of the anthemia is filled with black paint.

COMMENTARY - BIBLIOGRAPHY: Unpublished.
The vase has the characteristic slender shape of lekythoi by the Haimon P. which follow, in terms of decoration and shape, the tradition of the Workshop of the Diosphos P. The main difference between the two is that, according to the rules, the kernels of the anthemia of the Diosphos P. are filled with red paint and their drawing is more careful. The Megaira P. also appropriated the same type of decoration. For the decoration see *ABL* 133 and 160-161 and Kurtz 1975, 150ff. For comparable examples of lekythoi see Παπασπυρίδη - Κυπαρίσσης 1927/28, 91, fig. 1 (amongst vases found in a tomb on Stadiou Street) and *CVA* Mainz 1, 40-41, pl. 39, 1 (15) (similar decoration on different shape of lekythos from the Workshop of the Megaira P.).

H.S.

337

339 **BLACK-FIGURE PSYKTER (TYPE B)**
500-475 B.C.

INV. NO. A 15242.
H. 0.155, B.D. 0.071, M.D. 0.063 M.

Complete, joined together from many sherds.

Komos scene. On side A, to the left a young varviton-player and to the right a bearded reveller, who executes a dance movement. Both are naked, apart from their himatia which fall in a relaxed fashion about their shoulders and arms. On side B, another pair of revellers is depicted. The clean-shaven reveller on the left is holding a large rhyton in his left hand, whilst the bearded one to the right is dancing. Climbing plants with schematic ivy leaves fill the background of the scene on both sides. The pictori-

339 a

al metopes are crowned by schematic tongue decoration and framed by a vertical, double row of black dots linked by a dash. Depicted with thin applied, off-white paint, now fugitive at many points, are the bands which embellish the hair of the revellers, the dot rosettes which ornament their himatia and the funnel of the horn.

COMMENTARY - BIBLIOGRAPHY: Unpublished. The cooler belongs to type B which has double vertical tubular handles and a flat base. For the shape see Drougou 1975, while for typological parallels see *Agora* XII, pl. 2, no. 38. For the komos see Μαραγκού 1995, 136-137, no. 19 [Καραμπατέα]. Recently see Schwarz 1997 and Miller 1999. For the varviton-player see Μιχαηλίδης 1982, 73-74. The σχήματα were the spontaneous poses, positions or expressions which the dancer took while executing the dance and which interrupted his flow, that is his step and movement. The δεῖξις (demonstration) that is the combination of the σχῆμα and the φορά with different gestures, depicts different states of man, animals, things. For the naming of the components of the dance see Lawler 1984, 27-28 and Μιχαηλίδης 1982, 302-303, 350.

G.K.

339 a

340 TERRACOTTA FIGURINE OF HORSE AND RIDER
500-475 B.C.

INV. NO. E 1016.
H. 0.093, L. 0.109 M.

The upper part of the horse's body together with the rider, as well as the three legs of the animal are mended. Flaking on one side and chips over the whole surface. Soft, rosy clay with mica.
White slip mainly on the animal's body and applied red on the rider's torso. Vertical red lines on the side of its legs reach the endings. The horse is rendered stationary with legs firm and the head up.

The rider, with head raised, is touching the neck of the animal.

COMMENTARY - BIBLIOGRAPHY: Unpublished.
For the type see no. 325 and the similar no. 326. For typological parallels see *Kerameikos* XV, 170, no. 542, pl. 96.

Th.K.

341 TERRACOTTA FIGURINE OF HORSE AND RIDER
500-475 B.C.

INV. NO. E 1018.
H. 0.107, MAX.L. 0.122 M.

Complete. The left hind leg and part of the tail are mended. Chipped and flaking on the surface. Soft, grey-brown clay, with mica.
The rider firmly placed on the back of the horse is holding the neck of the animal with disproportionately large hands; the horse is depicted with spread out legs, firm head, shaking tale behind, mane in relief. The rider's face is mould-made. The physiognomy is depicted plastically as are the screwed ringlets framing his head. Traces of black and white slip over the whole group. The mantle of the rider and the mane of the horse have been rendered with applied red paint. Two red bands on the neck with black paint in the interstices to indicate the reins. Red lines indicate the fingers of the rider's hands; the sides of the animal are rendered in the same way.

COMMENTARY - BIBLIOGRAPHY: Unpublished.
The type is known from Rhodes, see *BMC* I, no. 104, pl. 20 (510-490 B.C.) and *CIRh* IV, 117, no. 10, fig. 113 (470 B.C.); likewise, from Boeotia see *BMC* I, nos. 804-805, pl. 109 and from Attica see *Kerameikos* XV, 171, no. 548, pl. 97.2 (1st half of 5th c. B.C., with bibliography). See also Winter 1903, I, 36,6 and 37,4. The Boeotian type in *BMC* I, 215, no. 804, pl. 109, is closest.

Th.K.

342 TERRACOTTA BOVINE FIGURINE
500-475 B.C.

INV. NO. E 1017.
H. 0.074, MAX.L. 0.11 M.

Complete. The tail mended, chipped ears, flaking and cracking all over the surface. Grey-brown clay, traces of white and black slip all over the figurine. Applied red on the back, ears, muzzle and neck.
The horns and neck are roundly rendered. The animal has a firm head and stretched legs. Its tail falls downwards with a slight incline to the left.

COMMENTARY - BIBLIOGRAPHY: Unpublished.
See no. 330.

Th.K.

340, 341

342, 343

343 TERRACOTTA FIGURINE OF A PIG
500-475 B.C.

INV. NO. E 1019.
H. 0.055, L. 0.085 M.

The front right leg is missing. The hind left is mended and has a small chip. Flaking. Brown-red clay. White slip over the entire surface.

The ears, eyes, back and the tail, raised upwards slightly and falling to the right, are indicated plastically. The legs of the animal are long. The muzzle, the back and the tail have applied reddish paint.

COMMENTARY - BIBLIOGRAPHY: Unpublished.
See no. 329 (with bibliography) and no. 369.

Th.K.

344

344 TERRACOTTA GROUP OF FEMALE MONKEY WITH HER YOUNG
500-475 B.C.

INV. NO. 1020.
H. 0.087, B.D. 0.046 M.

Part of the end of the left leg of the female monkey and of the left hand of the baby are missing. The left hand and leg of the mother and the head and left hand of the baby are mended. The surface is chipped and flaking. Brown clay. White and rosy slip on the whole surface.

The figures are placed on a flat, circular base. The mother is sitting on a rock, has a long torso and legs bent and close together. She is holding her baby tenderly around the waist and the legs, while the baby leans and touches her head encircling it with his right arm. It seems as though he has fallen asleep.

COMMENTARY - BIBLIOGRAPHY: Unpublished.
See Bloesch 1974, 30, no. 176, pl. 28 (similar); Winter 1903, I, 224, 1. For a variation on the type see McDermott 1938, 184, no. 142; *ClRh* IV, 262-263, tomb 132, fig. 287 and 289; *Lindos* I, 470, no. 1904, pl. 85; Liepmann 1975, 44, no. T15 (fat bellied with young monkey; end of 6th c. B.C.); *BMC* I, no. 796, pl. 107 (squatting monkey with a stone on his shoulders). Similar groups were usual votives in shrines of a female deity during the Classical and Archaic periods; they are also found in graves of young children and have been interpreted as maternal symbols; see Hatzisteliou-Price 1969, 110.

Th.K.

345 TERRACOTTA FIGURE OF A NAKED SQUATTING SILENUS
500-475 B.C.

INV. NO. E 1022.
H. 0.08, MAX.L. 0.04 M.

Intact. Flaking and damaged. It comes from a much-used mould. Red slip over the whole surface.

The Silen, bearded and ithyphallic, supports his elbows on his knees and has his hands on his large hemispherical stomach. His horse-legs, apart, at the same time form a strong base for the figure. Leaning slightly to the right with

345

his large head right on his shoulders, he has a broad face with almost human features: almond-shaped eyes, raised arches of the eyebrows, human (not animal) ears, half-open mouth with a fleshy lower lip and a moustache above the upper lip.

COMMENTARY - BIBLIOGRAPHY: Unpublished.

It is considered an older ithyphallic type of Bess of Rhodian origin, which is found in differing variations from the late 6th c. to 470-460 B.C. on Rhodes but also in Attica, Boeotia, Macedonia, the Aegean islands and Magna Graecia. Its presence in the graves of young children and women is interpreted as the symbol of male fertility with apotropaic and magical powers. For the type see Winter 1903, I, 215,4; Bol - Kotera 1986, 47, no. 23; Schmidt 1994, 43, no. 37, pl. 10; *Kerameikos* XV, 77, n. 134-135. For the interpretation of the type see Schmaltz 1974, 31ff. About its presence in graves see Peredolskaja 1964, 29; Μυλωνάς 1975, Α, 65, grave no. Βρ.-ειδ. 13, Β, pl. 215β. For typological parallels see *Kerameikos* XV, 78, no. 239, pl. 48.1,2.

Th.K.

From tomb 632

346 BLACK-FIGURE WHITE-GROUND
ALABASTRON
500-475 B.C.

INV. NO. A 15458.
H. 0.172, M.D. 0.045 M.

Intact, mouth mended. Chips mainly on the rim, flakes and cracks.

On the main zone, on the cream slip, three bands of black-figure, multi-leaved encircled palmettes. Added violet colour emphasises the heart of each palmette. The zone is crowned by six dotted bands and tongue-pattern. The black glaze of the lower part of the vase is interrupted by a reserved band and three violet lines. Shoulder, neck and the underside of the rim are covered with black glaze.

COMMENTARY - BIBLIOGRAPHY: Unpublished.

For the Workshop of the Diosphos P. see commentary on no. 289. For black-figure, white-ground alabastra, see *Agora* XXX, 48-50 and Wehgartner 1983, 112-134 (esp. 113, n. 21). For the shape and the system of the subsidiary decoration cf. a black-figure, white-ground alabastron in Oxford, Ashmolean Museum, no. 1919.35, attributed to the Diosphos P. by E. Haspels; see also *ABL* 100-101 and 237, no. 11 and Boardman 1980, 172, fig. 268. Cf. also white alabastron with black-figure palmettes attributed to the Diosphos P. in Gerona, no. 9, see Mertens 1977, 95, no. 10, 97 pl. XIV.2 (=*ABL* 237, 117). For the alabastra of the Workshop of the Dios-

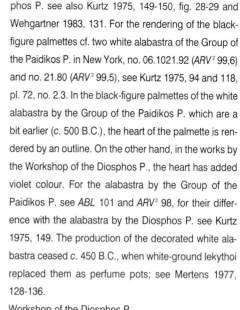

phos P. see also Kurtz 1975, 149-150, fig. 28-29 and Wehgartner 1983, 131. For the rendering of the black-figure palmettes cf. two white alabastra of the Group of the Paidikos P. in New York, no. 06.1021.92 (*ARV²* 99,6) and no. 21.80 (*ARV²* 99,5), see Kurtz 1975, 94 and 118, pl. 72, no. 2.3. In the black-figure palmettes of the white alabastra by the Group of the Paidikos P. which are a bit earlier (*c.* 500 B.C.), the heart of the palmette is rendered by an outline. On the other hand, in the works by the Workshop of the Diosphos P., the heart has added violet colour. For the alabastra by the Group of the Paidikos P. see *ABL* 101 and *ARV²* 98, for their difference with the alabastra by the Diosphos P. see Kurtz 1975, 149. The production of the decorated white alabastra ceased *c.* 450 B.C., when white-ground lekythoi replaced them as perfume pots; see Mertens 1977, 128-136.

Workshop of the Diosphos P.

G.K.

347

347 BLACK-GLAZED PYXIS WITH LID
500-480 B.C.

INV. NO. A 15248.
H. 0.12, M.D. 0.104, B.D. 0.064 M.

Mended from several pieces and restored on the lid. Many chips on the ring, joining the base with the main body and on the surface of the vase. Brownish red clay. Wide, ring base, hemispherical body, lid slightly convex, vertical side walls and acorn-shaped handle.

Black glaze on the vase, apart from the vertical and horizontal surface of the base and the bottom which has a conical knob. The rim and the groove of the lid remain unglazed. Reserved band on the rim of the lid as well as in the edge of the upper surface. The reserved handle is circled by black bands. Traces of thin red ochre (miltos) on the rim of the body and the lid.

COMMENTARY - BIBLIOGRAPHY: Unpublished.

It belongs to the type of lekanis-pyxis or the type of the handleless lekanis; see *Agora* XII, 172. It is considered to be a toiletry pot and is often found in burials, as a burial offering. For closer parallels see *Kerameikos* IX, pl. 44,16 and *Agora* XII, pl. 42, 1269 (with earlier bibliography).

I.T.-D.

348 BLACK-GLAZED FEEDER WITH STRAINER
480-470 B.C.

INV. NO. A 15326.
H. 0.054, MAX.D. 0.072, B.D. 0.042 M.

Complete, with flakes on the glaze. Light brown clay. The body is concave, a characteristic which is visibly diminished toward the base, while there is a sloping lip that is offset from the body. Horseshoe, cylindrical handle set diagonally in the middle of the vase where the horizontal, cylindrical spout stems from; the top of the strainer is slightly concave.

The whole vase is in black glaze, apart from the interior, the top of the strainer, the steep walls of the base and its underside, the inner face of the handles and the area of the body at the level of the lower handle-attachments which are reserved.

COMMENTARY - BIBLIOGRAPHY: Unpublished.

The feeder with strainer of this type is a usual burial offering in children's graves, since it is the vase that was mainly used for feeding infants. Several examples come from children's burials in the cemetery of Kerameikos, where its evolution in terms of typology is depicted; see *Kerameikos* IX, 5, pl. 80. The shape of this feeder appears older than the larger and more conical feeders from the Kerameikos, see *Kerameikos* IX, 141 no. 229.4, pl. 54 (closest parallel as far as the outline is concerned), 126, no. 152.9, pl. 41 and 123, no. 239.1, pl.

60 (nearest to the details). Cf. also *CIRh* IV, 121, fig. 111 (from Kameiros) and *CVA* Rodi (1) [Italia 9] III He pl. 1, 3. For feeders in general see *Agora* XII, 161, nos. 1197-1199, pl. 39, fig. 11 and recently Collin-Bouffier in *Céramique* 1999, 91-96.

E.B.-V.

349 MINIATURE SKYPHOS OF THE CORINTHIAN TYPE
480-470 B.C.

INV. NO. A 15327.
H. 0.036, M.D. 0.054, B.D. 0.024 M.

Complete. Mended with chips and fading glaze. Brown clay. Body slightly curved and conical, horizontal, round loop handles, ring base.

The reserved zone at the handle area is decorated with degenerated Z-shaped ornament among black bands. Black dots on the reserved handles. The base, of similar colour, has a nipple knob on the centre of its underside.

COMMENTARY - BIBLIOGRAPHY: Unpublished.

This is a common type of vase and is often found in the cemetery of the Athenian Kerameikos as a burial offering. For the type, in the category of miniatures, see *Agora* XII, 185 and 333, nos. 1377, 1378, pl. 45, where other typological parallels are mentioned. For the most recent parallel see *Kerameikos* IX, 94, no. 31.6, pl. 47 (from a pot burial of the early 5th c. B.C.).

E.B.-V.

348

349

350 STONE CASE FOR CINERARY URN
500-470 B.C.

INV. NO. Λ 5776.
H. 0.48, W. 0.93 (LOWER) - 1 (UPPER), TH. 1.03,
D. OF DEPRESSION 0.29, D. OF LID 0.58, TH. OF LID 0.035 M.

Case of solid limestone, square in section
with a gradual narrowing of its width at
the lower part. Chipped on the surface
and traces of incrustations and of a patina. Roughly worked with clear traces of a
pointed tool. On the upper surface there
is a deep cylindrical cutting with marks of
a chisel and point. The cutting is covered
with a marble, discoid lid with a bevelled
edge. Traces of a pointed tool on the surfaces of the lid.

COMMENTARY - BIBLIOGRAPHY: Unpublished.
The bronze cinerary urn no. 351 was placed inside the
cutting. Regarding this method of burial cf. Kurtz -
Boardman 1994, 93, pl. 23 (bronze ash-urn from the
Kerameikos, found containing ashes wrapped in purple
cloth, inside a wooden box placed in a stone case).
Also, see *Kerameikos* VII₁, 83-84 (cauldron in limestone
case); Έργο ΥΠΠΟ 1998, 123 (bronze urn in marble
case from the necropolis of Thasos; 4th c. B.C.); Orsi
1906, 323, fig. 240 (burial of the 5th c. B.C.).

N.S.

351 BRONZE CAULDRON
500-470 B.C.

INV. NO. Δ 7172.
H. 0.27, MAX.D. 0.377, M.D. 0.21, D. OF LID 0.236, D. OF LIP
OF LID 0.025 M.

Complete. Bronze with dark green pati-na and cracking on the body of the vase. The original golden-brown surface is pre-served on some parts of the lid.

The body is almost hemispherical with a flattened shoulder and narrow, hori-zontal rim, slightly raised. Round the periphery of the rim, on top of the shoul-der, are soldered with lead four reels, semicircular in section, in opposite pairs and decorated with five pairs of relief rings at regular intervals. Two of them, diametrically opposed, on the left and right, are perforated lengthwise to take the elliptical loop handles. The latter are decorated with a relief ring in their middle. The lid of the brazier looks like a shield with wide horizontal rim and slightly con-cave body. Four bronze nails – nailed obliquely into the middle of each reel – secured it to the rim of the cauldron.

COMMENTARY - BIBLIOGRAPHY: Unpublished.
For the type of cauldron cf. Μπέσιος - Παππά (n.p.d.), 66, AM Πυ538 (500-480 B.C.). The example of the lid of this particular cauldron is characteristic, both in terms of type and details – broad rim without perfora-tions etc. – and in the way it is used. For the interpre-tation of comparable objects (usually clay), which are sometimes found in tombs and have until now been considered shields, when it is more often a question of lids, plates or other types of utensil, see Σταμπολίδης 1998, 114-116; Stampolidis 1998a, 80-82; *idem* 1998b, 182-183.

N.S.

352 ALABASTRON
480-470 B.C.

INV. NO. Δ 7145.
H. 0.148, M.D. 0.044, INT. M.D. 0.018 M.

Made of alabaster. A large part of the body is missing. It has a wide, flat lip. The pseudo-handles appear as unpierced lugs. The convex edge of the body has been made from a separate piece of alabaster. The green colour on the rim and the body is due to the adjoining bronze urn (lebes) of the tomb 608.

COMMENTARY - BIBLIOGRAPHY: Unpublished.
This shape appears in Attica in the mid 6th c. B.C., and is quite popular until the end of the 5th c. B.C. Its use as a perfume pot is confirmed by written sources and the fact that it often appears in pottery, where scenes of women using cosmetics are depicted. It was therefore a rather popular burial offering in women's tombs. In order to be carried, the vessel was suspended by thin straps slipped around the handles or the neck. When not in use, it was hung or put in a special box called ἀλαβαστ(ρ)οθήκη (alabastron case), (Poll. 1, 21). It is believed that the material and the shape of the alabastron come from Egypt. It has been reported that its name derives from the Egyptian phrase a-la-baste (vessel of the Goddess Bastet).
For a similar alabastron of 480 B.C. see *Kerameikos* XII, 82, no. 10, fig. 21. For the alabastra made of alabaster see Amyx 1958, 213ff. For alabastra of the 2nd quarter of the 5th c. B.C. see Τιβέριος 1984, 23-24, with extensive bibliography. For other alabastra from the excavations of the Kerameikos see Knigge 1966, 128, fig. 16, 133, no. 27, pl. 55 and Willemsen 1977, pl. 55. Generally, for the alabaster alabastron, the source of its material and other related matters, see Coleman-Carter 1998, esp. 757-769 and *KdA*, 14, no. 13 (same as far as the edge of the vase made from separate piece of alabastron is concerned). See Zaphiropoulou 1973, 614, nos. 22-31, fig. 18-19, 633ff.

E.B.-V.

353 BLACK-GLAZED LEKYTHOS (SECONDARY TYPE)
480-470 B.C.

INV. NO. A 15249.
H. 0.147, M.D. 0.03, MAX.D. 0.048, B.D. 0.04 M.

Almost intact, mended at the neck. Flakes. Brownish red clay. The neck, shoulder, underside of the handle and the base on its resting surface are reserved. Calyx-shaped mouth, strap handle, discoid base. On the shoulder there is a lotus pattern, with alternate black and white ray pattern. Thin black lines circling the lower part of the neck. Violet colour on the rim of the mouth, double violet line below the shoulder, violet line on the lower part of the body, at the junction with the foot and on the edge of the foot.

COMMENTARY - BIBLIOGRAPHY: Unpublished.
This type of black-glazed lekythos is well known from the Athenian Agora and the Kerameikos as well as from the excavations of many cemeteries in Attica. The majority of these vases date to the 1st half of the 5th c. B.C., and more precisely its 2nd quarter. For a lekythos with similar decoration see *Agora* XII, 314, no. 1114, pl. 38 (c. 500 B.C.). For the shape and decoration see *Kerameikos* IX, 178, no. E44.2, pl. 90 (480-470 B.C.). Cf. also *Agora* XII, 153, pl. 38; *Kerameikos* XII, 33-38; more recently Πωλογιώργη 1993-94, 258-260, pl. 39α-γ, with bibliography.

E.B.-V.

354 BLACK-GLAZED ARYBALLOS
480-470 B.C.

INV. NO. A 15251.
H. 0.081, M.D. 0.041, B.D. 0.05 M.

Complete. On the shiny black glaze there are chips. Red-brown clay. Globular body, depressed. The mouth is hemispherical, with the top of the lip reserved.
Strap handle, low discoid base, reserved on the front and on the resting surface.

COMMENTARY - BIBLIOGRAPHY: Unpublished.
The aryballoi – small oil containers used by athletes in the gymnasia to spread oil on their body – are distinguished in two types according to shape: the Corinthian, with discoid mouth, one handle and no base, and the Attic, with hemispherical mouth, two handles and flat base. No. 354 appears to be a combination of both: the shape belongs to the Attic type, but its han-

352

dle is Corinthian. Generally, the type of the black-glazed aryballos is not particularly popular in Attica. It is not found in the excavations of the Agora and in the, so far, published finds of the excavations in the Kerameikos.

For a similar example, but with two handles, see *CVA* Heidelberg (4), 174, no. 66.2, pl. 183.5, with bibliography. For a parallel closer to the shape see Αλεξανδρή 1989, no. 59 (with two handles and spherical body with no base, in NM [Κακαρούγκα-Στασινοπούλου]). For a similar see *CVA* Würzburg (2), pl. 30.5. All parallels date in the early 5th c. B.C. Judging by its shape alone, this aryballos may be compared to the red-figure aryballos in the NM, a well-known work of art by Douris, dating *c.* 480 B.C.; also see Robertson 1992, 92, fig. 85. For aryballoi in general see Hommel 1978, 3-50; Beazley 1927/28, 193ff.; Richter - Milne 1937, 16. For black-glazed aryballoi see also *Agora* XII, 152, n. 10 and Simon 1975, 161 [Hölscher].

E.B.-V.

355 BLACK-GLAZED PYXIS
480-470 B.C.

INV. NO. A 15250.
H. 0.059, M.D. 0.12, B.D. 0.079 M.

Intact. Few chips on the mouth and its inside. Light brown clay. Lid missing. Hemispherical body. The rim has a groove for the fitting of the lid. Wide ring base. Rim and base reserved. On the bottom of the base a conical projection with black dot.

COMMENTARY - BIBLIOGRAPHY: Unpublished.
The term pyxis referred to a wooden box with lid used mainly by women as a jewellery case or a cosmetics box. The name came from the material of which they were made, boxwood, in Greek *pyxos* (modern Greek *pyxari* or *tsimisiri*). No. 355 typologically belongs among the pyxides no. 1267 and 1272 from the Athenian Agora, which date at 525-500 B.C. and the 2nd quarter of the 5th c. B.C., respectively. See *Agora* XII, 172, pl. 42. Also *Kerameikos* IX, 126, no. 154.5, pl. 83 (470/60 B.C.) and 140, no. 222.1, pl. 83 (2nd quarter of 5th c. B.C.). For a similar pyxis from the N.P. Goulandris Collection see Μαραγκού 1985, 110, no. 154 (460 B.C.). For the type of this pyxis see *Kerameikos* IX, 54 and *Agora* XII, 172-173.

E.B.-V.

353, 354, 355

356 BLACK-GLAZED PHIALE MESOMPHALOS
500-450 B.C.

INV. NO. A 15243.
H. 0.033, M.D. 0.14 M.

Intact. Small part of the rim restored. A roughly made base, concave on the resting surface creating a low rounded boss at the centre of the bottom. Shallow bowl. Flat rim, slightly sloping outwards with suspension hole. The boss is reserved and outlined in violet.

COMMENTARY - BIBLIOGRAPHY: Unpublished.
The phiale is considered a libation vessel, but was also used as a drinking vessel. Clay phialae imitate metal work, mainly bronze or silver, and rarely gold. It was imported in Greece from the East during the Geometric period and appeared as a clay vessel in the mid 7th c. B.C., becoming popular ever since in the Attic pottery, see Kurtz 1975 117, n. 6. The phiale is well known from farewell scenes on Attic pottery. It may well have symbolised safe return. For parallels see *Agora* XII, pl. 23, 552 and p. 105ff. (with relevant bibliography). For the shape see Luschey 1932.

I.T.-D.

357 TERRACOTTA FIGURINE OF HORSE AND RIDER
500-450 B.C.

INV. NO. E 1021.
H. 0.088, MAX.L. 0.085 M.

Complete. Slip flaking on the surface. Soft, brown clay with mica. Traces of a white slip all over the surface of the group. The clothing of the horseman is rendered in red. The horse gear is indicated with black and red bands around its body and neck.

The group, handmade, expresses concisely but with clarity in the impetuosity of the scene, the idea of free gallop. The horseman, with a pointed beard and his head held up and back, holds tightly onto the horse's neck with his two broad, short arms. The short-bodied horse has his head up, tail in the air and legs straight. The mane is rendered plastically.

COMMENTARY - BIBLIOGRAPHY: Unpublished.
This type, especially widespread in Boeotia in the 6th c. B.C. decorated with painted bands, continues without many changes in Attica, especially in the Kerameikos, in the early 5th c. B.C. with a series of groups similar to no. 357 (see also nos. 325-326). The type is completed with a new version in which the face of the horseman is made in a mould (see no. 341). For this type see Winter 1903, I, 7 and 25 and *Kerameikos* XV, 164, n. 295-297, with earlier bibliography. For typolog-

ical parallels see *Kerameikos* XV, 170, nos. 545-546, pl. 96-97 (1st half of 5th c. B.C.; with small differences in the rendering of the horse's head).

Th.K.

358 BLACK-GLAZED SKYPHOS (TYPE B)
480-450 B.C.

INV. NO. A 15325.
H. 0.058, B.D. 0.038, M.D. 0.072 M.

Intact. Slight chips on the mouth and flakes on the body on the outside and the inside, as well as in the base. Ring base, one vertical strap handle and one loop handle.

The entire vase is covered in black glaze, apart from the resting surface underneath the base which is reserved. The latter is decorated with a black band, small circle in the middle, the centre of which is defined with a black dot.

COMMENTARY - BIBLIOGRAPHY: Unpublished.

The skyphos was the most common drinking vessel in Attic pottery and became especially popular in the 6th-4th c. B.C. This example belongs to type B, see *Agora* XII, 86. For similar specimens see *Kerameikos* IX, pl. 41, 7; *Agora* XII, pl. 17, 362; Boulter 1953, pl. 73, 2; *CVA* Vienne, Kunsthistorisches Museum (Bd 1), pl. 44.

I.T.-D.

358

359 TERRACOTTA FIGURINE OF A RECLINING MAN
c. 450 B.C.

INV. NO. E 1033.
H. 0.069, L. OF BASE 0.072 M.

Restored from many fragments and with flaking surface; small pieces are missing. Brown-grey clay with obvious traces of fire on the surface; the core is rosy. Traces of white slip and red paint all over the surface.

The bearded man, reclining on a low bed-like base to the left, is depicted in a concise way. He is wearing an himation which leaves his chest uncovered. His left arm is supported by his elbow on a pillow and is covered by the himation, while the right arm rests on the knee of his bent right leg. His hair is parted in the middle. The facial features are difficult to make out. The figure comes from a used mould. Under the base, there is an air hole. Boeotian.

COMMENTARY - BIBLIOGRAPHY: Unpublished.
The type, originating from Rhodian prototypes, is found in many regions (Samos, Thrace, Boeotia, Sicily, South Italy) in shrines and tombs, mainly from the 6th to the middle of the 5th c. B.C. The figure is often depicted with drinking vessels and represents a symposiast at a private or sacred meal. Many such figures come from the shrine of the Kaveiroi at Thebes. For the reclining figure type in Archaic plastic art see Fehr 1971, nos. 496-525 (figurines). On the Boeotian type and its meaning see Winter 1903, I, 193,2; Schmaltz 1974, 90-94; Paul 1959, 66, no. 30, pl. 13; Pfisterer-Haas 1996, 12, no. 5. For the East Greek type see Simon 1989, 158-159, no. 252, pl. 99 (Froning) with extensive bibliography. For a typological parallel see *Olynthus* XIV, 222, no. 238, pl. 95; Schmaltz 1974, 92, no. 237, pl. 19; Pfisterer-Haas 1996, 12, no. 5.

Th.K.

359

360

360 TERRACOTTA FIGURINE OF A RECLINING WOMAN
c. 450 B.C.

INV. NO. 1028.
H. 0.105, L. 0.122 M.

A few parts missing and restored. Mended from many fragments especially on main side. Chipped and flaking. Rosy clay. White slip on the main side and traces of red paint on the figure – originally it would have been completely painted red. The main side is made in a mould, the back handmade.

The frontal figure is depicted naked (?) reclining on a rectangular, bed-like base. Her left arm is supported by her elbow on a pillow while her right hand is resting on the knee of her bent right leg. The hair is wrapped in a sakos except the locks on the forehead and the temples, which are parted in the middle in two solid masses. The head is small and the facial features hardly discernible. The figure is usually interpreted as that of a young hetaira.

COMMENTARY - BIBLIOGRAPHY: Unpublished.
See *Kerameikos* XV, 36, no. 117, pl. 24. 1,2 (with bibliography); Σίνδος 1985, 35, no. 41 (with bibliography); Winter 1903, I, 191,4; *Corinth* XV₂, 104, n. 3. For the interpretation see Rohde 1968, 17, 40f, no. 13 (goddess, not hetaira); Hoffmann 1961, 10, no. 31 (escort to the dead for the life beyond).

Th.K.

361 TERRACOTTA FIGURINE OF AN ENTHRONED WOMAN

c. 450 B.C.

INV. NO. E 1025.
H. 0.13 M.

Complete. Mended at the neck and the footstool. Chipped and flaking. Brown clay. Traces of white slip all over the surface, red paint on the clothing; red bands on the edges of the sides of the throne, and black on the himation which covers the head. Strong traces of burning.

The figure is depicted seated on a throne, in a strict en face posture, with the hands attached to the hips and the feet resting on the low footstool. She is wearing a long chiton with no folds and an himation which covers the head, falls symmetrically on the shoulders and is held in her hands on the knees. The feet are visible under the hem of the chiton. The uniform locks of hair on the forehead, parted in the middle, are covered with a low garland. The facial features are depicted plastically, the eyeballs, the eyebrow arches, the thin lips. It comes from a much used mould. Small air hole underneath.

COMMENTARY - BIBLIOGRAPHY: Unpublished.
The type, common in Rhodes, Attica, Boeotia, Olynthos, is produced from an Ionic-Rhodian prototype. In Attica, it is often produced in local workshops; it may have been originally created in a Rhodian mould. See *Kerameikos* XV, 32 and n. 61, 63 (with bibliography) and 33-34, nos. 103 and 105, pl. 22.1,2, respectively. For the interpretation of the figure and the meaning of its presence in tombs see *Kerameikos* XV, 25 and Bol - Kotera 1986, 68, no. 37. For typological parallels see Κόκκου-Βυριδή 1999, 241, nos. 213-214, pl. 50 (2nd quarter of 5th c. B.C.; perhaps from the same mould).

Th.K.

362 TERRACOTTA FIGURINE OF ENTHRONED
FEMALE FIGURE
c. 450 B.C.

INV. NO. E 1027.
H. 0.155 M.

Small part of the front left support of the throne is missing. The head and the lower part of the figure are mended. Chipped and flaking. Brown clay, reddish-brown in places. White slip all over. Traces of black paint on the himation.

Young slender woman, en face, is seated on a wide throne with a tall back, which widens towards the top. She is wearing a long chiton and himation, which covers her left arm, the lower torso and the hips, and has her feet on a low footstool. The right arm is brought bent to the breast holding an object not clearly discernible (flower or bird). The hair is wrapped in a sakos, which splits the head into three zones leaving a small part of the hair on the top of the head uncovered. The facial features, the eyeballs, the tight lips, the long nose are plastically rendered.

COMMENTARY - BIBLIOGRAPHY: Unpublished.
For the enthroned female figure type see Winter 1903, I, 72, 9; Higgins 1967, 74, fig. 24 and pl. 30c; Poulsen 1937, 56-58, fig. 34-35; Mollard-Besques 1954, I, 120, C233, pl. 86; Simon 1989, 169, no. 171, pl. 104 (Froning). For the sakos see *Kerameikos* XV, 17, no. 40, pl. 11.3.

Th.K.

363 TERRACOTTA FIGURINE OF A STANDING WOMAN
c. 450 B.C.

INV. NO. E 1026.
H. 0.122 M.

Intact, chipped and flaking. Brown clay. Traces of white slip all over, black paint on the hair, red and black on the chiton and himation. Strong traces of burning on the surface. The front is made in a mould. The inside is hollow and there is an air hole in the base.

The small figure is standing, en face, on a rectangular base and is bringing her left leg slightly forward. The dress is rendered concisely. She is wearing a long chiton belted at the waist (a double band is discernible, painted in purple, the ends of which are folded and hang down) and a long himation which she holds with her left hand; on her head she wears a bonnet. Her right hand, bent on her breast, is holding a flower (?) which would have been painted. The locks of hair on the forehead, parted in the middle, are covered by a low garland. The facial features are indicated plastically.

COMMENTARY - BIBLIOGRAPHY: Unpublished.
The type is a creation of the Attic workshop with variations in Rhodes and Boeotia. See *Kerameikos* XV, 15, no. 36, pl. 9.1-3, with earlier bibliography (Rhodian or Attic; 470-460 B.C.); Leyenaar-Plaisier 1979, 31, no. 48, pl. 9 (Boeotian). For typological parallels see *Kerameikos* XV, 15, no. 36, pl. 9.1-3 (perhaps from the same mould).

Th.K.

364 HEAD AND PART OF THE TORSO OF A TERRACOTTA FEMALE FIGURINE
c. 450 B.C.

INV. NO. E 1035.
MAX.H. 0.094 M.

The front part of the body is broken. Strong traces of burning. Traces of white slip. The face in strict frontal view. The hair, parted in the middle, frames the narrow forehead while at the back it is wrapped in a sakos. The facial features are plastically rendered.

COMMENTARY - BIBLIOGRAPHY: Unpublished.
It probably belongs to a figurine of a standing woman; see *BMC* I, 172, no. 671, pl. 88. For the head see *BMC* I, 179, no. 672, pl. 89.

Th.K.

363

364

365 TERRACOTTA BUST OF A WOMAN
c. 450 B.C.

INV. NO. E 1032.
H. 0.148 M.

Mended from many fragments. Small chips, mainly on the lower right part of the main side. Flaking surface. Brown clay; white slip all over, traces of red and light blue paint in places are all that is left of the decoration. Mould-made, hollow inside, it has an elliptical perforation in the lower part.

The type presents the body from the waist up. The figure is wearing a Doric peplos, open on the right side, with an over-fold, below which the breasts are depicted. The arms are stuck onto the torso. The edge of the peplos round the neck is highlighted with light blue fugitive paint. The hair is wrapped in a sakos, pointed at the back, apart from two rows of wavy locks parted in the middle, which crown the narrow forehead and temples. Traces of red paint are discernible on the hair, the sakos and the lips.

COMMENTARY - BIBLIOGRAPHY: Unpublished. On the peplos-wearing bust type see Winter 1903, 63, 5; Poulsen 1937, 50-52, fig. 28-29; *BMC* I, 181-183, nos. 678, 679, 682, pl. 89; Mollard-Besques 1954, I, 83, nos. C10, C11, pl. 56; Simon 1989, 169, no. 672 (Froning); *Kerameikos* XV, 13-14, 18-20, nos. 45-49, pl. 12-13 (with an exhaustive discussion on the type and earlier bibliography); see Μπόνιας 1998, 201, no. 491, pl. 51 (with bibliography). For the head see Schürmann 1989, 36-37, no. 71, pl. 15; Leyenaar-Plaisier 1979, 15-16, no. 15, pl. 3 (for the significance). Earlier on, the peplos-wearing busts had been interpreted as dolls (Poulsen), others believe they represent Demeter or Persephone (Mollard-Besques, Leyenaar-Plaisier) or Nymphs or Graces (Froning). They are most probably associated with beliefs on worship or magic of the dead, since they are usually found in tombs of children and women, often with clay images of hands (*Kerameikos* VII, 128 and *Kerameikos* XV, 14) as in the offering ditch at the KERAMEIKOS Station (see no. 367). They all come from the same Attic workshop.

Th.K.

365

366 HEAD OF A TERRACOTTA FEMALE FIGURE
c. 450 B.C.

INV. NO. E 1034.
MAX.H. 0.072 M.

The head, the neck and part of the back are preserved. The nose is broken. Brown clay. White slip all over but flaking in places.
The face is oval and en face. The hair is wrapped in a sakos, except for a row of wavy locks, parted in the middle, which crown the forehead and the temples. The eyeballs, the arched eyebrows, the eyelids and the chin are plastically rendered.

COMMENTARY - BIBLIOGRAPHY: Unpublished.
For typological parallels see *Kerameikos* XV, 19, no. 48, pl. 13.3 and no. 45, pl. 12.2, 3 (with the sakos shaped differently at the back).

Th.K.

366

367 TERRACOTTA MODELS OF A RIGHT AND A LEFT HAND
c. 450 B.C.

INV. NOS. E 1029 AND E 1030.
L. 0.11 M.

Complete. The left is mended from two fragments; flaking surface. Rosy clay, white slip.
The palm is shown open and stretched in line with the forearm, with the fingers close together except the thumb. The forearm is hollow, the palm solid.

COMMENTARY - BIBLIOGRAPHY: Unpublished.
On this type see *Kerameikos* XV, 20-21, nos. 52-54 and 55, pl. 13.6 and 12.4; *BMC* I, 183 nos. 687-690, pl. 90 and lately Μπόνιας 1998, 204, no. 505, pl. 58 (with earlier bibliography). Their presence in tombs is related to the magic associated with the dead; see Kübler 1935, 273, fig. 6. The stretched fingers are interpreted as a gesture of protection or of apotropaic character; see Karo 1943, pl. 24. On the sacred or even magical symbolism of these objects see *Délos* XXIII, 98-101, nos. 230-235, pl. 25.

Th.K.

368 SHIN AND FOOT OF A DOLL
c. 450 B.C.

INV. NO. E 1036.
H. 0.047, L. OF LEG 0.016 M.

Complete. Brown clay, traces of white slip. Handmade.
The upper part is flattened and has a horizontal perforation for suspending the shin from the thighs. The toes are not indicated.

COMMENTARY - BIBLIOGRAPHY: Unpublished.
For the type see *Kerameikos* XV, 51, n. 94, with earlier bibliography. Dolls, a kind of a toy in the hands of small children, especially girls, were offered to a female deity after childhood or, in the case of premature death, they were placed as grave gifts in the tombs of small children; see Buschor 1939, 24-25. From the earlier bibliography, the article of Dörig 1958, 41-52 remains very important as well as that of McElderkin 1930, 450-470. For the interpretation see Bauchhens 1973, 1-13. For typological parallels see *Kerameikos* XV, 54, no. 152, pl. 30.8 (beginning of 4th c. B.C.); *BMC* I, 260, no. 959, pl.135 or 265, no. 973, pl. 137 (4th c. B.C.); *Corinth* XV₂,

151, no. XX:27, 28, 29, pl. 31; *Olynthus* XIV, 234, no. 298, pl. 99 (end of 5th - beginning of 4th c. B.C.).

Th.K.

369 TERRACOTTA FIGURINE OF A PIG
c. 450 B.C.

INV. NO. E 1031.
H. 0.046, L. 0.084 M.

Complete with small chips and flaking. Brownish red-grey clay as a result of burning. White slip.
The ears, back and tail are plastically rendered. Underneath, there is an air hole.

COMMENTARY - BIBLIOGRAPHY: Unpublished.
Cf. no. 329 (with bibliography) and no. 343.

Th.K.

370 SMALL TERRACOTTA MODEL OF A STOOL
5th c. B.C.

INV. NO. E 1037.
H. 0.02, L. 0.031, W. 0.026 M.

Complete.
The small stool, Π-shaped, is supported on two solid sides with wavy profiles.

COMMENTARY - BIBLIOGRAPHY: Unpublished.
For the name and usage see Richter 1966, 47 (βάθρον, θράνον, θρανίδιον, ἴκρια). For the small model of a stool from the Potters' Quarter at Corinth see Richter 1966, fig. 273.

Th.K.

371

371 RED-FIGURE LEKYTHOS (MAIN TYPE)
450-440 B.C.

INV. NO. A 15429.
H. 0.275, B.D. 0.059, M.D. 0.056,
D. AT SHOULDER LEVEL 0. 095 M.

Complete. Mended from many pieces and restored. Large chips and flakes, mainly on the scene. Traces of red ochre (miltos) on the shoulder, handle, and the external, vertical surface of the foot.

On the left, a woman is depicted playing the double-flute, seated on a chair. Her hair is pulled up, over the neck, in a bun (krovylos). She is wearing a long chiton and an himation around her waist, hanging from her right thigh. On the right, a female dancer, listening to the flute's music, is performing a twirl (strovilos). She is wearing a short chiton that swirls with the movement of her body. In her extended hands she holds rattles (krotala).

Relief line is used to render the outlines and the main anatomical details of the figures and folds in their drapery. Dilute glaze is used to enhance the details of the chair. The bands, holding both figures' hair, are rendered with added, thin white colour. Faded traces of a rough sketch can be detected on the flute player's thighs. The scene is framed by a band of interrupted meander to the right, framed by cross squares. The ground line is defined by means of a band of simple meander facing right. The shoulder, which is reserved, is decorated with black-figure palmettes, a characteristic of the Workshop of the Achilles P., along with Ionic moulding on the junction of the neck with the shoulder.

COMMENTARY - BIBLIOGRAPHY: Unpublished.

This scene is almost a replica of another on a Nolan-type amphora by the Sabouroff P. in Syracuse, no. 21151, see Καββαδίας 2000, cat. no. 113. For the models (paradeigmata) used by painters see Τιβέριος 1981, 134-150. The decoration of the shoulder is characteristic of the Workshop of the Achilles P. The black-figure palmette belongs to type IIB in Kurtz 1975, 43-44 and pl. 19-20. See also Oakley 1997, 73-78 (for the shape and the decoration of the Achillean lekythoi).

For the Sabouroff P. see commentary on no. 236. For the term στρόβιλος (twirl) (and σοβάς or κυκλοσοβεῖν) see Roos 1951. For similar scenes see Beck 1975, 58-60, fig. 374-395, pl. 76-78 and Pomeroy 1985, 47-138. Cf. the red-figure lekythoi by the Bowdoin P. in Basel, Antikenmuseum und Sammlung Ludwig, no. 1944.2699 (ARV² 682,112 and Addenda², 279) and in Würzburg, the Kisselef Collection, no. K 1860, see Simon 1989, no. 151. Brommer 1989, 487 believes that this dance is identified with "γέρανος". For the dancers' social status see Oakley 1990, 37, 257. For the flute see Μιχαηλίδης 1982, 61-70 and for the rattles (κρόταλα or κρέμβαλα), which produced a sound (ρόμβος) that accompanied the flute, see Μιχαηλίδης 1982, 175-176. See also recently, Landels 1999, 24-26 (for the flute) and 83 (for the rattles).
Sabouroff P.

G.K.

372   BLACK-FIGURE WHITE-GROUND LEKYTHOS
450-425 B.C.

INV. NO. A 15212.
H. 0.144, M.D. 0.027, B.D. 0.035 M.

Intact, slightly flaked. Brownish red clay. Discoid base, cylindrical body that becomes narrower toward the foot, vertical strap handle, calyx-shaped mouth.
Black glaze on the inside and outside of the rim, on the outside of the handle, the lower part of the body and the surface of the foot. Cream slip covers the main body, which is decorated by a horizontal stalk of opposed pairs of alternate ivy leaves and its fruit. It is outlined above by a chequerboard pattern and below by a black line. Below the main scene on the black glaze, there are three, reserved, parallel lines. At the beginning of the neck, thin black lines and a row of black rays on the shoulder.

COMMENTARY - BIBLIOGRAPHY: Unpublished.
The lekythos is one of the better known vases in burials, as an offering to the deceased. It appears in the beginning of the 6th c. B.C., and is especially popular in the 5th c. B.C. No. 372 belongs to the Workshop of the P. of the Megaira (Beldam Workshop); see Kurtz, pl. 71d (similar). See also Μυλωνάς 1975, Γ, pl. 204α, B17-56; *Corinth* XIII, pl. 55,7; Schlörb-Vierneisel 1966, pl. 26,55,4.

I.T.-D.

373   BLACK-GLAZED LEKYTHOS (SECONDARY TYPE)
450-425 B.C.

INV. NO. A 15213.
H. 0.119, B.D. 0.032, M.D. 0.028 M.

Intact. Small chips on the handle and flakes on the rim. Brown clay. Discoid base, globular body, vertical strap handle, echinus mouth. Shiny black glaze covers the vase, the mouth, the outer surface of the handle and the upper part of the foot.
On the base of the reserved neck, small lines and a schematised ray-pattern on the shoulder. On the rim's surface a reserved band. The resting surface of the vase is also reserved, on the centre of which there is a small cavity.

COMMENTARY - BIBLIOGRAPHY: Unpublished.
An extremely popular Attic vase of the 5th c. B.C.; similar specimens have repeatedly been found in Athenian cemeteries. It belongs to the group of black-glazed (black-bodied) lekythoi that were produced by the same workshops as the black-figure, red-figure and white-ground lekythoi. See Kurtz 1975, 115. For typological parallels see *Agora* XII, 153, pl. 38; *CVA* Stuttgart, pl. 25,8 (KAS 107); Πωλογιώργη 1993-94, 258-260, pl. 39α-γ (with earlier bibliography).

I.T.-D.

372

373

374

374 CORINTHIAN KOTYLISKE
450-425 B.C.

INV. NO. A 15214.
H. 0.05, M.D. 0.064, B.D. 0.033 M.

Complete. Foot mended and many flakes on the handles, the interior and exterior of the vase. Pale brown clay. Conical ring base, horizontal loop handles.
Red glaze on the interior and exterior of the vase and on the resting surface of the foot, due to uneven firing. Red band outlines the part of the body beneath the handles. The lower part of the body and the upper part of the foot are reserved.

COMMENTARY - BIBLIOGRAPHY: Unpublished.
The kotyle, a drinking vessel, is a shape that appeared first in Corinth, and derived from the Corinthian skyphos. It was soon adopted by Athenian potters who used it until the mid 5th c. B.C., when it started to disappear. For parallels see *Kerameikos* IX, pl. 54,168 and

Corinth XIII, pl. 52, no. 344-3. For the miniature Corinthian vases see *Perachora* II, 290ff.

I.T.-D.

375 BLACK-GLAZED LEKANIS WITH LID
450-425 B.C.

INV. NO. A 15211.
H. 0.121, M.D. 0.124, B.D. 0.068 M.

Intact. Small chips on the lid's handle and the rim. Red-brown clay. Ring base, hemispherical body, horizontal strap handles, with lugs on the side. The handle of the lid is cylindrical, ending in a disc with a cavity in the centre. Shiny black glaze covers the vase. The vertical side of the handle's disc is reserved, along with two concentric bands on the upper surface and around the disc's cavity. The lid's flange, the lip, the underside of the handles along with the resting surface

of the foot are also reserved; the latter is decorated with two concentric, reserved circles and a black circle in the centre.

COMMENTARY - BIBLIOGRAPHY: Unpublished.
The lekanis is a common type in Attic pottery, occurring since the 6th c. B.C. It is mainly considered as a cosmetics vase; see *Agora* XII, 165-167. For similar examples see Schneider-Hermann 1975, 43-44, no. 110; Richter - Milne 1937, fig. 150; *CVA* Karlsrhue, pl. 35,14; *CVA* Oxford 1, Great Britain 3, pl. XLVIII, 17.

I.T.-D.

375

376 TREFOIL-MOUTHED BLACK-GLAZED OENOCHOE WITH IMPRESSED DECORATION
440-430 B.C.

INV. NO. A 15451.
H. 0.073, B.D. 0.046 M.

The handle and large part of the mouth missing. The trefoil mouth is mended. Chips on the foot and flakes.

The main body of the vase is decorated with impressed, vertical grooves which are alternately joined in the lower part with arches. A panel in the centre of side A, however, is decorated in the middle with a horizontal band of an impressed tongue-pattern framed up and down by three pairs of palmettes. The upper part and the ground of the panel are defined by horizontal bands of impressed tongue-pattern, on which upright and hanging palmettes are based. The area beneath the handle is decorated with four, suc-

cessive rows of impressed tongue-pattern. The handle's base is framed by two impressed upright palmettes. The junction between the neck and the main body of the vase is enhanced by a thin band of impressed semicircles.

COMMENTARY - BIBLIOGRAPHY: Unpublished.
For the combination of impressed tongue-pattern and palmettes see *Agora* XII, 74, pl. 47, no. 204.

G.K.

377 WHITE-GROUND LEKYTHOS (SECONDARY TYPE - ATL)
440-430 B.C.

INV. NO. A 15450.
H. 0.143, B.D. 0.041, M.D. 0.033,
D. AT SHOULDER LEVEL 0.049 M.

Intact. Small chips mainly on the mouth and flakes on the walls of the vase.

At the centre of the scene, a funerary monument on a broad base with two red bands. On the left side of the tomb, a young man in right profile. He wears an himation and his right hand is placed on the waist while he is drawing his slightly bent leg to the back.

The scene is crowned by a band of Z-shaped ornaments. The outline of the tomb and the young man is rendered with shiny glaze. The two red bands, the hem and the details of the himation are rendered in a matt red paint, along with the Z-shaped ornament that crowns the scene. The shoulder, reserved, is decorated by a black-glaze ray pattern, while the junction of the neck is enhanced by a schematised tongue-pattern.

COMMENTARY - BIBLIOGRAPHY: Unpublished.
For the shape of the lekythos and the Workshop of the Tymbos P. see commentary on no. 231. Cf. a lekythos from the Kerameikos (Kerameikos Museum, no. 1108), see Felten 1976, 81, cat. no. 9, pl. 25. For the type of the tumulus see Nakayama 1982, 37-40 and 189 (type GH-II-13). For archaeological remains of tumuli see Σκιλάρντι 1975, 86-95; lately Mersch 1996, 27-35 and Kistler 1998. Bands, usually red, were the commonest ornament of tomb stelai and tumuli, see Pfanner 1977.

They were often painted on the stele itself, as in Vergina, see Σαατσόγλου-Παλιαδέλη 1984, 191ff. and *eadem* 1988.
Workshop of the Tymbos P.

G.K.

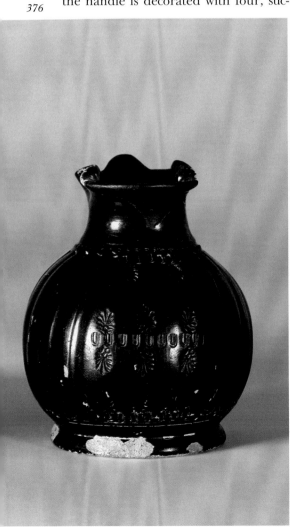

376

377

378   BLACK-GLAZED CYLINDRICAL PYXIS WITH LID
450-425 B.C.

INV. NO. A 15257.
H. (INCL. LID) 0.04, M.D. 0.05, B.D. 0.063, MAX.D. 0.055 M.

Intact with flakes. Grey clay, due to bad firing. The lid is cylindrical, convex on the upper part, with tall, slightly convex side wall. The body of the vase is shallow with a discoid base with deep groove close to the edge. On the base centre, a small lug. The lid has a horizontal disc on the upper part, decorated with two, concentric reserved circles with central dot. The vertical side wall of the lid is outlined by a black band, that is surrounded up and down by reserved bands.

COMMENTARY - BIBLIOGRAPHY: Unpublished.

No. 378 is a powder pyxis. Generally for the type see *Agora* XII, 173 (with bibliography) and 327, no. 1294, pl. 43 (similar example). For general information on pyxides see commentary on no. 355.

E.B.-V.

379   BLACK-GLAZED SALT-CELLAR
450-425 B.C.

INV. NO. A 15256.
H. 0.028, M.D. 0.054, B.D. 0.039 M.

Intact with chips and flakes. Red-brown clay. The echinus body has an in-curving rim. The body's contour is slightly conical, inwardly convex on the upper part. Flat base, that forms a ring around the resting surface.

COMMENTARY - BIBLIOGRAPHY: Unpublished.

Generally for this type see *Agora* XII, 136 and 300, no. 192, pl. 34 (closer to the type and dimensions). For a similar example see *Kerameikos* IX, 134, no. 198.2, pl. 82 and 57.3 (2nd quarter of 5th c. B.C.).

E.B.-V.

380 TERRACOTTA FIGURINE OF A STANDING WOMAN
450-425 B.C.

INV. NO. E 1024.
H. (INCL. BASE) 0.211, H. (EXCL. BASE) 0.19, L. OF BASE 0.055, W. 0.045 M.

Complete. Joined at the neck and the level of the thighs. Part of the left hand is missing. Chipped, flaking and with strong traces of burning. Clay grey from the fire. White slip covers the whole front part.

The figure is standing on the left leg, en face, on a tall rectangular base. The relaxed right leg is bent forward. She is wearing a Doric peplos open on the right side with an over-fold and both arms hang down against the body. The wavy hair, parted in the middle, crowns the low forehead and temples and is adorned with a low garland, while long locks in relief fall on the shoulders. The facial features are plastically indicated, the arched eyebrows and the half open mouth with a heart-shaped upper lip. Hollow inside. Large air hole in the base.

COMMENTARY - BIBLIOGRAPHY: Unpublished.
This type was created in Attica in 460-450 B.C.; many examples come from the Acropolis of Athens and other areas, while local imitations are known from Boeotia, Rhodes and elsewhere. The Attic examples are distinguished by the excellent work, the exact rendering of the clothing, the perfection of the facial features. For this type, the study of Poulsen 1937, 51ff. remains basic; see also Winter 1903, I, 63, 1a-b and Higgins 1967, 73, pl. 30. For typological parallels see Poulsen 1937, 55, fig. 33. For the head see *Kerameikos* XV, 19, no. 47 (Halbfigur), pl. 13.4,5; Leyenaar-Plaisier 1979, 15, no. 14, pl. 3; Higgins 1967, 74, 30A. For Boeotian examples see Schmidt 1994, 51, no. 50, pl. 13a; Schilardi 1977, 530, no. 463, pl. 58-59; *BMC* I, 180, no. 673, pl. 88.

Th.K.

381 TERRACOTTA FIGURINE OF A STANDING WOMAN
450-425 B.C.

INV. NO. E 1023.
H. 0.097 M.

Intact except a small chip off base. Burnt. Concave underside of base. Grey clay because of intense burning.

A young woman, perhaps a young girl, with himation is standing en face on a low four-sided base with the left leg slightly bent forward. Both arms are bent under the himation; the right is on the breast, while the left is at the waist. Wavy locks of hair frame the face. The facial features are difficult to make out. Careless workmanship.

COMMENTARY - BIBLIOGRAPHY: Unpublished.
For a similar figurine see *Kerameikos* XV, 21, no. 58, pl. 14.3 (perhaps from the same mould but a later generation of figurines).

Th.K.

381

382 WHITE-GROUND LEKYTHOS (MAIN TYPE)
c. 440-430 B.C.

INV. NO. A 15479.
H. 0.278, B.D. 0.057 (0.05 THE RESTING RING),
D. AT SHOULDER LEVEL 0.079 M.

Mended from many pieces. Small parts of the mouth and body missing. Traces of fire mainly on the shoulder and on the male figure.

At the centre of the scene is a tall funerary stele with a pediment, set on two-stepped base. On the left, a young man is standing in right profile, extending his slightly bent arm. He is wrapped, apart from his right shoulder, in a red himation, the colour of which has been affected by the fire. On the right, a kneeling mourner in left profile, apart from her head which is shown in three-quarter view. She holds her left hand on her head, while stretching her right hand down to the stele. Her garment has almost disappeared. The outlines are rendered with gilded glaze. The meander band crown-

ing the scene, as well as the vegetal pattern on the shoulder (palmette) have disappeared.

COMMENTARY - BIBLIOGRAPHY: Unpublished.
For the P. of Munich 2335 and the kneeling mourner see commentary on no. 232 and for the "visitation to the tomb" see lekythos no. 237. The dead youth is approaching the stele, the meeting point with the world of the living, and with his right hand is making a conversational or a greeting gesture to the mourner. For this gesture see Olmos 1980, 97. According to the established savoir-vivre, the himation should not cover the youth's right shoulder. For the way in which the himation was worn see Ρωμαίος 1955, 10. This stele belongs to the type B-II, as specified in Nakayama 1982, 74-75, pl. 11. A closer stylistic parallel is the white-ground lekythos by the P. of Munich 2335 in the NM, no. 1947 (*ARV*² 1168, 133; *Addenda*² 338).
P. of Munich 2335.

G.K.

this pelike see an example in Copenhagen, originally from Athens; see *CVA* Copenhagen (1/6) III, pl. 176, 1-2. Cf. also the black-glazed pelike with lid, no. 17602 in the NM. For the development of the type, and bibliography, see *Agora* XII, 49-51. For pelikai in general see Becker 1977.

E.B.-V.

384 WHITE-GROUND LEKYTHOS
430-426 B.C.

INV. NO. A 15302.
PRES.H. 0.202, MAX.D. 0.07, B.D. 0.05 M.

The upper part of the neck, the mouth and the handle missing. Chips, flakes in parts. Faded colours. Red-brown clay. On the shoulder a floral pattern of palmettes, volutes and tendrils. On the upper part of the body, a band of meander running right, interrupted in the middle by an X in matt outline. In the middle of the scene, a rectangular grave stele, on a two-stepped base with a three-part finial. On the left, a young woman in profile, wrapped in himation, is walking towards the stele, with her head low. Another woman in three-quarter view, with her head in right profile, wearing a peplos with traces of yellowish glaze, her hair in a bun (krovylos) and extending her right arm behind the stele, which conceals it. Traces of red ribbons on the stele as well as red colour on the first and the third part of its finial.

COMMENTARY - BIBLIOGRAPHY: Unpublished.

This lekythos depicts a well-known subject in the white-ground lekythoi of the 2nd half of the 5th c. B.C., the "visitation to the tomb". This grave stele belongs to the sub-category AV2 of Nakayama 1982. The scene, although rendered rather hastily, has managed to project successfully the sentiments of the depicted figures and especially the sadness of the figure on the left. The "cut off" hand of the figure on the right is a well-known pattern employed by the Reed P. (e.g. *CVA* Tübingen (5) no. 7313, pl. 31); the details of the face, the translucence and the folds of the garment on the right figure all attribute this lekythos to the prolific Reed P., who worked in the last quarter of the 5th c. B.C. The figures, however, show the childishness of the figures of the Bird P. So, in this lekythos one can see stylistic

383 BLACK-GLAZED PELIKE WITH LID
430-426 B.C.

INV. NO. A 15282.
H. (EXCL. LID) 0.15, H. (INCL. LID) 0.18, B.D. 0.082, M.D. 0.081, D. OF LID 0.096 M.

Mended. Two handles and small part of the lid missing. Chips and flakes occasionally. Red-brown clay. The neck is tall, the vase has a continuous curve and a discoid base. The rim of the lid is rather tall, with convergent walls.

COMMENTARY - BIBLIOGRAPHY: Unpublished.
The pelike is generally considered to have been an oil vessel, although it was put to other uses as well, e.g. as a burial urn. In many ways, it appears to have been similar to the amphora. The shape of the pelike appeared in Attic pottery in the late 6th c. B.C. Usually, these vases were decorated in black- or red-figure technique, while they also appear in black glaze, though not as often. According to the typology proposed by the excavators of the Athenian Agora, this pelike belongs to the 3rd class (covered pelike). For a similar type see *Agora* XII, 50, no. 25, pl. 2. For shape and size close to

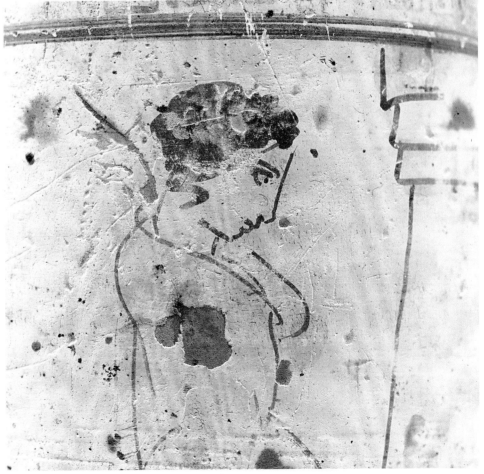

384 α

relation between the Reed and the Bird P., well known in other instances. For the figure on the right see *CVA* Copenhagen (5), III.1, pl. 173, 3a-b, while for the head of this same figure, see white-ground lekythos no. 19273 in NM (see Kardara 1960, 158, pl. 40-41). For the figure on the left cf. Παπασπυρίδη 1923, 122, fig. 6a; *CVA* Japan (2), pl. B.7, and *CVA* Berlin (8) pl. 17, 1-2. For grave stelai on white-ground lekythoi see Nakayama 1982. Generally for white-ground lekythoi see Kurtz 1975; Felten 1976, 77ff.; Τζάχου-Αλεξανδρή 1997b, 303-365; *eadem* 1998, with bibliography.

E.B.-V.

385 WHITE-GROUND LEKYTHOS
430-426 B.C.

INV. NO. A 15293.
PRES.H. 0.29, MAX.D. 0.054, D. AT SHOULDER LEVEL 0.084 M.

The foot is missing. Mended with restored parts on the neck, the shoulder and the body. Faded colours, surface worn. Red-brown clay.
On the shoulder, floral pattern of palmettes with alternating matt black and red leaves, enhanced with tendrils. On the upper part of the body, a band of meander running right of matt outline. At the centre of the scene, a long stele reaches to the beginning of the shoulder, and the meander band. The stele on a two-stepped base is decorated in its upper half with a large four-leaf pattern,

383

385

387

389

which has a pair of antithetic S-shaped volutes on its centre. On the left and right side of the stele, one can see parts of other grave monuments, supposedly in the background of the scene. On the left, a woman is walking towards the stele, extending her left arm, which is concealed from the monument. Her head is in profile, her torso in three-quarter view. She is wearing a peplos belted in the waist, and in her right hand she is probably carrying a torch with ribbons hanging. The garment's hems are emphasised with a red band. The young man on the right of the stele is leaning on his right leg, his head in profile, while his relaxed left leg is crossed behind him with the body shown frontally, his bent right arm placed on the tomb, holding two spears in his left hand. He is dressed as a traveller: chlamys, boots and petasos on his back.

COMMENTARY - BIBLIOGRAPHY: Unpublished.
For the figure of the young man see lekythoi 535 and 536 in Frankfurt (*CVA* Frankfurt am Main (4), 40, pl. 20. 1-21.7). For the female figure see the white-ground lekythoi nos. 14515 and 1848 in NM (Παπασπυρίδη 1923, 123, fig. 3a-b) as well as the woman on the lekythos no. 334 in Palermo (*CVA* Palermo, no. 334, pl. 8, 1-2) and in 361 in Tokyo (*CVA* Japan (2), pl. B). For the rare and quite peculiar four-leaf ornament of the stele cf. the lekythos no. 1897, 172a in Glasgow, a work that is obviously by the same painter (*CVA* Great Britain (18), 34, pl. 33.5,5,6,7). This pattern does not depict an existing finial, confirming those who believe that the imaginary rendering of the grave is often found in vases of this period. See Shapiro 1987, 655.
The above mentioned vases are works by the Reed P., to whom we also attribute this vase. The most acceptable date of the work of the Reed P. is mainly the period 420-410 B.C. This vase, however, is among others of the same workshop, a find from the mass burial. The dead of this burial were the victims of pestilence either in 430/29 B.C., when the disease first started, or in 427/6 B.C. when it broke out again (Thuc. II 47.3-54). Therefore, the vase, that has to be dated between 430-427/6 B.C., brings to this period the beginning of the Reed P.'s work. Generally, for the bibliography on the white-ground lekythoi, see no. 384.

E.B.-V.

386 WHITE-GROUND LEKYTHOS
430 B.C.

INV. NO. A 15295.
PRES.H. 0.18, MAX.D. 0.067, B.D. 0.057 M.

The neck and the handle missing. Chips and flakes in parts. Faded matt red outline. On the shoulder, faded matt palmettes. On the upper part of the body, a horizontal band of faded meander between lines of shiny outline. At the centre of the scene, a grave stele on a two-stepped base, which is crowned by acanthus leaves. On the left, a male figure is turning to the stele, leaning his left arm on a spear. The figure on the right, a female, with her hair in a bun, is standing with her right, bent leg on the stele step, holding a basket. On both figures, there are traces of reddish paint.

384

386

388

390

COMMENTARY - BIBLIOGRAPHY: Unpublished.
The subject of the depiction is the "visitation to the tomb" with two figures. The dead man appears to be the young man who is depicted as a departing traveller. The scene is calm, with the sadness being evident on the face of the dead. The acanthus in finials as well as the basket are often found in the iconography of the white-ground lekythoi, regardless of workshop. The condition of the lekythos today, due to the faded colours and the worn surface, makes a stylistic approach to the scene more difficult. The young man's figure has similarities with a figure in a white-ground lekythos in Berlin, which is attributed by I. Wehgartner to the P. of Munich 2335. See CVA Berlin (8), pl. 17, 1-2. It must be pointed out that there is a general similarity in the figures with the work of the Bird P. The stylistic relation between those two painters is well known. The figures on our lekythos are closer, in terms of details, to the Circle of the P. of Munich 2335. For the white-ground lekythoi see the general bibliography in no. 384. For the P. of Munich 2335 see Τιβέριος 1989. For the basket see Schelp 1975.

E.B.-V.

387   RED-FIGURE LEKYTHOS
c. 430 B.C.

INV. NO. A 15281.
PRES.H. 0.17, D. AT SHOULDER LEVEL 0.068, B.D. 0.05 M.

The neck with mouth and a small piece on side B of the vase are missing. Chips, flakes in parts. Brown clay. The body, almost cylindrical, is tapering to an S-contour on the discoid base.
On side A of the vase, a pair is depicted in a departure scene. On the left, the woman is wearing a peplos, her hair in a bun, and has a phiale in her right hand. On the right, the young man is wearing a petasos and chlamys buckled on his left shoulder which covers almost the entire body, leaving his right arm free, with which he is holding a spear. The scene is crowned by a band of meander running right, while the ground over which the figures are standing, is defined by a simple, reserved band. The shoulder is decorated with three black palmettes, enriched with volutes. The palmette in the centre is reversed.

COMMENTARY - BIBLIOGRAPHY: Unpublished.
This is a departure scene, a very popular subject in the 5th c. iconography. For a similar depiction of this subject in the 3rd quarter of the 5th c. B.C., when this vase is dated, see Lezzi-Hafter 1988, pl. 66a (tondo of a kylix by the Calliope P.). The offering from a woman in front of a man who seems to depart is made for the safe return of the traveller or the warrior at home, while there is the opinion that the offering in these scenes is made for the prosperity of the house; see Hollein 1988 151-157 and Killet 1994, 81-86. The female figure on the lekythos can be paralleled – as far as the rendering of the head (hair, face, neck) and her pose are concerned – with the female figure on the lekythos no. 12343 in Basel, which is attributed to the Klügmann P.; see CVA Basel (3), III.12343, pl. 30.3-4, 33.2. The red-figure lekythos from the Kerameikos could be attributed to the Workshop of the Klügmann P., and is probably a late work of the same painter. For the painter see lately Zoroglu 1999, 141-145.

E.B.-V.

388   RED-FIGURE SQUAT LEKYTHOS
430-426 B.C.

INV. NO. A 15265.
·H. 0.112, M.D. 0.032, MAX.D. 0.065, B.D. 0.05 M.

Complete. Mended with few chips. Red-brown clay. The mouth is calyx-shaped, the neck is short and there is a clay projection at the join with the shoulder. The body is rather elongated and cylindrical, with a wide, ring base. Strap handle. Female figure on the left, clad in a long chiton and himation on a reserved band. On her right, extended arm she is holding a piece of cloth. Hair gathered in a bun, leaving her earring to show.

COMMENTARY - BIBLIOGRAPHY: Unpublished.
This category of squat lekythoi, with scenes depicting a single woman, is rather usual in the 2nd half of the 5th c. B.C. and until the end of the century. These figures seem to relate to scenes depicting women's quarters (gynaikonites) and wedding preparations (epaulia). The shape belongs to the type VI A as in Rudolph 1971, 28, 90, pl. XII 4,5 and dates between 440-425 B.C. Furthermore, in terms of form and iconography, this lekythos belongs to the category SL as in Sabetai 1993, 212-213 which dates in 430-420 B.C. For similar types see lekythos 2509 in Zurich (CVA Zurich (1), III, 1 no. 2509, pl. 24, 11-12), by a different vase-painter. For a type of similar iconography see Lezzi-Hafter 1988, pl. 124, 197e and CVA Torino (3) III, 1, pl. 12,4. No. 388 is stylistically very close to the lekythos no. 167 in the Kisselef Collection in Würzburg, which is related to the group of the P. of the Bathing Women.

E.B.-V.

389   RED-FIGURE CHOUS
430-426 B.C.

INV. NO. A 15272.
H. 0.066, MAX.D. 0.064, B.D. 0.049 M.

Mended on the neck, handle missing. Few chips. Red-brown clay. The vase is small, trefoil-mouthed, with the middle lobe, a bit larger than the others. Globular body, broad ring base.
The picture panel is defined on the right and on the left by two vertical reserved bands, while over and under it there is a band of Ionic moulding. Two facing, naked boys, one leg bent, are playing, holding in their hands raised ribbons, with a ball tied to their end. The hair is in long locks, held up in the forehead by a white band with ivy leaves. Diagonally to the chest, under the armpit, one can see the "periamma", the magic amulet that brings luck to children, a well-known iconographic detail in scenes of children on choes. Between the children two Maltese dogs, taking part in the game.

COMMENTARY - BIBLIOGRAPHY: Unpublished.
The chous, the most popular type of oenochoe of the last third of the 5th c. B.C., is a usual funeral offering in children's tombs in the years of the Peloponnesian War, and its frequent presence has been connected with the children's death rate because of the pestilence. This shape is connected with the Anthesteria and especially with the second day of the celebration, the Day of the Choes, even though it has been said that, due to the fact that they were only produced for a short period of time, they were unlikely to be officially connected to the Anthesteria.
What is interesting about this chous is that this specific game is depicted here for the first time. The two children hold a strap or a rope with a ball fastened to the end. They either hurl the ball as far as they can by whirling the strap, or holding the strap by the end they

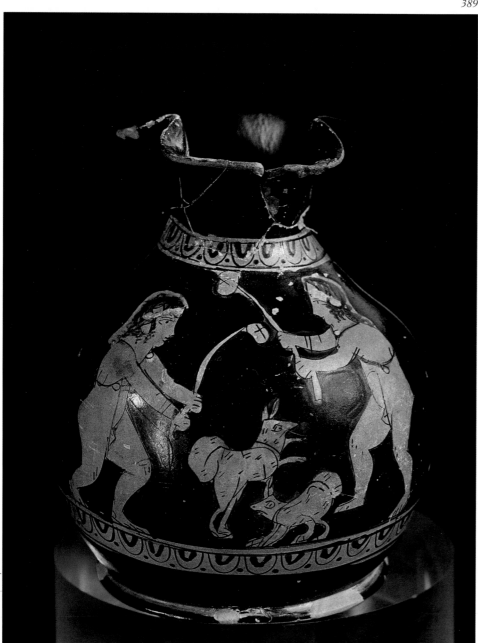

Flat base, reserved on its resting surface, with two black, concentric circles on the underside. The two-part handle begins at the rim and ends on the shoulder of the vase.

COMMENTARY - BIBLIOGRAPHY: Unpublished.

This vase, a quite popular drinking cup in the 2nd half of the 5th c. B.C., was known in antiquity as a "kothon" (Ath. XI, 483b), which Beazley classified as a "mug", within the class of oenochoae. For the name referring to this shape see Scheibler 1968. Indeed, the vase combines elements of a cup and a jug. Thus, kothon was often used by soldiers and travellers, since its shape facilitated both drawing and drinking water. This type of cup is also known as the "Pheidias cup", from a vase bearing the signature of the great artist himself on the base. See *OF* V, 169ff., esp. 176.

Similar vases come from the Athenian Agora (see *Agora* XII, 203) and from the Kerameikos, like the one from the burial enclosure of Hegeso, in the 3rd quarter of the 5th c. B.C. (Kübler 1938, 799, 57b), or the burial of the Korkyreian proxenoi in 433/2 B.C. (see Knigge 1972, nos. 4-5, fig. 23.1 and 24.1). Cf. *Kerameikos* IX, pl. 112.4, 113.4. For other parallels see Schilardi 1977, 166ff., no. 75, pl. 19 (from the Thespeian Polyandreion) and *CVA* Mainz (2) 71, pl. 50.

E.B.-V.

throw the ball in the air. In both cases, the dogs try to catch the ball, as one can see from their pose. The vase-painter has managed to depict the tension of the game in the faces and the bodies of the children as well as in the lively motion of their small dogs. For a closer iconographic parallel on how the figures are composed together see the vase from the excavation at Aiolou Street, *ADelt* 18 (1963) Chronika, pl. 32δ. For the style of execution see the chous from Athens, in London, British Museum, no. 1929.10-16.2, (*ARV*[2] 1320,1) which is attributed to the Group of Athens 12144. In this same group probably belongs the chous from the Kerameikos. For games in antiquity see Schmidt 1971. For this breed of dogs, which were called "μελιταῖα κυνάρια" (Strabo C 277), meaning Maltese dogs, see recently Zlotogorska 1997, esp. 71-117. Generally for choes see Van Hoorn 1951; Bažant

1975, 72-28; Rühfel 1984b, 125-174; Hamilton 1992; *APP* 1997, 473-490 [Τζάχου-Αλεξανδρή].

E.B.-V.

390 BLACK-GLAZED KOTHON
430-426 B.C.

INV. NO. A 15286.
H. 0.084, B.D. 0.055, M.D. 0.082 M.

Complete. Mended with a few chips and flakes. Red-brown clay. The neck has concave walls. The area between the neck and the body is emphasised by a thin relief band with relief dotting. Globular body, with thick, vertical grooves.

391 BLACK-GLAZED POINTED AMPHORISKOS
430-400 B.C.

INV. NO. A 15315.
H. 0.19, M.D. 0.036, MAX.D. 0.08 M.

Body and neck mended and one handle restored. Cracks on the body of the vase. Flakes mainly on the neck, the handles and the shoulder. Black shiny glaze all over. Thin, knob-shaped foot, ovoid body, arch-shaped, cylindrical vertical handles, cylindrical neck, calyx-shaped mouth, slightly projecting, in-turned rim, flat on the upper surface. At the body-foot join, a plastic ring.

A meander band divides the vase's body in two parts, which bear a vertical, tongue-pattern, grooved decoration. In the area from the shoulder to the base of the neck, three meander bands, with an Ionic moulding and impressed small lines, as well as two shallow rings.

COMMENTARY - BIBLIOGRAPHY: Unpublished.
The miniature amphoriskoi of this shape are found from 440 B.C. onwards and go on until the beginning of the 4th c. B.C. They are vessels containing perfumed oils, with their use defining not only the size but also the shape of the rim; see *Agora* XII, 316, no. 1150, pl. 39. For the decoration, which is thought to have been imported from Corinth, see Καπετανάκη 1973, 154ff. For the shape see also Schlörb-Vierneisel 1966, 49, pl. 40,3 no. 100 (HS 163), 1; see also *Corinth* XIII, 272, no. 421-3, pl. 71 and Vogeikoff 1994, 56, no. 41 (with bibliography).

V.O.

393 WHITE-GROUND LEKYTHOS (MAIN TYPE)
c. 420 B.C.

INV. NO. A 15480.
PRES.H. 0.256, B.D. 0.06, D. AT SHOULDER LEVEL 0.08 M.

Part of the neck and mouth is missing. The foot and the handle are mended. Large chip on the upper, right side of the scene. The meander band above the scene is faded. The palmettes decorating the vase's shoulder are also mainly faded. The outlines are rendered with matt red colour. Traces of a preliminary sketch on the back of the female figure.

In the centre of the scene, a large grave stele with pedimental finial, decorated with fillets tied around it. On the left, a woman in right profile, is seated on a rock in a three-quarter view. Her right hand is on her thigh. In her bent, outstretched left arm she is holding out a large pyxis to the young man on the right. The young man on the right is leaning loosely on his staff, while his himation is wrapped on and hanging from his left forearm. The young man is extending his right hand, tentatively, towards the pyxis.

Added colours are richly applied on the vase. The tondo and the main acroterion of the pedimental finial are rendered with red wash, along with some red fillets adorning the stele. The lower part of the woman's chiton is rendered with green (χιτὼν βατραχιοῦς) and some of the fillets decorating the stele are rendered with azure colour.

392 BRONZE ARROWHEADS
430-420 B.C.

INV. NO. Δ 7160Α-ΑΓ.
H. 0.012-0.025, D. OF SHAFT HOLE 0.0045-0.005 M.

Intact. On some, holes of corrosion can be observed.

Thirty-three bronze arrowheads of pyramidal shape (three facets). Incisions highlight the ends of the wings. On some of the arrowheads, the cylinder of the shaft exceeds the wings, while on others they are the same length.

COMMENTARY - BIBLIOGRAPHY: Unpublished.
Vermeule - Comstock 1972, 416-417, nos. 599-600; Walters 1899, nos. 2797-2815; *Olynthus* X, 378-411, nos. 2071-2096, pl. 125-126 (no. 2139, with inv. no. 38.50, is a mould for making arrowheads); *Corinth* XII, 199-200, nos. 1512-1521, pl. 91 (5th-4th c. B.C.); *Antikenmuseum* 1988, 193, no. 35 (from house 25 at Priene).

N.S.

392

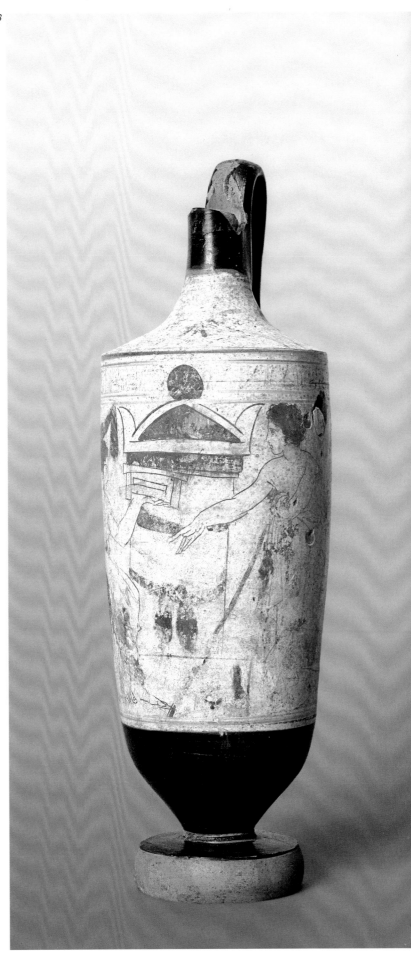

COMMENTARY - BIBLIOGRAPHY: Unpublished.
The painter, who has skilfully managed to increase and reduce the thickness of his line whenever needed, has used his brush to successfully render the body's volume as well as the third dimension. Their drawing skills combined with the use of many added colours have associated the Group R artists with works of the great art at the end of the 5th c. B.C., especially with the famous painter Parrhasios. For the Group R see *ARV²* 1376, 1383-1384, 1390, 1692; *Para* 485, 524; *Addenda²* 371-372; Kurtz 1975, 58-62. Cf. also a lekythos of the Group R in Basel, Antikenmuseum und Sammlung Ludwig, no. Kä 413 (*ARV²* 1383,6, *CVA* Basel 79-81, pl. 51.3-4 and 51.3-3 [Schlehoverova]). The stele belongs to type B-V-26 till B-V-37 of Nakayama 1982, 77-78 and 224-226. For the connection between the Group R and Parrhasios see Παπασπυρί-δη 1923, 142-143 and Robertson 1992, 252-253. For the young man's pose see the commentary on no. 237 and for the "conversation" gesture see Neumann 1965, 23-37. For the woman seated on the rock see commentary on no. 118. For the use of pyxides in the burial ceremony, their depiction on white-ground lekythoi and the symbolism of these objects as the "limit and the end" of life, see Brümmer 1985, 154-158 and Lissarague 1995. For the terms referring to the coloured garments see Miller 1989. For the fillets see commentary on no. 377.

Group R.

G.K.

---

394 RED-FIGURE SQUAT LEKYTHOS
c. 420 B.C.

INV. NO. A 15534.
H. 0.142, B.D. 0.072, M.D. 0.036, MAX.D. 0.083 M.

Complete. Chips and flakes mainly on the scene. Orange-reddish clay. Ring base, with reserved band on the side and the resting surface also reserved, almost globular body, neck offset on its base, calyx-shaped mouth with flat rim. Shiny black glaze covers the body of the vase.
A woman is depicted seated on a chair in profile to the right. She is wearing a long chiton amply folded and himation. On her thighs, turning to her, an Eros his knees bent, and large, upraised wings that are rendered with black dots and horizontal lines. On his head a ribbon of added white colour. His hands are outstretched forward and it seems that he was offering an article to the woman, probably a ribbon. The ground line of the scene is rendered with a simple reserved band.

COMMENTARY - BIBLIOGRAPHY: Unpublished.
This is an Attic shape, the use of which was particularly widespread during the 2nd half of the 5th and the early 4th c. B.C. Basic study for the shape is Rudolph 1971. Generally for the squat lekythoi and the shape see *Agora* XXX, 47-48.
The scene is part of a group of women's subjects that flourished from the 5th c. onwards, and it is possibly connected with the worship of Aphodite, with similar scenes that survive through the 4th c. B.C., see Schefold 1981, 43, fig. 47. The depiction of seated women is a usual subject in the squat lekythoi iconography, along with the subject of gift offering to women from Erotes which was often connected to scenes from wedding preparations, the epaulia; see Oakley - Sinos 1993, 38ff.; Vérilhac - Vial 1998, 324 and 359-360. It is most probably an offer to an unmarried woman. For the painters of the red-figure squat lekythoi see *ARV²*, 1362ff. and 1210, 71 (for a similar depiction of a woman with Eros on a skyphos). For the subject see *LIMC* III.1, 935ff. Also see Langlotz 1954. For a similar iconographic example, where Eros is depicted with Helen, see Ghali-Kahil 1955, 178, pl. XXIX, no. 3.

H.S.

394

395 RED-FIGURE SQUAT LEKYTHOS
425-400 B.C.

INV. NO. A 15218.
H. 0.22, B.D. 0.049, M.D. 0.0415, MAX.D. 0.069 M.

Intact. Chips mainly on the mouth and handle and flakes on the body. Light brown pure clay. Discoid base, with two steps, a simple reserved grooved ring, which is covered in the upper part with black glaze and a black band round the lower part of it, while the resting surface is preserved and carries a concave, conical moulding. Cylindrical body, narrower to the foot, neck and shoulder reserved. On the base of the neck, small lines and on the sloping shoulder, black-figure ray-pattern. Strap handle with black ridge, calyx-shaped mouth with black glaze, with reserved flat rim and reserved groove on its base. On the rim, the neck, the shoulder and the base traces of red ochre (miltos) are preserved.

The scene depicts a young man, standing in left profile holding with his right hand a spear with black-figure decoration just above the middle, while his left arm, bent to the waist, is concealed by the chlamys, which is held on his right shoulder and opens at the front to reveal his naked body. At the back of his neck hangs a petasos, the hat that protects from the sun, and on his feet, tall boots. The neck and the larger part of the body are rendered with outline. Traces of a preliminary sketch and relief lines. The anatomic details and the hair are barely depicted. The scene is framed above and below by a band of Ionic moulding.

396

397

395

398

COMMENTARY - BIBLIOGRAPHY: Unpublished.
The shape follows the tradition of the Category 6L and the Group 16 of Palermo; see Cook 1984, 149-152. The same shape was used by the L.M. P. See *CVA* Palermo-Collezione Mormino (I), III, I, pl. 7, nos. 6-7. The subject of the young man with petasos, chlamys and krepides is quite popular in Attic vase-painting of this period and also in earlier years. Athenian cavalrymen, travellers and hunters were dressed in this way; see Losfeld 1991, 171ff. and Rich 1861, s.v. Crepida (κρηπίς), 201-202. As far as the style is concerned, it is probably connected to the Chania P., who is barely known and his work dates at the last decades of the 5th c. B.C. The features of the young man's face have obvious similarities with those of the Amazon on the lekythos from Polyrrheneia (see Von Bothmer 1957, pl. 86, no. 4), the fingers are similar to those from the lekythos from Kamarina (see *Monumenti Antichi* II, 909, fig. 105). The painter has decorated the same shape of lekythoi and, in at least one case, has placed over and under the scene bands of Ionic moulding, see *EAA*, II, 306. On this lekythos, the similarities are evident in the foot. Generally his figures are characterised by heavy, almost stark members. For the painter see *ARV*² 1369. For the red-figure lekythoi of that period see Campenon 1994, 87-88, pl. 15.

H.S.

396 RED-FIGURE SQUAT LEKYTHOS
425-400 B.C.

INV. NO. A 15215.
H. 0.14, B.D. 0.062, M.D. 0.039, MAX.D. 0.079 M.

Complete. Mended on the neck, with chips on the mouth, the handle and the body and with flakes. Yellowish clay. Ring base, globular depressed and elongated body, covered with black glaze which is in parts reddish due to misfiring. The neck at the base is set off from the shoulder, strap handle and calyx-shaped mouth by a grooved ring at the join with the neck.

A woman stands in profile to the right. She wears a long, multi-folded chiton and an himation, leaving the upper right part of the body and the arm uncovered; it is draped over the left shoulder, hanging down at the back. The head is slightly inclined forward, and the hair is gathered at the nape in a bun, with small, free locks of hair at the side. In her right

hand, she is holding a folded cloth, decorated with alternate bands of thin lines and dots, while with her left hand she is lifting her himation, ready to move forward. In the field behind the figure, a reserved ring, probably a schematised rendering of a ribbon and in front of it a tendril with a schematised lotus bud. This work is rather hastily and not elaborately rendered.

COMMENTARY - BIBLIOGRAPHY: Unpublished.
As a subject, this scene is connected with women's everyday life. The depiction of standing or seated women on lekythoi is especially popular in Attic vase-painting during the 2nd half of the 5th c. B.C. Apparently, the scene is connected with the offering of cloth to the dead, a custom depicted on white-ground lekythoi, see Pekridou-Gorecki 1989, 136-138 and Losfeld 1991, 312ff. The rendering of the hair with loose, wavy locks on the temples and the ear area and a richly folded chiton, all refer to workshops of the last decades of the 5th c. B.C., a style that was established from the Workshop of the Meidias P. Generally for the squat lekythoi see no. 394. For the ring and the tendril see *CVA* Berlin 8, 63 (with relevant bibliography).

H.S.

397 RED-FIGURE SQUAT LEKYTHOS
425-400 B.C.

INV. NO. A 15217.
H. 0.08, B.D. 0.051, MAX.D. 0.057, M.D. 0.029 M.

Complete, slightly flaked. Orange clay. Ring base with reserved underside where there are traces of red ochre (miltos), hemispherical squat body, the neck on the base is set off from the body, strap handle, echinus mouth covered with black glaze, the bottom of which is outlined by a grooved ring.

A sphinx sits to the right with wings and the front left leg raised. The hair gathered on the neck is adorned with a red band (taenia). The wings are rendered by black dots, small oblique lines and relief outline. A double band of Ionic moulding forms the ground line.

COMMENTARY - BIBLIOGRAPHY: Unpublished.
The sphinx is a popular theme in Attic pottery and especially in the late black-figure style where it was

frequently used to illustrate the myth of the Theban Sphinx by the Haimon P., see no. 336. In the 2nd half of the 5th c. B.C., it is often depicted on red-figure squat lekythoi. The theme's interpretation varies, since the sphinx is connected both to the Olympian gods and to Hades. Most probably, it was a funerary theme, due to the fact that similar vases were often found in graves. See Simon 1989, nos. 163-164 (for depictions of sphinxes) and no. 165 (for the workshops and the use of squat lekythoi). For similar squat lekythoi depicting sphinxes see Giudice *et al.* 1992, 196, no. E146; *CVA* Sweden 3, 100, pl. 35, 9-10; Simon 1989, no. 158, pl. 70. For squat lekythoi and the painters see commentary on no. 394.

H.S.

398 BLACK-GLAZED RIBBED SQUAT LEKYTHOS
425-400 B.C.

INV. NO. A 15216.
H. 0.07, B.D. 0.0385, MAX.D. 0.046, M.D. 0.0225 M.

Complete. Small chip on the rim and flakes mainly on the foot and on the interior of the mouth and the handle. Red-brown clay. The vase is covered with shiny black glaze. Ring base with grooved ring at the edge, with reserved and slightly convex resting surface. Depressed, globular body, decorated with impressed leave-shaped triangles filled with oblique vertical lines, short neck offset from the body, vertical strap handle, calyx-shaped mouth.

COMMENTARY - BIBLIOGRAPHY: Unpublished.
The decoration of this vase has evolved the decoration on squat lekythoi with vertical ribs, whose use began probably in the 3rd quarter of the 5th c. B.C. and is considered to be an imitation of metallic vases, see Talcott 1935, 509. This decoration is frequently complemented by stamped concentric circles. For similar decoration in squat lekythoi and in a small prochous see respectively *CVA* Pologne 2 - Collections de Cracovie, pl. 14, 6 and Μυλωνάς 1975, A, tomb Z 17, 263, no. 414, Γ, pl. 317α. For the vertical ribs on squat lekythoi see *Agora* XII, 1135-1141, 315, pl. 38, nos. 1129-1131; for other examples of this type see Talcott 1935, 476, pl. 1, nos. 50-51; Corbett 1949, 326, pl. 91, no. 43; Φιλιππάκη 1953-54, 109-110, fig. 9(2).

H.S.

399 BONE IMPLEMENT (SPATULA)
425-400 B.C.

INV. NO. Δ 7168.
MAX.PRES.L. 0.092, DIM. OF HANDLE 0.004 × 0.005,
W. OF BODY 0.01-0.011 M.

Mended from three parts. The end of the handle is chipped; flaking and cracked on the surface. Blue-green colour, because of proximity to oxidised bronze objects, while it also bears traces of rust from contact with an iron object.
Handle of rectangular section, tongue-shaped body, becoming gradually thinner towards its end. At the junction of main body and handle are two triangular decorative projections.

COMMENTARY - BIBLIOGRAPHY: Unpublished.
See *Corinth* XII, 181-182, no. 1335, pl. 82, esp. 185-186, no. 1355, pl. 83 (early 5th c. B.C.); Richter 1953, 451, no. 1757; Walters 1899, 315, no. 2344. For many examples see *Antikenmuseum* 1988, 267, no. 4.

N.S.

400 BONE IMPLEMENT (SPATULA)
425-400 B.C.

INV. NO. Δ 7168A.
MAX.PRES.L. 0.0835, DIM. OF HANDLE 0.0035 × 0.004,
W. OF BODY 0.0085 M.

Cf. no. 399; here, however, the handle is almost cylindrical and there are no triangular projections.

COMMENTARY - BIBLIOGRAPHY: Unpublished.
See no. 399.

N.S.

401 BONE BEAD
425-400 B.C.

INV. NO. Δ 7168B.
L. 0.011, MAX.D. 0.008, D. OF PERFORATION 0.004 M.

Complete with slight cracks on the surface. Blue-green colour. Body which looks like a small barrel and has a perforation, cylindrical in section, along its axis.

COMMENTARY - BIBLIOGRAPHY: Unpublished.
Cf. *Corinth* XII, 295, nos. 2507-2510, pl. 122 (Hellenistic - Byzantine period) and no. 2511 (clay bead of the Hellenistic period).

N.S.

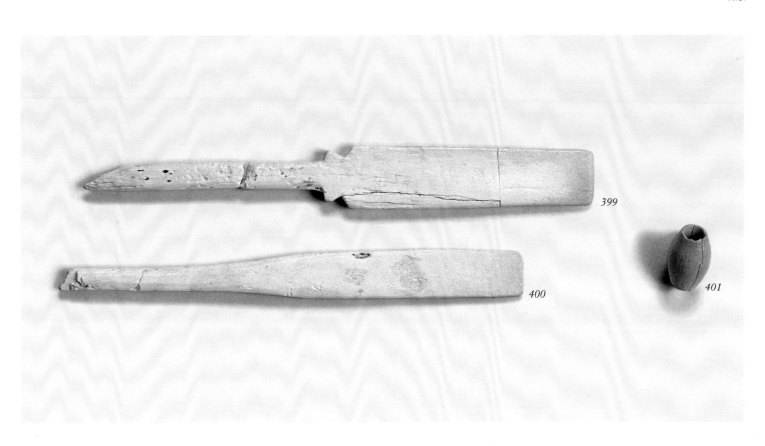

399

400

401

402 KNUCKLE-BONES

INV. NO. Δ 7141.
L. 0.035-0.023 M.

131 knuckle-bones, mainly of ovicaprids. Sixty-four have traces of polishing, one is perforated while attempts have been made to perforate six of them. Two preserve traces of grooving, while the rest are all unworked. Very few carry traces of burning.

In antiquity, the flattened surface was called ὕπτιος or hollow, πρανής or curved and the narrow one κῷος = "Coan" and χίος="Chian". When the specimens preserve traces of tooling, these are mostly to be found on the πρανής and κῷος sides. On the perforated one the perforation is between the κῷος and the χίος sides. At least four preserve traces of the tool, a knife, used to cut them from the bone.

COMMENTARY - BIBLIOGRAPHY: Unpublished.
Knuckle-bones (astragaloi), a children's game, are usually found as offerings in children's burials or in shrines. They have been depicted in sculpture and in painting and in some cases were covered in metal, like gold, silver or lead (see Amandry 1984, 347ff.), while in others, their shape had been imitated by working a different material, such as stone or clay. In general, for knuckle-bones and their depiction on a funeral stele see Hampe 1951.

H.S.

403 BLACK-GLAZED SQUAT LEKYTHOS WITH IMPRESSED DECORATION
425-400 B.C.

INV. NO. A 15220.
H. 0.12, B.D. 0.06, MAX.D. 0.073, M.D. 0.035 M.

Part of the neck and body missing. Mended with chips, flakes and restored in a few areas. Light brown clay. Ring base covered on the upper surface with black glaze. The band outlining its side and the resting surface which preserves some traces of red ochre (miltos) are reserved. Depressed, globular and elongated body, covered with shiny black glaze with shades of different colour due to misfiring, neck offset from the body, vertical strap handle. Calyx-shaped mouth with flat rim.

The body is decorated with bands of impressed vertical palmettes, facing up or down. The palmettes facing down are connected at their base with leaves in a horizontal arrangement with the top facing right. On the shoulder, a band of simple impressed palmettes facing down.

COMMENTARY - BIBLIOGRAPHY: Unpublished.
This type of decoration is often found in black-glazed amphoriskoi of this period, but also in other shapes of mainly open vases and was created after the middle of the 5th c. B.C., from earlier models and it has been

402

said that it was influenced by the sculptural decoration of the Acropolis monuments, see Καπετανάκη 1973, 152-155. For similar examples of decoration in squat lekythoi see Schaal 1923, pl. 58, i and Μυλωνάς 1975, A, Tomb B27, 61-62, no. 87, B, pl. 213. Generally for impressed decoration on black-glazed vases see *Agora* XII, 22ff., 155-156 and bibliography in *CVA* Heidelberg 4, 71-72. For similar decoration in vases combined with impressed figures see Sparkes 1968, 3-16, pl. 1-8.

H.S.

404 LID OF A CYLINDRICAL PYXIS
425-400 B.C.

INV. NO. A 15221.
H. 0.03, M.D. 0.06 M.

Complete. Mended, chipped and restored in a small part of the upper surface. Pure, orange clay. It belonged to a pyxis type D. Cylindrical body, black-glazed with reserved parts and reserved underside. The upper surface is flat, decorated with a black dot in the middle, framed by two concentric black and reserved circles. A wide, reserved, grooved ring goes round the edge of the flat surface while a reserved band circles the junction of the convex with the vertical side of the lid and the edge.

COMMENTARY - BIBLIOGRAPHY: Unpublished.
This type of pyxis is often found in the 3rd and last quarters of the 5th c. B.C., and is definitely not a standard for accurate dating; it was also widely used during the 4th c. B.C. In this case, according to the context of the grave, it dates to the last quarter of the 5th c. B.C. For similar examples of the 2nd and 3rd quarters of the century see *Agora* XII, 327, pl. 43, nos. 1294 and 1296; *CVA* Stuttgart 1, 42-43, pl. 37, no. 4; Lullies 1955, 42, pl. 33, no. 103; Buschor 1959, 20, fig. 13 left; *Ashmolean Museum* 1967, 108, no. 405, pl. LVI. For this type see *Agora* XII, 177-178.

H.S.

405 BLACK-GLAZED LAMP
425-400 B.C.

INV. NO. Δ 7143.
H. 0.025, B.D. 0.048, MAX.D. 0.073, M.D. 0.046 M.

Intact with chips and flakes. Light brown clay. Low and flat discoid base, with the resting surface reserved, with a wash of dilute glaze in the colour of clay. Low body with continuous convex wall and in-curving rim. Large filling hole, small nozzle with fire hole. Horizontal strap handle. Except for the foot, the lamp is covered in shiny, black glaze.

COMMENTARY - BIBLIOGRAPHY: Unpublished.
It is the characteristic shape of a group of lamps at the end of the 5th c. B.C., which were certainly used until the mid 4th c. B.C., with parallels from the Athenian Agora; it belongs to the type 21C, see *Agora* IV, 48, pl. 6 and 34, no. 171 and in the Kerameikos, where it corresponds to the category Rundsculterlampen 1. Glatter Rand, offener Körper (lamps with round shoulder), see *Kerameikos* XI, 24, no. 61, pl. 14-15.

H.S.

403

404

405

406 RED-FIGURE CHOUS
c. 420 B.C.

INV. NO. A 15435.
H. 0.113, B.D. 0.066, MAX.D. 0.091 M.

Intact. Chips on the rim and flakes. Brown clay with irregular firing. Discoid base, spherical body, broad neck rounding up to a wide trefoil mouth. Vertical strap handle, which stems from the mouth and ends on the body. On the main face of the vase, a trapezoidal panel is defined up and down by bands of two-row Ionic moulding with dots and two lines vertical to the pattern on the side. The vase is covered with shiny black glaze. The edge of the base and its concave resting surface are reserved as well as two thin rings at the join of the base to the body.

On the panel, a child is depicted performing a dancing movement to the left. His left hand reaches forward and the right one is bent behind his neck. The right leg is forward, the left one slightly bent back. The anatomical details in the body are defined by slightly relief lines and there was possibly a peri-amma (amulet). The outline of the head is reserved and around it there is a band, which was initially painted with added white colour. The hair is in small wavy locks. On the left end of the panel, in front of the child, a table is depicted with sweets, while at the right end, behind the child, four objects have been placed, that are very worn, and only a chous and a roller-wheel toy can be identified.

COMMENTARY - BIBLIOGRAPHY: Unpublished.
This vase belongs to the category of the small choes with child scenes and is found in the last quarter of the 5th and the beginning of the 4th c. B.C. In terms of shape, it belongs, according to Beazley, to the category no. 3 of oenochoae. The choes are thought to be connected with the festival of Anthesteria and with Dionysos as well as with the wreathing ceremony of three-year-old children which occurred during the festival, where they were offered the vase as a gift. This opinion has been questioned.

For the scene and the child's pose see *Agora* XXX, 246-247, no. 739, pl. 78 and generally for the shape 41-42. Generally for choes and the festival of the Anthesteria see *LIMC*, III.1, s.v. Dionysos, 414ff. and esp. 418-419; Van Hoorn 1951, 38 (for dancing scenes); Parke 1977; Hamilton 1992 (with a survey of previous interpretations on shape and iconography); Green 1971, 189-228 (mainly for the development of the shape); Green 1972, 6-7. For the roller-cart, a common children's toy in Classical Athens, see Aristoph., *Clouds*, ll. 861-864, 878-880.

H.S.

406, 407

407 BLACK-GLAZED PYXIS WITH LID
425-400 B.C.

INV. NO. A 15434.
H. (EXCL. LID) 0.055, H. (INCL. LID) 0.096, B.D. 0.068,
M.D. 0.092, D. OF LID 0.10 M.

Intact with chips and flakes. Red-brown clay. Ring base, concave on the resting surface with conical lug in the centre, hemispherical body with a flange on the upper part that forms a band for the lid. Lid with convex upper surface and two-partite knob-handle. The vase is covered with shiny black glaze, apart from the lid's interior and the resting surface of the foot that have traces of red ochre (miltos).

COMMENTARY - BIBLIOGRAPHY: Unpublished.
This type of pyxis has been found in the 3rd and 4th quarters of the 5th c. B.C. For the shape see Noble 1988, 70. For the possibility that the vase was named in antiquity "κυλιχνίς" see Milne 1939, 247-254. For similar examples see *Kerameikos* IX, 154, no. 301, 2 (HW23), pl. 66 and Μυλωνάς 1975, B, 62, no. 681, Γ, pl. 344α.

H.S.

From tomb 116

408 RED-FIGURE SQUAT LEKYTHOS
c. 420 B.C.

INV. NO. A 15329.
H. 0.182, B.D. 0.082, M.D. 0.045 M.

Mended from many pieces, with restorations and many chips in the body. Ring base, almost globular body, with offset neck at the join with the body, vertical strap handle, calyx-mouth with flat rim. Shiny black glaze covers the body.
A woman is depicted, seated on a chair to the right. In front of her a naked young man with a chlamys and a petasos at the back of his neck. With his left hand he is holding a spear and a box from which he has taken a round object that he is offering to the woman. The scene is framed by an Ionic moulding below the picture and a tongue-pattern above, which decorates half the neck.

COMMENTARY - BIBLIOGRAPHY: Unpublished.
This is another type of lekythos, that appears at the end of the Archaic period and is especially popular during the 2nd half of the 5th c. B.C. mainly as a grave offering; see *Agora* XII, 153. It is presented as a perfume pot, in many scenes, see Richter 1935, 99-101. For the shape see *Agora* XII, 1122. The representation of seated woman with standing man is a common subject in the iconography of the squat lekythoi. This vase possibly shows a scene from everyday life, depicting the offering of a (love) gift; see Sutton 1981, 378. One cannot exclude the case of the scene being the well-known myth of Polyneikes and Eriphyle; see *LIMC* III.1, s.v. Eriphyle, 843-846. According to the myth, Polyneikes offers an ornament, the necklace of Harmony, to Eriphyle in order to convince her husband Amphiaraos to take part in the expedition of the Seven against Thebes. It is a work by the vase-painter Aeson, see *ARV*² 1174 and *Addenda* 339; see also Τιβέριος 1996, 328-329.

I.T.-D.

408

408

409 RED-FIGURE PELIKE
End of 5th c. B.C.

INV. NO. A 15255.
H. 0.29, B.D. 0.15, MAX.D. 0.23, M.D. 0.17 M.

Part of one handle and of the neck missing. The rest of the neck, the handles
and the back side are mended. Chips
and flakes where there is added white
colour. Red-brown clay. Uneven firing on
one side.
On the front of the vase, three figures
standing. The middle one depicts a naked,
bearded Satyr standing frontally; his
head, with an ivy wreath, turns to the
right. With his bent left hand he is holding an upright thyrsos, while his right
one hangs down loosely. He is flanked
by two women turning towards him. The
left one, a Maenad, wears a peplos and
has long hair reaching to her shoulder.
She holds up a torch in her left hand and
an oenochoe in her slightly bent right one.
The flame of the torch is rendered with
added white colour. The figure on the
right has her hair in a bun. She is wearing
a long chiton and himation, which conceals her left arm, while she holds up her
right one. All three figures are crowned
with a wreath rendered with added white.
On side B of the vase, two young men,
each wearing an himation, stand facing
each other. The first one is holding out
a strigil and the second one a staff in his
right hand. Between them a short pillar. In the background, the lower part
of a lyre. Both scenes are framed by a
band of ivy leaves above and an Ionic
moulding below. A double palmette on
both handles.

COMMENTARY - BIBLIOGRAPHY: Unpublished.
The main side of the vase refers to the big thematic
circle of Dionysiac themes, while on side B there is a
well-known subject in the iconography of large vases
of the 5th and the 4th c. B.C.: that depicting two or
three male figures wearing himatia. For similar scenes
see CVA France 28, Musée du Louvre, pl. 41/31 and pl.
59/4; CVA Baltimore 1, pl. 24/2; Γιούρη 1965, 153-170,
pl. 73; Δρούγου 1982, 85 and 91, n. 5.

V.O.

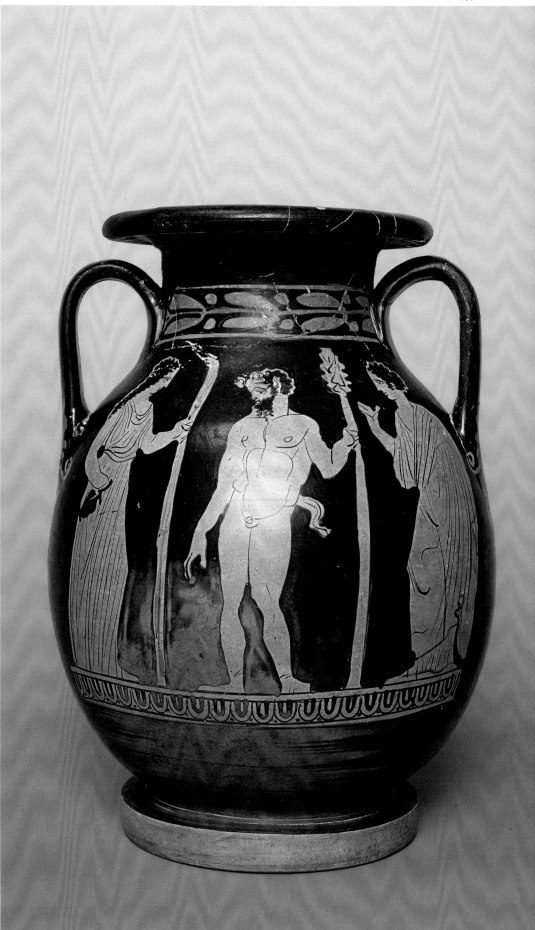

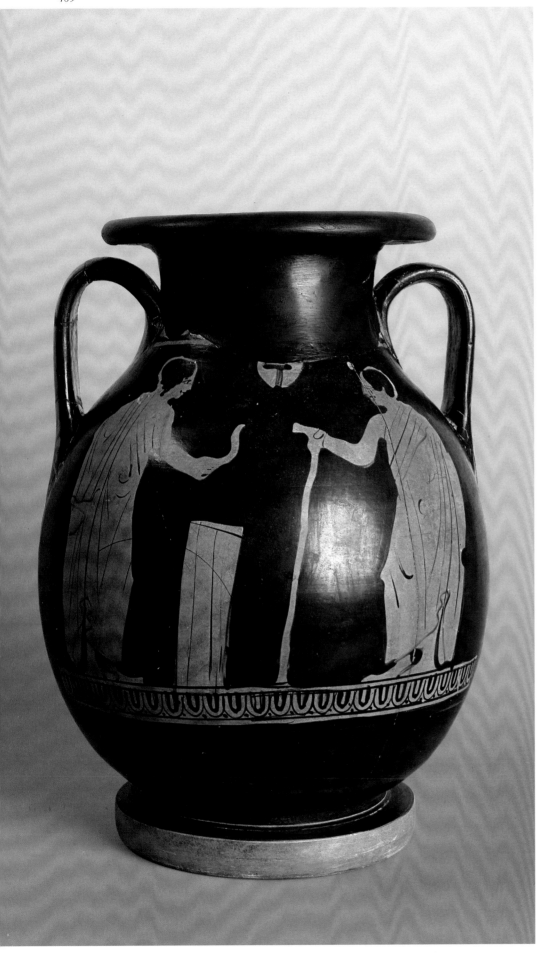

410 FRAGMENT OF A RED-FIGURE LOUTROPHOROS

c. 410 B.C.

INV. NO. A 15369.
MAX.PRES.H. 0.27, MAX.PRES.W. 0.34 M.

Part of the main body and shoulder of a loutrophoros is preserved as well as the base of one handle. Mended from six pieces. Many chips and flakes, mainly on the added white. Red-brown clay.

A young naked warrior is shown being attacked by two Amazons. He wears a helmet and holds a spear in his right hand and a shield in his left hand, which is covered by his draped himation. The interior of the shield can be seen with a tendril around the edge. Across his chest, the dotted strap of the sword.

The Amazon on the left, preserved from the waist down, wears an eastern garment; she is turned to the right and aims at the warrior with her bow. Between the two figures, a laurel bush with the leaves rendered in added white. The same

colour is used for the crest and strap of the warrior's helmet, as well as for the Amazon's arrow.

The mounted Amazon on the right, who is not preserved in the scene, is piercing the warrior's side with her spear. The warrior, weak as he is, cannot hold the shield firmly and tries to defend himself by striding to the left, at the same time stabbing the horse's chest with his spear. A small part of the horse's head, chest, right front leg and part of the left one are preserved. Relief line and dilute glaze are used to render the muscles of the man and the horse, and a faint preliminary sketch can be made out, mainly on the horse. The scene is framed below by a running meander running interrupted by checker-board squares, while the shoulder is decorated with a tongue-pattern.

COMMENTARY - BIBLIOGRAPHY: Unpublished.

The type of vase our fragment comes from is a loutrophoros-hydria. The loutrophoros in antiquity had a double function: for carrying water from the Kallirrhoe spring for the bridal bath, and for use as a grave marker for those who died single. See Richter - Milne 1937, 5 and Beazley 1932, 5.

The Athenian Amazon battle is depicted, a battle which took place between the Amazons and the Athenians, an especially popular subject in vase-painting and in sculpture. Apparently, the depiction of the laurel, which is in a prominent position in the scene, indicates the exact place of the battle which, according to the myth, was close to the temple of Apollo Delphinios; see Plut., *Theseus,* 27. Generally for the Amazon battles see Von Bothmer 1957 and Matheson 1992, 234ff. (with recent bibliography). Work by the Aristophanes P.; see *ARV*[2] 1318-1319; *Addenda*[2] 363; Τιβέριος 1996, 330.

I.T.-D.

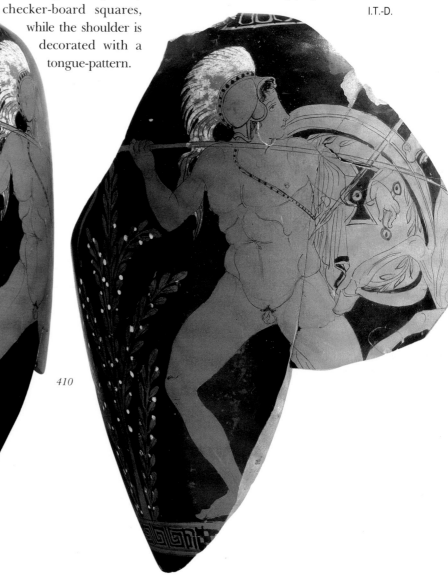

410

411

From tomb 407

411 BONE BEADS
Early 4th c. B.C.

INV. NO. Δ 7142.
D. 0.017-0.02, D. OF PERFORATION 0.006-0.0066 M.

Eleven bone ring-shaped beads from a necklace.

COMMENTARY - BIBLIOGRAPHY: Unpublished.
The beads were found together with a black-glazed skyphos of 380 B.C. Beads of this type made of stone or bone are the most common form of jewellery as early as the Neolithic period. For similar beads of the Classical period see *Perachora* II, 518, pl. 194 F9-11 and 411, pl. 187 and *Kerameikos* XI, pl. 86,6.

M.D.Th.

Tomb 945

412 SQUAT "PALMETTE" LEKYTHOS
400-375 B.C.

INV. NO. A 15473.
H. 0.076, B.D. 0.034 M.D. 0.027 M.

Intact. Chips on the calyx-shaped mouth, the main body (below the handle) and the base. Flakes on the palmette. Uneven firing, especially on the back side of the vase.
The front is decorated with a panel containing a multi-leafed palmette, roughly sketched in red-figure.

COMMENTARY - BIBLIOGRAPHY: Unpublished.
The first examples of the small "palmette" squat lekythoi appear at the end of the 5th c. B.C. and are usually found as burial offerings during the 4th c. B.C., see Καλτσάς 1998, 29, n. 30-31. For the shape see *Agora* XII, 316 and 154, no. 1138, pl. 38. For the squat

lekythos in general see Rudolph 1971. See also *Eretria* IX, 61-62 and 117, no. S118, pl. 47. For a parallel from the Kerameikos see Schlörb-Vierneisel 1966, 66, no. 1241 (tomb HS 99), pl. 46.3. Also, see *Olynthus* XIII, 146, pl. 103, no. 101.

G.K.

413 BLACK-GLAZED SQUAT LEKYTHOS
400-375 B.C.

INV. NO. A 15474.
H. 0.06, B.D. 0.028, M.D. 0.024 M.

Intact. Flakes and chips on the vase. Uneven firing, especially on the lower part of the vase.

COMMENTARY - BIBLIOGRAPHY: Unpublished.
See also the commentary on no. 412. As far as the shape is concerned see *Agora* XII, 316 and 154, pl. 38, no. 1139. For the same type from the Kerameikos cf. Schlörb-Vierneisel 1966, 68, no. 128.1 (tomb HS 99), pl. 46.6.

G.K.

414 BLACK-GLAZED SQUAT LEKYTHOS
400-375 B.C.

INV. NO. A 15475.
H. 0.06, B.D. 0.028, M.D. 0.024 M.

Intact. Flakes and chips on the vase. Uneven firing, especially on the lower part of the vase.

COMMENTARY - BIBLIOGRAPHY: Unpublished.
See commentary on nos. 412 and 413.

G.K.

415 WHITE ALABASTRON
400-375 B.C.

INV. NO. A 15477.
H. 0.192, M.D. 0.015, M.D. (INCL. RIM) 0.064 M.

Complete. Mended. The mouth is restored. In some parts, especially in the
lower half of the vase, the white slip is
flaked.

COMMENTARY - BIBLIOGRAPHY: Unpublished.
For the shape see *Agora* XXIII, 47-48 and *Agora* XXX
48-50. See also Mertens 1977, 128-136 and Wehgartner
1983, 112-114, with bibliography. The alabastra were
perfume bottles which were put in graves as burial
offerings. On the use of the alabastron in general see
Angermeier 1936; *Neue Pauly,* I, s.v. Alabastron, Parfüm-
gefäß [Scheibler]. For the type and use of the alabastron in the Archaic and the Classical period see Θέ-

μελης - Τουράτσογλου 1997, 42-43 and 168-169, n.
178. The vase has an ovoid body, narrow neck, wide
rim and two small lugs just below the shoulder. The
white clay alabastra imitate the stone (alabaster) or
metal examples imported from the East. See Özgen -
Öztürk 1996, 55-56, 121-125, cat. nos. 75-78 and 131,
cat. no. 86. For alabaster alabastra see Boulter 1963,
121, no. D9, pl. 39 and 124-125, nos. G2, G3, G4, pl.
45 and Dörig 1972, cat. no. 251. Despite the fact that
the decorated white alabastra disappear after 450 B.C.
(see commentary on no. 346), the plain white alabastra
carry on to the 4th c. B.C. For the influence of exotic
materials on Attic white-ground pottery see Vickers
1984. For the texture of the chalk-white slip see Noll -
Holm - Born 1973, 122-123.

G.K.

415, 416

416 WHITE ALABASTRON
400-375 B.C.

INV. NO. A 15478.
H. 0.22, M.D. 0.018, M.D. (INCL. RIM) 0.065 M.

Complete. Mended. Mouth restored. Several chips and flakes of the white slip on the vase.

COMMENTARY - BIBLIOGRAPHY: Unpublished.
See commentary on no. 415.

G.K.

417 BLACK-GLAZED PYXIS WITH LID
400-375 B.C.

INV. NO. A 15476.
H. (INCL. LID) 0.08, H. (EXCL. LID) 0.077, D. OF LID 0.106, M.D. 0.092 M.

Intact. Chips and flakes mainly on the underside of the vase and the edge of the lid.
Concentric, reserved bands appear on the lower part of the vase and the underside of the ring base. The upper surface of the lid is decorated with concentric reserved circles, an incised one on the brim and two on the centre, where there is a suspension hole for the metallic ring, now lost.

COMMENTARY - BIBLIOGRAPHY: Unpublished.
Pyxides were used by women to store powders and toiletries. For their typology see Roberts 1978; *Agora* XXX, 51-54; Wehgartner 1983, 136-137. This particular pyxis with the upward and slightly convex walls is more similar to type B than to type C; cf. *Agora* XII, 174-175, no. 1291, pl. 43. For a similar type, slightly earlier (end of 5th c. B.C.), see *Agora* XII, 327, no. 1291, pl. 43 (type B pyxis).

G.K.

417

418 BLACK-GLAZED TREFOIL-MOUTHED
OENOCHOE
400-375 B.C.

INV. NO. A 15252.
H. 0.138, B.D. 0.044, MAX.D. 0.081, M.D. 0.061 M.

Complete. Mended in the upper part of the body. Chips and flakes. Discoid base, broader body towards the well-shaped neck, slender neck. Cylindrical handle. Shiny black glaze, that gave the impression of a metallic surface, apart from the foot which is reserved. The body becomes narrower from the base of the handle downwards and is decorated, from the shoulder until just over the foot, with vertical relief ribs. The handle springs from the shoulder and rests on the trefoil mouth.

COMMENTARY - BIBLIOGRAPHY: Unpublished.
This vase belongs to type 2 of the trefoil-mouthed oenochoae and began to take shape at the end of the 6th or the beginning of the 5th c. B.C.; see *Agora* XII, 60, no. 104, pl. 5.

V.O.

419 BLACK-GLAZED LAMP
400-375 B.C.

INV. NO. Δ 7146.
H. 0.042, B.D. 0.042, TOTAL L. 0.126, D. OF FILLING HOLE 0.022 M.

Chips on the upper surface of the tip of the nozzle and on parts of the body and the foot. Shiny black glaze giving the impression of a metallic surface, from which the low, discoid base is exempt. Curved body. Large horizontal strap handle, enclosing the shoulder in the shape of the letter Ω. Small filling hole and traces of red colour in the groove that surrounds it. Black glaze in the interior and small knob in the centre of the base.

COMMENTARY - BIBLIOGRAPHY: Unpublished.
Very few lamps of this type have been found in the late finds from Olynthos, showing that they were established before 348 B.C. Their dating is based both on the typological evolution of Group "24C" of the Athenian Agora, and on their resemblance with type "25A Prime" that peaks in the 2nd half of the 4th and the 3rd c. B.C., as well as in the finds from the Athenian Agora. See *Kerameikos* XI, no. 81, pl. 16, 17 (380-370 B.C.); *Corinth* IV$_2$, type VII; Knigge 1970, pl. 44a; *Agora* IV, 67, type 25A, no. 269, pl. 9,38; Lyon-Caen 1986, 35, no. 33.

V.O.

418, 419

420 TERRACOTTA FIGURINE OF A COMIC ACTOR
c. 350 B.C.

INV. NO. E 1040.
H. 0.093 M.

Intact. Brown-red clay. White slip on surface of main side, flaking in places.
The figure is shown frontally supported
on its left leg on top of a low imperfectly
formed base. The relaxed, slightly bent,
right leg is pulled back. The actor is wearing a full-length chiton, belted high up
and an himation which falls from the left
shoulder, is twisted around the swollen
belly and covers the left arm which is bent
towards the waist. He is pulling up the
himation with his raised right arm, in a
revealing gesture. The head is turned
slightly towards the left. The hair, untied
on the shoulders, is rendered with red
paint. He is wearing a face-mask which
highlights the physiognomy.

COMMENTARY - BIBLIOGRAPHY: Unpublished.
Figurines of actors of Ancient and Middle Comedy are
numerous and are rendered as caricatures of women
nearing childbirth. They date to 400-330 B.C.; see
Bieber 1961a, 40-41, no. 160 (Ancient Comedy), 47, no.
192 (Middle Comedy). For the type see Winter 1903, II,
421,9. For typological parallels see *BMC* I, 401, no.
1530, pl. 206 (from Cyrenaica); Schürmann 1989, 102,
no. 356, pl. 62 (from Sicily; 350-325 B.C.); Muller 1996,
430-431, nos. 1087-1090, pl. 134 (from Thasos).

Th.K.

420

421 BLACK-GLAZED HYDRISKE
c. 350 B.C.

INV. NO. A 15444.
H. 0.112, B.D. 0.03, MAX.D. 0.061, M.D. 0.036 M.

Complete. Many chips and flakes. Shiny black glaze all over the vase, apart from the reserved resting surface. Stepped base with traces of irregular firing. Piriform body with tall neck. On the shoulder, there are two horizontal handles bent upwards adjacent to the body. Tall neck and rim, formed by a plastic sloping ring.

COMMENTARY - BIBLIOGRAPHY: Unpublished.
For the typology of the miniature hydriae see Pfrommer 1983, 80ff.

V.O.

422 MINIATURE BLACK-GLAZED PERFUME BOTTLE
325-300 B.C.

INV. NO. A 15400.
H. 0.064, B.D. 0.021, MAX.D. 0.041, M.D. 0.017 M.

Complete. Chips and flakes on the body and the base. Low, discoid base that is reserved. Ovoid body. Around the base of the neck, a low thin groove. Rim with plastic downward sloping ring.

COMMENTARY - BIBLIOGRAPHY: Unpublished.
This type of vase was widely spread in the last quarter of the 4th c. B.C. until the end of the Hellenistic period, and also until the end of late antiquity: the well-known unguentarium. For its name in general see *Labraunda* II, 1, 24-25. From stratigraphical observations by Schlörb-Vierneisel in the Kerameikos cemetery, we conclude that the black-glazed perfume bottles preceded those made of grey clay; see Schlörb-Vierneisel 1966, 87, no. 150 (HS 7), pl. 53, 6 (325-300 B.C.) and *Agora* XXIX, 177, no. 1167, fig. 72, pl. 85 (325-300 B.C.). The article of Anderson-Stojanović 1987 is also seminal.

V.O.

423 BLACK-GLAZED PERFUME BOTTLE
325-300 B.C.

INV. NO. A 15401.
H. 0.10, B.D. 0.027, MAX.D. 0.067, M.D. 0.023 M.

Intact. Chips and flakes on the body and base. Globular body with discoid base and ring-shaped sloping mouth. On the perimeter of the base of the neck, three incised, concentric reserved grooves.

COMMENTARY - BIBLIOGRAPHY: Unpublished.
Cf. no. 422. See also *Agora* XXIX, no. 1163, pl. 85 (325-300 B.C.) and Schlörb-Vierneisel 1966, 90, no. 156, pl. 53,5 (HS 90) (4th quarter of 4th c. B.C.).

V.O.

421

424 BLACK-GLAZED KANTHAROS
325-300 B.C.

INV. NO. A 15402.
H. 0.075, B.D. 0.047, M.D. 0.083 M.

Intact. Very few chips and flakes. Shiny black glaze, traces of uneven firing on one side. Ring grooved base with very low stem. Hemispherical body, broad cylindrical neck with simple, thin mouth that is slightly offset. Strap handles with spurs on the shoulder (spurred handles). On the bottom, stamped decoration of four palmettes in a cross within a circle of rouletting.

COMMENTARY - BIBLIOGRAPHY: Unpublished.
This was an especially popular drinking vessel from the 6th c. onwards, whose shape with its simple, thin lip was the latest evolution in the form of this particular vase. It is rarely found in the 1st half of the 4th c. B.C., while the Athenian Agora has examples of this type from 350 B.C. onwards. See *Agora* XII₁, 117 and 122. The earlier kantharoi have an internal impressed decoration of palmettes and small lines. In terms of shape, the kantharos survives during the Hellenistic period; see *Agora* XXIX₁, 83. For typological parallels see *Agora* XXIX₂, no. 8, fig. 4, pl. 1, 2 (325-300 B.C.).

V.O.

425 BLACK-GLAZED KANTHAROS
325-300 B.C.

INV. NO. A 15403.
H. 0.08, B.D. 0.046, M.D. 0.078 M.

Complete. Mended from many pieces. Chips and flakes. Traces of irregular firing on one side. Conical base of two unequal, successive rings with very low stem and concave resting surface. Hemispherical body, broad, cylindrical neck with plain rim. Flattened handles with pointed spurs. Stamped decoration on the bottom with palmettes in a cross, circled by fine rouletting.

COMMENTARY - BIBLIOGRAPHY: Unpublished.
Cf. no. 424.

V.O.

425, 424

426 ASH-URN WITH LID
325-300 B.C.

INV. NO. A 15367.
H. 0.244, H. (INCL. LID) 0.295, B.D. 0.167, MAX.D. 0.235,
M.D. 0.018 M.

Complete, part of the base restored. Red-brown clay. Flaked glaze on the vase, while the lid has preserved, with a few chips and flakes, its shiny black glaze. Red glaze on the interior. Ring base, globular body, horizontal handles bent upwards with nipple-shaped lugs on the side. Below the rim, a projecting flange for the lid. Conical lid with vertical, slightly convex wall on its base and ring handle. The only decoration is the red concentric bands which decorate underside flat surface.

COMMENTARY - BIBLIOGRAPHY: Unpublished.
For the shape see Vanderpool 1966, pl. 72.

V.O.

427 MINIATURE BLACK-GLAZED PERFUME BOTTLE
325-300 B.C.

INV. NO. A 15364.
H. 0.063, B.D. 0.023, M.D. 0.023, MAX.D. 0.04 M.

Intact with flakes. Discoid base, pear-shaped body, plastic sloping rim. Shiny black glaze on the vase, apart from the resting surface of the foot. Traces of uneven firing.

COMMENTARY - BIBLIOGRAPHY: Unpublished.
Most of the Athenian perfume bottles were made of fine, grey clay which was not porous and was suited for storing valuable liquids for a long period of time. The advantage of this particular material made the use of the black-glazed perfume bottles, after the early Hellenistic times, rather scarce. See *Agora* XXIX, 176, no. 1167, fig. 72, pl. 85. Cf. also nos. 422 and 423.

V.O.

428 BLACK-GLAZED SKYPHOS
325-300 B.C.

INV. NO. A 15363.
H. 0.06, B.D. 0.025, MAX.D. 0.053, M.D. 0.039 M.

Intact. Flakes on a large part of the vase. Ring base with a slight projection on the centre of the outside. Piriform body. Horseshoe-shaped handles. Incurving rim. Black glaze on the vase.

COMMENTARY - BIBLIOGRAPHY: Unpublished.
See *Agora* XII, no. 327, pl. 15 and Margreiter 1988, 74, no. 253, pl. 23.

V.O.

429 MINIATURE SINGLE-HANDLED SKYPHOS
325-300 B.C.

INV. NO. A 15361.
H. 0.018, B.D. 0.023, M.D. 0.039 M.

The handle is restored. Chips on the rim, flakes. Shiny black glaze on the surface of the vase. Ring base with small projection in the centre, on the outside.

COMMENTARY - BIBLIOGRAPHY: Unpublished.
This type of vase, like the skyphos, was extremely popular, since they were used as drinking vessels or as food bowls during the 4th c. B.C. In the 3rd c. B.C., they evolve into handleless small bowls (skyphidia). Perhaps they were attributed the name "kanastron" or "kanasthon" or "tryblion" by the ancient Athenians; see *Agora* XII, 124, no. 762, pl. 31 (350-325 B.C.) and *Agora* XXIX, no. 857, fig. 58, pl. 71.

V.O.

430 BLACK-GLAZED SINGLE-HANDLED
SKYPHIDION
325-300 B.C.

INV. NO. A 15365.
H. 0.019, B.D. 0.023, M.D. 0.042 M.

Intact. Flakes on the handle and in the body. Ring base with small projection on the centre, on the outside. Shallow open body with out-curving rim. Horseshoe-shaped handle.

COMMENTARY - BIBLIOGRAPHY: Unpublished.
Cf. no. 429. Also see *Agora* XII, 126, no. 762, pl. 31 and *Agora* XXIX, 155, no. 857, fig. 58.

V.O.

431 MINIATURE PLATE (PINAKION)
325-300 B.C.

INV. NO. A 15362.
H. 0.012, B.D. 0.03, M.D. 0.042 M.

Complete. The biggest part of the vase flaked. Chips. Discoid base, shallow open body. Thick walls. Flat, out-curving rim.

COMMENTARY-BIBLIOGRAPHY: Unpublished.
Similar vases from the Athenian Agora appear at the end of the 5th or the beginning of the 4th c. B.C. The earlier ones are black-glazed becoming rarer after 325 B.C. See *Agora* XXIX, 215, no. 1471, fig. 87.

V.O.

432 LEKANIS
End of 4th c. B.C.

INV. NO. A 15368.
H. 0.14, B.D. 0.125, M.D. 0.293 M.

Mended and restored. Traces of uneven firing. Buff clay with small inclusions and other added mixtures. Low ring base. Conical body. Reserved handles of cylindrical section root exactly below the flat rim. On the interior, a decoration of three red bands.

COMMENTARY - BIBLIOGRAPHY: Unpublished.
Open household pot, a common domestic item. In Athens it was particularly popular especially from 525 until 300 B.C. See *Agora* XII, no. 1819, pl. 85.

V.O.

433 MINIATURE BLACK-GLAZED KALYX
325-300 B.C.

INV. NO. A 15366
H. 0.024, M.D. 0.032 M.

Intact with flakes and slightly chipped. Barely existing base with flat resting surface. Calyx-shaped body with neck ending in open mouth.

COMMENTARY - BIBLIOGRAPHY: Unpublished.
For the shape see *Agora* XII, 121-122, no. 692, pl. 28 and no. 1398, pl. 45; Ρωμιοπούλου 1964, 101, fig. 10α-γ; Πατσιαδά 1983, 174, no. 107, pl. 65α.

V.O.

434 MINIATURE LAMP
325-300 B.C.

INV. NO. Δ 7153.
H. 0.03, L. 0.06, D. OF FILLING HOLE 0.018, B.D. 0.025 M.

Intact. Pure, yellow-brown clay, with soapy texture, unglazed. Discoid base, globular body, nozzle with rounded edge and small filling hole. On its edge, black glaze. On the inside, black glaze. Small pierced lug on the shoulder. On the outside of the base, red glaze.

COMMENTARY - BIBLIOGRAPHY: Unpublished.
This lamp, according to Howland, belongs to type "25B Prime", see *Agora* IV, no. 319, pl. 11, 39, which corresponds to VII of Corinth. Its handy shape and ease of manufacture, made it very popular from the 3rd quarter of the 4th until the 2nd quarter of the 3rd c. B.C. For the shape see also *Kerameikos* XI, nos. 143-144, pl. 26-27 (3rd-4th quarter of 4th c. B.C.); Davidson 1934, 55-56, no. 67 (type VII), fig. 24 (end of 4th c. B.C.); Δρούγου 1992, type ΠΛ3, globular unglazed lamps, 40-42, no. 50, fig. 4 (end of 4th - beginning of 3rd c. B.C.).

V.O.

435 UNGLAZED POINTED AMPHORISKOS
3rd c. B.C.

INV. NO. A 15396.
H. 0.129, M.D. 0.023, MAX.D. 0.064 M.

Complete, mended at the rim. Globular body. Plastic, knob-shaped end. Handles cylindrical in section, which spring just below the low, plastic ring of the lip, and are adjacent to the wider part of the body. From the red-painted inside of the lip, a drop of paint has dripped onto the outside.

COMMENTARY - BIBLIOGRAPHY: Unpublished.
For the shape see *CVA* USA 3, no. 20, pl. XIX.

V.O.

436 UNGLAZED POINTED AMPHORISKOS
3rd c. B.C.

INV. NO. A 15399.
H. 0.253, MAX.D. 0.104, M.D. 0.043 M.

Intact, small chip on the knob. Impure clay with inclusions and other added mixtures. Conical knob, angular at the join to the body with a flat end. Long, pear-shaped body. Tall neck, tapering to a plastic ring-shaped out-curving lip. Tall handles that spring just below the ring of the rim and are adjacent to the vase's shoulder.

COMMENTARY - BIBLIOGRAPHY: Unpublished.
This type of amphora is Thasian. For the shape see *CVA* Deutschland 29, pl. 93, 2; for typological parallels see Ρωμιοπούλου 1989, 37, pl. 21 and Χρυσοστόμου 1998β, 36, no. 1, pl. 11.

V.O.

435, 436

437 LAGYNOS
3rd c. B.C.

INV. NO. A 15397.
H. 0.126, B.D. 0.048, MAX.D. 0.084, M.D. 0.031 M.

Complete. Mended from many pieces and restored in some parts of the body, with several chips and flakes. The vase's surface has a whitish glaze. Ring base, spherical body, tall cylindrical neck, ring-shaped rim, slightly everted. Strap handle with a right angle bent. Its back is rendered plastically.

Black band round the base and at the join with the neck. On the body, the same black band is framed above and below by two faded parallel lines. The edge and the inside of it are black, while a horizontal black line defines the upper part of the handle.

COMMENTARY - BIBLIOGRAPHY: Unpublished.

The lagynos is one of the most characteristic Hellenistic vases and as far as dating is concerned is one of the most puzzling. See Γιαννικουρή et al. 1990, 175. Two shapes can be distinguished: a) vases with a bi-conical body and b) vases with a globular body. This lagynos from the Kerameikos belongs to the second group, and is also characterised as globular, see Καλτσάς 1983, 37. From the 2nd c. B.C. onwards, the lagynos probably replaced the oenochoe becoming a more advanced, globular, version of the older type. For the shape and terminology see the Leroux 1913 study, and the publication of *Labraunda* II, 1, 17-19. See also Metzger 1994, 73-75, pl. 36-37 and *Agora* XXIX$_1$, 227ff., no. 1514, fig. 90, pl. 116. For small-size globular lagynoi see also Gräpler 1997, 87, no. 114/4, fig. 154, 165.

V.O.

438 BLACK-GLAZED MASTOID PHIALE
250-200 B.C.

INV. NO. A 15398.
H. 0.051, M.D. 0.106, B.D. 0.025 M.

Complete. Mended from many pieces and restored to a large extent. Many chips and flakes of the black glaze and of the added white colour. Traces of uneven firing.

On the outside, the discoid base is defined by a pair of successive concentric incised grooves, which are repeated in the middle of the body. On the inside below the slightly flaring rim, an incised groove. The centre of the bottom is decorated with an incised medallion with four rays in a star, which in parts preserve added dilute white paint. At the extension of the rays, pairs of horizontal irregular parallel red strokes.

COMMENTARY - BIBLIOGRAPHY Unpublished.

The type of the plain mastoid footless phiale, which was used as a drinking vessel, can be found throughout the 3rd c. B.C. in Athens and in other areas. The vases with painted decoration on the interior, appear as new shapes at the beginning of the Hellenistic period; see *Agora* XXIX$_1$, 110, n. 113. They can be divided into two groups: a) phialae with a plain rim and conical body and b) phialae with a hemispherical body and an everted rim. The difference in the shape of these vases serves as a criterion for accurately dating them. The shape continues to be found in the 2nd c. B.C., but not after 175 B.C., as one can conclude from the finds of the Athenian Agora. For the shape see *Agora* XXIX, no. 361, fig. 22, pl. 35 (240-220 B.C.); for the decoration on the interior see *Agora* XXIX, nos. 363, 364, pl. 35 (240-220 B.C.) and Rotroff 1991, no. 84, fig. 17, pl. 35.

V.O.

438, 437

439 PLEMOCHOE (KERNOS)
400-350 B.C.

INV. NO. A 15404.
H. 0.109, M.D. 0.108, B.D. 0.062 M.

Complete, mended in the rim. Chipped. Pink clay with added mixtures and other inclusions. Ring base, low conical foot. The junction of the foot and the conical body is enhanced by a plastic ring. Between the body and the shoulder a horizontal plastic ring where the handles with pairs of holes are. Over it, the shoulder of the vase in the shape of a spherical band and out-curving rim.

COMMENTARY - BIBLIOGRAPHY: Unpublished.
The term "kernos" has been attributed to vases that mainly come from the temple of Eleusis and from the Athenian Agora (see Pollitt 1979, 205ff.) and they are connected to the cult of Demeter, Rhea and Cybele. These vases are found in two types: a) the simple "kernos", like the vases in this exhibition, and b) the composite type, with one central vase surrounded by many kotyliskai. The small differences that are seen in the shape of the small kernoi cannot be considered a criterion for dating the vases.
In a thorough and extensive study of these vases, Brommer (1980), suggested very convincingly that the term plemochoe should be used for the simple type and the term kernos for the more complex one. This view has also been expressed by M.M. Miles, whose latest research (*Agora* XXXI, 95) concerns finds from the Athenian Eleusinion temple. For parallels see Pollitt 1979, fig. 1 (with earlier bibliography); Jones 1982, pl. 6; Bakalakis 1991, 117, fig. 6; *Agora* XXXI, pl. 18a, 19b. For the complex type see *Agora* XII, no. 1364, pl. 44.

V.O.

440 PLEMOCHOE (KERNOS)
400-350 B.C.

INV. NO. A 15405.
H. 0.074, M.D. 0.09, B.D. 0.047 M.

Complete. Parts of the rim and the restored flat ring missing. Red-brown clay with inclusions and mica. Conical foot and body, out-curving rim. Pairs of holes on the handles. Traces of red colour on the inside.

COMMENTARY - BIBLIOGRAPHY: Unpublished.
Cf. no. 439.

V.O.

441 PLEMOCHOE (KERNOS)
400-350 B.C.

INV. NO. A 15406.
H. 0.072, M.D. 0.076, B.D. 0.044 M.

Complete. Chips on the rim and the flat ring. Reddish clay with many added mixtures. Ring base, conical foot.

COMMENTARY - BIBLIOGRAPHY: Unpublished.
Cf. no. 439.

V.O.

442 PLEMOCHOE (KERNOS)
400-350 B.C.

INV. NO. A 15407.
H. 0.07, M.D. 0.073, B.D. 0.044 M.

Complete, restored in the rim and the flat ring. Buff clay. Ring base with low, cylindrical foot. Conical body. Traces of black glaze.

COMMENTARY - BIBLIOGRAPHY: Unpublished.
Cf. no. 439.

V.O.

443   LID OF A BLACK-FIGURE PELIKE
500-450 B.C.

INV. NO. A 15370.
H. 0.085, D. 0.103 M.

Complete. The handle is restored with cracks. Brown clay. The side, vertical wall is slightly convex, with shiny glaze and traces of uneven firing. A band of violet in the projecting, low ring of the base. Violet also circles the base and top of the handle. The black-glazed knob is in the shape of a pomegranate.

The depiction covers the upper surface of the lid: three octopuses extend around the knob. Between them, three blank spaces with one, two and three dolphins respectively. Added white colour on the head and body of the octopuses.

COMMENTARY - BIBLIOGRAPHY: Unpublished. For similar shapes see Roberts 1978, fig. 9a, c. For depictions of octopuses in various vases see *CVA* Berlin 7, pl. 26, 3; *ABL*, pl. 50; *Agora* XXIII, 186, no. 659, pl. 63 (with relevant bibliography); *CVA* J.P.Getty, 13, no. 18, pl. 397.2,4-6.

V.O.

443

444 PLASTIC TREFOIL-MOUTHED OENOCHOE
Mid 4th c. B.C.

INV. NO. E 1042.
H. 0.273, B.D. 0.092, M.D. 0.03-0.037 M.

Incomplete, mended. The arms are broken at the level of the elbows. Incomplete, mended base. The glaze and slip are partly chipped. Pink brown clay. Tall, echinus foot tapered on the upper part. The back of the vase is a black-glazed trefoil-mouthed oenochoe with cylindrical neck and vertical strap handle with a vertical rib.

The front of the vase is an upright standing woman, wearing a long chiton (or peplos) and himation, and standing on her straight left leg with her right one behind. The himation has thick folds and seems to be doubled over at the back and

444

above her breast. The back and neck of the woman are covered by a mantle, the hem of which is left loose on the left, at the level of the feet. At the shoulders, behind the mantle, imprints of wings as they begin to form. The way the garments are rendered poses questions. It is likely that ornaments were later added to the front part of the vase, like the fold of drapery on the breast and the wavy hem below the left arm, in order to obtain a more elaborate result. The arms are missing, but the traces of the broken parts reveal that the left one was parallel to the body, while the right one was bent in order to hold the mantle. The head is slightly tilted to the left, the hair is rendered with small, wavy grooves held on the back of the head with a wreath. An earring can be made out above the left cheek.

The whole vase and the foot, apart from the back of the black-glazed oenochoe, has a white slip and the details are rendered with various colours (yellow for the hair and red on the ribbon that binds, and red and azure for the shoes and upper part of the base).

COMMENTARY - BIBLIOGRAPHY: Unpublished.

Plastic oenochoae or lekythoi were made as votive or burial offerings initially in Athens around 400 B.C., and their production lasted until 320 B.C. There are imitations later in Boeotia, Olynthos and in Campania. Due to their impressive effect, they were considered luxury vases and were a sought-after export product in foreign markets such as South Russia. The type of this particular vase is found for the first time as a plastic vase. The wings indicate that it is probably a Nike, one of the most common subjects. Most probably, it is a winged female figure.

For similar vases see Trumpf-Lyritzaki 1969, 7, 9, 10, pl. 3, no. 10 (Nike in NM from the Cyrenaica; beginning of 4th c. B.C.), pl. 4a, no. 13 (Nike in the Kerameikos Museum) and no. 17 (Nike in the British Museum from Athens; middle of 4th c. B.C.); Williams 1978, 379-401, pl. 91, nos. 2-4 (late 5th - early 4th c. B.C.); *BMC* II, 59, pl. 39, no. 1703 (from Athens; 3rd quarter of 4th c. B.C.); Köster 1926, pl. 33 (Nike from Eretria); Breitenstein 1941, 29, pl. 30, nos. 274 (4th c. B.C.); Mollard-Besques 1986, IV.1, 143-144, pl.155d-f, no. D4111-4114; *Olynthus* VII, 101-102, pl. 54-55, nos. 395-396.

O.Z.

445 MARBLE FUNERARY SIREN
340-330 B.C.

INV. NO. Λ 5773.
H. 0.44, MAX.W. 0.255 M.

Pentelic marble. Missing the head and upper part of the neck, the right arm and a fragment of the breast and shoulder-blade, the right wing, a fragment of the left and the legs immediately below the knees. Chipped on the fingers of the left hand and small amount of damage to the surface.

The Siren is shown naked with her left hand touching her breast. Behind the legs, part of the tail is preserved. The body is rendered in a rather flat manner, without many anatomical details.

COMMENTARY - BIBLIOGRAPHY: Unpublished.

The Siren is an old subject in various works of art, see Biers 1999, 135-144. For representations in plastic art and particularly on grave stelai see Diepolder 1965, 29-30 and Woysh - Meautis 1982, 91-99. On grave stelai, it appears in the 4th c. B.C. (see Cook 1969, 65ff., pl. 40-45) and is interpreted as a spirit which weeps and shows sympathy for the dead. For Sirens see Rolley 1994, 41. This specific work is the creation of an Attic workshop. For parallels see Collignon 1911, 216-225; Vedder 1985, 65-73, fig. 46, 49; Hofstetter 1990, 152, A213, fig. 34.

T.K.

446 MARBLE PEDIMENTAL GRAVE STELE
350-325 B.C.

INV. NO. Λ 5775.
H. 0.545, PRES.W. 0.285, TH. 0.044 M.

Pentelic marble. Most of it is preserved. The back is roughly worked with a pointed chisel.

The relief, shallow representation is inside a rectangular field. On the left, a standing female figure, dressed in a chiton and himation which also covers her head, is turning to the right and receives the female figure sitting on a stool in the centre, dressed in the same manner and resting her feet on a foot-stool. Behind her, a smaller female figure can be seen dressed in a sleeved chiton and watching the reception.

Below the pediment of the stele is the carved inscription: ΜΙΚΑ ΙΠΠΟΚΛΕΟ ΕΡΕ-ΤΡΙΚΗ.

COMMENTARY - BIBLIOGRAPHY: Unpublished.
The stele type has a broad distribution in Attica. For the shape see Conze 1893, I, pl. XLII:120. For its architectural form see Κώστογλου-Δεσποίνη 1979, 92ff.
On the interpretation of the representation the following may be noted: the central figure is the dead Mika from Eretria; the left figure is, most probably, a relative who is grieving for the loss of the dead girl, while the third figure is a maid who sympathises in grief. The known subject of reception on grave monuments reaches its highest expression in the last quarter of the 4th c. B.C. and shows the communication between the dead and the living, as well as the bonds of love that join them despite the fact of death; see Schmaltz 1983, 15ff., 24-58, where he follows the views of scholars concerning the reception from the time of Winckelmann to the present day. See also Pemberton 1989, 45-50. For comparable representations of receptions see Clairmont 1993, III, 143-144, pl. 3321; Hamiaux 1996, 196, Ma 793, 193; Scholl 1996, 131, pl. 25; Conze 1893, I, pl. LXXXIV.

T.K.

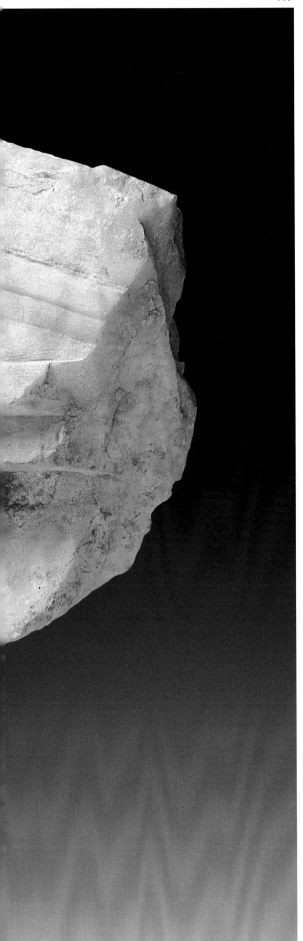

447 MARBLE RELIEF PEDIMENTAL STELE
350-325 B.C.

INV. NO. M 4521.
H. 0.29, W. 0.45, W. OF JAMBS 0.06, RELIEF PROJECTION 0.043,
DEPTH OF FIELD 0.026, H. OF LETTERS 0.01-0.02 M.

Pentelic marble. The upper part of the stele is preserved almost complete. The field is worked with a rasp, while the back is roughly worked with a pick.

The pediment is not free but incorporated in the triangular ending of the stele. It is rendered with a relief cornice and anthemion akroteria and is supported on relief jambs with an intermediate epistyle. A deep blue paint, flaking in places, covers the background of the relief field. Of the representation, only the head of a young girl is preserved, which is depicted in three-quarter view and has a slight inclination down and to the right. The hair, roughly worked, is rendered with many details. A garland with a triangular ending decorates the upper part of the forehead, while the face is smooth, carefully worked in its details and expression.

On the epistyle is carved the name of the dead girl with scattered lettering: IEP[Ω]. Only part of the last letter (Ω) is preserved.

COMMENTARY - BIBLIOGRAPHY: Unpublished.

For the architectural form of the stele there are a good number of parallels; see Hamiaux 1996, 157. The strong colour in the background of the representation is also found elsewhere; see Σαατσόγλου-Παλιαδέλη 1984, 97-98 and 180-182; Ανδρόνικος 1994, 126-128; Richter 1944, 321-333. For other figures which are related in manner of depiction see Diepolder 1965, 42, 37; Conze 1900, 42, fig. 880. On the garland see Krug 1968, type Ala; Σίνδος 1985, 78, no. 111.

The name Ιερώ does not help to identify the figure depicted with other known figures; see Osborne - Byrne 1994, 233.

T.K.

448 MARBLE HEAD OF A KORE
2nd-1st c. B.C.

INV. NO. M 3711.
TOTAL H. 0.064, H. OF HEAD 0.055 M.

White, fine-grained island marble. The hair, right side of the face and neck are chipped. Oval face with tall forehead. The mouth is very small and the nose is thin. Under the eyebrows in the shape of a wide arch, the large eyes project; the right is unworked. The execution of the hair is half finished. Combed upwards in gentle waves into an unworked bun, in front of which runs a shallow groove. There is a fold on the neck.

COMMENTARY - BIBLIOGRAPHY: Unpublished.

In sculpture, hair of this type usually characterises Aphrodite (Fuchs 1963, no. 44, pl. 54), as does the horizontal fold on the neck which should not be seen as a sign of age but of beauty.

P.Z.

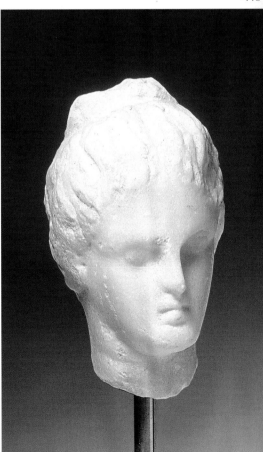

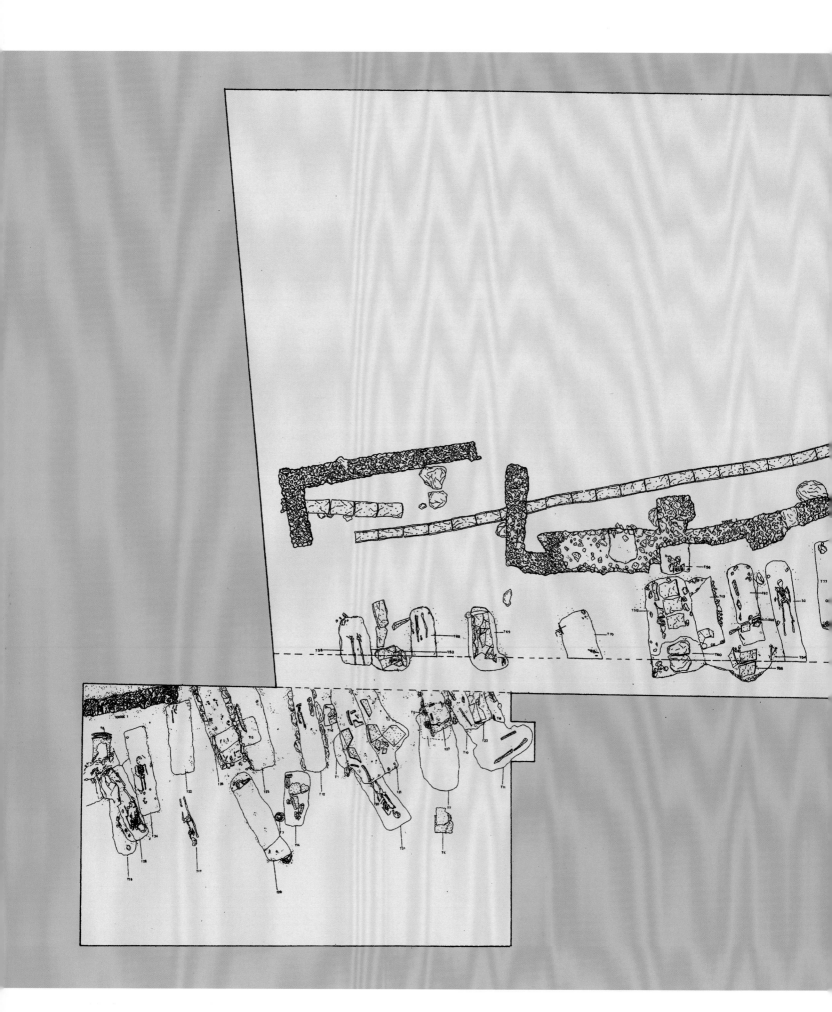

IAKHOU Shaft

An exploratory excavation was carried out on the 360 sq.m. site of the IAKHOU Shaft which lies alongside the verge of the Iera Odos close to its junction with Pireos Street. An enclosure wall running more or less in an E-W direction, forty-nine graves, two conduits and a foundation composed of river pebbles post-dating the other finds were brought to light.

A wall 15 m. in length and 0.50-0.80 m. in width and extending in both directions was found at a depth of 1.30 m. below the surface of the present-day road. It encloses a roadside cemetery that developed beside the southern edge of the ancient Sacred Way which passes a few metres north of the excavation site.

The Sacred Way is known to have started from the Sacred Gate, and thence to have proceeded to Kerameikos and finally to have reached Eleusis[1]. Various monuments, graves and shrines flanked it throughout its length. It is known also that following the building of the Themistoclean walls an old law was enforced that did not allow the establishment of cemeteries in residential districts. In consequence the most suitable sites for the development of the vast cemeteries were considered to be the strips of land beside roadways which, according to the sources, were bordered by imposing private and public tomb monuments (Paus. I, 29, 1). In addition, this position was chosen for practical reasons. For one thing the monuments would be visible to all and for another they would be easily accessible. Contrary, however, to all expectations and to travellers' accounts that imposing tomb monuments would be found on the verges of the Sacred Way immediately after its starting-point, in the sector closest to Kerameikos, only simple graves were discovered with offerings of vases characteristic of similar graves of the time[2].

This was precisely the picture presented by the excavation of the IAKHOU shaft. Constructed of medium-size rough stones bonded with earth, the enclosure wall has small buttresses built against its exterior. Judging by the pottery and small columns immured in it, the wall dates to the Roman occupation. Forty-nine graves were excavated within it, of which 22 were covered with flat tiles and 6 with pitched tiles, 8 were cist graves, 7 pit burials, 1 burial in a re-used terracotta beehive, 1 a pot burial and 4 were destroyed to the point of being unrecognisable. Most of them had a N-S alignment and had been violated and robbed by subsequent intrusions attested to by the discovery of the foundations of more recent structures which existed prior to the widening of the road. The only graves that can be dated with certitude are the shaft graves whose offerings are of Roman date. In constructing some of these fragments of grave stelai or complete stelai were re-used (see no. 450). Among the more representative forms of vases found in a fragmentary state in the fills and the graves are lekythoi, Megarian skyphoi, small tablets, perfume flasks and Hellenistic and Roman household pottery as well as sherds of Byzantine date. A variety of marble fragments, small grave columns and grave stelai were also recovered. Prominent among the marble finds is an inscribed 3rd c. B.C. stele recording an honorific decree issued by a religious association honouring the overseer of a sanctuary belonging to a Benevolent Goddess. Clearly it comes from a sanctuary in the immediate vicinity, most probably from the Sanctuary of Ariste and Kalliste[3].

Before the exploratory excavation of the site of the IAKHOU shaft was made, a sector of a burial enclosure and thirty graves were discovered where work similarly connected with the shaft was in progress on the north pavement of the Iera Odos at the level of premises no. 38 and over an area of about 120 sq.m. The enclosure is the continuation of the one at the IAKHOU shaft already mentioned; it contained thirty graves of various types: 3 covered with pitched tiles and 15 with flat tiles, 9 pit burials and 3 pan burials which date mainly to the Roman age. The excavation of this site ceased before it was completed for technical reasons that concerned the M.R.A. Nonetheless the graves have been conserved under a covering of earth with a view to their excavation being resumed at a future time and to a greater depth. Since the KERAMEIKOS Station was abandoned in order to preserve and protect the Kerameikos archaeological site and was re-located further to the south, there was no need for the IAKHOU Shaft which was to have been an adjunct of this particular Station. Consequently it is not considered essential to continue the investigation, at least not in the form of a rescue dig.

IOANNA TSIRIGOTI-DRAKOTOU

2. IAKHOU Shaft. Grave stele no. 450 upon discovery.

3. IAKHOU Shaft. Part of the cemetery.

2

NOTES

1. On the course of the Sacred Way see Τσιριγώτη-Δρακωτού 1987, 24-27; *eadem* 1992, 28-32; *eadem* 1999.

2. See Πλάτωνος - Χατζηπούλιου 1984, 11-14.

3. These are two early local deities, later assimilated to Artemis (Paus. I, 29, 2). See Τσιριγώτη-Δρακωτού 1996.

449 BRONZE MIRROR
425-400 B.C.

INV. NO. Δ 7161.
D. 0.16, H. (INCL. HANDLE) 0.245, D. OF LOOP 0.027-0.031,
TH. OF LOOP 0.05 M.

Bronze, with heavy oxidisation and dark green patina. The original golden-brown surface is preserved in places.

The disc of the mirror has a low perimeter lip on one side. The same surface is decorated with slightly raised surfaces of the edge of a circle, double or triple, which divide the disc into three zones of almost equal width. At the centre, there is a relief, spherical swelling with a depression. The handle is attached to the edge of the disc, which is in the form of a flower calyx, out of which sprouts a heart-shaped ivy leaf decorated with shallow engraving on its edge. The elongated end of the calyx – nearly square in section – probably fitted into a strong wooden or bone stem. Directly opposite the calyx handle, a smaller ivy leaf with similar engraved decoration is attached, of which the strap ending is bent over to hold an elliptical suspension loop. The back of the disc is very smooth, at least where the original surface is preserved.

COMMENTARY - BIBLIOGRAPHY: Unpublished.
Cf. Oberländer 1967, nos. 199-236; Boulter 1963, 119, pl. 37.B12 (= Oberländer 1967, no. 234; mirror from a burial in Lenorman Street; about 460-450 B.C.); *SCE* II, 331, no. 23 and *SCE* IV₂, 145, fig. 25, 2 and 5 (= Oberländer 1967, no. 202; from Marion, Cyprus, with concentric circles and suspension loop and handle in the shape of ivy); *Kerameikos* XIV, 36, no. 24.15, pl. 34.5 (2nd quarter of 4th c. B.C.); *Olynthus* X, 172, no. 516, pl. 31 (with concentric circles; early 4th c. B.C.); *Corinth* XII, 182, no. 1308, pl. 81 (5th-4th c. B.C.).

N.S.

449

450 MARBLE GRAVE PEDIMENTAL STELE OF ELEKTRA
End of 2nd c. A.D.

INV. NO. Λ 5774.
H. 1.30, W. 0.51, TH. 0.099 M.

Pentelic marble. Complete; recomposed from two fragments. It has small chips in places, especially on the lowest part. The front surface is worked using a rasp and flat chisel, while the back and the insertion strut are roughly worked using a pointed tool. Left and right, on each upper side, there is a socket with an iron nail sunk in lead.

The stele is slender, narrowing slightly towards the top. On the lower part of the stele inside an arched opening supported by jambs, the relief representation is rendered. A standing female figure en face occupies the centre, wearing a chiton and multi-folded himation, with her weight on the left leg, the right one relaxed and bent at the knee. On her left is a small female figure in low relief wearing a long, sleeved chiton. She turns to the central figure holding her left arm below her breast while the right one is probably placed on an object (incense burner?).

Left and right of the arched opening, two

450

longs to a later use of the stele reads: ΑΡΣΙΝΟΗ ΕΡΜΟΚΡΑΤΟΥ ΕΚ ΠΗΛΗΚΩΝ. The stele is crowned with a pediment and akroteria. In the middle of the tympanum, a relief acanthus is depicted with a light stalk which ends in an open flower

COMMENTARY - BIBLIOGRAPHY: Unpublished.

For the type of stele with an apsidal niche see Mühsam 1953, 70-103 and Couilloud 1974 (with earlier bibliography). It belongs to the architectural type 3, drawing 7 of Von Moock 1998. The standing female figure belongs to the so-called "Maiden of Herculaneum" type, which is very widespread from the 1st c. B.C. until late antiquity. The main study on the "Matron" and "Maiden" of Herculaneum types is Bieber 1977. For comparable representations see Von Moock 1998, 109, no. 134, pl. 17a, c, d, 133, no. 259, pl. 38d, 39a-b. For the hair-style, which is common and well known, see Von Moock 1998, 36-38. The poppy flower indicates early death; see Von Moock 1998, 78, n. 935. For the incense burner see Firatli 1964, 33 and Dentzer 1982, 324, 524-525, n. 825.

For the name of dead Elektra see Bechtel 1917, 578; for the name of her father Epagathos see Osborne - Byrne 1994, 143-144. The place of origin of dead Electra was the deme of Alopeke, which belonged to the Antiochid tribe and is identified with the present-day suburb of Daphne; see Traill 1975. The position and the careless writing of the second inscription confirm to the reuse of the stele in a later period. For the name Arsinoe in Attica see Osborne - Byrne 1994, 65 and Bechtel 1917, 578. For the name Hermokrates see Osborne - Byrne 1994, 159. The deme of Pelekoi was near present-day Chasia; see Traill 1975, 47.

T.K.

451 THREE BONE PINS
1st-2nd c. A.D.

INV. NO. Δ 7170A-Γ.
A. L. 0.14, MAX. D. 0.005 M.
B. L. 0.12, MAX. D. 0.006 M.
Γ. L. 0.142, MAX. D. 0.004, D. OF HEAD 0.005 M.

The pointed end of pin (α) is chipped. At the top are traces of a lengthways hole, in which remains of a bone peg can be seen, perhaps part of a decorative sphere.
Of pin (β) only a discoid base carved all round is preserved, which formed part of the decorative sphere that topped it.
Pin (γ) is complete, with the decorative sphere slightly damaged.
The first two belong to the same type with a larger diameter on the upper part immediately below the decorative sphere, while the third becomes thicker at two thirds of its length and tapers below the decorative sphere.

COMMENTARY - BIBLIOGRAPHY: Unpublished.

See *Corinth* XII, 282-285, nos. 2291-2339, pl. 118-119 (Hellenistic period and later); *Délos* XVIII, 277-279, no. 725, pl. 85; Πωλογιώργη 1998, 38, pl. 9γ (2nd c. A.D.).

N.S.

closed poppy flowers are rendered in low relief. On the broad surfaces immediately above the apse, there are two rosettes left and right, while two inscriptions occupy the rest of the surface, which belong to different chronological phases.
The first, which is the earliest, reads as follows: ΗΛΕΚΤΡΑ ΕΠΑΓΑΘΟΥ ΑΛΩΠΕ-ΚΗΘΕΝ ΧΑΙΡΕ. The second which be-

451

452 MARBLE MEMORIAL STELE
420-400 B.C.

INV. NO. M 4551.
H. 2.10, W. 0.82-0.89, TH. 0.255-0.268 M.

452

Inscribed stele of excellent-quality Pentelic marble, with lists of names of Athenian cavalry who fell in battles of the Peloponnesian War. The upper part is decorated with a relief representation of a battle scene of a horseman with foot-soldiers. At the top, a rectangular dowel hole (0.135 × 0.08 × 0.08 m.), for inserting the pedimental capping, and below, a rectangular plug (0.09 × 0.285 × 0.15 m.), broken at one end, which was for fixing the stele onto its base. It is very well preserved with some damage, chipping and flaking, chiefly on the sides, the moulding and the representation where the figures of the standing foot-soldier and the horseman have particularly suffered, whilst the inscribed section has remained virtually untouched and the decipherment is unhampered. The front surface of the stele has been polished with crystalline sand, the back is coarsely worked with a thick point, and on the sides, which have been polished with a flat implement, the marks of a claw chisel can be distinguished as well as over the whole background of the representation.

The upper part is separated from the rest of the stele by a moulding (h. 0.09 m.), which is continued onto the narrow sides. It "supports" a relief representation with the battle scene of a horseman against two foot-soldiers, one of whom is already wounded and has fallen to the ground. The landscape is indicated by the rocky elevations on the ground where the figures are in action, as well as by the rock on the far right, from which the horse of another rider is emerging moving at a gallop with half-open mouth, thus showing the continuity of action. The rearing horse takes centre stage with its two front legs ready to trample the wounded man, who, half lying down, supports himself with his right elbow on a low rock trying to protect himself both from the horse and its rider. The Athenian horseman, with a broad-brimmed hat (petasos), is sitting on his himation, which can be distinguished on top of the horse's back, holding the reins in his left hand and a spear in his raised right, which is being readied to spear his fallen opponent. The left part of the scene is taken up by the figure of the attacking hoplite with his Boeotian hat. Legs wide apart, he stands his ground with his right leg stretched out and he, also, balances himself on the low rock on which his fallen comrade leans whom he wants to protect. He is naked and bare-foot, and, between his body and left arm holding a shield. His cloak, twisted around, is indicated in relief. The part blowing above his back and right shoulder was painted, as grooves on the surface of the marble indicate. Certainly colour played a major role in the representation, and the spear of the rider was also painted, whilst the weapons held in the right hands of both foot-soldiers were of metal, as indicated by the perforations for securing them.

0.47 m. below the moulding, the first inscription is engraved in 21 lines in the pre-Euclid script with letters characteristic of the last quarter of the 5th c. B.C. The letters are 0.012 to 0.015 m. high, and the line spacing is 0.019 to 0.02 m. The names of nineteen Athenian cavalry are listed and a mounted archer, a "hippotoxotes" is mentioned below. These fell, as we are informed by two lines which precede the list, in the battles of Tanagra and Spartolos in Chalkidiki, both in the first decade of the Peloponnesian War. The names are arranged in lines in two columns divided according to the tribal system of Classical Athens (ten tribes in all). The second, eleven-line long inscription was engraved later in the area between the moulding and the first inscription, in the Ionic script with letters 0.016 to 0.019 m. high, likewise in lines but more carelessly inscribed, in uneven line spacings. This is a list of names in two columns of a further twelve fallen Athenian cavalry from five tribes; the eight men from the Oineid tribe are listed below their tribe name – which has been engraved in the middle with slightly larger letters 0.022 to 0.024 m. high – in two columns of five and three names respectively, whilst in the remaining space, the names of four more men divided according to their tribes are in-

scribed, continuing on in lines but with close line-spacing. The text above is probably linked to these, a four-lined inscription in an elegiac couplet, which praises the distinguished bravery of the cavalry who fought against the foot-soldiers, Ἀλκάθοο παρὰ τείχεσιν, that is in a battle at Megara. The elegy is the last item to have been inscribed on the stele, immediately beneath the moulding, and a little obliquely towards the top, with letters likewise of the Ionic script, small in size up to 0.012 m., without always strictly observing the line arrangement, and with small line-spacing of 0.005 m. due to the cramped area.

COMMENTARY - BIBLIOGRAPHY: Unpublished (forth. in the *Πεπραγμένα της Α΄ Επιστημονικής Ημερίδος της Γ΄ Εφορείας, 1996).*

The stele, a memorial from the Demosion Sema, was found in 1995 in the excavation for the PALAIOLOGOU Shaft, in the region of the Larissa Railway Station, in secondary use, as it had most probably been used as a cover for a marble sarcophagus, the remains of which were found there together with other destroyed tombs and an inscribed funerary column of advanced Hellenistic date (Παρλαμά 1990-91, 536). The proximity of the find spot of this important testimony of Athenian history to the ancient road to the Hippios Kolonos, and the discovery in 1948 in the same area by the Larissa Station of the large well-known relief with the representation of a horse (NM, no. 4464; Schuchardt

1978, 75-99, pl. 41-49) allows further inquiry into the subject of the monuments of the Demosion Sema and their relationship to this famous road. The stele from the PALAIOLOGOU Shaft must have been set up around 420 B.C. with the relief and the first inscription in the pre-Euclid script, where the dead cavalrymen of the battles of Tanagra and Spartolos are commemorated. The representation portrays the sacrifice of the chosen few of the Athenian cavalry corps, reproducing the theme of the conflict of the horseman with two foot-soldiers, of whom one, already wounded and half fallen or stretched out on the ground, tries to protect himself, while the other shields him while attacking the enemy, attempting to knock the adversary off his mount. The place where the scene is played out, part of the landscape of the battle, is forcefully indicated by the high rock to the right of which emerges the head

foot-soldier grasping his shield, the preserved figures of the rider and the half-reclining foot-soldier are depicted precisely as on the stele no. 452. The same subject of rider with two foot-soldiers is also presented on the relief of another fine memorial from the Demosion Sema, NM, no. 2744, from the beginning of the 4th c. B.C., listing Athenian cavalry who fell at Corinth and Boeotia (Travlos 1988, fig. 422).

The first inscription of the stele no. 452, contemporary with the engraving of the relief, was cut at a considerably large distance, 0.47 m. below the moulding. This shows that, either the space was deliberately left vacant to accommodate a new inscription soon afterwards, a common practice on monuments of this kind (Κριτζάς 1989, 172-173 and n. 14), or it initially bore painted decoration (a wreath trimmed with ribbons?) which was removed when the second inscription in

line-spacing from the last name of cavalry, only the ending ON is preserved, because this is where the greatest damage to the surface of the slab has been noted. The men mentioned in tribal order are three from the Erectheid, two from the Aigeid, three from the Pandionid, two from the Leontid and two from the Akamantid in the left hand column of the list, and in the right, one from the Oineid, two from the Kekropid, one from the Hippothontid, one from the Aiantid and two from the Antiochid. The cutting of the letters is very careful as also is the justification, apart from one example, probably a mistake on the part of the engraver; also the length of the word ΗΙΠΠΟΘΟΝΤΙΔΟΣ forces it to be shifted with the starting letter outside, without affecting the justification of the rest. Quite separate from the justification is the title and name of the mounted archer. Of the two battles commemorated, the battle of

452

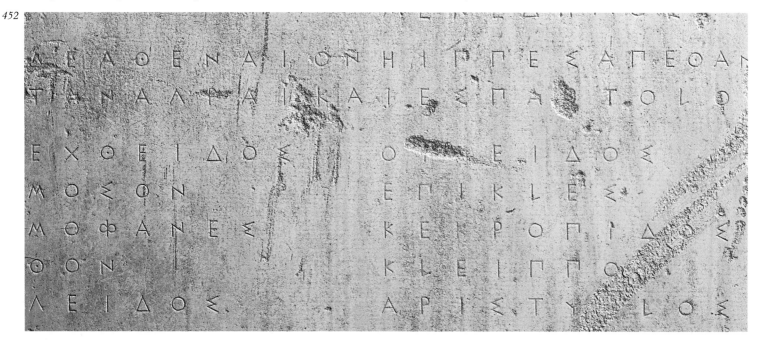

and front legs of the second horse, and by the rocky elevation of the ground where the fallen warrior is propped up and the fighting foot-soldier stands. The Athenian rider dominates the centre where he is always depicted as victor in these representations. The closest parallels for the scene on the stele of the PALAIOLOGOU Shaft are to be found in a corresponding group from the frieze of the temple of Athena Nike on the Acropolis (Ridgway 1981, 93, fig. 56 and 57) which is dated to the same period. A further, and more pertinent comparison may be made with the figures of the upper zone of the slightly later relief of Pythodorus (Eleusis Museum, no. 5101; op.cit., also with regard to the "landscape reliefs", 135, 156, fig. 99. Cf. Andrewes - Lewis 1957, 177-180 and Hölscher 1973, 99-101). On the latter, which is broken on both sides, preserving the second horse and only the left arm of the fighting

the Ionic script was inscribed. It is easy to distinguish the part of this re-used surface (0.35 x 0.65 m.), which is rather coarse and is obviously surrounded by a frame of polished marble surface. The names and the elegiac couplet of this second inscription are not confined only to the prepared area, but occupy the whole extent of the available space. The nineteen names of cavalry in the first list, which are inscribed in two columns below the two-lined epigraph ΗΟΙΔΕ ΑΘΕΝΑΙΟΝ ΗΙΠΠΕΣ ΑΠΕΘΑΝΟ(Ν) / ΕΝ ΤΑΝΑΓΡΑΙ ΚΑΙ Ε ΣΠΑΡΤΟΛΟ(Ι) ("These Athenian cavalry men died at Tanagra and Spartolos") are known in Attic prosopography (Kirchner 1901-1903 and Osborne - Byrne 1994, II) and are immediately recognisable, as only the first letter in four of them is missing. From the name of the mounted archer which is inscribed separately beneath the left column of the list and at a greater distance than one

Spartolos is easy to identify since there was only one at Spartolos in Chalchidiki, that of 429/8 (Thuc. II, 79, Diod. XII, 47.3, cf. CAH V, 399) where the Athenians, with 2,000 hoplites and 200 cavalry, suffered a dreadful defeat. The battle of Tanagra is most probably that of 426 (Thuc. III, 91 and Diod. XII, 65. 1-5), a victorious battle for the Athenians, which has been described as a "prelude" to that of 424 at Delion "in Tanagra" (Thuc. IV, 76.4). In this latter battle, the Athenians and the cavalry corps in the hilly expanse where the enemy had been marshalled, suffered a terrible defeat once more with nearly 1,000 slain, amongst which the fallen cavalry would probably have been more than the nineteen which are referred to along with those of Spartolos on the stele. Certainly, however, not even the battle of Delion can be ruled out, which happened in Tanagran territory, a battle in which the presence of Athenian cavalry is clearly attested (Thuc. IV, 94) whilst this is not the case with the battle of 426 BC. Pausanias, on the other hand, in his discussion of the Demosion Sema mentions: "those who fell at Delion on the land of Tanagra were also buried here..." (I, 29, 13); it is, however, known that the Albani relief (dated to 430-425 B.C.) has been connected with the commemoration of the battle of Delion. The relief is a representation of a rider fighting against a foot-soldier and has been considered as the first of a series where this subject is depicted (Ridgway 1981, 144-145, fig. 104).

The second inscription on the upper part of the inscribed surface of the stele was engraved in the Ionic script. It lists the names of twelve more Athenian cavalry from five tribes, in two columns, and the four-lined elegy. The names and tribe names are also inscribed in lines, and with an attempt to maintain a correspondence with the first inscription. However, the engraving is more careless, marked by a general lack of order; this is because the stele was standing in a vertical position while being engraved, and the fact that the new inscription was added in two successive stages, even though within a short period of time. It is obviously the work of the same cutter, and very probably the same who engraved the elegy in which, since the space was limited, the letters are smaller and closer together. There is internal justification, but all in all it is not in keeping with the rest. The list commemorates eight men from the Oineid tribe who were probably inscribed first in two columns, and four more who were inserted a little later: the Erectheids left, below the five of the Oineid, the Aigeid, the Pandionid and the Kekropid tribes in the right column. The names in this later engraving, which are likewise common in Attic prosopography, are crammed, the line-spaces narrow and the justification not always regular, as the space was limited and the engraver wanted to emphasise the names of the clans to which the dead belonged by using slightly bigger letters, and at the same time to leave a small space between them and the older inscription. The battle in which these men fell is indirectly indicated by the four-lined stanza above, which adds yet another brilliant elegy to the series of funerary epigrams. The poem, with the awe-inspiring image of Ares whom the Athenian cavalry dared to confront fighting by the walls of Alkathos, "... οἱ δ' ἀρετῆς ἐθέλοντες ἔχεν λόγον ἔξοχον", is a work by a great poet, and might be attributed to Euripides. We believe that the reference to the walls of the Megarian acropolis of Alkathos, the founding hero of the city, does not leave any doubt that we are dealing with a battle in the region of Megara, one of a series of great conflicts between the two cities during the Peloponnesian War. The specific battle should not be sought amongst those of the Archidameian War (431-421 B.C.), when the Athenians invaded every year the Megaris region, with cavalry and their entire army, until Nisaia finally submitted to the Athenians (Thuc. II, 31,3), since then, the fallen men must have been honoured together with those of the first inscription, since, the yearly Athenian campaigns were suspended after the capture of Nisaia in 426 B.C. We believe that we are dealing with the conflict of 409/8 B.C. when, on the pretext of retaking Nisaia from the Megarians, the Athenians dispatched a force of 1,000 foot-soldiers and 400 cavalry. After a valiant fight, the Athenians managed to overpower their adversaries, even though they were far more numerous (Diod. XIII, 65.1-2). This was an important victory, since it was achieved against an army superior in numbers, formed by the combined forces of Megara and Sparta. It is very likely that this battle should be identified with the place of sacrifice of the twelve men listed in the second inscription of the stele, whose bravery and daring is honoured in the elegy; this is further supported by the use of the Ionic script, which was certainly in use in the years 409/8 – its usage is in fact known earlier on private monuments – and its establishment in 403 was nothing more than the sanctioning of its use. Finally, mention should be made here of stele no. 118 of the Megara Collection, a public monument with a list of fallen, also dated to the last quarter of the 5th c. B.C., which has also been linked with the battle of 409/8 BC (Κριτζάς 1989, 166ff. and esp. 175).

L.P.

CHRONOLOGICAL CHART

PERIOD	DATES
Early Helladic	3600-2050 B.C.
Middle Helladic	2050-1600 B.C.
Late Helladic	1600-1065 B.C.
Sub-Mycenaean	1065-1015 B.C.
Proto-Geometric	1000-900 B.C.
Early Geometric	900-850 B.C.
Middle Geometric	850-770 B.C.
Late Geometric	770-700 B.C.
Proto-Corinthian	700-600 B.C.
Archaic period	700-480 B.C.
Classical period	480-323 B.C.
Hellenistic period	323-31 B.C.
Roman period	31 B.C.-A.D. 312
Late Roman period (west)	4th-6th c. A.D.
Early Christian period (east)	4th-6th c. A.D.
Byzantine period	6th-15th c. A.D.

ABBREVIATIONS

ANCIENT AUTHORS

Arist.	Aristotle
Aristoph.	Aristophanes
Ath.	Athenaios
Diod.	Diodorus
Harp.	Harpokration
Lyc.	Lycurgus
Paus.	Pausanias
Pl.	Plato
Plut.	Plutarch
Poll.	Pollux
Thuc.	Thucydides

CHRONOLOGICAL PERIODS

c.	century
EH	Early Helladic
LG	Late Geometric
LH	Late Helladic
MG	Middle Geometric
MH	Middle Helladic
PC	Proto-Corinthian
PG	Proto-Geometric
SubM	Sub-Mycenaean

DIMENSIONS

b.d.	base diameter
cm.	centimetre(s)
d.	diameter
dim.	dimensions
excl.	excluding
ext.	external
gr.	gram(s)
h.	height
ha.	hectares
incl.	including
int.	internal
l.	length
lb.(s)	pound(s)
m.	metre(s)
max.	maximum
m.d.	mouth diameter
min.	minimum
pres.	preserved
sq.m.	square metre(s)
th.	thickness
w.	width
wt.	weight

VARIOUS

A.D.	*anno domini*
B.C.	before Christ
c.	*circa*
cat. no.(s.)	catalogue number(s)
cf.	confer
col.	column
ed.(s.)	editor(s)
esp.	especially
et al.	*et alii*
etc.	*et cetera*
ff.	folios, following
fig.	figure
forth.	forthcoming
inv.	inventory
1./11.	line(s)
M.R.A.	Metropolitan Railway of Athens
n.	note
n.p.d.	no publication date
NM	National Museum, Athens
no.(s.)	number(s)
obv.	obverse
op.cit.	*opus citatum*
P.	Painter
p.	page
par.	paragraph
pl.	plate
rev.	reverse
s.v.	*sub verbo*
to l.	to the left
to r.	to the right

ABBREVIATIONS OF JOURNALS AND SERIES OF PUBLICATIONS

AA   *Archäologischer Anzeiger*

AAA   *Athens Annals of Archaeology*

AArch   *Acta Archaeologica*

ADelt   *Αρχαιολογικόν Δελτίον*

AEphem   *Αρχαιολογική Εφημερίς*

AErgoMak   *Το Αρχαιολογικό Έργο στη Μακεδονία και Θράκη*

AJA   *American Journal of Archaeology*

AM   *Mitteilungen des Deutschen Archäologischen Instituts. Athenische Abteilung*

AnnStorAnt   *Annali del Seminario di studi del mondo classico, Sezione di archeologia e storia antica, Napoli*

AntK   *Antike Kunst*

AntPl   *Antike Plastik*

ASAtene   *Annuario della Scuola Archeologica di Atene e delle Missioni italiane in Oriente*

BABesch   *Bulletin Antieke Beschaving*

BAR   *British Archaeological Reports*

BCH   *Bulletin de Correspondance Hellénique*

BerlWPr   *Berliner Winckelmanns Programm*

BICS   *Bulletin of the Institute of Classical Studies*

BMusHongr   *Bulletin du Musée hongrois des beaux-arts*

Boreas   *Münstersche Beiträge zur Archäologie*

BSA   *Annual of the British School at Athens*

CAH   *Cambridge Ancient History*

ClQ   *Classical Quarterly*

ClRh   *Clara Rhodos*

CVA   *Corpus Vasorum Antiquorum*

DeltChrA-Etair   *Δελτίον της Χριστιανικής Αρχαιολογικής Εταιρείας*

Διαχρονία   *Περιοδική έκδοση του Συλλόγου Μεταπτυχιακών Φοιτητών Ιστορίας-Αρχαιολογίας Εθνικού και Καποδιστριακού Πανεπιστημίου Αθηνών*

EAA   *Enciclopedia dell'Arte Antica*

EAD   *Exploration Archéologique de Délos*

EpistEpet-Thess   *Επιστημονική Επετηρίδα της Φιλοσοφικής Σχολής του Αριστοτελείου Πανεπιστημίου Θεσσαλονίκης*

GettyJ   *The J. Paul Getty Museum Journal*

HefteABern   *Hefte des Archäologischen Seminars der Universität, Bern*

Hesperia   *Hesperia, Journal of the American School of Classical Studies at Athens*

Ηόρος   *Ηόρος: ένα αρχαιογνωστικό περιοδικό*

HSCPh   *Harvard Studies in Classical Philology*

IstMitt   *Mitteilungen des Deutschen Archäologischen Instituts. Istanbuler Abteilung*

JdI   *Jahrbuch des Deutschen Archäologischen Instituts*

JIAN   *Journal International d'Archéologie Numismatique*

JbKuSamml-BadWürt   *Jarbuch der Staatlichen Kunstsammlungen in Baden-Württemberg*

JEA   *Journal of Egyptian Archaeology*

JGS   *Journal of Glass Studies*

JHS   *Journal of Hellenic Studies*

JRS   *Journal of Roman Studies*

Kerameus   *Forschungen zur Antiken Keramik. II. Reihe*

Kernos   *Revue internationale et pluridisciplinaire de religion grecque antique, Liège*

LIMC   *Lexicon Iconographicum Mythologiae Classicae*

MetrMusJ   *Metropolitan Museum Journal*

OF   *Olympische Forschungen*

ÖJh   *Jahreshefte des Österreichischen Archäologischen Instituts in Wien*

Prakt   *Πεπραγμένα της εν Αθήναις Αρχαιολογικής Εταιρείας*

RA   *Revue Archéologique*

RE   *Paulys Realencyklopädie der classischen Altertumswissenschaft*

RendLincei   *Atti dell'Accademia nazionale dei Lincei, Rendiconti*

SBHeidelberg   *Sitzungsberichte der Heidelberger Akademie der Wissenschaften, philosophisch-historische Klasse*

SEG   *Supplementum Epigraphicum Graecum*

SIMA   *Studies in Mediterranean Archaeology*

SNG   *Sylloge Nummorum Graecorum*

ZPE   *Zeitschrift für Papyrologie und Epigraphik*

ABBREVIATIONS - BIBLIOGRAPHY

ABV: Beazley J.D., *Attic Black-Figure Vase-Painters*, Oxford 1956

ABL: Haspels E., *Attic Black-Figured Lekythoi*, Paris 1936

Addenda²: Carpenter T.H., *Beazley Addenda, Additional References to ABV, ARV² & Paralipomena*, Oxford 1989²

AGDS II: *Antike Gemmen in Deutschen Sammlungen*, II. Staatliche Museen Preußischer Kulturbesitz Antikenabteilung, Berlin (ed. E. Zwierlein-Diehl), 1969

AGDS III: *Antike Gemmen in Deutschen Sammlungen* III. Braunschweig, Göttingen, Kasel (ed. P. Zazoff), 1970

AGDS IV: *Antike Gemmen in Deutschen Sammlungen* IV. Hannover, Kestner-Museum. Hamburg, Museum für Kunst und Gewerbe (ed. P. Zazoff), 1975

AGDS Nürnberg: *Antike Gemmen in Deutschen Sammlungen*. Die antiken Gemmen der Sammlung Friedrich Julius Rudolf Bergau im Germanischen Nationalmuseum, Nürnberg (ed. C. Weiß), 1996

Agora I: Harrison E., *The Athenian Agora*, I. *Portrait Sculpture*, Princeton 1953

Agora IV: Howland R.H., *The Athenian Agora*, IV. *Greek Lamps and their Survivals*, Princeton 1958

Agora V: Robinson H.S., *The Athenian Agora*, V. *Pottery of the Roman Period*, Princeton 1959

Agora VI: Grandjouan C., *The Athenian Agora*, VI. *Terracottas and Plastic Lamps of the Roman Period*, Princeton 1961

Agora VII: Perlzweig J., *The Athenian Agora*, VII. *Lamps of the Roman Period*, Princeton 1961

Agora VIII: Brann E., *The Athenian Agora*, VIII. *Late Geometric and Protoattic Pottery, Mid 8th to Late 7th Century B.C.*, Princeton 1962

Agora X: Lang M. - Crosby M., *The Athenian Agora*, X. *Weights, Measures and Tokens*, Princeton 1964

Agora XI: Harrison E., *The Athenian Agora*, XI. *Archaic and Archaistic Sculpture*, Princeton 1965

Agora XII: Sparkes B.A. - Talcott L., *The Athenian Agora*, XII. *Black and Plain Pottery of the 6th, 5th and 4th Centuries B.C.*, Princeton 1970

Agora XIX: Lalonde G.V. - Langdon G.V. - Walbank M.B., *The Athenian Agora*, XIX. *Inscriptions - Horoi - Poletai Records - Leases of Public Lands*, Princeton 1991

Agora XXII: Rotroff S.I., *The Athenian Agora*, XXII. *Hellenistic Pottery: Athenian and Imported Moldmade Bowls*, Princeton 1982

Agora XXIII: Moore M.B. - Philippides M.Z.P., *The Athenian Agora*, XXIII. *Attic Black-Figured Pottery*, Princeton 1986

Agora XXVI: Kroll J.H., *The Athenian Agora*, XXVI. *The Greek Coins*, Princeton 1993

Agora XXVIII: Boegenhold A.L. *et al.*, *The Athenian Agora*, XXVIII. *The Lawcourts at Athens. Sites, Buildings, Equipment, Procedure and Testimonia*, Princeton 1995

Agora XXIX: Rotroff S.I., *The Athenian Agora*, XXIX. *Athenian and Imported Wheelmade Table Ware and Related Material*, Princeton 1997

Agora XXX: Moore M.B., *The Athenian Agora*, XXX. *Attic Red-Figured and White Ground Pottery*, Princeton 1997

Agora XXXI: Miles M.M., *The Athenian Agora*, XXXI. *The City Eleusinion*, Princeton 1998

Αηδόνια 1996: *Ο Θησαυρός των Αηδονιών*, Exhibition Catalogue, Athens 1996

ΑΚΑΜΑΤΗΣ 1993: Ακαμάτης Ι.Μ., *Πήλινες μήτρες αγγείων από την Πέλλα. Συμβολή στη μελέτη της ελληνιστικής κεραμικής*, Athens 1993

ΑΛΕΞΑΝΔΡΗ 1972: Αλεξανδρή Ο., Ζάππειον - Λεωφόρος Βασ. Όλγας (έργα Δήμου), *ADelt* 27 (1972) Chronika, 107

ΑΛΕΞΑΝΔΡΗ 1973: Αλεξανδρή Ο., Λεωφόρος Βασ. Κων/νου, οδός Δραγάτση, Κολοκοτρώνη και Βασ. Γεωργίου, *ADelt* 29 (1973-1974) Chronika, 146-149

ΑΛΕΞΑΝΔΡΗ 1976: Αλεξανδρή Ο., Οδός Αριστείδου 5, *ADelt* 31 (1976) Chronika, 27

ΑΛΕΞΑΝΔΡΗ 1989: Αλεξανδρή Ο. (ed.), *Το πνεύμα και το σώμα. Οι αθλητικοί αγώνες στην αρχαία Ελλάδα*, Exhibition Catalogue, 1989

ALPÖZEN - BERKAYA - ÖZDAS 1995: Alpözen T. - Berkaya B. - Özdas A., *Commercial Amphoras of the Bodrum Museum of Underwater Archaeology*, Bodrum 1995

Alt-Ägina II.1: Smetana-Scherrer R., *Spätklassische und hellenistische Keramik, Alt-Ägina*, II.1, Mainz am Rhein 1982

AMANDRY 1984: Amandry P., Os et coquilles, *L'Antre corycien* II, *BCH* Suppl. IX, 1984, 347-380

AMOURETTI 1986: Amouretti M.C., *Le pain et l'huile dans la Grèce antique, Annales Littéraires de l'Université de Besançon* 328, Paris 1986

AMYX 1958: Amyx D., The Attic Stelai, III, *Hesperia* 27 (1958) 163-310

ANDERSON-STOJANOVIĆ 1987: Anderson-Stojanović V.R., The Chronology and Function of Ceramic Unguentaria, *AJA* 91 (1987) 105-122

ΑΝΔΡΕΙΩΜΕΝΟΥ 1977: Ανδρειωμένου Α., Νεκροταφείο της αρχαίας Ακραιφίας, *AAA* X (1977) 273-282

ANDREWES - LEWIS 1975: Andrewes A. - Lewis D.M., *JHS* 77 (1957) 177-180

ΑΝΔΡΟΝΙΚΟΣ 1955: Ανδρόνικος Μ., Ελληνιστικός τάφος Βέροιας, *AEphem* 1955, 22-50

ΑΝΔΡΟΝΙΚΟΣ 1994: Ανδρόνικος Μ., *Βεργίνα*, II, *Ο τάφος της Περσεφόνης*, 1994

ANGERMEIER 1936: Angermeier H.E., *Das Alabastron. Ein Beitrag zur Lekythen-Forschung*, Gießen 1936

Antikenmuseum 1988: *Antikenmuseum Berlin, Die Ausgestellten Werken*, Berlin 1988

APP 1995: Oakley J. (ed.), *Athenian Potters and Painters*. Catalogue of the Exhibit. December 1, 1994 - March 1, 1995, Gennadius Library, Athens 1995

APP 1997: Oakley J. - Coulson W.D.E. - Palagia O. (eds.), *Athenian Potters and Painters. The Conference Proceedings*, Oxford 1997

ARV²: Beazley J.D., *Attic Red-Figure Vase-Painters*, Oxford 1963²

Αρχαία Μακεδονία 1988: *Αρχαία Μακεδονία*. Exhibition Catalogue, 1988

Ashmolean Museum 1967: *Select Exhibition of Sir John and Lady Beazley's Gifts to the Ashmolean Museum 1912-1966*, London 1967

ATHUSAKI 1970: Athusaki K., Drei weissgrundige Lekythen, *AM* 85 (1970) 45-53

ΑΤΖΑΚΑ 1987: Ατζακά Π., *Βυζαντινά Μνημεία* 7, *Σύνταγμα των παλαιοχριστιανικών ψηφιδωτών της Ελλάδος, II. Στερεά Ελλάς και Πελοπόννησος*, Thessaloniki 1987

ΑΤΖΑΚΑ 1998: Ατζακά Π., *Βυζαντινά Μνημεία* 9, *Σύνταγμα των παλαιοχριστιανικών ψηφιδωτών της Θεσσαλονίκης*, III, Thessaloniki 1998

BAILEY 1975: Bailey D.M., *A Catalogue of the Lamps in the British Museum*, I. *Greek, Hellenistic and Early Roman Pottery Lamps*, London 1975

BAILEY 1988: Bailey D.M., *A Catalogue of the Lamps in the British Museum*, III. *Roman Provincial Lamps*, London 1988

BAIN 1991: Bain D., Six Greek Verbs of Sexual Congress, *ClQ* 41 (1991) 51-77

BAKALAKIS 1991: Bakalakis G., Les kernoi éleusiniens, *Kernos* 4 (1991) 105-117

ΒΑΛΑΒΑΝΗΣ 1991: Βαλαβάνης Π., *Παναθηναϊκοί αμφορείς από την Ερέτρια. Συμβολή στην αττική αγγειογραφία του 4ον αι. π.Χ.*, Athens 1991

BARR-SHARRAR - BORZA 1982: Barr-Sharrar B. - Borza E.V., *Symposium Series* I. *Macedonian Metal Vases in Perspective, National Gallery of Art, Washington*, Studies in the History of Art, 10, 1982

BASCH 1987: Basch L., *Le musée imaginaire de la Marine Antique*, 1987

BAUCHHENS 1973: Bauchhens Chr., Zwei Terrakotten aus Kleinasien, *AA* 1973, 1-13

BAUDAIN *et al.* 1994: Baudain C. - Liau B. - Long L., Une cargaison de bronze hellénistique, *Archaeonautica* 12 (1994) 61-87

BAŽANT 1975: Bažant S., Iconography of Choes Reconsidered, *Listy Filologické* 98 (1975) 72-78

BEAZLEY 1927/28: Beazley J.D., Aryballos, *BSA* 29 (1927/28) 193ff.

BEAZLEY 1932: Beazley J.D., Battle-Loutrophoros, *MetrMusJ* 23 (1932) 5-22

BEAZLEY 1939a: Beazley J.D., Excavations at Al Mina, Sueidia II, *JHS* 59 (1939)

BEAZLEY 1939b: Beazley J., Excavations at Al Mina, Sueidia III. The Red-Figured Vases, *JHS* 59 (1939) 1-44

BEAZLEY 1940-45: Beazley J., Miniature Panathenaics, *BSA* 41 (1940-45) 10-21

BECATTI 1965: Becatti G., La mosaïque gréco-romaine, in *Colloques internationaux du Centre National de la Recherche Scientifique*, Paris 1965, 112-118

BECATTI 1974: Becatti G., *Meidias*, 1974

BECHTEL 1917: Bechtel F., *Die historischen Personennamen des Griechischen bis zur Kaiserzeit*, 1917

BECK 1975: Beck A., *Album of Greek Education. The Greeks at School and Play*, Sydney 1975

BECKER 1977: Becker R.M., *Formen attischer Peliken*, 1977

BEMMANN 1994: Bemmann K., *Füllhörner in klassischer und hellenistischer Zeit*, 1994

BENNETT - ELTON 1898: Bennett R. - Elton J., *History of Corn Milling*, London 1898

BENSON 1970: Benson J.L., *Horse, Bird and Man. The Origins of Greek Painting*, Amherst 1970

BENTON 1953: Benton S., Further Excavations at Aetos, *BSA* 48 (1953) 255-368

ΒΕΡΣΑΚΗΣ 1912: Βερσάκης Φ., Μνημεία των νοτίων προπόδων της Ακροπόλεως, *AEphem* 1912, 173-182

BIAGIO-SIMONA 1991: Biagio-Simona S., *I vetri Romani provenienti della terra dell'Attuale Contone Ticino*, I, Locarno 1991

BIEBER 1961a: Bieber M., *The History of Greek and Roman Theatre*, Princeton 1961

BIEBER 1961b: Bieber M., *The Sculpture of the Hellenistic Age*, 1961

BIEBER 1977: Bieber M., *The Copies of Herculaneum Women*, 1977

BIERS 1999: Biers W., Plastic Seirenes from Corinth, *Hesperia* 68 (1999) 135-146

BLECH 1982: Blech M., *Studien zum Kranz bei den Griechen*, Berlin - New York 1982

BLISS - MCALISTER 1902: Bliss F.J. - McAlister R.A.S., *Excavations in Palestine 1898-1900*, London 1902

BLOESCH 1974: Bloesch H., *Das Tier in der Antike, 400 Werke ägyptischer, griechischer, etruskischer und römischer Kunst im privaten offentlichen Besitz. Ausstellung Archäologisches Institut der Universität Zürich 21.9-17.11.1974*

BLONDÉ 1983: Blondé F., *Greek Lamps of Thorikos*, Gent 1983

BMC I, II: Higgins R.A., *Catalogue of the Terracottas in the Department of Greek and Roman Antiquities, British Museum* I-II, London 1954-1959

BMC III: Poole R.S., *British Museum. A Catalogue of the Greek Coins*, III. *The Tauric Chersonese, Sarmatia, Dacia, Moesia, Thrace*, 1877

BNP I: Morrisson C., *Catalogue des monnaies byzantines de la Bibliothèque Nationale*, I. *D'Anastase Ier à Justinien II (491-711)*, Paris 1970

BOARDMAN 1974: Boardman J., *Athenian Black Figure Vases*, 1974

BOARDMAN 1978: Boardman J., *Athenian Black Figure Vases*, 1978²

BOARDMAN 1980: Boardman J., *Αθηναϊκά μελανόμορφα αγγεία* (Gr. tr.), Athens 1980

BOARDMAN 1985: Boardman J., *Athenian Red Figure Vases. The Classical Period*, 1985

BOARDMAN 1988: Boardman J., Sex Differentiation in Grave Vases, *AnnStorAnt* 10 (1988) 171-179

BOARDMAN 1990: Boardman J., Symposion Furniture, in *Sympotica, A Symposium on the Symposion*, Oxford 1990, 122-135

BOARDMAN 1993: Boardman J., *The Oxford History of Classical Art*, 1993

BÖTTGER 1992: Böttger B., Die kaiserzeitlichen und spätantiken Amphoren aus dem Kerameikos, *AM* 107 (1992) 315-381

BÖHLAU 1887: Böhlau J., Frühattischen Vasen, *JdI* 2 (1887) 33-66

BOHEN 1988: Bohen B., *Die geometrischen Pyxiden*, Berlin 1988

ΒΟΚΟΤΟΠΟΥΛΟΥ 1986: Βοκοτοπούλου Ι., *Βίτσα. Τα νεκροταφεία μιας μολοσσικής κώμης*, Athens 1986

BOL - KOTERA 1986: Bol P.C. - Kotera E., *Antike Bildwerke* III. *Bildwerke aus Terrakotta aus mykenischer bis römischer Zeit*, Frankfurt 1986

BORBOUDAKIS *et al.* 1983: Borboudakis M. - Gallas K. - Wessel K., *Byzantinisches Kreta*, München 1983

ΒΟΡΔΟΣ - ΤΣΑΡΔΑΚΑ - ΧΑΤΖΗΔΑΝΙΗΛ 1997: Βόρδος Α. - Τσαρδάκα Δ. - Χατζηδανιήλ Κ., Κλειστό σύνολο κεραμικής από το πηγάδι του οικοπέδου Κ. Λημναίου στην Επάνω Σκάλα Μυτιλήνης, in *Δ΄ Επιστημονική Συνάντηση για την Ελληνιστική Κεραμική*, Athens 1997, 233-240

BORELL - RITTIG 1998: Borell B. - Rittig D., *Orientalische und griechische Bronzereliefs aus Olympia*, OF XXVII, 1998

BOTTINI 1966: Bottini B., Les Lydia du Musée d'Art et d'Histoire de Genève, *AntK* 1966, 138-143

BOULTER 1953: Boulter C., Pottery of the Mid-Fifth Century from a Well in the Athenian Agora, *Hesperia* 22 (1953) 59-115

BOULTER 1963: Boulter C., Graves in Lenormant Street, Athens, *Hesperia* 32 (1963) 113-137

BOVON 1966: Bovon A., *Lampes d'Argos, Etudes Péloponnésiennes* V, Paris 1966

BOVON - BRUNEAU 1966: Bovon A. - Bruneau Ph., Huiliers hellénistiques, *BCH* 90 (1966) 131-143

BRANN 1960: Brann E., Late Geometric Well Groups from the Athenian Agora, *Hesperia* 29 (1960) 402-416

BRANN 1961a: Brann E., Late Geometric Well Groups from the Athenian Agora, *Hesperia* 30 (1961) 93-146

BRANN 1961b: Brann E., Protoattic Well Groups from the Athenian Agora, *Hesperia* 30 (1961) 305-379

BRAUN 1970: Braun K., Der Dipylon-Brunnen B1, Die Funde, *AM* 85 (1970) 129-269

BRAUN 1991: Braun K., Frühhellenistische Brandgräber aus dem Theonichosbezirk, in *Γ΄ Επιστημονική Συνάντηση για την Ελληνιστική Κεραμική*, Thessaloniki 1991, 23-34

BRECKENRIDGE 1959: Breckenridge J.D., *The Numismatic Iconography of Justinian II*, American Numismatic Society (Museum Notes and Monographs 144), New York 1959

BREITENSTEIN 1941: Breitenstein N., *Catalogue of the Terracottas, Danish National Museum*, 1941

BREITFELD-VON EICKSTEDT 1997: Breitfeld-Von Eickstedt D., Die Lekanis vom 6.-4. Jh. v.Chr. Beobachtungen zur Form und Entwicklung einer Vasengattung, in *APP* 1997, 55-61

BROMMER 1973: Brommer F., *Vasenlisten zur griechischen Heldensage*, Marburg 1973³

BROMMER 1974: Brommer F., *Herakles. Die zwölf Taten des Helden in antiker Kunst und Literatur*, Darmstadt 1974

BROMMER 1980: Brommer F., Plemochoe, *AA* 1980, 544-549

BROMMER 1989: Brommer F., Antike Tänze, *AA* 1989, 483-494

BRONEER 1962: Broneer O., Excavations at Isthmia 1959-1960, *Hesperia* 31 (1962) 1-25

BRØNDSTED 1928: Brøndsted J., *La Basilique de Cinq Martyres à Kapljuc, Recherches à Salone*, Copenhague 1928

BROWNLEE 1995: Brownlee A.B., Attic Black Figure from Corinth: III, *Hesperia* 64 (1995) 337-382

BRÜCKNER - PERNICE 1893: Brückner A. - Pernice E., Ein attischer Friedhof, *AM* 18 (1893) 73-191

BRÜMMER 1985: Brümmer E., Griechische Truhenbehälte, *JdI* 100 (1985) 1-168

BRUNEAU 1969: Bruneau Ph., Prolongements de la technique des mosaïques de galets en Grèce, *BCH* 93 (1969) 308-332

BRUNEAU 1970: Bruneau Ph., Tombes d'Argos, *BCH* 94 (1970) 437-531

BRUNEAU 1977: Bruneau Ph., Lampes corinthiennes II, *BCH* 101 (1977) 249-275

BRUNNSÅKER 1971: Brunnsåker St., *The Tyrant-Slayers of Kritios and Nesiotis*, Stockholm 1971

BUCHHOLZ 1966: Buchholz H.G., Tönerne Rasseln aus Zypern, *AA* 1966, 140-151

BUDDE - NICKOLS 1964: Budde L. - Nickols R., *A Catalogue of the Greek and Roman Sculpture in the Fitzwilliam Museum Cambridge*, 1964

BUITRON-OLIVER 1995: Buitron-Oliver D., *Douris, Kerameus* 9, Mainz am Rhein 1995

BULAS 1932: Bulas C., Etude sur une classe de vases à décor en forme des réseau ou d'écailles, *BCH* 56 (1932) 388-398

BURN 1987: Burn L., *The Meidias Painter*, 1987

BURR 1933a: Burr D., The Terracotta Figurines, *Hesperia* 2 (1933) 184-194

BURR 1933b: Burr D., A Geometric House and a Protoattic Votive Deposit, *Hesperia* 2 (1933) 542-640

BUSCHOR 1939: Buschor E., *Grab eines attischen Mädchens*, 1939

BUSCHOR 1959: Buschor E., *Grab eines attischen Mädchens*, München 1959

CAMBELL 1968: Cambell L., *Mithraic Iconography and Ideology*, Leiden 1968

CAMBELL 1979: Cambell S., Roman Mosaic Workshops in Turkey, *AJA* 83 (1979) 287-292

CAMERON 1979: Cameron F., *Greek Bronze Hand-Mirrors in South Italy*, Oxford 1979

CAMP 1986: Camp J.M., *The Athenian Agora*, London 1986

CAMPENON 1994: Campenon Chr., *La céramique attique à figures rouges autour de 400 av. J.-C.*, Paris 1994

CARPENTER 1997: Carpenter Th., *Dionysos Imagery in Fifth Century Athens*, Oxford 1997

CASKEY - AMANDRY 1952: Caskey L. - Amandry P., Investigations at the Heraion of Argos 1949, *Hesperia* 21 (1952) 165-221

CASKEY 1960: Caskey J.L., The Early Helladic Period in the Argolid, *Hesperia* 29 (1960) 285-303

CAVANAGH - MEE 1998: Cavanagh W. - Mee C., *A Private Place: Death in Prehistoric Greece*, SIMA 125, 1998

Céramique 1999: *Céramique et peinture grecques. Modes d'emploi*, Rencontres de l'Ecole du Louvre, 1999

CHAVANE 1975: Chavane M.J., *Les petits objets, Salamine de Chypre* VI, Paris 1975

ΓΙΑΛΟΥΡΗΣ 1982: Γιαλούρης Ν. (ed.), *Ιστορία των Ολυμπιακών αγώνων*, 1982

ΓΙΑΛΟΥΡΗΣ 1994: Γιαλούρης Ν., *Ελληνική τέχνη. Αρχαία γλυπτά*, 1994

ΓΙΑΝΝΙΚΟΥΡΗ *et al.* 1990: Γιαννικουρή Α. - Φιλήμονος Μ. - Πατσιαδά Β., Χρονολογικά προβλήματα γραπτής κεραμικής από τη Ρόδο, in *Β΄ Επιστημονική Συνάντηση για την Ελληνιστική Κεραμεική*, Athens 1990, 172-184

ΓΙΑΝΝΙΚΟΥΡΗ 1999: Γιαννικουρή Α., Το Ιερό της Δήμητρος στην πόλη της Ρόδου, in *Πρακτικά του Διεθνούς Επιστημονικού Συνεδρίου: Ρόδος 2.400 χρόνια*, Α΄, Athens 1999, 63-72.

ΓΙΟΥΡΗ 1965: Γιούρη Ευ., Αττικά ερυθρόμορφα αγγεία του 4ου π.Χ. αι., *ADelt* 20 (1965) Meletai, 153-170

CLAIRMONT 1970: Clairmont Chr., *Gravestone and Epigram: Greek Memorials from the Archaic and Classical Periods*, Mainz 1970

CLAIRMONT 1993: Clairmont Chr., *Classical Attic Tombstones*, 3, Kilchberg 1993

CLEMENT 1971: Clement P., Isthmia Excavations, *ADelt* 26 (1971) Chronika, 101-111

COLDSTREAM 1968: Coldstream J.N., *Greek Geometric Pottery*, London 1968

COLDSTREAM 1977: Coldstream J.N., *Geometric Greece*, London 1977 (Gr. tr., Athens 1997)

COLEMAN-CARTER 1998: Coleman-Carter J., *The Chora of Metaponto. The Necropoleis II*, 1998

COLLIGNON 1911: Collignon M., *Les statues funéraires dans l'art grec*, Paris 1911

CONZE 1893: Conze A., *Die attische Grabreliefs* I, Berlin 1893

CONZE 1900: Conze A., *Die attische Grabreliefs* II.1, Berlin 1900

CONZE 1911-22: Conze A., *Die attische Grabreliefs* IV, 1911-1922

COOK 1934/35: Cook J.M., Protoattic Pottery, *BSA* 35 (1934/35) 165-219

COOK 1947: Cook J.M., Athenian Workshops Around 700, *BSA* 42 (1947) 139-155

COOK 1969: Cook B.F., An Attic Grave Stele in New York, *AntPl* IX (1969) 65 κ.ε.

COOK 1984: Cook B.F., Class 6L: A Minor Workshop of Red Figured Lekythoi, in *Ancient Greek and Related Pottery, Proceedings of the International Vase Symposium*, Allard Pierson Series, 8, Amsterdam 1984, 149-152

CORBETT 1949: Corbett P., Attic Pottery of the Later Fifth Century from the Athenian Agora, *Hesperia* 18 (1949) 298-351

Corinth IV₂: Broneer O., *Corinth* IV₂. *Terracotta Lamps*, Cambridge Mass. 1930

Corinth VII₁: Weinberg S.S., *Corinth* VII₁. *The Geometric and Orientalizing Pottery*, Cambridge Mass. 1943

Corinth VII₃: Edwards G.R., *Corinth* VII₃. *Corinthian Hellenistic Pottery*, Princeton 1975

Corinth VII₄: Herbert S., *Corinth* VII₄. *The Red-Figure Pottery*, Princeton 1977

Corinth XII: Davidson G.R., *Corinth* XII. *The Minor Objects*, Princeton 1952

Corinth XIII: Blegen C.W. - Palmer H. - Young R.S., *Corinth* XIII. *The North Cemetery*, Princeton 1964

Corinth XV₂: Newhall-Stillwell A., *Corinth* XV₂. *The Potter's Quarter. The Terracottas*, Princeton 1952

Corinth XVIII₂: Warner-Slane K., *Corinth* XVIII₂. *The Sanctuary of Demeter and Kore. The Roman Pottery and Lamps*, Princeton 1990

COUILLOUD 1974: Couilloud M. Th., *Caractères des monuments funéraires*, *BCH* 98 (1974) 397-498

COURBIN 1966: Courbin P., *La céramique géometrique de l'Argolide*, Paris 1966

COURBY 1922: Courby A., *Les vases grecs à reliefs*, Paris 1922

ΓΡΑΜΜΕΝΟΣ - ΤΙΒΕΡΙΟΣ 1984: Γραμμένος Δ. - Τιβέριος Μ., Νεκροταφείο του 5ου αι. π.Χ. στην αρχαία Άργιλο, *ADelt* 39 (1984) Meletai, 1-47

CUMMER - SCHÖFIELD 1984: Cummer W.W. - Schöfield El., *Ayia Irini: House A'. Keos* III, Mainz am Rhein 1984

CURTIUS 1903: Curtius L., *Die antike Herme*, Leipzig 1903

DAREMBERG - SAGLIO: Daremberg Ch. - Saglio E., *Dictionnaire des antiquités grecques et romaines d'après les textes et les monuments*, Paris 1877-1919

DAVIDSON 1934: Davidson G.R., *Small Objects from the Pnyx*. I, *Hesperia* Suppl. VII, 1934

DAVIDSON - OLIVER 1984: Davidson R.F. - Oliver A. Jr., *Ancient Greek and Roman Jewellery in the Brooklyn Museum*, 1984

DAVIDSON-WEINBERG - McCLELLAN 1992: Davidson-Weinberg G. - McClellan M., *Glass Vessels in Ancient Greece, Core-Formed Glass Vessels*, 1992

DAVISON 1961: Davison J.M., *Attic Workshops*, *Yale Classical Studies* 16, 1961

DAWKINS 1929: Dawkins R.M., *The Sanctuary of Artemis Orthia at Sparta*, London 1929

DE JULIIS 1984: de Juliis E. (ed.), *Gli Ori di Taranto di età ellenistica*, 1984

DELBRÜCK 1933: Delbrück R., *Spätantike Kaiserporträts*, 1933

DELLI PONTI 1973: delli Ponti G., *I bronzi del Museo Provinciale di Lecce*, Lecce 1973

Délos VIII: Chamonard J., *Le Quartier du Théâtre*, *EAD* VIII, Paris 1922/24

Délos XVIII: Deonna W., *Le mobilier délien*, *EAD* XVIII, Paris 1938

Délos XXIII: Laumonier A., *Les figurines de terre cuite*, *EAD* XXIII, Paris 1956

Délos XXVI: Bruneau Ph., *Les lampes*, *EAD* XXVI, Paris 1965

Délos XXVII: Bruneau Ph., *L'îlot de la Maison des Comédiens*, *EAD* XXVII, Paris 1970

Délos XXIX: Bruneau Ph., *Les mosaïques*, *EAD* XXIX, Paris 1972

Délos XXXI: Laumonier A., *La céramique hellénistique à reliefs. 1. Ateliers "Ioniens"*, *EAD* XXXI, Paris 1977

DENEAUVE 1969: Deneauve J., *Lampes de Carthage*, Paris 1969

DENOYELLE 1996: Denoyelle M., Le Peintre d'Analatos: Essai de synthèse et perspectives nouvelles, *AntK* 1996, 71-87

DENTZER 1982: Dentzer J.M., *Le motif du banquet couché dans le proche Orient et le monde grec du VIIe au IVe s. av. J.-Chr.*, 1982

DEPPERT-LIPPITZ 1985: Deppert-Lippitz B., *Goldschmuck der Römerzeit im Römisch-Germanischen Zentralmuseum*, 1985

DE RIDDER 1896: De Ridder A., *Catalogue des bronzes trouvés sur l'Acropole d'Athènes* (Bibliothèque des Ecoles Françaises d'Athènes et de Rome 74), Paris 1896

DESBOROUGH 1952: Desborough V.R.d'A., *Protogeometric Pottery*, Oxford 1952

DESBOROUGH 1954: Desborough V.R.d'A., Mycenae 1939-1953. Part V. Four Tombs, *BSA* 49 (1954) 258-266

DESBOROUGH 1972: Desborough V.R.d'A., *The Greek Dark Ages*, London 1972

ΔΕΣΠΙΝΗΣ 1963: Δεσπίνης Γ.Ι., Επιτύμβιοι Τράπεζαι μετ' αναγλύφων παραστάσεων, *AEphem* 1963, 47-68

ΔΕΣΠΙΝΗΣ 1975: Δεσπίνης Γ.Ι., *Ακρόλιθα*, 1975

DESPINIS 1994: Despinis G.I., Neues zu einem alten Fund, *AM* 109 (1994) 173-198

DESPINIS et al. 1997: Despinis G. - Stephanidou-Tiveriou T.H. - Voutiras E., *Catalogue of Sculpture in the Archaeological Museum of Thessaloniki*, 1997

ΔΕΣΠΟΤΟΠΟΥΛΟΣ 1940: Δεσποτόπουλος Θ.Π., Η οδοποιία εν Ελλάδι από των αρχαιοτάτων χρόνων μέχρι σήμερον, *Τεχνικά Χρονικά* 1940, 5-30

DIEPOLDER 1931: Diepolder H., *Die attischen Grabreliefs*, 1931

DIETZ 1991: Dietz S., *The Argolid at the Transition to the Mycenaean Age*, Copenhagen 1991

DOC II₂: Grierson Ph., *Catalogue of the Byzantine Coins in the Dumbarton Oaks Collection and in the Whittemore Collection* II₂. *Heraclius Constantine to Theodosius III (641-717)*, Washington 1968

DONDERER 1986: Donderer M., *Die Chronologie der römischen Mosaiken in Venetien und Istrien bis zur Zeit der Antoninen*, Berlin 1986

DÖRIG 1958: Dörig J., Von griechischen Puppen, *AntK* 1 (1958) 41-52.

DÖRIG 1972: Dörig J. (ed.), *Art Antique. Collections privées de Suisse Romande*, Genève 1972

DÖRPFELD 1888: Dörpfeld W., Die Stoa des Eumenes in Athen, *AM* 13 (1888) 100-102

DROUGOU 1975: Drougou St., *Der attische Psykter*, Würzburg 1975

ΔΡΟΥΓΟΥ - ΤΟΥΡΑΤΣΟΓΛΟΥ 1980: Δρούγου Στ. - Τουράτσογλου I., *Ελληνιστικοί λαξευτοί τάφοι Βεροίας*, Athens 1980

ΔΡΟΥΓΟΥ 1982: Δρούγου Στ., Ερυθρόμορφος κρατήρας του 4ου αι. από τη Βέροια. Ο ζωγράφος της Toya, *AEphem* 1982, 85-98

ΔΡΟΥΓΟΥ 1992: Δρούγου Στ., *Ανασκαφή Πέλλας 1957-1964. Οι πήλινοι λύχνοι*, Athens 1992

DUMOULIN 1994: Dumoulin D., *Antike Schildkröten*, Würzburg 1994

DUNAND 1973: Dunand Fr., *Le culte d'Isis dans le bassin oriental de la Méditerranée*, 1973

DUSENBERY 1967: Dusenbery E., Ancient Glass from the Cemeteries of Samothrace, *JGS* 9 (1967) 34-49

DYGGVE 1939: Dyggve Ej., *Zierarchitektur und Kleinfunde, Forschungen in Salona* III, Wien 1939

ECKSTEIN 1956: Eckstein F., Athleten-Hauben, *RM* 63 (1956) 90-95

EINGARTNER 1991: Eingartner J., *Isis und ihre Dienerinnen in der Kunst der römischen Kaiserzeit*, *Mnemosyne* Suppl. 115, 1991

ΕΛΕΥΘΕΡΑΤΟΥ forth.: Ελευθεράτου Στ., Δύο τελετουργικές πυρές από την ανασκαφή για το «Μετρό» στο οικόπεδο Μακρυγιάννη, *ADelt* 51-52 (1996-1997) Meletai (forth.)

ELIOT 1962: Eliot C.W.J., *Coastal Demes of Attica*, Toronto 1962

Ελληνικό κόσμημα 1997: *Το ελληνικό κόσμημα. 6.000 χρόνια παράδοση*, Athens 1997

EL SHAHAT 1983: El Shahat, *Η Ίσις και η ελληνιστική γυναικεία ενδυμασία στην Αίγυπτο* (Ph.D. thesis), Athens 1983

EMPEREUR - HESNARD 1987: Empereur J.Y. - Hesnard A., Les amphores hellénistiques, in P. Lévêque - J.P. Morel, *Céramiques hellénistiques et romaines*, II, 1987, 9-71

Ephesos IV: Vetters H., *Ephesos: vorläufiger Grabungsbericht 1970*, Wien 1971

Έργο ΥΠΠΟ 1998: *Το Έργο του Υπουργείου Πολιτισμού στον τομέα της πολιτιστικής κληρονομιάς* 2, 1998

Eretria IX: Gex K., *Rotfigurige und weissgrundige Keramik*, *Eretria* IX, Lausanne 1993

ESCHBACH 1986: Eschbach N., *Statuen auf panathenäischen Preisamphoren des 4. Jhs v.Chr.*, 1986

FAIDER-FEYTMANS 1952: Faider-Feytmans G., *Antiquités Mariemont*, 1952

FEHR 1971: Fehr B., *Orientalische und griechische Gelage*, Bonn 1971

FELTEN 1976: Felten F., Weissgrundige Lekythen aus dem athener Kerameikos, *AM* 91 (1976) 77-113

FIRATLI 1964: Firatli N., *Les stèles funéraires de Byzance gréco-romaine*, 1964

FITTA 1997: Fitta M., *Giochi e giocattoli nell'Antichità*, Milano 1997

Fouilles de Delphes V: Perdrizet P., *Monuments figurés, petits bronzes, terre cuites, antiquités diverses*, *Fouilles de Delphes* V, Paris 1908

FRANCISCIS 1963: de Franciscis A., *Il Museo Nazionale di Napoli*, 1963

FRANZIUS 1973: Franzius G., *Tänzer und Tänze in der archaischen Vasenmalerei* (Ph.D. thesis), Göttingen 1973

FUCHS 1963: Fuchs W., *Das Schiffsfund von Mahdia*, 1963

FUCHS 1974: Fuchs O., *Der attische Adel im Spiegel der Kalosinschriften (480-410 v.Chr.)*, Wien 1974

FUCHS 1978: Fuchs W., Unerkannte Hekate-Heiligtümer, in *Greece and Italy in the Classical World, Acta of the XIth International Congress of Classical Archaeology*, London 1978, 229

FULLERTON 1986: Fullerton M.D., The Location and Archaism of the Hekate Epipyrgidia, *AA* 1986, 669- 675

GALINIER 1996: Galinier C., *La production du Peintre de Sappho dans l'atelier des Peintres de Sappho et de Diosphos: parcours d'un artisan à figures noires parmi les ateliers athéniens de la fin de l'archaïsme* (Ph.D. thesis), Lille 1996

GALINIER 1998: Galinier C., Héraclès entre bêtes et dieux dans l'atelier des Peintres de Sappho et de Diosphos, in C. Bonnet - C. Jourdain-Annequin - V. Pirenne-Delforge (eds.), *Le Bestiaire d'Héraclès. IIIᵉ Rencontre héracléenne, Kernos* Suppl. 7, 1998, 75-85

GALINIER 1999: Galinier C., Les Peintres de Sappho et de Diosphos, structure d'atelier, in Villanueva-Puig (ed.), *Céramique et peintre grecques. Modes d'emploi, Actes du Colloque international*, Ecole du Louvre 26-28 Avril 1995, Paris 1999, 181-186

GARLAND 1985: Garland R., *The Greek Way of Death*, Ithaca - New York 1985

GHALI-KAHIL 1955: Ghali-Kahil L., *Les enlèvements et le retour d'Hélène dans les textes et les documents figurés*, Paris 1955

GIGLIOLI 1922: Giglioli G.Q., La corsa della fiaccola ad Atene, *RendLincei* 31 (1922) 315-335

GIUDICE *et al.* 1992: Giudice F. - Tusa S. - Tusa V., *La collezione archeologica del Banco di Sicilia, Museo de la Fondazione Mormino del Banco di Sicilia*, Palermo 1992

Glories of the Past 1990: Von Bothmer D. (ed.), *Glories of the Past. Ancient Art from the Shelby White and Leon Levy Collection*, 1990

GOODENOUGH 1954: Goodenough E.R., *Jewish Symbols in the Greco-Roman Period*, 5, New York 1954

GOODENOUGH 1953-1968: Goodenough E.R., *Jewish Symbols in the Greco-Roman Period*, 7, New York 1953-1968

GRABOW 1998: Grabow E., *Schlagenbilder in der griechischen schwarzfigurigen Vasenkunst*, Münster 1998

GRACE 1961: Grace V., *Amphoras and the Ancient Wine Trade*, American School of Classical Studies, Picture Book, 6, 1961

GRÄPLER 1997: Gräpler D., *Tonfiguren im Grab. Fundkontexte hellenistischer Terrakotten aus der Nekropole von Tarent*, München 1997

GRAY 1974: Gray D., Seewesen, *Archäologia Homerica* IG, 1974

GREEN 1970: Green J.R., A Series of Added Red-Figure Choes, *AA* 1970, 475-487

GREEN 1971: Green J.R., Choes of the Later Fifth Century B.C., *BSA* 66 (1971) 189-228

GREEN 1972: Green J.R., Oinochoe, *BICS* 19 (1972) 1-16

GREENWALT 1920: Greenwalt C.H., Lydian Poterry of the 6th century B.C., *AM* 45 (1920) 163-170

GREIFENHAGEN 1975: Greifenhagen A., *Schmuckarbeiten in Edelmetal*, II, 1975

GRIERSON - MAYS 1992: Grierson Ph. - Mays M., *Catalogue of Late Roman Coins in Dumbarton Oaks Collection and in the Whittemore Collection*, 1992

GROSE 1989: Grose D.F., *The Toledo Museum of Art. Early Ancient Glass*, Toledo 1989

ΖΑΦΕΙΡΟΠΟΥΛΟΥ 1981: Ζαφειροπούλου Φ., *Προβλήματα της μηλιακής αγγειογραφίας*, Thessaloniki 1981

ΖΑΦΕΙΡΟΠΟΥΛΟΥ 1998: Ζαφειροπούλου Φ., *Δήλος*, Athens 1998

HACKENS 1976: Hackens T., *Museum of Art, Providence Rhode Island. Catalogue of the Classical Jewellery*, 1976

HAGER-WEIGEL 1997: Hager-Weigel E., *Griechische Akrolith Statuen des 5. und 4. Jhs v.Chr.*, Bonn 1997

HAMIAUX 1996: Hamiaux M., *Louvre I, Les sculptures grecques*, 1996

HAMILTON 1992: Hamilton R., *Choes and Anthesteria, Athenian Iconography and Ritual*, Michigan 1992

HAMPE 1936: Hampe R., *Frühe griechische Sagenbilder in Boötien*, 1936

HAMPE 1951: Hampe R., *Die Stele aus Pharsalos im Louvre, BerlWPr* 1951

HARDEN 1936: Harden D.B., *Roman Glass from Karamis Found by the University of Michigan Archaeological Expedition in Egypt 1924-1929*, Michigan 1936

HARDEN 1981: Harden D.B., *Catalogue of the Greek and Roman Glass in the British Museum*, London 1981

HASPELS 1927/28: Haspels E., How the Aryballos Was Suspended, *JHS* 29 (1927/28) 216-223

HASPELS 1972: Haspels E., Le Peintre de Diosphos, *RA* 1972, 103-109

HATZISTELIOU-PRICE 1969: Hatzisteliou-Price Th., The Type of the Crouching Child and 'Temple Boy', *BSA* 64 (1969) 95-111

HAYES 1997: Hayes J.W., *Handbook of the Mediterranean Roman Pottery*, London 1997

HAYNES 1974: Haynes S., *Etruscan Bronze Utensils*, London 1974

HEESEN 1996: Heesen P., *The J.L. Theodor Collection of Attic Black-Figure Vases*, Allard Pierson Series, 10, Amsterdam 1996

HELLMAN 1987: Hellman M.Chr., *Lampes antiques de la Bibliothèque Nationale*, I, *Collection Froehner*, Paris 1987

HERMANN 1900: Hermann P., Erwerbungen der Antikensammlung in Deutschland. II. Dresden. 2. Thongefäße, *AA* 1900, 110-113

HIESEL 1967: Hiesel G., *Samische Steingeräte*, Hamburg 1967

HIGGINS 1961: Higgins R.A., *Greek and Roman Jewellery*, 1961

HIGGINS 1967: Higgins R.A., *Greek Terracottas*, London 1967

HOFFMANN 1961: Hoffmann H., *Kunst des Altertums im Hamburg*, 1961

HOFFMANN 1997: Hoffmann H., *Sotades. Symbols of Immortality on Greek Vases*, Oxford 1997

HOFSTETTER 1990: Hofstetter E., *Sirenen im archaischen und klassischen Griechenland*, Würzburg 1990

HOLLEIN 1988: Hollein H.G., *Bürger Bild und Bildwelt der attischen Demokratie auf den rotfigurigen Vasen des 6.-4. Jhs v.Chr.*, Darmstadt 1988

HÖLSCHER 1973: Hölscher T., *Griechische Historienbilder des 5. und des 4. Jahrh. v.Chr. Würzburg*, 1973, 99-101

HOMMEL 1978: Hommel H., Bocksbeutel und Aryballos, Philologische Beiträge zur Urgeschichte und Gefäßformen, *SBHeidelberg* 2 (1978) 3-50

HORNBOSTEL 1973: Hornbostel W., *Serapis*, 1973

HOWATSON 1996: Howatson M.C., *The Oxford Companion to Classical Litterature* (Gr. tr.), Thessaloniki-Athens 1996

HÜLTSCH 1882: Hültsch F., *Griechische Metrologie*, Berlin 1882

ΘΕΜΕΛΗΣ 1989: Θέμελης Π., Βάθρο αναθήματος στη Βενδίδα, *Ηόρος* 7 (1989) 23-29

ΘΕΜΕΛΗΣ - ΤΟΥΡΑΤΣΟΓΛΟΥ 1997: Θέμελης Π. - Τουράτσογλου Ι., *Οι τάφοι του Δερβενίου*, 1997

ΘΡΕΨΙΑΔΗΣ 1960: Θρεψιάδης Ι., Ανασκαφή οικοπέδου ΟΔΕΠ (οδός Βουλής και Μητροπόλεως), Ανασκαφαί λεωφόρου Πανεπιστημίου, *ADelt* 16 (1960) Chronika, 22-29

ΘΡΕΨΙΑΔΗΣ - ΤΡΑΥΛΟΣ 1961/62: Θρεψιάδης Ι. - Τραυλός Ι., Ανασκαφαί νοτίως του Ολυμπιείου (1961), *ADelt* 17 (1961/62) Chronika, 9-14

ΘΡΕΨΙΑΔΗΣ 1971: Θρεψιάδης Ι., Ανασκαφαί και τυχαία ευρήματα Αττικής, Βοιωτίας και Ευβοίας, *AEphem* 1971, Chronika, 8-38

ΘΡΕΨΙΑΔΗΣ 1973: Θρεψιάδης Ι., Ανασκαφικαί έρευναι Αττικής και Βοιωτίας, *AEphem* 1973, Chronika, 54-86

ΙΓΝΑΤΙΑΔΟΥ 1990-95: Ιγνατιάδου Δ., Χειροποίητα γυάλινα αγγεία από το αρχαίο νεκροταφείο Θερμής (Σέδες), *AAA* XXIII-XXVIII (1990-1995) 223-233

ID: Coupry J., *Inscriptions de Délos*, Paris 1972

IG²: Kirchner J., *Inscriptiones Graecae* II², Berlin 1927

ISINGS 1957: Isings C., *Roman Glass from Dated Finds*, Groningen 1957

Isthmia III: Broneer O., *Isthmia* III. *Terracotta Lamps*, Princeton 1977

JACOBSTAHL 1931: Jacobstahl P., *Die melische Reliefs*, 1931

JACQUEMIN 1984: Jacquemin A., Céramique des époques archaïque, classique et hellénistique, *L'Antre corycien* II, *BCH* Suppl. IX, 1984, 166-175

JANSSEN 1989: Janssen J. - Janssen R., *Egyptian Household Animals*, Great Britain 1989

Jemen 1998/99: Von Wilfried Seipel, *Jemen, Kunst und Archäologie im Land der Königin von Saba*, Wien 1998/99

JENKINS 1978: Jenkins R.J.H., *Daedalika. A Study of Dorian Plastic Art in the Seventh Century B.C.*, Cambridge 1978²

JOHANSEN 1951: Johansen K.F., *The Attic Grave Reliefs*, 1951

JORDAN - ROTROFF 1999: Jordan D.R. - Rotroff S.I., A Curse in a Chytridion: A Contribution to the Study of Athenian Pyres, *Hesperia* 68 (1999) 147-154

JUDEICH 1931: Judeich W., *Topographie von Athen*, München 1931

JÜTHNER 1965-1968: Jüthner J., *Die athletischen Leibesübungen der Griechen*, I-II, 1965-1968

ΚΑΒΒΑΔΙΑΣ 1997: Καββαδίας Γ., Ο Θησέας και ο Μαραθώνιος Ταύρος. Παρατηρήσεις σε ένα νέο αττικό ερυθρόμορφο κιονωτό κρατήρα από το Άργος, in *APP* 1997, 309-317

ΚΑΒΒΑΔΙΑΣ 2000: Καββαδίας Γ., *Ο ζωγράφος του Sabouroff*, Athens 2000

KABUS-PREISSHOFEN 1989: Kabus-Preisshofen R., *Die hellenistische Plastik der Insel Kos, AM* 1989 Bh. 14

ΚΑΛΛΙΓΑΣ 1989: Καλλιγάς Π.Γ., in Αλεξανδρή 1989

ΚΑΛΛΙΓΑΣ 1994-95: Καλλιγάς Π.Γ., Η Αθηναϊκή Ακρόπολη το 1835, *ADelt* 49-50 (1994-1995) Meletai, 23-42

ΚΑΛΛΙΠΟΛΙΤΗΣ 1963: Καλλιπολίτης Β., Ανασκαφή τάφων Αναγυρούντος, *ADelt* 18 (1963) 120ff.

ΚΑΛΤΣΑΣ 1983: Καλτσάς Ν., Από τα ελληνιστικά νεκροταφεία της Πύλου, *ADelt* 38 (1983) Meletai, 1-77

ΚΑΛΤΣΑΣ 1998: Καλτσάς Ν., *Άκανθος* I. *Η ανασκαφή στο νεκροταφείο κατά το 1979*, Athens 1998

ΚΑΜΠΙΤΟΓΛΟΥ 1991: Καμπίτογλου Α., *Αρχαιολογικό Μουσείο Άνδρου. Οδηγός*, Athens 1991

ΚΑΜΠΟΥΡΟΓΛΟΥ 1931: Καμπούρογλου Δ., *Αι Αθήναι κατά τα έτη 1775-1795*, Athens 1931

ΚΑΠΕΤΑΝΑΚΗ 1973: Καπετανάκη Π., Μελαμβαφείς αμφορίσκοι εξ Αθηνών, *AAA* VI (1973) 152-155

ΚΑΡΑΓΙΩΡΓΑ-ΣΤΑΘΑΚΟΠΟΥΛΟΥ 1988: Καράγιωργα-Σταθακοπούλου Θ., Δημόσια έργα και ανασκαφές στην Αθήνα τα τελευταία 5 χρόνια, *Ηόρος* 6 (1988) 87-108

KARDARA 1960: Kardara Chr., Four White Lekythoi in the National Museum of Athens, *BSA* 55 (1960) 149-158

KARDULIAS - RUNNELS 1995: Kardulias P.N. - Runnels C.N., The Lithic Artifacts: Flaked Stone and Other Nonflaked Lithics, in C.N. Runnels - D.J. Pullen - S. Langdon (eds.), *Artifact and Assemblage. The Find from a Regional Survey of the Southern Argolid, Greece*, I, California 1995, 115ff.

KARIVIERI 1996: Karivieri A., *The Athenian Lamp Industry in Late Antiquity*, Helsinki 1996

KARO 1943: Karo C., *An Attic Cemetery: Excavations in the Kerameikos at Athens*, Philadelphia 1943

KAROUZOU 1951: Karouzou S., Attic Bronze Mirrors, in G.E. Mylonas (ed.), *Studies Presented to D.M. Robinson*, St. Louis 1951, 565-587

KAROUZOU 1962: Karouzou S., Scènes de Palestre, *BCH* 86 (1962) 430-466

KAROUZOU 1979: Karouzou S., Autour d'une oenochoé de Toulouse, *AAA* XII (1979) 127ff.

ΚΑΤΑΚΗΣ 1997: Κατάκης Σ., Φιλημάτιον Τερεντία χρηστή χαίρε, *AM* 112 (1997) 318-334

KATER-STIBBES 1973: Kater-Stibbes G.J.F., Preliminary Catalogue of Serapis Monuments, *EPRO* 36 (1973)

KdA: Hornbostel W. (ed.), *Kunst der Antike. Schätze aus norddeutschem Privatbesitz*, Mainz 1979²

KEAY 1984: Keay S.J., *Late Roman Amphorae in the Western Mediterranean, BAR* 1984

KEMP-LINDEMANN 1975: Kemp-Lindemann D., *Darstellungen des Achilleus in der griechischen und römischen Kunst*, Frankfurt - Bern 1975

Kenchreai V: Williams H., *Kenchreai V, The Lamps*, 1981

KENNER 1939: Kenner H., Flügelfrau und Flügeldämonen, *ÖJh* 31 (1939) 81-95

KENT 1948: Kent J.H., The Temple Estates of Delos, Rheneia and Mykonos, *Hesperia* 17 (1948) 243-338

Kerameikos I: Kraiker W. - Kübler K., *Kerameikos* I. *Die Nekropolen des 12. bis 10. Jhs v.Chr.*, Berlin 1939

Kerameikos IV: Kübler K., *Kerameikos* IV. *Neufunde aus der Nekropole des 11. und 10. Jhs v.Chr.*, Berlin 1943

Kerameikos V₁: Kübler K., *Kerameikos* V₁. *Die Nekropolen des 10. bis 8. Jhs v.Chr.*, Berlin 1959

Kerameikos VI₂: Kübler K., *Kerameikos* VI₂. *Die Nekropolen des späten 8. bis frühen 6. Jhs v.Chr.*, Berlin 1959

Kerameikos IX: Knigge U., *Kerameikos* IX. *Der Südhügel Kerameikos. Ergebnisse der Ausgrabungen*, Berlin 1976

Kerameikos XI: Scheibler I., *Kerameikos* XI. *Griechische Lampen*, Berlin 1976

Kerameikos XII: Koenigs W. - Knigge U. - Mallwitz A., *Kerameikos* XII. *Rundbauten im Kerameikos*, Berlin 1980

Kerameikos XIV: Kovascovics W.K., *Kerameikos* XIV. *Die Eckterrasse an der Gräberstraße des Kerameikos*, Berlin 1990

Kerameikos XV: Schlörb-Vierneisel B., *Kerameikos* XV. *Die figürlichen Terrakotten* I. *Spätmykenisch bis späthellenistisch*, München 1997

KERÉNYI 1966: Kerényi K., *Die Mythologie der Griechen*, 1966 (Gr. tr. 1974)

KEULS 1993: Keuls E., *The Reign of the Phallus*, 1993

KILLET 1994: Killet H., *Zur Ikonographie der Frau auf attischen Vasen archaisher und klassischer Zeit*, 1994

KILMER 1993: Kilmer M., *Greek Erotica on Attic Red Figure Vases*, 1993

KIRCHNER 1901-1903: Kirchner J., *Prosopographia Attica* A-K, *Louvre, Les sculptures grecques* I, 1901-1903

KIRCHNER 1948: Kirchner J., *Imagines Inscriptionum Atticarum*, 1948

KIRK 1949: Kirk G.S., Ships on Geometric Vases, *BSA* 44 (1949) 93ff.

KISS 1975: Kiss Z., *L'iconographie des princes Julio-Claudiens au temps d'Auguste et de Tibère*, 1975

KISTLER 1998: Kistler E., *Die "Opferrine-Zeremonie", Bankettideologie am Grab, Orientalisierumg und Formierung einer Adelsgesellschaft in Athen*, Stuttgart 1998

KLEIN 1932: Klein A.E., *Child Life in Greek Art*, 1932

KLEINER 1975: Kleiner F.S., *Greek and Roman Coins in the Athenian Agora*, Princeton 1975

KNIGGE 1966: Knigge U., Eridanos Nekropole, *AM* 81 (1966) 112-134

KNIGGE 1970: Knigge U., Kerameikos 1968-1969, *ADelt* 25 (1970) Chronika, 31-39

KNIGGE 1972: Knigge U., Untersuchungen bei den Gesandtenstelen im Kerameikos zu Athen, *AA* 87 (1972) 584-629

KNIGGE - KOVASCOVICS 1981: Knigge U. - Kovascovics W., Kerameikos: Tätigkeitsbericht 1979, *AA* 1981, 385-396

KNIGGE - VON FREYTAG 1987: Knigge U. - Von Freytag B., Ausgrabungen im Kerameikos 1983-1985, *AA* 1987, 481-499

KNIGGE 1990: Knigge U., *Ο Κεραμεικός της Αθήνας. Ιστορία, μνημεία, ανασκαφές*, Athens 1990

KNIGGE 1993: Knigge U., Die Ausgrabungen im Kerameikos 1990/91, *AA* 1993, 125-140

KOCH 1984: Koch G., Zum Grabrelief der Helena, *GettyJ* 12 (1984) 59-72

ΚΟΚΚΟΥ-ΒΥΡΙΔΗ 1999: Κόκκου-Βυριδή Κ., *Πρώιμες πυρές θυσιών στο Τελεστήριο της Ελευσίνας*, Athens 1999

KOKULA 1984: Kokula G., *Marmorlutrophoren, AM* Bh. 10, 1984

ΚΟΡΡΕΣ 1980: Κορρές Μ., Στοά του Ευμένους, *ADelt* 35 (1980) Chronika, 18-20

ΚΟΡΡΕΣ 1984: Κορρές Μ., Bauplanung und Bautheorie der Antike, *Diskussionen für archäologischen Bauforschung*, 4, Berlin 1984, 201-207

KOPTH-KONTH 1993-94: Κόρτη-Κόντη Στ., Το δένδρο στις μυθολογικές παραστάσεις των μελανόμορφων και πρώιμων ερυθρόμορφων αττικών αγγείων, 570-460 π.Χ., *Εγνατία* 4 (1993-94) 7-70

KÖSTER 1926: Köster A., *Die griechischen Terrakotten*, Berlin 1926

ΚΟΥΜΑΝΟΥΔΗΣ 1889: Κουμανούδης Στ., Εργασίαι προς Ν. και Δ. του Ζαππείου Μεγάρου, παρά το Β. πεζοπάτιον της λεωφόρου Όλγας, *Prakt* 1889, 8-18

KOZLOFF - MITTEN 1988: Kozloff A.P. - Mitten D.G., *The Gods' Delight; the Human Figure in Classical Bronze*, Cleveland 1988

KRAUS 1960: Kraus Th., *Hekate. Studien zu Wesen und Bild der Göttin in Kleinasien und Griechenland*, Heidelberg 1960

KRIEGER 1973: Krieger X., *Der Kampf zwischen Peleus und Thetis in der griechischen Vasenmalerei*, 1973

ΚΡΙΤΖΑΣ 1989: Κριτζάς Χ., Κατάλογος πεσόντων από τα Μέγαρα, *Φίλια Έπη εις Γ. Μυλωνάν*, Γ', 1989, 167-187

KROLL 1972: Kroll J.H., *Athenian Bronze Allotment Plates*, Cambridge Mass., 1972

KROLL 1979: Kroll J.H., A Chronology of Early Athenian Bronze Coinage, ca. 350-250 B.C., in *Greek Numismatics and Archaeology. Essays in Honor of Margaret Thompson*, Belgium 1979

KRUG 1968: Krug A., *Binden in der griechischen Kunst*, 1968

ΚΡΥΣΤΑΛΛΗ-ΒΟΤΣΗ 1976: Κρυστάλλη-Βότση Κ., Αυστηρορρυθμικό κεφάλι κούρου από την Κόρινθο, *AEphem* 1976, 182-193

KÜBLER 1934: Kübler K., Ausgrabungen im Kerameikos 1933/34, *AA* 1934, 219ff.

KÜBLER 1935: Kübler K., Ausgrabungen im Kerameikos, *AA* 1935, 260-300

KÜBLER 1938: Kübler K., Ausgrabungen im Kerameikos I, *AA* 1938, 586-606

KÜBLER 1952: Kübler K., Zum Formwandel in der spätantiken attischen Tonplastik, *JdI* 67 (1952) 99-145

KULOV 1999: Kulov I., Graves from the Roman Period near the Village of Banichan, Gotse Delchev District (Southwestern Bulgaria), *Archaeologia Bulgarica* 1 (1999) 61-69

KUNISCH 1998: Kunisch N., *Ornamente geometrischer Vasen. Ein Kompendium*, Köln - Wien 1998

Kunst der Schale 1990: Vierneisel K. - Kaeser B., *Kunst der Schale. Kultur des Trinkens*, München 1990

KUNZE 1930: Kunze E., Zu den Anhängen des griechischen Plastik, *AM* 55 (1930) 141-162

KUNZE 1950: Kunze E., *Archaische Schildbänder. Ein Beitrag zur frühgriechischen Bildgeschichte und Sagenüberlieferung*, *OF*, II, 1950

KURTZ 1975: Kurtz D.C., *Athenian White Lekythoi. Patterns and Painters*, Oxford 1975

KURTZ - BOARDMAN 1971: Kurtz D. - Boardman J., *Greek Burial Customs*, 1971

KURTZ - BOARDMAN 1985: Kurtz D. - Boardman J., *Tod und Jenseits bei den Griechen*, Mainz 1985

KURTZ - BOARDMAN 1994: Kurtz D. - Boardman J., *Έθιμα ταφής στον αρχαίο ελληνικό κόσμο* (Gr. tr.), Athens 1994

ΚΥΠΑΡΙΣΣΗΣ 1924/25: Κυπαρίσσης Ν., Αι ανασκαφαί των Βασιλικών Σταύλων, *ADelt* 9 (1924/25), Supplement, 68-72

KYRIELEIS 1975: Kyrieleis H., *Bildnisse der Ptolemäer*, Berlin 1975

ΚΩΝΣΤΑΝΤΙΝΙΔΗΣ 1902: Κωνσταντινίδης Α., *Μέγα Λεξικόν της Ελληνικής Γλώσσης*, Athens 1902

ΚΩΣΤΟΓΛΟΥ-ΔΕΣΠΟΙΝΗ 1979: Κώστογλου-Δεσποίνη Αικ., *Προβλήματα της παριανής πλαστικής του 5ου αι. π.Χ.*, Thessaloniki 1979

Labraunda II,1: Hellström P., *Pottery of Classical and Later Date, Terracottas, Lamps and Glass. Labraunda: Swedish Excavations and Researches* II,1, Lund 1965

LANDELS 1999: Landels J., *Music in Ancient Greece and Rome*, London - New York 1999

LANG 1968: Lang M., *Excavations of the Athenian Agora*, Picture Books, 11, "Waterworks in the Athenian Agora", American School of Classical Studies at Athens, Princeton, New Jersey 1968

LANGLOTZ 1954: Langlotz E., *Aphrodite in den Gärten*, 1954

LANGLOTZ 1967: Langlotz E., *Frühgriechische Bildhauerschulen*, Nürnberg 1967

LANGLOTZ 1968: Langlotz E., *Griechische Vasen in Würzburg*, 1968

LASER 1987: Laser S., Sport und Spiel, *Archäologia Homerica*, T., 1987

LAURENT 1898: Laurent M., L'Achille voilé dans les peintures de vases grecs, *RA* 1898, 152-186

LAWLER 1984: Lawler L., *Ο χορός στην αρχαία Ελλάδα*, Athens 1984

LAWRENCE 1925: Lawrence A., Greek Sculpture in Ptolemaic Egypt, *JEA* 2 (1925) 179-190

Lefkandi I: Popham M.R. - Sackett L.H. - Themelis P., *Lefkandi* I. *The Iron Age Settlement - The Cemeteries*, *BSA* Suppl. 11, 1980

Lefkandi III: Popham M.R. - Lemos I.S., *Lefkandi* III. *The Toumba Cemeteries. The Excavations of 1981, 1984, 1986 and 1992-1994*, *BSA* Suppl. 24, 1996

LEMOS 1997: Lemos A., Athenian Black-Figure: Rhodes Revisited, in *APP* 1997, 457-468

LÉVÊQUE 1952: Lévêque P., *Les antiquités égyptiennes, grecques, étrusques et gallo-romaines du Musée de Mariemont*, Bruxelles 1952

LEYENAAR-PLAISIER 1979: Leyenaar-Plaisier P.G., *Les terres cuites grecques et romaines. Catalogue de la Collection du Musée National des Antiquités à Leiden*, 1979

LEZZI-HAFTER 1988: Lezzi-Hafter A., *Der Eretria Maler*, 1988

LICHT 1942: Licht H., *Sexual Life in Ancient Greece*, London 1942

LIDDELL - SCOTT 1953: Liddell H.G. - Scott R., *A Greek-English Lexicon*, Oxford 1953

LIEPMANN 1975: Liepmann U., *Griechische Terrakotten, Bronzen, Skulpturen, Bildkatalog des Kestner-Museums*, Hannover XII, 1975

ΛΙΛΙΜΠΑΚΗ-ΑΚΑΜΑΤΗ 1994: Λιλιμπάκη-Ακαμάτη Μ., *Λαξευτοί θαλαμωτοί τάφοι Πέλλας*, Athens 1994

ΛΙΛΙΜΠΑΚΗ-ΑΚΑΜΑΤΗ 1989-91: Λιλιμπάκη-Ακαμάτη Μ., Ανατολικό νεκροταφείο της Πέλλας, *ADelt* 44-46 (1989-1991) Meletai, 73-152

Lindos I: Blinkenberg Ch., *Les petits objets*, *Lindos* I, Berlin 1931

Lindos III₂: Dyggve Ej., *Lindos. Fouilles de l'Acropole 1902-1014 et 1952*, *Lindos* III₂, Berlin 1960

LISSARRAGUE 1987: Lissarrague F., Les Satyres et le monde animal, in *Symposium Ancient Greek and Related Potters*, 1987

LISSARRAGUE 1990: Lissarrague F., *L'autre guerrier*, Paris-Rome 1990

LISSARRAGUE 1991: Lissarrague F., Femmes au figure, in G. Duby - M. Perrot (eds.), *Histoire des femmes en Occident*, Evreux 1991, 159-251

LISSARRAGUE 1995: Lissarrague F., Women, Boxes, Containers: Some Signs and Metaphors, in *Pandora*, 91-101

LLOYD-MORGAN 1975: Lloyd-Morgan G., A Note on Some Mirrors in the Museo Archeologico, Brescia, *Commentari dell'Ateneo di Brescia* 174 (1975) 107-116

LLOYD-MORGAN 1981: Lloyd-Morgan G., *Description of the Collections in the Rijksmuseum G.M. Kam at Nijmegen*, IX. *The Mirrors*, Nijmegen 1981

LOSFELD 1991: Losfeld G., *Essai sur le costume grec*, Paris 1991

LRBC I-II: Carson R.A.G. - Hill P.V. - Kent J.P.C., *Late Roman Bronze Coinage*, I-II, London 1960

LUCE 1924: Luce S.B., Studies of Exploits of Heracles on Vases, *AJA* 28 (1924) 296-325

LULLIES 1931: Lullies R., *Die Typen der griechischen Herme*, Königsberger Kunstgeschichtliche Forschungen 3, 1931

LULLIES 1955: Lullies R., *Eine Sammlung griechischer Kleinkunst*, München 1955

LUSCHEY 1932: Luschey H., *Die Phiale*, 1932

LYON-CAEN 1986: Lyon-Caen Chr., *Catalogue des lampes en terre cuite grecques et chrétiennes, Musée du Louvre*, 1986

ΜΑΚΡΗ - ΤΣΑΚΟΣ - ΒΑΒΥΛΟΠΟΥΛΟΥ 1987-88: Μακρή Ε. - Τσάκος Κ. - Βαβυλοπούλου-Χαριτωνίδου Α., Το Ριζόκαστρο. Σωζόμενα υπολείμματα: νέες παρατηρήσεις και επαναχρονολόγηση, *DeltChrAEtair* Δ', ΙΔ' (1987-1988) 329-363

MALAISE 1922: Malaise M., A propos de l'iconographie "canonique" d'Isis et des femmes vouées à son culte, *Kernos* 5 (1992) 329-346

MALLWITZ - HERMANN 1980: Mallwitz A. - Hermann H.V., *Die Funde aus Olympia*, 1980

ΜΑΝΑΚΙΔΟΥ 1994: Μανακίδου Ε., *Παραστάσεις με άρματα (8ος-5ος αι. π.Χ.). Παρατηρήσεις στην εικονογραφία τους*, Thessaloniki 1994

ΜΑΡΑΓΚΟΥ 1985: Μαραγκού Λ., *Αρχαία ελληνική τέχνη. Συλλογή Ν.Π. Γουλανδρή*, Athens 1985

ΜΑΡΑΓΚΟΥ 1995: Μαραγκού Λ. (ed.), *Αρχαία ελληνική τέχνη από τη Συλλογή Σταύρου Σ. Νιάρχου*, Athens 1995

MARCADÉ 1969: Marcadé J., *Au Musée de Délos*, Paris 1969

MARCADÉ 1996: Marcadé J. (ed.), *Sculptures déliennes*, Paris 1996

MARGREITER 1988: Margreiter I., *Die Kleinfunde aus dem Apollon-Heiligtum, Alt-Ägina* II.3 (eds. H. Walter - E. Walter-Karydi), Mainz am Rhein 1988

ΜΑΡΚΟΥΛΑΚΗ - ΚΙΝΔΕΛΗ 1982: Μαρκουλάκη Ε.-Κινδελή-Νινιού Β., Ελληνιστικός λαξευτός τάφος Χανίων. Ανασκαφή οικοπέδου Μαθιουλάκη, *ADelt* 37 (1982) Meletai, 71-118

MARWITZ 1979: Marwitz H., Eine Strigilis, *AntK* 22 (1979) 72-81

MATHESON 1992: Matheson S.B., *Polygnotos and Vase Painting in Classical Athens*, 1992

MATTUSH 1996: Mattush C.C. (ed.), *The Fire of Hephaistos; Large Classical Bronzes from North American Collections*, Cambridge Mass. 1996

MAY 1991: May R., Les jeux d'osselets, in *Jouer dans l'Antiquité*, Marseille 1991, 100ff.

McDERMOTT 1938: McDermott W.C., *The Ape in Antiquity*, 1938

McELDERKIN 1930: McElderkin K., Jointed Dolls in Antiquity, *AJA* 34 (1930) 450-470

McKESSON-CAMP 1979: McKesson-Camp J., *The Water Supply of Ancient Athens from 3000 to 86 B.C.*, 1979

McNALLY 1969: McNally S., An Attic Geometric Vase in the Collection of Mt. Holyoke College, *AJA* 73 (1969) 459-464

MELVILLE-JONES 1986: Melville-Jones J., *A Dictionary of Ancient Greek Coins*, London 1986

MELVILLE-JONES 1990: Melville-Jones J., *A Dictionary of Ancient Roman Coins*, London 1990

MERKELBACH 1995: Merkelbach R., *Isis-Regina, Zeus-Sarapis: die griechisch-ägyptische Religion nach den Quellen dargestellt*, Stuttgart - Leipzig 1995

MERKER 1973: Merker G., *The Hellenistic Sculpture of Rhodes*, SIMA 40, 1973

MERSCH 1996: Mersch A., *Studien zur Siedlungsgeschichte Attikas von 950 bis 400 v.Chr.*, Frankfurt 1996

MERTENS 1977: Mertens J., *Attic White-Ground. Its Development on Shapes Other than Lekythoi*, New York 1977

METZGER 1971: Metzger I., Piraeus-Zisterne, *ADelt* 26 (1971) Meletai, 41-94

METZGER 1994: Metzger I.R., Ein hellenistisches Grabmonument in Eretria, in *Γ' Επιστημονική Συνάντηση για την Ελληνιστική Κεραμική*, Athens 1994

MEURER 1909: Meurer M., *Vergleichende Formenlehre des Ornamentes und der Pflanze*, Dresden 1909

MIB III: Hahn W., *Moneta Imperii Byzantini III: Von Heraclius bis Leo III./Alleinregierung (610-720)*, Wien 1981

MILLEKER 1988: Milleker E., *The Statue of Apollo Lykeios in Athens*, 1988

MILLER 1974: Miller S.G., Menon's Cistern, *Hesperia* 43 (1974) 194-245

MILLER 1979: Miller St., Excavations at Nemea 1978, *Hesperia* 48 (1979) 73-103

MILLER 1989: Miller M., The Ependytes in Classical Athens, *Hesperia* 58 (1989) 313-329

MILLER 1999: Miller M., Re-examining Transvestism in Archaic and Classical Athens. The Zewadski Stamnos, *AJA* 103 (1999) 223-253

MILNE 1939: Milne M., Kylichnis, *AJA* 64 (1939), 247-254

ΜΙΧΑΗΛΙΔΗΣ 1982: Μιχαηλίδης Σ., *Εγκυκλοπαίδεια της αρχαίας ελληνικής μουσικής*, Athens 1982

MOLLARD-BESQUES 1954, 1963, 1972, 1986: Mollard-Besques S., *Musée National du Louvre, Catalogue raisonné des figurines et reliefs en terre-cuite grecs, étrusques et romains* I, 1954, II, 1963, III, 1972, IV, 1986

MOLINIER 1914: Molinier S., *Les "maisons sacrées" de Délos au temps de l'independance de l'île (315-166 av. J.-C.)*, Paris 1914

MOON 1981: Moon W., *Greek Vase Painting in Midwestern Collections*, Chicago 1981

MORAW 1998: Moraw S., *Die Mänade in der attischen Vasenmalerei des 6. und 5. Jhs v.Chr.*, Mainz 1998

MORET 1984: Moret J.M., *Oedipe, la Sphinx et les Thébains. Essai de mythologie iconographique*, Genève 1984

MORITZ 1958: Moritz L.A., *Grain Mills and Flour in Classical Antiquity*, Oxford 1958

MORRIS 1982: Morris S., A Middle Protoattic Workshop from Aigina and its Historical Background, *HSCPh* 86 (1982) 285-286

MORRISON - WILLIAMS 1968: Morrison J.S. - Williams R.T., *Greek Oared Ships 900-322 B.C.*, 1968

MORROW 1985: Morrow K.D., *Greek Footwear and the Dating of Sculpture*, Madison 1985

ΜΟΣΧΟΝΗΣΙΩΤΗ 1992: Μοσχονησιώτη Σ., Νεκροταφείο στον Άγ. Μάμαντα, *AErgoMak* 3 (1992) 351-356

MOUNTJOY 1981: Mountjoy P., *Four Early Mycenaean Wells from the South Slope of the Acropolis at Athens, Miscellanea Graeca*, Gent 1981

MOUNTJOY 1986: Mountjoy P.A., *Mycenaean Decorated Pottery. A Guide to Identification*, SIMA 73, 1986

MOUNTJOY 1988: Mountjoy P.A., LH IIIC Late Versus Submycenaean. The Kerameikos Pompeion Cemetery Reviewed, *JdI* 103 (1988) 1-33

MOUNTJOY 1995: Mountjoy P.A, *Mycenaean Athens*, SIMA 1995

MOUNTJOY 1999: Mountjoy P.A., *Regional Mycenaean Decorated Pottery*, I-II, 1999

ΜΠΑΖΙΩΤΟΠΟΥΛΟΥ-ΒΑΛΑΒΑΝΗ 1994: Μπαζιωτοπούλου-Βαλαβάνη Ε., Ανασκαφές σε αθηναϊκά κεραμεικά εργαστήρια αρχαϊκών και κλασικών χρόνων, in W.D.E. Coulson *et al.* (eds.), *The Archaeology of Athens and Attica under the Democracy*, 1994, 45-54

ΜΠΑΖΙΩΤΟΠΟΥΛΟΥ - ΔΡΑΚΩΤΟΥ 1994: Μπαζιωτοπούλου Ε. - Δρακωτού Ι., 3. ΜΕΤΡΟ Αθηνών, Ανασκαφή Σταθμού Κεραμεικός, *ADelt* 49 (1994) Chronika, 34-36

ΜΠΕΣΙΟΣ - ΠΑΠΠΑ (n.p.d.): Μπέσιος Μ. - Παππά Μ., *Πύδνα* (n.p.d.).

ΜΠΟΝΙΑΣ 1998: Μπόνιας Ζ., *Ένα αγροτικό Ιερό στις Αιγιές Λακωνίας*, Athens 1998

ΜΠΟΣΝΑΚΗΣ 1998: Μποσνάκης Δ., *Οι αιγυπτιακές θεότητες στη Ρόδο και την Κω από τους ελληνιστικούς χρόνους μέχρι τη Ρωμαιοκρατία*, Athens 1998

ΜΥΛΩΝΑΣ 1931-32: Μυλωνάς Γ., Ανασκαφή ρωμαϊκού βαλανείου προ των παλαιών Ανακτόρων, *ADelt* 14 (1931-32) Supplement, 41-48

MYLONAS 1959: Mylonas G.E., *Aghios Kosmas. An Early Bronze Age Settlement and Cemetery in Attica*, Princeton 1959

MYLONAS 1961: Mylonas G.E., *Eleusis and the Eleusinian Mysteries*, Princeton 1961

ΜΥΛΩΝΑΣ 1973: Μυλωνάς Γ.Ε., *Ο Ταφικός Κύκλος Β των Μυκηνών*, Α-Β, 1973

ΜΥΛΩΝΑΣ 1975: Μυλωνάς Γ.Ε., *Το Δυτικόν νεκροταφείον της Ελευσίνος*, Α-Γ, 1975

MULLER 1996: Muller, A., *Les terres cuites votives du Thesmophorion: de l'atelier au sanctuaire, Etudes Thasiennes* XVII, Paris 1996

MÜHSAM 1953: Mühsam H., *Attic Grave Reliefs from the Roman Period*, Berytus 10-11 (1953)

Münzen und Medaillen 1964: Attische schwarzfigurige Vasen, Münzen und Medaillen, November 1964, Basel

Mythen und Menschen 1997: Mythen und Menschen. Griechische Vasenkunst aus einer deutschen Privatsammlung, Mainz 1997

NACHBAUR 1998: Nachbaur G., Zwei Schalenfragmente von Onesimos, *ÖJh* 67 (1998) 97-108

NAKAYAMA 1982: Nakayama N., *Untersuchung der auf weissgrundigen Lekythen dargestellten Grabmäler* (Ph.D thesis), Freiburg 1982

NEILS 1992: Neils J., The Morgantina Phormiskos, *AJA* 96 (1992) 225-235

NEUGEBAUER 1921: Neugebauer K.A., *Asklepios*, 1921

NEUMANN 1965: Neumann G., *Gesten und Gebärden in der griechischen Kunst*, Berlin 1965

NICHOLSON 1968: Nicholson F., *Ancient Life in Miniature. An Exhibition of Classical Terracottas from Private Collections in England*, Birmingham 1968

NICOLE 1908: Nicole G., *Meidias*, 1908

NILSSON 1967: Nilsson M.P., *Geschichte der griechischen Religion* I, 1967[3]

NOBLE 1988: Noble J., *The Techniques of Painted Attic Pottery*, London 1988 (revised edition)

NOLL - HOLM - BORN 1973: Noll W. - Holm R. - Born L., Material und Techniken antiker Vasenmalerei, *JbKuSammlBadWürt* 10 (1973) 103-126

ΝΤΑΤΣΟΥΛΗ-ΣΤΑΥΡΙΔΗ 1984: Ντάτσουλη-Σταυρίδη Α., Ρωμαϊκά γλυπτά από το Εθνικό Μουσείο, *AEphem* 1984, 161-190

ΝΤΑΤΣΟΥΛΗ-ΣΤΑΥΡΙΔΗ 1985: Ντάτσουλη-Σταυρίδη Α., *Ρωμαϊκά πορτραίτα στο Εθνικό Αρχαιολογικό Μουσείο Αθηνών*, 1985

OAKLEY 1988: Oakley J., Attic Red-Figured Skyphoi of Corinthian Shape, *Hesperia* 57 (1988) 165-191

OAKLEY 1990: Oakley J., *The Phiale Painter*, Mainz 1990

OAKLEY - SINOS 1993: Oakley J. - Sinos R., *The Wedding in Ancient Athens*, Madison, Wisconsin 1993

OAKLEY 1997: Oakley J., *The Achilles Painter*, Mainz 1997

OBERLÄNDER 1967: Oberländer P., *Griechische Handspiegel*, Hamburg 1967

ΟΙΚΟΝΟΜΙΔΟΥ 1996: Οικονομίδου Μ., *Ελληνική τέχνη, Αρχαία νομίσματα*, Athens 1996

OLIVER-SMITH 1964: Oliver-Smith P.E., Representations of Aeolic Capital on Greek Vases Before 400 B.C., in *Essays in Memory of Karl Lehmann*, 1964, 232-241

OLIVER-SMITH 1981: Oliver-Smith P.E., *Architectural Elements on Greek Vases Before 400 B.C.*, Ann Arbor 1981.

OLMOS 1980: Olmos R.R., *Catalogo de los vasos griegos en el Museo arqueologico nacional*, I. *Las Lecitos aticas de fondo blanco*, Madrid 1980

Olynthus II: Robinson D.M., *Architecture and Sculpture. Excavations at Olynthus* II, Baltimore 1930

Olynthus IV: Robinson D.M., *The Terracottas of Olynthus Found in 1928*, Olynthus IV, Baltimore 1931

Olynthus V: Robinson D.M., *Mosaics, Vases and Lamps of Olynthus 1928-1931*, Olynthus V, Baltimore 1932

Olynthus VII: Robinson D.M., *The Terracottas of Olynthus Found in 1931*, Olynthus VII, Baltimore 1933

Olynthus XIV: Robinson D.M., *Terracottas, Lamps and Coins Found in 1934 and 1938*, Olynthus XIV, Baltimore 1952

ORSI 1906: Orsi P., *Gela; Scavi del 1900-1905*, Roma 1906

OSBORNE - BYRNE 1994: Osborne M.J. - Byrne S., *Lexicon of Greek Personal Names*, II. *Attica*, 1994

OSBORNE - BYRNE 1996: Osborne M.J. - Byrne S., *The Foreign Residents of Athens*, 1996

ÖZGEN - ÖZTÜRK 1996: Özgen I. - Öztürk J. (eds.), *The Lydian Treasure. Heritage Recovered*, Istanbul 1996

PALAGIA - COULSON 1998: Palagia O. - Coulson W. (eds.), *Regional Schools in Hellenistic Sculpture*, 1998

ΠΑΛΑΙΟΚΡΑΣΣΑ 1980: Παλαιοκρασσά Λ., Τα αρχαία γλυπτά της συλλογής στη Χώρα της Άνδρου, *AEphem* 1980, 18-32

Pandora: Reeder E. (ed.), *Pandora. Women in Classical Greece*, Walters Art Gallery, Baltimore and Princeton 1995

ΠΑΝΤΟΣ 1973: Πάντος Π., Επιγραφαί παρά την Αγοράν των Αθηνών, *AEphem* 1973, 175-188

ΠΑΝΤΟΣ 1992: Πάντος Π., Αρχαιολογικά ευρήματα από την ΝΔ. Αινίδα-Περιβόλι Φθιώτιδος, in *Διεθνές Συνέδριο για την Αρχαία Θεσσαλία στη μνήμη Δημήτρη Ρ. Θεοχάρη*, 1992, 414-421

PAPADOPOULOS 1995: Papadopoulos J., A Pergamene Cup with σχήματα συνουσιαστικά, in A. Cambitoglou - E.G.D. Robinson (eds.), *Classical Art in the Nicholson Museum, Sydney*, Mainz 1995, 223-235

ΠΑΠΑΠΟΣΤΟΛΟΥ 1977: Παπαποστόλου Ι.Α., Ελληνιστικοί τάφοι της Πάτρας Ι, *ADelt* 32 (1977) Meletai, 281-343

ΠΑΠΑΠΟΣΤΟΛΟΥ 1983: Παπαποστόλου Ι.Α., Κτερίσματα ταφής σε ρωμαϊκό μαυσωλείο στην Πάτρα, *AEphem* 1983, Meletai, 1-34

ΠΑΠΑΠΟΣΤΟΛΟΥ 1990: Παπαποστόλου Ι.Α., Κοσμήματα Πατρών και Δύμης, *AEphem* 1990, Meletai, 83-139

ΠΑΠΑΣΠΥΡΙΔΗ 1923: Παπασπυρίδη Σ., Ο "τεχνίτης των καλάμων" των λευκών ληκύθων, *ADelt* 8 (1923) Meletai, 117-146

ΠΑΠΑΣΠΥΡΙΔΗ - ΚΥΠΑΡΙΣΣΗΣ 1927/28: Παπασπυρίδη Σ. - Κυπαρίσσης Ν., Νέα λήκυθος του Δούριδος, *ADelt* 11 (1927/28) 91-110

ΠΑΠΑΣΠΥΡΙΔΗ-ΚΑΡΟΥΖΟΥ 1933-35: Παπασπυρίδη-Καρούζου Σ., Ανασκαφή τάφων του Άργους, *ADelt* 15 (1933-35) 16-53

ΠΑΠΑΧΑΤΖΗΣ 1974: Παπαχατζής Ν., *Παυσανίου Ελλάδος Περιήγησις. Αττικά*, Athens 1974

ΠΑΠΟΥΤΣΑΚΗ-ΣΕΡΜΠΕΤΗ 1983: Παπουτσάκη-Σερμπέτη, *Ο Ζωγράφος της Providence*, Athens 1983

Para: Beazley J.D., *Paralipomena*, Oxford 1971

PARKE 1977: Parke H.W., *Festivals of the Athenians*, Ithaca 1977

ΠΑΡΛΑΜΑ 1990-91: Παρλαμά Λ., Ο Μητροπολιτικός Σιδηρόδρομος και οι αρχαιότητες των Αθηνών, *Ηόρος* 8-9 (1990-1991) 231-245

ΠΑΡΛΑΜΑ 1992-98: Παρλαμά Λ., Αθήνα 1993-1995, από τις ανασκαφές του Μητροπολιτικού Σιδηροδρόμου, *Ηόρος* 10-12 (1992-1998) 521-544

PATRUCCO 1972: Patrucco R., *Lo sport nella Grecia antica*, 1972

ΠΑΤΣΙΑΔΑ 1983: Πατσιαδά Β., Κεραμική του τύπου της "Δυτικής κλιτύος" από τη Ρόδο, *ADelt* 38 (1983) Meletai, 105-210

PAUL 1959: Paul E., *Antike Welt in Ton. Griechische und römische Terrakotten des Archäologischen Instituts in Leipzig*, Leipzig 1959

PEACOCK - WILLIAMS 1986: Peacock D.P.S. - Williams D.F., *Amphorae and the Roman Economy. An Introductory Guide*, London - New York 1986

PEKRIDOU-GORECKI 1989: Pekridou-Gorecki A., *Mode im antiken Griechenland: Textile Fertigung und Kleidung*, München 1989 (Gr. edition 1993)

ΠΕΛΕΚΑΝΙΔΗΣ 1974: Πελεκανίδης Σ., *Βυζαντινά Μνημεία* I. *Σύνταγμα των παλαιοχριστιανικών ψηφιδωτών της Ελλάδος* I. *Νησιωτική Ελλάς*, Thessaloniki 1974

ΠΕΛΕΚΙΔΗΣ 1916: Πελεκίδης Σ., Ανασκαφή Φαλήρου, *ΑΔ* 2 (1916) 13-64

PÉLÉKIDIS 1962: Pélékidis C., *Histoire de l'Ephébie attique des origines à 31 av. J.-Chr.*, Paris 1962

PEMBERTON 1989: Pemberton G., *The Dexiosis on Attic Gravestones, Mediterranean Archaeology* 2, 1989

ΠΕΝΝΑ 1996: Πέννα Β., Η ζωή στις βυζαντινές πόλεις της Πελοποννήσου: η νομισματική μαρτυρία (8ος-12ος αι. μ.Χ.), in *Μνήμη Martin J. Price* (Βιβλιοθήκη της Ελληνικής Νομισματικής Εταιρείας, 5), Athens 1996

Perachora II: Payne H., *Perachora. The Sanctuaries of Hera Akraia and Limenia*, II, Oxford 1962

PEREDOLSKAJA 1964: Peredolskaja A.A., *Attische Tonfiguren aus einem südrussischen Grab, AntK* Bh. 2, 1964

PERNICE 1894: Pernice E., *Griechische Gewichte*, Berlin 1894

ΠΕΤΡΑΚΟΣ 1968: Πετράκος Β., *Ο Ωρωπός και το Ιερόν του Αμφιαράου*, Athens 1968

ΠΕΤΡΑΚΟΣ 1969: Πετράκος Β., Αρχαιότητες και μνημεία νήσων Αιγαίου, *ADelt* 24 (1969) Chronika, 368-371

ΠΕΤΡΑΚΟΣ 1991: Πετράκος Β., Ανασκαφή Ραμνούντος, *Prakt* 1991, 1-63

ΠΕΤΡΑΚΟΣ 1998: Πετράκος Β., Η ανασκαφή του Κεραμεικού από την Αρχαιολογική Εταιρεία, *Ο Μέντωρ* 48 (1998) 119-207

PETROCHEILOS 1996: Petrocheilos I., Frühe Phaleron-Oinochoen, *AM* 111 (1996) 45-64

ΠΕΤΡΟΝΩΤΗΣ 1986: Πετρονώτης Α., *Ελληνική παραδοσιακή αρχιτεκτονική, Αρκαδία*, 1986

PFANNER 1977: Pfanner M., Zur Schmückung griechischer Grabstelen, *HefteABern* 3 (1977) 5-15

PFISTERER-HAAS 1996: Pfisterer-Haas S., *Antike Terrakotten, Leipziger Universitätsverlag*, 1996 (Kleine Reihe des Antikenmuseum der Universität Leipzig, 3)

PFROMMER 1983: Pfrommer M., Zur Typologie der Miniaturhydrien Humeitepe, *IstMitt* 33 (1983) 79-89

PFROMMER 1987: Pfrommer M., *Studien zur alexandrinischen Toreutik frühhellenistischer Zeit*, Berlin 1987

PFUHL 1903: Pfuhl E., Der archaische Friedhof am Stadtberge von Thera, *AM* 28 (1903) 1ff.

PFUHL 1923: Pfuhl E., *Malerei und Zeichnung der Griechen*, München 1923

PICARD 1944/45: Picard Ch., Statues et ex-votos du «Stibadeion» dionysiaque de Délos, *BCH* 69 (1944/45) 240-270

PICARD 1954: Picard Ch., *Manuel d'archéologie grecque. La sculpture*, IV, 1954

ΠΙΚΟΥΛΑΣ 1991: Πίκουλας Κ., Ανιχνεύοντας αρχαίους δρόμους, in *International Colloquium "Land Routes in Greece from Prehistoric to Post-Byzantine Times"*, Athens 23-25/5/1991

ΠΙΤΤΑΚΗΣ 1860: Πιττάκης Κ.Σ., Επιγραφή εξ Αθηνών, *AEphem* 1860, 2102

PLANTZOS 1999: Plantzos D., *Hellenistic Engraved Gems*, Oxford 1999

PLASSART 1912: Plassart A., Fouilles de Délos, *BCH* 36 (1912) 387-435, 661-666

ΠΛΑΤΩΝ 1964: Πλάτων Ν., Εργασίαι διαμορφώσεως και τακτοποιήσεως του αρχαιολογικού χώρου Ακροπόλεως, *ADelt* 19 (1964) Chronika, 30-32

ΠΛΑΤΩΝ 1965: Πλάτων Ν., Εργασίαι διαμορφώσεως και τακτοποιήσεως του αρχαιολογικού χώρου Ακροπόλεως, *ADelt* 20 (1965) Chronika, 22-34

ΠΛΑΤΩΝΟΣ - ΧΑΤΖΗΠΟΥΛΙΟΥ 1984: Πλάτωνος Μ. - Χατζηπούλιου Ε., Ιερά Οδός, *ADelt* 39 (1984) Chronika, 11-14

PLATZ-HORSTER 1976: Platz-Horster G., *Antike Gläser. Ausstellung im Antike Museum*, 1976

POLACCO 1954: Polacco L., Cronologia del portico presso l'Odeo di Erode Attico e il "Porticus Eumenicae", *Memorie Ist. Veneto* XXXI.2, Venezia 1954, 719-724

POLIAKOFF 1987: Poliakoff M., *Compact Sports in the Ancient World*, 1987

POLLITT 1979: Pollitt J.J., Kernoi from the Athenian Agora, *Hesperia* 48 (1979) 205-233

POMEROY 1985: Pomeroy S., *Frauenleben im klassischen Altertum*, Stuttgart 1985

POULSEN 1937: Poulsen V.H., Der Strenge Stil. Studien zur Geschichte der griechischen Plastik 480-450, *AArch* 8 (1937) 1ff.

ΠΟΥΠΑΚΗ 1998: Πουπάκη Ειρ., Ο μύλος στην κλασική αρχαιότητα. Συμβολή στη μελέτη της τυπολογίας και της χρήσης ενός σημαντικού λίθινου σκεύους για αγροτικές εργασίες, *Διαχρονία* 3/4 (1998) 132-171

PRITCHETT 1980: Pritchett W.K., *Studies in Ancient Greek Topography* III, *Classical Studies* 22, 1980

PRUDHOMMEAU 1965: Prudhommeau G., *La danse grecque antique*, Paris 1965

PRYCE 1928: Pryce C.N., *Catalogue of Sculpture in the British Museum*, I², 1928

PÜLZ 1991: Pülz St., Eine Lekythos des Tymbos Malers, *AA* 1991, 367-370

ΠΩΛΟΓΙΩΡΓΗ 1988: Πωλογιώργη Μ.Ι., Τάφοι του Ωρωπού, *ADelt* 43 (1988) Meletai, 114-138

ΠΩΛΟΓΙΩΡΓΗ 1993-94: Πωλογιώργη Μ.Ι., Λήκυθοι του Αρχαιολογικού Μουσείου Πειραιώς, *Αρχαιογνωσία* 8 (1993-94) 257-276

ΠΩΛΟΓΙΩΡΓΗ 1995: Πωλογιώργη Μ.Ι., Παιδική ταφή στην Ηλιούπολη, *AEphem* 1995, 231-245

ΠΩΛΟΓΙΩΡΓΗ 1998: Πωλογιώργη Μ.Ι., *Μνημεία του Δυτικού Νεκροταφείου του Ωρωπού*, Athens 1998

ΠΩΛΟΓΙΩΡΓΗ forth.: Πωλογιώργη Μ.Ι., Διός κούρος επί ελεφαντίνου πλακιδίου, στον *Τιμητικό τόμο για την επίτιμο Έφορο Αρχαιοτήτων Ο. Τζάχου-Αλεξανδρή* (forth.)

REILLY 1989: Reilly J., Many Brides: "Mistress and Maid" on Athenian Lekythoi, *Hesperia* 58 (1989) 417ff.

REINACH 1917: Reinach S., *Catalogue illustré des antiquités nationales au Château de Saint-Germain-en-Laye*, I, Paris 1917

RIC: Roman Imperial Coinage, London, I-X, 1926-1994

ΡΗΓΙΝΟΣ 1994: Ρήγινος Γ., Κεραμική από τη Δυτική Ήπειρο. Κιβωτιόσχημος τάφος Θεσπρωτίας, in *Δ' Επιστημονική Συνάντηση για την Ελληνιστική Κεραμική*, Mytilene 1994, 93-109

RICH 1861: Rich A., *Dictionnaire des antiquités romaines et grecques*, Paris 1861

RICHARDS-MANTZOYΛINOY 1981: Richards-Μαντζουλίνου Ε., Η φυτική διακόσμηση των κλασικών χρόνων, *AAA* XIV (1981) 208-229

RICHTER 1915: Richter G.M.A., *Metropolitan Museum. Greek, Etruscan and Roman Bronzes*, New York 1915

RICHTER - MILNE 1937: Richter G.M.A. - Milne M.J., *Shapes and Names of Athenian Vases*, 1937

RICHTER 1944: Richter G.M.A., Polychromy in Greek Sculpture, *AJA* 48 (1944) 321-333

RICHTER 1950: Richter G.M.A., *The Sculpture and Sculptors of the Greeks*, 1950

RICHTER 1953: Richter G.M.A., *Metropolitan Museum of Art. Handbook of the Greek Collection*, Harvard 1953

RICHTER 1966: Richter G.M.A., *The Furniture of the Greeks, Etruscans and Romans*, 1966

RICHTER 1971: Richter G.M.A., *The Engraved Gems of the Romans*, 1971

RIDGWAY 1970: Ridgway B.S., *The Severe Style in Greek Sculpture*, Princeton 1970

RIDGWAY 1981: Ridgway B.S., *Fifth Century Styles in Greek Sculpture*, 1981

ROBERTS 1978: Roberts S.R., *The Attic Pyxis*, Chicago 1978

ROBERTSON 1971: Robertson A.S., *Roman Imperial Coins in the Hunter Coin Cabinet*, II, 1971

ROBERTSON 1978: Robertson A.S., *Roman Imperial Coins in the Hunter Coin Cabinet*, IV, Glasgow 1978

ROBERTSON 1982: Robertson A.S., *Roman Imperial Coins in the Hunter Coin Cabinet*, V, New York 1982

ROBERTSON 1992: Robertson M., *The Art of Vase-Painting in Classical Athens*, Cambridge 1992

ROBINSON - FLUCK 1937: Robinson D.M. - Fluck E.J., *A Study of the Greek Love-Names*, Baltimore 1937

ROHDE 1968: Rohde E., *Griechische Terrakotten*, 1968

ROLLEY 1983: Rolley Cl., *Les bronzes grecs*, Fribourg 1983

ROLLEY 1994: Rolley Cl., *La sculpture grecque*, Paris 1994

ROMBOS 1988: Rombos T., *The Iconography of the Attic Late Geometric II Pottery*, Jonsered 1988

ROOS 1951: Roos E., *Die tragische Orchestik im Zerrbild der altattischen Komödie*, Stockholm 1951

ΡΟΣ 1832-33: Ρος Λ., *Αναμνήσεις και ανακοινώσεις από την Ελλάδα (1832-1833)*, Ξένοι περιηγητές στον ελληνικό χώρο, 3 (commentary: T. Vournas), Athens 1976

ROSE 1997: Rose C.B., *Dynastic Commemoration and Imperial Portraiture in the Julio-Claudian Period*, 1997

ROTROFF 1983: Rotroff I.S., Three Cistern Systems on the Kolonos Agoraios, *Hesperia* 52 (1983) 257-297

ROTROFF 1984a: Rotroff I.S., The Origins and Chronology of Hellenistic Gray Unguentaria, *AJA* 88 (1984) 258

ROTROFF 1984b: Rotroff I.S., Spool Saltcellars in the Athenian Agora, *Hesperia* 53 (1984) 343-354

ROTROFF 1991: Rotroff I.S., Attic West Slope Vase Painting, *Hesperia* 60 (1991) 59-102

RUDOLPH 1971: Rudolph W., *Die Bauchlekythos; ein Beitrag zur Formgeschichte der attischen Keramik des 5. Jhs v.Chr.*, Bloomington 1971

RÜHFEL 1984a: Rühfel H., *Das Kind in der griechischen Kunst*, Mainz 1984

RÜHFEL 1984b: Rühfel H., *Kinderleben im klassischen Athen*, Mainz 1984

RUNNELS 1988: Runnels C.N., Early Bronze Age Stone Mortars from the Southern Argolid, *Hesperia* 57 (1988) 257-272

RUTKOWSKI 1979: Rutkowski B., Griechische Kandelaber, *JdI* 94 (1979) 211ff.

ΡΩΜΑΙΟΣ 1955: Ρωμαίος Κ., Εικών αρχαίου σχολείου, *Μικρά Μελετήματα*, Thessaloniki 1955

ΡΩΜΙΟΠΟΥΛΟΥ 1964: Ρωμιοπούλου Κ., Αγγεία του 4ου π.Χ. αιώνος εκ των ανασκαφών της Αμφιπόλεως, *AEphem* 1964, 91-104

ΡΩΜΙΟΠΟΥΛΟΥ 1989: Ρωμιοπούλου Κ., Κλειστά ταφικά σύνολα υστεροκλασικών χρόνων από τη Θεσσαλονίκη, in *Φίλια Έπη εις Γ. Μυλωνάν*, Γ', 1989, 194-218

ΣΑΑΤΣΟΓΛΟΥ-ΠΑΛΙΑΔΕΛΗ 1984: Σαατσόγλου-Παλιαδέλη Χρ., *Τα επιτάφια μνημεία από τη Μεγάλη Τούμπα της Βεργίνας* (Ph.D. thesis), *EpistEpetThess* 50, Thessaloniki 1984

ΣΑΑΤΣΟΓΛΟΥ-ΠΑΛΙΑΔΕΛΗ 1988: Σαατσόγλου-Παλιαδέλη Χρ., Νέα στοιχεία για την τεχνική των γραπτών στηλών της Βεργίνας, *AErgoMak* 2 (1988) 137-145

SABETAI 1993: Sabetai V., *The Washing Painter*, 1993

SACKETT - COCKING 1992: Sackett L.H. - Cocking J., Other Finds in Stone, Clay and Faience, in L.H. Sackett (ed.), *Knossos. Excavation at the Unexplored Mansion* II, *BSA* Suppl. 21, 1992

Samos XVIII: Jarosch V., *Samische Tonfiguren des 10. bis 7. Jhrs v.Chr. aus dem Heraion von Samos*, Samos XVIII, Bonn 1994

ΣΑΪΤΑΣ 1992: Σαΐτας Γ., *Ελληνική παραδοσιακή αρχιτεκτονική*, Μάνη, 1992

ΣΒΟΡΩΝΟΣ 1913: Σβορώνος I.N., Κατάλογος δωρεάς Καραπάνου, Συλλογή γλυπτών λίθων, *JIAN* 15 (1913) 157-184

SCE II: Gjerstad E., *The Swedish Cyprus Expedition*, II, *Finds and Results of the Excavations in Cyprus 1927-1931*, 1934

SCE IV₂: Gjerstad E., *The Swedish Cyprus Expedition*, IV₂, *The Cypro-geometric, Cypro-archaic and Cypro-classical Periods*, 1948

SCHAAL 1923: Schaal H., *Griechische Vasen aus Frankfurter Sammlungen*, Frankfurt 1923

SCHÄDLER 1996: Schädler U., Spielen mit Astragalen, *AA* 1996, 61-73

SCHÄFER 1997: Schäfer A., *Unterhaltung beim griechischen Symposion. Darbietung, Spiele und Wettkäpfe von homerischer bis in spätklassische Zeit*, Mainz 1997

SCHAUENBURG 1953: Schauenburg K., Pluton und Dionysos, *JdI* 68 (1953) 38-72

SCHAUENBURG 1972: Schauenburg K., Unteritalische Alabastra, *JdI* 87 (1972) 258-298

SCHEFOLD 1981: Schefold K., *Die Göttersage in der klassischen und hellenistischen Kunst*, München 1981

SCHEIBLER 1964: Scheibler I., Exaleiptra, *JdI* 79 (1964) 72-108

SCHEIBLER 1968: Scheibler I., Kothon-Exaleiptron. Addenda, *AA* 83 (1968) 389-397

SCHEIBLER 1992: Scheibler I., *Ελληνική κεραμική* (Gr. tr.), 1992

SCHELP 1975: Schelp J., *Das Kanoun, der griechische Opferkorb*, Würzburg 1975

SCHILARDI 1977: Schilardi D., *The Thespian Polyandrion (424 B.C.). The Excavations and the Finds from a Thespian State Burial*, 1977

SCHLÖRB-VIERNEISEL 1966: Schlörb-Vierneisel B., Eridanos Nekropole, *AM* 81 (1966) 4-111

SCHMALTZ 1974: Schmaltz B., *Terrakotten aus dem Kabirenheiligtum von Theben. Das Kabirenheiligtum bei Theben*, V, Berlin 1974

SCHMALTZ 1983: Schmaltz B., *Griechische Grabreliefs*, 1983

SCHMIDT 1971: Schmidt E.H., *Spielzeug und Spiele der Kinder in klassischer Altertum*, 1971

SCHMIDT 1994: Schmidt E., *Katalog der antiken Terrakotten. Martin von Wagner Museum der Universität Würzburg, Teil. 1. Die figürlichen Terrakotten*, 1994

SCHNEIDER-HERMANN 1975: Schneider-Hermann G., *Eine Niederländische Studiensammlung Antiker Kunst*, *BABesch* Suppl. I, 1975

SCHOLL 1996: Scholl A., *Die attischen Bildfeldstelen des 4. Jhs v.Chr. Untersuchungen zu den kleinformatigen Grabreliefs im spätklassischen Athen*, *AM* Bh. 17, 1996

SCHÖNE 1987: Schöne A., *Der Thiasos. Ein ikonographische Untersuchung über das Gefolge des Dionysos in der attischen Vasenmalerei des 6. und 5. Jhs v.Chr.*, Göteborg 1987

SCHRECKENBERG 1960: Schreckenberg H., *ΔΡΑΜΑ. Von Verben der griechischen Tragödie aus dem Tanz*, Wübung 1960

SCHRÖDER 1989: Schröder St., *Römische Bacchusbilder in der Tradition des Apollon Lykeios. Studien zur Bildformulierung und Bildbedeutung in späthellenistisch-römischer Zeit*, 1989

SCHUCHARDT 1978: Schuchardt W.H., Relief mit Pferd und Negerknaben im Nationalmuseum in Athen, N.M. 4464, *AntPl* XVII (1978) 75ff.

SCHÜRMANN 1989: Schürmann W., *Katalog der antiken Terrakotten im Badischen Landesmuseum, Karlsruhe*, *SIMA* 84, 1989

SCHWABACHER 1941: Schwabacher W., Hellenistische Reliefkeramik im Kerameikos, *AJA* 45 (1941) 182-228

SCHWARZ 1997: Schwarz G., Komostänzer in Graz. Eine archäologische Spurensuche, in *Festschrift für Thuri Lorenz zum 65. Geburtstag*, Wien 1997, 125-128

SCHWEITZER 1961: Schweitzer B., *Mythische Hochzeiten*, Heidelberg 1961

SCIALLANO - SIBELLA 1994: Sciallano M. - Sibella P., *Amphores. Comment les identifier?*, 1994²

SEGALL 1938: Segall B., *Katalog der Goldschmiedearbeiten*, 1938

SELTMAN 1955: Seltman C., *Greek Coins*, London 1955

SHAPIRO 1981: Shapiro A., Courtship Scenes in Attic Vase-Painting, *AJA* 85 (1981) 133-143

SHAPIRO 1987: Shapiro A., Kalos - Inscriptions with Patronymic, *ZPE* 68 (1987) 107-118

SHAPIRO 1991: Shapiro A., The Iconography of Mourning in Athenian Art, *AJA* 95 (1991) 629-652

SHAPIRO - PICÓN - SCOTT 1995: Shapiro A. - Picón C. - Scott G.D., *Greek Vases in the San Antonio Museum of Art*, San Antonio 1995

SHEAR 1930: Shear T.L, Excavations in the North Cemetery at Corinth in 1930, *AJA* 34 (1930) 403-431

SHEAR 1938: Shear T.L, The Campaign of 1937, *Hesperia* 7 (1938) 311-362

SHEAR 1973: Shear T.L., The Athenian Agora. Excavation of 1971 and 1972, *Hesperia* 42 (1973) 121-179, 359-407

SHEAR 1984: Shear T.L., The Athenian Agora. Excavation of 1980-1982, *Hesperia* 53 (1984) 1-57

SHEEDY 1992: Sheedy K., The Late Geometric Hydria and the Advent of the Protoattic Style, *AM* 107 (1992) 11-28

SHEER 1940: Sheer L., The Campaign of 1939, *Hesperia* 9 (1940) 261-307

ΣΗΜΑΝΤΩΝΗ-ΜΠΟΥΡΝΙΑ 1997: Σημαντώνη-Μπουρνιά Ε., *Αρχαιολογία των πρώιμων ελληνικών χρόνων*, Athens 1997

SIEBERT 1978: Siebert G., *Recherches sur les ateliers de bols à reliefs du Péloponnèse à l'époque hellénistique*, Paris 1978

SIMON 1963: Simon E., Polygnotan Paintings and the Niobid Painter, *AJA* 67 (1963) 43-62

SIMON 1975: Simon E., *Führer durch die Antikenabteilung der Martin v. Wagner Museum der Universität Würzburg*, 1975

SIMON 1983: Simon E., *Festivals of Attica. An Archaeological Commentary*, 1983

SIMON 1985a: Simon E., *Die Götter der Griechen*, 3, München 1985

SIMON 1985b: Simon E. Hekate in Athen, *AM* 100 (1985) 271-284

SIMON 1989: Simon E., *Die Sammlung Kisselef im Martin von Wagner Museum der Universität Würzburg, II, Minoische und Griechische Antiken*, München 1989

SIMON et al. 1997: Simon E. et al., *Mythen und Menschen. Griechische Vasenkunst aus einer deutschen Privatsammlung*, Mainz 1997, 48-50

Σίνδος 1985: *Σίνδος*, Exhibition Catalogue, Athens 1985

SINN 1977: Sinn U., *Antike Terrakotten. Vollständiger Katalog der Staatliche Kunstsammlungen Kassel 8*, 1977

ΣΚΙΑΣ 1898: Σκιάς Ν., *Πανάρχαία Ελευσινιακή νεκρόπολις*, *AEphem* 1898, 29-122

ΣΚΙΑΣ 1918: Σκιάς Α., Το παρά την Φυλήν άντρον του Πανός, *AEphem* 1918, 1-28

ΣΚΙΛΑΡΝΤΙ 1975: Σκιλάρντι Δ., Ανασκαφή παρά τα Μακρά Τείχη και η οινοχόη του Ταύρου, *AEphem* 1975, 66-149

SMITH 1981: Smith R.R.R., Greeks, Foreigners and Roman Republican Portrait, *JRS* 71 (1981) 24-38

SMITH 1991: Smith R.R.R., *Hellenistic Sculpture*, 1991

SMITHSON 1961: Smithson E., The Protogeometric Cemetery at Nea Ionia, 1949, *Hesperia* 30 (1961) 147-178

SNODGRASS 1971: Snodgrass A., *The Dark Age of Greece*, Edinburgh 1971

SPARKES 1968: Sparkes B.A., Black Perseus, *AntK* II,1 (1968) 3-16

SPARKES 1975: Sparkes B.A., Illustrating Aristophanes, *JHS* 1975, 122-135

ΣΠΑΘΑΡΗ - ΧΑΤΖΙΩΤΗ 1983: Σπαθάρη Ε. - Χατζιώτη Μ., Λεωφόρος Βασ. Σοφίας και Ηρώδου του Αττικού 2, *ADelt* 38 (1983) Chronika, 23-25

STÄHLER 1983: Stähler K., *Eine Sammlung griechischer Vasen*, Münster 1983

STAMBAUGH 1972: Stambaugh J.E., Sarapis under the Early Ptolemies, *EPRO* 25, Leiden 1972

ΣΤΑΜΠΟΛΙΔΗΣ 1992: Σταμπολίδης Ν., *Τα σφραγίσματα της Δήλου. 2Α. Ο Ερωτικός κύκλος*, 1992

ΣΤΑΜΠΟΛΙΔΗΣ 1994: Σταμπολίδης Ν., *Ελεύθερνα III.2, Από τη γεωμετρική και αρχαϊκή νεκρόπολη. Ταφικές πυρές και ομηρικά έπη*, Athens 1994

ΣΤΑΜΠΟΛΙΔΗΣ 1996: Σταμπολίδης Ν., *Ελεύθερνα III.3, "Αντίποινα". Συμβολή στη μελέτη των ηθών και των εθίμων της γεωμετρικής-αρχαϊκής περιόδου*, 1996

ΣΤΑΜΠΟΛΙΔΗΣ - ΚΑΡΕΤΣΟΥ 1998: Σταμπολίδης Ν. - Καρέτσου Α. (eds.), *Ανατολική Μεσόγειος. Κύπρος, Δωδεκάνησα, Κρήτη. 16ος-6ος αι. π.Χ.*, Herakleion 1998

STAMPOLIDIS 1998a: Stampolidis N., in Stampolidis N. - Karetsou A. (eds.), *Eastern Mediterranean, Cyprus - Dodecanese - Crete, 16th-6th Century B.C.*, Herakleion 1998, 68-100

STAMPOLIDIS 1998b: Stampolidis N., in Karageorghis V. - Stampolidis N. (eds.), *Eastern Mediterranean, Proceedings of the International Symposium*, ·Athens 1998, 175-185

STANSBURY-O'DONNELL 1990: Stansbury-O'Donnell M., Polygnotos's Nekyia: A Reconstruction and Analysis, *AJA* 94 (1990) 213-235

ΣΤΑΥΡΟΠΟΥΛΟΣ 1958: Σταυρόπουλλος Φ., Ανασκαφή Αρχαίας Ακαδήμειας, *Prakt* 1958, 5-13

STEINHART 1996: Steinhart M., *Töpferkunst und Meisterzeichnung*, Mainz 1996

ΣΤΕΦΑΝΙΔΟΥ-ΤΙΒΕΡΙΟΥ 1985: Στεφανίδου-Τιβερίου Θ., *Τραπεζοφόρα του Μουσείου Θεσσαλονίκης*, 1985

STEWART 1979: Stewart A.F., *Attica Studies in Athenian Sculpture of the Hellenistic Age*, London 1979

STEWART 1990: Stewart A.F., *Greek Sculpture*, 1990

STEWART 1997: Stewart A.F., *Art, Desire and the Body in Ancient Greece*, Cambridge 1997

STORCK - TEAGUE 1952: Storck J. - Teague W.D., *Flour for Man's Bread. A History of Milling*, Minnesota 1952

STRONG 1966: Strong D.E., *Greek and Roman Gold and Silver Plate*, London - New York 1966

STUPPERICH 1979: Stupperich R., Weißgrundige Lekythen in Münster, *Boreas* 2 (1979) 209-222

STYRENIUS 1967: Styrenius C.G., *Submycenaean Studies*, Lund 1967

SUTTON 1981: Sutton R.F., *The Interaction Between Men and Women Portrayed on Attic Red-Figure Pottery*, University of North Carolina at Chapel Hill, 1981

SZABO 1975: Szabo M., Attelages de chevaux archaïques en terre cuite en Attique et en Béotie, *BMusHongr* 45 (1975) 7ff.

SZABO 1994: Szabo M., Archaic Terracottas of Boetia, *Studia Archeologica* 67, Roma 1994

TALCOTT 1935: Talcott L., Pottery from a Fifth Century Well, *Hesperia* 4 (1935) 477-523

TESTA 1989: Testa A., *Candelabri et Thymiateria*, 1989

ΤΖΑΒΕΛΛΑ-EVJEN 1984: Τζαβέλλα-Evjen X., *Λιθαρές*, Athens 1984

ΤΖΑΧΟΥ-ΑΛΕΞΑΝΔΡΗ 1987: Τζάχου-Αλεξανδρή Ο., Contribution to the Knowledge of 8th Cent. B.C. Ship Representations, in *Tropis* II (1987) 333-361

ΤΖΑΧΟΥ-ΑΛΕΞΑΝΔΡΗ 1997a: Τζάχου-Αλεξανδρή Ο., Απεικονίσεις των Ανθεστηρίων και ο χους της οδού Πειραιώς του ζ. της Ερέτριας, in *APP* 1997, 473-490

ΤΖΑΧΟΥ-ΑΛΕΞΑΝΔΡΗ 1997b: Τζάχου-Αλεξανδρή Ο., Δίδυμο ταφικό μνημείο του ζ. του Αχιλλέως, in *Έπαινος Ιω. Κ. Παπαδημητρίου*, 1997, 303-365

ΤΖΑΧΟΥ-ΑΛΕΞΑΝΔΡΗ 1998: Τζάχου-Αλεξανδρή Ο., *Λευκές λήκυθοι του ζωγράφου του Αχιλλέως στο Εθνικό Αρχαιολογικό Μουσείο*, Athens 1998

THEMELIS 1979: Themelis P., Ausgrabungen in Kallipolis (Ost-Aetolien) 1977-1978, *AAA* XXII (1979) 245-279

THOMPSON 1933: Thompson H.A., Terracotta Lamps, *Hesperia* 2 (1933) 195-215

THOMPSON 1934: Thompson H.A., Two Centuries of Hellenistic Pottery, *Hesperia* 3 (1934) 311-480

THOMPSON 1940: Thompson M., Some Unpublished Bronze Money of the Early Eighth Century, *Hesperia* 9 (1940) 358-380

THOMPSON 1947: Thompson H.A., The Excavation of the Athenian Agora 1940-1946, *Hesperia* 16 (1947) 193-213

THOMPSON - WYCHERLEY 1972: Thompson H. A. - Wycherley R.E., *The Agora of Athens*, Princeton 1972

ΤΙΒΕΡΙΟΣ 1981: Τιβέριος Μ., *Προβλήματα της μελανόμορφης αττικής κεραμικής*, Thessaloniki 1981

ΤΙΒΕΡΙΟΣ 1984: Τιβέριος Μ. - Γραμμένος Δ., Ανασκαφή ενός νεκροταφείου στην Αρχαία Άργιλο, *ADelt* 39 (1984) Meletai, 1-47

ΤΙΒΕΡΙΟΣ 1985: Τιβέριος Μ., *Μία "Κρίσις των όπλων" του ζ. του Συλέα. Παρατηρήσεις σε ερμηνευτικά θέματα και στις σχέσεις εικονογραφίας και πολιτικής κατά την υστεροαρχαϊκή και πρώιμη κλασική περίοδ*ο, Athens 1985

ΤΙΒΕΡΙΟΣ 1989: Τιβέριος Μ., *Περίκλεια Παναθήναια. Ένας κρατήρας του Ζωγράφου του Μονάχου 2335*, Thessaloniki 1989

ΤΙΒΕΡΙΟΣ 1996: Τιβέριος Μ., *Ελληνική τέχνη. Αρχαία αγγεία*, 1996

TINTH 1983: Tinth T.T., Serapis debout, *EPRO* 46 (1983)

TÖLLE-KASTENBEIN 1994: Tölle-Kastenbein R., *Das archaische Wasserleitungsnetz für Athen*, Mainz 1994

TOSTO 1999: Tosto V., *The Black-Figure Pottery Signed ΝΙΚΟΣΘΕΝΕΣ ΕΠΟΙΕΣΕΝ*, Allard Pierson Series, 11, Amsterdam 1999

TOYNBEE 1934: Toynbee J.M.C., *The Hadrianic School*, Cambridge 1934

ΤΟΥΡΑΤΣΟΓΛΟΥ 1986: Τουράτσογλου Ι., Το ξίφος της Βεροίας: Συμβολή στη Μακεδονική οπλοποιία των ύστερων κλασικών χρόνων, in *Αρχαία Μακεδονία IV. Δ΄ Διεθνές Συμπόσιο, Θεσσαλονίκη 21-25 Σεπτεμβρίου 1983*, Thessaloniki 1986, 611-650

TOURATSOGLOU 1988: Touratsoglou I., *Die Münzstätte von Thessaloniki in der römischen Kaiserzeit (32/31 v.Chr. bis 268 n.Chr.)*, Berlin - New York 1988

ΤΟΥΡΑΤΣΟΓΛΟΥ 1996: Τουράτσογλου Ι., in *Νομίσματα και Νομισματική*, Athens 1996

TRACY 1994: Tracy S.V., IG II² 1195 and Agathe Tyche in Attica, *Hesperia* 63 (1994) 241-244

TRAILL 1975: Traill J., *The Political Organization of Attica. A Study of the Demes. Trittyes and Phylai*, *Hesperia* Suppl. XIV, 1975

ΤΡΑΥΛΟΣ 1960: Τραυλός Ι., *Πολεοδομική εξέλιξις των Αθηνών*, Athens 1960

TRAVLOS 1971: Travlos I., *Pictorial Dictionary of Ancient Athens*, London 1971

TRAVLOS 1988: Travlos I., *Bildlexikon zur Topographie des antiken Attika*, Tübingen 1988

TRÉHEUX 1952: Tréheux J., Etudes d'épigraphie délienne, *BCH* 76 (1952) 562-595

ΤΡΙΑΝΘ 1977: Τριάντη Ι., Αρχαϊκές ερμαϊκές στήλες, *ADelt* 32 (1977) Meletai, 116-122

Tropis II: *2nd International Symposium on Ship Construction in Antiquity*, Delphi 1987 (ed. H. Tzalas)

Tropis V: *5th International Symposium on Ship Construction in Antiquity*, 1999 (ed. H. Tzalas)

TRUMPF-LYRITZAKI 1969: Trumpf-Lyritzaki M., *Griechische Figurenvasen des Reichen Stils und der späten Klassik*, 1969

ΤΣΑΚΟΣ 1977: Τσάκος Κ., Ελληνιστικοί λαξευτοί τάφοι στη Σάμο, *ADelt* 32 (1977) Meletai, 344-420

ΤΣΑΚΟΣ 1986: Τσάκος Κ., Μακρυγιάννη. Κτίριο Weiler, *ADelt* 41 (1986) Chronika, 11-15

ΤΣΙΡΙΓΩΤΗ-ΔΡΑΚΩΤΟΥ 1987: Τσιριγώτη-Δρακωτού Ι., Ιερά Οδός, *ADelt* 42 (1987) Chronika, 24-28

ΤΣΙΡΙΓΩΤΗ-ΔΡΑΚΩΤΟΥ 1992: Τσιριγώτη-Δρακωτού Ι., Η πορεία της Ιεράς Οδού και η σημασία της, *Αρχαιολογία* 43 (1992) 28-32

ΤΣΙΡΙΓΩΤΗ-ΔΡΑΚΩΤΟΥ 1996: Τσιριγώτη-Δρακωτού Ι., Τιμητικό ψήφισμα από την Ιερά Οδό, *Α΄ Επιστημονική Ημερίδα της Γ΄ ΕΠΚΑ*, Μάρτιος 1996, Proceedings (forth.)

ΤΣΙΡΙΓΩΤΗ-ΔΡΑΚΩΤΟΥ 1999: Τσιριγώτη-Δρακωτού Ι., Ιερά Οδός: ειδήσεις από τις νεώτερες ανασκαφές, in *Β΄ Επιστημονική Ημερίδα της Γ΄ ΕΠΚΑ*, Ιανουάριος 1999, Proceedings (forth.)

URE 1927: Ure A.D., *Sixth and Fifth Century Pottery from Rhitsona*, London 1927.

ΦΙΛΑΔΕΛΦΕΥΣ 1920-21: Φιλαδελφεύς Α., Ανασκαφή παρά το χωρίον Σπάτα, *ADelt* 6 (1920-1921) 131-138

ΦΙΛΗΜΟΝΟΣ-ΤΣΟΠΟΤΟΥ 1980: Φιλήμονος-Τσοποτού Μ., Νισυριακά Ι, *ΑΔ* 35 (1980) Meletai, 60-87

ΦΙΛΙΠΠΑΚΗ 1953-54: Φιλιππάκη Β., Αττικός τάφος της τελευταίας τριακονταετίας του 5ου αι. π.Χ., *AEphem* 1953-54, Γ΄, 98-110

ΧΑΡΙΤΩΝΙΔΗΣ 1935: Χαριτωνίδης Χ., *Απόρρητα*, Thessaloniki 1935

ΧΑΡΙΤΩΝΙΔΗΣ 1958: Χαριτωνίδης Σ., Ανασκαφαί κλασικών τάφων παρά την πλατείαν Συντάγματος, *AEphem* 1958, 1-152

ΧΡΥΣΟΣΤΟΜΟΥ 1998a: Χρυσοστόμου Π., *Μακεδονικοί τάφοι Πέλλας I, Τάφος Β΄ ο ασύλητος*, Athens 1998

ΧΡΥΣΟΣΤΟΜΟΥ 1998b: Χρυσοστόμου Π., *Η θεσσαλική θεά Εν(ν)οδία ή Φεραία θεά*, Athens 1998

VAGALINSKI 1992: Vagalinski L., Roman Bronze Strigils and Rings for them from Trace (1st-3rd cent. AD), in N. Mols *et al.* (eds.), *Acta of the 2nd International Congress on Ancient Bronzes*, Nijmegen 1992, 435-443

VANDERHOEVEN n.p.d.: Vanderhoeven M., *Verres romaines (Ier-IIIème siècle) de Musées Curtius et de Verre à Liège*, n.p.d.

VANDERPOOL *et al.* 1962: Vanderpool E. - McCredie J.R. - Steinberg A., Koroni. A Ptolemaic Camp on the East Coast of Attica, *Hesperia* 31 (1962) 26-61

VANDERPOOL 1966: Vanderpool E., Some Attic Inscriptions, *Hesperia* 35 (1966) 274-283

VAN HOORN 1951: Van Hoorn G., *Choes and Anthesteria*, 1951

VANHOVE 1992: Vanhove D., *Le sport dans la Grèce antique*, 1992

Vases à mémoire 1988: Landes C. - Laurens A.-F. (eds.), *Vases à mémoire. Les collections de céramique grecque dans le Midi de la France*, 1988

VEDDER 1985: Vedder U., *Untersuchungen zur plastischen Ausstattung attischer Grabanlagen des 4. Jhs v.Chr.*, 1985

Veder Greco 1988: Franchi dell'Orto L. - Franchi R. (eds.), *Veder Greco. Le necropoli di Agrigento*, Rome 1988

VÉRILHAC - VIAL 1998: Vérilhac A.M. - Vial C., *Le mariage grec*, *BCH* Suppl. 32, 1998

VERMEULE - COMSTOCK 1972: Vermeule C. - Comstock M., *Greek, Etruscan and Roman Bronzes in the Museum of Fine Arts Boston*, Greenwich 1972

VEYNE *et al.* 1998: Veyne P. - Lissarrague Fr. - Frontisi-Doucroux Fr., *Les mystères du Gynécée*, Paris 1998

VIALE 1921/22: Viale V., Il portico detto di Eumene, *ASAtene* IV/V (1921/22) 13-32

VIAN 1951: Vian F., *Répertoire des Gigantomachies figurées dans l'art grec et romain*, Paris 1951

VICKERS 1984: Vickers M., The Influence of Exotic Materials on Attic White-Ground Pottery, in H.A.G. Brijder (ed.), *Ancient Greek and Related Pottery. Proceedings of the International Vase Symposium in Amsterdam, April 1984*, Amsterdam 1984, 12-15

VIDAL-NAQUET 1983: Vidal-Naquet P., *Ο μαύρος κυνηγός*, Athens 1983

VIERNEISEL 1961: Vierneisel K., Neue Tonfiguren aus dem Heraion von Samos, *AM* 76 (1961) 25-59

VIERNEISEL 1978: Vierneisel K. (ed.), *Römisches im Antikenmuseum*, Berlin 1978

VOGEIKOFF 1994: Vogeikoff N., *Hellenistic Pottery from the South Slope of the Athenian Acropolis* (Ph.D. thesis, Bryn Mawr College), 1994

VOIGTLÄNDER 1982: Voigtländer W., Funde aus der Insula westlich des Bouleuterion in Milet, *IstMitt* 32 (1982) 30-173

VOLLENWEIDER 1979: Vollenweider M.L., *Catalogue raisonnée des sceaux, cylindres, intailles et camées*, II, 1976-1979

VOLLENWEIDER 1984: Vollenweider M.L., *Deliciae Leonis. Antike geschnittene Steine und Ringe aus einer Privatsammlung*, 1984

VON BISSING 1936-37: Von Bissing F.W., Sul tipo di sistri trovati nel Tervere, *BSA* 9 (1936-37) 211-224

VON BOTHMER 1957: Von Bothmer D., *Amazons in Greek Art*, Oxford 1957

VON MOOCK 1998: Von Moock D., *Die figürlichen Grabstelen Attikas in der Kaiserzeit*, 1998

VON SCHNEIDER 1892: Von Schneider R., Neuere Erwerbungen der Antiken Sammlung des Österreichischen Kaiserhauses in Wien, *JdI* 1892, 170-174

VORBERG 1988: Vorberg G., *Glossarium eroticum*, Main 1988

VORSTER 1983: Vorster C., *Griechische Kinderstatuen*, Köln 1983

WALDHAUER 1914: Waldhauer O., *Kaiserlichte Hermitage. Die antiken Tonlampen*, St. Petersburg 1914

WALKER - BIERBRIER 1997: Walker S. - Bierbrier M., *Ancient Faces. Mummy Portraits from Roman Egypt. Catalogue of Roman Portrait in the British Museum*, IV, 1997

WALLENSTEIN 1971: Wallenstein K., *Korinthische Plastik des 7. und 6. Jhs v.Chr.*, Bonn 1971

WALTER-KARYDI 1987: Walter-Karydi E., *Die äginetische Bildhauerschule, Werke und schriftliche Quellen, Alt-Ägina* II.2, Mainz am Rhein 1987

WALTER-KARYDI 1997: Walter-Karydi E., Aigina versus Athens? The Case of the Protoattic Pottery on Aigina, in *APP* 1997, 385-394

WALTERS 1899: Walters H., *Catalogue of the Bronzes, Greek, Roman and Etruscan, in the Department of Greek and Roman Antiquities, British Museum*, London, The Trustees, 1899

WALTERS 1979: Walters E., Two Attic Grave Reliefs of the Roman Period, *AAA* XII (1979) 212-221

WALTERS 1988: Walters E., *Attic Grave Reliefs that Represent Women in the Dress of Isis, Hesperia* Suppl. 22, 1988

WARDEN 1990: Warden P.G., The Small Finds, in D. White (ed.), *The Extramural Sanctuary of Demeter and Persephone at Cyrene, Libya. Final Reports* IV, Philadelphia 1990

WEDDE 1999: Wedde M., Decked Vessels in Early Greek Ship Architecture, in *Tropis* V, 1999

WEHGARTNER 1983: Wehgartner I., *Attisch weissgrundige Keramik*, Mainz 1983

WEHGARTNER 1989: Wehgartner I., Man Leaning on his Stick. Zu Bild und Inschrift eines attischen Salbgefäß, *Würzburg (N.F.)* 15 (1989) 223-231

WEINBERG 1949: Weinberg S.S., Investigations at Corinth 1947-1948, *Hesperia* 18 (1949) 148-157

WHITE 1963: White D., Survey of Millstones from Morgantina, *AJA* 67 (1963) 199-206

WHITEHEAD 1986: Whitehead D., *The Demes of Attica 508-250 B.C. A Political and Social Study*, 1986

WHITLEY 1994: Whitley J., Protoattic Pottery: A Contextual Approach, in I. Morris (ed.), *Classical Greece: Ancient Histories and Modern Archaeologies*, Cambridge 1994, 51-70

WIEGAND - SCHRADER 1904: Wiegand T. - Schrader H., *Priene*, Berlin 1904

WILLEMSEN 1977: Willemsen F., Zu den Lakedämoniergräbern im Kerameikos, *AM* 92 (1977) 117-157

WILLERS 1967: Willers D., Zum Hermes Propylaios des Alkamenes, *JdI* 82 (1967) 37ff.

WILLERS 1975: Willers D., *Hekate Epipyrgidia, AM* Bh. 4, 1975

WILLIAMS 1958: Williams R.T., Greek Ships on Two Levels, *JHS* 88 (1958) 121ff.

WILLIAMS 1978: Williams E.R., Figurine Vases from the Athenian Agora, *Hesperia* 47 (1978) 379-401

WILLIAMS 1982: Williams C., Zeus and Other Deities. Notes on Two Archaistic Piers, *Hesperia* Suppl. XX, 1982, 175-181

WILLIAMS 1991: Williams D., *The Drawing of the Human Figure on Early Red-Figure Vases, New Perspectives in Early Greek Art*, Studies in the History of Art, 32 (ed. D. Buitron-Oliver), Washington 1991

WINTER 1903: Winter F., *Die antiken Terrakotten III 1:2 Die Typen der figürlichen Terrakotten.* I-II, 1903

WITT 1971: Witt R.E., *Isis in the Graeco-Roman World*, 1971

WOOLEY 1938: Wooley C., Excavation at Al Mina, Suedia II, *JHS* 58 (1938) 133-170

WOYSH-MEAUTIS 1982: Woysh-Meautis D., *La représentation des animaux*, 1982

WREDE 1985: Wrede H., *Die antike Herme, Trierer Beiträge zur Altertumskunde* 1, Mainz am Rhein 1985

WRIGHT 1982: Wright J.C., Excavations at Tsoungiza (Archaia Nemea) 1981, *Hesperia* 51 (1982) 375-397

YADIN 1963: Yadin Y., *Finds from the Bar Kokhba Period in the Cave of Letters*, Jerusalem 1963

YADIN 1972: Yadin Y., *Bar Kokhba*, Jerusalem 1972

YOUNG 1938: Young R.S., Pottery from a 7th Century Well, *Hesperia* 7 (1938) 414ff.

YOUNG 1939: Young R.S., *Late Geometric Graves and a Seventh Century Well, Hesperia* Suppl. II, 1939

YOUNG 1942: Young R.S., Graves from the Phaleron Cemetery, *AJA* 46 (1942) 23-57

YOUNG 1951: Young R.S., Sepulture Intra Urbem, *Hesperia* 20 (1951) 67-134

YOUNG 1956: Young J.H., Roads in South Attica, *Antiquity* 30 (1956) 94-97

ZAPHIROPOULOU 1973: Zaphiropoulou F., Vases et autres objets de marbre de Rhenée, *BCH* Suppl. I, 1973, 601-636

ZILLER 1877: Ziller E., Untersuchungen über die antiken Wasserleitungen Athens, *AM* 2 (1877) 107-131

ZIMMER 1987: Zimmer G., *Spiegel im Antikenmuseum*, Berlin 1987

ZIMMERMANN 1998: Zimmermann N., Beziehungen zwischen Ton und Metallgefäßen spätklassischer und frühhellenistischer Zeit, *International Archäologia* 20 (1998)

ZLOTOGORSKA 1997: Zlotogorska M., *Darstellungen von Hunden auf griechischen Grabreliefs*, 1997

ZOROGLU 1999: Zoroglu L., Zwei Lekythoi des Klügmann-Malers aus Kelenderis, *AA* 1999, 141-145

413

PHOTOGRAPHIC ARCHIVES

3rd and 1st Ephorates of Prehistoric and Classical Antiquities, DAI Athens (p. 266-267), ATTIKO METRO S.A. (p. 27, 148)

COMPUTER PROCESSING OF ILLUSTRATIONS: PANOS STAMATAS

COMPUTER PROCESSING OF TEXT: ELENI VALMA

COLOURS SEPARATION: SELECTOR

MONTAGE - PRINTING: A. PETROULAKIS S.A.

BINDING: G. MOUTSIS

PAPER: ZANDERS 135 gr. MEGA GLOSS